American Home and Family Series

BARCLAY-CHAMPION-BRINKLEY-FUNDERBURK: TEEN GUIDE TO HOMEMAKING
CARSON: HOW YOU LOOK AND DRESS
CARSON-RAMEE: HOW YOU PLAN AND PREPARE MEALS
HURLOCK: CHILD GROWTH AND DEVELOPMENT
LANDIS: YOUR MARRIAGE AND FAMILY LIVING
MORTON-GEUTHER-GUTHRIE: THE HOME—ITS FURNISHINGS AND EQUIPMENT
SHANK-FITCH-CHAPMAN-SICKLER: GUIDE TO MODERN MEALS
STURM-GRIESER: GUIDE TO MODERN CLOTHING
(OTHER TITLES IN PROCESS)

About the Authors

JEANNE HAYDEN BRINKLEY—Teacher-Educator, School of Home Economics, the Florida State University, Tallahassee, Florida. Mrs. Brinkley's professional experiences include: Occupational Consultant, Home Economics, for the State of Florida; Acting Assistant Director, Home Economics, State of Florida; home economics teacher in Orlando, Florida; and County Supervisor of Home Economics Education for Orange County, Florida. She has served as a member or chairman of numerous state curriculum and vocational workshops and on textbook criteria and accreditation committees.

The late MARION S. BARCLAY served as Supervisor of Home Economics Education in Hillsborough County, Florida. Mrs. Barclay's professional experiences include: Home Economics teaching in high schools in Elgin, Illinois, Tampa, Florida, and the P. M. Yonge Laboratory School of the University of Florida; editor and consultant for curriculum materials at the University of Florida and Florida State University; editor or co-editor for three state curriculum guides, and author of numerous articles published in educational journals.

KATHLEEN WAGNER FUNDERBURK—Curriculum Consultant, Home Economics Education, Department of Education, State of Florida, Tallahassee. Mrs. Funderburk's professional roles include: Teacher at the elementary, junior and senior high school, and adult levels; Home Economics Consultant to the Florida Junior Colleges; participant in and director of state curriculum projects, including the development of a K-12 Vocational Home Economics System for Florida; and participant in evaluations made for the Southern Association of Colleges and Secondary Schools.

FRANCES CHAMPION—Director, Home Economics (retired), Department of Education, State of Florida, Tallahassee. Miss Champion's professional experiences include: Teaching in Georgia High Schools, Emory University, University of Georgia, and Georgia State College; City Supervisor of Home Economics at Columbus, Georgia; Assistant State Supervisor of Home Economics Education for the State of Georgia; Assistant National Advisor for the Future Homemakers of America, Washington, D.C.; and Home Economics Editor for various publications.

Webster Division, McGraw-Hill Book Company

New York
St. Louis
San Francisco
Düsseldorf
London
Mexico
Montreal
New Delhi
Panama
Singapore
Sydney
Toronto

Teen Guide to Homemaking THIRD EDITION

Marion S. Barclay FORMERLY SUPERVISOR OF HOME ECONOMICS EDUCATION, HILLSBOROUGH COUNTY, FLORIDA

Frances Champion DIRECTOR, HOME ECONOMICS, (RETIRED), DEPARTMENT OF EDUCATION, STATE OF FLORIDA, TALLAHASSEE

Jeanne Hayden Brinkley TEACHER–EDUCATOR, SCHOOL OF HOME ECONOMICS, THE FLORIDA STATE UNIVERSITY, TALLAHASSEE, FLORIDA

Kathleen W. Funderburk CURRICULUM CONSULTANT, HOME ECONOMICS EDUCATION, DEPARTMENT OF EDUCATION, STATE OF FLORIDA, TALLAHASSEE

Side column material, pre-chapter and post-chapter tests prepared by
Dr. Valerie M. Chamberlain
ASSOCIATE PROFESSOR, COLLEGE OF HOME ECONOMICS, TEXAS TECH UNIVERSITY, LUBBOCK, TEXAS

TEEN GUIDE TO HOMEMAKING

Copyright © 1972, 1967, 1961, by McGraw-Hill, Inc. All rights reserved. Printed in the United States of America. No part of this publication may be reproduced, stored in a retrieval system, or transmitted, in any form or by any means, electronic, mechanical, photocopying, recording, or otherwise, without prior written permission of the publisher.

07-003644-6

8 9 10 DODO 1 0 9 8 7 6 5

IN CONSULTATION WITH

Patricia J. Thompson—Adjunct Lecturer, Department of Family and Consumer Studies, Herbert H. Lehman College, City University of New York.

Mrs. Leilani Peck, Home Economist and Staff Writer, ARA Services, Inc., Research and Food Standards Department, Philadelphia, Pennsylvania

Editorial Direction—Margie S. Jennings
Art Production—Richard O'Leary
Design—Silvia Walters and Helen Williams
Drawings—Edward S. Barclay and Helios Studios
Editing and Styling—Sue S. Watson
Production Supervision—Bert Henke and Richard E. Shaw
Cover Design—A batik by Lynn Titleman
Photographs for unit opening pages provided courtesy of Oneida Silversmiths; Clairol Inc.; Viking Sewing Machine Company; Farley Manning Associates, Inc.; Chesebrough-Pond's Inc.; Kraft Kitchens; and the Aluminum Association

Preface

Each generation of teen-agers has characteristics which tend to set it apart from all previous ones. Teen-agers of the 70's seem unique in their ability to question and in their ability to understand.

As a group, today's teen-agers seem to be genuinely interested in others. They want to look below the surface of their fellow human beings to gain an insight into the thoughts and actions of others. Teen-agers are not totally impressed by appearances or material goods. Rather, they tend to become interested in each person as an individual. This awareness has brought a type of kinship, a willingness to care about people as people. It asserts itself in various forms. The willingness of teen-agers to volunteer as helpers in reading clinics, as Candy Stripers in hospitals, or as junior leaders or athletic coaches of young children are but a few examples of ways teen-agers show their interest in others. Their concern leads them to be interested in their own environment. They understand that only if resources are used intelligently will these same resources continue to be available for the people in whom they are interested.

Information is channeled to teen-agers by the school system as well as by newspapers, radio, and television. This constant input of facts helps to enlarge the scope of subject matter on which they are informed.

Today's teen-agers are capable of learning that an upheaval has occurred in the surface of the earth or in the world's political structure. But to them, a fact is only a starting point. They want to know what caused the upheaval, the eventual results they can expect, and the likelihood of its recurrence. This generation of teen-agers can assimilate facts, as have their predecessors. But they seem unique in their ability to develop patterns of logical reasoning through their serious questioning of existing systems. This ability to reason logically places the teen-ager of the 70's in an enviable position. He can realistically relate to the world as it exists while he idealistically searches for ways to improve it.

Teen-agers of the 70's understand that much remains to be done in areas of interpersonal relationships and environment. However, perhaps more than any previous group they have been able to effectively combine idealism with realism. They understand that whether they live in one of the great inner city areas, the suburbs, or in relatively rural regions of the country, the crux of successful living lies in the building of successful interpersonal relationships in a socially and hygienically sound environment.

The third edition of TEEN GUIDE TO HOMEMAKING recognizes the wide range of the modern teen-agers' interests and experiences. An effort has been

Acknowledgments:
The authors of TEEN GUIDE TO HOMEMAKING acknowledge the counsel and help of the following individuals who made significant contributions to this text by providing up-to-date information or ideas for student activities, using the recipes in their classrooms, or by evaluating the manuscript:
Miss Allie E. Ferguson, Administrator, and **Miss Francies Thomas, Miss Virginia Leslie, Miss Lucy Lang,** and **Miss Pauline Willoughby,** Area Supervisors of Home Economics for the Florida State Department of Education.
Dean Hortense Glenn and **Dr. Hazel Stevens, Dr. Helen Cate,** and **Dr. Ruth Dales,** School of Home Economics, The Florida State University, Tallahassee.
Miss Margie Lowrance, State Supervisor, Home and Family Life Education, State Coordinating Council for Occupational Education, Olympia, Washington.
Mrs. Ethel Washington, Supervisor, Home Economics Education, Detroit Public Schools, Detroit, Michigan.
Mrs. Louise Harmon, Supervisor, and **Mrs. Dorothy B. Hunter,** Teacher Specialist, Home Economics, Montgomery County Schools, Rockville, Maryland.
Mrs. Barbara Wood, Elizabeth Cobb Junior School, Tallahassee, Florida.

Mrs. Emma H. Morgan, Duncan-Fletcher Junior High School, Jacksonville Beach, Florida.
Mrs. Wanda Montgomery, Edward H. White Senior High School, Jacksonville, Florida.
Mrs. Gladys Hendren, Holly Hill Junior High School, Holly Hill, Florida.
Mrs. Amanda Johnson Powell, Conway Junior High School, Orlando, Florida.
Mrs. Lillian Johnson, Zephyrhills High School, Zephyrhills, Florida.
Mrs. Emma Lou Harvey, Zephyrhills High School, Zephyrhills, Florida.
Mrs. Estelle Patchin, Lakeland Junior High School, Lakeland, Florida.
Mrs. Marilyn McKinley, Reading Teacher, Borden, Indiana.
Miss Gail Trapnell, Consultant in Distributive Education, Florida State Department of Education.
Miss Elizabeth Dickenson, Florida Agricultural Extension, Clothing and Textile Specialist, Retired, University of Florida, Gainesville.
Mrs. Koleen Haire, Belle Vue Middle School, Tallahassee, Florida.
Miss Mary Cook, Port Saint Joe High School, Port Saint Joe, Florida.
Mrs. Louise Converse, Venice High School, Venice, Florida.
Miss Jane Ashe, Marathon Senior High School, Marathon, Florida.
Miss Kanella Kermode, Charlotte Junior-Senior High, Punta Gorda, Florida.
Mrs. Eileen S. Moore, Home Economics Department Head, Ribault High School, Jacksonville, Florida.

made to approach the broad concepts involved in successful family living from the viewpoint of the concerned teen-ager who has become involved in the problems of the world around him.

The third edition of this widely used text considers the effects of decisions on the lives of those who make them. It is understood that each person now lives and, for that matter, will continue to live in some kind of family group. The decisions which are made within his home will lead either toward happiness or dissension. *That teen-agers learn to understand and accept the results of their own decisions is the underlying theme of the book.*

This text, like Home Economics as a discipline within the educational system, concerns itself with the development of the total individual. In order to cover a many faceted subject, basic areas are presented in each unit. They include: Part I—YOUR RELATIONSHIPS—which deals with the area of *Human Development and the Family;* Part II—YOUR HOME and Part III—YOUR RESOURCES—which when coupled cover at appropriate levels the areas of *Home Management and Family Economics* and *Housing and Interior Design;* Part V—YOUR CLOTHES—which considers necessary decisions in the area of *Textiles and Clothing;* and Part VI—YOUR FOODS—which deals with the results of decisions made in the area of *Foods and Nutrition.* To complete this comprehensive text, special units have been incorporated which offer a look at YOUR HOME ECONOMICS DEPARTMENT—Part IV and YOUR RECIPES—Part VII, which is composed of student-tested recipes.

There seems to be a real desire on the part of many of today's teen-agers to learn how to spend to best advantage whatever money they have available. There is also a desire to begin thinking about jobs for which they have special aptitude, talent, or interest. Both *consumer education* and *vocational education* have been covered in each unit of the text at levels appropriate for students in their early to mid-teens.

Consumership is presented from the viewpoint of *buying wisely,* considering needs before wants. Special areas where teen-agers are likely to spend money are emphasized. Clothes, food, general school expenses, and the expenses involved with the teen-ager's social life are given special consideration. Laws protecting the consumer and the consumer's responsibilities are also discussed.

It is understood that many students will end their formal educations when they are old enough to enter the world of work. Others have goals which include post high school or perhaps a college education. Consideration has been given to vocational information which will be of interest to each of these groups. Jobs and professions are described so that students can have brief glimpses at many types of work. The insignia calls attention to job descriptions so they are easily recognized as they appear throughout the text. These descriptions will help students determine whether or not they have an interest in, or an aptitude for, a given occupation.

The third-column material in the new edition of TEEN GUIDE TO HOMEMAKING has been written for student involvement. Each activity is written in a manner which will encourage student participation. In general, third-column material which carries the insignia ⚒ leads students to want to participate in classroom or home-centered *activities*. Columns which are marked ℰ can be considered *enrichment* materials which add to the *information* provided in the text itself. Columns marked ⓔ deal largely with *attitudes*. Debates, discussions, and thought-producing activities to which students can react emotionally are often included.

The third-column activities cover a broad range of interest- and ability-centered learning experiences. This variety provides for each student several activities which may be of particular interest.

Bulletin board ideas have been provided in each unit. Simple and educational in content, the directions are worded so that artistically inclined students can prepare them with little or no help from the teacher.

A testing program has been incorporated into the third edition of TEEN GUIDE TO HOMEMAKING. An introductory test precedes each chapter. It is designed to increase the student's interest in learning and to give him an idea of his basic understanding of the subject. A more comprehensive test follows each chapter. By taking both the pretest and posttest, the student can determine his own progress.

Studied sequentially or by unit, TEEN GUIDE TO HOMEMAKING provides for comprehensive learning in Home Economics. The use and application of the pre- and posttesting program, the text itself, and the involvement-oriented third-column materials allow each student to grow at his own rate. Thus each can grasp at his individual level the concepts through which successful family living can become a *matter of decision* for teenagers and their families.

Miss Nancy Rehak, Ft. Myers High School, Ft. Myers, Florida.
Miss Judith Rickel, Henderson High School, Decatur, Georgia.
Mrs. Marilee Walther, Florida State University, Tallahassee.
Miss Katie Barrineau, Supervisor, Home Economics Education, Escambia County Schools, Pensacola, Florida.
Mrs. Elizabeth Barclay, Seminole Senior High School, Seminole, Florida.
Miss Lois Bray, Hillsborough High School, Tampa, Florida.
Mrs. Idalyne Lawhon, Director of Nursing Services, American National Red Cross, Tampa, Florida.
Mrs. Kathryn Martin, Sertoma Sheltered Workshop, MacDonald Training Center, Tampa, Florida.
Walter C. Funderburk, chemist, Food Laboratory, Florida Department of Agriculture and Consumer Services.
Dr. Edward K. Walker, Optometrist, Tallahassee, Florida.
Special acknowledgment is given to **Carol, Nancy,** and **Paul Funderburk** for photographic research.

1
Your Relationships

Chapter 1 Teen-agers in today's world 15
  The world you live in • Your
  teen-age environment • Teen-age roles

Chapter 2 Relationships in today's families 25
  How families differ • How families change
  The seven c's of family living

Chapter 3 Your self-concept 41
  What is a teen-ager? • Basic human needs
  Individual differences
  Steps toward achieving maturity

Chapter 4 Your image 59
  The importance of communication
  Manners and mannerisms
  Aids to personal attractiveness
  The impact of image

Chapter 5 Your future 77
  Your opportunities • Setting future goals
  Your widening circle of friends
  Your social growth
  Your vocational growth

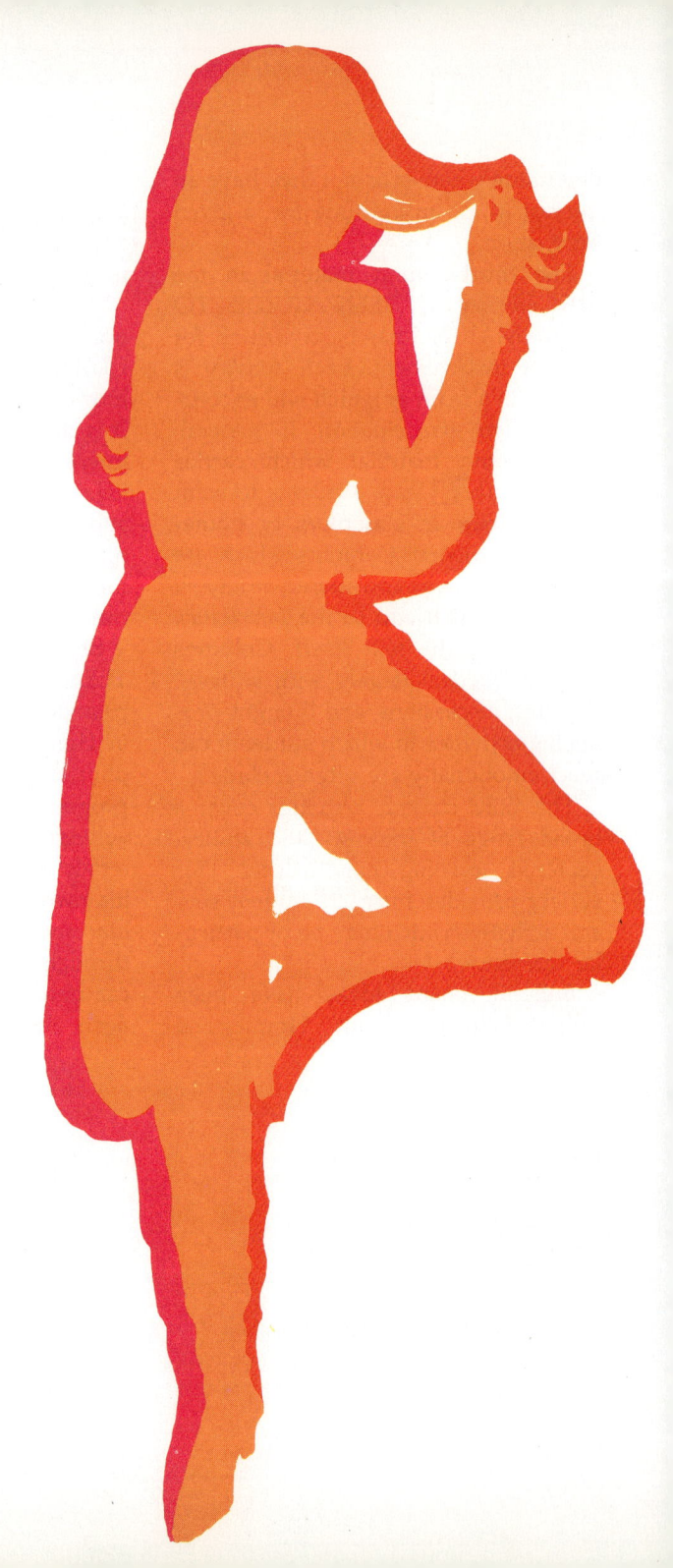

2
Your Home and Family

Chapter 6 Using your home for family living 99
The home meets physical needs • The home meets mental and emotional needs • The role of parents Roles of brothers and sisters • The role of older family members • Family sharing

Chapter 7 Centering the home around growing children 121
The pattern of growth • The special needs of children • Taking responsibility for children

Chapter 8 Managing the problems of family living 147
Problem solving in home management Comfort, convenience, privacy, and efficiency Health and safety

Chapter 9 Managing the household tasks of family living 167
Organizing for efficiency • Daily care Weekly care • Seasonal care Outdoor improvement tasks

3
Your Resources

Chapter 10 Managing your resources 185
Kinds of resources • Resources work as a team • Using your resources to reach your goals • The results of management

Chapter 11 Using your time, energy, and money 195
Attitudes about time • Managing your time • Attitudes about energy • Managing your energy resources • Attitudes about money • Managing your money

Chapter 12 Making consumer decisions 215
Spending money • Consumer responsibilities • Consumer protection • Types of buying Where to buy • How to pay Business-consumer interaction

4
Your Home Economics Department 236
Looking at the department
Improving the department
Caring for the department

5
Your Clothes

Chapter 13   Choosing clothes for you
             and your activities   255
   Develop a plan • Choose clothes for attractiveness
   Choose clothes for appropriateness • Choose clothes for wearability
   Choose clothes for enjoyment

Chapter 14   Buying clothes for
             use and fashion   271
   Laws protecting consumers
   Making quality judgments
   Buying outerwear • Buying undergarments
   Buying accessories

Chapter 15   Maintaining your clothes
             for attractiveness   295
   Daily care • Weekly care • Seasonal care

Chapter 16   Planning projects to
             match your ability   309
   Sharing the clothing construction center
   Selecting sewing equipment
   Choosing a project • Selecting fabric
   Using the sewing machine

Chapter 17   Creating clothes to
             wear and enjoy   331
   Selecting a pattern
   Choosing fabric to suit the pattern
   Preparation for sewing
   Assembling a garment

6
Your Foods

Chapter 18 Choosing food for health and vitality 359
A guide to nutrition • The effects of nutrition on health
What are calories? • What are nutrients? • Water in the diet
Nutrition—product of history, hope of the future

Chapter 19 Buying food for economy and convenience 375
Why food costs differ • Consumer information and protection
Shopping for food • Buying food for good nutrition

Chapter 20 Managing meals at home or school 391
Getting acquainted with the kitchen • Planning
interesting meals • Meal preparation

Chapter 21 Preparing protein foods 407
Principles of protein cookery • Meat • Fish • Poultry • Eggs

Chapter 22 Preparing milk and milk-rich foods 419
Milk in the menu • Principles of milk cookery • Cheese

Chapter 23 Preparing fruits and vegetables 427
Available forms of fruits and vegetables
Principles for cooking fruits and vegetables
Principles for preserving fruits and vegetables
Principles for serving raw fruits and vegetables

Chapter 24 Preparing cereal products 439
Types of cereal foods • Principles of cereal cookery

Chapter 25 Preparing energy foods 449
Types of foods • Principles of cookery

Chapter 26 Enjoying food with family and friends 459
Choosing and using tableware • Table manners
Types of meal service • Cleaning

7
Your Recipes 478

Protein foods • Milk-rich foods • Fruits and
vegetables • Cereal foods • Energy foods

Bibliography 514
Index 516

1
Your Relationships

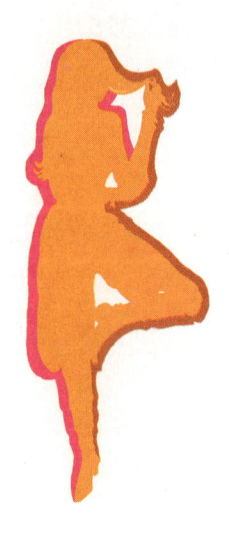

Chapter 1   Teen-agers in today's world
Chapter 2   Relationships in today's families
Chapter 3   Your self-concept
Chapter 4   Your image
Chapter 5   Your future

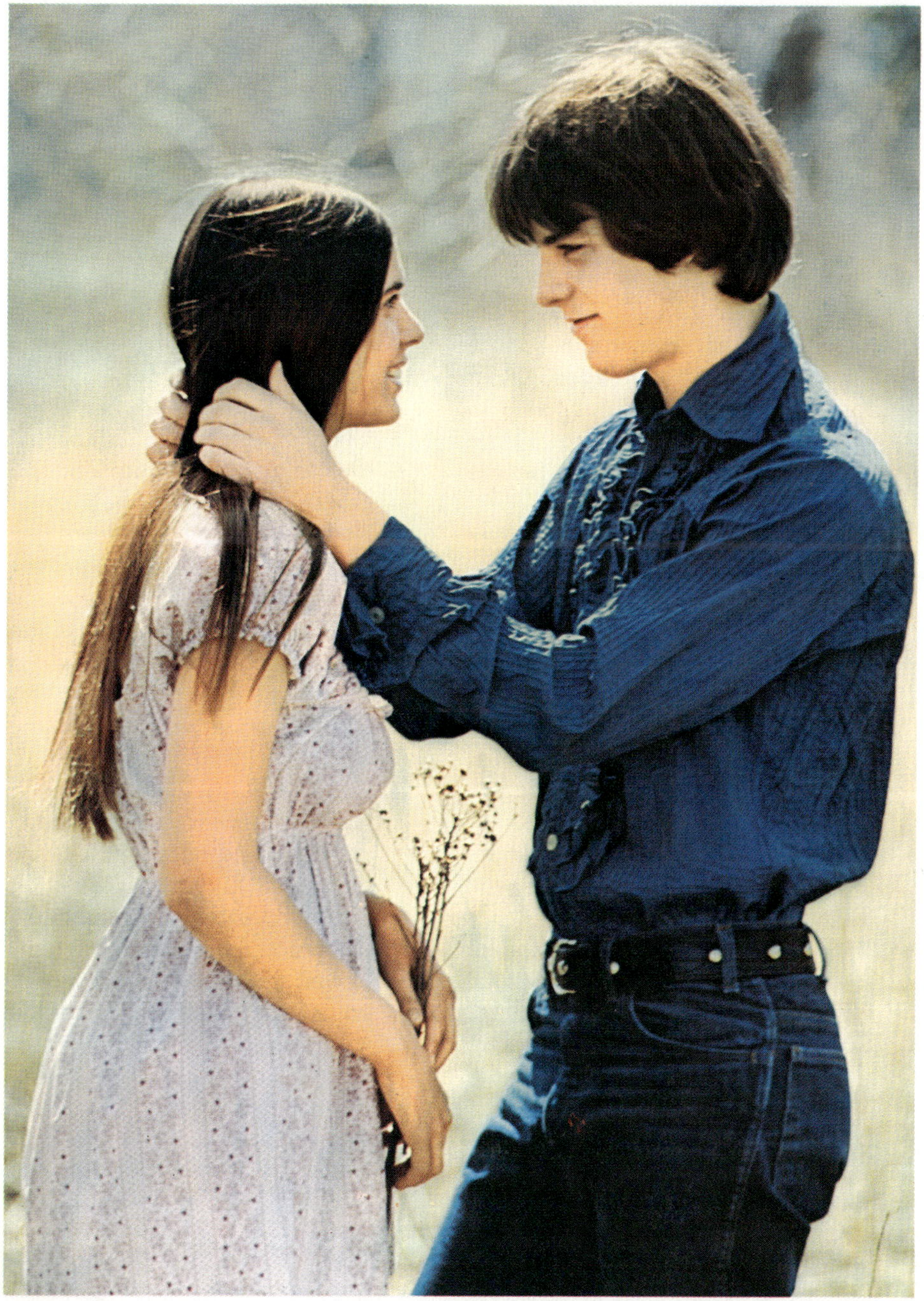

1 CHAPTER PRETEST

Number from 1 to 25. Beside each number indicate whether the corresponding statement is true or false. *Do not* write in this book.

1. Available knowledge has doubled in the past 10 years.
2. World events can have an immediate effect on people in many parts of the earth.
3. Your environment is limited to your home and your school.
4. TV and radio have made it possible for events from around the world to be reported in individual homes.
5. A teen-ager's life is simpler today than it was 10 years ago.
6. The world supply of natural resources is unlimited.
7. Communities differ in the opportunities they offer teen-agers for their growth and development.
8. Citizenship includes responsibilities as well as privileges.
9. A person's technical environment includes the industry and machines which surround him.
10. Ideally, in a family, each individual is concerned about the personal growth and development of others within the family.
11. How well a teen-ager fits into his world today is related to how well he can expect to fill his adult roles in the future.
12. A teen-ager can learn from his friends how to get along with others.
13. When people have the privilege of religious freedom they also have the responsibility to be tolerant of religious beliefs different from their own.
14. Men's and women's roles are more distinct and separate than in the past.
15. Worthwhile goals and values usually include concern for the welfare of other people.
16. Taking part in school activities provides a person with the opportunity to grow socially, emotionally, and mentally.
17. Boys usually mature at an earlier age than girls.
18. More girls than boys die at birth and during the first year of life.
19. Women have a longer life expectancy than men.
20. What you learn in your classes at school is limited to what you read and study.
21. Families today are less dependent upon others than in the past.
22. The social pressures on youth today are greater than they were on the youth of previous generations.
23. Examples of community resources are libraries, schools, recreation centers, hospitals, and parks.
24. The waste of resources in one nation of the world can have an effect on people in distant countries.
25. Citizenship begins when a person is 18 years old.

Give the following information on a separate sheet of paper.

1. Give 3 examples which show that the community in which a person grows up can affect his life.
2. List 3 ways in which a teen-ager can show good citizenship.
3. Give 2 examples of goods which are available to the consumer today that were unavailable 5 years ago.
4. List 2 services available to the consumer today that were unavailable 5 years ago.
5. Give 3 reasons why more women are employed outside the home today than 10 years ago.
6. List 3 occupations in which men are much more frequently employed than women. For each occupation listed give one reason why there are more men than women in this field.
7. List 3 occupations in which women are much more frequently employed than men. For each occupation listed give one reason why.

CHAPTER 1

Teen-agers in today's world

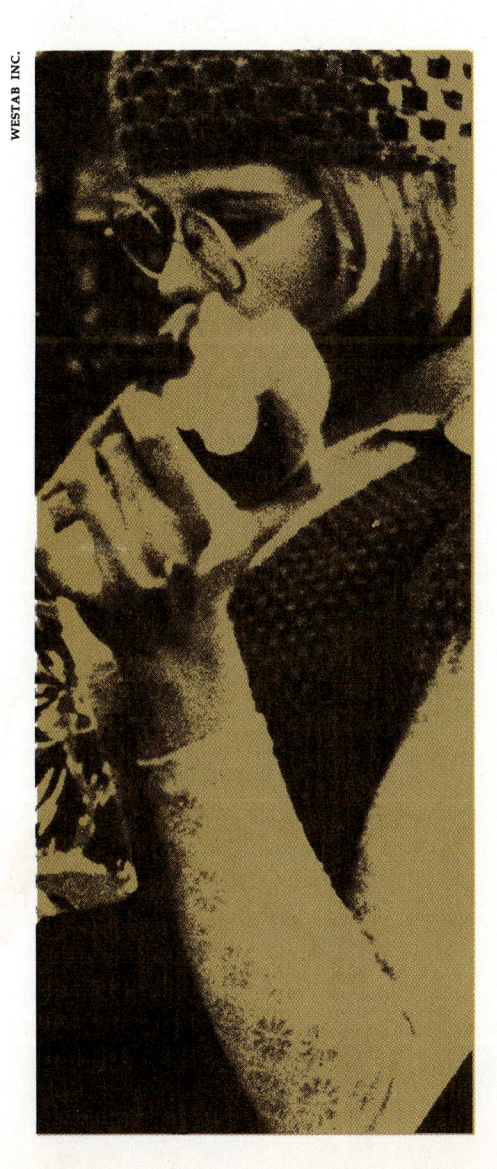

Traditionally the teen-ager's world was limited to his home, his family, and his neighborhood. The world beyond was off limits. Events moved at a slow pace. There seemed to be lots of time to do the things teen-agers enjoyed. There was time to think, to try and fail, and to try again. There was time to dream.

Now the teen-ager's world is changed. Available information doubles every few years. In order to survive in this fast-moving world of changing technology, the teen-ager has been forced to step up his pace of living. He has, of necessity, become a fast-moving individual. He is successful to the degree that he is able to adapt himself to the pace set by the world around him.

The world you live in

Today, you may listen to a transistor radio made in Japan. You may walk in shoes made in Spain or Italy. You may wear a shirt or blouse made in Taiwan. You may listen to English, French, or German records. You pick up ideas from all over the world. While building your own set of values and determining your own goals, you must somehow

List three examples of social pressures, tensions, or frustrations which are greater for the teen-ager today than in earlier times. Why do you think these pressures and tensions have increased?

Give examples from books, short stories, or television programs which illustrate how different people cope with modern-day social pressures and frustrations. Discuss these from the standpoint of mature and immature reactions to the situations.

Invite a person who has lived in another country to talk about the privileges and responsibilities of teen-agers in that country. Suggest that the visitor and students prepare for a question and answer session when the talk is completed. Judging from what you are able to learn in the discussion, do you feel that teen-age pressures and tensions are a local, national, or worldwide situation?

Distinguish between natural, human, and technical resources.

Explain the meaning of the expression, *No man is an island.* In what ways are you dependent on others? How are others dependent on you?

Give examples to illustrate the quotation, *Knowledge doubles every few years.*

Write a brief report on one of the following:
1. Special areas in which scientists have made outstanding discoveries during the past few years.
2. Technological improvements which have made space experiments possible.
3. Recent advancements in the field of medicine.
4. The effects of recent technical advancements on household equipment.
5. Goods and services which are available today that were not available ten years ago.

manage to fit into a world as well as into a neighborhood.

TV brings you people, places, and ideas from every corner of the globe and the space beyond. At no earlier time in history has the teen-ager's world been so complex or so exciting as now.

A WORLD OF HAPPENINGS

News travels fast. A political event or economic change taking place in Europe, the Middle East, or Asia today can influence your life tomorrow. A war declared in any part of the world may send young people into military service. A failure of a food crop in another nation may affect the price you pay for food. The indifference of a single government to the traffic of dangerous drugs can have tragic consequences for many young people in a number of countries. Carelessness in the use of natural resources of the land or sea affects individuals all over the earth.

A WORLD OF OPPORTUNITY

There is work to be done in today's world. There are people to house, to feed, and to clothe. There is a natural environment to protect. The vast resources of our planet can no longer be taken for granted. Many are being used up. Others are being wasted or destroyed. As the population increases, social pressure, tension, and frustration mount. In the struggle for a better environment for all, you will share with an ever-rising number of people an ever-increasing number of human problems. Perhaps the greatest opportunity presented to today's teen-agers is the chance to prove that they can live peacefully together.

A WORLD OF CHALLENGE

At one time, teen-agers were content to live in a special world of their own, prepared for them by others. This is no longer true. Today's teen-agers know that important events happen daily. You and other teen-agers are a part of the *real* world. You know problems exist. You want to join others who share your feelings, interests, and enthusiasm in working for world improvements.

As a group, teen-agers are conspicuous. They have a life style of their own. They have their own fads. They have their own language, tastes, and heroes. Events involving teen-agers appear regularly in the daily news reports. As a teen-ager, you may be annoyed when the news seems to emphasize only the bad things teen-agers do. In common with most teens, you have probably developed worthwhile goals and values which include the welfare of others.

Your teen-age environment

Your environment is all the people, things, and events that surround

COURTESY GIRL SCOUTS OF THE U.S.A.

Recreation areas provided by business and government as well as home surroundings are parts of your teen-age environment.

COURTESY MONSANTO COMPANY

Write the word ENVIRONMENT on a chalkboard by arranging the letters in a vertical line. Beside each list several things which affect your total environment. For example . . .

E Events, experiences

N Neighborhoods (and neighbors), natural resources

V Values, vapors, vehicles

I

R

O

N

M

E

N

T

Collect articles from newspapers and magazines about events in distant places which may have an effect on you as an individual. Give examples to illustrate how these events may affect your life.

17

Using different time periods, discuss the effect of the *times* (war, peace, depression, inflation, high interest rates) on a teen-ager's life.

Read real estate advertising to determine what seems to make people want to rent or buy in a certain neighborhood.

List recreational resources in your community which are available during different seasons of the year.

List local opportunities for people your age to become involved in some type of community service. Tell about some of the types of community service in which you or some of your friends have participated. In what ways did this work give satisfaction or a feeling of accomplishment?

Discuss community goods and services that families could use which are available without spending money. Include the services offered by mental health clinics, welfare agencies, and recreational centers.

you. There is a natural environment of plants, animals, and weather. There is a human environment of people. And there is a technical environment of chemicals, industry, and machines. Each of these—nature, people, and technology—fits into the total environment necessary for modern living.

Your teen environment, while fast-moving, remains basically one of home and family, school and friends. You are a member of a community. People in a community have much in common. As a member of a youth group, you may already be involved in some form of community service. As a young citizen, you are protected by the law. You also have a responsibility to learn which rules and regulations apply to you and the reasons behind them. As a modern teen, you are a citizen of your country and a member of the world community. Each community is strong in relation to the strength of its individual citizens.

YOUR FAMILY

Perhaps you are becoming more aware of the relationships within your family and the relationships of your family within the community. You know that a family is more than a group of people living together under the same roof. Ideally, it is a group, usually related by blood or marriage, who work together for an environment in which each can experience personal growth.

No two families look, act, or feel exactly alike. In some families there are strong family ties. Family members enjoy each other's company and enjoy doing things together. The people who live in such families share warm feelings of love and loyalty. Other families with equally warm feelings allow each member to go his own way in finding meaningful activities. In still other families there may be little closeness between family members. No matter what type your family is, as a family member, you have something to give to and something to gain from others in your family.

YOUR RELIGIOUS GROUP

If you are a member of a religious group, you have certain responsibilities to those with whom you worship. You will note that many teen-agers gain inner strength from their religion. It becomes a steadying force in life's stormy moments of indecision.

In Canada and the United States, as in most countries of the Western world, religious freedom includes religious tolerance. This tolerance includes the understanding of extremely active religious participation on the part of some, and the practice of no religion at all by others. Still other people substitute ethics for deity in their religious lives.

YOUR COMMUNITY

The country in which you are born, the section of the country, the state, and even the town or city in which you live affect your thinking. Your speech, your ideas, your dress, and your social attitudes are all affected by your community.

Communities differ. Some are urban. Some are suburban. Others remain rural. They differ in how much opportunity they offer their young people for various types of growth. In some places, schools and colleges are the centers of community life. Some towns and cities have youth centers or other recreational facilities especially for young people. Some communities are sports towns where home teams are enthusiastically supported. Others heavily support musical events, art museums, and libraries where young people learn to appreciate the world's culture.

The opportunities for education, for work, for social growth, for health, and for recreation are among the most important community resources. What organizations in your community offer such services to teen-agers?

YOUR NATION

As a citizen, you have certain responsibilities. Each citizen is expected to obey the law. In a system that allows for differences of opinion, your right to express your opinion brings the responsibility to respect the rights of others as they express theirs.

An interested citizen generally wants to learn about government at every level. A teen-ager can participate in government through volunteer work with the political party of his choice. Being a citizen of a country, however, includes more than being active in politics. Through active participation in groups working to improve your environment, the safety of your neighborhood, or the spirit of your school, you are practicing sound national citizenship.

Discuss specific examples which illustrate how the section of the country in which a person is reared may influence his life. Tell about differences you have observed in the dress, speech, and activities of people from different areas.

Name three ways your community has influenced your thinking.

Teen-agers frequently find their lifetime occupation while working with projects supported by their local communities.

COURTESY CARL G. KARSCH, PRESBYTERIAN LIFE

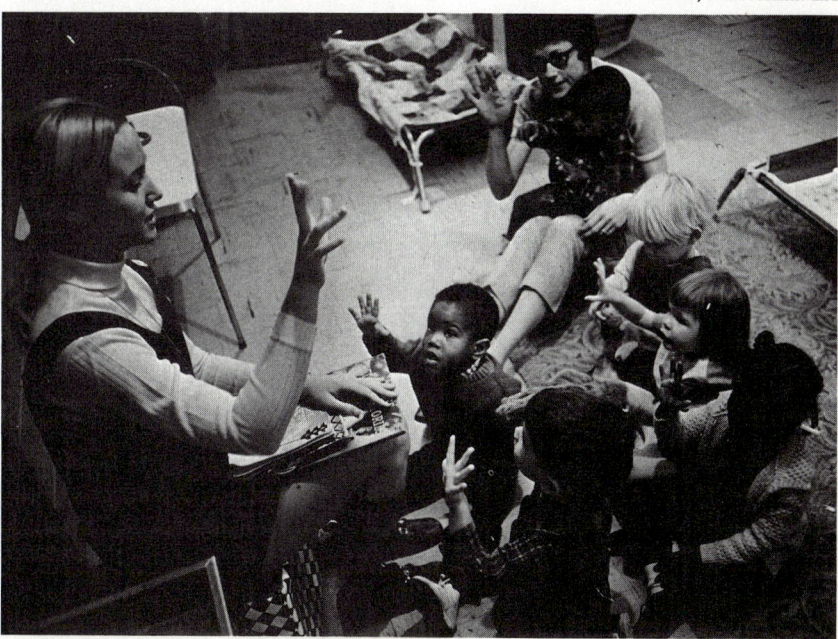

19

List occupations in which men are more frequently employed than women. List occupations in which women are more numerous than men. Give reasons why these differences exist. Which of these reasons are most valid and why?

Tell about a woman who is employed in a *man's job.* Tell about a man who is employed in an occupation which is most often held by women. What was your reaction when you heard that this person was working in this area? Why did you react in this way? What problems do you think people may face in working in jobs thought to be foreign to their sex roles? How can such problems be overcome?

Bulletin board IDEA
Title: *Your Sea of Opportunities*
Directions: Place the silhouettes of 6 fishes on the bulletin board with bubbles rising to the top of the blue background. On each fish write one of the following:
    Home and Family
    Religious Group
    School   Community
    Nation   World

YOUR WORLD

As you move toward independence as an adult, you will begin to see how interdependent people are; that is, how they must lean on one another. The earth, air, sky, and water are all shared, even though nations set up boundaries between themselves. As problems are compounded by an increasing world population, you will be expected to make increased contributions toward world improvement. Consider what some of these contributions might be.

Teen-age roles

In everything you do, you take on a *role,* a way of acting that seems to you to fit the situation. Your ability to fit into society will be determined by how well you can play your various roles. The roles you play well as a teen-ager are an indication of the types of roles you can fill successfully as an adult.

AS A MEMBER OF YOUR SEX GROUP

From the moment the attending doctor or midwife announces, "It's a boy" or "It's a girl," a human being is treated as a member of that sex. This one factor has lifelong impact on each person. From the moment you can first remember, you thought of yourself as son or daughter, brother or sister, nephew or niece, grandson or granddaughter. At one time it was popular to speak of women as the weaker sex. Research has shown, however, that more boys than girls die at birth and in the first year of life. Girls mature a year or two ahead of boys. Further, women, as a group, live longer than men. Consider how being a boy or a girl has influenced the way you think about yourself.

In the past, certain work was *man's work* while other tasks were called *woman's work.* Since much housework has become a matter of push buttons, chemicals, and equipment, ideas of work roles have become less important. The satisfaction a person derives from his job and the happiness of a family have become more important than the work performed.

A boy's roles

Although boys and girls do many of the same things, some behavior is considered appropriate for boys that is not appropriate for girls. Every culture is different, but in most countries boys, not girls, enter military combat training. Boys play football. Boys work as miners rather than as secretaries and telephone operators. You can probably think of many other things that are expected of boys and men. Most important, as a husband and father, a man's role will entail obligations, responsibilities, and privileges in relation to his wife and children.

As boys and girls mature, they find joy in fulfilling their roles as males or females.

COURTESY INGENUE MAGAZINE

A girl's roles

At one time, a woman's job was generally home-based. Today, many women combine marriage with work outside the home. What reasons are behind the woman's new role in the world of work? Among the most important is the availability of many labor-saving devices in the home. Too, many women find fulfillment in working roles, as well as in their roles as wives and mothers. The need for extra income also sends many women into the labor force. Nevertheless, it remains true, and probably always will, that the aim of most girls is to learn to successfully play their roles as wives and mothers.

AS A FAMILY MEMBER

Each teen-ager has a role to perform within his own family. He can be aided in this role by learning more about his own feelings and the feelings of other family members. He can then better enjoy the relationships within the family, or, if

Discuss the advantages of belonging to one or two organizations and being an active member of each. Compare these to the advantages of belonging to a larger number of organizations while being relatively inactive in each. What is a *joiner?* Why are some people joiners while others are not?

Complete a research project on a school organization you think you would like to join. Talk to the sponsor and some of the members. Ask about the cost of the club in time, effort, and money. Determine what would be expected of you as a member and what you could expect to gain by joining.

Discuss the qualities needed by a person if he is to be a good club leader.

List responsibilities and privileges of a citizen at home, at school, and in the community.

Compare effective school membership for students with good citizenship for adults.

Discuss the results of the attitude *Let George do it.*

Plan a *K and C* week (Kindness and consideration). Draw a classmate's name from a grab bag. Do not tell anyone whose name you drew. For one week try to show this person considerations and acts of kindness. At the end of the week, try to guess each others' secret K and C partners.

Plan and carry out a *school courtesy week*. Determine rules to be observed in the classroom, hallways, lunchroom, and at school events. Discuss examples of good and poor school spirit observed during this week.

necessary, he can work to improve them. Each family tends to offer privileges to its members along with responsibilities. Both privileges and responsibilities increase as a teenager matures. What responsibilities do you accept at home? What privileges do you want which you can enjoy while fulfilling your role as a teen-age member of the family?

AS A STUDENT

The teen-ager's major role in school is that of student. He learns to follow regulations as he grows both socially and mentally. As he enjoys such student activities as school publications, athletic events, and student government, the teen-ager is learning to live in the larger world beyond the school. As he follows the school regulations concerning attendance, safety, and the use of such study aids as the library, the teen-ager learns to cooperate within the community. As he studies, he is finding areas of special interest which may help him choose meaningful work in the future.

To a certain degree, a young person closes some doors as he opens others. For instance, an outstanding young singer may be encouraged to forget football, for which he has little natural aptitude anyway. Perhaps this is wise. However, by continuing to be interested in all types of activities, at least as a spectator, many doors can be left partially open for later roles which a person may play.

In what ways do *your* school roles open doors to the worlds of challenge and opportunity which lie beyond the school? How do your school roles help you prepare for activities in the world of work which becomes increasingly important as you continue to grow?

AS A FRIEND

The teens are usually thought of as a friendly time. Many teen-age activities, combined with the teen-ager's growing ability to do things on his own, offer special opportunities for forming lasting friendships. The role of friend can give

Within his own family a teen-ager often finds himself between the make-believe world of childhood and the young adult world of serious decision making.

COURTESY LIVE BETTER ELECTRICALLY PROGRAM—EDISON ELECTRIC INSTITUTE

a teen-ager a chance to grow in his understanding of other people. As a friend, he can test his attitudes and ideas on others. Friendship can help the teen-ager understand the kind of person he is. He can learn to see himself as others do. Friendship also gives him confidence in himself and in his ability to get along with others.

What are your responsibilities in your role as a teen-age friend? In what ways can friendship help you learn from others?

AS A CITIZEN

What are the responsibilities of the teen-age citizen? This question confuses some young people, because they think citizenship begins when a person is old enough to vote. This is not true. Instead, citizenship begins the day a person is born. A citizen can begin early to make useful contributions to the home, the community, the nation, or the world. What contributions are you ready to make today? What contributions will you be ready to make next year, or when you are an adult?

As a teen-ager, you fill many roles. These roles help you to grow as a member of your own sex group, your family, your school, and the world beyond. The effort you put forth to play each of these roles will largely determine the contributions you make to the world in which you live.

COURTESY INGENUE MAGAZINE

Friendships offer opportunities for teen-agers to understand one another on a one-to-one basis.

Sometimes acting in fun and sometimes working seriously, the teen-ager shows awareness of his responsibilities as a citizen.

COURTESY SIMPLICITY PATTERN CO. INC.

1 CHAPTER POSTTEST

Fill in the blank in each sentence with the *best* word to complete the statement. *Do not* write in this book.

1. In everything you do, you take on a way of acting which is called a(an) ___(1)___ .
2. Part of the process of growing up includes learning to spend money wisely for goods and ___(2)___ which are available to the consumer.
3. World-wide careless use of natural ___(3)___ can affect your daily life.
4. One of the greatest concerns facing people today is the problem of the continually increasing world ___(4)___ .
5. All the people, events, and things that surround you make up your ___(5)___ .
6. A person can be successful and happy if he is able to ___(6)___ to the people and events of the world around him.
7. It is generally evident between the ages of 12 and 14 that girls ___(7)___ at an earlier age than boys.
8. In recent years men's and women's ___(8)___ in life have become much more flexible and less clearly defined.
9. As a teen-ager grows up and gains privileges, he is also expected to assume ___(9)___ .
10. Regardless of his age, a person who is making worthwhile contributions to his home and his community is a good ___(10)___ .

Give the following information on a separate sheet of paper.

1. List 5 ways in which teen-agers' lives have changed in your community in the past 5 years.
2. Give 3 examples to show how a recent political event or economic change in another part of the world has had an effect on people who live in your community.
3. Give 2 examples to illustrate that world news travels quickly.
4. List 5 characteristics of students who are good school citizens.
5. Give 5 examples of behavior in which boys and girls differ.
6. Give 2 examples to illustrate that many women assume responsibilities today which were considered *men's work* in the past.
7. Give 2 examples to illustrate that many men assume responsibilities today which were considered *women's work* in the past.

2 CHAPTER PRETEST

Fill in the blank in each sentence with the *best* word or words to complete the statement. *Do not* use a word which already appears in the sentence. *Do not* write in this book.

1. The basic social unit in our society is the ___(1)___ .
2. A family in which either the mother or father makes the decisions, controls the money, and establishes the rules is an example of a(an) ___(2)___ family.
3. The ideals which influence the decisions you make and the goals which you set for yourself are called your ___(3)___ .
4. Family units pass through various stages of the ___(4)___ .
5. In the United States at least one out of every ___(5)___ families moves every year.
6. The need human beings have to love and to be loved is a basic ___(6)___ need.
7. Listening is an important part of ___(7)___ which contributes to a healthy family atmosphere.
8. When family members share the work to be done and respect the rights of others, there is a spirit of ___(8)___ .
9. If you are truthful, honest, and dependable, others will trust you and have ___(9)___ in you.
10. Being concerned and thoughtful about the rights and feelings of other family members shows that you are a(an) ___(10)___ person.

24

CHAPTER 2

Relationships in today's families

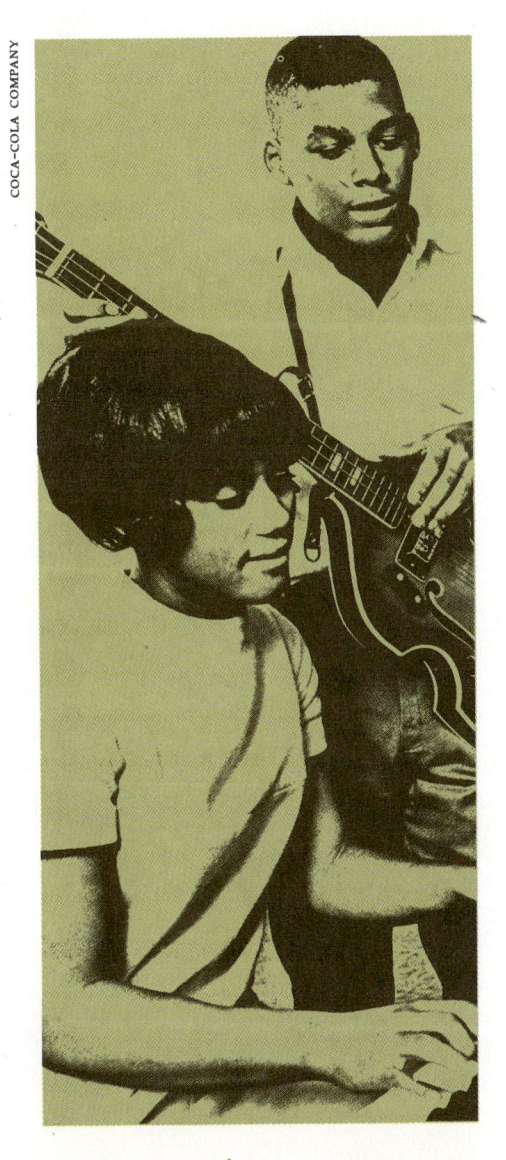

Suppose you were given the assignment of describing a typical family that might be found anywhere in the world. What would you say? Would you include a mother and a father, two or three children, maybe a dog or a cat? You need only look around your own neighborhood to see that this is just one version of a family.

If you look beyond home base to include all of the world's families, you notice that the family is the basic social unit. Every family does indeed have a core of parents and children. However, sometimes many relatives cluster around this *core family.* Aunts, uncles, and grandparents may all live as a group with the parents and their children. In some cultures, there are several wives. In others, everyone in the community is considered a relative and is treated as a sister or a brother.

Not long ago, it was common in this country to find several generations living together in a single household. Each person had a special role to play in the family, and each was necessary to the welfare of the whole group. This large household of people is called an

Make a study of the housing used in various parts of the world. You may wish to include the extended family houses of China and India, the Chinese sampan, and the homes of tribal people such as the American Indians, African pygmies, Lapps, and Eskimos. You may use pictures or specific floor plans in your study. Discuss how these forms of housing affect the daily life and family living of the people who use them.

Explain the statement, *The smallest molecule of a society is the family.*

Report on some of the organized services which are available to help families in your community.

Invite a foreign-born mother of one of your classmates or a foreign-born teacher to visit your class. Ask your guest to tell about differences in family life in the two countries.

On a map, locate the birthplace of each grandparent of every class member. Discuss how differences in the place of birth can affect an individual.

Show pictures of families in a variety of situations and circumstances. Suggest some of the values which are important to each of the families pictured. Tell how you were able to determine their values.

Write to a pen pal in another city or country. Try to learn about family life in your pen pal's part of the world. Report interesting facts to your class.

Organize sides for a debate, Pro and Con: *Families are becoming outdated.*

Pretend that you and your family are moving to another planet and will not return. Make a list of things you will do during your last 24 hours on earth. What does this show about your values?

Bulletin board IDEA
Title: *Keys to Happy Family Living*
Directions: Cut out seven keys. Label each with one of the C's of family living. Mount these around a picture of a happy-looking family.

COURTESY ARTEX HOBBY PRODUCTS, INC.

The core family includes parents and their children.

extended family. Although the extended family is still found in many parts of the world and in some parts of our country, the *core, or nuclear, family* is most common in modern America. In fact, the reason houses are much smaller today than a century ago is that the families which occupy them are also smaller.

How families differ

Think for a moment about the many different families in your community. Do you know a widower and teen-age son who live alone? Or a divorced mother and two children? Or a mother and stepfather and daughter? Or a fatherless family with eight children? None of these examples fits the common idea of the average American family. Yet they are families, many of them very happy ones. You may have become so used to the idea of both parents and their children living together that you overlook the countless combinations of related people who live together sharing common resources, customs, goals, and values. Each in its own way is functioning as a family, the basic social unit in our society.

Families are as different as the people in them. As you think about *who* lives together in a family, think also about *what* it is that draws a family together. Do resources, customs, goals, and values set your family apart from the one next door, or across the country, or around the world?

RESOURCES

Families have different groups of resources. Their incomes vary. The family with a three-thousand-dollar annual income lives quite differently from the one with a thirty-thousand-dollar annual income. Their possessions are quite different, too. Perhaps one family has inherited a great deal of furniture or dishes from grandparents who have moved to smaller quarters. Another family may not care for a great many possessions.

Families also differ in the talents and skills their members possess. Perhaps one family has members who can contribute lovely pieces of art or handmade clothing to the family's well-being. Another family may be capable of earning money with which to buy similar articles. Resources differ from family to family, but energy, skills, talents, and attitudes often contribute as much to family happiness as the dollars family members can earn.

CUSTOMS AND TRADITIONS

As long as man has maintained a home life, he has established certain traditions and customs which have helped to bind his family together and give it special meaning. For example, in pioneer western America, a passing stranger was often greeted with a warm invitation to stay for dinner. On special occasions in Russia, guests are greeted at the door with a loaf of bread and a mound of salt. The hostess offers the guests pieces of the bread, which they then dip into the salt. Her greeting is, *"Dobro pojalorat,"* which means, "Welcome with good will."

While some customs vary according to country, others depend upon the family's religious beliefs. Religion often determines such customs as the blessing said before meals, the food which is eaten, and even the family's activities.

Then there are customs which are special to the individual family, such as the ways birthdays and holidays are celebrated. Such customs might seem pointless or very serious. Perhaps you take them so for granted in your everyday life that you cannot easily call to mind just what customs you do follow. Can you, for example, think of five customs that your family has? Compare your list with those of others in the class. Are your customs a result of your nationality, the area where you live, your religious beliefs, or are they special to your family alone? Whatever your customs may be, they help to form a bond between family members.

GOALS AND VALUES

Most families have family goals. Your family may be planning to

Tell the class about a tradition or custom observed in your family. If possible, find out how it originated. Discuss the ways in which family members cooperate to preserve the tradition.

Make a report to your class about customs and traditions in another country which seem interesting or strange. Assign to one class member a report on peculiar customs and traditions observed by certain groups within the United States.

Describe interesting ways in which certain of your neighbors traditionally celebrate special occasions.

Complete sentences similar to the following:
Some women like to work outside the home because . . .
When a wife works outside the home, her husband must make adjustments such as . . .
When mothers work, children . . .
Analyze how your own values and goals influenced the way you completed each sentence.

List some of your goals. Describe how your family's values have influenced the choices of goals on your list.

Read or listen to recordings of short passages from biographies or autobiographies. List some of the values expressed. For each value listed, discuss whether it was influenced primarily by the home, friends, school, or community. Defend your decisions.

Write a paragraph describing how a certain person, experience, or event has influenced your values.

Make a list of your wishes. Rank these in order of importance. Analyze how your wishes and desires are related to your values.

Bulletin board IDEA
Title: *Focus on Families*
Directions: Find or sketch cartoons or collect pictures which suggest authoritarian, permissive, and democratic families. Discuss why each drawing or picture suggests a particular type of family life pattern. After you have discussed these illustrations, select the most interesting ones. Arrange the selected illustrations so they appear to be in a picture frame on the bulletin board.

COURTESY CLEARASIL

Time for personal development is offered to each child in most modern families.

paint several rooms of your home or to buy trundle beds so that you and a very young sister can share your bedroom with a certain degree of privacy. Or you may all be concerned about seeing to it that each child finishes school with a good education. The goals which your entire family share may involve no one else, or they may be far-reaching enough to affect others. For example, a home improvement project may affect the comfort and happiness of your family and close friends. But your family's plans to give you an education to become a teacher, nurse, or mechanic will probably be an asset to the whole community.

No two families have exactly the same goals. There may be four families in your neighborhood with the same amount of income. Yet they will probably spend their money quite differently. The Carsons might plan to spend some of their money on a summer vacation. The Wrights might decide to buy a new car. The Stines might be planning for a new baby. And the Cerniks might be saving for retirement. What makes families and individuals use money for such different purposes? How do goals give directions to a family's plans?

If you think of your goals as *where* you are going, then your values are *why* you are going that way. Values are your ideals, what you consider most important in life. By the time you started school, you had already developed a sense of right and wrong behavior by following the examples set by your family. In school and among friends, you have been exposed to many other values and may have begun to doubt some of the things you had accepted all along. You are now faced with some important decisions. You are beginning to set about the serious task of choosing the values which will guide you in all of your decision making and goal setting throughout life. Most of your values—for example, ideas about honesty, love, privacy, respect, patriotism, and responsibility—are affected by other family members. But your friends, teachers, movies, television, magazines, books, and various organizations also influence your thinking. It is the blending of your values with those of other family members which finally determines your family's set of values.

FAMILY PATTERNS

Families differ in their ideas of how to bring up children. At one time, family patterns were fairly clearcut. With changing times and changing roles of men and women, family patterns have changed, too. They reflect the changes in relationships between husbands and wives and between parents and children. Families are often classified according to the source of family authority. There are families where the father is clearly the head of the home. In others, the mother heads the home. In many societies, one or the other is the customary form of family life. In modern America, permissive and democratic families have developed.

The authoritarian family

Have you seen pictures of the typical *patriarchal*, or father-ruled, family? The father is sitting. His wife and children stand. If there are very young children, the mother may be sitting as she holds a young child for the picture. The picture leaves no doubt about who is boss. The father in this type of family makes all the family decisions. He controls the money. He, and he alone, has the last word in family affairs. Although less frequently found than in earlier centuries, some very happy modern families operate on this principle.

Another form of authoritarian family also exists. The *matriarchal*, or mother-ruled, family may seem to be different from the family just described. In general, however, the family pattern is the same except that the powers of the mother and father are reversed. It is the mother who makes the final family decision.

The permissive family

In some families, there appears to be a pattern of *everyone for himself* or *anything goes*. These are called *permissive* families. Such families are often an outgrowth of the desire to let each family member be free to make his own decisions. Studies show that in such families, if there are no rules at all, children have a hard time growing up with a positive self-concept.

The democratic family

A family often mirrors the larger society around it. Our democratic form of civil government reflects itself in a democratic form of family

Collect pictures of families in various stages of the family life cycle. Identify the stage of the family life cycle shown in each picture. Be able to defend your choices.

Role-play situations which illustrate authoritarian, permissive, and democratic families. Discuss the strengths and weaknesses of each type of family as shown by the role-playing situations.

Bulletin board IDEA
Title: *Bill of Rights for the Democratic Family*
Directions: Use appropriate pictures with the following titles:
Respect for Individuality (Illustration might show a teen-ager shopping for clothes or personal items.)
Financial Independence (Illustration might show a teen-age baby-sitter or a teen-ager doing other work for income.)
Mutual Cooperation (Illustration might show family members working together or discussing a problem.)

Describe a fictional family from a story or a TV show. Tell whether this family is authoritarian, permissive, or democratic. Explain why you classified this family as you did.

Discuss how stages in the family life cycle may overlap in some families. Give examples to illustrate your explanation. If your family is going through more than one stage of the family life cycle at this time, give some examples from your home life which are typical of two or more stages.

Describe a family you know which fits the authoritarian, permissive, or democratic pattern of family life. Be sure to protect the privacy of the family you are describing. *Do not* use real names and avoid special details which clearly define this family. As you describe the family, tell some things which illustrate why you think this family fits the pattern you have chosen.

COURTESY COCA-COLA COMPANY

The democratic family searches for outlets through which each member may develop personal talents or skills.

government. In such families, the family tries to teach its young members how to take responsibility for their actions. Ideally, this is done at the appropriate age and level of maturity for each family member. In achieving family goals, each member may offer a different talent, skill, or resource. Cooperative efforts tend to yield desired family goals. When a set of realistic rules is developed and followed, such families can be happy ones.

How families change

Once formed, a family does not always remain the same. Some

changes happen in the family itself. The membership changes through birth, growth, marriage, death, or divorce. Most changes come about as part of a series of natural events called *the family life cycle.* These changes can be expected. Understanding something about the family life cycle can help a family plan for future needs.

Family changes occur through forces outside the family. For example, the economy of the country has helped to bring about a change in the roles played by different family members.

THE FAMILY LIFE CYCLE

You may already have shared in certain important family events, such as a wedding, a baptism, a confirmation, or a bar mitzvah. A silver or golden wedding anniversary may have taken place. Such events can be expected to occur as families pass through certain stages of *the family life cycle.* In a simple way, these stages can be described as the *Young Married Stage,* the *Founding Family Stage,* the *Growing Family Stage,* the *Teen-age Stage,* the *Launching Stage,* and the *Empty-nest Stage.* Families in each stage share certain problems. As young marrieds, a couple sets up a new home. At this stage a husband and wife usually acquire the basic household furnishings and equipment they need to start a home. During this stage, both husband and wife may work. When they have their first baby, they enter the Founding Family Stage. New investments in baby clothing, equipment, and furniture are needed. With a new baby, the mother may not be able to hold a job outside the home. Also, she may want to care for her baby more than she wants outside work. If more children are born, the family enters the Growing Family Stage. This stage tends to keep both parents extremely busy. When children start to school, the household schedule usually takes on an even more hectic pattern. When

During the *Founding Family Stage* both parents are extremely busy providing for the physical and emotional needs of their child.

COURTESY THE EMKO COMPANY

Match the items in List A with those they describe in List B. Use a choice from List B only once. *Do not write in this book.*

List A: *Typical events or situations*

A Children approximately 13 to 18 years old with developing interests outside the home.
B Couple usually acquires basic household furnishings and equipment. The wife may have a job.
C Children leave home for college, work, or marriage.
D First baby is born. Couple invests in equipment needed by the baby.
E Additional children may be born and the oldest child may start to school.
F Couple prepares for retirement.

List B: *Stages in the family life cycle*

1 Young married
2 Founding family
3 Growing family
4 Teen-age
5 Launching
6 Empty nest

Find newspaper and magazine articles which support the following statements about changes in family life.
1. An increasing number of mothers are employed outside the home.
2. School-age children have poor eating habits.
3. Families are becoming smaller.
4. The number of one-parent families is increasing.
5. The amount of time spent for family recreation is increasing.
6. The number of people treated for mental illnesses is on the increase.
7. Juvenile delinquency is increasing.
8. Individuals can expect to live longer today than in the past.

Ask a working mother to talk to the class about ways in which she uses her abilities to manage two jobs.

Bulletin board IDEA
Title: *Yesterday . . . Today*
Directions: Mount pictures which show how women's roles have changed. You may include pictures which compare out-of-date equipment with this year's models.

children enter the teens, the family enters the Teen-age Stage. Your family is probably in that stage now. In the Teen-age Stage, children develop varied interests outside the home. Once children leave their parents' home for more education or to start families of their own, the Launching Stage has been reached. When all children have left home, the parents are left with an Empty Nest. Children are no longer the center of family attention. New problems and new interests concern the parents as they prepare for retirement.

Each person who marries will in his lifetime share a part in at least two cycles: that of the family he grows up in and that of the family he starts when he marries. In each stage, the family must make new adjustments. It will face new problems. It will have new standards to meet. It will set new goals. New decisions will have to be made.

Although all families pass through similar stages of the family cycle, no two go through the same stages in the same way. Some families may skip a stage, or backtrack, or even overlap stages. A childless couple, for example, will go through fewer stages than a family with children. If a couple with grown children ready to be launched has a new baby, that couple will repeat several stages. If one parent dies and the other remarries, there will be overlapping and perhaps some

backtracking in the cycle. The same is true if parents divorce and remarry.

What stage in the family life cycle has your family reached? How is life in the family different now than in the previous stage? What new needs does your family have? What adjustments need to be made?

CHANGING ROLES

To do the work of a family, parents and children form a team. Each member of the family team has a different role to perform. In many families the father provides the main financial support. The major portion of the mother's time and interest is devoted to homemaking and child care. But more and more women today combine marriage with outside employment. So men and women share many of the tasks that must be performed to keep a home running smoothly.

As a family reaches the Teen-age Stage, many of the tasks earlier performed by parents are taken over by teen-agers. Can you sense change in your family? What tasks can you now assume that were previously more than you could manage?

The Industrial Revolution has brought about profound changes in family life. Before the Industrial Revolution, more families lived on farms than in cities. A family could produce almost all of what it needed in the way of food, clothing, and shelter. In addition, families were largely responsible for educating their children. Daughters learned the role of mother-homemaker, and sons learned the role of father-husband in the home setting. Each family member, including many other relatives in the household, was important. Each had definite duties. Children were real assets because they could be put to work. In a large family there were more hands to pitch in and help.

Few families today fit this description. After the Industrial Revolution, many families left farms in search of work in towns and cities. As a result of these moves, individual families produced less for themselves. They began to depend more on outsiders to produce food, housing, and clothing. They looked to the community to provide jobs, education, and entertainment. This was the beginning of the *family consumer group.* No longer were children seen merely as extensions of the family. Children became accepted as individuals in their own right. Children no longer followed in their parents' footsteps as a matter of course. They began to select their mates for personal rather than family reasons. They began to select careers in line with their own abilities and interests.

OUTSIDE FORCES IN CHANGE
There are many outside forces that make modern families entirely different from those of other times. These changes occur at all stages of the family life cycle. Families are affected by political, economic, and social events. At best, families have only a limited control over these happenings. A declaration of war, a strike, a company move, or changed social standards all influence the quality of family life. What current events are affecting your family? Do you consider the changes minor or major?

MOBILITY
Each year one family out of every five moves. Often this means adapting to a new community and a whole new way of life. Reasons for such moves include new job opportunities, the lure of faraway places, a desire to get a new start,

Explain each of the following statements in your own words. Give an example to illustrate each explanation.
1 In this century, the family has changed from a *producing unit* to a *consuming unit.*
2 Individuals and families are becoming more mobile than in the past.
3 Male and female roles are changing and are becoming more flexible.
4 TV and radio have a great influence on families as well as on individuals.
5 The family has shifted from a rather self-sufficient unit to one which is dependent on outside community resources.

In a mobile society, successful families quickly adapt to a new environment while remembering happy experiences from the past.

COURTESY UNITED VAN LINES

Make a booklet similar to those given out by a moving company. In the booklet, give suggestions for making a move as smooth as possible. The following examples will help.
1. Explain to the children why the move is being made.
2. Let children keep some of their old toys. Perhaps they can help pack them.
3. Allow neighborhood children to play in the new home while it is being settled.
4. If the move is to a strange area, read about the new community ahead of time.
5. Obtain pictures of the new community. Picture postcards may be one source. If possible, get a picture of the new home.
6. Do as much as possible ahead of the actual moving day.

Justify your own list of suggestions, as well as those above.

Bulletin board IDEA
Title: *Family Climate—Keep It Warm*
Directions: Make the title in red letters against a bright yellow background. Add a cutout of a warm, friendly-looking sun. Place the sun so that it is smiling down on pictures of families doing things together.

COURTESY MAZOLA CORN OIL

Families who live some distance from close relatives can add to their children's security by making friends among older residents in their new neighborhood.

and climate and health factors. Since these moves usually mean leaving relatives behind, parents and children are more dependent upon one another for companionship and security and less dependent upon a large group of relatives. There is likely to be more conflict between parents and children in a mobile core family than in extended families, in which children answer to several relatives. Knowing the tendency toward conflict in a small family unit, it is important for both parents and children to develop bonds of closeness. The wise transplanted family learns to talk easily together. Often they find substitute grandparents, aunts, and cousins.

The seven c's of family living

Do you know a family that really enjoy each other? What makes their relationship so special? Family relations are improved by the seven c's of family living: cooperation, communication, confidence, concern, commitment, companionship, and consideration. The seven c's are a good key to getting along with other people, too.

COOPERATION
In family living, cooperation means that every person has a position and fulfills the duties it implies. At the same time, he respects other members of his family. Family cooperation is a two-way deal: You give a little; you take a little. Everybody benefits. You show cooperation when you arrive at meals on time, when you do your share of home duties without being reminded, and when you take other people's wants and needs as seriously as your own. To show a spirit of cooperation, you can pitch in on some of your parents' projects. Perhaps you can share in do-it-yourself home improvements or neighborhood charity drives. You can volunteer to help with your brother's homework or to repair your sister's toy. You can stay out of the way when older brothers

Family cooperation implies that each member will pull his share of the load in projects planned by the family.

COURTESY DUTCH BOY PAINTS

and sisters entertain. You can give in without sulking when you are overruled in a family decision. If you are willing to cooperate with other family members, you can expect to find them cooperating more with you.

COMMUNICATION
In a healthy family atmosphere, the channels of communications are always open. Two-way communication helps a family avoid misunderstandings and hurt feelings. Instead of tuning out his parents when they discuss a subject he would prefer they ignore, the fair-minded teen-ager listens. He may not always agree, but communications fail unless everyone, including parents, has the right to be heard. If you ask for help when you need it, your family may be more likely to save words of advice for those times.

Some families keep communication lines open by setting aside a special time when everyone can get together to exchange ideas and contribute to decision making. Other families get together casually as problems come up. However they go about it, a family needs to get problems out in the open. When

Make a list of basic rules for girls and boys your age which you think could be reasonably established by parents. Discuss the reasons why rules are different in different homes. Discuss mature ways in which teen-agers may try to change rules if they think they are unfair.

Discuss *I didn't ask to be born* as an attitude affecting family life.

Spend five minutes making a list of things your parents do for you and a list of things you do for your parents. Which list is longer? Why?

Discuss the possible reasons why parents or friends make unfair comparisons between children.

Tell about special occasions which you have particularly enjoyed with your family. Analyze the reasons why these were especially enjoyable experiences.

Prepare a brief report which describes the family life of a family in a book you have read. Tell whether you would like to be a member of this family. Give reasons to support your choice.

SCRAMBLE GAME

Unscramble the seven C's of family living, one letter to each square. *Do not* write in this book.

C T O O O R P I E N A

T I O O N A N S I D C E R

M M O O N N C C I I U T A

E C N E D I F N O C

C I I P P N N O O A H S M

R O N C C E N

T M M M E N C I O T

Now arrange the shaded letters to form another word which begins with C. This word tells of something you and your family have if you have seven other C's.

The Seven C's of Family Living are found on pages 34 through 37.

Communication is easy when family members are interested in each other's activities.

COURTESY HOOVER

a decision affects the whole family, a democratic family tries to find ways to consider each member's needs. Can you remember a time when you found yourself willing to go along with a decision simply because you had a part in making it?

CONFIDENCE

The confidence other members of the family have in you grows as you show that you are honest, trustworthy, and dependable. Be truthful. Actually, telling the truth is easier than lying since one lie starts a chain reaction. It's hard to remember a lie and to make a group of lies consistent and logical. Once you have been caught in a lie, part of the confidence others have placed in you is lost.

Learn to keep family secrets. You show maturity when you respect family privacy. Learn to distinguish between what is and what is not private family business. Perhaps you have laughed at the embarrassing stories young children tell about their families. But part of growing up is realizing what is better left unsaid to people outside the family. Why confide family problems to friends when this practice causes hurts that are hard to heal? When you need to confide in someone outside your family, turn to a professionally trained counselor. The counselor may be a minister, social worker, school counselor, or youth-group leader. Such a person can be trusted to treat your family problems confidentially.

CONCERN

The concern which family members show for one another is an indication of the strength of a family. Often there isn't much you can do in a physical way to help when troubles arise within the family group. But the way you show your willingness to understand when the going gets rough for any family member is a mark of your value as a family member.

Perhaps there is a bully on the street who has convinced your

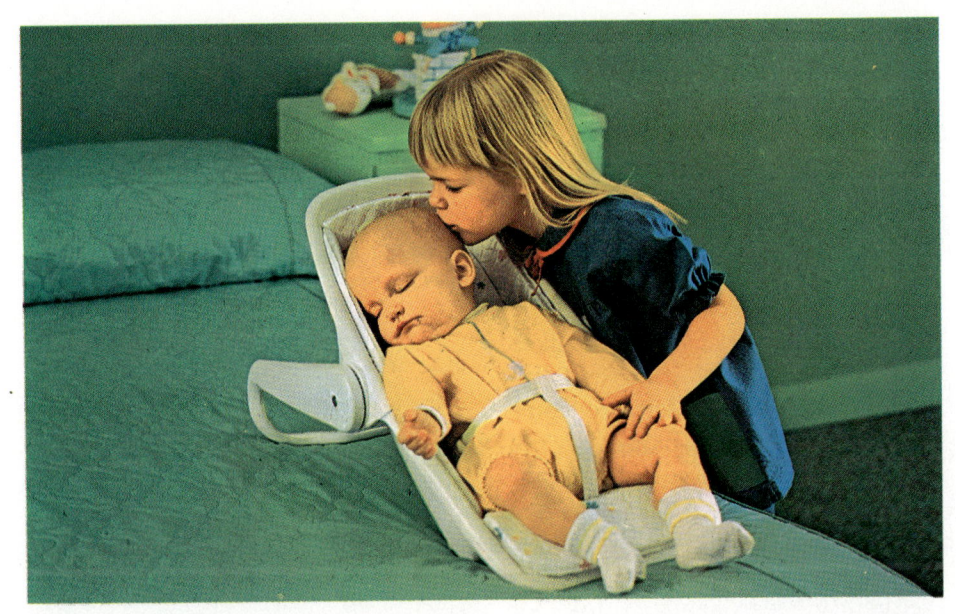

Concern for other family members can be learned very early in life.

five-year-old brother that a step outside the front door means certain death. Perhaps your older sister has broken an engagement after wedding gifts have arrived. Perhaps your father finds that his new boss is almost impossible to work for, or your mother is grieving over the loss of her parents. Maybe your brother can't find summer work or failed to pass his exam for a driver's license. Any member of a family may from time to time find that his load is too heavy to bear alone. At such times it is the loving concern shown by other family members which makes each one feel that he is a worthwhile part of the family.

COMMITMENT

Commitment is the acceptance of a charge, or trust. In family life this means the acceptance of lifetime concern for other family members. It means acceptance of all the burdens and joys which come to the family.

Parents generally understand that commitment is necessary for happy family living. Perhaps some parents are at fault when, in their efforts to make life happy for their children, they try to hide the difficult periods through which the family must pass. In general, all children, and particularly teen-agers, want to know the facts when problems

Suggest some of the reasons why parents worry about their teen-age children. Suggest ways in which teenagers can help their parents overcome these worries.

List as many ways as possible to get along well with others. To help you begin, think of a person with whom you would especially like to get along better.

Suggest ways in which you can show your parents and your brothers and sisters that you care about them. Discuss the ways in which parents express affections toward their children. Discuss the reasons for the many differences in the way people show they care about others.

List five things which give you the greatest happiness in your home. List three things which cause you the most worry. *Do not* sign your list. Combine the lists of all the class members. Discuss the most frequently mentioned items. Make suggestions for lessening the causes of worry.

37

Make a list of suggestions for getting along well with your parents. Include items such as these:

Try to put yourself in the place of your parents and to understand their point of view in home situations.

Express affection for your parents, and let them see that you mean it.

Show pride in your parents in front of your friends. Do your share of the work around the home.

Do your best with the educational opportunities your parents give you.

Be loyal and honest in family matters.

Tell your parents about your experiences in school or social life, and show interest in their hobbies and activities.

Ask your parents to join you in some of your activities.

Extend to your parents the same courtesies you would to people outside the family.

Ask your parents to let you share in decisions on such matters as the hours you keep and how you spend your time and money. Then follow the decisions and be willing to tell your parents what your plans are.

beset their family. If money is short, if there is a possible move to a distant city, if one of their parents is seriously ill, or if there is an unexpected financial setback, they deserve to know. Most teen-agers are understanding and want to help in such times.

There is no room in a happy family for a *loner*. Everybody likes to feel independent to an extent. But in family groups which are committed to the well-being of the family, everyone pulls together during life's stormy seasons.

COMPANIONSHIP
Frequently teen-agers think of companionship as the pairing off of two people into a friendship arrangement. They see their parents as companions and feel they must look beyond the family circle for companionship. Of course, in one way this is right. Teen-agers often must look beyond home base for teen-age companions. Certainly in the search for a lifetime marriage partner, many friendships outside the home are usually desirable.

There is a companionship within the home, however, which members of happy families experience. Can you remember a confidential talk you had with your mother as the two of you worked to get the evening meal on the table? Do you remember a giggling party one night, long after your parents were asleep, when your older sister ex-

COURTESY ALBERTO-CULVER COMPANY

Consideration can be shown through careful attention to correspondence when you are away from home.

plained to you some of the facts of teen-age growth which were bothering you? Do you remember comforting your father simply by being there and understanding while your mother was desperately ill? Perhaps you remember quietly listening while your lonely divorced mother told you some of the background of your family's problems. Do you remember teaming with your little brother and promising to plead for a puppy he wanted very badly?

Certainly there is companionship in family life. And the family which excludes children from this form of companionship misses a great deal of the happiness family life can bring.

CONSIDERATION

Consideration, as applied to family living, simply means that family members are thoughtful of the rights and feelings of others. Perhaps if there is one place where teen-agers as a group fall down in their contribution to family living, it is in consideration. And probably this failing is caused by thoughtlessness. Most teen-agers do not intend to be inconsiderate.

Have you ever behaved in any of the following ways? Your parents have been planning a big night for months, and you have agreed to stay at home with a young brother or sister. At the last moment you get a chance to go to a very special event. You do stay at home as agreed, but you make things so miserable that your parents' evening is ruined.

Perhaps this has happened to you: You get a chance to be cheer leader and find the cost of a uniform and transportation to the games may be well over a hundred dollars, money your family doesn't have. You find yourself making your parents miserable by crying far into the night over your personal disappointment, never thinking that they may feel as badly as you over your heartbreak.

Has this ever happened to you? Your brother refuses to hear alarm clocks. He oversleeps and misses his bus to school or to work. He gets in trouble, and you tell him that it serves him right.

Do you see yourself in any of these situations? Certainly not, if you are doing your part to help make yours a happy family. The considerate person is able to sympathize with others who are in trouble, but his concern is even deeper than sympathy. He has *empathy*. This means that he can understand how other family members feel. Such consideration, when practiced, contributes to family happiness now. Too, it gives each child within the family a good springboard from which to bound successfully into the uneven stream of life.

Make a list of typical problems teen-agers have with their parents and other members of their families. Role-play typical situations in class. Offer solutions for the problems brought out in the role playing.

Display pictures showing various family situations where members seem happy, unhappy, angry, fearful, anxious, etc. Suggest possible reasons for these emotions.

Role-play some of the following situations, trying to work out solutions to family problems:

1 Grandmother is critical of the way granddaughter dresses.
2 Great-aunt Mary lives with her daughter, son-in-law, and grandchildren. She has little to do with her time.
3 Grandfather goes to bed at nine o'clock and objects to the noise made by his teen-age grandchildren.

2 CHAPTER POSTTEST

Match the *descriptions* given in List A with the *types of families* given in List B. Use a family type from List B only once. *Do not* write in this book.

List A: Descriptions

A A large household of people with several generations living together
B A family made up only of parents and their children
C A family in which almost anything is allowed and in which there are few rules
D The mother rules and makes the major family decisions
E The father rules and is the final authority
F Family members cooperate in making decisions, and each individual family member is expected to be responsible for his actions.

List B: Types of families

1 Core
2 Democratic
3 Extended
4 Matriarchal
5 Patriarchal
6 Permissive

Complete the crossword puzzle using the seven C's of family living. On a separate sheet of paper, fill in the spaces numbered ACROSS 1 and 6 and the spaces numbered DOWN 1, 2, 3, 4, and 5.

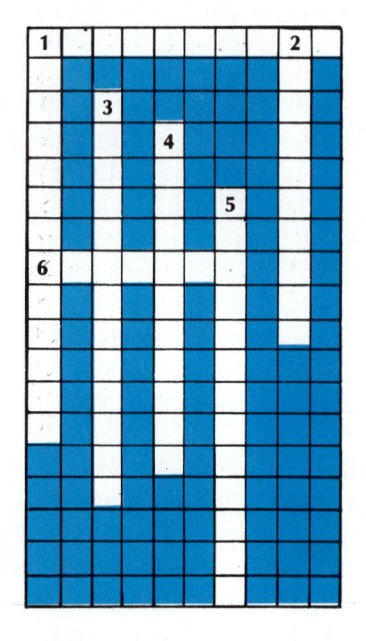

ACROSS

1 Involves being able to keep a secret so that people trust you.
6 Involves your interest in and care for other people.

DOWN

1 Involves listening and getting problems out in the open.
2 Involves the acceptance of a lifetime of family togetherness during periods of joy and sorrow.
3 Involves the enjoyment which comes from the company of other family members.
4 Involves give-and-take and doing your share of work.
5 Involves being thoughtful of the rights and feelings of others.

3 CHAPTER PRETEST

Fill in the blank in each sentence with the *best* word to complete the statement. *Do not* use a word which already appears in the sentence. *Do not* write in this book.

1 The way in which you view yourself is called your ___(1)___.
2 The period during which a child matures into an adult, normally occurring during the teen-age years, is called ___(2)___.
3 Basic human needs are divided into physical, emotional, social, and ___(3)___ needs.
4 As a person matures and grows away from his family circle, he is gaining ___(4)___.
5 Measles and mumps are examples of ___(5)___ diseases.
6 The shape and contour of your face, eyes, nose, ears, and mouth are examples of ___(6)___ characteristics.
7 A person who is able to adjust and adapt to his environment as it actually exists, rather than as he wishes it would be, is said to be ___(7)___.
8 The three basic emotions are love, fear, and ___(8)___.
9 Inborn abilities in mechanics, mathematics, or foreign languages are called ___(9)___.
10 An inborn ability which is highly developed through training and practice is called a(an) ___(10)___.

CHAPTER 3

Your self-concept

Each person sees himself in his own way. Your view of yourself is called your *self-concept*. This self-concept has developed from the time you were born. It is at the center of your personality. It influences everything you think and say and do. All of your traits are, in a sense, screened through your self-concept before other people see them. Your attitude toward yourself is reflected by it. A strong self-concept shows confidence in yourself and your abilities. A weak self-concept makes it hard to become the best person you can become. When you understand this, you can take steps to strengthen your personality.

An ideal home is one where each person is accepted as he *is* and for *what* he is. A feeling of acceptance is important in the building of a healthy self-concept. When a person feels rejected, he is likely to feel uneasy and unhappy. If he does not receive emotional support at home, he must look elsewhere for help and guidance. Often he can find this help in school or club activities. Adults involved in providing these activities are interested in helping young people become secure and self-accepting.

Describe someone you know who seems to have a strong self-concept without being conceited. Keeping his or her name a secret, list the personality traits which this person possesses.

Describe someone you know who seems to have a weak self-concept. List the personality traits which this person possesses.

Compare the traits in these two lists which affect the relationships these two people have with others. Which person seems to get along better with other people? Give reasons why you think this is true.

Draw cartoons or collect pictures to illustrate *Adolescence is . . .* For example:

Adolescence is when you laugh at a joke, even if you do not understand it.

Adolescence is when your date isn't ready and you are forced to visit with her parents whom you have never met.

Draw stick figures, sketch cartoons, or make a chart showing the types of love different people experience in a lifetime. Begin with the self-love of the infant which grows into love for parents. Show how love usually broadens to include a country, friends, a marriage partner, and a family.

What is a teen-ager?

The Industrial Revolution, which ushered in the age of machines, changed the way man lived. Prior to this time, no emphasis was placed on the teen years. Young people went from childhood to adulthood with very little fuss. They simply went to work. Children as young as six years old frequently labored long hours on farms or in factories.

Cruel child-labor practices were among the first abuses of children to be corrected by law. Increased production with machinery made it possible for goods to be produced by a smaller number of workers. As a result, laws were enacted which gave children time to develop into healthy adults. This growing time allowed a group to develop who are known as *teen-agers*. This group of people are often called *adolescents*. Adolescence is defined as the period of life during which a child matures into an adult.

Basic human needs

As a human being, you share certain basic needs with other people. These include needs which are physical, emotional, mental, and social by nature. The things a man needs are provided by his *environment*. Since your environment consists of all the people, places, things, and events around you, it is these surroundings which must provide your needs.

PHYSICAL NEEDS

To stay alive, you need a steady supply of air and water. For life to continue, you need food, shelter, sleep and rest, and space in which to move. The more adequately these needs are met, the more easily the *real* you, the person within your body, can develop the special qualities of an individual person.

In a social situation, teen-agers are offered opportunities for recreation while learning how to get along with one another.

COURTESY MIDOL

In a simpler time, man could perhaps turn to nature's abundance and survive. Today he must plan, work, and cooperate with others to get from his environment the things he needs in order to live.

EMOTIONAL, MENTAL, AND SOCIAL NEEDS

Have you heard the saying that man cannot live by bread alone? This means that, for man to find life rewarding, his whole being must be fed as well as his stomach. Needs are similar in all human beings. They can be met, however, in different ways. If a person's basic needs are not met to some degree, his life is hardly worth living. For example, babies who are cared for physically, but who receive no love (emotional care), are slow to develop. They have very little desire to learn. Their will to live is related to how well their emotional needs are met. Mental and social growth also depend on the attention a person receives.

Man has many needs. Some are simply physical. Most needs, however, are combined ones. When met, they help him grow emotionally, mentally, and socially into a complete person.

Love

Much has been said about the need for love. Yet love means different things to different people at different times in each of their lives. With proper care and guidance, a person grows in his ability to love in much the same way he grows in size and weight. To a helpless baby, love means prompt attention to his needs. Love is shown in the way he is held and cared for. Even a small baby knows when he is wanted. Through love, he develops his sense of trust. Kind attention tells him that he is worthwhile. It helps prepare him for social growth and learning. Without love, he cannot

Describe the different types of love most people experience in a lifetime. Look up *love* in the dictionary to find its many meanings.

Make a transparency by drawing on an acetate sheet a series of circles, each surrounding the one before. Label each circle to show how love can grow and broaden.

Social growth is evident when teen-agers can enjoy working together toward a worthwhile goal.

COURTESY MIDOL

43

Write a paragraph concerning someone you know which shows that he or she is not growing up emotionally.

Tell about an incident in which you know that you did not act your age.

Discuss ways in which a person's emotions might affect his physical growth.

Present short skits to show childish behavior in teen-agers.

Discuss the following questions:
1. What TV programs do you now enjoy that you did not enjoy when you were younger? Why?
2. Which TV programs do you no longer enjoy that you did at one time? Why?

Discuss how your taste for food has changed as you have grown older.

List the event which you consider the most important during each of the last five years. Tell why each event was important to you.

form the framework into which the pieces of his personality must fit.

The young child needs love, too. So do teen-agers. And how about your parents? Do people outgrow their need for love?

Acceptance

To know that someone accepts you as you are is necessary for good emotional health. Some people are hard to love. But you can accept them for what they are. Every person needs to feel he is a member of the human race. He may be different and his ideas may seem strange. Even so, he needs friends and associates who accept him as a person.

Appreciation

Each person needs to feel that he has done something on his own. He needs to feel that what he has done is appreciated. Unless he feels that his efforts bring some rewards, he will soon give up trying. Rewards can come in such forms as money, praise, good grades, and prizes. In whatever form, their importance to the individual is that the rewards strengthen his personality and stimulate his will to try.

Security

For a person to make the most of himself, he must feel safe and secure. He needs to feel that the things and people important to him will be there when he needs them. If they are not, he will feel afraid. Fear that causes a person to stop trying will make it hard for him to grow into a healthy, well-adjusted person.

Variety

Human beings are naturally curious. They are quickly bored. They need to experience variety, or change. This need can be met through creative work. It can also be met through the imaginative use of leisure time. It can be expressed in the choice of food, clothing, and housing.

Independence

To become truly grown up, a person must gain a degree of independence. Achieving independence is a gradual process of separating what is *you* from what is *your family*. You gain independence from your family little by little. From childhood on, you have been allowed to do certain things on your own, to go places without your family, and to make some of your own decisions. As you enter your teens, you are even more concerned about stepping up that move toward independence.

An independent person can provide for himself the things that others once provided for him. To achieve independence, he must recognize his basic needs and find socially acceptable ways to meet them. Among the things he must acquire for himself are food, clothing, and shelter. These basic necessities are not free. Work must be performed. Someone has had to work to provide these necessities in the past. As a teen-ager takes over work which was earlier done by others, he moves another step toward independence.

Do you want total independence? Since each person must depend on his environment for survival, he can never be completely independent. Nor is total independence desirable. Perhaps the goal of teen-agers should be eventual economic independence. Since a person never outgrows his need for love, total emotional independence may never come.

Meaningful communication
As people mature, they ask themselves questions about life and its various meanings. They need to feel that there is more to life than mere existence. They feel a need to share their thoughts with others and learn what others think. This sharing of thoughts and accepting of new ideas is a part of the growth pattern of the teen-ager as he reaches toward maturity.

Individual differences

In 1830 there were 1 billion people in the whole world. By 1930 there were 2 billion. By 1960 there were 3 billion. During 1970 the world's population grew to some 3½ billion persons. At this rate, by the time you are a parent of teen-agers around the year 2000, there will be 7 billion people in the world. Yet with billions of people on the earth, there is something special about each person. Of the 3½ billion people in the world today, the over 200 million in the United States, and the millions or thousands of people in your state or city, there is only one *you*. You are one of many in your school. You are one of perhaps twenty or thirty in your classroom. You are one of several people in your family. Out of all these people, you are an individual, one of a kind.

COURTESY MODESS

A degree of independence can be gained by developing salable job skills.

Suggest ways, in addition to those given below, in which you can show your parents that you are growing up and can assume responsibility.
1 Clean up your home after you and your friends have had fun.
2 Return home when your parents expect you. If the time that you are expected home seems unreasonably early, talk things over with your parents. Perhaps a compromise can be made, but once an appointed time is set, keep the schedule.
3 Have a good time entertaining your friends at home without disturbing your family or the neighbors with too much noise.

Bulletin board IDEA
Title: *Little Things Can Mean So Much*
Directions: Mount pictures which depict the tenderness a mother shows her baby, the affection family members feel for each other, the gift a child has made, or any other ideas which are appropriate.

COURTESY KIMBERLY CLARK CORPORATION

COURTESY SIMPLICITY PATTERN CO., INC.

Discuss the relationship between a teen-ager's growing independence from his family and his responsibility toward his family. Divide a sheet of paper into two columns. In the left-hand column list the kinds of independence you would like to have. In the right-hand column list the responsibilities which you should assume for each type of independence gained. For example . . .

Choose my own clothes	Keep clothing costs within the family budget
	Buy clothes which can be used with others already in my wardrobe
	Consider quality and care when buying

Bulletin board IDEA
Title: *From Tiny Acorns*
Directions: Make a large tree from poster or construction paper. On the paper acorns which are hanging from branches and lying on the ground write such words as friends, acceptance, responsibility, independence—results of emotional maturity.

COURTESY COCA-COLA COMPANY

A person's self-concept grows as he understands the reactions of others to his ideas.

The sum of all the things that make you an individual is called your personality. Many of the characteristics that you possess were inherited from your parents. They were passed along to you at birth. They are called *inherited characteristics*. You developed others as you grew up. They are called *acquired characteristics*. You can acquire new characteristics as long as you live. The wise person tries to acquire those characteristics which will make him a more useful, happier person.

People have much in common, but it is their differences that cause them to be individuals. Even identical twins do not have the same acquired characteristics. Knowing how people differ from one another will help you to understand them better.

PHYSICAL MAKEUP

Every boy and girl inherits certain traits from parents, grandparents, and even more distant ancestors. Carried in the sex cells, these characteristics set down certain lines of development for each person. While these traits may be influenced by the environment, they can never be completely changed. From babyhood on, however, a person's development depends on the food, housing, and care he receives. Thus, environment and heredity combine to create an individual with special characteristics. For example, heredity determines that your body can grow only so tall. But you need proper food, rest, and exercise if you are to reach that height.

Body build and muscle shapes
Your body shape—height and breadth—is determined by both your bone structure and your muscular development. Barring illness, accident, or injury, you will grow according to a pattern set by heredity.

Heredity controls the growth and shape of your bones and muscles. It also determines where fat will be deposited. This is why certain body types seem to run in families. Proper nutrition can influence weight. Exercise can change appearance by providing muscle tone and by trimming excess fat. Even though all these conditions affect it, your body is still shaped by inherited traits. You will only grow to the height determined by heredity. Your bone shapes were determined before your birth.

Each person is a unique combination of traits he inherits from his parents and traits he acquires from the people and events which surround him.

COURTESY THE GREYHOUND CORPORATION

Give an example which illustrates your understanding of each of the following types of maturity:
1 Chronological: *how old a person is in months and years*
2 Physical: *how developed a person's body is*
3 Intellectual: *how grown-up a person is in his thinking*
4 Emotional: *how grown-up a person is in the way he expresses his feelings*
5 Social: *how well a person gets along with others*
List characteristics for each type of maturity listed above.

Describe a person who is mature in one way but immature in other ways. For example, describe a person who is . . .
1 Intellectually mature and socially immature
2 Chronologically mature and emotionally immature
3 Socially mature and physically immature

Defend the statement: *Some teen-agers are not really adolescents.*

Classify the following characteristics as being *primarily* inherited or *primarily* acquired:
Your values
Your sex (male or female)
Your physical resemblance to ancestors
Your fears and anxieties
Your manner of speech
Your eye color
Your eating habits
Your ability to get along with others
Your color-blindness or lack of it
Your skill in sewing
Your mental capacity
Your potential height

Make a general statement about the effect inherited and acquired characteristics have on the total development of a person.

Make a report to your class on current articles which deal with the following subjects:
1 Pro and Con: Left-handedness is an inherited characteristic.
2 Pro and Con: Genius is an inherited characteristic.

Strength and endurance
Strength depends on the development and coordination of muscles. In the teens, coordination may be hard to establish for a time because of different rates of growth for different parts of the body. Some people who develop good coordination of the large muscles may make good athletes. Other people develop good coordination of small muscles. They may become skilled at working with tools or at playing some musical instrument.

Endurance, as thought of in relation to good health, is the ability to withstand fatigue. If good health continues, this is a quality that improves with practice. Physical endurance is particularly important during the teens.

Even though teen-agers seem to have boundless energy, they are subject to considerable physical stress. A schedule which includes school, recreation, sports, and sometimes work is a heavy one. But teen-agers like to keep busy. In their search for useful activities, many are turning their talents toward social services, such as volunteer hospital work and reading and play clinics in densely settled housing areas. However, when young people participate in so many activities, they need to take certain precautions to prevent physical stress. Energy must be continually renewed through good food, exercise, and sleep and rest.

Allergies
The body of each human being is made up of a cell combination unlike that of any other person. Because of this difference, each person reacts differently to his environment. The person who is extremely sensitive to substances in the environment is said to be *allergic* to them.

Although any person may be allergic to a specific substance, allergies tend to run in families. They are still another of your possible inherited traits. Allergies may be suspected if sneezing, hives, stomach upsets, watery eyes, or other symptoms of discomfort occur when you come in contact with certain substances.

Allergies are among the most difficult to identify of all personal discomforts. It may take a long series of tests by a doctor to find the cause of these symptoms. Often a person can make a correct guess at what causes allergic reactions just by observation. Such guesses may be verified by a doctor's tests. Awareness of the symptoms and causes of allergy can cut down unnecessary discomfort.

Inherited and contracted diseases
Most people have some physical flaws, or handicaps. The seriousness of such a handicap depends to some degree upon the individual's attitude toward it. Minor handicaps are generally handicaps only to the ex-

tent that a person allows them to be. Of course, there are cases where babies are born with defects which require immediate attention. Otherwise, such children may be hampered in living happy, productive lives.

For the most part, with the help of modern science, people can learn to live with diseases. This is true of both inherited and contracted diseases. For example, there is medicine to control diabetes, for which some people inherit a tendency. There is medicine to control tuberculosis, a contracted disease. Childhood diseases can generally be handled with preventive inoculations.

Appearance
A person's general appearance is a combination of inherited and acquired characteristics. Facial features and the color of skin, hair, and eyes are all controlled by inheritance. However, the overall attractiveness of a person's appearance is controlled through acquired habits of health and grooming.

MENTAL MAKEUP
The human brain is a mass of nerve cells. Its complexity may never be fully understood. It is known, however, that the brain is the center of human thought. The brain makes it possible to learn from experience. Your mental capacity contributes much to determining the kind of person you are. Learning ability, talents, skills, and attitudes are all the product of the brain. Some mental qualities are inherited. Others are acquired. The goal of the wise teen-ager is to combine his inherited mental powers with those he can acquire for favorable mental growth.

Intelligence
The ability to learn is called *intelligence*. Each person is different from others in his mental ability. However, no one develops his brain to capacity. In most any person you might think of, there is still room for mental growth.

COURTESY SIMPLICITY PATTERN CO. INC.

The person who feels accepted tends to develop a healthy self-concept and a good personality.

Give examples to illustrate ways that the following qualities might be learned from a person's parents:
Loyalty
Honesty
Self-respect
Sportsmanship
Tolerance
Orderliness
Dependability
Courtesy
Unselfishness
Cheerfulness
Consideration for others
Promptness
Friendliness
Tactfulness

Choose one of the above traits and list all the possible ways you can think of to develop it. Through a class discussion, add your ideas to those of your classmates.

Take part in a brief panel discussion on the topic *What are the advantages of growing up in a large (or small) family?*

Discuss the ways in which a person's height, weight, body build, or a particular physical characteristic might affect his happiness or his success in life.

Determine one special ability or talent of each of the students in your class. Discuss ways in which these abilities or talents might be used for class, school, home, or community projects.

Determine one of your best characteristics which makes you a unique individual, unlike anyone else. Make a sketch, drawing, or cartoon which illustrates this point about yourself.

List and explain in your own words the steps toward achieving maturity.

Distinguish between abilities, talents, and skills.

List several ways in which you were dependent on your family two years ago but are now quite independent. Discuss the reasons why you have been able to assume greater independence in these areas.

Answer these questions to determine your own mental, emotional, and social growth:
1 Are you working in school to the best of your ability?
2 Are you able to control your emotions?
3 Do you work well with other people?
4 Do you have many friends?

There are different learning areas. Not everyone is good in math. Not everyone has a good memory. Not everyone can see space relations in the same way. People vary in the learning areas in which they are strongest and weakest. That is why each person's ability to learn is special. The quality of your brain power is inherited. But how much brain power you will develop is up to you. In what areas can you develop more effectively?

Aptitudes and talents
An inborn ability is called an *aptitude*. People have different aptitudes. Some people have mechanical aptitudes. They work well with engines and machines. Some are able to solve math problems easily. They have a mathematical aptitude. Some people have a way with words or languages. They are said to have a verbal aptitude.

There are tests to help identify aptitudes. If you learn what you can expect to do well, you will be better able to make sound decisions in your choice of education or job.

A marked aptitude is called a *talent*. Some people have an ear for music or an eye for color. They are fortunate to have been born with this special talent.

Most talents are developed through training and practice. It is important to identify your talents early so that they can be developed while you have time for learning.

Skills
Modern living involves learning many skills. Skills are perfected by practice. People can develop skill even when they have neither an aptitude nor a talent. It may take a great deal of effort, but a skill can be developed. Learning a salable skill in the teens can help prepare for economic independence. Combining a talent and a skill can result in outstanding achievements.

EMOTIONAL MAKEUP
Notice the many types of people among your friends and schoolmates. Some are happy-go-lucky. Some always seem to be worried. Some are kind and generous. Some are critical and hard to please. These people are different in their emotional makeup. How did they get this way?

A number of causes and effects build any given personality. People are born different. Too, the basic needs for physical, mental, and emotional attention have been well met for some people, while others are less fortunate. Since the emotional makeup is caused by the interaction of heredity and environment, a stable emotional makeup is caused by a good mixture of the two.

An attitude is a learned way of looking at things, people, and actions. Each person has a special set of attitudes toward himself, people, customs, and events. Your likes and

A person's self-confidence is shown in his ability to form lasting friendships.

dislikes reveal your attitudes. You learn these attitudes from your family and friends.

Most of your actions are based on your attitudes. Positive attitudes which show self-confidence will be a great help when you are trying to make decisions. On the other hand, negative attitudes often reflect fear, or insecurity. The fear of failure brought on by negative attitudes may make it hard for you to make good decisions or to get along well with other people.

Most feelings can be regarded as some form or some combination of the three basic emotions: love, anger, and fear. Each basic emotion has its place in human life. Love can make you tolerant and understanding. Anger can make you go out and strive to overcome obstacles. Fear can help you avoid danger. No one needs to be ashamed of how he feels. But each person is responsible to himself and to others for how he expresses his feelings. During the teens, you will need to increase your ability to deal with your feelings in socially acceptable ways.

When a person is frustrated in his basic need for love and acceptance, he may feel angry at everyone and everything. This kind of anger is called *hostility*. He is angry at others

Write an autobiography. Describe the earliest recollections you have of your family, your friends, and your home. Try to include as many experiences as you can that may have affected you as a person.

From the experience of class members who have lived elsewhere, compare the recreational opportunities in various communities and in the place where you now live. Compile separate lists of the advantages your community offers for the physical, mental, social, and moral growth of its youth.

Make a research project centering around movie or TV personalities who have capitalized on a physical characteristic which could have been considered a handicap.

Make a report on individuals who have made great achievements in spite of difficult problems. Franklin Roosevelt, Abraham Lincoln, and Helen Keller are a few examples. Why were these people able to overcome their obstacles?

Suggest ways, in addition to those given below, in which you can help your parents know your friends.
1. Have your friends come to your home for various occasions—a regular family meal, a picnic supper in the park, or an informal party.
2. Ask your parents to attend an event at school at which some of your friends will be present.
3. Ask your parents to provide transportation to an out-of-town athletic activity.
4. Tell your parents about interesting activities and plans your friends may have.
5. Discuss with your parents the problems you are having with a certain friend.
6. Explain to your parents why you and your friends do certain things. For example, you might explain that when you dress differently from others you feel that you don't fit into your group.

Bulletin board IDEA
Title: *Trapped?*
Directions: Use a toy mouse and a mouse trap. Underneath write: *Make the Most of Your Opportunities.*

because he is angry with himself. When he strengthens himself through his own efforts, these feelings are usually reduced. Often doing something well makes a person feel less hostile, or even happy, toward himself. Can you think of possible accomplishments which would improve a teen-ager's self-concept?

A person who is afraid that he is not getting the love he needs experiences *jealousy*. Jealousy, a hard emotion to deal with, is frequently found between brothers and sisters within a family. A jealous person is his own worst enemy. He must convince himself that he is a worthwhile person.

Teen-agers experience many new emotions foreign to childhood. Moods of loneliness or sadness, followed by periods of extreme happiness, are all a part of growing up. But it is sometimes difficult to cope with the ups-and-downs of adolescence. This is especially so if one can remember the long smooth-running years of a happy childhood.

Teen-age independence often causes a good deal of emotional stress. For example, you may feel extremely happy with the independence gained from money earned by working. But the lost security of leaning on your parents for the money needed may tug at you, removing much of the joy independence brings. Your wish to make many friends may conflict with your desire for a steady date. Your desire for good grades may conflict with your wish to be popular.

Very few teen-agers are strong enough to go it alone at such times. When emotional stresses occur, you may need someone with whom to talk over your problems. There are many professional people who are able to help you cope with emotional stress. In addition to your parents and family, it is often wise to talk with a trusted clergyman, social worker, or guidance counselor.

Steps toward achieving maturity

Becoming a mature person takes time and effort on your part. Maturity is achieved gradually, over a long period of time. To be sure, people share basic needs, but they want different things. Each has his own special emotional makeup. People differ in how soon and how well their wants and needs can be met. Each must learn to make good choices, choices which will satisfy his needs and wants in socially acceptable ways.

MAKING DECISIONS

Sooner than you might want to believe, you and others like you will be making some of the world's major decisions. The know-how you gain early in making simple decisions will help you to make those bigger decisions wisely. For example, at this time you can make some decisions about friends, food, clothing, school, money, and behavior. These decisions will all have a bearing on your life and also on the lives of other people. To make the most of your teen years, you will want to better understand yourself and others. Understanding is a first step to making wise decisions.

Separating wants from needs
You understand that each person has basic *needs.* But you know that people not only need but also *want* certain things, too. Perhaps the wanted object is a car, a record, or a piece of clothing. No one can have everything he wants. Many wants are created by advertising and by pressure from other people. You must learn how to separate these wants from *real needs.*

IDENTIFYING YOUR VALUES
The things near and dear to you are the things you value. Some people value success, while others value popularity, loyalty, sincerity, or generosity. Many value independence and freedom. No one is born with a set of values. He acquires it through learning. Values are learned from parents, family, religious group, friends, and teachers. Values may also be learned from movies, TV, magazines, and books. They help you decide just how important something is to you. A sound set of values is a great help in guiding your life. Your values can change as you gain in experience and wisdom. It is probable, however, that some of the values you learned early in life will be with you always. What values are guiding your life today? What values would you expect to guide you in the future?

CHOOSING YOUR GOALS
A *goal* is something in the future toward which a person is willing to

COURTESY ST. LOUIS DISTRICT DAIRY COUNCIL

Most teen-agers are able to translate the facts they understand into wise decisions when choices are to be made.

Display in class a bar of soap, a dollar bill, a bunch of carrots, a new dress, a living room lamp, and a rug. Write down the name of the item you would choose if only one could be taken. In short phrases or sentences tell why particular items were chosen. Summarize the results by finding which items were chosen most and least frequently. What might you learn about people from the choices which they made?

Pretend that you are stranded on an isolated island. What are the things that you wish you had done before this happened? What do your thoughts tell you about your values and goals?

Bulletin board IDEA
Title: *Is Your Personality in Full Bloom?*
Directions: Use flowers made from tissue paper or cut from construction paper. In the centers of the flowers write:
   Sense of humor
   Understanding
   Reliability
   Consideration
   Cheerfulness
   Trustworthiness

Read the following incidents and decide what you would do in each situation. Discuss the values which influenced your decision in each case.

You are a student assistant in the school office. The secretary has given you a final examination to proofread and duplicate. It is your homemaking exam. The secretary does not realize that it is a test for one of your classes.

Your parents have gone away for the weekend and have left you at home with your older sister. They have asked you not to have any friends over while they are away. Bill and John come over to the house on Saturday night while your sister is out. The boys say that they only want to come in for a little while to play records and talk.

Two teen-age girls, Susan and Patty, have just returned from a party. Some of their friends got drunk at the party. Susan didn't drink any and Patty has accused her of being afraid to try it.

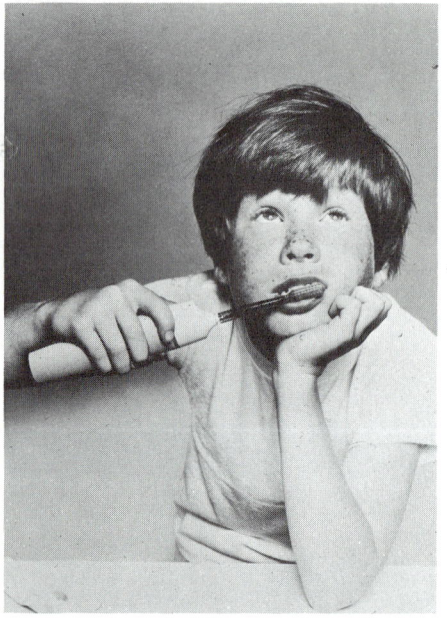

COURTESY SUNBEAM APPLIANCE COMPANY, DIVISION OF SUNBEAM CORPORATION

A child needs to learn to put the daily chores of living before the fun of playing.

work. Goals give your life direction by making you act. When you reach one goal, you can strive for another. Reaching goals is one way to meet your need for achievement and independence. Which goals have you achieved thus far in your life? Which goals have you set that will help you achieve independence?

POSTPONING GRATIFICATION

Wants and needs cannot always be met promptly. In fact, there are many wants and needs that cannot be met without long-range planning. There are few instant solutions to problems. Some things are worth waiting for and working for. You can't be an instant athlete or an instant concert pianist.

Real satisfaction in living comes through effort and a willingness to plan. For example, you may have a friend who feels he or she must have a certain sweater. Your friend has $3, but the sweater costs $6. What can your friend do? He has a number of choices. He can leave a $3 deposit, ask the clerk to lay away the sweater, and then set about getting the other $3. He may decide to gratify this need instantly by borrowing the money. He might even be tempted to shoplift. What would a mature person do?

Making adjustments

No one gets his own way all the time. There are some things in life you can't change. Circumstances require people to adjust and often to compromise. You can waste a lot of time and energy if you don't face this fact. Adjustment does not always mean doing things the other person's way. It often means changing your way of doing things in order to reach sound goals. Sometimes you may have to substitute one goal for another.

ACCEPTING RESPONSIBILITY

When you were a child, many things were decided for you. Now you are expected to make choices. You are expected to solve problems.

You have grown to a point where you want to stand on your own two feet. Right now you know what you *do not* want: too much advice, early curfews, and a long list of rules. But do you know what you *do* want? Are you ready to take full responsibility for your behavior? Is it still more comfortable to let your family make some of the decisions for you? Rebellion, to a certain extent, is a part of teen-age growth, but independence is not simply a rejection of all adult values and authority. Rather, mature independence is the ability to make decisions based on your own values and to follow them.

Do you think independence is achieved just by moving out of your family home? Unless you are prepared to meet basic needs, you will soon learn the difference between independence and self-deception. There are many teen-agers who are independent while living at home. There are others who may be hundreds of miles away at college, working, or married who are still emotionally dependent and homesick.

On the basis of all your experiences and knowledge collected through childhood and in the teen years, you can begin to set your own standards. You can begin to develop your own values, set your own goals, make your own decisions, and accept responsibility for your actions.

LEARNING FROM FAILURES AND SUCCESSES

Everyone is bound to encounter failure and defeat at times. Such experiences are a part of life. It is what you learn from these experiences that is really important. Many people have even turned one kind of failure into a success of another kind. Some teen-agers have difficulty in adjusting to their new, more adult roles. They may get into trouble of various kinds. But a failure can be the beginning of a success if it is handled correctly.

Have you heard the adage *nothing succeeds like success?* It is also true that what appears to be *overnight success* is usually the result of years of hard work. The satisfaction gained from success is a spur to further achievement. Learn from your failures. Build on your successes. No one is a *born loser*. Losers are self-made.

UNDERSTANDING YOURSELF

There are many parts to your total self-concept. Body, mind, and spirit blend together to make the one and only *you*. Is it any wonder that some people call their personality a puzzle? But like a puzzle, the personality is understood when all the parts are fitted together and you see the whole picture, your own self-concept. This understanding of yourself will allow you to make wise decisions as you fit together your values, standards, and goals to build a sound philosophy of life.

Finish this story: As Mary joined Pam for their walk to school, Pam said irritably, "We were both supposed to wear our red skirts today."

"I . . . I'm sorry," Mary answered. "I changed my mind."

As the two girls walked on, Pam remarked, "Mother said I can get the pair of shoes like yours. Let's go downtown after school to get them."

"Pam, I can't, not *today*," Mary blurted. For just a moment she wished she could run away.

Pam stopped and stared at her. "Why not today?"

Mary felt more and more like running away as she admitted, "Polly Smith asked me to go home with her after school."

Pam looked at Mary in confusion. "Why didn't you tell *me*? Mother would probably have let me go, too."

In complete misery now, Mary replied, "I didn't think of it."

Mary was very upset because she and Pam had been best friends since the first grade and were still good friends. They had shared many good times together. How could she make other friends without hurting Pam's feelings?

3 CHAPTER POSTTEST

Fill in the blank in each sentence with the *best* word to complete the statement. *Do not* use a word which already appears in the sentence. *Do not* write in this book.

1. Your self-concept begins to develop when you are ___(1)___.
2. A strong self-concept indicates that you have ___(2)___ in yourself and your abilities.
3. Food, clothing, and shelter are a part of your ___(3)___ needs.
4. When love, acceptance, appreciation, and security exist in a home, the ___(4)___ needs of the family members are probably met.
5. Your natural hair color is an example of a(an) ___(5)___ characteristic.
6. A person who is very sensitive to certain substances in his surroundings is said to have ___(6)___.
7. Each person is unlike any other because of the combined effects of his heredity and ___(7)___.
8. Your ability to learn is called your ___(8)___.
9. Your appearance is determined by both your inherited and your ___(9)___ characteristics.
10. A marked aptitude is called a(an) ___(10)___.
11. When a person is frustrated in his need for love and acceptance and is angry with everyone, everything, and especially with himself, he is said to be ___(11)___.
12. When a person resents and envies the attention and affection another receives, he is probably also ___(12)___.
13. The way you look at your surroundings, your actions, and your self-concept reflect a positive or negative ___(13)___ toward life.
14. The future things for which you are willing to work hard and for which you are willing to postpone desires are your ___(14)___.
15. The things which are important to you that guide your life are your ___(15)___.

Match the *illustrations* given in List A with the *types of maturity* given in List B. Use each type of maturity given in List B only once.

List A: **Illustrations**

A How many birthdays you have had
B How mature your body is
C How mature your relationships with other people are
D How grown-up your reasoning and thinking are
E How well you control your feelings

List B: **Types of maturity**

1 Chronological
2 Emotional
3 Intellectual
4 Physical
5 Social

4 CHAPTER PRETEST

Fill in the blank in each sentence with the *best* word to complete the statement. *Do not* write in this book.

1. Posture, facial expressions, and gestures are forms of body language, or ___(1)___ communication.
2. Biting nails, twisting hair, and chewing on pencils are annoying mannerisms, or ___(2)___, which suggest a lack of self-confidence.
3. Posture, personal care or grooming, clothing selection, sleep, and a sensible ___(3)___ are all necessary for an attractive personal appearance.
4. A product used to stop body odors by reducing the normal flow of perspiration is a(an) ___(4)___.
5. The most common teen-age eye defect is ___(5)___.
6. A doctor who specializes in the care and treatment of the skin is a(an) ___(6)___.
7. By the time a person reaches twenty years of age, the supply of ___(7)___ to the hair and skin decreases.
8. The most important consideration in preventing and lessening blackheads and other skin blemishes is ___(8)___.
9. If the total length of your foot is 8½ inches, your stockings or hose should measure at least ___(9)___ inches from heel to toe.

CHAPTER 4

Your image

Most people care a great deal about how other people react toward them, but many do not understand the reasons behind some of these reactions. Such people do not realize that their own looks and actions are the cause of most of the reactions of others toward them. In general, people like those who present a *positive image*. If you think well of yourself, you can present such an image without seeming overbearing or conceited.

A positive image can also be presented by displaying thoughtfulness toward others. People who think well of themselves can easily be kind to others. On the other hand, those who are curt, rude, or surly may reflect a lack of self-confidence and self-esteem. Impolite people often do not like themselves. Their negative self-concepts result in images which others do not like. Your relationships with other people can be good or bad, depending on the image you present.

Can a person improve his image if he feels that he needs to? He certainly can. A person can learn to communicate acceptably and develop a happy disposition. If he is

Discuss the importance of first impressions. List five things which cause your first impressions of a person. As a class, combine your lists. Determine which traits are mentioned most frequently. Discuss the reasons why these points are important.

Tell about a situation when your first impression of a person changed later. Discuss the reasons why. Make conclusions about the effect of impressions on lasting friendships.

Bulletin board IDEA
Title: *Feather Your Nest With . . .*
Directions: Use pictures or cut-outs of two birds, one sitting on a nest. Around them write words such as these:
    Friendliness
    Politeness
    Cheerfulness
    Courteousness
    Thoughtfulness

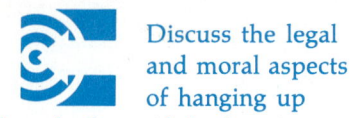

Discuss the legal and moral aspects of hanging up the telephone if the line is needed for an emergency.

Explain how the following suggestions will help you develop acceptable telephone behavior:
1. Answer the telephone quickly. After saying, "Hello," you may say something like, "This is the Browns' residence."
2. Identify yourself if the call is for you by saying, "This is Connie," or "This is she."
3. If the call is not for you, answer, "Just a moment, I'll call him."
4. Dial carefully. Let the telephone ring long enough so that the person called will have time to answer.
5. Limit the length of your telephone calls.
6. Make your calls at a time that will be convenient to your family as well as to the person you are calling.
7. The person who makes the telephone call is usually the one who should end it.
8. If you share a party line, be very careful not to inconvenience or annoy other people on your line.

also careful with his personal habits and appearance, he will present a positive image. It is this positive image which makes for the birth of lasting friendships.

The importance of communication

Of all the skills a person develops during his teen years, it is the skill of communication that is most effective in presenting his image to others. Communication is a two-way arrangement between a sender and a receiver. That means that you need to listen as well as to talk. There are many forms of communication. Speaking, or verbal communication, is only one. Writing is another. How well you communicate depends on your skill with writing, the spoken language, gestures, facial expressions, and voice tones. There are certain communication barriers such as shyness and fear. Awareness of these barriers will help you overcome them.

VERBAL
Teen-agers often have a vocabulary of their own. Their private language sets them apart from adults. Each generation of teen-agers seems to develop its own version of the spoken language. Teen-age slang is usually short-lived. It is constantly changing. It serves one important purpose, however. It unifies the teen-age group.

To many teen-agers, the most important people in the world are other teen-agers. But since young people must talk with grown-ups as well as each other, they usually develop two kinds of conversation, one which adults understand and another to which their own group can relate.

Using the telephone
If they have the opportunity, many teen-agers spend a great deal of time talking on the telephone. Parents often wonder how teen-agers can find so much to talk about. One explanation may be that the telephone answers the need for closeness in communication without close physical contact. Since many teen-agers find communications of a personal nature too difficult to handle along with eye-to-eye contact, the telephone becomes for them a valuable tool.

The telephone is a family resource, however, and everyone should have a fair chance to use it. The teen-ager who monopolizes the phone may be holding up calls that are important to other members of the family. He shows maturity when he controls the length of his conversations and times them so they do not interfere with the telephone needs of other family members. He must be doubly careful if his family's phone is a part of a party system. When several families are involved, considerate teen-agers limit telephone calls to business only.

NONVERBAL

Body language is a term sometimes used to refer to nonverbal communication. People communicate in nonverbal ways through touch and facial expressions. A pat on the shoulder or a sincere look of sympathy may communicate more to a person in trouble than any words could. But just as nonverbal communication can express kindness, it can also express negative feelings. A frown or a look of disapproval are nonverbal communications you have experienced. Turning your back or refusing to shake hands are also negative forms of communication. What other nonverbal forms can you think of? When you consider that your actions often express your thoughts, do you see new importance in controlling them?

WRITTEN

With the telephone so handy, many teen-agers rarely write social notes. But the written word remains an important form of communication. Out of courtesy to the sender, social correspondence should be answered. No matter how pleasant your note may be, if you wait too long to send it, the delay shows your lack of appreciation. A few well-chosen words mailed promptly can show appreciation for gifts or other kindnesses. A brief card or note sent to a shut-in can help him during days that seem endless. Letters to pen pals or to relatives or friends in other countries can strengthen ties you wish to keep strong.

BARRIERS TO COMMUNICATION

Unfortunately, communication is not always easy. It can be made difficult by a number of barriers.

Often emotional barriers interfere. For instance, a person who has grown up in a family that does not allow children to express themselves may speak and listen only with great difficulty. Too, a person who has been made to feel stupid

COURTESY WHAT'S NEW IN HOME ECONOMICS

Teen-agers say with their dress as well as their language that they are a member of their own special generation.

Perform short silent skits which demonstrate types of nonverbal communication. Discuss how the actors in these skits communicated through their posture, facial expression, or gestures.

View part of a movie with the sound turned off. Discuss what you think was happening. What led you to make these conclusions? Replay the section of the movie with the sound turned on to see how well the actors communicated without verbal language.

Discuss the meaning of the statement, *It's not what you say, but how you say it.* Give examples to illustrate the truth of the statement. Then say one word or phrase in a variety of ways to give it different meanings. Say *no* so that it means emphatically *no,* so that it means *maybe,* and so that it actually means *yes.* Discuss the importance of voice inflection and voice pitch.

Bulletin board IDEA
Title: *Is This Your Hang-up?*
Directions: Around the black silhouette of a telephone write suggestions for good telephone etiquette.

Discuss speech impediments, handicaps, and accents which may make it difficult to communicate verbally with others. Suggest ways to make communication easier in these situations. Discuss other types of handicaps such as mental retardation, cultural deprivation, and cerebral palsy which may cause communication problems. Suggest ways in which you can help handicapped people feel more at ease in their efforts to communicate with you.

for things he has said may remain quiet in self-defense. If no one has listened to him during childhood, he may have lost his desire to listen to others.

There are physical barriers to communication. A person who is hard of hearing or who has a speech impediment needs patience and consideration from others. Educational differences may make it hard for people to speak easily together. In this situation, good will on both sides is required to establish lasting lines of communication.

In this nation and throughout the world, there are many cultures. For example, Eastern and Western civilizations have different ways of looking at problems and different ways of expressing thoughts and feelings. Sometimes these cultural differences bring communication to a dead end. If it is to resume, both sides must move to restore it. It is helpful to be aware of cultural differences. Respect for another person's point of view, no matter how different from your own, is necessary if barriers are to be overcome.

Manners and mannerisms

Your manners and mannerisms tell others a great deal about you. Are you a fidgeter? Do you speak harshly before you take time to think? Do you burst out in giggles for no reason? Do you chew the end of your pencil when you study? Most people develop manners and mannerisms that they may not be aware of. Many of these are the result of nervousness or uncertainty. Such personal mannerisms as a broad grin and a firm handshake attract people. Other mannerisms may turn them away.

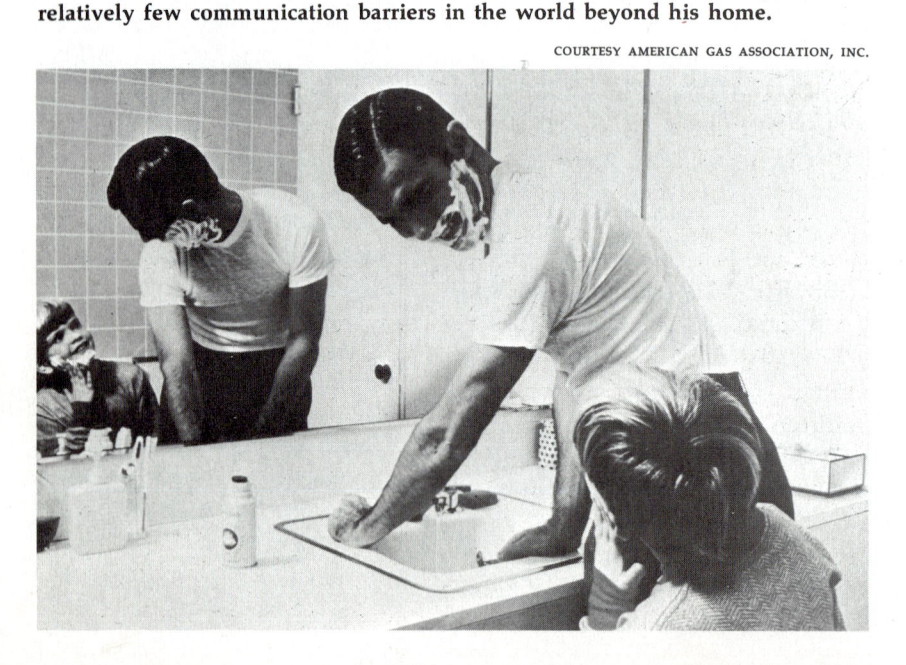

PUBLIC CONDUCT

The words *please* and *thank you* are chain-reaction words. People usually react positively to them. Your awareness of the feelings of others is an indication of your maturity.

Young people, being full of energy and good humor, are often

The child who grows up in an emotionally healthy home situation tends to find relatively few communication barriers in the world beyond his home.

COURTESY AMERICAN GAS ASSOCIATION, INC.

noisy. Most understanding adults would not want them to be different. When the public behavior of teen-agers interferes with the rights and comfort of others, however, there may be good reason for adults to be annoyed.

In most public places, the noise and confusion levels are generally quite high. Thoughtfulness can help reduce such noise levels. Teen-agers can avoid shouting, screaming, shoving, or playing their transistor radios loudly in public areas. Such activities are generally accepted when teen-agers choose the right time and place to display their high spirits.

Courtesies to salesclerks, service employees, and older people are further signs of a teen-ager's continuing growth toward maturity. His understanding of the difficulties others must face marks him as a teen-ager who is considerate.

FACIAL EXPRESSIONS

One of the first things people notice about you as an individual is your facial expression. It can reveal many of your attitudes. Are you smiling? Are you frowning? Are you relaxed? Are you tense? Try to expect good things to happen. This kind of thinking will show itself in your facial expression.

PERSONAL MANNERISMS

Even the most attractive person can ruin the effect of a good appearance

COURTESY MIDOL

Courtesy suggests that teen-agers will make an effort to choose a suitable time and place for their joyful, noisy activities.

by developing unpleasant mannerisms. Such habits as tugging at clothes, constant hair combing, fussing with accessories, or frequent peeks into the nearest mirror all suggest a lack of self-confidence. Biting nails, snapping gum, and sniffing unnecessarily are other personal habits that can soon annoy people and lead them to avoid your company.

PERSONAL PROBLEMS

Some young people, because of boredom, a negative self-concept, or pressure from others have turned to the use of cigarettes, alcohol, or drugs. All three products introduce harmful chemicals into the body that affect body functions. While tobacco appears to damage only the

In addition to *please, thank you,* and *I'm sorry,* list other chain-reaction words which show a person's consideration and regard for others.

Demonstrate and then discuss mannerisms and personal habits which indicate both strong and weak self-concepts.

Select a picture of someone's hands. Describe the person whose hands are pictured. What does this tell you about the importance of your hands in creating an image?

Suggest ways to overcome nail biting. Tell about a method which was successful for you, a friend, or a member of your family. Discuss the reasons why some people bite their nails.

Discuss the reasons why some teen-agers try smoking, drinking alcoholic beverages, or using drugs. Discuss the harmful effects of these practices. Draw conclusions about the personalities of teen-agers who do these things and the effects that these practices have on their acceptance by others.

Make a weekly schedule for good grooming, including those things which should be done daily. Prepare a class chart and have it duplicated. Check your good grooming practices on the chart at the beginning of each class period. This may be continued for approximately two weeks.

Make a collection of newspaper and magazine advertisements for grooming aids. Discuss the statements made in the advertisements. What appeal is made to the consumer? Try to determine whether the advertising is factual or emotionalized.

Work in small committees to arrange a display. Give an explanation of one unusual type of grooming article. If possible have several examples of each item and give the advantages and disadvantages of each.

Make your own deodorant by mixing and blending equal amounts of talcum powder and baking soda. Apply as often as needed.

physical body, alcohol and drugs affect mental processes as well.

Young people offer different reasons for experimenting in these dangerous areas, but those who use them seem to have three characteristics in common. They want to feel accepted, they want to feel important, and they want to feel grown up. They fail to realize that maturity is the result of personal growth. Substitute routes to maturity are bound to fail. Once established, such habits are damaging to physical and mental health. Their effects may be long-lasting. Every young person owes it to himself to learn the facts about tobacco, alcohol, and drug abuse. At the same time, he should search for successful ways to become a secure and confident adult.

Aids to personal attractiveness

If you, like most teen-agers, are interested in improving your attractiveness, check your general health habits. Posture, exercise, diet, rest, and personal care are all important aids to appearance. Cosmetics and attractive clothes become effective only after good health habits are established.

POSTURE

Have you ever carefully observed a beauty contest on TV? Notice how the winner demonstrates correct posture when walking. Her head is high, her shoulders are erect, her back is straight, and her hips are tucked in. When she walks, her legs swing forward from the hips rather than from the knees. With knees flexed and toes pointed straight ahead, she moves forward with an easy motion. She avoids coming down hard on her heels, but rather touches her heel to the ground lightly and shifts her weight forward smoothly on the ball of her foot. As she walks, she keeps her knees so close together that they almost touch at every step.

Posture is a chain reaction. If the shoulders slump, the stomach is thrust forward. Then a person's clothes hang wrong, and it is impossible to walk gracefully.

Perhaps the easiest way to get your body aligned properly is to imagine that you are suspended in air, with your feet barely touching the floor. To achieve good posture while standing, take hold of your hair directly above the ears and pull up. Straighten yourself up in the direction you are pulling your hair. Now relax your knees so that they rock easily and are not locked into place. Pull. Can you feel your head assuming an upright position? Now return your arms to your sides and look at yourself in a mirror. Study both your front and side views to see if you look better. Do you feel better? Do you feel your shoulders straighten? Is your rib cage lifted out of your waistline? Are your hips tucked under? Do you feel taller?

Your posture when you bend or stoop to pick up something from a low position can be either awkward or graceful. Avoid bending from the waist to reach the floor unless you are doing exercises. Rather, bend your knees and keep your back as straight as possible. Then as you lift or stand, the strain is on your strong leg muscles rather than on your back. This motion is not only more graceful but also helps protect your back from injuries.

Your sitting posture is as important as your walking posture. As you prepare to sit down, feel for the edge of the chair or couch with the back of one leg. Then keep your back straight as you sit. Lower your body to the front edge of the chair and slide back after you are seated. You will find that you look and feel graceful. As you slide back in the chair, place your hands on the front edge next to your hips, raise your weight slightly with your arms, and slip backward. If you keep the base of your spine against the back of the chair, you will find it difficult to slump. You can place your feet in various graceful positions if you remember to keep your knees and ankles close together.

As you rise from a chair, go through the sitting motions in reverse. Move your body forward to the front edge of the chair by placing your hands on the edge of the chair next to your hips and raising your body slightly as you move forward. When your body weight is fairly well centered over your feet, raise your body with your thigh muscles.

EXERCISE

Exercise is a desirable health practice. Taken regularly and correctly it adds to your overall attractiveness. Exercise develops the body muscles. It stimulates the appetite and aids the processes of digestion and elimination. Exercise in clean air helps you fill your lungs with

Play *Posture Raid*. Each day while you are studying this unit your teacher may designate three students who may call out *Posture Raid* any time during that class period. When one of the students calls this, everyone must freeze without changing his position at all. Several students may be called upon to analyze their posture. Also, students displaying good posture may be noted.

Exercise is important for maintaining the stamina necessary for the rapid pace of teen-age living.

COURTESY COMMERCE BANCSHARES, INC.

Act out the following skit while one student reads the script. Be sure to practice before performing for the class. (This demonstration may be presented by using a bright light as a projector.)

Listen folks, and let me talk
About the ways that ladies walk,
Illustrating all in jest,
Posture bad and at its best.
Several models will appear
Who by posture make it clear
The bad results when women fair
Do not know or do not care.

With a slinky backward crouch,
Enters model *Sarah Slouch*.
Down with head and down with seat,
Here is Sarah, all complete.
Saggy shoulders, sunken chest,
Her diaphragm looks quite depressed.

Next we ask to introduce
Suzie Swayback on the loose.
She's full of curves and simple graces,
But Suzie curves in funny places.
Did you know her hollow spine
Makes her rump stick out behind?
From their chins down to their shoes,
Aren't you sorry for swayback Sues?

the oxygen you need for good health.

There are many ways to get the exercise you need. Walking is a good exercise for most people, young or old. Teen-age boys and girls can exercise regularly by taking part in sports and various kinds of dances. If your health is good, jogging and gymnastics help to maintain muscle tone and to trim excess weight.

Most teen-agers are in a period of rapid growth. Sometimes their bodies grow faster than their hearts and circulatory systems. For this reason, they should have a doctor's permission before engaging in interschool competitive sports such as basketball or football. Don't overlook your everyday activities as useful forms of exercise. The errands you run, the household tasks you perform, and the special chores you carry out provide useful forms of exercise.

CLEANLINESS

Body cleanliness is a *must* for good health and good looks. For cleanliness, lather the entire body with mild soap and water. Follow a sudsy bath with some kind of clear-water rinse. Dry the body quickly and completely by rubbing briskly with a clean bath towel. The pores of the skin are cleaned by a daily bath, sponge bath, or shower. Bathing removes perspiration and helps prevent body odor.

COURTESY WINTHROP LABORATORIES

A daily bath with soap and water followed by the use of some type of deodorant is important for the active teen-ager.

Deodorants and antiperspirants

Because the body perspires constantly and perspiration contains waste material, body odor can be a problem even when a daily bath is taken. Both deodorants and antiperspirants can help solve body odor problems.

Deodorants stop odors while allowing perspiration to flow normally. In order for them to be effective against odor-producing bacteria, they must be applied to clean skin. Deodorants cannot be expected to be effective if applied to an unbathed body.

66

Deodorants may be obtained in powder, cream, stick, or liquid spray-on forms. Read the label carefully, and follow the directions for using the form of deodorant you have chosen. You may wish to try different kinds of deodorants to find one that is especially effective for you. Because the body sometimes builds up a resistance to a particular deodorant, try changing brands occasionally.

Usually deodorants are considered to be underarm protective agents. However, since foot odors can also be very offensive, particularly among teen-age boys, special applications can be bought to prevent foot odors. The insides of shoes can be swabbed with rubbing alcohol after wearing to further cut down on foot odors.

Antiperspirants are used to reduce the flow of perspiration as well as to prevent odors. Since many teen-agers are bothered by a heavy flow of perspiration during periods of tension, antiperspirants are very effective. They help a person avoid the embarrassment caused when heavy underarm circles show on his clothing. Antiperspirants should be used only according to directions given on the label to avoid irritating the skin or damaging the clothing.

Since offenders seldom know when they have offensive odors, it is wise for all teen-agers to bathe or shower and use deodorants or antiperspirants daily. This is a very important practice for girls to follow during the days of their regular menstrual flow. Special powders and sprays are available which offer added protection during this time.

NUTRITION

Lack of pep, a blotchy complexion, dull-looking hair, and extra pounds can be the results of poor eating habits. This is not a promising start for someone who wants to be attractive. Changes in food habits can improve appearance. For good looks, include at least two servings of meat and four servings each of

Good nutrition is basic to good looks and good health.

COURTESY TANG INSTANT BREAKFAST DRINK

Now meet *Helen,* round and plump,
Famous for her camel's *Hump.*
Lots of ladies look like that
When they're lazy and they're fat.
Can she not stand tall and straight
Just because of what she ate?
Humps belong on camels, madam.
Ladies are not meant to have them.

Parades, of course, are lots of fun.
Do you look like you're in one?
Sally Stiff, the crazy nut,
Has a military strut.
From her toes to top of head,
She's so stiff she might be dead.
Perhaps the army likes her kind.
The guy who does is surely blind.

For easy, simple, natural grace,
Polly Posture sets the pace.
Head and body all aligned,
Every movement is refined.
As she walks into the light,
Her whole appearance brings delight.
Suppose that you were in her spot,
You'd look like Polly, would you not?

Discuss the following list of aids to getting a good night's sleep. Be able to explain why each direction will help you.
1. Follow a schedule so that you go to bed at approximately the same time every night.
2. Take some exercise every day.
3. Avoid excitement just before bedtime.
4. Try to forget your troubles when you go to bed.
5. Refrain from eating foods which are difficult to digest just before going to bed. If a snack is desired, eat something light and nutritious.
6. Have enough, but not too much, covering.
7. Wear a loose fitting and comfortable sleeping garment.
8. Arrange for good ventilation in the room.
9. Darken the room and, if possible, shut out irritating noises.

Bulletin board IDEA
Title: *The most important thing YOU wear is your expression*
Directions: Mount pictures of people who have a happy facial expression.

milk, cereals, and fruits and vegetables in your daily diet.

ELIMINATION
An important health practice is the establishment of regular habits for body elimination. A bowel movement at regular intervals is part of a good health routine.

SLEEP AND REST
Your body requires daily rest, relaxation, and sleep if it is to grow as it should. Sleep and rest also help you to be alert, lively, and agreeable. When you sleep, your whole body is at rest. The heart beats more slowly, and all body processes are slowed. During sleep, the body rids itself of waste materials. After proper sleep and rest, you are refreshed and ready for activity.

CARE OF THE EYES
Eyes are attractive when they are clear and sparkling. Healthful living habits add to their beauty. But since eyes are used for seeing, your chief concern is to keep them in good working order. Unfortunately, people often do not realize the priceless value of their eyes until they have allowed them to become damaged.

Approximately one-fourth of the American teen-age population has defective vision which needs attention. Nearsightedness is the most common teen-age eye defect. While not an actual disease, nearsightedness hinders a person from reading assignments on the chalkboard and causes difficulties with other essential parts of his schoolwork. In order to see, nearsighted people often squint and develop a worried, unattractive frown. Certainly if you need glasses for nearsightedness or any other reason, you should make arrangements to get and wear them.

By the time people reach their midteens, they are usually responsible enough to wear contact lenses. Glasses or contacts, whatever your choice, if you suspect any kind of eye defect, consult a competent eye doctor, called an ophthalmologist. Other specialists who make eye examinations and fit glasses are called optometrists. Opticians grind lenses and make glasses.

CARE OF THE TEETH
In a way, your teeth are much like your eyes. While noticed for the way they add to or detract from your looks, they make a definite contribution to your health. Oral hygiene helps reduce decay of the teeth, unpleasant breath, and possible diseases of the mouth and gums. Sound teeth, free of cavities, are due primarily to a good diet, regular and effective tooth brushing, and periodic dental checkups.

During the formation and growth of teeth, which ends when a person is about eighteen years of age, the food he eats affects the strength of his teeth. For the maintenance of healthy teeth, good food continues to be necessary. Daily care is also essential. Since tooth decay frequently occurs when food clings and ferments between the teeth, you should form the habit of brushing the teeth as soon as possible after eating. When this is impossible, at least rinse your mouth with water.

Your toothbrush should have a flat brushing surface and bristles soft enough to encourage vigorous brushing. If possible, use two brushes alternately, allowing time for each to dry between uses.

The cleansing agent may be a powder or a paste that you buy, or it may be a homemade mixture of salt and baking soda. Whatever kind of dentifrice you use, remember that while paste or powder helps clean the teeth, brushing itself does most of the cleaning.

CARE OF THE HAIR
Hair is most attractive when it is kept clean and well brushed and when care is taken to shape it for the individual face and head. A large part of the millions of dollars spent in the United States each year on beauty aids is spent in hair-styling salons. However, the simple hair styles which look best on teen-agers can be cared for at home economically and effectively.

Daily care
Daily brushing with a stiff-bristled brush will help keep hair shining

COURTESY AMERICAN GAS ASSOCIATION, INC.

Shampoo your hair as often as is necessary to remove oil and dandruff.

with its own natural luster. Brushing removes dust from the hair, massages the scalp, removes dandruff, and distributes the oil evenly. Massaging with the fingertips is another good way to stimulate blood circulation in the scalp, further helping to keep the hair healthy. It is body oil that gives teen-age hair its youthful appearance and high gloss. Enjoy this glossiness while you can. As you grow older, even as early as in the twenties, the body's supply of oil to the hair and skin will lessen. The hair will become less glossy.

It is important that your brush and comb be cleaned frequently, at least as often as you wash your hair. Your hairbrush and comb should not be used by other people, nor

List habits of good eye care which you can practice. The following items will help you start your list.
1 Tilt material you are reading at approximately the same angle that you tilt your head.
2 When you are reading, glance at a distant object occasionally to rest your eyes.
3 Do not look directly into bright lights.
4 Sit at least 7 feet away from a TV set and have a light on in the room when watching. It is especially important to sit some distance from a colored set.

Brush your teeth correctly. Be sure to follow these practices:
1 Place the bristles of the toothbrush against the gums at the start of each stroke. Brush from the gums to the edges of the teeth.
2 Clean the inside surfaces of the teeth in the same way as the outer surfaces.
3 Scrub the chewing edges of the teeth.
4 Use dental floss to clean between the teeth.
5 Massage the gums for at least one minute each day. Use the rubber tip of the toothbrush or your fingers.

Demonstrate the proper way to wash your hair.
Be able to explain why each of the following steps is necessary.
1 Brush and comb your hair thoroughly.
2 Wet your hair with warm water.
3 Lather your hair with a commercial shampoo (or use a soap jelly made by dissolving pieces of mild soap in warm water). Avoid rubbing bar soap directly on your hair.
4 Massage the lather thoroughly into your hair and scalp. Use your finger tips rather than your fingernails.
5 Rinse with running water.
6 Repeat steps 3 through 5. (Omit if your hair is dry.)
7 Be sure the final rinse is thorough. Clean, thoroughly rinsed hair will squeak when pulled through the fingers.
8 Use a clean towel to blot up the excess water.

Demonstrate how to wash hair when running water is not available.

Demonstrate how to clean your brush and combs. Tell why it is important to clean all of them at the same time that you shampoo your hair.

should you use theirs. Diseases of the hair and scalp can be carried from person to person by using a common comb or brush.

Shampooing

Hair should be shampooed at least every week, or as frequently as is necessary to keep it sweet-smelling, clean, and lustrous. The need for a shampoo depends upon your surroundings, your activities, and the amount of oil in your hair. It does not harm the hair to shampoo it frequently if mild shampoo is used and the hair is rinsed thoroughly. Teen-agers with skin problems often wash their hair every day. Daily washing helps remove the oil and dirt which irritate the skin as the hair brushes against it.

After rinsing your hair, blot it with a towel. When it is almost dry, set it in some style which looks well on you. Allow it to dry before going out. It is in bad taste to appear in public with your hair in rollers, even when the rollers are covered with a scarf.

Styling

Both boys and girls are interested in finding a hair style suited to them. The shape of the face and the features determine what arrangement is most becoming. No matter what style you choose, it will look better if your hair is clean, well brushed, and generally well cared for.

Teen-age hair problems

Typical teen-age hair problems include hair which is too oily, too dry, too thin, too thick, too fine, too coarse, dull-looking, or lifeless. No matter what the exact problem, regular brushing and systematic washing tend to improve the condition. Hair which is too thick can be thinned during cutting, while thin hair tends to look thicker if cut short.

Hair growing on a girl's lower legs and underarms can be removed by shaving. Light hair on the upper lip can be bleached with peroxide. Dark facial hair can be removed electrically by your doctor or by a person he recommends.

CARE OF THE FACE

In addition to a daily bath to cleanse the entire body, the face requires special attention. Whether your face is oily, dry, or normal, it needs care.

Daily care

Wash your face at least once and preferably two or three times a day to remove the dirt which clings to the surface oils.

Girls may find creams helpful to their skin and effective when used to remove makeup. While cream does not take the place of soap and water for cleansing, it may be applied gently before washing, especially if your skin is dry. Baby oil can be used to remove makeup. A little cream or oil rubbed in very lightly after washing the face will help to prevent chapping and roughness.

Teen-age skin problems
A clear, smooth complexion is a part of good looks. Unfortunately, many teen-agers have difficulty in keeping their skins free from blackheads and pimples. While skin blemishes can cause embarrassment, they are not a sign of bad blood or necessarily of a lack of cleanliness. In the early teen years there are many physical and psychological changes taking place. The glands which control the supply of oil to the skin, especially of the face, back, and shoulders, become very active. The extra amounts of oil, if not removed from the openings of the glands, can cause blackheads. If the oil accumulates below the surface of the skin, whiteheads form. These oil-plugged gland openings can become infected and cause troublesome pimples.

To help prevent skin blemishes, teen-agers must give special attention to skin cleanliness. Thorough cleansing with warm suds to remove surface oil is necessary, in severe cases as often as four or five times a day. Soap should be carefully rinsed away after every application.

Other factors which are likely to cause skin blemishes are poor diet, poor habits of health and body hygiene, and nervous tension and worry.

The young person with facial skin problems needs to consider his daily living habits. Is he getting enough sleep, having enough vigorous exercise, and eating a sensible diet? Is he passing up sweet soft drinks, desserts, and fatty foods? In their place is he substituting lean meat, vegetables, and fresh fruits? Does he drink plenty of liquid, six to eight glasses daily?

Picking the face will irritate the skin and make blemishes worse. Keep fingers, soiled handkerchiefs,

Most teen-age skin problems can be avoided by regular and thorough cleaning of the face with soap and warm water.

COURTESY WINTHROP LABORATORIES

Determine the shape of your face. This may be done by pulling your hair completely back and outlining your face on a mirror with soap. Be sure to clean the mirror afterward. Divide the class into groups—those with round-shaped faces together, those with long-shaped faces together, etc. The groups can decide which types of hair styles and necklines are most becoming on them. Each group may select one girl who can demonstrate a flattering neckline and hairdo on the following day.

Choose pictures of a variety of hair styles from the most casual to the most elaborate. Include pictures of hair styles for men and boys. Describe the personality of a person who might wear a certain hair style.

Make a transparency by drawing various face shapes on acetate. On separate sheets, draw different hair styles. Try the hair styles on the different face shapes. Decide which are the most and which are the least becoming. Tell why a particular hair style is flattering to a particular face shape. Discuss factors such as height, texture of the hair, length of the neck, and current fashions in relation to hair styles.

Demonstrate the proper way to wash your face. Be able to explain each of these steps:
1 Wash your face and neck with a lather made from warm water and a mild soap. Apply the lather with your freshly washed hands or a soft, clean washcloth.
2 As you apply the lather, gently rub your face, using an upward and circular motion. Be sure to reach the creases in the skin around the nose, corners of the eyes, and ears. Be careful also to clean to the hairline around the forehead, ears, and back of the neck.
3 Thoroughly rinse away the soap.
4 Pat your face dry with a clean, soft towel.

Demonstrate the procedure followed to remove problem blackheads from your face:
1 Scrub the skin well with soap and water.
2 Apply a towel that has been dipped and wrung from very hot water.
3 With clean hands and a tissue, gently press out the clogged material.
4 Sponge the skin with clean cold water, pat with an ice cube, or apply lotion.

and dirty powder puffs away from your face. If skin trouble persists in spite of your best efforts, see a doctor. He may refer you to a dermatologist, a doctor who specializes in the treatment of skin problems.

Cosmetics

If makeup is used, it should be applied to a clean skin and, even then, lightly. Since fashions in makeup tend to change rapidly, many teenage girls prefer to use very little or no makeup at all. Excessive makeup on eyes, lips, or cheeks is unattractive for school wear.

In selecting any preparation for skin, hair, or eyes, make a careful choice of brands. To find out which ones are best for you, try out several brands. Information found on labels or given by consumer reports should be considered. Regardless of the brand, choose colors which blend with your personal skin tone.

Your eyebrows frame your eyes. The most attractive eyebrows are smooth and natural looking. If necessary, a girl may smooth the shape by plucking hairs from the lower edge of the brows. An eyebrow pencil may be used with light, short strokes to supplement thin brows. Rubbing the eyebrows with petroleum jelly will help to keep them smooth.

If you would like to have your eyelashes appear longer, apply petroleum jelly to them. For special parties, you may wish to use more elaborate eye makeup. If you use eye makeup, be careful not to use too much and to apply it skillfully.

CARE OF HANDS AND FINGERNAILS

Your hands are in sight most of the time. To be attractive, they must be clean. Fingernails and cuticles require daily attention as well as a weekly manicure.

Daily care

Wash your hands frequently, many, many times a day: before and after meals; after working, playing, or handling anything that is dirty; before working in the kitchen or starting to sew; and after going to the bathroom. Use a mild soap and water. Rinse and dry your hands completely so that they will remain smooth and soft. A hand lotion, rubbed or patted into the skin, will help prevent dryness and chapping.

Well-kept fingernails are an essential part of well-cared-for hands. Nails can be attractive if treated with care. Do not bite them or use them as tools to dig, scrape, or pry. Keep them clean by scrubbing them with a soft brush. Your cuticles will stay soft if you push them into place with the towel each time you wash your hands. You can also use an oil or cuticle cream at night.

Manicuring the fingernails

The complete care of your nails includes a weekly manicure. Necessary equipment includes an emery board, perhaps a nail file, a soft orangewood stick, and warm, soapy water. You may wish to use cuticle oil and nail polish. Work on a glass-topped, or otherwise well-protected, table. To avoid accidents, never use your lap. Avoid using nail polish unless you can give your hands such constant care that you never appear in public with chipped, poorly-cared-for polish. Nail polish may be used for any special party occasion, however, if removed when it begins to chip.

Fingernail problems

Have you ever asked yourself what to do about the habit of nail biting? Keeping nails in good condition, filing rough edges, and softening the cuticle are positive ways to combat the nail-biting habit. Hangnails can be prevented by caring for the cuticles. Brittle nails or splitting nails may be a sign of poor nutrition and should be discussed with a doctor.

CARE OF THE FEET AND TOENAILS

People frequently mention being exhausted without noticing that only their feet are tired. Since the feet must support the entire weight of the body while a person is standing or walking, it is very important that they receive constant care. Care includes daily cleansing and checking for fungus growth and toenail problems. It also includes the general attention given to properly fitted shoes and hose.

Daily care

Feet should be cared for daily. Because perspiration is trapped in shoes and stockings, feet need to be washed daily with mild soap and warm water and dried well, especially between the toes. Occasionally the feet should be massaged with a cream or oil to prevent roughness or chapping. A deodorant foot powder applied to the feet will help to prevent offensive odor.

Discuss proper shoe care in relation to the prevention of foot problems. Include such procedures as the use of a shoe horn when putting on shoes, proper shoe storage, proper methods of cleaning various types of shoes, the care to be given to wet shoes, and the importance of shoe repairs. Explain how each of these will help prevent foot problems.

With occasional professional help, a girl can learn to manage her own hair, eyebrows, and nails for beauty and good health.

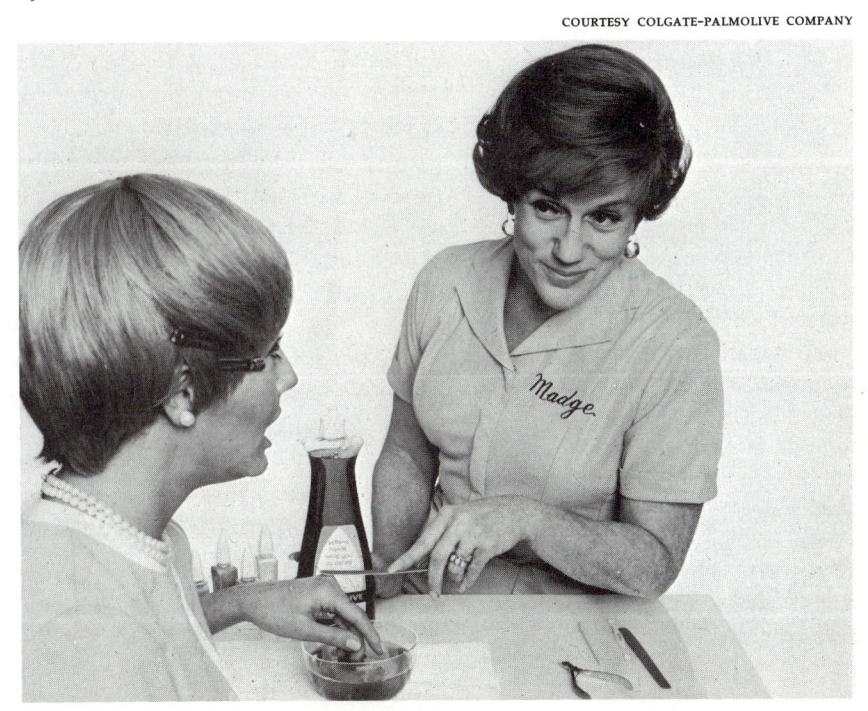

COURTESY COLGATE-PALMOLIVE COMPANY

Demonstrate the correct procedures for giving a manicure. Be able to explain each step.
1 Remove old nail polish.
2 Clean under the nails with an orangewood stick wrapped in cotton. Moisten the cotton with soapy water.
3 Shape the ends of the nails with an emery board, using short strokes toward the center of the nail.
4 Push back the skin at the base of the nails with the orangewood stick.
5 Wash and dry the hands and nails thoroughly.
6 Apply nail polish, if desired.

Your career
Cosmetologist

Duties: Provides beauty services for customers. Suggests coiffures according to physical features of patron and current styles, or determines coiffure from instruction of patron. May shape and color eyebrows or eyelashes, suggest makeup, remove unwanted hair, or care for fingernails and toenails. May massage face or neck.
Where employed: Department stores, specialty shops, or beauty shops. Can be self-employed.

Keep a constant watch for fungus growth between the toes. Infections such as athlete's foot can usually be controlled by using drugstore preparations. Stubborn infection should be called to the attention of a doctor.

Toenail care is important to both health and appearance. The appearance of the toenails is especially important with sandals or bare feet. Keep the nails carefully trimmed and the cuticles pushed back. If you use nail polish on your toenails, check daily to be sure it is not chipped or worn off.

Toenail and foot problems
Toenails should receive regular care in order to prevent serious foot problems. File or cut the nails straight across the top, and push back the cuticles gently.

Ingrown toenails are usually caused by wearing shoes or stockings that are too short or shoes that are too narrow. Ingrown toenails are painful and may cause serious infections. An obvious remedy is to wear shoes and stockings that fit properly. Immediate relief can be had by soaking the feet in hot water and placing a bit of absorbent cotton under the corner of the infected nail. If pain continues, consult a doctor.

Other foot troubles, such as corns, calluses, and blisters, are caused by poorly fitting shoes. Choose shoes that provide ventilation for the feet as well as support for walking and standing. It is a mistake to choose shoes only on the basis of style.

Fashion sometimes decrees such extreme styles as spike heels or pointed toes. Cramming your feet into uncomfortable shoes can cause long-lasting damage. Think of comfort and support first. Then choose a style that is becoming. If the shoes fit when they are purchased, they will wear evenly and retain their lines.

Stockings, pantyhose, and socks should be long enough and wide enough so that the feet are not cramped. Poorly fitting hose can cause such foot troubles as bunions and ingrown toenails. The length of your foot determines the size of hose to buy. For instance, a size 9 stocking is 9 inches long. Your stockings should be at least ½ inch longer than the total length of your foot. If your foot length is 9 inches, you will probably wear a size 9½ stocking. Consider shrinkage problems connected with all hosiery, especially stretch hose or hose which will be dried with heat in a drier.

The impact of image

Many teen-agers fight accepting the importance of their image. To them it seems that their friends know what they really are like. Friends, they feel, will understand if they have poor habits of speech or dress. Friends will overlook annoying manners or mannerisms. Friends will look beneath their personal appearance to the real person inside.

Are such teen-agers reasoning correctly, or are they deceiving themselves? Can you remember wanting to comfort your little brother who had been shoved around by the neighborhood bully, but having to clean him off first because he was too messy to touch? Can you remember wanting to throw your arms around your dad's neck when he got home from a hard day's work in the out-of-doors, but deciding you'd wait until he washed up first. Did you ever want to comfort your mother but decide from the expression on her face and the tone of her voice that it was no time for conversation? These are people you love. They are part of your family. Yet you reject them temporarily because of the impact of their image.

Happy people live in the world as it exists. While they strive for improvements, they understand that people are accepted or rejected, at least to a degree, at face value.

Are you satisfied with your image? Are you accepted? What is acceptance worth to you? Can an image be changed overnight? What changes can come quickly? Which are the changes that will take some time? What is the price? Are you willing to pay it?

In every aspect of life, decisions must be made. Goals must be set. The carry-through tasks must be begun. Evaluation is necessary from time to time. Long practice periods are quickly forgotten when worthwhile goals are reached.

COURTESY MIDOL

Your image is a combination of your physical appearance, dress, manners, mannerisms, and habits.

Prepare a booklet which is a guide to good grooming for teen-age boys and girls. Include articles and pictures which suggest cosmetics for various skin tones.

Make a good grooming kit. Discuss the advantages and disadvantages of each of the items in the kit. Decide which items are essential and which items might be considered luxuries. Suggest substitute items which are less expensive than original items in the kit.

Your career
Cosmetics and toiletries salesperson

Duties: Sells cosmetics and toiletries such as skin creams, hair preparations, and lipstick. Explains beneficial properties of preparations. Demonstrates methods of application to the customer. Suggests shades or varieties of makeup to suit customer's complexion. May weigh and mix facial powders, according to an established formula, to obtain desired shade. Arranges sales displays. **Where employed:** Department stores, specialty shops, and beauty shops. Can be self-employed.

4 CHAPTER POSTTEST

Match the *descriptions* given in List A with the *types of specialists* given in List B. Use a specialist given in List B only once. *Do not* write in this book.

List A: **Descriptions**

A A person who specializes in the care and treatment of the skin
B A person who specializes in the care and treatment of the eyes
C A person who makes and fits glasses and grinds lenses
D A person who specializes in the care and treatment of the teeth and gums
E A person who specializes in general health care

List B: **Type of specialist**

1 Dentist
2 Dermatologist
3 Family doctor
4 Ophthalmologist or oculist
5 Optician

Fill in the blank in each sentence with the *best* word or words to complete the statement.

1 A product which is used to reduce body odors while allowing perspiration to flow normally is a(an) __(1)__.
2 In the daily care of your teeth it is the __(2)__ that is vital in cleaning them.
3 Pimples and blackheads are caused by __(3)__ which has not been removed from the openings of the glands.
4 Brittle or splitting nails are usually the result of poor __(4)__.
5 The growth of fungus between the toes may result in a common infection known as __(5)__.
6 The painful condition caused by wearing shoes or stockings that are too short or shoes that are too narrow is called __(6)__ toenail.
7 People are accepted or rejected, at least to a degree, at face __(7)__.

Give the following information on a separate sheet of paper.

1 List 5 forms of nonverbal communication.
2 List 3 barriers to effective communication.
3 List 5 mannerisms or habits which suggest a lack of self-confidence.
4 Give examples of 3 chain-reaction words which have a positive effect on other people.
5 List 4 general rules to follow for an attractive complexion which are also guidelines for overall good health.
6 List 5 characteristics which contribute toward making a positive impression on others.

5 CHAPTER PRETEST

Fill in the blank in each sentence with the *best* word to complete the statement. *Do not* use a word which already appears in the sentence. *Do not* write in this book.

1 A person who has tact, can make introductions smoothly, and is able to communicate easily with others has acquired __(1)__ skills which are helpful throughout life.
2 Friends help you fulfill your basic needs for love, appreciation, security, variety, independence, and __(2)__.
3 Manners, or rules of behavior for social situations, are referred to as __(3)__.
4 A closed circle of people who limit their friendships outside the group is a(an) __(4)__.
5 When 2 boys and 2 girls pair off and go out together it is called a(an) __(5)__ date.
6 If you can listen and are able to get your date to talk about his interests, you are considered a good __(6)__.
7 Your progress toward selecting a satisfying lifetime job, occupation, profession, or trade refers to your __(7)__ growth.
8 The purpose of a job is to produce goods or __(8)__.
9 In choosing a job which you can do successfully you need to consider your aptitudes, abilities, talents, and __(9)__.

CHAPTER 5

Your future

If there is anything certain about the teen years, it is the fact that each person must do his own job of growing up. You are on your own when it comes to making the most of yourself and your opportunities. When you were a child, other people carried the main responsibility for your welfare. Now you will be taking an increasingly greater share of the responsibility.

Whether you are a boy or a girl, you need to develop salable job skills. You also need to develop and improve your social skills. No matter how ready other people are to help you, you must develop these skills for yourself.

Your opportunities

The teen years are social years. Teen-agers enjoy parties, sports events, and other forms of entertainment. Maturity for most teen-agers also brings an interest in vocational opportunities. They begin to grow interested in working for money. The two interests seem to go hand in hand. Work provides money which may be used in part to finance interesting forms of social entertainment.

Duplicate a list of ten values; for example honesty, loyalty, responsibility and patriotism. Ask each student to number them in order of importance to him. Collect and tabulate the data. Prepare a graph, chart, or bulletin board that shows the results. Discuss the following:

1 What influence do values have on a person's goals?
2 Why are values different for different people?
3 How does a person acquire his values?

Bulletin board IDEA
Title: *STAIRWAY of Opportunities*
SOCIAL
VOCATIONAL
EDUCATIONAL

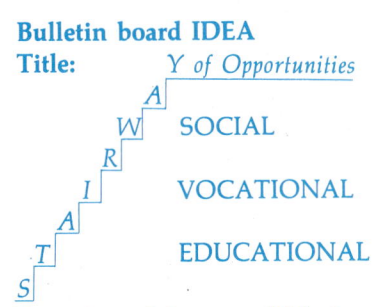

Directions: Mount and label three appropriate pictures showing social, vocational, and educational opportunities for teen-agers.

Present skits demonstrating good manners at home and in public places such as grocery stores, theaters, and ball parks.

Present skits dealing with situations in which poor manners were displayed. (Examples: gossiping, talking with one member of a group while excluding others, showing noisy and boisterous behavior when such is inappropriate.) Present the skits a second time, displaying acceptable behavior.

Your career
House mother

Duties: Acts as house manager, advisor, and chaperon. May order supplies, plan menus, or determine need for maintenance, repairs, and furnishings. Assigns rooms, assists in planning recreational activities, and supervises work and study programs. May chaperon group-sponsored trips and social functions.
Where employed: Boarding schools, college housing areas, children's homes, and similar establishments.

SOCIAL OPPORTUNITIES

The teen-age practice of frequently getting together with others leads to social growth. Parties and dates are important aspects of the teen-age social scene. Some teens envy their friends who seem to have a natural ability to act with assurance as guests or as hosts or hostesses, to make introductions smoothly, or to carry on meaningful boy-girl conversations. Actually, basic social skills such as these do not require a special natural talent. They can be learned by the teen-ager who will make the effort to practice them.

If you have both boys and girls among your friends during your teen years, you will have many chances to develop a more interesting personality. For example, you can learn to talk about the hobbies and interests that other boys and girls enjoy. In order to talk easily, you will probably need to learn something about such things as fishing and other outdoor sports and games, cooking, model making, ham radio operation, record collections, and car repairs.

Boy-girl friendships help you to appreciate the friendships that adulthood will bring. They also give you a basis of comparison and an understanding of people. These friendships will prepare you for the

Boy-girl friendships offer teen-agers a chance to understand and appreciate each other.

COURTESY BILL STUART AND YARDLEY OF LONDON, INC.

selection of a mate when you are ready for marriage.

VOCATIONAL OPPORTUNITIES

With many new interests, the teen-ager may begin to earn some of his own money. Laws tend to limit the hours and conditions under which teen-agers can work. But the teen who wants a summer job or after-school work will usually find opportunities in restaurants, supermarkets, stores, and many other businesses. Sitting with children, working in yards, cleaning swimming pools, running errands, and operating paper routes are popular jobs among young teens.

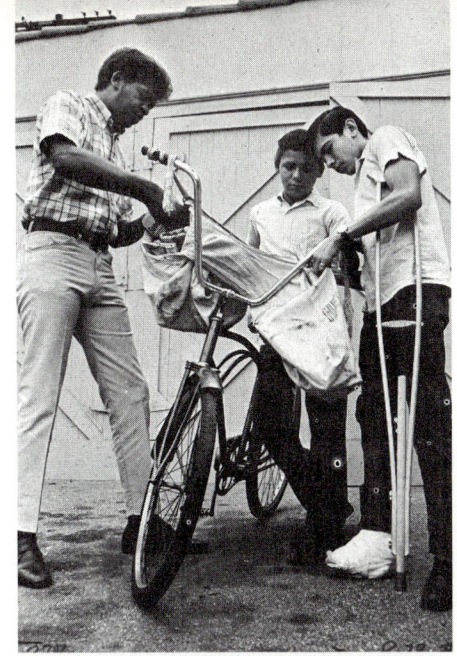

COURTESY PACE PROGRAMS, INC.

A paper route can provide work experience and income for young teen-agers.

Baby-sitting is a service which frequently provides teen-agers an opportunity for earned income.

COURTESY FUTURE HOMEMAKERS OF AMERICA

Write your resolutions for the year. For each item given below write an appropriate resolution. A few are given as examples.

A is for Aptitudes—
   I'll find mine and develop them.
B is for Brushes—
   I'll keep my hair brush clean.
C is for Clothing care—
   I'll keep my clothes picked up every day.
D is for Dental care—
   I'll brush morning and night and after meals when possible.
E is for Eye care—
F is for Future—
G is for Goals—
H is for Health—
I is for Ideals—
J is for Judgment—
K is for Knowledge—
L is for Lips—
M is for Morals—
N is for Nutrition—
O is for Organization—
P is for Posture—
Q is for Quizzes—
R is for Room—
S is for Skin care—
T is for Table manners—
U is for Undergarments—
V is for Vocations—
W is for Walking—
X is for X-rays—
Y is for You—
Z is for Zeal—

List resources available in your school and community for personal and vocational guidance and counseling.

List both school and community organizations which provide experiences which could help you choose an occupation.

Investigate financial aid programs available to a high school student to help him further his education. Find out how a person can qualify and apply for such assistance.

Some teen-agers are eligible for special learn-while-you-earn, or work-study, programs. These programs allow them to earn varying amounts of money while they complete their educations.

SOURCES OF ASSISTANCE
Today's teen-agers find that many people are ready to help them along the road to a satisfying life. Once, teen-agers had only their families to rely on. People turned to grandparents, uncles, cousins, and distant relatives when they needed help or advice. With the increased mobility of modern families, it has been necessary to combine family and community resources so that teen-agers may be given assistance in finding the opportunities which are available.

Parents and other family members
As in former times, ties remain strong in many families. In such families, parents are the logical people for teen-agers to ask when they need advice. You are fortunate if you have family members who can offer good advice and guidance concerning your future.

Once there were family businesses and family trades. Young people went into the family employment pool as a matter of course. Today, a carpenter's son may become an astronaut, and a bank president's son may prefer to work in a garage. Some families find it hard to accept departures from family traditions. But more and more people are recognizing the fact that each person needs a job which is satisfying to him rather than pleasing to his elders.

Friends
Some of your friends may know you almost as well as your family does. You can try out new ideas on them. You can share your thoughts and feelings, too. You can be very honest with a good friend. While friends your own age may not have had enough experience to offer

Good friends can talk about their problems as they work together.

COURTESY WHAT'S NEW IN HOME ECONOMICS

sound advice for your future, they can provide real encouragement when you have a problem. Both encouragement and guidance may be offered by a teen-ager's older friends. Perhaps an older neighbor or a family friend can make helpful suggestions concerning a social or vocational problem.

Teachers
People usually become teachers because they want to share their knowledge and because they want to help young people. If you find a teacher who seems to understand you particularly well, talk with him freely. Teachers may be easy to approach in such informal situations as physical education classes or laboratories in science, home economics, and industrial arts. Most teachers are more than willing to give assistance. Although teachers are considered to be specialists in the field of mental growth, they are interested in your social and vocational growth as well. Call on them when you need advice or assistance.

Counselors
There are many kinds of counselors who can help you plan for your future. First, there is your school guidance counselor. Your counselor can help you review your school record and arrange for tests that can identify your aptitudes and skills. Leaders of youth groups have wide experience with young people. If

COURTESY OF THE SELMER DIVISION OF THE MAGNAVOX COMPANY

Teachers usually choose to be teachers because they like to work with young people.

you have been a 4-H-er, Scout, Future Farmer, Future Homemaker, Future Teacher, or a member of a similar group, you know leaders to whom you can turn with confidence. Let them know if you need help.

Social service workers and community aides are trained to help you in many areas. Whether your problems are concerned with physical, mental, or social growth, feel free to ask for help when it is needed.

Other professional leaders
Doctors, dentists, and nurses can help with personal problems as well

As a class, list on the chalkboard the qualities desired in a friend. Develop them into a check list entitled *How good a friend am I?* Using a scale such as 1 = poor, 2 = fair, 3 = good, 4 = very good, and 5 = excellent, rate yourself. For the three friendship qualities on which you rated the lowest, make a definite plan for improvement. Report your progress toward strengthening these points. Your friendship check list might include points such as these . . .

Dependability—I can be depended upon to do what is expected of me.

Loyalty—I am loyal to my friends, never talking behind their backs.

Tact—I say things without hurting others' feelings.

Bulletin board IDEA
Title: *What are you cut out to be?*
Directions: Make a row of cut out paper dolls from newspaper, newsprint, or other suitable lightweight paper by folding and cutting it. Cut so that the figures will be joined when the paper is unfolded. Border the display with the row of figures. Below the title mount pictures of people engaged in a variety of jobs.

81

Divide a sheet of paper into two vertical columns. In the left-hand column list traits you like your friends to have. In the right-hand column list traits you would want an employee to possess if you were in the position of hiring workers. Compare the lists. Draw conclusions concerning the relationship of the two lists.

Discuss the merits of this statement, *If I have 10 real friends by the time I'm 80 years old, I'll be a rich person.*

Pretend that you are going to the moon for 6 months. You may take one boy and one girl with you. Who would they be? Why?

Your career
Dietitian for nursery school

Duties: Plans, prepares, and serves meals and snacks for small children. Has a knowledge of nutritional value of foods and general food preferences of children of various ages.
Where employed: Public nursery schools, churches, large department stores, shopping centers or malls, and privately owned nursery schools.

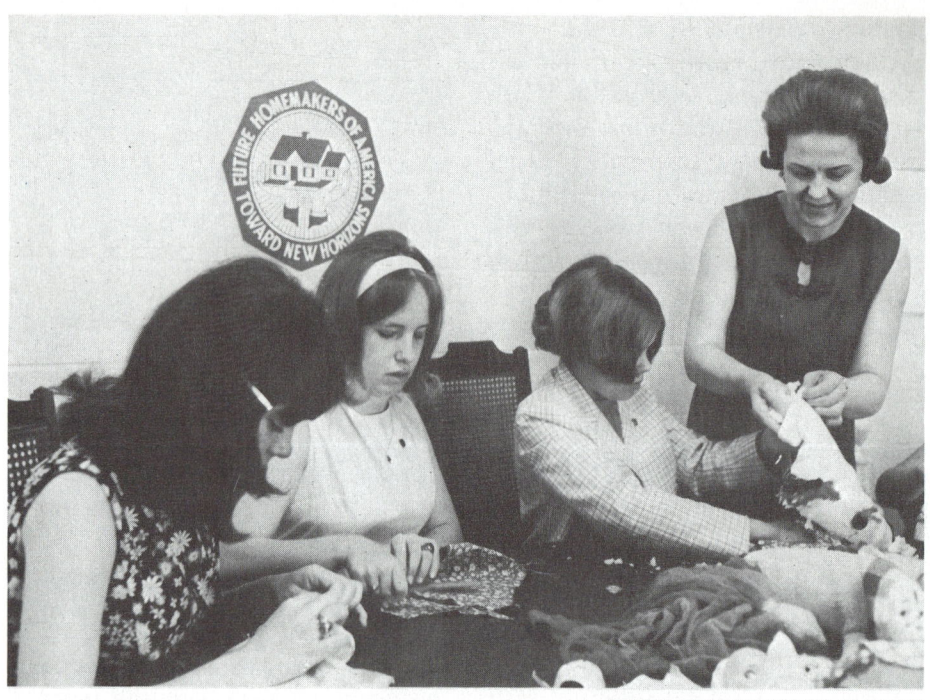

Club sponsors are generally people with whom you can work easily.

as with health problems. Many personal concerns can be handled through better nutrition, better health care, and counseling. Such worrisome conditions as underweight, overweight, and skin infections are problems a teen-ager need not try to cope with alone. Consult a doctor or your school nurse about these conditions as well as any long-lasting sign of ill health such as sleeplessness, poor appetite, stomach upsets, or lasting feelings of depression. As these problems are faced and dealt with in constructive ways, you will find yourself gaining in assurance, wisdom, and maturity.

Setting future goals

When you understand yourself, and when you know your opportunities and your available sources of assistance, you can begin to move in the direction you want to go. The courses you elect in school, the books you read, the friends you make, and the after-school employment you accept can each lead toward the life style and job choices you make for yourself.

PERSONAL GOALS

What kind of a person do you want to be? Confident? Competent? Considerate? Interesting? Well-liked? Responsible? These are goals worth striving toward. Much of the personal shaping you give to your life takes place between your twelfth and twentieth birthdays. Both your social activities and the things you learn in school aid in this development. Do you want a successful marriage, a good education, close friends, or useful accomplishments? All of these are worthwhile.

OCCUPATIONAL GOALS

What job would you choose for a lifetime occupation? Would you rather work with ideas, people, or things? All work has value, both to the person who accomplishes it and to the society that benefits from it. Since work is an outlet for purposeful living, everyone needs some kind of job.

A lifetime occupation is a serious matter. Today, there are many new jobs which have developed during your lifetime. There are also thousands of time-honored jobs from which to choose. One of these occupations is the right one for you. Although it may not please your best friend or other members of your family, choose a job which you like and can do well.

Avoid choosing your lifetime occupation by accident, since the happiness or misery of a lifetime is tied very closely to the satisfaction you find in working. The symbol which appears throughout this book, may show you job opportunities which are of special interest to you.

Your widening circle of friends

As a person grows up, he needs to establish relationships outside his home. You will continue to love your family and want to be with

Tape record conversations held with several boys who are considered leaders in the school. Ask them to comment on the qualities they like and dislike in girls. Replay the tapes so that the class may discuss the points made. If this plan is not workable, some class members may interview the boys asking them the same questions and reporting to the class.

Simple at-home parties for two or more couples offer girls the opportunity to bear part of the expense of dating.

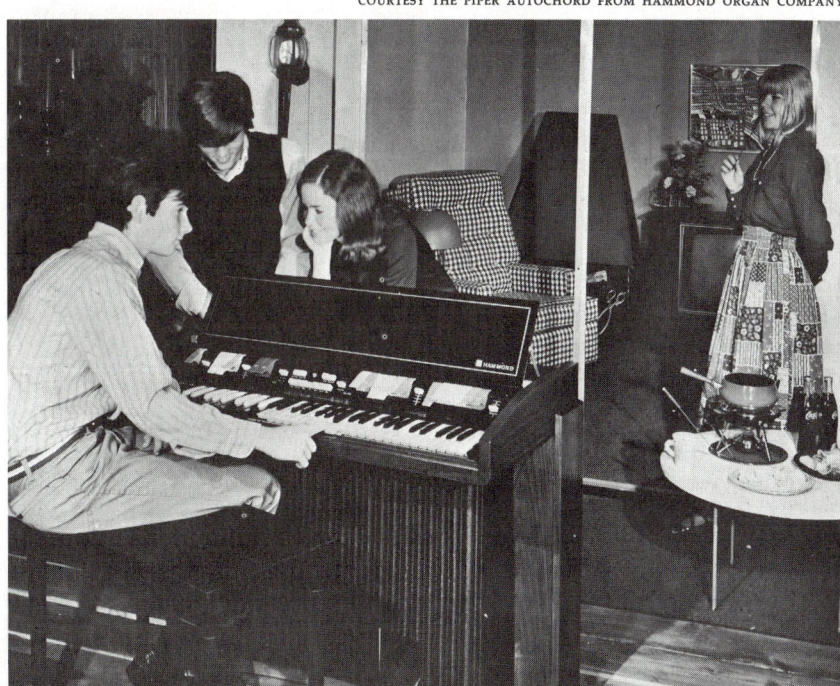

COURTESY THE PIPER AUTOCHORD FROM HAMMOND ORGAN COMPANY

83

Write the word FRIENDSHIP on the chalkboard by arranging the letters in a vertical line. Beside each letter write words which describe the kinds of friends you like to have. For example . . .
F Friendly, forgiving, frank
R Reliable, reassuring
I Interesting
E
N
D
S
H
I
P

Redo the graph substituting words which describe people you do *not* want as your friends.

Your career
Landscape gardener

Duties: Plans and executes small scale landscaping operations and maintains grounds and landscape of private residences or business areas. Prepares and grades terrain, applies fertilizer, seeds and sods lawns, locates and plants shrubs, trees, and flowers selected by property owner or himself.
Where employed: Landscape nursery, greenhouse, or may be self-employed.

them. You also will want friends of your own with whom to share some of your hopes, problems, experiences, and secrets. With friends you can enlarge upon common interests, gain new experiences, and enjoy old and new hobbies.

Has it occurred to you that others just like you are looking for true and lasting friendships? Just as you are sometimes critical of others, so, too, are others deciding whether or not you are worthy of their friendships.

MAKING AND KEEPING FRIENDS
Most people agree that friendships are important, but some people don't seem to know how to make friends. Friendship is earned and must be deserved. Most teen-agers agree that good friends have certain traits in common. What do you look for in a friend? Loyalty? Dependability? Truthfulness? Sincerity? Tolerance? Openness and honesty seem to be among the most important traits a friend can have.

Friends are people who enjoy being together. They help each other when there is trouble. Do you possess the following set of traits? Can they be strengthened with effort?
1. I can be depended upon to finish those jobs I agree to do.
2. I make only promises I can keep.
3. I am sincere and have a genuine interest in others.
4. I am tactful and considerate of the feelings of others.
5. I look for things to praise rather than to criticize.
6. I am honest and loyal, not revealing secrets or confidences.
7. I respect others' belongings. I seldom borrow, I take good care of borrowed items, and I return them promptly.

Friendships are likely to begin in the neighborhood or at school. If you are friendly and relaxed and treat all people in a considerate way, you will attract friends. Friendship is not a thing to be bought. A person who tries to impress others with his possessions will not attract sincere friendships.

It takes time to make a real friend. If you are new in a neighborhood and feel unaccepted, be patient. Friendships worth having are worth waiting for and working toward. Enter into the kinds of activities which interest you. It is natural for people to select their friends from among those who enjoy the same kinds of activities which they themselves like. Similar standards of conduct also attract people to one another. You may need to evaluate a new friend's actions before deciding whether to continue a friendly association.

Friendships need not be ended when people move. You can keep your friendships through letters, cards, or visits.

VALUES OF FRIENDSHIPS

Friendships can enrich a person's life by what he gives as well as by what he gets. Friends make each other feel like worthwhile people. They accept each other. In so doing, they fulfill each other's basic need for acceptance. A wide variety of friends usually helps to make a person more interesting. In many communities there are students who have lived overseas. Friendships with such young people can be a means of encouraging world fellowship and understanding.

It is important to have friends of both sexes. It is equally important to be aware of the problems involved with being a member of a *clique*, a closed circle, within your school. A clique often bands together for status reasons, but the general student body may consider members of cliques to be snobs. As a result, young people in the closed circle lose many opportunities to form valuable new friendships among interesting students outside the group.

Your social growth

Social growth pertains to growth in the area of human relationships. Whether you are learning to live with your family, schoolmates, or casual acquaintances, you are experiencing social growth. Boy-girl relationships eventually become the area of social growth in which teen-agers are most keenly interested.

The difference in the rate of social maturity between boys and girls is rather clearly pronounced by the time they become teen-agers. The fact that girls become interested in dating before boys of the same age frequently causes problems. Boys who work happily in mixed groups to complete class projects tend to prefer the company of boys for social occasions. This can make girls feel unnecessarily rejected.

Teen-agers are wise who accept the fact that there is a real differ-

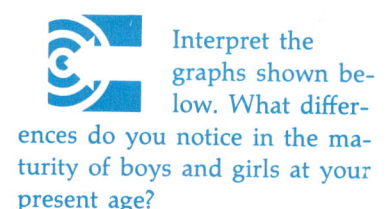

COURTESY MIDOL

Most teen-agers enjoy activities which include a group of people their own age.

Interpret the graphs shown below. What differences do you notice in the maturity of boys and girls at your present age?

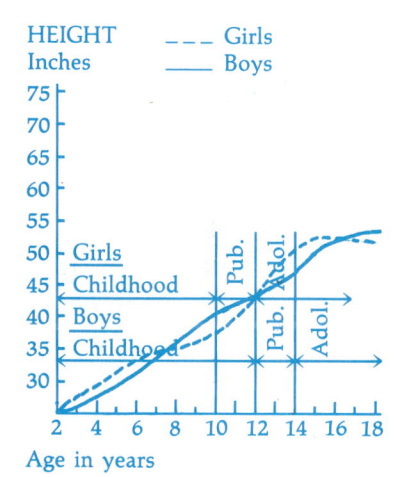

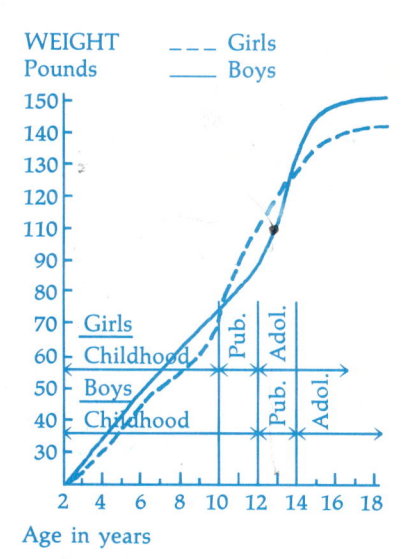

HEIGHT --- Girls
Inches ___ Boys

Age in years

WEIGHT --- Girls
Pounds ___ Boys

Age in years

Pub. = Puberty,
Adol. = Adolescence

85

Plan and give *mini-skits* which show correct and incorrect ways for a boy to ask a girl to go to a party. Plan skits which show correct and incorrect ways for a girl to accept and refuse invitations.

Practice mock situations in which a girl and boy on a date order refreshments in a restaurant. Discuss the difficulties girls face when boys do not give them directives concerning the type of meal and acceptable cost of food to order. Also discuss the results of a girl's overspending in a dating situation.

Bulletin board IDEA
Title: *Fishing for a Date? Check Your Bait.*
Directions: Placing a large picture of a teen-ager on a bulletin board, mount a stick near him which resembles a fishing pole. Dangle a piece of string and a hook from the pole. To the hook attach streamers which describe traits of a good dating partner. For instance, print on the streamers such words as polite, thoughtful, punctual, and good conversationalist.

ence in dating readiness between boys and girls during the early teens. To allow for normal social growth of both boys and girls, try having group functions and group activities. In just a few months or years, most boys will think girls are generally quite wonderful. No longer will they resent the attention girls give them.

Certain customs have grown up around the dating involved with social growth. Local customs differ, but in general a few standard rules apply. In the beginning, girls and boys simply appear at the same social events. Grown-ups usually see that they are safely transported to and from such occasions.

As teen-agers begin to take a special interest in one another, the rules change. Boys begin inviting girls to special functions. The girl must then accept or reject the invitation. Whether her answer is *yes* or *no,* her attitude can be considerate. Both boys and girls should have an understanding with their parents about the time they will be home after a date, and there should be an arrangement to inform both families of any changes in these plans.

GROUP DATING
Group dating is usually the first sign of boy-girl social interest. A group of boys and girls may plan an outing. They may arrange to swim, bowl, skate, or hike. The number of boys and girls may or may not be equal. In such a group, everyone can have a good time. School events and those sponsored by other organizations provide opportunities for young teens to learn how to get along easily with members of the opposite sex. When group activities are planned, each individual usually pays his own way. However, when a group of boys and girls go to a park or a beach to cook their dinner and spend the evening, the food may be furnished by the girls and the transportation by the boys. Music from a portable radio or record player may be their entertainment.

DOUBLE-DATING
After a certain amount of experience in group dating, two girls and two boys may plan a double date. A double date is most enjoyable when both couples are about the same age and share the same interests. Activities enjoyed by larger groups are also suitable for double dates. The difference is that each boy usually assumes the financial obligation of one girl, unless a pay-your-own-way arrangement is the local teen-age custom. When expenses are to be shared on a date, the fact should be made clear in advance.

Sometimes double-daters will join a larger group to share the fun of a local party. The presence of others helps beginning daters to feel more at ease.

SINGLE-DATING

As teen-agers mature, they occasionally go on single dates, social occasions which include only two people. At other times they may prefer to join another couple or a group. As a rule, single-dating is not practiced by young teen-agers. Since so much of the fun of dating is the sharing of happy conversation, many teen-agers tend to date in groups.

GOING STEADY

A *steady* arrangement, where one boy and one girl date each other exclusively, sometimes follows single-dating. To some teen-agers, this dating arrangement gives the assurance of a dating partner. It does cut down, however, on opportunities to meet other boys and girls. Going steady also has the disadvantage that, if one member tires of the arrangement, the other may be very hurt and confused.

The attitudes of families toward steady dating arrangements vary. Some families approve heartily of their young daughters going with only one boy. They feel they can trust his judgment in choosing places to go and in getting their daughter safely home again. Other families definitely disapprove of the idea of steady dating. They feel that teen-agers are likely to become emotionally involved with each other long before serious ideas of marriage can be considered.

Wise teen-agers learn to go along with their parents' wishes. When they give their parents the opportunity to trust them, rules are usually loosened to the point that dating can be fun.

DATING ETIQUETTE

Successful teen-age dating takes at least two thoughtful people. They are careful in their asking for and accepting dates. They are careful to keep their parents informed of their

Practice making introductions. Include examples which illustrate introducing:
A friend from school and your mother
A teacher and your grandmother
A man and a woman
Two of your friends, one a boy and one a girl

When her parents approve, a girl can occasionally invite her date for an at-home snack or an evening of entertainment.

COURTESY MIKASA CHINA

Suggest places to go and things to do in your community for group, double, and single dates. Include activities which cost little or no money.

List the advantages and disadvantages of group, double, and single dates. Discuss the reasons why many young teenagers prefer to begin dating in groups.

List the advantages and disadvantages of going steady. Discuss how going steady can mean different things to different people. Give examples to illustrate how going steady has different meanings in different communities.

Make a list of the girl's responsibilities on a date and another list of the boy's responsibilities on a date.

Read letters concerning dating problems which appear in the women's section of the daily newspaper. Write replies to the letters as if you were a columnist. Share some of the best replies with the class. Discuss why the suggestions offered were good advice.

plans. They are careful to dress in an acceptable manner and to help their dating partner have a good time.

Planning entertainment

Occasionally good times happen almost on the spur of the moment. In general, however, it is safer to make plans in advance. That way, both daters are dressed appropriately for the planned event. Can you think of anything more likely to get a date started wrong than to have the boy show up in dungarees when the girl is wearing her new party dress?

A boy and girl can have fun on a blind date if the plans have been made by friends who know both of them. For instance, you may have a cousin or friend arrive at your home unexpectedly. If you have already made dating plans, it is all right to consult your date about finding someone to make up a foursome. Plans for this type of date might include a movie and an after-movie snack. Such a plan allows you to help a friend entertain your guest who is a stranger to him.

When couples know each other well, shared interests often make the best basis for a successful date. For example, couples who enjoy ice skating may have fun on a skating date. The date might be rather disappointing, however, if only the girl can skate. Sometimes at the close of an especially enjoyable occasion, arrangements may be made for a future date.

Asking for a date

When a boy asks a girl for a date, both should be clear about the plans. Asking a girl what she is doing Friday night can be an embarrassing question at best for both parties. A far better approach would be, "Can you go with me to the basketball game Friday night?" The girl can easily accept or reject such an invitation without being forced to admit that she has nothing else to do.

A boy can ask for a date in person or he can call on the telephone. If friends live far apart, plans can be made by letter. If a girl invites a boy to a dance or a party, she may prefer to do so in writing.

Accepting a date

A girl or boy has an obligation to make a prompt decision concerning an invitation. It is unfair to keep a person dangling in hopes that something better may turn up. If a girl must check with her parents before accepting an invitation, she should tell the boy rather than hedge. Boys understand that many girls have family regulations. They usually appreciate the concern for each other shown by a girl and her family. Both boys and girls are wise to decline invitations with kindness, giving a reason which will spare the other person's feelings.

Dressing for a date

Because parties, ball games, movies, and other teen-age functions are run on a time schedule, courtesy requires that a girl be dressed and ready when a boy calls for her. This means that a girl will be dressed appropriately for the occasion, have her hair combed, and have her makeup on. For a school party she might wear a new dress, an attractive pants suit, or whatever is suggested by those who establish the school's dress code. For a date to go to the movies, she might dress a little more specially than for school. Neatness, cleanliness, and simplicity are always in good taste.

A boy, too, should make an effort to be appropriately dressed for a date. Soiled, rumpled clothing shows lack of self-respect and lack of respect for his date. Slacks, sport shirts, and sweaters or jackets are good selections for informal parties or movie dates. A suit or a sport coat and pants with a shirt and tie are right for meals at special restaurants or special parties.

Both boys and girls should avoid appearing in public in conspicuous clothing. Clothing that is not suited to the wearer or appropriate to the occasion can make a person feel ill at ease. When a girl wears a dress that is fitted too snugly or cut rather low, she may cause embarrassment for both herself and her dating partner. Similarly, a boy may be conspicuous if he wears a suit and tie to a party where the other guests are wearing sport clothes.

Gaining family approval

Parents are responsible for their children until the children are launched into lives of their own. When parents ask about young people's dating plans, they are usually showing responsible interest and concern, rather than interference. Thoughtful teen-agers respond to this interest by telling their

COURTESY GAY GIBSON

A moment spent informing parents of changed plans is a courtesy which encourages parent–teen-age understandings.

Divide the chalkboard into 3 vertical columns. Label the left-hand column *friend,* the middle column *date,* and the right-hand column *mate.* Brainstorm to list the qualities desired in each kind of companion. Discuss the reasons for the similarities and differences in the lists.

Tell about an experience when either a boy or girl was dressed inappropriately for a particular occasion. Discuss the ways in which this situation might have been avoided.

Use a tape recorder to hear how your voice sounds to others. Make suggestions for improving your voice and enunciation.

Let someone in the class who has a flair for the dramatic, present a monologue in which he or she is trying to carry on a conversation with a shy member of the opposite sex. Afterwards, suggest questions this person might have asked to stimulate the conversation and to draw out the untalkative person. Discuss the types of questions which should be avoided such as those which are too personal, too difficult, or require only a yes or no answer.

List occupations which exist today which were unheard of in your grandparents' day. List occupations which were important in the past for which there is no longer any demand. What caused these changes?

List possible part-time job opportunities for teen-agers in various types of seasonal work associated with holidays, harvest times, tourist seasons, sports events, and special festivals or local celebrations.

Your career
Bridal consultant

Duties: Advises prospective brides on various phases of wedding planning, such as attire of wedding party and selection of trousseau. Advises bride on selection of silver pattern, china, glassware, stationery, invitations, flowers, and catering service. May attend rehearsals and wedding ceremony to give advice on etiquette.
Where employed: A large department store, a tuxedo and wedding gown rental company, an exclusive women's specialty shop, or may be self-employed.

parents where they are going, how they will get there, and when they plan to return home.

A considerate boy arrives at the girl's home at the time set for the date. He always calls for her at the door. If he has not met her parents, she will invite him in and introduce them. In using the commonly accepted form of introduction, the girl presents the boy to her parents, saying, "Mother and Dad, this is George Butler." She may mention her parents' last name if it is different from her own. It is the responsibility of the girl's parents to tell the boy what time they expect her to return home. The girl and boy must respect her parents' wishes in this matter.

It is not proper for a girl to invite a boy into the house for any length of time if a parent or another responsible adult is not at home. With her parents' permission, she can invite her date in for a snack after he brings her home. An at-home snack is one way the girl can balance out the heavy expenses a boy must bear when dating.

Dating behavior
On a date for which a boy has extended the invitation, he takes care of the expenses involved. Since the boy's finances may be limited, the girl who is considerate in her suggestions for entertainment and food will usually find herself sought after. If two people are congenial, such inexpensive functions as school activities and neighborhood gatherings can be enjoyable. Overspending seldom adds to the success of a date.

Having arranged a date, the boy and girl together are responsible for making the event enjoyable. If they join others, each should be sure the other is having a good time. Activities should be continual so that embarrassing silences do not occur. Keeping the conversational ball rolling is the responsibility of both parties. Conversation is not a monologue, with one person doing all the talking, but a dialogue in which two people take part.

Some girls feel that they do not know what to talk about when they are with boys. And boys feel the same way about girls. Here is where a little knowledge of many things and the development of many interests can be important. Ask questions until you find the interests of your dating partner. At the same time, be willing to answer your partner's questions in an interesting manner. If you help your partner talk about his or her interests, you are sure to be considered a good conversationalist.

Avoid the mistake of talking about yourself exclusively, especially on dates. That sort of conversation can be very tiresome. Equally boring and in poor taste are descriptions of what happened on other occasions or on other dates.

It is the girl's responsibility to keep track of the time and to say when it is time to go home. This may not be easy when a group is having fun, because the hours have a way of slipping by. However, this part of the date remains the girl's responsibility.

Your ability to be a good date depends on your *friendship quotient*. It is determined by how well you get along with others and how pleasantly you adjust to group decisions. Being a good date, however, does not mean that you must disregard your own values or your own code of behavior. The decision of another person or the crowd is not always the best one for you. You need to decide when to go along with a plan and when to use your own judgment as to your actions.

If it is necessary, as it may be, for one party to break a date, he or she must be honest and tell the other the reason, expressing regret. A date is not to be broken to accept another date. Dates should be broken only in a case of emergency.

Your vocational growth

Growth, as most people view it, means getting taller, or heavier, or bigger in some way. From a vocational point of view, growth doesn't come about in this manner. Vocational growth is measured in the education, attitudes, and skills you are acquiring.

In a social situation, activities are centered around people. Your ability to get along well with people is also important in work situations. However, the emphasis is changed. The purpose of a job is to produce goods or services. It is your ability to adjust your thinking away from yourself and to the job at hand which determines your readiness for vocational undertakings.

THE ECONOMICS OF YOUR JOB CHOICE

It is difficult to think of a job which requires no education or skill. As the world of work continues to become more technical, special training is necessary for most any job. Of course, there is a relationship between education and earning power. However, with the push in our society for a good education for every child, perhaps some people have been educated in the wrong direction. It is possible that too many people are being educated for what is called *professional* work and too few are training to become *skilled* workers.

Perhaps you are facing vocational choices at a time when there is a change in the total thinking which affects the world of work. Today may be the time when each person can choose and train for a job he likes. His income may be based on the *quality* of his work rather than his *choice of occupation*. What kind of work would you like?

Answer this letter as if you were Joe's long-time friend:

Dear old Buddy,
I wish I could see you and talk over something very important. You always have a level head and give good advice. Boy, could I use some now. Here is the situation—I have been offered a job. It is a good job, $2.10 an hour, down at Donavan's garage. They need someone immediately and tell me that they don't care if I have a high school diploma or not since they are so short-handed. They tell me I can learn mechanics while I am working. Just think, I can earn close to $100 a week. What I couldn't do with that. That's the score. Should I stick with school or grab this opportunity? I must decide soon or the job will be gone. Please answer right away.

As ever,
Joe

List opportunities in your community for boys and girls your age to make money.

CAREERS IN HOME ECONOMICS

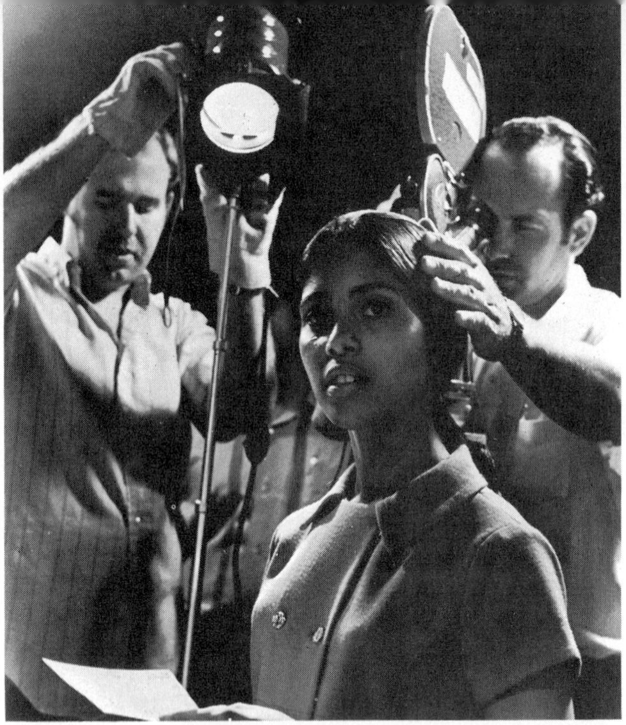

COURTESY MCGRAW-HILL CLOTHING CONSTRUCTION FILM LOOPS

Modeling

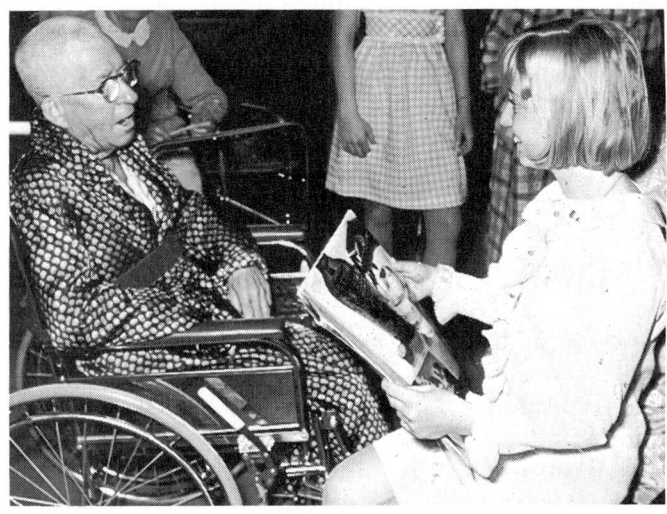

COURTESY FUTURE HOMEMAKERS OF AMERICA

Social work

COURTESY GIRL SCOUTS OF THE U.S.A.

Interior design

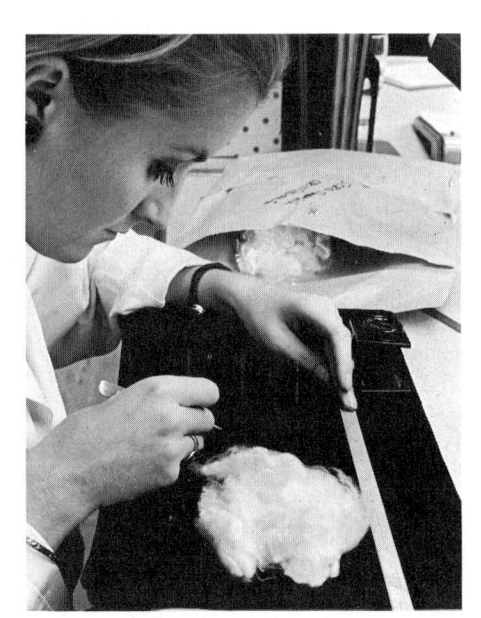

COURTESY CELANESE FIBERS MARKETING COMPANY

Foods or textile research

POSSIBLE JOB CHOICES
You have something of value to offer to society. It is time to think seriously about the things you can offer as well as the opportunities available. It may be too early for setting your final vocational goal, but it is wise to begin thinking of things you would like to do. Consider your talents and aptitudes as you think of possible job choices. Try to be sensible in choosing a job which you can do successfully.

By now you have noticed occupations briefly presented in the side column of this book. When you read about an occupation which particularly interests you, search in your school library for facts concerning that occupation. Ask your teacher or counselor for information or help as you begin to think about your future in the world of work.

Check yourself
As you consider your occupation of the future, think of the work habits and attitudes you are developing which will help you make a success of your life's work. Check the statements listed on the following chart. Your ability to honestly say *yes* in relation to the job of your choice indicates your growth toward vocational success.

TYING PRESENT TO FUTURE
As you continue to study home economics, you will become aware of many job opportunities in this field. As a young teen-ager, you may make a general study of the various areas within home economics. In advanced courses you may study a single field in greater detail.

Home economics is divided into five large areas. They include:
1 Human development and the family
2 Home management and family economics
3 Foods and nutrition
4 Textiles and clothing
5 Housing and interior design

In each of these five areas there are a number of jobs which require various amounts of formal education. You might enjoy working with troubled families. Perhaps your interests are in working with small children. Perhaps you would like to work in a hospital kitchen or in a restaurant or school cafeteria. Perhaps your interests lie in the fields of foods or textile research. Perhaps you would prefer to design clothing or to work in the field of merchandising. Perhaps you would like to work with architects to build efficient housing. Or perhaps you would like to work with furniture, colors, and fabrics in the field of interior decoration. Whatever your choice, there are opportunities at many levels in every field.

These are only a few of the many opportunities from which both boys and girls can choose their lifetime occupations. The occupation you choose may determine whether you

Invite a school counselor to come to class to discuss occupational opportunities in your local area and in the state. Ask him about the type of education and training required to fill one of these positions. He may also discuss the approximate costs involved in attending a junior college, private or state college or university, business school, or a vocational-technical school.

Invite a person from the local state employment office to come to class to discuss the employment situation in your community. Discuss the effects of the local employment situation on teen-agers and their families.

Your career
Visiting homemaker

Duties: Goes into a home to assume the responsibilities of the homemaker without outside direction. This may be a temporary or long-range position.
Where employed: In homes where illness or death have deprived the family of the mother's services.

Divide the class into five buzz groups. Let each group take one of the following areas of home economics and brainstorm for occupational opportunities in that field:

Human Development and the Family
Home Management and Family Economics
Foods and Nutrition
Textiles and Clothing
Housing and Interior Design

List for the class the occupations mentioned in each area. Ask the class as a whole to suggest additional opportunities in each of these fields.

Interview people employed in occupations relating to the 5 areas of home economics. Develop a list of qualifications for people engaged in each of these occupations.

Bulletin board IDEA
Title: *Star Studded Careers in Home Economics*
Directions: Make five large stars from aluminum foil. From each star, cut out letters to form the names of occupations in the five areas of home economics. Mount the stars on a bright blue background. Replace with new stars featuring different careers.

Check your salable work habits

1. I have a real desire to learn new skills and new ways of doing things.
2. I am neat in my personal appearance and my personal work habits.
3. I am punctual.
4. I can apply myself to a job without being easily bored or distracted.
5. I can work under pressure, when necessary, without becoming nervous and upset.
6. I can adapt to new and unexpected situations.
7. I have confidence in my own abilities.
8. I have a sense of duty and responsibility.
9. I can cooperate with fellow workers.
10. I can gain the friendship and respect of fellow workers.
11. I can cooperate with supervision and management.
12. I can follow directions willingly and without argument because I respect authority.
13. I can understand instructions and carry them out accurately.
14. I can accept criticism without feeling hurt.
15. I can work without constant supervision.
16. I ask questions about things I don't understand.
17. I can complete a job once I start it.
18. I am a pleasant person to work with.
19. I like people.

How did you do? If you answered *yes* to most of the statements, you will probably be a good employee.

will work while finishing high school or whether you will continue your education at a technical or community college or university. In fairness to yourself, try to get the best education common sense will allow you to obtain. Each person's educational goals are affected by his family's financial situation and his own ability to learn. Yet, there is some form of education or training suitable for every person who wants it.

As early as possible, decide what you would like to do. Learn the requirements necessary for work in that field. Your day-to-day actions can easily determine the degree of success you will have in your chosen occupation.

CHAPTER 5 POSTTEST

Number from 1 to 20. Beside each number indicate if the corresponding statement is true or false. *Do not* write in this book.

1. The satisfaction a person finds in his occupation has an effect on his overall happiness in life.
2. Some people try to buy friendship with material possessions.
3. It is unreasonable for parents of teen-agers to expect their children to be home from a party at a predetermined time.
4. Double dating has some advantages that single dating does not have.
5. Going steady can give a person a sense of security.
6. A good way for a boy to ask a girl for a date is to inquire, "Are you busy on Saturday night?"
7. When a boy asks a girl for a date, he should tell her where they will be going.
8. It is socially acceptable for a girl to break a date with one boy to accept a date with another.
9. It is acceptable etiquette for a boy to remain in the car and blow the horn to indicate to his date that he is there.
10. After a boy calls for a girl, she should take 5 to 10 minutes to finish getting ready so that she will not appear overly eager.
11. Sloppy dress may indicate a lack of respect for your date as well as a lack of self-respect.
12. The best way for a girl to introduce a boy to her parents is to say, "Bill, I'd like you to meet my mother and father."
13. On a date, it is poor taste to talk about dates you have had with other people.
14. On a date, it is the girl's responsibility to keep track of the time and to say when it is time to go home.
15. A blind date is correctly arranged by others without the two people involved knowing anything about the situation.
16. Dating contributes to preparation for marriage.
17. Vocational growth is achieved only through occupational training.
18. Occupations in the fields of home economics are limited to women only.
19. Generally, the higher a person's level of education, the greater is his overall lifetime income.
20. Because there will be new and different job opportunities when you are out of school, there are no advantages in planning and preparing for your job of the future now while you have support from family and teachers.

Match the *related words* in list A with the *descriptive terms* in List B. Use a term from List B only once.

List A: **Related words**

A Good education, successful marriage, useful and satisfying occupation
B Sincerity, honesty, loyalty, reliability
C Actions and behavior
D A circle of friends which tends to exclude others
E Employment skills

List B: **Descriptive terms**

1. Clique
2. Personal goals
3. Standards of conduct
4. Values
5. Vocational growth

Give the following information on a separate sheet of paper.

1. List 4 sources of vocational guidance.
2. Give 3 disadvantages to going steady in the early teens.
3. List 8 salable work habits which would be assets in any occupation.
4. List 5 courtesies, or rules of etiquette, to be followed in accepting or rejecting an invitation.

2
Your Home and Family

Chapter 6   Using your home for family living
Chapter 7   Centering the home around growing children
Chapter 8   Managing the problems of family living
Chapter 9   Managing the household tasks of family living

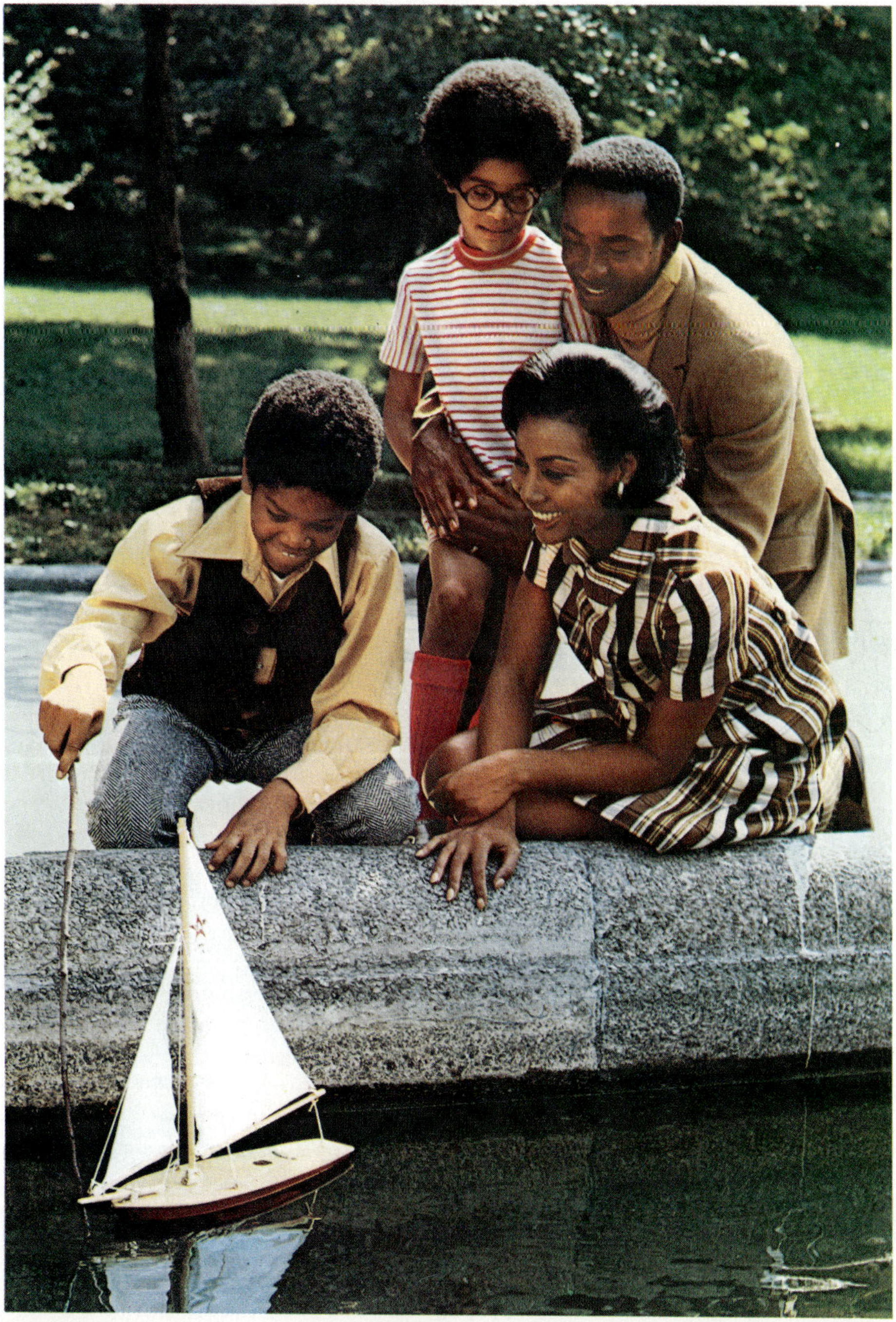

CHAPTER 6 PRETEST

Number from 1 to 32. Beside each number indicate if the corresponding statement is true or false. *Do not* write in this book.

1. One of the most important needs which can be met in a home is the need for security.
2. The security a person feels is caused by a large income and many material possessions.
3. People in a family can be related by blood, marriage, or the process of adoption.
4. A person's responsibilities lessen when he marries.
5. When a mother goes to work outside the home, there is no need for a change in home duties carried by the family.
6. In most families, the mother makes the greatest number of decisions concerning the spending of the family income.
7. A child's role in the family depends in part upon his age and maturity, his sex, the size of the family, and his position in the family.
8. A child tends to be more self-reliant as he grows older.
9. Being the middle child in a family of three brothers and sisters is ideal, because there are no disadvantages to this position.
10. A greater degree of maturity is usually expected of the youngest child than was expected of his brothers and sisters when they were his age.
11. An only child is more likely to be independent than is a child the same age who has younger brothers and sisters.
12. Identical twins have identical personalities.
13. Occasional arguing and quarreling among teen-age brothers and sisters is quite common.
14. A feeling of uselessness is an emotion which may accompany old age unless younger family members provide opportunities for older people to contribute to family well-being.
15. A three-generation family can be a happy one.
16. Listening may be one of the most valuable contributions a teen-ager can make to the life of an older person.
17. Because teen-agers develop many interests outside the home, there is no longer any reason to share in family activities.
18. In developing happy family relationships, the number of activities shared by family members is more important than the quality of the experiences.
19. A family's resources include attitudes, talents, and skills.
20. The way in which a family spends its money may be more important than the amount of money they have to spend.
21. Most spending plans make provision for buying some things the family wants as well as for the things they need.
22. A family might save money by doing things for themselves instead of buying the services of other people to do the same jobs.
23. Family disagreements may be lessened by making arrangements in advance for sharing responsibilities for work to be done.
24. The amount of fun a family has is related to the amount of money spent for recreation.
25. In most homes, it would be customary for a teen-ager to consult his mother before he asked a friend to stay for dinner.
26. If some of his parents' friends come for a visit unexpectedly, a teen-ager has no responsibility for making them feel welcome.
27. An emergency shelf of convenience foods can be very helpful when you are entertaining guests who had not been expected.
28. There are some advantages to entertaining guests on the spur of the moment.
29. It is poor manners for several friends to pool their resources to get one gift for a mutual friend.
30. In selecting a gift for a friend, the most important consideration is that you spend at least as much as your friend spent for the last present he gave you.
31. All gifts should be given in wrapped packages.
32. A gift received through the mail should be acknowledged by a thank-you note.

CHAPTER 6

Using your home for family living

A home is more than a house. It is the combination of all the materials, talents, skills, activities, feelings, and hopes which a group of people draws upon to build itself into a family. Think of what a home can offer: physical protection; mental, emotional, and spiritual guidance; love, security, and a sense of belonging. These provide a background through which a family helps its young members prepare for adulthood. In fact, it is this kind of background which makes a happy, meaningful home for anyone who lives there.

The home meets physical needs

Food, clothing, and shelter are basic and necessary for normal development. But if a child is to grow into a well-rounded adult, basics are not enough. Quality enters in. Within the home, each child needs to receive *nourishing* food, *appropriate* clothing, and *clean, dry* shelter. The home which meets each of these needs adds further meaning to life if it does so in a spirit of love. In what ways does your home add meaning to your life?

Make a list of those concerns, problems, and worries which your parents have. Then list your own concerns, problems, and worries. Compare the lists. Draw conclusions from having made this comparison.

Make a list of household duties and chores which you think it is fair and right for parents to expect of a teenager. Discuss why the class members' lists vary.

Give examples you have noticed which show that men's roles and women's roles have changed in your lifetime.

Bulletin board IDEA
Title: *What Is a Homemaker?*
Directions: Determine the services a homemaker performs for her family. Then find pictures that represent a homemaker acting in the role of nurse, counselor, cook, decorator, or other homemaker roles. Arrange the pictures around the title. Change the pictures from time to time.

Decide which of the following you consider essential for happy family life. Discuss your decisions in class. *Do not write in this book.*

1. The parents provide the children with plenty of spending money.
2. The mother does most of the work, and the children have no home responsibilities.
3. All family members speak English.
4. The parents require that the children be good athletes, good musicians, and good students.
5. Plans are made which allow for all family members, including very young ones, to have some experiences away from home.
6. The home is located in the best section of town.
7. The parents encourage the children to share and to be cooperative.
8. Rest and relaxation are planned for all family members.
9. Family members are encouraged to have friends their own age.
10. The family is interested in helping each member do at least one worthwhile thing well.
11. Each child has a room of his own.

The home meets mental and emotional needs

The home which provides love and security offers its members a chance to open their minds for mental and emotional growth. People who can talk and be listened to at home begin this development quite early. If they are given a chance to go to school and are allowed to attend social group activities, mental and emotional needs can be met in slightly different environments. Through activities at home or those approved by the family, young people grow at a more rapid pace than if neglected by older family members.

One of the most important things a home can offer its members is a feeling of security. When a family member is accepted for what he is, he is able to develop easily as a secure member of the family group. In modern society, many young people are accepted into a home other than their natural one. If they are accepted for what they are, generally there soon develops a close family relationship between all of those who live together.

The security a home gives is not just financial or material in nature. It also includes the assurance you feel when there is a special spot that only you can fill. Perhaps only a person who has lived alone for a long time can appreciate to the full extent the security of a home. He knows what is missing in a life where there is no family to turn to for advice, comfort, appreciation, or understanding.

You may take your home for granted now, not realizing its true value. You may feel that your family doesn't understand you very well. But even when there is some quarreling and bickering at home, the family circle is the place where most young people feel more secure and more loved than in any other group. To them, the home offers stability never again found until they build homes of their own.

The role of parents

Have you ever stopped to consider the role your parents play as parents? In a world that is changing as rapidly as ours, their responsibilities are many and sometimes heavy. Financial pressures, the day-to-day grind of a job, illness, or personal problems may make them worried and tense at times. Often they are tired. Still, they must go on with the job of being a parent and continue with their other activities as well.

Many of their responsibilities are rewarding. Parents are happy to see the growth and development of their children. Most of them enjoy their family's achievements and find pleasure in being with their children. By showing pride in your parents' achievements at work or at

COURTESY GENERAL FOODS KITCHENS

A mother frequently fills the roles of both wage earner and homemaker in today's society.

12. The family generally enjoys doing things together.
13. The family provides opportunities for the children to make money by helping around the house.
14. The father earns a big salary.
15. The girls' dresses are always bought in a store.
16. The parents express their love for their children through their actions.
17. The family always eats in a dining room.
18. The family's food is nutritious.
19. The house is up-to-date and modern with the newest types of equipment.
20. The father is employed in a professional occupation.
21. Some parts of the house are warm, dry, and comfortable.
22. The family goes regularly to a doctor or to a clinic.
23. The mother has a career outside the home.
24. The family members are proud of each others' accomplishments.

Why are there no right and wrong responses to this checklist?

Why do the class members consider different factors essential for happy family living?

home, you can make life seem more rewarding to them.

BEING A PARENT

The job of parenthood is, in a sense, the most responsible job a person ever accepts. With parenthood comes the responsibility for the growth and well-being of a child, whether natural or adopted. The outcome of a life rests to a large degree in the hands of parents. Imagine what your life would be like if your parents were not on the job every day. Then consider the many ways in which you are dependent upon them and the many responsibilities they have.

Providing for the family

Most families try to provide for their children's physical needs, as well as to give the protection, guidance, love, and security their children require. Parents, or parent substitutes, need to be on hand so the children can talk over problems with them in the hope of making

COURTESY COCA-COLA COMPANY

Most parents attach great importance to the security and social development of their children.

wise decisions. At the same time they can make an effort to steer the family along a smooth course, hopefully preventing small irritations from becoming major problems. They also must handle day-to-day tasks as they plan ahead for their family's future.

Personal problems of parents
Parents are expected to set a good example. Often, however, this is difficult because adults have problems as serious as those of their children. Sometimes teen-agers forget that their parents have many of the same problems they have and also many of the same desires. Parents may be facing problems such as getting along with each other, helping their own aging parents or other relatives, and handling heavy social obligations. They may have worries about unemployment, personal appearance, health, or other things that they never mention. As a teen-ager begins to understand that each person has problems which are important to him, the tensions within his home tend to ease.

In families where parents do not get along well with each other, teen-agers can be cooperative and understanding. The teen-ager's cooperation is even more important in situations where parents are separated. The parents may be divorced, and children may live with one parent and a stepfather or stepmother. Such a situation may call for more understanding than a teen-ager can give unless he gets the help of a trusted outside person.

In your relations with your parents, it is essential that you try to understand their side of any matter. Also, try to explain your side so that they can understand your way of thinking. A certain amount of give-and-take is necessary in happy parent-child relationships.

Changing family roles
It takes time, money, energy, and patience to rear a family. Someone must supply the money. Someone must make sure that the everyday necessities are there. Someone must care for the sick. Someone must supervise and guide growing children. In today's changing society, many families must decide who will be responsible for each of these tasks.

The father's role includes financial, child-care, and family-leadership responsibilities. Even when the mother works, if there is a father in the home, he is usually the major wage earner. The father has a special role in rearing and caring for children and helping them to learn their adult roles. He is a family leader and projects this image to the children.

Many homes change when the mother goes to work to increase the family's income. The change often includes a change in the father's

Observe your family and note the times and places where difficulties arise. Suggest ways in which changes can be made to improve each situation.

Show your parents these courtesies:
Address them by the titles they prefer such as *Mother, Father, Mom,* or *Dad.*
Always introduce your friends to your parents.
Stand when your parents introduce you to one of their friends, and acknowledge the introduction, repeating the person's name.
Answer politely the questions your parents' friends ask you —even though at times they may seem foolish.
When a parent gets the facts wrong in telling about something, avoid correcting him in front of others.
Do not argue, especially in public, when a parent says *No.*
In a restaurant, wait for your mother to place her order first.
Be a cheerful and pleasant companion.
Show good manners and respect, treating your mother like a lady and your father like a gentleman.

Read a biography or part of a biography of a famous person such as Franklin Roosevelt, Elizabeth Barrett Browning, or George Washington Carver. Tell the rest of the class about some of the environmental handicaps of his or her early years. Discuss his achievements. List the personal characteristics he had which made him a highly respected person. Why was he able to achieve greatness in spite of his early environment?

Using other well-known people, give examples to show how they have overcome environmental handicaps to live productive lives.

Listen to an appropriate short dramatic reading from *God's Little Acre* or *The Grapes of Wrath*. Discuss the effects of environment on the interpersonal relationships of the people who have been characterized.

Relate incidents you have observed, have read about, or have seen on TV in which a family cooperated to work out a conflict.

Plan a home experience for improving yourself as a family member. Carry out your plan for one month. Report the results to your teacher orally or in a brief written summary.

COURTESY WESTINGHOUSE ELECTRIC CORPORATION

Fathers and children frequently perform tasks formerly considered to be only a mother's responsibility.

role. In order to make the mother's life a bearable one, he takes on many of the tasks she performed earlier. It is not at all unusual to see a father and his children buying the family's weekly supply of groceries. Nor is it strange to see him doing the family laundry at the local laundromat.

Most men understand that society has changed so that the survival of families, even at a modest level, often requires two pay checks. If a wife is to continue to be a companion to the husband and children while she works outside the home, then the father's cooperation in carrying out household tasks is necessary.

The mother's role usually includes the major responsibility for the smooth running of the household, whether or not she works outside the home. Until she is absent from home or ill, her family may not realize the wide variety of tasks and advisory roles a mother regularly assumes.

In most homes, the mother tries to see that the family income, from whatever source, is wisely spent. She makes most of the decisions concerning family buying. In addition, she is often expected to be the family's cook, driver, gardener, nurse, laundress, and seamstress.

She is expected to train the young, listen sympathetically to the problems of each family member, and provide necessary encouragement and support to her family.

The many demands of a mother's role may result in physical and emotional strain and fatigue. She needs the cooperation and understanding of the rest of the family. She also needs to feel that she is appreciated rather than taken for granted.

If the mother is employed outside the home, there is even more need for family understanding and cooperation. The family is to be admired whose members volunteer to do many of the things the mother would do if she were at home all of the time. When she comes home from work, she may be too tired to take part in some of the household activities. At such times the rest of the family can give her special consideration and assistance. It is a cooperative, understanding attitude which is most helpful when a mother is expected to work both at home and away.

Roles of brothers and sisters

There are advantages and disadvantages in being one of several children. Each child plays a role in his family. The roles may vary, depending on the position of the child in the family and on the size of the family. If you are a member of such a family, there may be times when you depend on the warmth of your relationship with your brothers or sisters. Then there may be times when you get tired of having brothers and sisters and wish you could be completely free of them. Some teen-agers feel guilty when they are annoyed to this point. It is not unusual to feel an-

Role-play situations which show conflicts caused by the age or sex of brothers and sisters or their varying interests. Situations might include:
Use of the telephone
Use of makeup
Use of family possessions
Use and amount of allowance
Freedom to choose clothing
Family chores
Age to begin dating

One of a teen-ager's greatest contributions to a happy family is the ability to understand and support his parents when problems arise.

COURTESY DR. PEPPER COMPANY

Divide the class into four groups. Place in one group those students who are the oldest child in their family, in another group those who are the youngest, in another group those who are middle children, and in another group those who are the only child. In these groups, discuss the advantages and disadvantages of that particular position in the family. Report the results of these discussions to the entire class. What general conclusions can be made?

Suggest ways in which an expectant mother can prepare an older child for the arrival of a new baby. Suggest things the mother and other family members can do after the new baby has come home which will give an older child a sense of security.

Discuss the advantages and disadvantages of being the only boy in a family of all girls and the only girl in a family of all boys.

Write Golden Rules for *Getting Along with* _____. Choose someone in your family with whom you would like to improve your relationship.

noyed with those with whom you must associate. Even your best friend would probably irritate you if you lived and worked together in the same home day after day.

CHILDREN IN A FAMILY ARE DIFFERENT

Within a family the oldest child, the middle child, and the youngest child frequently have very different traits, values, and goals. The *only child* in a family may take an entirely different outlook on life from that of children in larger families. Twins, while often quite different from one another, share a companionship different from that held between any other family members.

In large families, children soon learn to share with others. There are likely to be some differences in the way each is affected by his position in the family.

The oldest child

The oldest child was an only child until his younger brother or sister was born. He received the undivided attention of his parents until younger brothers and sisters joined the family. Sometimes an improperly handled oldest child never fully accepts his brothers and sisters. He resents the fact that his parents' attention must be shared with others. As a rule, however, he outgrows this resentment. He is happy in helping with the younger children and may assume many more responsibilities than they do. As a result, he may become quite self-reliant. At the same time he may tend to be bossy toward younger brothers and sisters. Of course, because he is older, it is likely that he will have some special privileges along with special responsibilities.

The middle child

Sometimes it seems that the middle child has a difficult place in the family. He may envy or try to do the things done by the oldest child in the family. At the same time he may seek for the kind of attention being given to a younger brother or sister. There are advantages in his family position, however. He is often spared some of the mistakes made by parents in working with the first child in the family. Too, he is likely to grow out of babyhood sooner than if he were the youngest child.

The youngest child

Sometimes the youngest child may have too much done for him. His parents often do not expect of him as much as they expected of his older brothers and sisters at the same ages. Brothers and sisters tend to help him out of difficult situations. They may think of him as a baby, even when he is old enough to do many things for himself. On the other hand, he has brothers and sisters to act as playmates and to show him how to do things. Generally, he grows up feeling accepted as an important member of the family group. Nevertheless, he needs to be aware, as he moves into circles beyond the home, that he may have never carried his full share of responsibilities.

The only child
Although the only child does not have brother-sister problems, he may have other, more serious difficulties. His parents are more likely to continue to consider him their baby. He may find it difficult to become independent as he grows up. He may also lack companions of his own age, spending too much time with parents and other adults. He may also be lonely and wish for the companionship of brothers and sisters which his friends enjoy.

Of course, there are also a number of advantages in being an only child. The parents are able to give him individual attention and, if he needs it, a larger share of the family dollar. He does not need to compete with brothers and sisters for recognition by others.

Twins
Some twins look so much alike that it may be difficult to tell which is which. Others may look entirely different. Twins may seem to enjoy having everything alike—their toys, their clothes, and their daily routine. As they grow older, though,

Children within a family generally learn to adapt to a family situation, whether they are an *only* child or one of several.

Get approval to visit a home for elderly people. Prepare refreshments to take and plan some form of entertainment. Perhaps some students would like to return to the home later to visit with, read to, or write letters for the residents.

Invite a grandparent who gets along well in a three-generation family to come to class. Ask him or her to discuss the adjustments which were necessary for happy family living in his particular household.

Visit a Golden Age Club in your community to demonstrate some special skill which would be of interest to the members. This may involve doing some kind of handicraft, making seasonal decorations, or demonstrating how to make inexpensive gifts and novelties.

Discuss and demonstrate the courtesies which younger people are expected to show to older people.

Suggest ways in which older people can be made to feel wanted and useful by contributing to the family's well-being.

they may wish to be treated as individuals and may develop personalities that are very different.

As young children, twins do not seem to need much attention from brothers and sisters or parents. They have each other for companionship. However, as they build their own personalities, they tend to separate into two individuals, each requiring that his physical, mental, and emotional needs be met.

QUARRELS BETWEEN CHILDREN

A survey made recently asked questions of boys and girls who had brothers or sisters. When asked about quarrels, 98 percent of the boys and 99 percent of the girls admitted that they had arguments at least now and then. The causes for brotherly and sisterly quarrels included these: (1) household chores and responsibilities; (2) favors by parents to one or another of the children in the family; (3) treatment of friends by a brother or sister; (4) borrowing and lending of personal possessions; and (5) caring for younger children in the family.

As in all relations, it usually isn't the obvious thing that causes a quarrel. A deeper problem may be triggered by something as simple as a friendly "hello" your younger sister gives to your best friend. Deeper problems may be caused by resentment, insecurity, envy, or anger with self. There is very often some jealousy between brothers and sisters. One of the children may be better looking or more popular or may earn better grades. Most jealousy will be outgrown in time. In any case, one way to play down hostile feelings toward brothers and sisters is to be proud of them. Act happy when your brother has made the team or your sister has been asked to model in a school fashion show. Generally, as they react to your interest in them, quarrels tend to become less frequent.

The role of older family members

Grandparents frequently play an active role in the total family situation. They may be comparatively young, vigorous people who have full-time jobs which will keep them busy for a number of years. They may have their own homes with teen-agers or young adult children of their own. Often, also, they may assume the care of a grandchild or grandchildren whose mother works. Some do part-time work or take part in community activities after retirement. If they are in good health, they may prefer to be quite independent, living alone and visiting only for short periods with their children's families.

Particularly when a grandparent or other elderly relative lives with the family, his role within the family becomes a source of joy or irritation. Children must understand the needs and problems peculiar to older people. Unless they do, difficulties usually develop.

CHANGES THAT ACCOMPANY OLD AGE

Men and women reaching retirement age today can expect to live longer than if they had lived a generation ago. This general lengthening of the life span causes them to be faced with many changes that go along with what people sometimes call the *golden years.*

People continually change physically, but this change is very pronounced during old age. Hearing and vision may be affected. It is not so easy for older people to move around as it once was. There may be frequent aches and pains. There may even be pains which are imagined.

Old people often need food that is easily chewed and digested. Sometimes they must be urged to drink milk and to eat fruits and vegetables. They may eat heavy breakfasts but prefer light lunches and early dinners.

A feeling of loneliness is frequently a part of old age. As a person grows older, he finds that many of his loved ones and old friends are gone. Younger people, with different interests and little free time, seldom stop to talk with him. As he becomes less active and as his hearing and eyesight become less keen, the older person may begin to lose contact with the world around him. Often he begins to feel helpless, or worse yet, useless. All of these aspects of old age may tend to complicate life in a home where three or more generations live together.

WELCOMING OLDER FAMILY MEMBERS

Often teen-agers can do more than anyone else to make the three-generation family a happy one. While rebellion at the thought of old folks about the house is very common among teen-agers, an acceptance of aged grandparents is a

COURTESY HUNT-WESSON FOODS, INC.

A grandparent can generally fit happily into a home when he is encouraged to feel like a useful part of the family.

Bulletin board IDEA
Title: *The Best Things in Life Are Free*
Directions: Mount pictures which show families having happy times together. Ask students to bring to class pictures which show the affection and warmth family members feel for each other. Change the pictures every few days.

109

Collect newspaper columns which contain letters concerned with teen-age–parent relationships. Divide into groups of three or four students. With only the letters in hand, let each group write an appropriate reply. Read the published letters and the students' replies to the rest of the class. Discuss these and then compare them with the columnists' answers.

thing to be admired. When teen-agers know that blanket rules and orders given out by grandparents can be softened by understanding parents, they usually can live with an unhappy situation. Often they learn to take lectures with a grain of salt. Such situations can actually weld parents and children more closely together.

Teen-agers who are mature enough to accept grandparents, sometimes even sharing a room with them, frequently find themselves admired by their own friends. Often friends will join them and their grandparents in playing dominoes, checkers, or similar games.

Many things can be done to make the three-generation family a happy one. Besides taking care of a grandparent's physical needs, teen-agers can give him companionship, consideration, and respect.

Older people may enjoy having you read to them or talk about things that happened during the day. Frequently all they need is someone who will listen. As you grow older, you will treasure firsthand stories of a childhood lived long ago, whether in this country or another. You may have read great novels by writers who, as children, enjoyed listening to adventure tales told by their elders.

An older person may enjoy being included in the family games. Although he may forget the rules, winning may make the whole day bright for a person who can no longer move about. Some grandparents enjoy gardening, woodworking, rug hooking, painting with oils or watercolors, or needlework. These activities may be even more meaningful for a grandparent if, while working with such hobbies, he feels he is teaching interesting skills to a beloved grandchild.

Older people may enjoy an occasional opportunity to baby-sit with young children. On the other hand, if the older person is not strong and the children are boisterous, other arrangements will be

Loneliness which accompanies old age is lessened when grandparents can exchange feelings of affection with their grandchildren.

COURTESY HUNT-WESSON FOODS, INC.

necessary. An elderly person's services are not to be used as a convenience. Through his years of loving service, he has earned a lifetime right to the family's affection and respect.

Family sharing

Most families first learn to share by sharing family activities. They also share resources such as money and possessions. Too, a family can share fun, friends, and special occasions. Of course, family responsibilities must also be shared by family members. Although each member need not share in every single family function, the happy family is generally bound together because it shares a *singleness of purpose.*

Sharing home duties offers an opportunity for sharing thoughts, ideas, and problems. For instance, working with mother in preparing meals gives a teen-ager a chance to talk about pleasant happenings at school, to tell about a perplexing situation with a friend, or to discuss future plans. Cleaning up after the meal presents an opportunity for those involved to share confidences, tell about funny experiences, or sing for the joy of singing.

As children become teen-agers, it is difficult for the family to share time together. Each person's private interests tend to pull him from the family group. However, with effort, each member may operate in his own circles of interest while the family remains close in spirit.

Usually the members of a family are proud of the part any one of them takes in community activities or any talent displayed in athletics, art, music, or dramatics. But with so many outside activities in progress, most families must make a real effort to find time for family functions.

Knowing their true and lasting value, many families make a strong effort to have family-centered activities. Often it is the quality of the shared experiences rather than the number of occasions shared which gives a family this sense of unity. Whether time spent together is used for hobbies, conversation, or community service, it is common interests shared together which weld a family into a strong unit.

SHARING FAMILY RESOURCES

A family's resources are made up of its material possessions as well as its talents, skills, attitudes, and health. Together they make it possible for people to live together as a family. While money is a necessary resource, another equally important one is the labor given by family members in producing necessary articles or in making the home run smoothly.

The family's money

Money usually comes to the family as wages earned by family mem-

---

Examine the expenditures made by several families over the same period of time. Determine each family's stage in the family life cycle. List some of the values and goals held by each of the families. Identify the expenditures which influenced you in drawing your conclusions.

Excluding outside employment, suggest ways in which you could indirectly add to your family's resources.

For various family situations, list the expenditures a family has if the mother is employed in addition to being a homemaker. Other than for the income, suggest reasons why some women work.

Your career
Homemaker's aide

Duties: Assists busy homemakers with routine cleaning, laundry, meal preparation, and child care responsibilities either on a full-time or part-time basis.
Where employed: Government agencies or private agencies. May be self-employed.

Plan a *Family Fun* activity which you can organize and manage. This might be a surprise for your family and something which would be enjoyed by all. For example, it might be preparing and serving Sunday breakfast, organizing a skating party, or baking a cake to celebrate a special occasion. Make your plans carefully and let your teacher check them. Tell when you plan to carry out your *Family Fun* project. Try not to tell your family that you are doing this for a school assignment.

After carrying out your project, make a brief report answering the following questions:
1. Were you able to carry out your original plan? If not, why not? If not, what did you do instead?
2. Was your planned activity really fun? Why, or why not?
3. Would you enjoy doing this again? Why, or why not?
4. Did you tell your family that this was a school assignment? If yes, did you have to tell and why? If no, explain why this made it a more enjoyable experience for you and the rest of your family.

bers. The way in which the family spends its money often makes the difference between a happy family and one which flounders. In happy families the income is used for necessities before frill items are purchased.

A family spending plan, or budget, helps a family spend its money wisely. A financial plan must include provision for the needs of the family. The usual items included are food, shelter, operating expenses, clothing, education and training for advancement, and savings. Most spending plans leave some money for things the family wants beyond the necessities.

For any spending plan to be successful, family cooperation is necessary. If expenses are greater than it seems they should be, everyone should try to find ways to cut down on spending. If the whole family has a fairly good idea of what the problem is, it is easier to share in the solution. Talking over the situation in an informal family discussion has worked out in many homes. When family members truly understand how the money is spent, cheerful cooperation is possible. It is useless, however, to expect family members to avoid spending when they do not know that a money problem exists.

Sometimes a family group can stretch their money by doing work themselves, rather than buying the services of others. Each family must make a decision as to how much of the work of maintaining the home is to be done or can be done by the members themselves. Too, they must decide how much they must have done or can afford to have done by others.

Many times a family starts on a cooperative labor plan, only to find that one or more members are unwilling or unable to carry their agreed-upon share of the load. Often in such cases it is better to back up and start over, hiring help for certain tasks if necessary. Sacrifices in other areas are then necessary. But when the choice is between things and family happiness, successful families put the family first.

The family's possessions
In a home where the rights of each person are respected and where no person behaves too selfishly, young people usually realize that they must take turns in using and caring for family property.

With older brothers and sisters, disagreements may center around use of the bathroom, the telephone, or the family car. With younger ones, sharing may involve such things as a bicycle, favorite books or games, or the TV set. It helps if the persons concerned are agreeable and reasonable in making arrangements in advance and in abiding by the schedules later. When there is

Outings which family members share together can be remembered and treasured for a lifetime.

a sincere effort to work out plans for sharing family possessions, bickering and quarreling are lessened.

SHARING FAMILY WORK

Consider the number of tasks that have to be done in any twenty-four-hour period to keep a family comfortable, well fed, and adequately clothed. The house has to be straightened and kept at a comfortable temperature. Food must be available, meals prepared and served, the table cleared, and the dishes washed. Proper clothing for each member has to be in readiness—that is, clean, in repair, and adequate for the weather and the activity.

Household tasks

As boys and girls mature, they begin to realize that providing clean clothes, hot, appetizing meals, and a neat home takes a great deal of effort. The sooner young people learn to share in household duties, the sooner a household with teenagers runs smoothly.

Make complete plans for celebrating a special family occasion such as a birthday, anniversary, graduation, holiday, or special achievement. Discuss the values which are gained from celebrations such as these. If possible, carry out your plans at home and tell the class about your celebration.

Divide the class into 5 or 6 buzz groups. Let each group list appropriate games and entertainment ideas for one of the following:
Birthday party for a friend
End-of-the-school-year party
Club Christmas party
After-the-game party
Anniversary party for grandparents
Get-acquainted party for a new family in the neighborhood

Role-play situations in which a hostess introduces her guests to each other, to her mother, and to her father.

Prepare a booklet of games to use in entertaining your friends or family. Get suggestions from the class. If you want to, you could make your booklet part of the home economics department's file.

Demonstrate ways to prepare in advance foods such as sandwiches, cookies, and cakes suitable for parties.

List foods your family would like to have on an emergency shelf and purchase these foods. Plan and prepare meals from the emergency shelf.

Collect and file recipes for use for emergency meals.

Discuss the type of help you need when giving a party at home.

Make a list of places to go in your community and activities that a family could enjoy as a group. Include inexpensive activities such as fishing, going to a museum, and having a picnic.

List indoor activities which can be fun for the entire family.

Bulletin board IDEA
Title: *A*

ROUND-UP

of good ideas for family fun
Directions: Display pictures of happy families doing things together.

The care of younger children
Looking after younger children is a family responsibility and one which may be accepted on a part-time basis by teen-agers in the family. Caring for younger brothers and sisters may mean that some of your free time is spent with them. You may be asked to feed them, put them to bed, or play with them. Sometimes more than one of the older children take turns with younger ones. Here is an opportunity for cooperation and even compromise. Usually child care can be fun rather than a chore if you develop a good attitude toward the assignment.

SHARING FAMILY FUN
Family members can have fun together. In a family that works and plays together, the parents and children learn to share and care.

Planning good times in the family
Even in the busiest of modern families, plans can be made for celebrations, holidays, and special events which enrich and strengthen relationships in the family. Family members who are not particularly fond of a majority decision in such matters are often those who enjoy an activity most. Perhaps part of their pleasure is derived by knowing that they are being cooperative family members.

The family's interests usually determine the activities planned for family fun. A sports-loving group might enjoy fishing or bowling together. A family which is less active physically might get more pleasure out of indoor games, a picnic, or a cook-out. If both the parents and children play musical instruments, such a family would doubtless enjoy playing or listening to music.

The equipment for family fun need not be expensive. The activities chosen should be those for which the space and equipment are available or easily secured. It isn't the equipment that makes the fun but the people who are involved. Outdoor cooking and eating, for instance, may be as simple as a hot-dog roast in the city park. A family can have just as much fun with simple equipment as with the most expensive kind.

Variety can add interest to family activities. Most people like to do something new and different occasionally. A new game or a picnic in a new spot may provide a change that the whole family enjoys. If you generally have family fun outdoors, try something indoors. If you are used to staying indoors, you might go to a ball game together. Suggest to the family that each person think of a new kind of activity which he would like to have the family try. From these you can decide on something which is fun for everyone.

Fun at home can be shared by all family members. They may choose to listen to records, play games, watch TV, or read together. Occasionally they may enjoy talking about something that interests all of them. In fact, some students who at school appear to be well informed on a current subject, may have formed their opinions while discussing the matter at home.

Children and parents may, with little or no forethought, find themselves producing unrehearsed skits, reciting poetry with dramatic effects, or harmonizing in group singing. It might naturally occur to a teen-ager to demonstrate a new dance step and to offer instruction to parents or younger family members during such an evening.

Fun away from home offers many possibilities for family activities. Eating popcorn together at a local stand or going to a museum or art gallery may be of special interest to some. Others may prefer a movie, a play, or a swim at a nearby beach. Any activity which gives parents and children a chance to enjoy being together is usually worthwhile.

Such family outings as picnics, school carnivals, and beach parties remembered a lifetime usually last only a few hours at the time. Longer outings may be planned which involve a weekend fishing trip, a camp-out in a state park, or a visit with relatives in another city. A vacation trip usually requires careful planning. Sometimes the family planning and fond remembrances are as much fun as the trip itself.

COURTESY WHAT'S NEW IN HOME ECONOMICS

Hospitality can be shown by family members of all ages.

SHARING FAMILY FRIENDS

Hospitality offers another way for having family fun. In a home where guests are made welcome, each family member feels free to invite his friends. Your brother may bring other boys in to watch TV. Your sister may ask her best friends over to talk. Your father may invite a couple from work home for the evening. At such times, try to consult your mother in the planning, so that everyone does not bring a guest at the same time.

Discuss your responsibilities when your parents have guests and your parents' responsibilities when you have guests.

Decide which of the following activities are essential parts of being a good party host or hostess:

Decide on the date, place, and kind of party.
Make advance arrangements for the place where the party will be given.
Plan the guest list very carefully.
Plan the refreshments and entertainment.
Purchase the supplies for the refreshments, favors, and decorations.
Send out or extend the invitations.
Prepare or make arrangements for the refreshments and decorations.
Greet each guest and make him feel welcome.
See that the guests are introduced to each other.
Tell something about the guests as you introduce them, to aid conversation.
Show an interest in all the guests and try to see that everyone has a good time.
See that everything is left in order at the end of the party.

List points which should be included in any invitation to a party. Write some invitations which include all of the points listed.

Invite some friends to your home. Show hospitality by engaging in some of the following activities:
Get them to talk about themselves, their interests, or their hobbies.
Ask them if they would like to watch TV, hear some music, play cards, or play a game.
Show them your hobby collection or recent photographs.
Show them something you have made.
Tell them about some school experiences, such as your courses, special events, or the school teams.
Discuss a play you have seen recently on TV, at the movies, or on the stage.
Talk about recent events which occurred in your community, in the nation, or in the world.
Tell about a book you have read recently and liked.
Have special entertainment planned, such as a record party, a picnic, or a luncheon.
Share in showing home movies or film slides of vacation trips or important family events.

In some homes it is the practice to have a special evening meal once a week. At this meal, family members may invite guests by taking turns. Of course, everyone makes a special effort to make the visitor happy so that he feels he is a guest of the entire family.

Welcoming guests of the family
Certainly you will want to share in making guests feel welcome. You may assist in the duties of the host or the hostess if your help is needed. If the guests are friends of your parents, try to take a minor role in the conversation. It is usually good manners to sit down and chat with them for a few minutes. However, if you see that you are interrupting a conversation, it is better to sit quietly. Perhaps you can add more to the hospitality of the hour by making coffee, preparing snacks, or quietly serving other needs of the guests.

If a friend of your parents arrives at the door when they are absent, explain that your parents are not at home and that you know they will regret having missed the visitor. If your parents have already told you to invite their friends to come in when they are away from home, you may do so. Ordinarily the friends will not accept, but if they do come in, ask them to make themselves comfortable with a book, magazine, or TV until your parents return.

Instant hospitality
When friends of the family drop in unexpectedly, the welcome you give them should be as sincere as if you had invited them for that particular day and hour.

If company interrupts an activity, the situation can be handled smoothly in a number of ways. You may stop what you were doing and entertain the guests, or, if another family member can take over, you may excuse yourself and continue your own activity. Probably most guests would enjoy chatting while you finish some small job you are in the midst of completing.

Food for the unexpected guest is always available if a special hospitality food supply is kept on hand. Here convenience foods come into their own. Many families have pre-planned menus for instant entertaining. Soups are often included among foods kept for such times. They can be served as soup or as sauces on other foods. A variety of canned and frozen meats and vegetables can be kept for casserole dishes. Eggs from the refrigerator might be used in a main dish such as an omelet or a soufflé. Packaged and homemade mixes can be used for biscuits, muffins, cakes, or other additions to an emergency meal. Ice cream is certainly a convenient dessert to have on hand for unexpected guests.

Spur-of-the-moment entertaining is often more fun than any other form of entertainment. Even if school books must be removed before a guest can sit down, everyone is more at ease because he realizes that the occasion is unplanned. It helps if materials for entertaining are close at hand. One advantage of unplanned entertaining is that no one is overtired because of long and tedious preparation.

You may be uncertain as to your responsibilities when guests drop by. If they are your guests, they are your responsibility. If they are family friends, the family as a unit should share in entertaining.

SHARING SPECIAL FAMILY OCCASIONS

The special days that are celebrated together by family members are often those remembered longest. Many teen-agers and adults recall happily the good times they had when birthdays, anniversaries, and holidays were occasions for family gatherings.

It is important to children that older family members share in the fun of these special good times. Whether they are trimming a Christmas tree or having a picnic on the Fourth of July, the event means more to children when others enjoy it too.

Celebrating special occasions

Families may be quite different in the ways they choose to observe a special occasion. In some families,

COURTESY KRAFT KITCHENS

Mothers and teen-age daughters often enjoy working together to give baby or bridal showers for close family friends.

each member is permitted to select just how his own birthday will be celebrated. One teen-ager may prefer a beach party, while another chooses to eat at a special restaurant.

Family parties can also celebrate special family honors. Perhaps a daughter has been chosen class representative to the student council. Perhaps a son makes the honor roll. Perhaps a father is promoted or gets a new job opportunity. Perhaps the baby learns how to walk. Any of these are occasions worthy of celebration in many families. Youngsters who grow up in such an

Pretend you have spent a week visiting with a friend. Write a bread-and-butter note of thanks for his or her hospitality.

Write both an acceptance note and a note of regret to an invitation for a weekend visit in the home of a friend.

Discuss the following statements and defend your position:
1 A written invitation is to be answered even if there is no RSVP on it.
2 You must bring your weekend hostess a gift.
3 If you are invited for a weekend and are having a good time, by all means stay longer.

List the responsibilities of a guest such as:
Acknowledges the invitation.
Arrives on time.
Leaves at the time suggested by the host or hostess.
Mingles with other guests.
Joins in the spirit of the party.
Makes no unnecessary work or trouble.
Offers to help the hostess.
Thanks the host or hostess for the hospitality.

Check the following list of safety precautions to follow when entertaining. Add other safety precautions which seem important to you.

1. Remove fragile articles from the party area.
2. Be sure that rugs are placed so that guests will not trip over them.
3. Be sure that none of the decorations or costumes used are flammable.
4. Protect furnishings and guests' clothes by placing a screen in front of a fireplace in which a fire is burning.
5. When entertaining a large number of people, be sure that the rooms are not so full of furniture that exits are blocked.
6. Exercise the utmost caution when cooking outdoors. Use lighter fluids only before the fire is lighted.
7. Be sure to have all walkways well lighted.
8. Prepare alternate plans which can be used if rain or other weather conditions interfere with planned outdoor entertainment.

atmosphere generally enjoy sharing their achievements with other family members.

In many families where the grandmother and grandfather are still living, the family has some special kind of observance of their wedding anniversary. Their children and grandchildren often plan to gather for an afternoon of visiting and invite old friends to share the happy time.

Decorating for special occasions
Although decorations are not required for a party, they make any occasion more festive. The trend is toward selecting decorations that are simple and inexpensive. Appropriateness and originality are also important considerations. Homemade decorations can be more original than the kind found in stores. They are usually less expensive.

Fresh flowers are always in good taste when used for adding a special touch to a family party. They are a colorful attraction as a table decoration or as an arrangement on a coffee table or a mantel above the fireplace.

Gifts for special occasions
A gift is an expression of the warm feelings of the giver. Presented within the family in a spirit of appreciation and affection, it is of value, not for what it costs, but rather because it is an expression of loving-kindness from one family member to another.

In choosing a gift, try to pick something that will be enjoyed by the person receiving it. Any mother's heart is touched when a tiny son gives her a baseball or a toy truck for her birthday. She knows he is giving her the best gift he can think of. However, as you mature, your gifts will represent less what you would want to have. They will be chosen to please the person receiving them.

It is not necessary, and often not a good idea, to buy costly gifts. Such gifts may cause embarrassment if the receiver cannot or does not want to feel obligated. Most people will especially enjoy an article that you have made yourself.

When the family knows that the person who is to receive their gifts wants a single large, expensive article, the members may pool their funds and get one gift.

Wrapping gifts in interesting and unusual ways can add to the fun of gift giving. The many unusual wrappings on the market make it easy to create attractive, personalized packages. Sometimes the most original wrappings and decorations are those that are made inexpensively at home from leftover wallpaper, funny papers, or other, similar wrappings.

In deciding how to wrap a gift, there are two considerations: what the gift is, and who is to receive it.

COURTESY BETTER HOMES AND GARDENS, © MEREDITH CORPORATION, 1965

Warm feelings can be expressed through gift wrappings as well as through the gift itself.

Gift wrappings for boys and men are generally quite tailored, while gift wrappings for women may be frilly or simple. Gifts for little girls may be wrapped in bright-colored paper with ribbons, or they may be almost flowerlike in their daintiness. Gifts such as flowers and fruits need no wrapping, although they may be specially packaged.

Delivering gifts in good condition requires careful wrapping. If you are wrapping a present to be mailed, it will be necessary to put it in a box. Use flat bows and decorations, and provide an outer covering of corrugated paper and heavy wrapping paper. The gifts that are to be delivered in person or by messenger may be wrapped with large bows, flower sprays, berries, or various other perishable decorations.

If you receive a gift, except within the immediate household, you are expected to send a thank-you note. Since a gift is more an *expression of feelings* than a *thing*, it is not worth hurting others' feelings by neglecting to acknowledge it.

Demonstrate wrapping gifts attractively and creatively. Include examples which use materials that would not have to be bought, such as old greeting cards, shelving paper, berries, greenery, or leaves.

Demonstrate wrapping a package for mailing.

Make and display some appropriate gifts for a weekend hostess.

Prepare attractively wrapped foods for holiday gifts such as plum puddings, fruit cakes, fancy cookies, candies, jellies, dried fruits, and fancy breads.

The week before a holiday vacation, let each student demonstrate to the class how to make a gift item or seasonal decoration of her choice. Emphasize the need to be well prepared and organized, perhaps having some steps already completed. The demonstration should be so clear that another student could make the item at home without written directions.

6 CHAPTER POSTTEST

Number from 1 to 10 on a piece of paper. Beside each number write the letter which corresponds to the *best* answer for that question. *Do not* write in this book.

1. Which of the following is a basic physical need?
   a Independence
   b Companionship
   c Food
   d Security
2. Which of the following is the most important emotional need provided by a home?
   a Security
   b Clothing
   c Shelter
   d Variety
3. Which child in a family is the most likely to be independent?
   a The youngest
   b The middle
   c The oldest
   d A twin
4. Which child in a family is the most likely to experience feelings of jealousy?
   a The youngest
   b The middle
   c The oldest
   d An only child
5. Which of the following is most likely to be the source of an argument between brothers and sisters?
   a Household chores
   b School work
   c Use of allowance
   d Use of leisure time at home
6. Which family member is likely to make the greatest number of consumer decisions?
   a Father   c Brother
   b Mother   d Sister
7. Which of the following is another name for a family spending plan?
   a Expense account
   b Mortgage
   c Budget
   d Standard of living
8. Which of the following is the most important consideration in selecting a gift for one of your friends?
   a It looks as if it cost more than it did.
   b It is something your friend would like to have.
   c It can be wrapped easily.
   d It is something you would like to have.
9. Which is *least* likely to change if the mother goes to work?
   a Total family income
   b Father's role
   c Mother's role
   d Children's attitudes toward school.
10. Which of the following is *not* a true statement?
    a People now live longer than they did in former generations.
    b Loneliness may accompany old age.
    c Physical changes are evident during a person's later years.
    d A three-generation family is of necessity an unhappy one.

7 CHAPTER PRETEST

Fill in the blank in each sentence with the *best* word to complete the statement. *Do not* write in this book.

1. A doctor who specializes in the care of expectant mothers and the delivery of babies is a(an) __(1)__.
2. Each stage of human growth contains __(2)__ tasks which the individual learns to perform before he moves successfully to the next stage.
3. The first year of a baby's life is generally referred to as __(3)__.
4. At the very early stages of a baby's life, his mental growth is closely related to his __(4)__ growth.
5. The ideas of *mine* and *yours* are not very important to the __(5)__ because he enjoys playing at the same time, rather than with, other children his age.
6. The child between 3 and 6 years of age is called a(an) __(6)__.
7. The purpose of discipline is to establish acceptable __(7)__.
8. Clothes designed with __(8)__ features encourage a child to dress and undress himself.
9. After a child is __(9)__ years old, he usually eats the same foods as the rest of the family.
10. The stage of development which marks the beginning of physical maturity is __(10)__.
11. One of a baby-sitter's chief concerns at bathtime is the __(11)__ of a young child.

CHAPTER 7

Centering the home around growing children

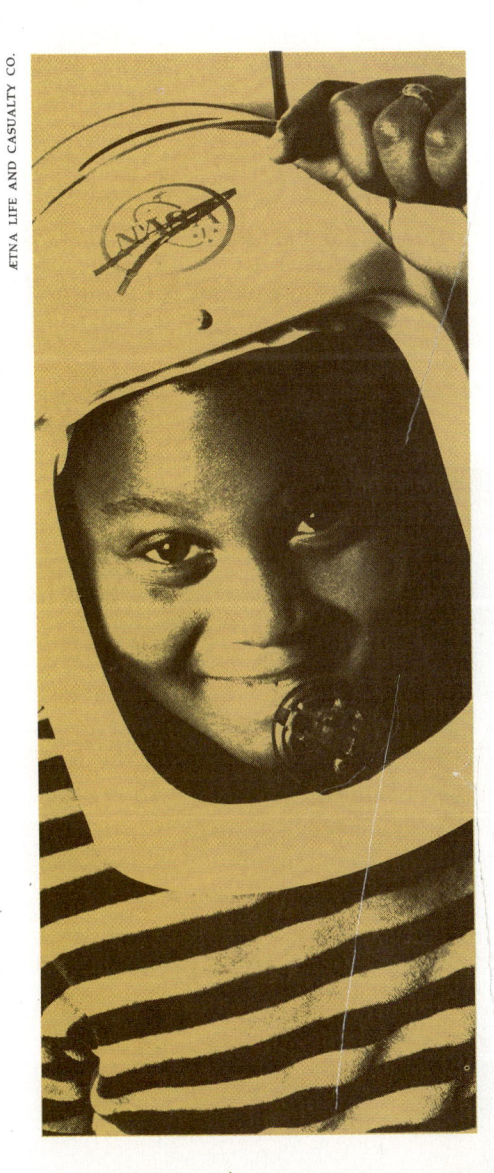

Have you ever said, "When *I* have children, I won't make them do this or that"? Most people *have* said such things from time to time, especially when it seemed very hard to learn a new skill. But as teen-agers mature, they often decide that their parents were right in their insistence that children learn certain things at certain ages.

Perhaps you have seen a young child run up to a friend to brag about his older brother's or sister's skill in some area. Although they may try to hide it, teen-agers are just as proud as they see their younger brothers and sisters learn to walk and talk or advance in school. Both the young child and the teen-agers are sharing the family's pleasure in the growth of its members. The interest family members take in one another helps to build strong, lasting family ties.

A new baby's arrival brings many changes in the operation of a household. Changes in family life begin even before the baby is born. As soon as a woman suspects she might be pregnant, she should make an appointment at a prenatal clinic or with her own doctor. A doctor who specializes in the care

Read the following poem and in one sentence tell what it means to you.

Children Learn What They Live
If a child lives with criticism,
 he learns to condemn.
If a child lives with hostility,
 he learns to fight.
If a child lives with ridicule,
 he learns to be shy.
If a child lives with jealousy,
 he learns to feel guilty.
If a child lives with tolerance,
 he learns to be patient.
If a child lives with encouragement, he learns confidence.
If a child lives with praise,
 he learns to appreciate.
If a child lives with fairness,
 he learns justice.
If a child lives with security,
 he learns to have faith.
If a child lives with approval,
 he learns to like himself.
If a child lives with acceptance,
 he learns to find love in the world.
 by Dorothy Law Nolte

Give in order the most obvious physical developmental tasks which a child accomplishes before he learns to walk. In other words, list the physical stages through which most children pass before they walk. Do you know a child who has skipped one of the usual stages? If so, which stage? Was he able to learn this skill later?

Make a chart showing the developmental levels usually achieved by children before reaching school age. On the left-hand side of the chart list in three rows the areas of development: Physical, Mental, and Social-emotional. Across the top of the chart label the three columns as follows: Infants, Toddlers, and Preschoolers. Fill in the nine squares with the appropriate information.

Bulletin board IDEA
Title: *A Child's Growth Is More than Luck*
Directions: Cut a large four-leaf clover from green construction paper. Write one of the following words on each leaf.
   Emotional
   Social
   Physical
   Mental
On the stem write *Growth*.

of expectant mothers and the delivery of babies is called an *obstetrician*. A mother who follows the doctor's directions during pregnancy gives herself and her baby an added chance for good health all of their lives. The doctor may suggest extra rest for the mother-to-be. She may need help with her regular duties before, as well as after, the baby arrives. Since much of the mother's time will be taken up with caring for the baby, other family members may have to take over some of her usual routine duties in the home. They may also be called upon to help with the care of the baby.

The physical, mental, and emotional development of the new baby, and of other family members, often depends on how well older family members understand natural growth factors.

The pattern of growth

Each of the students in your school has learned to perform certain tasks as he developed. For instance, each learned to sit, stand, walk, talk, read, and make friends. These are frequently called *developmental tasks*. A developmental task is a task which is presented at or about a certain time in a person's life. Successful achievement leads to happiness and success with later tasks. Failure leads to unhappiness in the person, disapproval by society, and difficulty with later tasks.

A baby accomplishes the developmental tasks when his muscles and his mind are ready for him to learn them. However, his family can help him learn these tasks. They can see that he has the food, exercise, and rest his muscles need to grow strong. They can also see that he has a chance to practice his skills.

Unless a child succeeds in learning the appropriate developmental tasks at each stage of growth, he does not have a firm foundation on which to build in the next stage. A person can learn some developmental tasks which were skipped earlier, but these are generally harder to learn during a later developmental stage. For example, the child who has learned to handle a pencil easily before he learns to write will learn to form letters more easily than a child who must learn to hold the pencil at the same time that he learns to make the letters.

A teen-ager who has never learned to control his temper doesn't need to go through the rest of his life acting like a toddler. But it will be much harder for him to learn this control than it would have been at an earlier age.

As you observe different children growing up, you will notice certain common growth patterns. However, the final results vary. Thus, most children learn to talk, but even within a single family they may not all talk alike. One child may talk all the time, while another prefers to listen. One child may prefer long sentences with many big words, while another speaks very simply.

As a person grows, the developmental stages leading to these final results move regularly from the simple to the complex, from similar tasks to very different tasks, and from general tasks to specific ones. As a child develops, former developmental tasks become parts of larger, final results. For example, a toddler learns to catch a rolled ball. He enjoys this skill for its own sake. If he grows up to become a member of the school baseball team, this early developmental task has become a forgotten part of all the skills he has learned which have earned him the position.

Some of these general patterns of growth are more noticeable in connection with the physical growth of a child, but they apply to mental and social growth as well. The family's ability to accept a child in whatever stage he has reached will make it much easier to help him grow and develop at his own pace. For example, it is useless to expect a child to learn to walk before his leg muscles have grown strong. Nor can he be expected to tie shoe strings before his fingers have mastered simple tasks such as building block houses. He will not learn much about talking until his mouth and throat muscles are developed adequately to control the delicate adjustments necessary for proper pronunciation of words.

Children are helped by encouragement. In working with them, try to make them feel good about their accomplishments and secure in your recognition of their personal needs. This may be your most important contribution to their physical, mental, and emotional growth.

Tell about a child you know (without naming him) who reached a certain developmental stage later than other people his age. Did this create any problems? Were the problems eventually overcome? How, and why?

The developmental tasks of childhood can be achieved as a child plays with his favorite toys.

COURTESY PLAYSKOOL TOYS

Identify well-known people who have achieved great success in life who as children were considered slow in some area of development. What lesson can be learned from the experiences of these people?

Post a large line graph showing the differences in girls' and boys' rates of growth. At what ages are the differences in their growth rates most noticeable? Why? (See page 85.)

List family activities which children particularly enjoy.

Discuss ways to help children form good social habits.

Explain the meaning of this statement: *A three-year-old plays at the same time as, rather than with, his friend.*

Give examples to illustrate that a child's interest span or period of concentration increases with age.

Bulletin board IDEA
Title: *Everybody Loves a Baby*
Directions: Around musical notes cut from construction paper, mount pictures of the class members when they were babies.

THE INFANT AND TODDLER

The first three years of a child's life are full of changes. The helpless newborn infant gains weight, grows in height and strength, and learns many of the basic skills that allow him to take care of himself.

A person generally grows more rapidly during the first year of his life than at any other time. Usually at the end of six months he weighs twice as much as he did when he was born, and at the end of a year his birth weight has tripled. He grows taller as well as heavier, gaining about 9 inches in height during his first year of life. Boys generally grow a little faster than girls during this period. They are likely to be taller and heavier than girls of the same age.

A young child's most rapid growth period occurs during his first year of life.

COURTESY SPERRY AND HUTCHINSON COMPANY

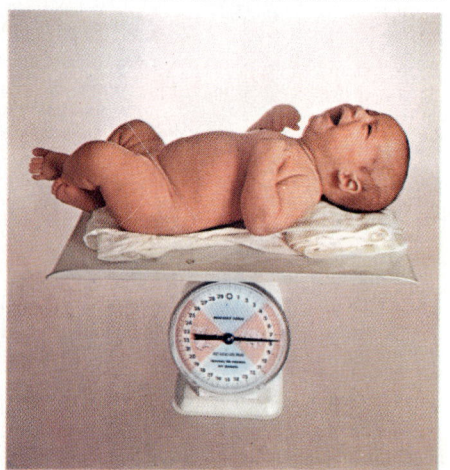

At the very early stages of a person's life, mental growth is clearly related to physical growth. Thus, it is very hard to separate the physical and mental development of the infant. For example, the newborn baby cannot focus his eyes. By the time he is about four weeks old, his eyes can follow a moving object, although it is not certain how well he can see it. A slightly older baby can turn his head as his eyes follow an object.

By the time the baby is able to creep, and then to walk, his curiosity is very evident. His mental growth is less obviously related to his physical development than during his first months of life. By the time he is three, the toddler knows a great deal about his family and the contents of his home. He is also very interested in objects outside his home. The toddler will explore the possibilities of an ant, a bee, a dog, or an automobile with equal curiosity. Unfortunately, he is not very alert to the dangers which this curiosity may involve. One of the real problems in training the older baby and the toddler lies in finding ways to encourage their curiosity, and thereby their mental growth, while protecting them from physical danger.

At first glance the infant may seem to lack any evidence of social development. But his awareness of others begins much earlier than many suppose. His first smiles may be for anyone who gives him attention. As long as the people around him take care of his physical needs, he remains happy. This happiness leads him to develop trust in others. As the baby grows older and is able to distinguish between the people who approach him, he may become shy and timid with strangers. This apparent setback in his social development is really a sign of his advancing mental growth. If he is allowed to become acquainted with strangers at his own pace, he will continue to develop trust in other people.

The toddler continues to grow in his awareness of other people. And as his awareness of others grows, his self-concept also develops. This awareness of self leads to other apparent setbacks in social development. As he tries to learn what he may and may not do, the toddler appears from time to time to be stubborn, selfish, shy, demanding, babyish, or bold. He needs time to learn how he may and may not behave with other people. It is not fair to judge him according to standards for older people. On the other hand, it is equally unfair to expect him to learn these limits by himself. He needs specific directions.

The older toddler enjoys other children. He is not ready to play with others in the same way that older children do. And he is not really ready to share toys. But two toddlers playing side by side with their own trucks seem to have much more fun than if each is playing alone. Their ideas of *mine* and *yours* are not very clear. They need to be watched in their play so that they do not hurt themselves or each other and so that they can be led away from any quarrels that may develop. Fortunately, a toddler's moods do not last very long.

THE PRESCHOOLER
A child between the ages of three and six is sometimes called a *preschooler*. The physical changes of a preschool child are not so rapid as were those of the infant or toddler.

COURTESY CLAIROL INC.

Parents who understand that a preschooler's physical growth rate slows down can use this time to promote mental and emotional growth.

Describe the physical characteristics of a newborn baby and of a one-year-old child. If someone in the class can draw well, have him sketch the babies described. The sketch may be made on a sheet of acetate or on the chalkboard. Compare the newborn baby and the one-year-old. If possible, bring to class actual photographs of children of the two ages.

Invite a panel of mothers to come to class. Select mothers who are in different stages of the family life cycle. Ask them to discuss the emotional adjustments and financial concerns of parents in their own particular stage.

List the values to be gained from studying child development.

Discuss the meanings of the following sayings. Try to form a sound opinion concerning each saying.
1 Spare the rod and spoil the child.
2 Children should be seen and not heard.
3 As a twig is bent, the tree is inclined.
4 He is a bad boy through and through.
Why do you think each saying is true, partially true, or untrue?

125

Tell a story about a young child which begins, "But, Mother, all I meant to do was . . ."

Follow these instructions:
1. Sit on a very low chair or stool pulled up to a regular-height table.
2. Use a very large serving spoon and a large mixing bowl.
3. Use the hand which you ordinarily do *not* use for eating.
4. Ask someone to tie a large towel around your neck as a bib.
5. Now eat cereal and milk from the bowl.

Compare the frustrations you feel to those of a young child as he learns to feed himself. This experiment should help you understand young children who are learning to do strange and difficult tasks.

Invite a mother to bring her baby to class. Ask her to demonstrate effective ways of dressing and undressing the child.

Ask the director of a recreation center to suggest occupational opportunities for a young person who is interested in working with children.

On the other hand, by the time a child is six years old, he has gone through several rapidly changing stages of mental and social development.

The preschooler experiences one of the slow-down periods of physical growth. Sometimes this natural slowing down upsets the preschooler's family. They anxiously consult the doctor to find out what is wrong. Although the preschooler's body does not change size as rapidly as it did during babyhood, his physical growth shows up in other ways. His muscles gain in strength, and he learns muscle coordination. The preschool child is ready to learn many physical skills which were beyond his earlier ability. This greater muscular control shows up as he runs, plays with wheeled toys, or throws a ball. His muscular control is also shown as he paints, builds with blocks, and plays house. These types of physical activity are also important to the mental and social growth of the preschooler.

The preschool child is even more curious about the world which surrounds him than is the toddler. His manner of approach to mental problems is different. While the toddler pokes and tastes and is generally active in his explorations, the preschooler takes time to think about things, to ask questions about them, and to seek out the relationships between them. This questioning and thinking is added to active investigation. It does not replace it. The development of a mental approach to mental problems is slow and uneven.

As the child's grasp of abstract ideas expands, he may seem to ask the same series of questions he asked earlier. Whenever the preschooler does this, either he is seeking reassurance that his ideas are indeed correct, or he is looking for new relationships on a more complicated level. Whatever his reason for asking, he needs direct answers to his questions.

The preschooler can give clear expression to his emotions and has not yet learned to hold in his feelings. For this reason he sometimes seems to be unnecessarily violent in his reactions. Although the preschool years are the years in which a child properly begins to learn to control his feelings, this learning process is long and complicated. It is usually better to accept the preschooler's outspoken reactions as being truly natural than to try to force him to show them in socially acceptable ways. While the preschooler's display of temper may be unpleasant, his outgoing expressions of love and joy more than make up for it.

The preschooler's social world expands rapidly from that of his family to that of his playmates. At first, like the toddler, he plays alongside a friend. By the age of

Muscular skills developed by the preschooler are frequently used to demonstrate his mental and social growth.

five, he readily engages in highly organized group play. Quarreling at this age is rather frequent, often very noisy and somewhat violent, but also brief. The preschooler can remember former disagreements, but in general he does not seek to do so. He does not carry a grudge. His disobedience of adults is his own idea rather than a response to a playmate's dare.

THE ELEMENTARY SCHOOL CHILD

From the ages of six through eleven or twelve, a person goes through an important stage of development that ends with the onset of *puberty*. Puberty is the stage of development that marks the beginning of physical maturity.

During the elementary school years, the rate of physical growth is quite slow. However, most boys

Prepare an oral report on one of the following topics. Present the report to class at the assigned time.
1. Desirable habits for children to develop
2. Teaching a child about work and responsibility
3. Influencing character development
4. Getting ready for a new baby
5. Working wives and mothers
6. Understanding and working with handicapped children
7. Adopting a child or the adopted child
8. Baby-sitting procedures
9. Guidance and discipline
10. Play as a means of development
11. Safety for children
12. Childhood diseases and protective health habits
13. Equipment and furnishings for a baby
14. Social-emotional development at a specific age

When possible, use pictures or examples to illustrate your report. Your report may be judged on the following points:
A. Accuracy of material presented
B. Coverage of topic
C. Interesting presentation
D. Review or summary

Read aloud the following story written in make-believe alphabet. Compare the way you read this story with the way a young child may read in a real alphabet.

See the Cat Run
yϕϕ   t#ϕ   (⊥t   /nu
yϕϕ   t#ϕ   x⊥t   (⊥t.
yϕϕ   t#ϕ   (⊥t   /nu.
/nu,   x⊥t   (⊥t,   /nu!
/nu   xo/   xnu.
/nuuvu2   vy   xnu.
vt   vy   xnu   to   /nu,
   vyu't   vt,   (⊥t?
#⊥+ϕ   xnu,   x⊥t   (⊥t.

Did you read the story in a monotone? Did you hesitate? Did you feel frustrated? If so, why? What conclusions can you make about the learning experiences of young children?

Code:
ϕ = e   x = f   2 = g
# = h   v = i   u = n
o = o   / = r   y = s
t = t   n = u   + = v
⊥ = a   (= c

List kinds of punishments you have observed for various types of misbehavior. Discuss the reactions of the children to the punishments used in these situations.

will double in muscular strength during their grade school years. Increase in strength is generally slower for girls than for boys.

Puberty brings a rapid change in the growth rate for both boys and girls. The pubertal period, reached earlier by girls than by boys, gives girls a brief lead in growth. A girl of eleven or twelve may be taller than boys of the same age, but a year or two later she may be shorter than these same boys.

The mental growth of the elementary school child is readily seen as he progresses through school. But his school reports and advancement should not be considered the only

When showing off what he has learned, the young school child may also show his family the emotional strength they have given him.

COURTESY ETHAN ALLEN AMERICAN TRADITIONAL INTERIORS

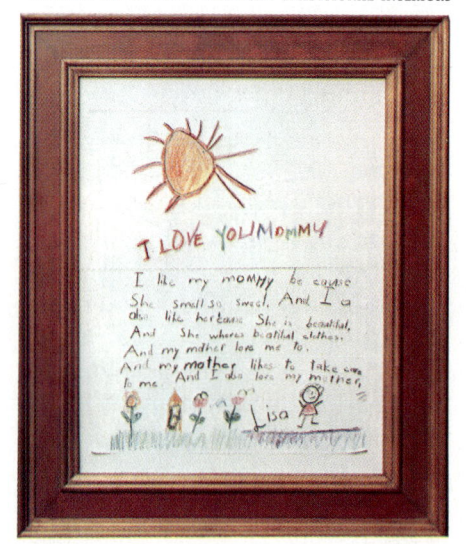

signs of his mental development. Group activities outside of school, family excursions, television programs, and library books all contribute to his mental growth. Throughout the elementary school years, children enthusiastically start a project, work on it for a short time, then turn to something else. At times they may return to the project or start a similar one on a more advanced level. At other times, the single part-project is enough. This type of behavior is a sign of the elementary school child's urge to explore, rather than an indication that he cannot carry through his own projects.

During the elementary school years, the child is more concerned with his contemporaries than with other people. Family opinion matters, but it loses its importance whenever it conflicts with the opinion of the *gang*. Although it may not seem to be so, this reliance on the gang is a sign of growing independence.

The elementary school child has learned a great deal about socially acceptable forms of behavior. He is able to adjust these to match a variety of situations, so that he may have *company manners, family manners, school manners,* and *playground manners.*

Although the occurrences are not frequent, quarreling is common throughout the elementary school years. These quarrels generally concern *differing ideas* or *positions of importance* rather than possessions. The elementary school child is more apt to remember his grievance and to stay mad than is a younger child, but he is capable of forgetting quickly. Although the gang and a best friend are very important during these years, there are frequent realignments of such relationships.

THE TEEN-AGER

The teen years are a period of change. Some changes are caused by the physical developments that begin with puberty. Others are caused by the teen-ager's widening horizons, which bring new knowledge, new responsibilities, and new privileges.

The second growth spurt in a person's life begins with the onset of puberty. Individual differences in development seem to be more noticeable during this time than during most of the earlier growth periods. Part of the concern over individual differences is caused by the fact that teen-agers have a strong urge to be just like their friends. Confusion results when individual differences in physical development occur.

The varying rates of growth of different parts of the body are especially apparent during the teens. Arms may be suddenly longer at one time, legs at another. The nose may lengthen to full adult size before the rest of the facial features

COURTESY TEENFORM, INC.

Both the physical and social growth of the early teen years tend to progress more smoothly when family members understand their importance.

mature. Muscles suddenly become stronger and more powerful.

These changes accompany the more obvious physical developments which indicate that the boy or girl is becoming a physically mature man or woman. Although signs of this maturing, such as the deepening voice of a boy or the developing breasts of a girl, are eagerly awaited, their actual occurrence may be embarrassing for the teen-ager. This is especially true when the changes appear to occur overnight.

List the advantages of nursery school attendance for a child. Discuss conditions under which a young child would probably profit most from attending nursery school.

Listen to a tape of kindergarten age children playing together. Discuss the portions of the tape which illustrate the social and emotional developmental level of children at this age.

Discuss the elementary school years as gang years for many children. List organizations which help elementary school age children feel that they are part of an acceptable group.

Your career
Children's clothes salesperson

Duties: Sells children's clothing and accessories. Keeps inventory of merchandise on hand. Builds or arranges displays. Performs stockkeeping duties. Advises customers of appropriateness of sizes and fabrics for given age groups. **Where employed:** Department stores, children's specialty shops, or catalogue order houses.

Borrow children's clothing items from a local store and bring them to class. Discuss the features of each garment from the standpoint of:
1 Ease of putting on and taking off the garment
2 Self-help features
3 Comfort
4 Washability and ease of care
5 Durability
6 Safety

Make clothing items for an infant or small child. Make these from usable clothes which are no longer worn.

Discuss why the following practices will encourage a child to want to dress himself:
Install low closet rods, shelves, and drawers that he can reach and use.
Provide clothing that he can fasten and unfasten easily.
Provide opportunities for him to practice buttoning and unbuttoning clothes, lacing shoes, and putting on mittens and socks.
Select clothes that he likes.
Encourage him to try to dress himself and show approval when he does.

Much of a teen-ager's strength seems to go into producing all these rapid physical developments and into learning how to handle his constantly differing size. Changes may occur so rapidly that the body requires extra rest and extra food in order to accommodate them. If the need for rest and for nourishment to aid growth is not understood, the teen-ager and his parents may begin to worry about his apparent lack of energy or his desire to overeat.

The teen-ager's search for independence may be marked by smoothness or intense disagreements with his family. Oddly enough, teen-agers are as apt to worry about a smooth adjustment to their growing independence as they are about unhappy adjustments. People cannot be in complete agreement with others and retain their own identities. The smoothness with which these disagreements are handled is often a sign of the growing maturity of the teen-ager. (See also Part 1.)

The special needs of children

If a child is to develop a good self-concept, someone must see that he has an opportunity to develop sound attitudes toward himself and others. Older brothers and sisters in a home need to realize that they have a natural position in which they can encourage or discourage a young child's development of these attitudes. If all family members practice the following, most youngsters develop a good self-concept.
1 Set a good example.
2 Respect and safeguard the rights of all family members.
3 Assure all family members of love and affection.
4 Understand and control personal emotions while helping the younger family members learn this control.
5 Give positive directions.
6 Help younger family members to help themselves.

Children are not miniature adults. Each developmental stage has its special needs as well as its special opportunities for learning. A child who is forced to take too much or too little responsibility for his own welfare is seriously disadvantaged. He may grow up to have a child's frustrated feelings in an adult's body.

Children's physical, mental, and emotional needs are very closely linked. Children need opportunities to grow and strengthen physically. They need opportunities to learn. They need opportunities to develop positive feelings about themselves and other people.

PHYSICAL NEEDS

A child's home is the place where his early physical needs are met. His chance to reach his full potential depends on how well his home meets these basic needs.

Shelter and furnishings

Infants and children through the elementary school years appear to pay little or no attention to shelter. Concerned adults must see that children are given protection from both extreme heat and cold. They must keep the child dry when it rains or snows. They must, to a degree, shelter him from wind and sunshine.

A young baby spends much of the twenty-four hours of the day sleeping. He needs a sleeping place of his own. At first this may be some sort of basket, replaced later by a crib, or a crib may be used from the beginning. The mattress must be firm and flat, and it should be covered with a rubber or plastic sheet under the surface sheet. A washable pad is placed on top. Pillows are not usually recommended for babies because they may affect the baby's posture and can cause smothering. All types of lightweight plastic should be *avoided completely,* as a baby is likely to smother if he pulls it over his face. Bed coverings should be warm, light in weight, and easily laundered. The room should be well ventilated and comfortably warm.

The small child pays more attention to the furniture in his home than he does to the building and rooms. Although he likes bright colors, he isn't interested in the quality of the furniture. He does notice the *size* of the furniture. If the family budget does not allow for specially sized furniture, a sturdy, lightweight climbing stool will help the small child reach full-sized beds, wash basins, and chairs. The same stool may serve as a necessary footrest for the child sitting in an adult chair.

Careful families check all home furnishings and materials for safety. Sharp corners, sharp or rough edges, or splintery surfaces can turn the young child's minor tumble into a major injury. Unsteady furniture can increase the chances for a fall. Small objects may be swallowed. Some paints are poisonous. Since it is almost impossible to keep the very young child from chewing any surface he can reach, it is necessary to remove such paint and to recover such surfaces with nonpoisonous paint.

Clothing

Today's clothing for children is made with comfort and activity in mind. As a child outgrows the size or need of certain items, other clothing can be chosen which is equally useful.

As a baby, the child needs plenty of diapers. They may be disposable or easy-wash ones, depending on the amount of money and time available for clothing and its care. He needs soft, warm, stretchy, washable cover-ups, or pajamas. Except for special occasions, the modern baby wears mainly these

Discuss why the following considerations will help a person buy children's clothing effectively:

Select clothes that fit comfortably, give the child freedom, and permit good posture.
Select clothes that are simple but well constructed and durable.
Select clothes that are easily cared for.
Choose clothes that are suited to the temperature.
Choose clothes that are light in weight.
Choose pretty, bright colors when possible.
Select clothes with durable fasteners that are located on the front of the garment.

Your career
Children's clothes designer

Duties: Designs clothes for children. Selects and advises on appropriateness of given fabrics, designs, trims, and colors for particular garments.
Where employed: Manufacturers of children's clothes or pattern manufacturing houses.

Collect pictures of furniture and equipment which can be adjusted to meet the needs of a growing child. Collect pictures of multi-purpose children's furnishings and tell how the items can be used to serve more than one need. Suggest useful substitute baby equipment such as a plastic dishpan for a bathtub or a drawer or wicker clothes basket for a bassinet.

Plan a typical family dinner menu, and vary it to meet the needs of a two-year-old child. Include foods which he could eat by himself. Plan other menus to meet the needs of children at different ages.

List facts you may have observed about young children's likes and dislikes about food such as:
1 Most children prefer mildly flavored foods rather than those which are strongly flavored or highly spiced.
2 Young children generally prefer foods served lukewarm rather than hot or cold.
3 Young children like to be able to pick up foods and eat with their fingers.

Make a scrapbook or joke book for the children's section of a hospital.

COURTESY THE WILLIAM CARTER COMPANY

Acceptable clothing for children is easy to put on, easy to remove, and easy to wash or clean.

two items. Both day and night, diapers are worn to keep him dry. Cover-ups are worn only if he needs them for warmth. Blankets or a snowsuit are used when he is taken out in cold weather. Plastic pants may be used at certain times to provide extra protection against dampness.

Toddlers and young children need clothing which is appropriate to the weather conditions where they live. Their clothing should help them remain cool in warm weather, but be warm enough to prevent them from becoming too chilly in other climates or seasons. It should also allow them to enjoy freedom of movement. At the same time, it must not be too large. Floppy pants legs and dangling sleeves are the cause of many childhood accidents, especially burns and falls. Equally important,

132

children's clothing should be chosen for easy care. Little good is derived from telling a child over and over, "Don't get your clothes dirty." Children must learn to be neat. But even more, they need to learn how to run and climb. They need to explore and satisfy their curiosity. These activities are likely to get children dirty. Sturdy clothes which launder easily can be kept reasonably neat.

As a child progresses through grade school, it is important that he be allowed to choose at least part of his own clothes. Since pressure from his gang is so important, he needs to have clothes pretty much like those of his school mates. If at all possible, the wise family finds ways to provide clothing to meet his social and emotional needs. For example, the flat-chested fifth-grade girl may need a new bra more than she needs a new dress. And the timid boy of the same age may need sneakers more than dress shoes.

Nutrition and food preparation

The basis of a child's future health is directly related to the food he eats. The food his mother ate before his birth and the food the child gets during the first months and years of his life determine much of his *physical* and *mental* development during his entire life.

Adults must be careful to buy food for children rather than for their own likes and dislikes. A child's taste is quite different from that of an older person. Generally, his foods should be only mildly flavored. It is best to avoid snack foods and to concentrate instead on good nutrition.

Because of the rapid growth a baby experiences during his first year of life, nutrition can hardly be overemphasized. A mother's own milk generally agrees with a young infant. It contains the nutrients the baby needs. Many doctors advise mothers to try to nurse their babies at least during early infancy.

There may be reasons, however, why a mother cannot or does not want to breast-feed her baby. In such cases, the baby is bottle-fed with a formula recommended by his doctor. A bottle-fed baby should be held in a position similar to the way he would be held if the mother were nursing him so that he may feel securely loved by his family.

For best growth and development, the baby must have other foods besides milk shortly after birth. Vitamins A and D are necessary. These and other vitamins are usually supplied as supplements. Since babies enjoy sucking, many are given fruit juice in a regular nursing bottle. Other usual supplements are well-cooked cereals and such fruits and vegetables as applesauce, bananas, sieved peas, carrots, beets, and potatoes. The sieved yolks of hard-cooked eggs and sieved meats are added later. For-

Demonstrate warming various kinds of baby bottles, testing the temperature of the contents, giving the bottle to a baby, and bubbling him.

Demonstrate giving a baby cereal from a spoon.

Plan a holiday party with games, refreshments, and student-made gifts for a local orphanage, school for retarded children, or child care center.

Discuss the occupational opportunities available to work with children in libraries, hospitals, children's sections of department stores, and toy stores.

Your career
Baby food specialist

Duties: Tests nutritional value, taste, and appearance of baby food. May plan menus for infants and small children. May assist in product package design or copy writing for advertisements.
Where employed: Manufacturing companies and government agencies; for example the Food and Drug Administration and the Consumer Protection and Environmental Health Service.

List points to look for in judging a nursery school. If possible, visit one and observe the children, teachers, equipment, toys, furnishings, and precautions taken for the children's safety.

Distinguish between an obstetrician and a pediatrician.

Make a chart showing recommended preventive shots for a child until he reaches school age.

tunately, the busy mother can buy these foods already prepared for the baby, thus saving many hours of her time.

By the end of his first year, a child is eating many foods besides a daily quart of milk. He usually learns how to drink from a cup and how to bite and chew regular foods. His efforts to feed himself should be encouraged. So should his interest in new foods. The child who has learned to eat and like a variety of foods has an early start toward good health.

In his third year the child will enjoy raw vegetables and fruits in addition to the cooked foods he has already learned to like. After he is three, he can eat the foods prepared for the family, provided they are not too rich, too hard to handle, or too difficult to chew and swallow. Rich desserts, fried foods, nuts, highly seasoned foods, hot breads, and beverages such as tea and coffee should not be given to a young child.

Protection from dangers

Until they have enough experience and judgment to look out for themselves, children need to be protected. They must be kept safe from physical harm and also from the emotional harm that results from too much teasing, ridicule, and sarcasm.

Adults must protect children from illness and diseases. They can best do this by following the advice of the specialist at a well-baby clinic, the family doctor, or a pediatrician, one who specializes in child care. Such doctors will help the family establish proper routines of rest and nutrition to meet the individual child's needs. They will also schedule preventive shots at the proper times so that childhood diseases can be avoided.

Every effort should be made to teach a young child safe behavior. You may do this by setting a good example, as well as by seeing that

Self-feeding is a happy experience for a child when he is praised for his successes and little is said about the food he spills.

COURTESY CARDINAL GLENNON MEMORIAL HOSPITAL FOR CHILDREN

he plays safely in safe areas. A child must be taught which activities are dangerous and how to avoid them. (See page 145.)

MENTAL NEEDS

At no time in his life will a human being have as much to learn as in early childhood. A child needs to have his mental growth stimulated. He needs people, books, toys, and other learning materials in his environment.

Learning self-care

The young child, if encouraged, usually wants to take care of himself. For example, at an early age, he wants to feed himself. At first he tends to use his fingers. In time, he wants to learn how to use regular eating tools. The skills of cutting, spreading, and spooning are difficult to learn. If a child, by the age of seven or eight, has learned to feed himself in a manner somewhat acceptable to adults, he is progressing at a reasonable rate.

When a child is interested in dressing himself, he should be permitted to do as much as he can. When adults lose patience and dress the child themselves to save time, they deprive him of a chance to learn. The child will enjoy trying to dress himself if the clothing is designed for self-help. Desirable features are simple designs, large buttons and buttonholes, and slide fasteners that can be easily reached and managed. The child can learn to put his clothes on hooks or in drawers if storage places are arranged low for his height.

Other ways in which a child is interested in self-help include combing his hair, brushing his teeth, turning on the water faucet to wash his hands, and going to the toilet alone. He also enjoys opening doors and walking up and down short flights of steps. You can help him become independent if you let him do for himself as much as he can and will. Too, when routine in such matters can be practiced, it adds to the child's personal security.

Toilet training involves many complicated learnings. The young

COURTESY COCA-COLA COMPANY

A parent's interest in a child's curiosity leads to early mental growth.

Using your left hand if you are right-handed and your right hand if you are left-handed and a stubby crayon, color a printed picture which is very small and detailed. What feelings do you experience? How do you think these feelings are similar to those that a young child experiences? Why were you asked to use the hand which you ordinarily would not use? How did the size of the picture you colored compare to the size of a picture a young child might be given to color? What have you learned from doing this that relates to the development of a young child?

List reasons why babies cry. If possible, make sound tapes of babies crying. Are there different cries? Can you identify cries of pain or hunger?

Bulletin board IDEA
Title: *I'm Expecting:*
 Love
 Security
 Guidance
 Physical care
Directions: Mount a large picture of a baby on one side of the bulletin board with the caption balancing the picture on the other side.

135

Observe a pre-school age child, other than your own brother or sister. Report to class your observations in three of the following situations:
1 At play
2 At mealtime
3 Being dressed or undressed
4 On a shopping trip or other outing
5 Going to bed for a nap or for the night

You may observe the child in nursery school, on a playground, in the neighborhood, in a store, or in his own home. You may use the same child for all three observations or you may use different children. In your report answer questions such as these:

A How old was the child? If you do not know for sure, how old do you think he was? What was he doing to help you judge his age?
B How did the child react to the situation? Why did he react this way?
C What provisions were made for letting the child do things for himself? Did he? Why or why not?

child needs time to master this task. Most children want to try but will seem to lose ground more than once before the habit of control is firmly established.

Far too much toilet training is done simply to get the approval of grandparents or family friends. Children are usually more relaxed and grown-up about the whole experience if allowed to more or less go it alone. Most youngsters are toilet-trained by the time they enter kindergarten. Toilet training varies widely from family to family. For this reason, when you are caring for young children, find out what is expected of them. Follow the family rules so the child will not become confused.

Play and playthings

Much of a child's learning takes place as he plays. Through play he develops an alert, imaginative mind as well as a strong body. The young child needs playthings with which he can learn to control and develop his body. They may also provide him with opportunities to practice the ideas he is developing. As he plays house or builds a town with blocks, he is trying out some of the relationships he has seen between the people and the things around him.

Children play differently from time to time. Sometimes they enjoy playing quietly; other times they are boisterous. They play with others, and they play alone. They need opportunities and equipment to aid them in all these types of play.

The tiny baby needs little or no equipment for active play. He plays as he kicks and pulls. As the child grows older, he needs equipment that will encourage him to use his large muscles. From large blocks, he progresses to wheeled toys, such as wagons, tricycles, and skates. Still later, he learns to use balancing boards, swings, slides, and climbing equipment. All of these playthings belong in the child's general environment. Families can furnish some of them. Other equipment is available in playgrounds, nurseries, or day-care centers. In one way or another, the child should be given the opportunity to learn through the use of a wide range of play equipment.

Playthings should be chosen for the child's use. For example, a small, cuddly doll that can be dressed and undressed aids in many kinds of learnings. On the other hand, a large beautifully dressed doll that must be placed on a shelf contributes little to a child's development.

Playthings must be safe, but they need not be expensive. An empty box which imagination can turn into a house, a car, an orbiting space ship, or a store can be more fun for a child than toys bought for every special purpose. In fact, simple toys are often better than complicated ones because they stimulate the imagination, encouraging the child to work out several ideas during a single play period. Playthings must be sturdy enough to survive rough handling. The older child likes to test out his strength by moving large objects. He needs toys which are strong enough to hold up his weight but light enough to move.

Games are enjoyed by very young children. A baby's first *game* may occur when an older person helps him to exercise by pulling him to a sitting position. The baby enjoys not only the muscular exercise but the companionship of the older person as well. Later, when he can sit up, the baby likes games of peekaboo. At about the same age, he enjoys the companionship of *retriever*, a game in which he deliberately drops a toy for the fun of having someone pick it up for him.

True social games do not develop until the late preschool years. The older preschool child enjoys complicated games of make-believe with other children of his own age and with older children and adults. These games can also be fun for older children. The older ones must remember, however, that the preschooler is not ready for formal rules.

Play space should be checked for safety on a regular basis. A child needs protection from danger while he satisfies his curiosity. Broken glass, rusty nails, and sharp metal edges can cause serious injuries.

COURTESY SOL LEITER AND THOMAS J. LIPTON, INC.

Children discover the real world through their make-believe world of play.

Play equipment must be kept in good repair and placed in proper positions.

Indoor play space should be provided for all children. Even the very young child can be given a safe corner for play. But because his play must be supervised and because his mother will want to be near him as she does her housework, a playpen can be a real convenience. It can be moved from room to room so that the older baby can go with his mother as she does

Select or write stories for children of varying ages. As a community service project, get permission to read these during a planned storytelling hour at the local library. Or read stories to children in the children's section of a hospital.

Interview a kindergarten teacher to find out what type of assistant she would find most valuable.

Your career
Kindergartner

Duties: Entertains children in nurseries maintained by department stores, country clubs, or similar establishments as a service to patrons. Performs many tasks such as reading aloud to children, organizing and participating in games or parties, and giving elementary lessons in arts or crafts.
Where employed: Family resort areas, large department stores, country clubs, and similar recreation areas.

Bring to class a favorite book of childhood days or one belonging to a younger brother or sister. Tell the class why you think it is suited for a particular age.

List *do's* and *don'ts* of telling stories to children. Add to the following list:
1. Make the story short.
2. For younger children, use facial expressions, motions, and expressive sounds.
3. If necessary, change the words in the story to simpler ones.
4. Avoid exciting, gruesome, or terrifying stories at bedtime.
5. Avoid stories with frightening endings.

Your career
Sitter services

Duties: Plays games, reads, entertains, and performs simple household services for invalids, elderly people, or children when other family members are not available.
Where employed: Government agencies or private agencies. May be self-employed.

COURTESY THE GREYHOUND CORPORATION

As a child grows in his awareness of others, he enjoys imitating adults while playing with friends his own age.

her daily tasks. The older child may use the living-room floor, the kitchen table, or the play area of sleeping quarters for his indoor play space.

Outdoor play is desirable when weather permits. It offers the child a chance to move freely as he uses up his apparently boundless energy to develop endurance, muscular strength, and coordination.

No matter where a child plays, it is important that he learn to put away his play materials when he is through with them. A box, a drawer, or open shelves should be provided for convenient toy storage. A similar storage space should be provided for larger outdoor equipment. The child will learn to care for his belongings more quickly if the storage areas are convenient to the play areas.

Language development
A child learns to talk by acquiring words and language patterns from the people around him. He also

learns to talk by having experiences which give him something to talk about. He learns to communicate through constant practice.

If older people anticipate the child's every wish, they deny him the opportunity to learn to speak. If people accept a child's baby talk without guiding him into correct speech patterns, they deny him a chance for conversational improvement. If people brush off a child's attempts to converse by giving him only *yes* or *no* answers or by indifferent listening, the child will have little chance to develop language skills.

If a child's home is a place where books are treasured and where reading is an accepted family activity, he will very soon acquire the family attitude. The very young child enjoys looking at the bright pictures in the sturdy books prepared for his age group. As he learns to talk, he takes pleasure in pointing to a picture and naming the objects it portrays. At the same age, he also enjoys having an older person tell him about the pictures as he turns the pages of a book.

In many families a daily period of time is set aside for the child to watch television. The wise family helps the child select programs which are appropriate to his development. They make sure that the child's natural interest in television does not interfere with his needs for other activities. Young children enjoy programs which are shared with older family members and talked about afterwards.

Young children generally enjoy music. There are many ways in which the alert family can encourage this interest. The toddler can be encouraged to march or drum to a favorite record. He can sing along with others.

SOCIAL AND EMOTIONAL NEEDS

To get along with others, children need to be taught basic social skills. They need to be guided so that they learn what is expected of them in the world outside their homes. The foundations of mental and emotional health are laid down in childhood.

Relationships

A child needs to learn that life is a matter of give-and-take. He can learn that sometimes he must be the giver, and he can learn to enjoy the giving. He must be taught to consider the feelings and desires of others. It is a fortunate child who learns to get along with other children and with adults outside his family.

Security

A child needs to be regarded seriously as a family member. His security is provided by the people who take care of him. If secure within his family group, he can be taught to cope with familiar situa-

Make play clay according to the following recipe. Discuss appropriate times and places for its use.
1 Mix one cup flour, one-half cup cornstarch, and one cup cold water in a large bowl.
2 Boil four cups water and one cup salt in a large-based pan.
3 Pour the boiling water mixture slowly into the flour mixture and stir.
4 Return this milky-looking mixture to the pan and stir over low heat until it thickens (three to five minutes).
5 Cool. Knead in four to five cups of flour until the play clay is soft, but not sticky.
6 Add color if desired. Separate into batches for different colors, using a different color powder paint for each batch.
7 Store in a covered crock, pottery jar, foil-lined tin, or tightly closed plastic bag.
This play clay is spongier and less drying to the hands than uncooked salt dough. Flour or water may be added from time to time for ease of handling.

◈ Defend the statement: *A teen-ager who has very few responsibilities is seriously disadvantaged.*

Discuss some of your own early childhood experiences when love and affection helped you.

Distinguish between discipline and punishment. Give examples to illustrate your understanding of the differences between the two. Write a definition for *effective discipline.*

➫ **Your career**
Nursemaid

Duties: Performs any combination of the following duties in caring for children: Observes and monitors play activities or amuses children by reading to or playing games with them. Prepares and serves meals or formulas. Sterilizes bottles and other equipment used for feeding infants. Dresses or assists children to dress. Bathes or helps children bathe. Accompanies children on walks or other outings.
Where employed: By private employment agencies or government agencies. May be self-employed.

COURTESY NATIONAL OAK FLOORING MANUFACTURERS' ASSOCIATION, INC.

Children can learn from their brothers and sisters that life is full of give-and-take.

tions as well as those that are new and different. When a child comes to you hurt or bewildered, let him know he can count on you.

Sometimes with the birth of a new brother or sister, a child loses his sense of security. He may be helped to overcome his loss by special attention which makes him feel that Mother still loves him. It is especially helpful if he can be honestly praised for his own growth and development. He will also be helped to understand and outgrow his jealousy if he is allowed to help care for the baby.

Discipline

Children need to understand that there are real limits in all aspects of daily life. They learn these limits most easily by following the examples set by older family members. Children imitate their older brothers and sisters as well as their parents. This places a great responsibility upon all the older members of the family. Older family members must follow the same rules for health and safety that they expect the younger family members to follow.

Firm rules and good reasons are important in establishing acceptable behavior patterns. A little child likes to be given specific help in behaving acceptably. When he is told only what *not* to do, he becomes stubborn and resentful. Often he is confused by such instructions. If you say, "No, that stove is hot. You will hurt yourself," a child will begin to see that rules of this type are made to protect him.

A young child must be expected to follow the rules. If necessary, he must be picked up and removed from a dangerous area. Some people fear that turning the child toward an acceptable activity is giving in to the child. Instead, this is an effective part of child rearing. Substituting a desirable activity for an unacceptable one clearly defines the limits of acceptable behavior. With proper training and practice, he can make desirable substitutions independently as he matures.

Punishment may sometimes be absolutely necessary. In such instances, it should be both positive and instructional. Related to the offense, it should be administered promptly and calmly. There should be no doubt in the child's mind as to why he is being punished. It should be his behavior, rather than the child himself, which punishment attacks.

Taking responsibility for children

You may already have had a chance to care for young children. Taking care of youngsters is a very responsible job. Little children look up to older children. To a toddler, a teen-ager is a grown-up.

WHEN ARE YOU READY?
It takes patience and understanding to deal with children. As a baby-sitter, you are in a position of great trust. Before you accept this responsibility, ask yourself whether you are prepared to act in an adult way. Can you keep calm? Can you be fair? Can you direct a child's interest from harmful to constructive play? Can you think straight in a real crisis and get the kind of help you need?

WHEN YOU ARE A BABY-SITTER
Your first experience with baby-sitting may have been at home when you were asked to mind younger brothers and sisters. You know the rules at home. You also know your family's routines and the family standards of child care. Families differ on whether family members are paid for baby-sitting. When you sit for others, you usually do so for pay. In assuming responsibility for other people's chil-

List the qualities you would want in a baby-sitter for your own child. Develop these into a checklist and rate yourself as a baby-sitter.

Form a panel composed of parents of small children and three student baby-sitters. Ask them to discuss what parents expect of the baby-sitter and what the sitter expects of the parents. Discuss pay, transportation, hours of employment, responsibilities to be assumed by the parents and by the sitter, and privileges and restrictions.

Make a guidebook for baby-sitters, summarizing facts dealing with the responsibilities of a baby-sitter.

Develop a form to fill out for each of the families for whom you baby-sit. Include the doctor's name and telephone number, the name and telephone number of a relative or friend to contact in an emergency, bedtime routine, and special things the children like.

Give skits which demonstrate the activities which are acceptable and unacceptable for young children just before bedtime.

View children's TV programs. Select programs appropriate for children of different ages. Make a list of suggestions for improving them and send it to the local television station.

Develop a checklist for judging TV programs for children of various ages. Watch some children's programs and rate them using the checklist. Develop devices for evaluating magazines, books, records, and movies for children.

Discuss what is meant by an educational toy, remembering that there are areas of education which are not a part of school. Discuss how a push-and-pull toy could be educational.

Make a checklist for evaluating toys for children at various ages. Bring some toys to class and evaluate them for:
Safety
Durability
Educational value, in the broadest sense

Suggest everyday household items which make good, safe substitute toys. Discuss why a child may not show interest in an expensive toy, but enjoy playing with a wooden spoon and cooking pan.

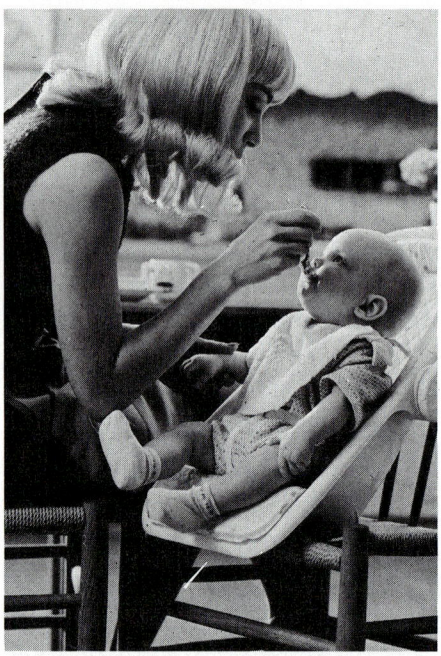

COURTESY COSCO HOUSEHOLD PRODUCTS, INC.

Baby-sitting with a young child may include feeding and dressing him as well as keeping him safe and happy.

dren, you need certain very definite preparation for the job. If you are a paid baby-sitter, you are expected to know what to do in any situation that may arise.

Baby-sitting is a part-time occupation chosen by many mature people as well as by teen-agers. It is more than sitting, certainly, and it involves having up-to-date information on child care, guidance, and health. Baby-sitting offers an opportunity for the teen-ager to earn money. Valuable, too, is the training obtained in making decisions, meeting emergencies, and learning how to get along with adults as well as children.

Baby-sitting may involve feeding and dressing a child, reading stories to him, playing out-of-doors, putting him to bed, or perhaps keeping a convalescent child quiet and amused. It is wise for younger teen-agers to accept only daytime or early evening assignments in homes of people already well known to the sitter.

While a knowledge of the behavior of your own brothers and sisters will be helpful in baby-sitting, the problems presented by other children may be different. Therefore, as a would-be baby-sitter, you need to know what type of behavior to expect from children of different ages. You should also know how to make financial and transportation arrangements, how to dress, and what to do after you arrive in a child's home.

CARING FOR A BABY

Even though you may not have complete charge of a baby very often, it is important for you to know how to take care of a baby. Babies usually cry because something is wrong. A mother soon learns to tell from the tone of her baby's cry whether he is thirsty, hungry, uncomfortable, sick, or merely seeking attention. When you are caring for a baby, the mother will generally tell you the types of crying to expect.

Holding the baby
A young baby's muscles are soft and relatively weak. He cannot hold his head up without help. To support his head and the upper part of his back, slip one hand under his head and place your other hand and arm under the lower part of his back. Then you can safely lift him to your shoulder, where his head will be securely supported by your body.

Pick the baby up by grasping his entire body, rather than his arms. Hold him firmly in your arms, either resting against your shoulder or cradled in your arms. This gives the baby the support that will make him feel secure. A young baby has an instinctive fear of falling.

Feeding the baby
In caring for a baby, you may need to feed him. Be sure that the mother has shown you how to hold the baby securely. Be careful not to rush the baby through the feeding, and be sure that he is well bubbled both during and after his feeding time.

You probably will not be asked to prepare the baby's formula. If you are asked to do this, you must be given the directions for sanitation, measuring the ingredients, mixing the formula, and storing the bottles. You must follow these directions exactly. Usually formula enough for a twenty-four-hour period is prepared at one time.

Washing and dressing the baby
You may be asked to give an older baby his bath. A bath should be fun for the baby. He must be watched constantly while being bathed, since he can slip so easily. Never leave him alone or unsupported for any reason. Even when he is old enough to sit alone, the baby is bathed in a comparatively small amount of water.

You may need to dress the baby while you are in charge of him. Babies of any age may feel uncomfortable if their clothes become wet and sticky. The baby's mother will have shown you where to find changes of clothing. Ask the mother to show you how she wants the diapers folded and fastened. As a safety precaution in pinning the diaper, place your fingers between the baby's body and the diaper before inserting the pin. Keep pins out of the baby's reach. Learn to clothe the baby with as little handling as possible. It disturbs babies to feel tied down as their arms and legs are being clothed or as the clothing is being placed over their heads.

Sleep and rest for the baby
When it is time for the baby to sleep, be sure that he is comfortable. Check his clothing to see that it is dry and that he is comfortably warm. Place him in his bed and adjust his covers according to the directions his mother has given you. Be sure that the baby is protected

Make a baby-sitting kit full of surprises. This might include crayons and paper, storybooks, puppets, or any other items which would interest the children for whom you baby-sit.

Make finger paint from soap flakes, liquid starch, and food coloring. Mix the three ingredients until the desired consistency and color are obtained.

Suggest inexpensive indoor play materials such as strings of uncooked macaroni for necklaces and graduated sizes of cans for put-together toys. Make some of these toys at home and bring them to school to show the class.

Make bibs from washcloths and old towels.

Make crib sheets and pads from worn sheets and bed pads.

Make a toy chest from cardboard cartons or vegetable crates. Cover it with pictures or adhesive material or paint it.

Bring to class old toys and repaint or repair them. Give them to children who have few toys and playthings.

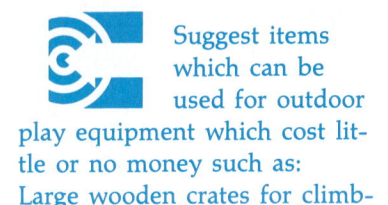

Suggest items which can be used for outdoor play equipment which cost little or no money such as:
Large wooden crates for climbing
Old tires for swinging
Large cable spools for rolling

from unusually bright lights and loud noises. Then leave him quietly so that he can doze off undisturbed. Be sure to remain within hearing distance so that you can go to him immediately if he needs you.

CARING FOR A YOUNG CHILD

Taking care of a young child is different in many ways from taking care of a baby. The young child needs someone to look after his physical needs, but as he grows and develops, he needs help in other ways as well. He must be guided in his play, protected from injury, and taught how to live with others. As his world expands, so grow the responsibilities of those who direct his development. Many teen-agers spend the summer months as effective companions for young children.

Feeding the young child

You may be asked to help a young child with his meal. If so, prepare his food according to his mother's directions. Be patient with the toddler if he is having trouble feeding himself. Help him if he needs help, but allow him to do what he can. Be sure to tell his returning parents just how much he has eaten.

Washing and grooming the young child

If you are asked to bathe a young child, make sure that he enjoys the experience. He needs a chance to splash, to play with soap and toys, and to use the washcloth. Although he enjoys washing himself, he probably will not do a very good job. A washcloth for each of you will allow you to bathe him while he enjoys his growing ability to take care of himself.

A young child can drown in only a few inches of water. If he turns on the hot-water tap while he is

A young child can be allowed to enjoy his bath while he is carefully watched by an older person.

COURTESY CULLIGAN INTERNATIONAL COMPANY

A baby-sitter's duties include guiding young charges away from dangerous activities as well as seeing that they are clean for mealtime and bedtime.

alone, he can be severely scalded. Your presence is needed both for his safety and for his security.

Help the child dress himself in the clothing his mother has provided for him. Remember to be patient. Be ready to help him when he needs help, but be careful not to take away his joy in being able to do things for himself.

It is not necessary for you to keep a young child shining clean every moment he is in your care. See that he washes his hands and face before eating, and help him brush his teeth afterward. He will naturally get messy during his activities. Let him enjoy his play. Then clean him up before he goes to bed.

Sleep and rest for the young child

In getting the child ready for bed and for sound, restful sleep, be sure that you do things in a relaxed manner. The toddler and the preschooler do not drop off to sleep as easily as a baby does. Allow children of these ages a chance to unwind. Perhaps a quiet story or song will help them relax. Be sure the toddler has his favorite toy with him if he usually sleeps with it. When you are certain the young child is comfortable, leave him to rest alone in his usual place. Remain free enough that you can go to him immediately if he needs help.

Role-play possible problem situations which may occur when you are baby-sitting. The following situations may help you think of others:
A child does not want to go to bed.
A child has wet his pants but does not want to change them.
A child cries when his parents leave.
Discuss the ways in which the baby-sitter handled the situation well. If appropriate, make suggestions for improving the situation. Use these suggestions in an instant replay.

Dramatize making friends with a child by role-playing good and poor ways to approach a child you have just met. After the dramatization, discuss the qualities that children like in their baby-sitters and in adults.

Bulletin board IDEA
Title: *Toys for Tots*
Directions: Use yarn to outline a drawing of a bookcase that has three shelves. Label the bottom shelf *one-year-old,* the middle shelf *two-year-old,* and the top shelf *three-year-old.* On each shelf tack toys or pictures of toys appropriate for children of that age.

7 CHAPTER POSTTEST

Number from 1 to 10 on a piece of paper. Beside each number write the letter corresponding with the answer which *best* completes the sentence. *Do not* write in this book.

1. A doctor who specializes in the care of children is a(an)...
   a. obstetrician.
   b. general practitioner.
   c. pediatrician.
   d. dermatologist.
2. An individual generally grows most rapidly in a physical sense during...
   a. the first year of life.
   b. the preschool years.
   c. the elementary school years.
   d. adolescence.
3. Accomplishing physical developmental tasks depends primarily upon...
   a. muscular growth, development, and coordination.
   b. an intellectually stimulating environment.
   c. social experiences.
   d. emotional maturity.
4. Social development in a baby is shown when he...
   a. cries.
   b. turns over.
   c. crawls.
   d. smiles.
5. Most young children prefer foods which are...
   a. strongly flavored.
   b. served very hot or very cold.
   c. highly seasoned.
   d. easily eaten with fingers.
6. A child between the ages of three and six usually...
   a. learns to control his emotions.
   b. is curious and asks questions.
   c. grows at an even and steady rate.
   d. pokes at things and puts them in his mouth.
7. Just before a young child goes to bed it is best to...
   a. play an active game.
   b. threaten that something bad will happen if he isn't good.
   c. read a pleasant story to him.
   d. watch an exciting TV show.
8. The time when the opinion of the gang is most important is usually during...
   a. the toddler stage.
   b. the preschool years.
   c. the elementary school years.
   d. the later adolescent years.
9. Effective discipline should involve...
   a. physical punishment.
   b. telling a child what he cannot do.
   c. establishing acceptable behavior.
   d. threatening the child.
10. The beginning of puberty usually occurs...
    a. at an earlier age for girls than for boys.
    b. at the same age for all boys.
    c. when emotional development begins.
    d. on one's thirteenth birthday.

8 CHAPTER PRETEST

Answer the following questions on a separate sheet of paper. *Do not* write in this book.

1. List in order the 7 steps in the *problem-solving approach* which may be used in any situation.
2. List 3 advantages in using the problem-solving approach to reach any difficult decision.
3. List 5 points to keep in mind when arranging furniture in any room.
4. List 10 questions which should be included on a checklist used to judge the safety of a home.
5. List 5 questions which should be included on a home storage efficiency checklist.
6. List 5 guidelines for a good family health program.
7. List 5 rules to follow in an emergency situation involving an accident or illness.
8. List 4 types of needs for which a comfortable home usually provides.
9. List 3 childhood diseases which can be prevented by inoculations.
10. Which childhood disease may cause birth defects in children if it is contracted by an expectant mother during the early months of pregnancy?
11. Which national association specializes in educating people of all ages in the area of first aid?

CHAPTER 8

Managing the problems of family living

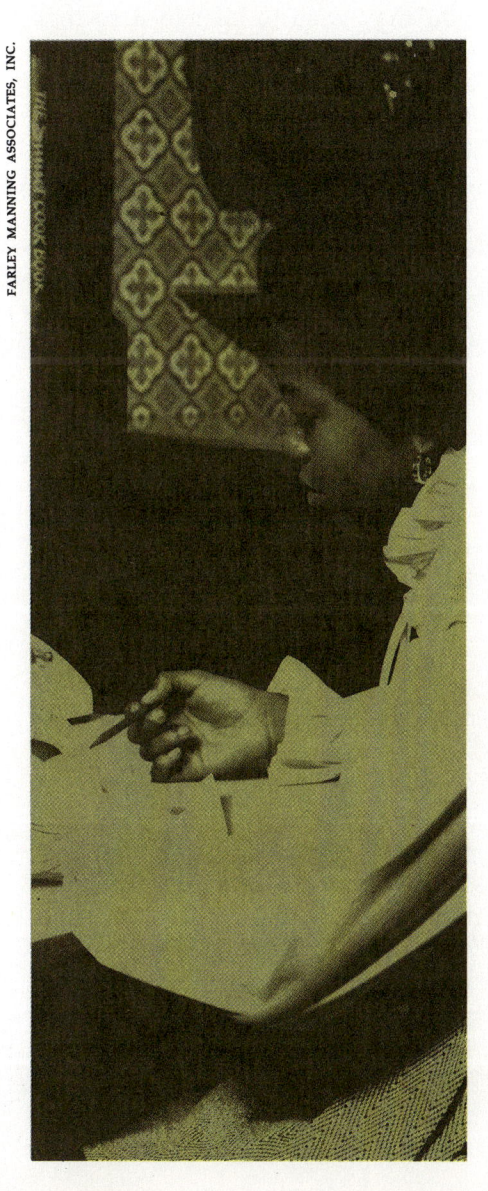

The main job of the home manager is to keep the family happy during the continual adjustments which the family must make. Planning is an essential part of management. But values must be determined and decisions made almost minute by minute. Knowledge used wisely in making on-the-spot decisions, or the application of common sense, has a tendency to make for happy family living.

Home management is involved in every aspect of family living. The abilities of family members to get along together or to adjust to new situations are management concerns. The day-in-day-out concern that family members be fed regularly is also a part of home management. So too is the problem of providing suitable clothing for every family member. When to paint, what equipment to buy, and where to live—these are matters of management. To keep the home warm during the winter, comfortably cool during the summer, and dry throughout the year calls for management. Too, the well-managed home, while kept neat enough for health and safety, is also planned for comfort, convenience, and privacy.

Recall times within the past week when you had decisions to make such as the choice of a dress to wear for a certain occasion, how to spend some of your money, or the choice between two things you wanted to do or places you wanted to go at the same time. Discuss the considerations that influenced you in making your decisions.

Answer the following questions about the way you make important decisions. *Do not write in this book.*
1 Do you think of the possible choices?
2 Do you then determine the advantages and disadvantages of each possible choice?
3 Do you consider carefully all of the alternatives?
4 Do you seek help at this point if you need it?
5 Do you decide whether or not your plan worked well?
6 When a decision is a good one, do you use it in similar situations unless there are new developments?

C Apply the problem-solving approach to one of your personal problems. Evaluate the results by answering the following questions:
1 Which decisions were the best and why?
2 How could the plan have been improved?
3 What did you learn by applying the problem-solving approach in this situation?

Relate an incident when you seemed to learn from making a mistake.

Problem solving in home management

How can you manage a home when the time comes that the responsibility falls on your shoulders? Every teen-ager at one time or another considers this question. Eventually, whether they realize it or not, successful home managers learn to use common sense. They learn to apply certain methods of problem solving to any problem, big or small.

There are a number of approaches to problem solving. Some approaches are less detailed than others. Some omit steps which are considered important in others. The following steps represent one approach to problem solving. As you become familiar with this approach, you may wish to change it so that it will better meet a given situation. In general, however, each step of this approach should be considered in the suggested order before a definite decision is made.

STATE THE PROBLEM
The first step, clearly stating the problem, is often one of the most difficult steps involved in clearing up a situation. You cannot reach an intelligent solution to a problem until you know exactly what it is. And you cannot know how to handle a situation unless you can relate it to your goals and values. Unfortunately, a first statement of the problem may overlook the real issues. For example, you may ask yourself, "Shall I buy this makeup?" If you are asking this question during a personal shopping trip, your question may mean, "Is the makeup a good buy for my purpose?" On the other hand, you may see the makeup while you are shopping for a gift for someone else. In this case, your question may mean, "Should I skimp on my gift selection in order to have the makeup?"

The following set of circumstances might describe a situation similar to one you have faced.

The problem of having clean, dry clothes for all family members is often solved when the family decides to buy home laundry equipment.

COURTESY LIVE BETTER ELECTRICALLY PROGRAM, EDISON ELECTRIC INSTITUTE

Sharon needs a new winter coat. But so does her brother Dan. The family resources will allow for the purchase of shoes for the entire family, some shirts, pants, and dresses. But there seems to be no workable way to fit two new winter coats into the overall clothing budget.

Few problems are simple. Most are made up of many related parts. Even the simple question, "What shall we have for dinner tonight?" involves at least four considerations. There is the need to meet the nutritional requirements of everyone in the family. There is the necessity for selecting food which fits within the family budget. There is the desire to choose food which individual family members enjoy. Also, there must be enough time and energy available for proper preparation of the selected foods.

COLLECT THE FACTS

Once the problem is clearly stated, you can begin to collect the facts which will help you make a wise decision. Sometimes this step can be as simple as organizing facts you know well. At other times you may need to look up all the facts. If the problem is simple, you may be able to organize the facts in your mind and make an immediate decision. If it is more complicated, you may prefer to write down the facts.

In Sharon's case, her family might explain to her that there is $150 available to buy winter clothes for her brother and herself. If she wrote down the facts of their needs and what similar articles had cost recently, she might have a set of facts and figures which looked something like this:

Need	Amount	Cost
Boy's shirts	4	$ 16.00
Wash pants	4	32.00
Blouses	2	12.00
Skirts	2	16.00
Boy's underwear	4 sets	8.00
Girl's underwear	4 sets	24.00
Boy's coat	1	30.00
Girl's coat	1	40.00
School shoes	2 pairs	30.00
Total estimated cost		$208.00
Available money		150.00
To be made up		$ 58.00

You may wish to organize facts into groups. There are facts about a problem itself. Your statement of the problem is the first of these. You may need to consider how the various possible solutions will affect the wants and needs of all the people involved. How do the other people feel about the situation? A judgment as to the importance of the

Present a skit showing a teenager faced with a difficult decision. Do not show the decision itself. Divide into small groups and decide which would be the best choice that the hero or heroine of the skit might make. What alternatives are there? What might be the consequences of each decision?

Ask the class to give several situations which suggest the need for the use of the problem-solving approach in arriving at a suitable plan of action. Divide into buzz-size groups and develop a problem-solving approach to these situations which seems likely to work well. Report back to the class and discuss the plans which have been proposed.

Bulletin board IDEA
Title: *Fiddle for Fun*
  But
  Act on Decisions
Directions: Use a picture of a fiddle, or violin. Write the steps in the problem-solving approach on pieces of paper which are mounted around the musical instrument.

Apply the problem-solving approach to one of the following situations. You will have to use your imagination in stating some of the factors which affect the situation.
1. Mary may choose one elective course this year. She may take art, chorus, band, or a foreign language.
2. John wants to buy a secondhand minibike which needs repair. Although he has been saving his money carefully, he is still $15 short of the selling price.
3. Bill wants to take guitar lessons. He also hopes to join a community basketball team. The team practices at the only time guitar lessons are given.

Bulletin board IDEA
Title: *Mr. Blueprint, Consider Our Needs*
Directions: Mount a house plan in the center of the board. Around it display pictures representing some of the following:
A newly married couple
A family with many children
An older couple
Several geographic locations
Hobbies and activities of family members

COURTESY VIKING SEWING MACHINE

By developing sewing skills, a girl can cut down on the cost of the clothes she needs and wants.

problem can be included with this group of facts.

Another group of facts consists of information relating to costs. Although most people consider the cost in money, they may overlook other costs. Some decisions may cost more time or energy than you can afford. Some decisions may require that someone give up a conflicting goal. Although the costs of inconvenience and dissatisfaction are hard to measure, they too must be considered as you search for a satisfactory solution.

A third group of facts concerns your resources. What is available to you to help meet your goals? Since costs and resources tend to be related, they are frequently thought of together. Thus, when you consider how much time an activity will take, you also consider how much time is available. There are certain resources which are frequently overlooked. For instance, do you have skills that will help you attain your goals? What substitutions can you make in order to reach a satisfactory decision?

At this point, Sharon might begin to reason out a list of possible solutions. They might include any of the following:
1. Mother can get the money we need. She can cut down on the cost of the food we eat. She and Dad don't really need to spend money on recreation. They're grown up now. Clothing is a real need. Our parents should not give to worthy causes right now. *We are their worthy causes.*
2. I can make my two skirts for $10 and save $6. But that is only $6. Would that help enough to count? Would the time used in sewing take away time needed for baby-sitting?
3. I can use my baby-sitting money for clothes instead of entertainment. But Dan makes money on yard work. Is it fair for me to make up

the $58 while he spends his money as usual?

4 Maybe, when we shop, we'll find good buys and it won't be necessary to spend $208.

CONSIDER THE ALTERNATIVES

The processes of clarifying the problem and gathering the necessary facts usually suggest alternative solutions. Are there other possible solutions you may have overlooked? Sometimes people overlook an obvious solution because they are concentrating too hard on the fact that a problem exists.

There is seldom a single, absolutely perfect solution for a problem. Consider the short-term and long-term results of each possible decision. Consider the advantages and disadvantages of each. You may need to gather additional facts or consult an expert in the field in order to be sure that you know all the advantages and disadvantages involved.

As you consider the possible solutions, you may discover that one particular choice seems to be the most attractive. Another choice may seem so distasteful you are ready to drop it immediately. Such likes and dislikes are an important part of the problem-solving process, but it is unwise to make them the *only* basis for choice. It is wiser to treat these feelings as part of the facts to be considered. The solution you like may not be the best solution. Perhaps you like it for only one reason. Would that part of the solution fit in with another solution? Checking the facts beyond the feelings may help you find a new alternative, better than any of your earlier ones.

Could some of Sharon's possible solutions to her problem be distasteful to other members of her family? For instance, would it be right to ask her parents to stop supporting research concerned with mental illness if one of them had been cured because of others' contributions to this cause? If her parents are trying to improve a set of shaky personal relations by doing something special together each

Apply these guidelines for good lighting of a study desk. List other useful guidelines.

Plan for adequate lighting.

Locate the light source above a point 15 inches to the left of the work center and 12 inches back from the front edge of the desk.

Position the bottom edge of the shade 15 inches from the desk top.

Choose a desk lamp which has an open top and a white inner surface.

Choose a shade which is partially or fully opaque.

Catering firms, snack bars, and restaurants offer part-time job opportunities where boys and girls can earn money for their personal expenses.

COURTESY HIBBING AREA TECHNICAL INSTITUTE

C Draw a before-and-after plan for the furniture in a teen-ager's bedroom. Tell why the second arrangement is more effective than the first. If your home situation allows, rearrange the furniture in your bedroom at home. Report the results of your project to the class.

Discuss the following set of guidelines for arranging bedroom furniture. Add others which you think might be helpful.
- Place large pieces of furniture so that they are parallel to the walls of the room rather than across corners.
- Put the dresser near the closet and in a place where the mirror is well lighted.
- Arrange a desk, desk chair, and desk lamp in a grouping near the location planned for bookshelves. A convenient electric outlet for the desk lamp is necessary to prevent accidents.
- Place a bed so that . . .
- It does not obstruct the passage through the room to the closet or hallway.
- There is enough space on the sides and at the foot to allow for easy movement around it.
- Light from the windows will not shine into a sleeper's eyes.

week, would she be asking too much to expect them to give up recreation? If making her own skirts and blouses means that a sewing machine must be purchased, is she solving any immediate problems? Perhaps only at this point would she consider talking over the problem with her brother. Maybe, by working together, they could both contribute to buying their school clothing for the year.

CONSIDER THE VALUES INVOLVED

In the previous steps, you have already made some value judgments. The importance of the problem and the list of costs involved in different solutions were probably determined by comparing the alternatives to individual or family values. The successful manager deliberately applies value scales at each step of the problem-solving process.

At this time a manager is wise to consider values again. A workable solution may be inappropriate to the total situation because it conflicts with a goal which is more valuable. Failure to consider all the values involved may result in the choice of an unsatisfactory solution.

In considering values, it is necessary to know what goals and ideals are important to all family members. It is also necessary to know the relative importance of the various items on this list. Finally, it is necessary to know where the family members differ from one another, both as to specific items on the list and also as to the relative importance of these items. Thus, Sharon's brother might not be willing to contribute to their fall wardrobe. In such a case, should Sharon be forced to contribute the entire needed $58? Or should Dan be expected to get by on less?

MAKE THE DECISION

In an ideal situation, the problem would now be solved. Ideally, the problem was clearly and fully stated. All the facts relating to the situation were gathered. All possible solutions were considered. Values were clearly defined. The one best solution is obvious.

Unfortunately, the ideal situation seldom exists. In a real situation you may find that you have had to define the problem more than once. You needed additional facts, found new solutions, and needed still more facts. At the end of this process, you are left with two or three workable solutions. The difficulty is apt to be a question of values. Sharon's problem may finally boil down to the fact that clothes are more important to her than to her brother. When each understands the other's values, they can usually make a good decision.

ACT ON THE DECISION

As soon as you have reached a decision, the solution you have selected becomes your plan of action. You should be ready to act on it immediately. If you delay your action, the problem may become more complicated. Remember your decision. In the rapid pace of modern life, few people can afford the luxury of solving the same problem every time it comes up. However, this does not mean that you must rush out helter-skelter to take action or that values never change. Be sure that you haven't forgotten any part of the problem. Have you considered the *what, who, when, where, why,* and *how* of the issue at stake? You probably need to add some detailed decisions concerning related smaller problems and actions. Once the major decision has been made, these smaller decisions tend to fall into place rather easily. But you must be certain that they have been thought of. The best decisions may fail unless all points are considered.

EVALUATE THE RESULTS

Even though many people omit this step, the problem-solving process is not really completed until you have evaluated the results. Review successful decisions to see why they were successful. Check to see whether some part of the plan could be improved. Similar decisions will be easier to make when you have learned the strengths and weaknesses of the previous plans you have made.

Sharon's plan to help by earning part of the money for her clothing, making some of the clothes, and shopping for high-quality clothing at low prices will probably work for her. She need not feel guilty if her brother prefers to go without his needed winter coat.

In spite of all efforts, there will be times when you choose the wrong solution. Successful people learn from such mistakes. Rather than hiding your mistakes or making excuses for them, review your unsuccessful plans to learn what mistakes were made. As you learn what happened and why it happened, you will be learning how to avoid such mistakes in the future. Once you have learned from your mistakes, move on to the next decision, ready to try again, this time more successfully.

Comfort, convenience, privacy, and efficiency

A comfortable home is a home which provides for the physical, mental, emotional, and social needs of each family member. A place is needed where everyone can gather to enjoy group activities. Each person needs a place where he can be alone when he wants quiet. In today's small homes, it may seem impossible to efficiently provide comfort, convenience, and privacy for everyone. How can the children in the family have privacy if they

Find pictures of multipurpose rooms—those that serve more than one purpose. Identify the activities for which each of these rooms seems to have been intended.

Plan a furniture arrangement for a living room, family room, or den which is convenient and has a good traffic pattern. Check the arrangement of the furniture in your home. If possible, rearrange the furniture in one room for the purpose of improving the traffic pattern.

Your career
Interior designer or decorator

Duties: Makes plans and furnishes interiors of houses, commercial and institutional buildings, hotels, clubs, ships, and theaters; or makes set decorations for television or motion pictures. Selects and plans the arrangement of furniture, draperies, floor coverings, wall coverings, paint, and other accessories. May work closely with the architect.
Where employed: May have his own business, or be employed by a large department store, a television or motion picture studio, or a commercial or industrial institution.

Using an area of the home economics department, make a study area and arrange one or more lamps to produce the best lighting effects for reading and other specified activities. Plan a work area in the foods laboratory by making the best use of the light available. Illustrate the effects of colored lamp shades on the lighting in a room.

Arrange doll furniture to show good and poor traffic patterns. Discuss the good and poor features of each arrangement from the standpoint of safety, convenience, and appearance.

must share the same room? How can the family provide space for quiet study if guests must be entertained during the study hour?

Most families have more usable space than they realize. Careful arrangement of the furnishings and wise use of available storage areas can add effectively to the useful living space in a home. Frequently a family is able to increase the comfort of the home simply by planning multiple uses for each area of the home. Thus, efficiently providing comfort, convenience, and privacy is a management problem. Like other management problems, its solution begins with the recognition of the needs of the specific family. Some needs are common to everyone. Others depend on individual situations.

Each family must provide for the physical needs of family members. Food, shelter, rest, and clothing needs take high priority. Health and safety also must be considered as basic needs. The exact way in which these needs are met will depend on the family. Providing a space for a hard-working father to stretch out and relax after work is a real need in many families. Providing space for someone to develop a talent or skill may be an equally real need in other families. Only when you know the requirements of your family can you plan to use your space most efficiently.

PLANNING FURNISHINGS FOR COMFORT, CONVENIENCE, AND PRIVACY

Once you know what needs must be met in your home, you are ready to consider how to arrange your furnishings so as to meet these needs. Can you plan a second use for one room? Moving just one or two pieces of furniture to another position can sometimes make the whole room more useful.

Perhaps a dining table can be moved from the center of the room to a wall. The room may then appear larger or the storage space may be more useful. If there is enough room at the table for family meals, the new arrangement may be a very

A room which is to be shared by several people can be planned to include space for study, hobbies, and sleep.

COURTESY ARMSTRONG FLOORING

wise one. Perhaps the change will give privacy for teen-age games or allow for the table to be used for study or hobby work.

Of course, rearranging the furniture in a room is not always as simple as moving one piece of furniture. Sometimes all the furniture must be rearranged in order to improve the comfort and usefulness of the room. Sometimes, too, one change suggests another, and one simple change leads to a complete rearrangement.

Furniture is often heavy and hard to move. It is wise to make careful plans before you actually begin to shift any furniture. Most people will remember to measure the furniture and the part of the room where it is to be placed, in order to be sure that the new arrangement will fit. There are other factors to consider also. Will the furniture be easy to use in its new position? Will the new use planned for the room fit in with the present uses of the room? Will the new furniture arrangement interfere with traffic patterns through the room? Does the new arrangement provide for storage needs?

As you plan new room arrangements, consider the types of furniture and the different ways of using each. Perhaps you are planning to use your bedroom for a study and sitting room. Arrange beds so they are easy to reach. Give thought to the ease with which they can be made each day. Plan the arrangement so that no furniture interferes with use of the chest or closet space. Even the neatest person will be tempted to pile things on the bed if it is difficult to reach the proper storage space.

New uses for a room must not conflict with the basic purposes of a room. For example, if you share a bedroom with a much younger child, you must consider his needs for rest before you plan to change your room into a bedroom-study-sitting room. It may be wiser to use the room as a playroom for the

COURTESY FORMICA CORPORATION

A bathroom used by several people can be divided into areas of privacy.

Make simple items of furniture that cost little or no money—bookshelves from boards and bricks or cement blocks, a night stand from a wooden crate, or a dressing table from items on hand. Finish these by painting or varnishing, covering with fabric, using an adhesive material, or by some other means which will make them attractive and serviceable. If you must spend money, keep a record of it.

Try different furniture arrangements in your bedroom. Which do you find most satisfactory? Why?

Make a floor plan for a bedroom to be shared by two sisters. Plan for the privacy, convenience, and comfort of each girl. You may plan to use room dividers, screens, hangings, or any other items which seem practical.

Set a lounging chair and floor lamp where they will be convenient and will help to give a feeling of good balance in a room.

Make something for your room or redecorate it, using one or more of the following ideas:
Recover a lamp shade.
Make pillows.
Hang pictures.
Dye scatter rugs.
Make a bulletin board.
Make a vanity dresser from an old table.

Make one of the following accessories for your closet:
Shoe bags
Covers for dresses
Padded hangers
Hat boxes covered with wallpaper or colorful fabric
Labeled shoe boxes for storing small things on the closet shelf

Bulletin board IDEA
Title: *Shelter Your Home from Fallout*

Directions: Mount pictures of storage accessory items such as pull-out shelves for pot lids; wall files for letters, notes and bills; vertical shelves for trays and cookie tins; racks for knives, spices, and kitchen tools; and caddies for records, towels, and clothes.

younger child as well as a bedroom for both of you. In this way, the extra activities in the room will not interfere with the basic sleeping patterns of either person. If this plan is carried out, you may decide to use the kitchen table for a study area. Check first, however, to see that your timing is appropriate. Homework does not belong in the kitchen while meals are being prepared. Perhaps the study area will need to be relocated.

Many plans for furniture arrangement are spoiled because of poor traffic patterns. Clear pathways from area to area are important for family safety. They also make family living more comfortable and convenient for everyone. Unless the furniture is carefully arranged, the natural pathways of the room can interrupt the activities of the people in the room. Suppose several comfortable chairs are arranged near the TV. The arrangement seems to be attractive and convenient. Several people can enjoy a program together. The chairs are placed so that people can visit together when the TV is not being used. The arrangement may turn out to be very inconvenient, however, if the TV program or the conversation is interrupted every time someone goes in or out of the room.

Unhappy situations result from careless furniture arrangements which interrupt the natural traffic flow. For example, no one likes to walk around the bed each time he needs to move from the closet to the dressing table. A coffee table in the path between the front door and the entrance to the next room can cause daily irritations. Is the dining table between the china cabinet and the kitchen? If so, serving meals and returning clean dishes to the china cabinet will be unnecessarily difficult.

As you arrange your furnishings, remember to include storage furniture to complete the arrangement. For example, if you are arranging an area for study, you need to include a shelf or cabinet for books. Storage for records should be included in your phonograph center.

ARRANGING STORAGE FOR EFFICIENCY

Well-planned storage areas contribute a great deal to family comfort. Unfortunately, the closets and cabinets which are built into a home often seem to be wrong for the storage needs of the family. With wise planning, however, you can usually provide convenient storage for all the items the family members use.

For efficient storage, try to plan so that items are stored close to the spot where they will be used. Suppose you plan to sew in your dining area. The storage areas in that room should contain the dishes you need for regular meals, as well as your sewing equipment. Such materials as cleaning supplies may be frequently needed in every part of the house. Your storage arrangements will be more convenient if you plan to keep such equipment together in a portable container which can be moved to the area where it is needed.

Once you have decided which items should be stored in each room, examine the available storage space. Consider the closets, cabinets, chests, shelves, and drawers in each room. How much storage space do you have? How deep or how shallow is each space? How easy is it to reach? Can you adjust the shelves so that some can accommodate tall objects and some smaller? Can you keep some of the smaller items together in a tray or box located in a larger storage space? Are you keeping items which are no longer useful?

As you fit family belongings into their storage areas, remember to keep the most frequently used items in the most easily reached places. Things like holiday decorations, which are used only once a year, can be stored in the most out-of-the-way places, such as the back of a high basement shelf.

If you still have a few items left over, can you provide some additional storage space? Perhaps you can buy an inexpensive chest of unpainted wood or corrugated paper. Perhaps you can add some shelves. Your new storage space need not be used for the leftover items. Use it in the best way possible. Perhaps you will decide to use existing storage space for problem items.

As you rearrange your storage, check for the safety of the stored items. If nearby plumbing should break, would the storage area be flooded out? Would this ruin some of the stored items? Is the heating system close to some storage areas? If so, be sure that heat-sensitive items and flammable items are not stored in these areas.

Make and carry out a plan for improving the storage in one area of your home. This may be in your own dresser drawers, your closet, or your desk. It may involve arranging for a place to hang your clothes or it may be concerned with reorganizing items in the kitchen cabinets. The project should fit your needs.

Well-planned storage areas provide for storage of items near areas where they will be used.

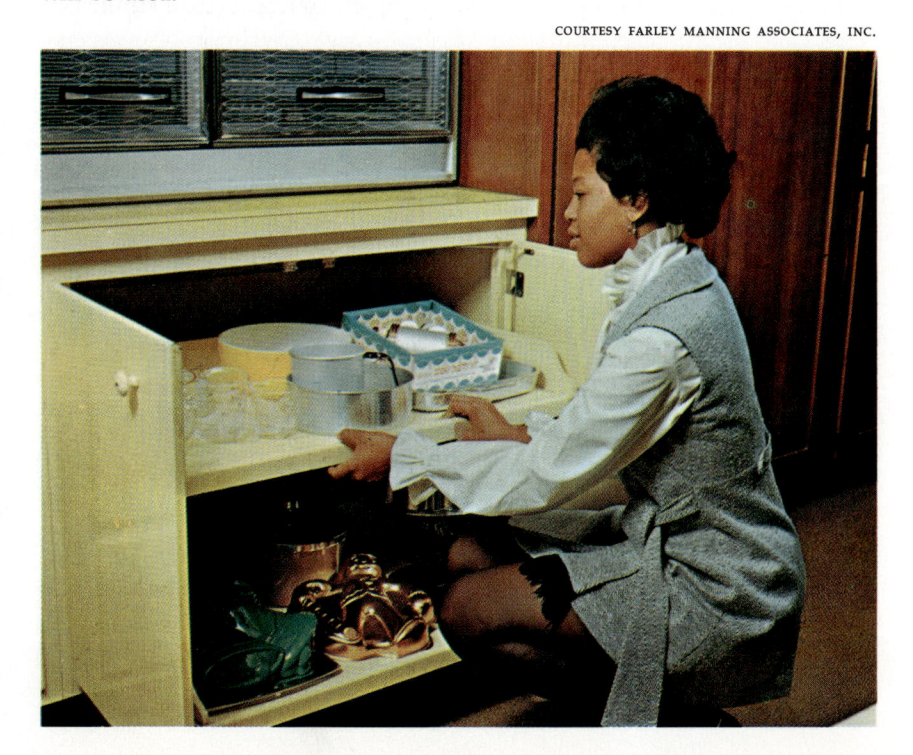

COURTESY FARLEY MANNING ASSOCIATES, INC.

Make a bookcase from bricks and boards according to the following directions:
1. Select smooth bricks. If desired, paint them to match the walls.
2. Stack them in two parallel rows.
3. Select a smooth board of the desired width and length. Paint it to match and place it over the bricks.
4. Stack more bricks and add more boards to make additional shelves.

Make some arrangement for hanging clothes. Use a curtain rod, broom handle, heavy rope, cane fishing pole, or other similar materials on hand.

Using available furniture in the home economics department, set up model arrangements of drawer and closet spaces. Suggest ways to make them attractive at very little expense.

Discuss the advantages and disadvantages of these storage aids and where each might be used.

Health and safety

Providing for the health and safety of all family members is a management problem. If family members are to remain healthy, certain needs must be met. Food and clothing must be provided. Adequate housing is necessary. The housing must provide proper heating and ventilation. It must also provide for proper disposal of wastes. For good health, there must be protection against pests. Finally, there must be provision for the emotional health of the family. The emotionally happy family will enjoy being together whether they are sharing necessary work or enjoying leisure time.

Wiring and furniture arrangements can be checked for safety when a room undergoes major cleaning or repairs.

COURTESY SEARS, ROEBUCK AND CO.

CHECKING THE HOME FOR SAFETY

Health and safety habits are often hard to establish. Most people know when an action is *not* safe. But it is easy to skip a safety practice simply to save a little time. Families who think of health and safety as management problems will generally avoid dangerous practices. They develop the habit of comparing long-term costs with the apparent convenience of skipping a safety practice. Family members can learn to ask themselves, "Can we afford the cost, in case this is the one time something goes wrong?"

There are two ways to ensure safe conditions around your home. First, check the home regularly to be sure that you and your family are continuing good safety habits. Safety-conscious families do this at least twice a year. Second, recheck safety factors whenever you rearrange furniture, buy a new appliance, or change your pattern of living in other ways which could affect health and safety.

Thinking through the following questions will help any family improve the safety conditions around their home.

1. Does the home meet fire safety regulations? Do family members clear away old papers and rags frequently enough for safety? Does the family store its belongings properly so as to prevent fires?

Are inflammable household items kept safely away from the kitchen range and the heating system? Are curtains and towels too close to the range? Does anyone in the family *ever* leave a fire untended? Does everyone *always* turn off all appliances as soon as he is through using them?

2 Is the electrical system safe? Is the wiring safe or has the insulation become frayed? Are the wires which connect the lamps and appliances plugged into one circuit? Can the appliances be rearranged so as to even out the load on the electric circuits? If not, can the lights and appliances be arranged so that they are used alternately? It may be annoying to unplug one appliance in order to use another, but less annoying than the high cost and danger of a fire.

3 Is the home free from factors which can cause falls? Is the furniture placed for safe movement? Are stairs, hallways, and other paths kept clear? Do all family members return all equipment to its proper place as soon as they stop using it? Are the floor boards and floor coverings smooth and skidproof? Is loose flooring repaired? Are there sturdy rails and handholds where they are needed? Do family members wipe up all spills immediately?

4 Are the storage areas safe? Are household poisons kept out of the reach of young family members? Are medicines stored where there is no possibility of their being picked up and used by mistake? Are cleaning supplies kept separate from food supplies and medicines separate from both? Does every family member know which bottle holds the medicine and which holds the candy? Are all containers put back where they belong as soon as they are used? Are all supplies clearly labeled?

5 Is the home free from other common causes of accidents? Do family members avoid spills? Are pans and hot dishes placed on the range or table so that the handles will not be bumped or reached by hands of young children? Are all items placed far enough from the edges of shelves, tables, and counter tops so that they will not get knocked off? Are hanging items securely fastened to the wall? Are they hung high and out of the way, or will they be bumped by passersby? Are doors which open out into traffic lanes kept tightly closed except when in use?

Make your room a safe place by following these suggestions. Add others you may think of.

1 Arrange the furniture in your room so that the passageways to the closet and to the hallway are clear.

2 Avoid placing clothing in the closet too near the closet light.

3 Store heavy boxes carefully; if they must be placed on the closet shelf, see that they are placed there securely.

4 Keep dresser drawers and closet doors closed.

5 Place dressing-table lamps and study lamps where they will not be knocked over and where their cords will not cause someone to trip or stumble over them.

6 Avoid using small scatter rugs on slippery floors unless they have nonskid backing on them.

7 In reaching high places in your room, as in painting, in hanging curtains, or in cleaning, use a sturdy ladder or stepstool rather than a chair.

8 Avoid entering your closet with a candle or match which is lighted.

Develop a rating scale or checklist for evaluating the safety of your home. Using the rating scale or list, check your home economics department for the safety factors which apply to it.

Sponsor safety slogans for a safer school. Using as many words as possible starting with the letter S, write safety slogans. Some of the words you might want to use are:

Samples	Smoke
Sane	Smother
Scheme	Solution
Search	Someone
Seek	Spark
Seems	Special
Sensible	Speed
Set	Standards
Simple	Strategy
Slip	Study
Slow	Suggest
Smart	Support

Bulletin board IDEA
Title: **S**afety **S**ense

Directions: Display appropriate articles and pictures of items such as knife racks, labels for poisons, and repaired electric cords.

MANAGING THE HOME FOR GOOD HEALTH

Among the greatest dangers to a family's health are the communicable diseases—that is, diseases which are transferred from one person to another. For instance, one family member can develop a case of the flu, and soon several family members are suffering from the same disease. There are certain health practices which help families prevent the spread of communicable diseases.

Most families seem to suffer their share of the usual childhood diseases, which start with one child and pass through the entire family. However, the diseases which are serious to very young children can be prevented by inoculation. Measles, whooping cough, diphtheria, mumps, smallpox, and polio can be prevented by inoculations. Chicken pox has generally been more a bother than a threat to life. It is the only one of the childhood diseases which remains untamed by science.

If older family members have passed through childhood without contracting measles, mumps, or German measles, they would be wise to get a preventive inoculation. These diseases are often very serious when contracted by adults, and German measles can cause birth defects if contracted by prospective mothers during the early months of pregnancy.

Regular visits to a clinic or the family doctor will ensure family members of receiving needed inoculations at the proper time. Regular medical and dental checkups also allow the specialists to notice and treat health problems which could become major difficulties if allowed to go untended. During regular health checkups, the medical specialists can also help the family plan to improve their general health practices.

Health studies indicate that good health requires adequate sleep and exercise. The health clinic worker or your family doctor can tell you what amounts of sleep and what types of exercise are best for individual family members. But even when a family knows these facts, a great deal of planning is required in order to see that the proper conditions of rest and exercise are provided for everyone.

For example, the family with a young child may need to plan a regular time each day for taking the child to the park for outdoor exercise. Yet the housework must also be done. The mother must plan her day so that she is not scrubbing floors or cooking a meal when it is time to go to the park.

Some families must plan carefully to encourage the TV addict or bookworm to take enough exercise. Often this can be accomplished by encouraging him to join in such community activities as scouting or other youth programs. Perhaps a family needs to plan family outings in order to encourage a stay-at-home to become more active.

Whatever the problem, the family who thinks of health as a management concern will find ways to improve the general family health program. Schedules can be rearranged to provide quiet daytime sleep for an adult who works at night. Careful plans can be made so that the food and clothing needs of each family member are met in ways that encourage the practice of good health habits.

Family patterns of housekeeping can be developed which aid in the health program. For instance, no matter where a family lives, insects and other household pests seem to be a continuing health problem. Each family member can learn to be responsible for housekeeping habits which help keep such pests away from the home. The toddler can be taught to close the screen door firmly behind him. Older family members can check to see that screens and screen doors are kept in good repair and that they fit tightly enough to keep out insects. If each family member learns to wipe up spills immediately, flies and cockroaches will be less likely to invade the home. Proper removal of waste food and paper will further discourage such pests. Even young children can be taught to keep waste containers firmly covered.

Health-conscious families know that good grooming habits are good health habits. Well-brushed hair and well-scrubbed hands and faces encourage good health. Everyone comes in contact with dangerous diseases frequently throughout life. People who neglect to brush their teeth or to wash and dry themselves carefully actually encourage disease germs and molds to grow. One careless family member can spread such a disease through the entire family.

Regular medical checkups and good health habits often prevent the development of serious illnesses.

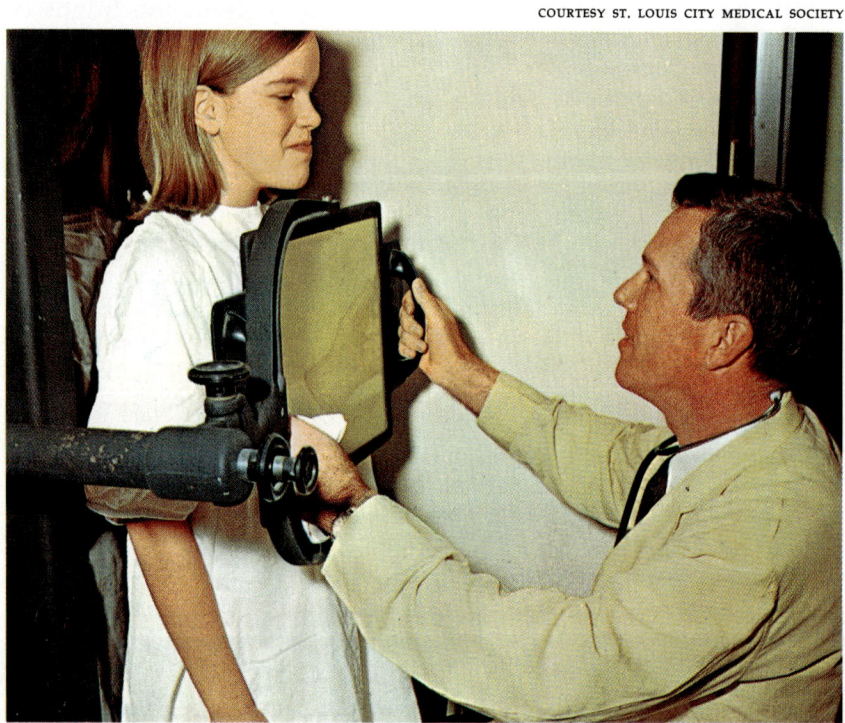

COURTESY ST. LOUIS CITY MEDICAL SOCIETY

Make a first aid kit appropriate for your home economics department, home, car, or boat. Some of these may be gift wrapped and given as gifts.

Plan and prepare a Safety Hazard Treasure Hunt for other class members. The person who finds the most hazards in a given time is the winner.

Suggest ways to maintain a good family health program. Take into consideration such factors as sanitation, adequate rest, and good nutrition.

Suggest ways of keeping children who are ill relatively quiet and happy. Suggest quiet activities and games for children of various ages.

Make a list of precautions to take in preventing the spread of communicable diseases.

Discuss what should be done in the following situations:
1. One of the members of your class falls to the floor, losing consciousness.
2. Your little brother cuts his finger. It appears to be a deep cut. You are the only person at home with him.
3. Your mother has fallen in the yard. She appears to have hurt her hip and it is very painful.

Bulletin board IDEA
Title: *Treat a Cold*
　　　　Like a Secret
　　　　Keep It to Yourself!
Directions: Use a large picture of a cartoon character who is covering his mouth and nose with a tissue.

HANDLING ILLNESSES IN THE HOME

No matter how good the general health program, sooner or later each family is likely to experience illness. It is important to be able to recognize the signs of illness. Often immediate medical advice will prevent the development of serious illness.

Reporting the illness

Illness is often first noticed when a person's facial expression changes. He may seem to be groggy or he may appear anxious. His face may be flushed or pale, dry or very moist. His skin may show a rash. His eyes may seem too bright or very dull.

Other easily noticed signs of illness include discharges from the nose or ears, sneezing, coughing, headaches, a sore throat, fever, pain, or nausea. The sick person may show a sudden change in appetite or in his pattern of elimination. He may complain of fatigue or general discomfort, or he may become quite irritable.

When you suspect that a family member is ill, get him to rest comfortably in bed. Do not give any medicine, not even aspirin, until after you have consulted the clinic or doctor. There may be grave danger in giving medicines without consulting a doctor.

It is usually wise to take the sick person's temperature with a clinical thermometer before calling the doctor. A clinical thermometer is a fragile instrument which requires careful handling. It should be stored in its case when not in use. Be sure you know how to use one before taking the temperature of anyone who may be ill. In order to prevent the spread of disease, disinfect the thermometer thoroughly before and after use.

When consulting the doctor, describe the conditions which make you suspect that the person is ill. Report the body temperature and the time you recorded it. It sometimes happens that the sick person has taken aspirin or a similar medicine for a headache or sore throat before anyone suspected a serious illness. If this has happened, be sure to tell the doctor how much medicine was taken and describe the time lapse between medication and the temperature check.

Caring for the sick

Most people who are seriously ill are cared for in the hospital. But many minor illnesses must be treated at home. Also, hospitals may allow a patient to return home while he is recovering from a serious illness or operation. Thus, every family needs to know how to care for people who must stay in bed for an extended period of time.

Even a minor illness will cause changes in regular household routines. Time which is ordinarily given to other tasks must be given to taking care of the patient. Each family must make the adjustments necessary to its own situation. Each family member generally accepts extra duties during the time of the illness.

Often a family may feel tempted to skip some of its regular cleaning during such a time. But cleanliness is even more important during an illness than during times of good health. This is especially true in the kitchen, the bathroom, the laundry, and the sickroom, where disease germs can multiply rapidly unless special precautions are taken.

Some tasks can be omitted or simplified. All members of the family must have good food and clean clothes. But simple meals and plain easy-care garments can be used instead of the special meals and more elaborate clothing which may have been planned. Cleaning tasks can be lightened in the less-used portions of the house, although they should not be omitted altogether. If the noise of the vacuum cleaner or floor polisher disturbs the patient, the floors may be cleaned with a mop until the patient is stronger.

The sickroom should be kept neat and cheerful at all times. Bright lights and loud noises may be especially disturbing to a feverish person. On the other hand, total dark and complete quiet can also be disturbing. Look for ways to brighten the room with soft lights and soothing sounds.

Medicines and sickroom supplies may be stored neatly on a tray in the sickroom or in a nearby bathroom or kitchen. Since illness can spread to other members of the family, be sure that supplies for a sick person are kept separate from other household items. Giving the patient the wrong medicine can have serious results. It is equally dangerous for another person to take the patient's medicine.

Discuss ways in which the following situations could be handled tactfully:
1 You have a very bad cold and a friend invites you to visit him in his home.
2 A friend asks to borrow your lipstick or comb.
3 A classmate offers you a bite of his apple.
4 You find a hair in your food when eating dinner at a friend's house.

The use of disposable dishes in the sick room can help cut down on the spread of communicable diseases.

COURTESY KAISER ALUMINUM

Follow these safety precautions when using small electric appliances. Add other safety precautions you are able to list.

1. Follow the manufacturer's directions in using any electric appliance.
2. Dry your hands thoroughly before connecting or disconnecting electrical equipment.
3. Never use more than one heating type appliance at a time on a given circuit.
4. Never connect electric appliances when standing on a wet surface.
5. Plug the cord into the appliance first, then into the wall outlet.
6. Always disconnect the cord from the wall outlet before removing it from the appliance—otherwise a *hot* plug will be exposed.
7. Grasp the plug rather than the cord when removing the cord from the outlet or the appliance.
8. Disconnect small appliances when not in use to avoid danger of shock or of accidentally touching the *on* switch.
9. Never let the cord dangle. It may cause the appliance to be pulled off the work area.

Any patient needs special attention given to his meals. Most illnesses take away his appetite for some time. The doctor will recommend foods which are appropriate for the patient. Be sure that his orders and recommendations are followed exactly. Poorly cooked foods are especially unappetizing when a person is ill. Arrange the food to please the eye as well as the taste. The extra attention given to the sick tray shows the patient how much the family cares for him.

As the patient begins to feel better, he may become restless. This recovery period is especially hard on a young child, but it is difficult for patients of every age. Sometimes the patient will be refreshed by being moved to another room for a short period each day. If the doctor approves, a friend may be invited for a short, cheerful visit. You must be certain that such visits do not overtire the patient. Reading aloud can be entertaining for older patients as well as preschoolers. A new simple game or project will also help a patient through this difficult recovery period.

EMERGENCY MEDICAL SUPPLIES AND FIRST AID

Your family will be better prepared to take care of home emergencies if plans have been made before emergencies arise. A well-stocked medicine cabinet will enable you to treat the minor cuts and burns that occur frequently. A knowledge of proper first-aid treatment will help you to know what to do and when to do it. Such knowledge may prevent minor emergencies from becoming major ones.

The home medicine cabinet

Drugs and supplies for emergencies should be stored in a separate place, away from toilet articles or food supplies. Medicines should be kept out of the reach of young children. Stock your medicine chest with the medicines and first-aid supplies recommended by your doctor. *The American National Red Cross* has prepared a list of supplies that are useful in common emergencies. Medicines that have been prescribed for a specific illness may be stored in the medicine cabinet during the illness. After an illness, it is usually wise to discard leftover medicine.

Check your medicine cabinet about once a month, as well as after any illness. Be sure that you have on hand a complete supply of the recommended medicines and first-aid supplies. Check to see that all packages are intact, that recommended medicines are still fresh enough to be useful, and that all supplies are clearly labeled.

Giving first aid

What *is* first aid? The American National Red Cross defines it as *the immediate and temporary care given the* victim of an accident or sudden illness until the services of a physician can be obtained.

There are many techniques in giving first aid which cannot be described in detail here. As a responsible member of your family, you need to learn first aid from a reliable source in your community. The Red Cross offers complete courses in first aid. Other sources of reliable instruction in your community may be the Boy Scouts, Girl Scouts, or Camp Fire Girls. Some hospitals offer first-aid courses. Schools supply first-aid instruction through Future Nurses Clubs, physical education classes, and health classes.

In any emergency, the immediate treatment given the patient generally has an effect on his recovery. It is better to do nothing than to do the wrong thing. On the other hand, if you know what to do in giving immediate care, you may help to save a life or to shorten an illness.

Many people become alarmed in an emergency. They rush to give immediate help. Unless you face the situation calmly and keep your head, you may do the wrong thing. Perhaps the first rule in first aid should be, "Don't do anything unless you know what has to be done." There are only three emergencies that cannot wait for the doctor's arrival. They are severe bleeding, stoppage of breath, and poisoning.

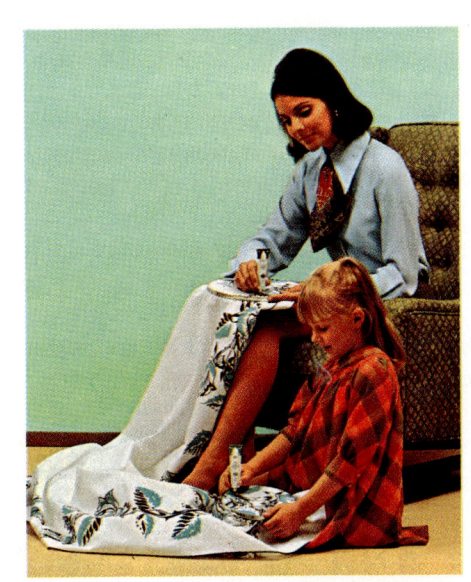

COURTESY ARTEX HOBBY PRODUCTS, INC.

Keeping the young child quiet is often one of the most important aids to his recuperation.

When an emergency occurs, you must decide at once whether or not to call a doctor. If you do, be sure to give him the address, the cause of the emergency, the patient's symptoms, and the nature of the attention already given. Do not move the patient. If the emergency victim is on his feet, have him lie down until the doctor arrives. You may cover any emergency patient lightly so as to keep his temperature even. Keep people from crowding around him. Anyone who is ill or in pain needs air and quiet. Under most circumstances this is all you can do or should do until the doctor arrives.

10 If it is necessary to scrape the batter down while the electric mixer is in operation, use a flexible rubber scraper as the stirring utensil.
11 Plug appliances into wall sockets made for such use. Wiring for lights is not made to carry current necessary to operate appliances.
12 Disconnect any appliance with exposed coils before cleaning it.
13 Never put a heating unit, electric motor, or electric cord in water, as this may cause a short circuit. (Electric appliances may be immersed in water up to the point indicated or completely immersed if the manufacturer's directions indicate.)
14 Allow hot appliances to cool before storing.
15 Never use an electric cord if the plug is loose or a screw or bolt has fallen out.
16 Avoid getting batter or liquid into the mechanism of an electric mixer.
17 Place a heat-resistant pad under the toaster, waffle baker, or coffee percolator.
18 Keep forks out of the electric toaster.

8 CHAPTER POSTTEST

Number from 1 to 26. Beside each number indicate if the corresponding statement is true or false. *Do not* write in this book.

1. Home management deals in part with planning for comfort, safety, and privacy in the home.
2. The problem-solving approach is used only in trying to solve very difficult problems.
3. The first step in the problem-solving approach is to state the problem.
4. The second step in the problem-solving approach is to consider the values involved.
5. Once a solution has been selected, it is best to delay action.
6. The most frequently omitted step in using the problem-solving approach is evaluating the results.
7. Planning to use an area of a home for several purposes is poor home management.
8. The needs of all family members should be considered when planning to use available space effectively.
9. The way furniture is arranged can make a room appear larger.
10. An example of a piece of multipurpose furniture is a sofa which opens out into a bed.
11. The traffic flow in a room needs to be considered in planning a new furniture arrangement.
12. A pot holder is best stored near the kitchen sink.
13. A flour sifter is most conveniently stored in or near the mixing center of the kitchen.
14. It is efficient to store Halloween decorations at eye level.
15. Providing for protection against insects in the home is part of a good family health program.
16. Pressurized cans of cleaning aids are best stored on a shelf inside the furnace closet door.
17. Good management involves making use of several kitchen appliances at the same time by the use of three-way plugs.
18. Medicines are best stored with food items such as spices and bottled extracts and syrups.
19. Diphtheria is a contracted disease.
20. There are preventive inoculations for mumps and diphtheria.
21. If an expectant mother has German measles during the early months of pregnancy the disease may cause birth defects in her baby.
22. Being tired and irritable and looking pale may be signs of illness.
23. A sick person with a poor appetite should be served heavy meals with rich foods.
24. Extra medicine left after an illness should be saved in case another family member needs it.
25. In case of a serious accident, one of the first things to do is to send for medical help.
26. An emergency patient should be kept lying down and as quiet as possible until the doctor arrives.

9 CHAPTER PRETEST

Fill in the blank in each sentence with the *best* word to complete the statement. *Do not* write in this book.

1. Putting books, toys, and clothes in their proper places is a(an) __(1)__ task that involves all the family.
2. It is especially important that fresh produce, dairy products, and __(2)__ be properly stored as soon as they are brought home.
3. The room which probably needs a thorough cleaning most frequently is the __(3)__.
4. Because they attract insect pests, food wastes should be removed from the kitchen at least __(4)__.
5. Cleaning kitchen cabinet doors, oven racks, and refrigerator shelves are tasks that are usually done __(5)__.
6. Washing outside windows and screens is a task that is usually done __(6)__.
7. In selecting carpeting for a kitchen or bathroom it is absolutely essential to find out if it is __(7)__.
8. Draperies and upholstered furniture can be dusted efficiently with a special __(8)__ which comes with most rod-type vacuum cleaners.
9. The last part of a room that should be cleaned is the __(9)__.
10. The way in which the outside of your home is kept usually gives a visitor his first __(10)__ of your home.

CHAPTER 9

Managing the household tasks of family living

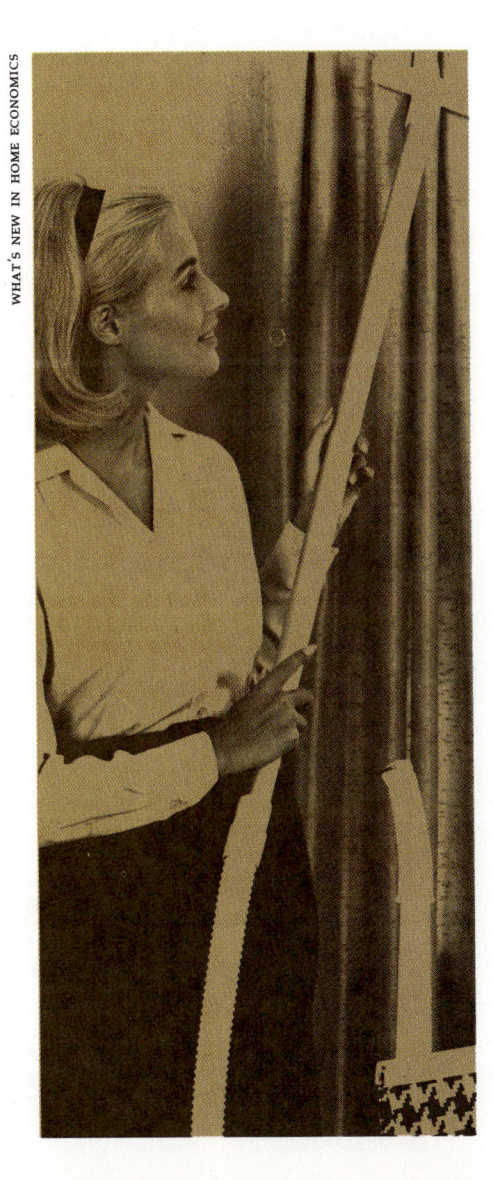

WHAT'S NEW IN HOME ECONOMICS

Have you ever seen a dusty furniture display in a shop window? Perhaps the furniture was expensive and well arranged, but the display was unattractive because someone had failed to provide it the necessary attention. Neglect gave the impression that nobody cared. Could it be that when a family neglects its home the same impression is given?

A well-kept home is the result of the wise use of time, energy, and money. No two families will have exactly the same amount of these basic resources available for household tasks. Equally important, each family has its own set of goals and values in housekeeping just as it has in other areas of family living. By learning to consider household tasks as problems in home management, a family can develop a program which fits its individual needs. As a responsible family member, you need to learn certain basic skills and facts which will help your family achieve housekeeping goals for family comfort.

Organizing for efficiency

Both cleanliness and neatness are required for the health and safety

Form debate teams and discuss the pros and cons of the following typical teen-age problems.
1 There is little value derived from expecting a busy teen-ager to assume the responsibilities for household tasks.
2 A teen-ager who works part-time deserves a lightened work load at home.
3 A teen-ager should be excused from his household tasks during the times when he has extra schoolwork.

Bulletin board IDEA
Title: *The A, B, C's of Home Management*
*A*dequate planning
*B*udgeting time, money, and energy
*C*ooperating within the family
Directions: Attach the main title near the top of the bulletin board. Print the three points which describe home management and fasten them below the title.

Make a survey of the household tasks done regularly by the class members. List the tasks done at home by the greatest number of students. List the other tasks in order of decreasing frequency. Discuss the ideas class members are learning in home economics which help them perform these tasks more efficiently.

of all family members. Household equipment and supplies need to be put away. So do toys and clothes. Have you ever been so tired from picking up that you skimped on necessary cleaning chores?

One way to be certain that your home remains neat and clean at all times is to plan a schedule for household tasks. Some tasks, such as picking up the clutter, are best handled on a daily basis. Other tasks need to be performed regularly each week. Still others need to be considered only once a month or once or twice a year.

In scheduling household tasks, a wise manager tries to arrange the work load for proper use of family resources. Job responsibilities can be assigned so that everyone in the family helps but still has free time for relaxation and recreation.

You may feel that a regular schedule of household tasks will trap you in jobs from which you can never escape. With a well-planned schedule, however, exactly the opposite is true. With or without a plan, certain jobs *must* be done. When you are without a plan, such duties actually interfere with other activities. With a plan, every family member knows when each task is to be done. There is less danger that the work load will get out of hand. Job responsibilities can be traded to meet special needs.

Good scheduling is not the whole answer to a well-cared-for home. Family members must look for other factors which make various jobs easier. For instance, do some jobs seem to be more difficult for your family than for others you know? If you find that it takes too long to dust or clean, perhaps some of the furniture is improperly located. Can you rearrange the room so that cleaning is easier? Could hobby items be arranged in a non-dust-catching display?

Perhaps you need new equipment to make household tasks easier. It

Organizing a room for comfort and convenience is a beginning point for effective housekeeping.

COURTESY ARMSTRONG FLOORING

may be something as simple as a new mop or something as expensive as a food mixer. It is easy to make mistakes when you consider buying new equipment. Some people buy so many gadgets to help with housework that it is more difficult to decide which gadget to use than to do the job without a gadget. Everything you buy must be kept somewhere, and housekeeping equipment costs money. Will it really help you enough to be worth the cost?

Daily care

The list of daily household chores is so long that some teen-agers feel it is impossible for anyone to do half the work. In every room of the home, small items must be picked up and returned to their proper places. Each room must be straightened. Beds must be made. Meals must be prepared, served, and cleared away. Wastes must be disposed of. Clothing must be cared for. Pets must be tended. House plants must be looked after.

This does indeed seem like an endless group of tasks. Yet many mothers do all the daily chores, take care of small children, and add one or two weekly chores each day. With only an occasional exception, they still have time and energy for relaxation and family recreation. These mothers have learned to combine skills and management techniques to simplify their housekeeping duties.

PICKING UP

A family can divide the pickup tasks so that the odds and ends of family living are in place when not in use. This plan points the way to simplified housekeeping. Each item has a special place where it is kept.

Every room of most homes contains many small items which are frequently used. Often these items are missing when they are needed. Much of the friction of family living is caused by such simple acts as forgetting to put items in their proper places. Time, energy, and good humor are lost simply because some family members fail to use available storage arrangements. Storage needs change from time to time. Does your home have a place for everything? Could there be some improvement?

Actually, putting things away as soon as you are through with them is a matter of habit. It is not too late to acquire this habit. The next time you find yourself dropping an item where you use it, remember how hard it is to search for lost belongings. It is not enough to remember to return the things you use. You must begin by planning to do more than your share.

Once a family has learned to cooperate in keeping small items where they belong, the task of keeping the home tidy becomes

List household tasks which are done daily, weekly, monthly, and seasonally. Which lists are the longest and which are the shortest? Why?

Make a schedule for doing the housekeeping tasks necessary in your own room or another specific room in your home. Schedule time to do daily, weekly, and monthly tasks. Follow this schedule for a month. Evaluate the results by determining the strengths and weaknesses of your plan. Consider your family's reactions. What circumstances made it necessary to change your schedule? Does a work schedule need to be somewhat flexible? Why?

List for each area of the home the supplies needed for effective cleaning of that area.

Design a Carry-all Cleaning Kit containing cleaning tools and supplies.

Think of a new way to use a common piece of household equipment that helps to conserve time, energy, or money.

Make an informative tag or label you would want to find on a particular piece of household equipment you might consider buying some day.

Show the class how to use various types of cleaning equipment. During the demonstrations, discuss the cost, care, and variety of uses of each piece of equipment. If possible, use different types of mops. Try to cooperate with a local dealer who can make available waste disposers and trash compactors.

simple. Many pickup tasks can be performed as family members go about other activities. It only takes a minute to smooth a cushion or straighten a curtain. A sweater or a game can be carried to an upstairs storage area each time you go to that part of the house. Such simple acts tend to give a home a cared-for look.

Keeping belongings in their proper place is a daily task which involves all of the family and each room that is used. Other tasks involved in keeping rooms straight will depend upon the main uses of each room. As a room is kept straightened each day, a good manager notes the areas which will soon need special attention. In this way, extra cleaning jobs can be scheduled as a part of the regular care.

CARING FOR THE KITCHEN AND DINING AREA

Meals are prepared in the kitchen and served in a dining area which may or may not be in the kitchen. The task of preparing meals is made easier when food and utensils are properly stored. Canned foods, staples, fresh produce, and meats should be put away as soon as they are brought into the house. Only in this way can food successfully retain the nutritive value it held at the time it was purchased. Meals can be prepared with a minimum of effort when each pot and pan and each type of food is always stored in a given place.

Because bacteria grow rapidly in food, cleanliness is especially important in the kitchen and dining area. Spilled food is easier to clean up immediately than at a later time. Sweep crumbs from the floor after each meal. Wash the surface of the oven and range top after each use. Wipe up food spills and splashes near the range, the refrigerator, the mixer, the can opener, and the sink. Wash the dishes and cooking utensils or store them in the dishwasher after each meal.

Food splashes can be wiped up in a moment immediately after they occur.

COURTESY FREEZE-DRIED SANKA COFFEE

Food wastes must be collected during food preparation and after each meal. They must be disposed of properly. Even in homes where there is a food-waste disposer, some provision must be made to prevent food wrappers from causing odors and attracting pests such as flies and cockroaches. Meat wrappers and ice-cream cartons frequently attract such pests. Rinse them before placing them in the kitchen trash container.

CARING FOR THE BATHROOM

It is easy to keep a bathroom in good order if each person who uses it checks its condition and tidies it after each use. Are towels and washcloths hung up neatly so they can air out and dry properly? Are toothbrushes, toothpaste, and other toilet articles returned to proper storage? Was the tub or washbasin cleaned after each use? Does the toilet bowl need cleaning? Are all water splashes carefully wiped up before you leave the bathroom?

At least once each day someone must check a bathroom for other needs. The wastebasket must be emptied regularly. Paper goods must be replenished. There may be a clothes hamper containing damp clothes which should be taken to the laundry area. Perhaps fresh towels or a clean bath mat is needed. The mirror needs to be checked for soap splashes and shined if necessary.

COURTESY FARLEY MANNING ASSOCIATES, INC.

Effective garbage storage areas provide for easy access and easy removal.

CARING FOR THE BEDROOMS

The family's bedrooms have two main uses. They provide a place for sleep. They are also the family dressing rooms. Sleeping comfort depends, to a degree, on whether the bedding is smooth and neat. Well-made beds also make the bedrooms look more attractive during the daytime hours. Clothing must also be put away each day.

CARING FOR THE HOME LIVING AREAS

The general living areas of the home require straightening each day. Family activities may cause

List the ways that a vacuum cleaner can be used to make housekeeping easy. Read the suggestions below and add others.

For cleaning draperies, shades, blinds, books, furniture, ornaments, picture frames, lamp shades, and shelves.

For cleaning the range drip pans and removing crumbs from the toaster.

For defrosting the refrigerator by blowing warm air on iced coils after attaching the hose to the vacuum blower outlet.

For cleaning linoleum or wood floors.

For cleaning mattresses, box springs, and closet shelves.

Bulletin board IDEA
Title: *Brush Up*
Directions: Attach to the bulletin board and label a variety of brushes used in homemaking. Some of the following might be used:
Vacuum cleaner attachment brushes
Vegetable brushes
Long-handled scrubbing brushes
Brushes for cleaning the bathroom
Clothes brushes

Clean the same room twice, allowing a week between cleanings. Follow these two procedures:
1. Clean the floor first, then dust the furniture, and clean the walls and drapes last.
2. Clean the walls and drapes first, dust the furniture, and clean the floor last.

Describe the differences in the cleanliness and appearance of the room after following each procedure. Check the room after three days. Which procedure seemed to be more effective after this lapse of time? Why?

special cleaning problems in these areas. For example, the floor in a frequently used entryway may need to be swept each day. Perhaps chairs located in front of the family TV set will require straightening and carpets will require cleaning more frequently than those located in other parts of the room.

There may be times when some special project should be left out in an unfinished state. This causes special housekeeping problems. But even if a painting must be left on the easel to dry, the rest of the painting materials may be put away. Perhaps the portable sewing machine should be left out, but the sewing project can be left neatly beside the machine, rather than scattered throughout the room.

Weekly care

In order to have a well-cared-for home, each room must be cleaned regularly. Just how often a thorough cleaning is required for each room depends on how the room is used, what type of dirt builds up in the room, and how much danger to general family health results from failure to clean the room.

WEEKLY CARE IN THE KITCHEN

In most homes every member of the family uses the kitchen each day. Meals and snacks are prepared, and many are eaten in the kitchen. Kitchens tend to accumulate stubborn soil such as food splashes, greasy or sticky finger marks, and spills. Because a clean kitchen is essential to good health, the kitchen probably needs a thorough cleaning more often than any other room of the house.

The floor, cabinets, counter tops, sink, and kitchen appliances such as the range and refrigerator require attention. Fortunately, modern cleaning products can be used with modern equipment to ensure clean kitchens with only a minimum of effort. Good detergents and polishes, when used on a regular basis, help to keep a kitchen healthfully clean.

Easy-care floors simplify cleaning tasks when accidents occur.

COURTESY WHAT'S NEW IN HOME ECONOMICS

Kitchen surfaces

Cabinets, walls, and counter surfaces may require weekly cleaning. An oily film of dirt usually builds up on these surfaces over a period of time. A range ventilator will help to avoid this buildup, especially if it is used each time cooking is done. When splashes and finger marks are wiped from kitchen surfaces as part of the daily chores, weekly cleaning may be unnecessary. Stains which can be wiped away in a moment when food is spilled may take concentrated effort and special cleaning solutions if allowed to dry and harden during the time lapse before weekly cleaning occurs.

Once a week, the most frequently used cabinet surfaces require a thorough cleaning. Other surfaces may be checked each week and cleaned whenever necessary. The exact cleaning methods used will depend on the type of surface. Paint, enamel, stainless steel, laminated plastic, and wood each require a special cleaning method. Use the method prescribed for your type of cabinets.

Check and clean when necessary the inside surfaces of cabinet shelving. Drawers and shelves require wiping and straightening as part of the regular cleaning program. It takes only a little extra time and effort to straighten one storage area each week. By doing this in regular rotation, all kitchen storage will be clean and fresh at all times.

Kitchen appliances

The type of weekly care necessary to keep a range clean and attractive depends greatly on the quality of daily care it receives. If spills are wiped up as they occur, there is little need for weekly cleaning. Unless the range is equipped with a self-cleaning oven, however, the racks and oven surfaces may need weekly attention. Surface burners, reflector bowls, and drip trays may also need a general cleaning on a weekly basis. Gas burners may need to be checked for clogged jets. A weekly inspection will show which parts of the range need to be cleaned. Follow the manufacturer's instructions for the best way to handle such cleaning.

The interior surfaces of the refrigerator require frequent cleaning to keep them free from odor. Careful daily care will make weekly care less difficult. Many refrigerators are equipped with swing-out or pull-out shelves which make it simple to wash the wall surfaces as needed. Shelves and storage drawers must also be washed regularly. Many families clean the refrigerator storage areas in rotation, doing one shelf or drawer each week. If spills are wiped up as they occur, this plan will keep the refrigerator clean at all times.

During the weekly inspection of the refrigerator, check to see that all food is in good condition. Small storage bowls and covered jars are

Divide the class into groups, each working on a certain problem. Compare and contrast various commercial products and various methods of doing common household tasks.

When comparing products and methods, consider the results, the cost, and the time and energy required to do the job. Summarize your findings in the form of recommendations. Include household tasks such as the following:
 Dusting furniture
 Cleaning windows and mirrors
 Shampooing rugs
 Cleaning ovens
 Cleaning and waxing floors

Assign other class groups to compare and contrast various types of equipment and tools.

Give the advantages and disadvantages of different types of the same item. Give instructions for use and care. Include such items as the following:
 Wet and dry mops
 Can openers
 Vacuum cleaners
 Electric blenders
 Outdoor grills

Follow these guidelines in caring for kitchen surfaces and equipment.

Wipe equipment and cabinet surfaces with a soft, clean, damp cloth or a sponge.

Use ordinary soap or detergent and water to clean stainless steel surfaces.

Remove accumulated grease with a mild cleaner.

Wipe up immediately foods spilled on vinyl plastic floor coverings. Wash these floors occasionally with mild detergent and warm water.

easily shoved aside and forgotten. If you look for forgotten food at least once a week and throw out unusable odds and ends, your refrigerator will work more efficiently. There will also be more available space for storage.

Unless you have a self-defrosting refrigerator, you will need to check from time to time to see if it will soon need defrosting. This check will allow you to plan ahead. You can schedule the defrosting job for a day when other household chores are comparatively light. Care of the freezer section of the refrigerator or of a separate freezer is similar to the care given to the refrigerator itself. Follow the cleaning directions which are given in your appliance booklet.

Kitchen floors

Modern kitchen floors are usually covered with a smooth-surfaced easy-to-clean floor covering, such as plastic tile or linoleum. With careful daily care, these floor surfaces remain in good condition from week to week. When floors become sticky or dirty, they can be thoroughly washed with a mild cleaning solution. A self-wringing cellulose-sponge mop, a string mop, or an ordinary sponge may be used for this mopping operation.

In some kitchens part or all of the floor is covered with washable carpeting made of synthetic fibers. With this carpeting, spills can be washed up as soon as they occur. A routine sweeping with a vacuum cleaner keeps such carpeting in good condition.

WEEKLY CARE OF THE BATHROOM

Weekly care of the bathroom is similar to the care of the kitchen. Some bathrooms have tile wall surfaces and floors. These surfaces may be treated in much the same way as kitchen floors and walls. Check to see if the tiles are made of a material which needs special care.

Such convenience appliances as self-cleaning ovens and self-defrosting refrigerators eliminate the need for many weekly cleaning chores.

COURTESY WESTINGHOUSE ELECTRIC CORPORATION

If the tub and washbasin are cleaned after each use, they need little extra weekly attention. Some families prefer to wash them with a disinfectant or special tub cleaner as part of the weekly care program. The toilet bowl requires at least weekly cleaning attention. Special products are available which help to simplify this job. Be sure the bowl brush, if used, is dried, aired, and returned to storage. The medicine cabinet and other bathroom storage areas may be inspected and cleaned on a rotation basis in much the same way as that recommended for kitchen storage areas. Bathroom carpets are cleaned in much the same way as are kitchen carpets. Most bathroom carpeting may be removed for washing or cleaning if the need arises.

WEEKLY CARE OF OTHER ROOMS

The room where the family gathers regularly for recreation may need to be cleaned as frequently as the kitchen and bathroom. Less frequently used rooms may need thorough cleaning less often, perhaps only now and then. Floor coverings and storage furniture similar to that in the kitchen can be cleaned in much the same way. Other furnishings in the general living areas must be dusted and perhaps polished. Hardwood floors need special care. Wax is usually recommended to protect such surfaces. Carpets in these rooms require occasional vacuuming. Such treatment will remove hidden dirt, helping carpets to wear longer.

Dusting need not be a difficult job. Many vacuum cleaners have dusting attachments which simplify the weekly cleaning chores. The upholstery nozzle can be used to remove dust from draperies and curtains, as well as from the surfaces and corners of upholstered furniture. The loosened dust is drawn into the vacuum cleaner instead of being scattered to other

COURTESY COLGATE-PALMOLIVE COMPANY

Most spots on carpets can be removed by applying special cleaning agents. The loosened soil can then be removed with a vacuum cleaner.

Block off the floor in the home economics laboratory into several sections. Try various types of floor waxes and cleaners on each section. Compare and contrast the sections of the floor 2 to 4 weeks later.

Use and care for the kitchen range by following these guidelines:

- For surface cooking, use flat-bottomed pans that fit the size of the surface units.
- Wash and scour drip pans where food and grease have spilled as soon as they are cool enough to handle.
- Avoid the use of scouring pads or powders on the enamel surfaces of the range. Use soap and water only after the range has cooled.
- Brush burned food from gas burners and electric units only after the units are completely cooled.
- Wash the porcelain interior of the range oven with soapy water or household ammonia water. When using a commercial oven cleaner, follow the manufacturer's directions exactly. An ammonia-soaked cloth left in the closed oven for several hours or overnight will loosen baked-on grease deposits and make oven cleaning easier to accomplish.

Suggest tasks which are necessary in the daily, weekly, and seasonal care of your room. Divide them into lists similar to the following:

In the morning:
Put away toilet articles and neatly arrange items on top of your dresser.
Hang up your sleeping garments.
Make the bed.

In the evening:
Replace any hobby or study materials you may have had out.
Hang up clothes that are to be worn again and put soiled clothes in the laundry storage area.
Put the room in order generally.

Weekly:
Straighten the contents of dresser drawers and closet.
Change the bed linen.
Clean mirrors.
Dust thoroughly.
Clean the floor.

Seasonally:
Clean upholstered furniture.
Polish wood furniture.
Clean and wax woodwork or wood floors.
Clean storage areas.
Wash windows.
Wash or dry-clean curtains or draperies.

parts of the room. The dusting brush can be used to dust tabletops and chair rungs. It is also helpful for removing the dust from the tops and backs of books in the bookshelves and for catching and removing dust and cobwebs from window blinds, walls, ceilings, and moldings. Special attachments are used to clean wide areas of the floor, as well as all carpeting. If a vacuum cleaner with rod-type cleaning attachments is available, it is seldom necessary to move the furniture in order to clean a room thoroughly.

Some room accessories and some types of furniture may need polishing as well as dusting. Specially treated dustcloths and furniture polishes are available for cleaning and polishing such furnishings in one operation. Small objects may be picked up for careful dusting. Dust the surface beneath them before setting the objects back in place. Mirrors and picture glass are usually checked in a routine weekly or biweekly cleaning program. Special cleaners are available which simplify the cleaning tasks that become apparent.

A specially treated dust mop may be useful for cleaning large areas of uncovered wood floors. Such mops apply a protective film to the floor surface as they remove the dust.

It is not necessary to own a large amount of special cleaning equipment in order to take advantage of modern housekeeping aids. Most products have more than one use. Read the labels carefully and select one or two polishes which will meet all your needs. Cloths for applying each polish and a clean, soft polishing rag can complete your polishing equipment. These cleaning aids may be kept together in one container so they can be easily carried to each room for its regular cleaning. Some vacuum cleaners provide storage for their attachments within the cleaner case. If the attachments must be kept separately, you may wish to plan storage for them along with the other cleaning supplies.

Weekly cleaning chores are easier when they are organized to prevent unnecessary work. Even with a vacuum-cleaner attachment, some dust from the tops of objects is likely to settle to the floor as you clean. If walls and draperies are cleaned first, then furniture tops and legs, and last the floor, all surfaces will be clean in just three trips through a room.

Bedrooms in regular use require one additional step during the weekly cleaning procedure. It is wise to change the bedding before other cleaning is done. Loose lint and dust will settle to the floor. While bedding is removed, use the vacuum-cleaner attachments to remove any noticeable dust or lint from the bed. When the bed has been made up, the rest of the room may be cleaned in the three-step method—first the walls and curtains, second the furniture tops and legs, and last the floors.

Seasonal care

Although old-fashioned spring and fall cleaning is no longer necessary, certain household tasks are still conveniently thought of as seasonal jobs. They may be required as often as once a month or only one to four times a year. If jobs of this type are carefully planned, they can usually be fitted into the regular cleaning routine without creating a heavy work load.

SPECIAL HOUSEKEEPING PROBLEMS

The walls and ceilings of a room gradually build up a film of dirt which can cause the whole room to look worn out. This dirt is often noticeable around the heating outlets or the windows. At least once a year, you will want to check each room to see if special cleaning is required.

Sometimes the walls can be cleaned. Most painted walls and some wallpapers can be washed. Wallpaper cleaners can be used to clean certain papered walls. At other times, the wall covering must be replaced rather than cleaned. Each family must determine its own needs. They must also decide whether they will hire someone to redecorate or whether they can do the job themselves.

Whatever the decision, this is a big job. The room must be upset. Furniture must be moved away from the walls. Curtains and draperies must be taken down. The carpet or flooring must be carefully covered.

It may be wise to combine wall cleaning or painting with other necessary cleaning jobs in order to avoid upsetting the room more than once. If the carpet or the draperies are to be sent out for cleaning, consider whether to have all forms of cleaning done at one time. Furniture

Beds should be vacuumed at regular intervals to remove lint and dust which have settled. Special spray products can be used to kill germs and odors.

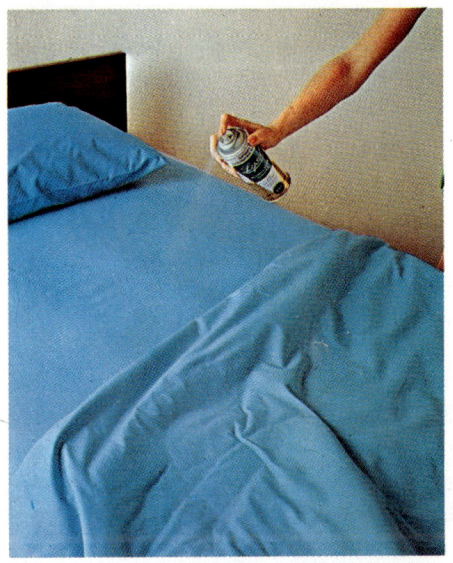

COURTESY LYSOL HOME SERVICE BUREAU

Clean and rearrange the drawers in your dresser or chest. Discuss why the following set of guidelines did or did not work well for you.
1. Take everything out of the drawers.
2. If the drawers are lined, remove soiled linings and throw them away.
3. Turn the drawers upside down on a paper, and shake or tap to remove dust.
4. Vacuum or wipe out the drawers with a slightly dampened dustcloth. Let them dry thoroughly.
5. If desired, reline the drawers.
6. Replace the articles in the drawers in an orderly fashion so they may be easily found when needed.

Demonstrate and practice making a bed by moving around it once only. Learn to miter corners of unfitted sheets. Have time trials or relay races to see who can make a bed quickest while meeting the standards previously established by the class.

Discuss some of the possible health effects of a sagging bed. Suggest ways in which a sagging bed can be made more firm.

Choose projects from the following list which might improve the appearance of your room:

1. Re-dye faded rugs, curtains, or bedspreads to brighten them.
2. Make throw pillows from old party dresses or draperies, leftover odds and ends of fabric you have at home, or from fabric samples which your home economics teacher may give you.
3. Make pillow cases from worn sheets.
4. Make a wastebasket out of a 2 gallon ice cream bucket. Paint or cover with adhesive material so that it makes an attractive addition to the room where it will be used. Ice cream stores will frequently give these buckets to you.
5. Make bookends from scrap lumber.
6. Braid an area rug from worn out nylon stockings and dye the rug a bright color.
7. Sew together different colored carpet samples to make an area rug. These carpet samples can also be glued to a heavy backing material or held together by a wide adhesive tape made for this purpose.

repairs may also be considered. The family may be planning to get new slipcovers or new upholstery. Perhaps this should be done now, especially if new paint or paper is being planned.

Of course, the family budget may not allow for doing all these special tasks at once. But even if you can do only one part of the job, it is wise to consider all of it before you start. In this way, you will be sure that your plans fit together. The most necessary jobs can be done first. Later the rest of the plans can be carried out with a minimum of confusion.

After the walls are cared for, and before the furniture is replaced, it may be wise to wash the windows both inside and out. Some hard-to-reach windows may be cleaned more easily when the furniture is moved than at any other time. Too, paint or paste splatters can be removed while painting ladders are still available.

You may plan to clean windows as part of the general wall cleaning, or they may be cleaned as a separate job. Either way, you will want to consider this job at least on a seasonal basis. It is not necessary to clean both sides of the windows at the same time, although many families find this convenient. Other families clean the inside window surfaces whenever necessary as part of the weekly cleaning. They wash the outside window surfaces only once or twice a year, perhaps when they adjust or replace screens or storm windows.

SEASONAL FLOOR CARE

Although daily and weekly cleaning will keep floors clean, most floors need special attention from time to time. Some vinyl floor covers do not require wax. However, most smooth-surfaced floors look better and wear longer if waxed occasionally. How often this is necessary depends on individual family needs. In families with small children, waxing the kitchen floor may be a weekly job. In other homes, it may be needed only two or three times a year.

A floor needs rewaxing whenever it remains dull after mopping. Many types of floor waxes are available. Some are self-polishing. Others must be applied and then buffed for a good finish. Some types of wax should never be used on certain types of flooring. Read the labels carefully, and choose a wax which will give the finish necessary for your floors. Be sure all the old wax is removed before applying the new wax. This can usually be done by washing the floor with a strong detergent cleaner.

Carpets require cleaning from time to time. A family may buy or rent special carpet cleaners to use for do-it-yourself cleaning, or a commercial carpet-cleaning firm may be hired. The best choice of cleaning methods depends on the type of carpeting, as well as on the family budget.

Many special pieces of equipment are available for floor care. Some of them are very expensive. Before your family decides to invest in special equipment such as a floor polisher or a rug shampooer, take time to consider its true worth to the family.

SEASONAL CARE OF APPLIANCES

Other seasonal chores are connected with the care of household equipment. Furnaces, water heaters, air conditioners, and similar appliances need special cleaning and servicing. Refrigerators and freezers may need defrosting and thorough cleaning. Follow the manufacturer's instructions or check with the utility companies in order to learn what care is needed to keep each piece of equipment in good working order.

SPECIAL STORAGE AREAS

The frequently used storage areas of the home can be kept clean and well organized as a part of the regular daily and weekly household chores. Storage areas for out-of-season items and keepsakes are frequently overlooked during this regular cleaning. These areas can be cleaned when the seasonal items are being removed and replaced.

During this cleaning process, it is important to examine the contents of the storage area. Are you keeping some items simply because you never thought to throw them away? Overcrowded storage areas can be dangerous to the health and safety of family members. Too, you may be pleasantly surprised to find how much easier it becomes to make seasonal changes once useless items are discarded.

Many communities supply a special collection service in order to help families get rid of bulky items which are no longer useful. Check to see if such a service is available to your community. If it is, plan the cleaning of basement, attic, and off-season-storage areas to coincide with the community clean-up week.

Special storage boxes and shelves allow for maximum storage in a small amount of closet space.

COURTESY SEARS, ROEBUCK AND COMPANY

Clean the closet in your bedroom or some other room of your home. Discuss why the following set of guidelines did or did not work well for you.
1   Remove all clothing and other articles.
2   Brush down the walls with a long-handled brush, a covered broom, or an appropriate vacuum-cleaner attachment.
3   Wash woodwork, doors, rods, and floor.
4   Spray the closet with insect spray and close the door for several hours, if necessary. Then air the closet for an hour or more.
5   Sort through the clothing you have taken out of the closet, and dispose of any unwearable articles.
6   Replace wearable articles in the closet.
7   Hang clothes up in this order if possible: best clothes which are worn only occasionally in the back, and everyday clothes nearest the door.
8   Store shoes off of the floor on racks, in shoe bags, or in shoe boxes.
9   Store hats in boxes.

Discuss ways in which students can help make their yards attractive. Carry out one project to improve the appearance of your own home, and tell the class about it. You might pick up litter, make a windowbox, or paint steps or porch furniture.

Take a tour of the outside of your school to determine a place that could be made more attractive with plants. Make a plan for a class improvement project. Start cuttings in class and eventually plant them as planned.

Start shrubbery cuttings in cans at school to be taken home and planted.

Ask the industrial arts teacher to demonstrate simple home repairs such as replacing plugs on electric cords, changing faucet washers, or putting on door catches or handles.

Outdoor improvement tasks

Some families live in cities, while others live on farms. Some rent their homes, and some own their homes. Homes are located in large buildings shared by many families and in single-family structures. In some homes a custodian is placed in charge of the outside work. In other homes family members must take care of these duties themselves. For these reasons, the specific duties involved in caring for the outside of the home vary from family to family. But whatever the situation, the neatness and safety of the approaches to the home are a part of each family's concern.

A clean, well-cared-for approach to your home is pleasing to friends and neighbors as they come to call. Too, the outside of your home gives strangers their first impression of your family. Even the young children in the family can learn to keep the sidewalks and hallways neat. Stray papers and trash can be picked up and discarded whenever they are noticed. Tools and toys can be placed where they belong. Those who pass are quick to recognize homes and neighborhoods where people are concerned with the appearance of their home.

Neatness outside the home involves more than picking up as you go along. Plants in yards or window boxes require routine care. Plant trimmings, scattered blossoms and leaves, and grass cuttings must be swept or raked up and discarded. Sidewalks may need to be swept and washed in summer or kept clear of ice and snow in winter.

Windows, doors, shutters, window boxes, railings, fences, and gutters must be kept clean and neat. They may require frequent attention. Because these areas of the home are exposed to many weather conditions, they may require painting for appearance and protection.

Care of the outside of the home affects family safety as well as the appearance of the home. Misplaced tools and toys may cause someone to receive a serious injury. Storm windows or screens that are not securely fastened can be hazards. Loose steps and handrails can also lead to serious accidents.

When you know just what duties must be performed to keep the outside of your home in good condition, you can organize them in much the same way as the indoor chores. Determine which tasks must be done each day, which may be done only once a week, and which may be placed on a seasonal basis. With planning, the outside of the home can be pleasant and inviting at all times.

CHAPTER 9 POSTTEST

On a separate sheet of paper copy the following list of household tasks. Beside each task indicate if it is usually done daily, weekly, or seasonally.

Make beds
Wash window screens
Clean oven racks and surfaces
Dispose of food wastes
Sweep crumbs from kitchen floor
Inspect and clean refrigerator
Care for pets
Hang up clothes
Shampoo rugs or carpets
Use brush to clean toilet bowls
Organize off-season-storage areas
Change sheets
Wash or dry-clean draperies
Trim or prune outdoor shrubbery

Number from 1 to 30. Beside each number indicate if the corresponding statement is true or false. *Do not write in this book.*

1. A home that looks neglected outside gives a visitor a poor impression of the family who lives there.
2. Household tasks are actually home management problems that need to be solved.
3. The health and safety of a family may be related to the neatness and cleanliness of the home.
4. Seasonal household tasks do not need to be included in a family cleaning plan or schedule.
5. A cleaning schedule helps you have a well-cared-for home.
6. Good management includes having a specific place where each household item is kept.
7. Once a storage plan has been made it should not be altered.
8. By the time a person is a teenager, it is too late for him to acquire the habit of putting things away when he is through with them.
9. Meals can be prepared with greater efficiency when tools and utensils are stored as near as possible to the place where they will be used.
10. All hobby materials and special projects should be completely put away at the end of the day.
11. If any room is cleaned regularly and thoroughly every week, that should be the only cleaning it ever needs.
12. Carpeting designed for kitchens is usually made of cotton or wool.
13. Furniture can be dusted with a vacuum-cleaner attachment designed for this purpose.
14. All uncarpeted floor surfaces should be waxed occasionally.
15. Remove old wax from floors before applying new wax.
16. In cleaning a bedroom, it is good management to make the bed before cleaning the floor.
17. Furniture should be dusted before vacuuming the walls and draperies in a room.
18. The floor should be cleaned before dusting the furniture in a room.
19. A complete and thorough spring and fall housecleaning of every room is necessary to ensure that a home is adequately clean.
20. It is a poor management technique to clean the inside of a window without cleaning the outside of it also.
21. Some furniture waxes need to be buffed to obtain a good finish.
22. Carpet cleaning equipment is available in most communities on a rental basis.
23. An electric polisher is a necessity for families with hardwood floors.
24. Overcrowded storage areas can create safety hazards.
25. For some families, it may be more economical to rent a lawn mower than to purchase one.
26. Painting outside railings, trim, and iron grill work is done only to make a home look attractive.
27. There are some outdoor tasks that may need to be done more frequently than once a week.
28. The room in the home in which cleanliness is most important is the living room.
29. Learning to put things back in their proper places after using them is a good habit.
30. Organizing a home for comfort, convenience, and safety is an important step toward efficient home management.

3
Your Resources

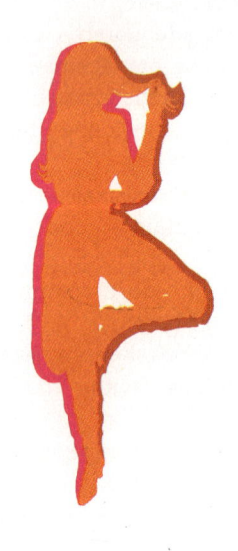

Chapter 10   Managing your resources
Chapter 11   Using your time, energy, and money
Chapter 12   Making consumer decisions

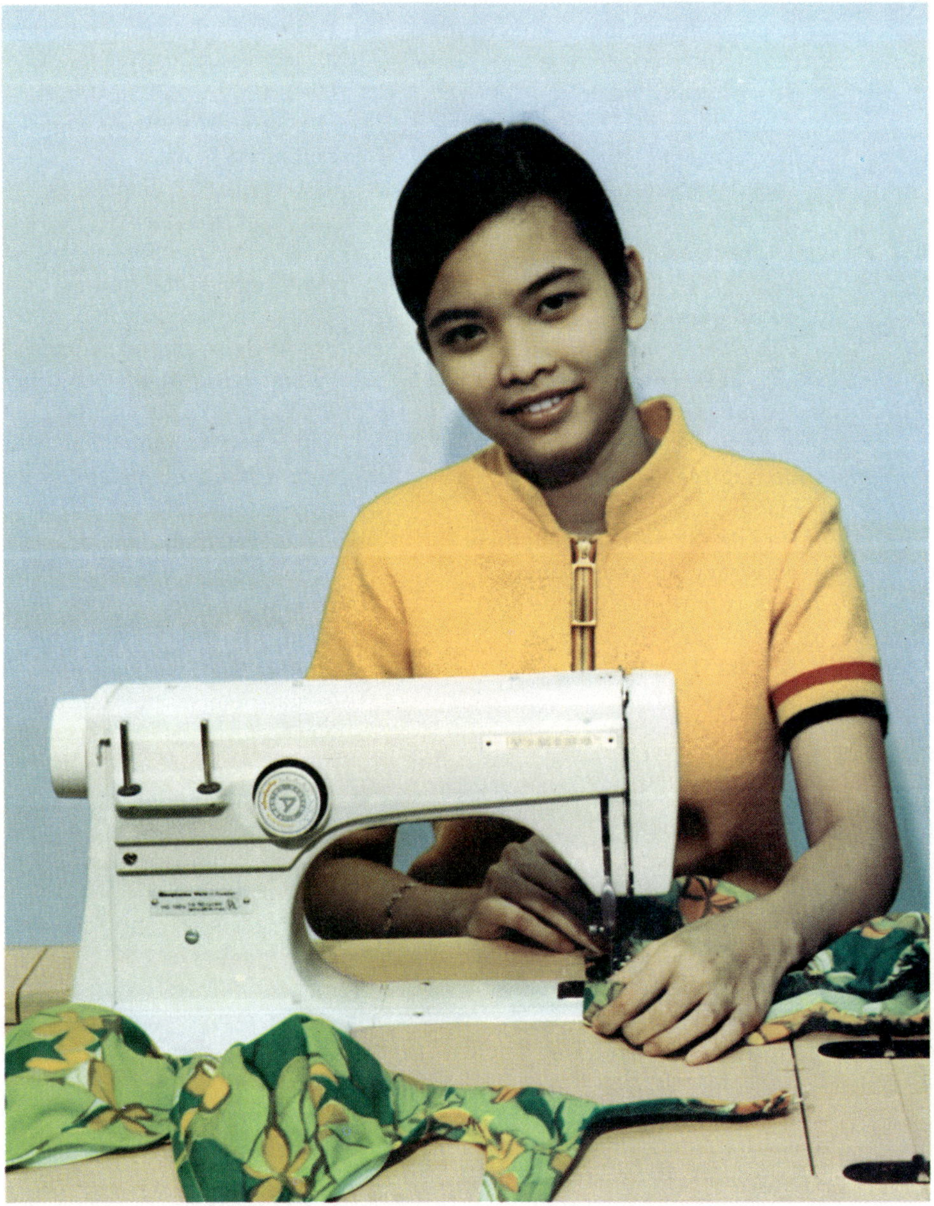

10 CHAPTER PRETEST

Number from 1 to 15 on a piece of paper. Beside each number write the letter which corresponds to the *best* answer for that question. *Do not* write in this book.

1. Which type of resource includes the open air, water, and forest lands?
   a. Human
   b. Material
   c. National
   d. Natural
2. Which type of resource includes your abilities, talents, and skills?
   a. Human
   b. Material
   c. National
   d. Natural
3. Which type of resource includes money, goods, industrial machinery, and factory equipment?
   a. Human
   b. Material
   c. National
   d. Natural
4. Which is likely to be a realistic long-range goal for the largest number of teen-age girls?
   a. To be a movie star
   b. To be a woman astronaut
   c. To be a successful wife and mother
   d. To be a fashion leader
5. If *money* is very limited, which is probably the best choice?
   a. To buy ready-made cookies in a bakery
   b. To buy partially prepared cookies that can be sliced and baked
   c. To buy and prepare a cookie mix
   d. To prepare cookies from basic ingredients
6. If *time* is very limited, which is probably the best choice?
   a. To buy ready-made cookies in a bakery
   b. To buy partially prepared cookies that can be sliced and baked
   c. To buy and prepare a cookie mix
   d. To prepare cookies from basic ingredients
7. Which is essential if you are to make the best use of your basic resources?
   a. Setting realistic goals
   b. Having a large income
   c. Having the newest equipment
   d. Satisfying all your wants
8. Which is most likely to be a *need* for the neighborhood paper boy?
   a. A color TV set
   b. A bicycle
   c. A football helmet
   d. An automobile
9. Which is most likely to be a *want* for a carpenter?
   a. An electric drill
   b. A level
   c. A saw
   d. A fishing pole
10. Which can best be measured by preestablished standards?
    a. Performance and achievement
    b. Goals and values
    c. Needs and wants
    d. Natural and human resources
11. Which is likely to have the *least* effect on an individual's behavior?
    a. His personal values
    b. His personal goals
    c. His basic human resources
    d. His score in a family game of dominoes
12. Under which circumstances are family roles *least* likely to change?
    a. When the mother begins to work outside the home
    b. When a new baby is born
    c. When the husband retires
    d. When one of the children changes from elementary to junior high school
13. Which is *least* likely to affect your energy resources?
    a. General health
    b. Daily activities and exercise
    c. Money income
    d. Food intake and diet
14. Which of the following is *not* a true statement about priorities?
    a. Needs usually take priority over wants.
    b. All teen-agers' priorities are the same.
    c. Setting priorities may be a difficult task.
    d. Some goals take priority over other goals.
15. Which of the following is *most* likely to occur when resources are unwisely managed?
    a. Dependence on others
    b. Attainment of goals
    c. Establishment of acceptable standards
    d. Establishment of desirable priorities

CHAPTER 10

Managing your resources

Do you know someone who is considered to be lucky by his friends? He seems to have a knack for getting the most out of life. He doesn't seem to be richer or smarter than other people, but he has reached many more of his goals than they have. Actually such a person is probably no more or no less lucky than his friends. His success is probably the result of wise *management* of his resources. You, too, have basic resources. What are they?

Kinds of resources

Your resources are all the things you have at your fingertips to help you reach your goals. There are many kinds of resources. You have heard of *natural resources,* such as air, water, land, timber, and space. You have also heard of *national resources,* such as factories, the labor force, and economic institutions. *Human resources* include abilities in the areas of energy, skills, aptitudes, intelligence, imagination, patience, and understanding. Human resources also include time and the goods and equipment produced by people. However, goods and equipment are

During the study of Part 3, make a notebook of new vocabulary words as they are introduced.

Use a special bulletin board throughout the study of Part 3 for the display of economic news, facts, and humor.

Read or listen to a recording of readings from *Mama's Bank Account.* Discuss the values that were held by the family and some of the goals for which they were striving. What were some of the resources used to achieve these goals?

Give examples from books, TV, or real life where people set unrealistic goals for themselves. Discuss why they seemed to be unrealistic goals. If these goals were not reached, what were the results? In some cases, why were people able to reach goals that seemed to be unrealistic? How can you apply this information to a decision you are now trying to make?

185

Divide the class into three groups for a race. In a specified length of time, let each group brainstorm to list as many ways as possible to save either time, energy, or money in doing household tasks. The group with the longest list is the winner. Share the ideas from all groups with the class and discuss them in relation to situations when each would be an effective course of action.

Ask a home-service representative to demonstrate the use and care of several labor-saving devices furnished in your home economics department.

Bulletin board IDEA
Title: *Financing the Family Life Cycle*
Directions: Divide a large white circle into pie-shaped segments, each to represent a stage in the family life cycle. Print the names of the various stages on the segments. Color each a different color. Mount them on a bulletin board. With colored yarn connect each wedge to a picture which describes a major expense of that stage of the cycle.

COURTESY GIRL SCOUTS OF THE U.S.A.

Natural resources can be used and enjoyed by a great number of people if wilderness areas are handled correctly.

more often called *material resources. Money*, too, is sometimes listed as a material resource.

Perhaps you are wondering how anyone can learn to manage all the things considered to be resources. Fortunately, you need to manage only a few basic resources. These include time, energy, and money. With them you can obtain the goods and services you need and want. Your talents and skills can be used to help you make effective use of these basic resources.

Resources work as a team

Resources rarely stand alone. They are related to each other. They can be used in combination, or they can be substituted for each other.

Sometimes a combination of resources can create a new resource. For example, a boy who uses his time and energy to develop the skill of painting can redecorate his family's home for much less money than if a painter were hired to do the job.

Wise use of basic resources depends on the amount of each resource available as well as on the goals to be reached. Everyone has the same amount of time. But each person differs from all others in the way he *needs* to spend time as well as in the way he *wants* to spend it. For example, the family with very little money may need to spend a great deal of time in cooking to stretch the food dollar. On the other hand, the high-income family may decide to buy quickly prepared meals to save time for recreation.

Not everyone has the same amount of energy to spend during each twenty-four hours. Each person's body makeup determines the maximum amount of energy available to him. Too, each person's general health, daily activities, emotional makeup, and other factors such as emergency situations combine to cause changes in his available energy resources. Also, of course, there are great differences in the amount of money various people have available.

As you plan to use your time, energy, and money, you may think of them one at a time, in combination with each other, or in place of each other. In managing these resources, it may be best to think of using them together or as substitutes for each other.

For example, a teen-aged girl who works after school may find it wise to spend money for ready-made clothes. Her outside job uses time and energy which cannot also be spent on sewing. The money she earns may be used as a substitute for time and energy. On the other hand, a mother who is at home most of the day may have more time and energy than money. She can afford to spend her time and energy resources making clothing for her family in order to save some of her available money for another use.

Human and material resources can be combined to change an unattractive area into a pleasing one.

PHOTOS COURTESY DOROTHY DEAN

Give an oral report in class completing one of the following statements. Be able to defend your statement with facts you have gained through study. *It may be good management for:*
1. A family to hire the laundry done if . . . .
2. Daughter to make her holiday dress if . . . .
3. Father to service the family car if . . . .
4. Son to hire someone to cut and edge the lawn if . . . .
5. Mother to use convenience foods if . . . .

Your career
Home-lighting adviser

Duties: Discusses with customers effective use of electric-lighting facilities in homes and suggests improvements in lighting or room arrangements. Demonstrates advantages of changes such as light rearrangement; bulbs suitable for reading, sewing, or other purposes; and use of reflectors. Suggests changes in color, decorations, and furnishings to increase light.
Where employed: Utility companies or electrical equipment houses.

◈ Make a list of six ways teen-agers are frequently tempted to waste their money. For each situation give a workable alternative.
Example: Overspending for party refreshments in order to have a nicer party than the one your friend gave last week.
Alternative: Set aside an exact amount to be spent on the party. Plan a menu and decorations which can be bought for no more than this amount.

Add to the following list other important reasons for learning to manage money effectively.
1 More quantity or higher quality can be bought for a given amount of money.
2 Parent–teen-age relationships often improve.
3 Money may be saved for large purchases.
4 Frustrations are lessened.

For one week, keep a record of the purchases you make before, during, and after school. Total the amount spent.
Would this total be enough to buy something you have been wanting? How can you manage your spending so that your school needs and some special wants are both satisfied?

COURTESY FRIGIDAIRE DIVISION OF GENERAL MOTORS

Energy can often be saved by arranging children's play areas near home work areas.

Although time, energy, and money are renewable to a certain extent, they can be used up. Many people forget that each is gone forever as soon as it is spent. This is just as true of time and energy as it is of money. It is fairly easy to see that you cannot spend the same dollar for a movie and for a new scarf. It is somewhat harder to realize that an hour spent visiting on the telephone cannot be used for homework.

In order to manage your basic resources wisely, you must learn to spend each to best advantage. Suppose you are asked to furnish a cake for a class party. You can buy a ready-made cake. You can make a cake from a mix. You can prepare a cake from flour, sugar, eggs, etc. No matter which you choose to do, you must spend some time, some energy, and some money for the cake. How can you spend two of your basic resources in order to save the third? How much of each basic resource is needed for your best choice? A ready-made cake would probably cost the most money and save the most time and energy. The cake prepared from basic ingredients would probably require the use of more time and energy, but it might cost the least money. The cake mix would require the use of small amounts of all three resources. If you have a short supply of money, make the cake at home. If your supply of time or energy is limited, buy the cake at the store. If you feel limited on all three resources, select the cake mix.

When you sense yourself being held back from making wise decisions because you lack a skill, begin to plan. Can you spend some free time and energy in developing a useful skill? For example, if it is hard to find ready-made clothes which fit well, you might decide to spend some of your basic resources in learning to sew. As your skill increases, you may be able to provide for your own clothing needs while saving time, energy, and money for other uses. In the meantime, a teen-aged girl might need a party dress. Her limited sewing skill might make it unwise for her to decide to make the dress herself. Instead, she might accept the responsibility for preparing the family meals for a few days. This would free her mother's time for sewing. Such a plan would solve the immediate clothing problem while allowing the girl time to develop a needed skill.

Sometimes you will find that you cannot use the basic resources of time, energy, and money to best advantage because you don't have a necessary piece of equipment. When this happens, you can choose the second best combination in order to achieve your immediate goal. For example, a family might choose to pay for the use of expensive equipment found in a nearby laundromat. However, they might become aware that such a practice takes one or two of their free evenings each week. A wise manager learns to watch for these situations. They can be a guide in the making of long-range plans which might include the purchase of home laundry equipment.

Using your resources to reach your goals

You cannot make wise use of your basic resources unless you know what your goals are. You must also understand your resources in order to select *realistic goals* for yourself. At first, it may seem fairly simple to select a number of lifetime goals. Perhaps you have planned to be a great leader who will make the world a better place to live. Perhaps you have dreamed of being famous or of owning many beautiful things. Ideals and imaginative dreams such as these can spur you on to real achievements, but they are probably not true goals.

It has been said that a person can do almost anything he wishes if he is willing to make the necessary sacrifices. But perhaps the sacrifices would be too great. A person might reach some goals only at the cost of personal and family happiness. To set unrealistic goals can lead to lifelong frustration. In order to choose realistic goals, learn to know your resources and to use them wisely. Learn to recognize the difference between dreams and possible achievements. Dreams are a very useful part of your experience as long as they are seasoned with reality.

INDIVIDUAL AND GROUP GOALS

You are living in a goal-oriented society. Individuals, families, communities, and nations are involved in planning for and reaching goals. Achieving a wisely chosen goal is a sign of progress. What goal is your family working toward? Perhaps you wish to take a special trip or find a better home. Each person in the family needs to give time, energy, or money to make this

Make a list of household tasks, study them, and experiment with ways of saving time, energy, and money as they are performed.

In your home economics department, look for ways in which furniture and equipment have been arranged to save time and energy.

Make a chart or a display showing some of the small ways in which a family may waste money.

Make a notebook of cartoons, clippings, magazine articles, and illustrations that show ways to save time and energy. Try to put one or more of these ideas into practice.

Bulletin board IDEA
Title: *Time Waits for No One*
Directions: Mount a clock face marked into quarter-hour periods. Between the 12 and 3 write EST, between the 3 and 6 write CST, between the 6 and 9 write MST, and between the 9 and 12 write PST. Ask the class members to think of timely sayings to fit each of the quarter-hour periods such as:
EST = Efficiency Saves Time
CST = Cooperation Saves Time
MST = Management Saves Time
PST = Patience Saves Time

As a class, list ten expenditures often made by students your age. Give the approximate cost of each expenditure. Consider the priority each item on the class list has for you. Rank the items from 1 to 10. Decide on a cut-off point which separates the things you consider important from those you could do without. Compare students' lists and discuss the reasons why they are different.

Suggest local opportunities for a teen-ager to add to the family's resources.

Discuss the following questions:
1 When might a teen-ager contribute to the money income of the family?
2 Why is it desirable for a teen-ager to know about household expenses?

Your career
Household items construction

Duties: Making accessories for the home such as slipcovers, draperies, pillows, curtains, or bedspreads.
Where employed: Specialty shops, upholstery shops, interior decoration shops. May be self-employed.

COURTESY THE NEW BOOK OF KNOWLEDGE

A child begins early in life to develop his long-range goal of language development and reading skills.

dream come true. When everyone takes part in the planning, the family can work more easily together as a unit.

LONG-RANGE AND SHORT-TERM GOALS

Many of a person's important goals in life will be reached only after years of planning and working. Such long-range goals are usually reached one step at a time. If you carefully consider each of these steps, you are planning short-term goals which fit your overall plan.

There are also short-term goals which are not related to your long-range goals. Both may be equally important. A wise manager learns to judge the value of all his goals. The immature person too often forgets to make such judgments. He may use up his resources to satisfy immediate desires. For instance, the boy who uses money which should be saved for education in order to buy flashy clothes may be giving up an important long-range goal in favor of a less-important short-term one.

ESTABLISHING PRIORITIES

A priority is the emphasis you place on a given item or situation. As you make both long-range and short-term plans, you will find that some take priority over others. There will be times when some of your goals conflict with others. In order to use your resources wisely, you must be able to choose the most important of the conflicting goals.

Setting priorities is a difficult task. The first astronauts probably had serious decisions to make when leaving their families in order to face the unknown dangers of space travel. Similar decisions must be made by a family that has to choose between living together in a distant city where the father has found an outstanding job opportunity and remaining at home because of seriously ill grandparents. To be together or to care for aging parents is a set of priority problems common in our complex society. Which goal would take priority in your family?

Perhaps priorities are not really different now than they were in the past. Pioneer families were faced with setting priorities between living in safe poverty or dangerous plenty. Do you think they set proper priorities?

Your life will be beset with conflicts. Often you may feel that no matter which way you turn, you end up going in the wrong direction. Learn to decide what is most important, and set out to reach that goal.

Consider your needs and wants

Your personal goals involve the things you yearn to be and to do and to have. These goals differ greatly from person to person. But all may be separated into those which satisfy *needs* and those which satisfy *wants*. For example, clothing is a need. But as teen-agers buy for this need, they often fulfill wants as well. A stylish extra-lightweight wrap which can be worn effectively only a few days in a season fulfills a want more than a need.

As times have changed, some goods and services which were once considered wants have become needs. For example, refrigeration is now considered a need for families in the United States. The individual situation also determines whether particular goods or services are needs or wants. Woodworking tools are a *need* for a carpenter. They help him provide for the basic physical needs for himself and his family. But the same tools must be considered a *want* for a salesman who enjoys woodworking as a hobby.

As you make plans, consider whether they will satisfy needs or wants. Both needs and wants are important to everyone. The wise manager first selects goals which will meet his basic physical, mental, and emotional needs. Leftover resources are used to satisfy his wants.

Compare two storybook characters' ambitions, abilities, talents, skills, and time and energy resources. Tell why you feel one character used his resources more wisely than did the other.

Give examples to show how *needs* and *wants* change for an individual as he grows older. Also give examples to show how some goods and services once considered *wants* are now considered *needs*.

A group often decides whether to aim at a short-term goal of fun or a long-range goal of skill development.

COURTESY XEROX CORPORATION

Plan and present a panel discussion on the topic: *How a teen-ager can prepare now for his job as a home manager later.* If possible, have both boys and girls on the panel. You might also invite some parents or perhaps some teachers from other classes to join the panel. If time allows, make a written evaluation of the discussion.

Consider your values

Values are the importance a person assigns to the needs of people and to ideals, things, and events. No matter how attractive a goal may seem, it will be a poor one if it is in serious conflict with a person's scale of values. Suppose you have been dreaming of being a fashion leader in your school. You know that such a goal would satisfy your basic need for recognition. You know you have a flair for selecting clothes. You realize you would need to spend more time and energy on personal grooming than you have done in the past. Clothes would also cost money. To be a fashion leader may be a realistic goal for you.

For many people, however, such a goal would be vain, or empty. Perhaps they value service to others more than they value their own personal image. A girl who feels this way might very well choose to spend her time and energy as a nurse's aide or a Scout leader. Such activities would be more in line with her value system.

These examples picture two sets of values. Neither is right or wrong. But both help to determine individual priorities. Popular teen-agers are seldom uninterested in their own appearance. Neither are they unaware of the needs of others. More realistic is the person who aspires toward both goals. But his *values* will help him determine which takes priority.

Consider your interests and abilities

What new hobbies or new skills do you wish you had time for? Teen-agers frequently become aware that they have a wide range of interests. It is often wise to make plans which will include time for their development. Even though other goals may become more important later on, such short-term goals as writing short stories, creating dried-flower

Creativity can be expressed through crafts or painting.

COURTESY SPINNERIN YARN COMPANY

arrangements, or learning a new game can introduce you to new activities or new friends.

Perhaps you have known a person who worked hard to make the team when he was better suited to be the bat boy. Such a person selected a goal without considering his abilities. He could be more helpful to his team and his school by being a good bat boy than by being a poor team member. Perhaps, too, you have known a girl who wanted to be a cheerleader. But she has never realized that successful cheerleaders spend hours in practice before appearing in front of a crowd. She may feel hurt because she was not chosen as part of the cheerleader squad. Successful people recognize their own abilities. They also realize that practice is necessary if their abilities are to be developed fully.

Eventually each person must select long-range goals from among his many interests. Most people have more ability in one or two areas than in others. A realistic and worthwhile short-term goal for you would be to recognize and develop your outstanding abilities.

SETTING STANDARDS

You have probably heard the word *standard* used in many ways. You have heard of a standard of living. You have heard of a standard of behavior. You may have heard of a standard of achievement and a standard test. A standard is a yardstick used to measure the outcome of an effort. Without a standard to go by, you have no way of knowing whether you are making wise use of your basic resources. Some standards are a personal measure. There are also standards set by society. These standards measure performance, satisfaction, and achievement. In the end, your own standards depend on your life goals and values.

The results of management

One of the goals most teen-agers seek is independence. It can be achieved through the wise management of resources. The typical teen-ager begins to want to *take charge* of his own life.

You know you are a one-of-a-kind person. Only you can determine what you are capable of achieving.

You must make your own decisions. Whether good or bad, you must accept the effects of your efforts. The end results are brought about by the use you make of your resources. When you can accept these results, blaming no one for the ups or downs that come with them, you are reaping the rewards of your management abilities.

Answer the following questions to determine whether or not you are managing your resources effectively. *Do not* write in this book.
Do you carry your share of the responsibilities in the groups to which you belong?
Do you usually get done what must be done without too much fuss and tension?
Is your life so well organized that you can take on extra duties at school or home when it is necessary?
Do you plan your daily life well enough that you have some time for recreation with your family?
Do you allow adequate time for personal grooming so that you do not have to be self-conscious about your appearance?
Do you make an effort to develop your talents, even if personal sacrifice is required?
Are you developing the technique of positive communication through your expression, your voice, your speech, and your listening habits?

10 CHAPTER POSTTEST

Fill in the blank in each sentence with the *best* word to complete the statement. *Do not* write in this book.

1. Water, land, and air are called ___(1)___ resources.
2. The educational institutions, factories, and economic institutions of a country are part of its ___(2)___ resources.
3. Goods, equipment, and currency are most often classified as ___(3)___ resources.
4. Peoples' aptitudes, abilities, and skills are ___(4)___ resources.
5. Your basic resources are your money, time, and ___(5)___.
6. The use of your basic resources depends on the amount of each resource available to you and on the ___(6)___ that you have set for yourself.
7. One basic resource that all people of all ages have in equal amounts is ___(7)___.
8. The wise and efficient use of one's basic resources is the result of intelligent planning and good ___(8)___.
9. An individual's diet and general health, as well as the amount of sleep and exercise that he gets, all affect his ___(9)___ level.
10. Using basic ingredients to make a wide variety of food products usually saves ___(10)___.
11. Using convenience foods to prepare family meals should help to conserve time and ___(11)___.
12. The importance or emphasis that you attach to a particular goal is the ___(12)___ that you give to that goal.
13. All goals can be separated into those that meet needs and those that satisfy ___(13)___.
14. A good manager first chooses goals that fulfill his basic mental, emotional, and ___(14)___ needs.
15. After basic needs have been met, leftover resources can be used to satisfy ___(15)___.
16. A person's most important goals in life, those that are reached one step at a time through a period of planning and work, are called ___(16)___ goals.
17. Regardless of how appealing a goal may be to an individual, it is not a good one if it is in conflict with his ___(17)___.
18. The basis, or rule, by which something is judged, is called a(an) ___(18)___.
19. Most teen-agers begin to take greater charge of their lives than they did previously, which is another way of saying that they are usually gaining more ___(19)___.
20. All of the things a person has to help him reach his goals are called ___(20)___.

11 CHAPTER PRETEST

Fill in the blank in each sentence with the *best* word to complete the statement. *Do not* write in this book.

1. A person's wants are influenced by his personal goals and ___(1)___.
2. A new, efficient way of performing some task may take longer at first if there are old and time-consuming ___(2)___ to break.
3. Individuals may vary considerably in their supply of ___(3)___ from one period in a day to another period within the same day.
4. A person's attitude toward money is often affected by the ___(4)___ of money available to him.
5. The first steps in making a savings plan are to list your available resources and all your ___(5)___.
6. A plan for spending and saving money to help reach your goals is called a(an) ___(6)___.
7. People who have developed a good savings program often use their savings to earn extra income in the form of rent, dividends, or ___(7)___ on investments.
8. A spending plan needs to be evaluated occasionally because a person's income and needs change more quickly than his ___(8)___.
9. Expenses which you cannot control are called ___(9)___ expenses.
10. Time schedules and spending plans should have some ___(10)___ to allow a person to meet unplanned situations.

CHAPTER 11

Using your time, energy, and money

Any large school system is likely to represent a wide cross section of society. The variation in its residents' resources usually covers a considerable range. For instance, the incomes of families in a community vary. To an extent, so do their amounts of free time and energy. Although many teen-agers do not fully understand that time and energy are resources, they are very aware of the amount of money their school friends have to spend. No matter what the varying amounts, teen-agers are flexible. They are usually highly successful in fitting together into a cooperative, happy group. Perhaps their flexibility is possible because teen-agers are able to look below the surface. Although they may not consider their own time and energy to be resources, they are aware that there are resources besides money. They understand that while one family may have a great deal of money, another has other resources which are equally important.

A typical school system may have Mark as one of its students. Mark may have two well-known, but very busy, parents. They may or may not be living together, and their income

Discuss incidents in which a person was offended because another could not change or adjust his time schedule for activities such as the following:
To talk at length on the telephone
To sit and visit
To go somewhere unexpectedly
Was the first person's annoyance justified? Why, or why not?

Tell about an experience when it took you or a member of your family an excessively long time to do something because of being tired or being preoccupied with some problem.

Discuss *tactful* ways in which some people indicate through their gestures and mannerisms: *It is time to leave, please.* Suggest ways, without hurting guests' feelings, in which you can indicate to them that it is time to go home.

◐ Write a make-believe story about a society where there are no clocks or time pieces. How do people manage their time?

Give examples to show why it is often necessary for a homemaker to allow for flexibility in her time schedule.

Make a plan for allowing part of your time to be used as a family resource.

Discuss how the way a person *needs* to spend his time can differ from how he *wants* to spend his time.

is very large. From their income, Mark may have any amount of money he decides to ask for. While he may buy anything he chooses, he knows it would be useless to ask for his parents' time or energy. These resources have been assigned to the making of more money or to the pursuit of their own interests.

Joe may attend the same school. Joe, his mother, and several brothers and sisters may live on welfare payments and the small amount of time and energy left over from their struggle for survival. Perhaps a worse situation must be faced by David, who has a working father who chooses not to share his earned wages with his family. Perhaps this family's money is supplied only through part-time jobs David and his mother can find.

These are the extremes. One boy's family provides money for his every *want* and *need,* but they are unwilling to contribute time or energy for his mental-emotional development. The other two boys have little of either time, energy, or money at their disposal because these basic resources are used for survival.

Fortunately, most modern school systems provide help for students whose basic resources are not supplied at home. Teachers, counselors, and school friends can spend time and energy helping a boy like Mark. Among school friends there are some who will give of their time and energy so that his life will have meaning. Joe and David can also find help. School lunches, dental and medical care, and help with transportation and school clothes are frequently available for students who need them. The ears of school nurses, principals, and understanding teachers are especially tuned for such needs. Even though your problems may seem too big to discuss, other students have problems of equal importance. Pride need not get in the way of a successful solution.

Most teen-agers fit somewhere between the two extremes. Although they may feel that they are short of one resource or another, most of them have some money.

In most school systems, students from a broad range of society learn to live and work together.

COURTESY ST. LOUIS DISTRICT DAIRY COUNCIL

They are allowed to use some of their family's time and energy as well as their own. In other words, they have a broad range of resources at their disposal. Their success lies in their ability to recognize time, energy, and money as real resources and to combine them for successful living.

Attitudes about time

When observing people, you have probably noticed that they have many different attitudes about time. Some people treat time with respect, knowing it is a valuable resource. Others abuse it. Some people cherish every minute, while others can't seem to wait for the hours to pass. Even the same person feels differently about time in different situations. Perhaps you feel that time flies as you try to include all your important activities in one day's schedule. On the other hand, you may feel that time drags while you wait for a certain telephone call. These differing feelings about time are based on your goals and interests.

There are many pressures for speed in modern life. There are also pressures for slow, careful activity which seem to contradict the pressures for speed. But how you feel about time at a particular moment is not so important as how you use the twenty-four hours you have at your disposal each day. Which of your actions show that you use time as a valuable resource?

Wise use of time before a party allows a girl to spend time with her guests when they arrive.

COURTESY FARLEY MANNING ASSOCIATES, INC.

Managing your time

Even though time is something that can't be seen, tasted, heard, or felt, it is real. Like other resources, it can be spent wisely or wasted through poor management. Those people who realize that time, like money, requires careful management have taken an important first step toward making wise use of their time.

Management of time, however, requires more than an understanding of its value. Successful time management requires a plan

Make a time schedule according to the suggestions below. After following the schedule for a few weeks, evaluate it for effectiveness.

1 Keep a record of the things you now do and the time required to do each. If you are planning a daily schedule, keep records for several school days and weekends. If you are planning a schedule for doing a particular thing, keep records of your work on two or three typical occasions.
2 Make a list of additional activities you feel you need to carry on within your available time. Estimate the time necessary for each activity.
3 Take a critical look at your activity list to see what other worthwhile things you can and want to do. Try planning to substitute them for current activities you consider less important.
4 Leave some unscheduled time.
5 After trying your schedule, make changes which will improve it.

Discuss the advantages of making a time schedule. Make a schedule just before you are responsible for an unusually heavy load of household tasks. Using the plan, carry out your duties. Did you find that the time schedule was helpful? Why, or why not?

Make a time schedule for a girl who is going to a very special school party on Friday night and must take care of necessary grooming needs after school that day. Remember to include items such as shoes, hose, hair, nails, makeup, mending, and pressing.

Bulletin board IDEA
Title: *There's an Art*
Directions: Cut a large paint palette from construction paper. On the palette make three large splotches of color. On each color write one of the words: *time, energy,* or *money.* Fasten the palette to a bulletin board below the title. Below the palette, finish the title with the words
To Drawing on Your Resources Wisely

for its use. Such a plan must be realistic. It must provide for needs before it can be concerned with wants. In making such a plan, you must also recognize your limitations, knowing that any plan will fail unless you are willing and able to follow it. The wise use of your time depends in part on the amount of self-discipline you are willing to exercise and on the habits you develop as you follow your plans.

PLANNING A TIME SCHEDULE
Busy people generally want to spend their time wisely. Many find that the best way to do this is to work by schedules. A schedule helps to ensure that there will be time allowed for each important activity each day. A plan may be quite general, or it may be worked out in detail.

List your activities
Each person must decide which type of activity plan will work for him. Perhaps the only help you need is the organization provided by noting your major activities in a notebook or on a desk calendar. Other people may prefer to list all activities, large and small.

Before making an elaborate time plan, you must determine your activities. List *all* activities for the day. Then check the list for forgotten items. Did you include personal grooming and care of clothes? Did you include all the activities that involve family and home responsibilities? Did you include classwork and time for study? Did you also list your other school-connected activities? Do you have a part-time job which must be included on the list? Did you note social activities? Did you include any special uses of your leisure time? For example, if you are planning to make a storage case for your room, you must remember to list this activity.

Next to each activity on your list, note the amount of time it will require. If you leave for school at eight o'clock each morning and get home at four o'clock each afternoon, you can list these exact times next to *School.* You will need to estimate the time for many of your activities. For example, you may be preparing a special school project at home. Next to this activity on your list, you can note that you expect to spend one hour between seven and eight o'clock for this project.

A carefully planned time schedule might become cramped by unexpected events. No one can tell ahead of time that heavy traffic or a rainstorm will cause a daily trip to take longer than usual. But a time schedule *can* allow extra time each day for the unexpected. Then, too, some activities themselves will take longer than you expected. You can't stop washing dishes halfway through the job because your schedule says it's time to stop. If you schedule your time wisely, you will be able to adjust your plan to take care of occasional poor time estimates.

Consider priorities
As you look over your list, it may seem that you have scheduled more activities than there is time for. This often happens to people who are learning to plan their time. One reason people spend their time unwisely is simply that they try to do too much.

Go back over your list and separate the activities which you *need* to include from those which you *want* to include. As you become more skillful in managing your time, you will discover that you have more leisure time. You will have learned to take care of your needs effectively. In the meantime, you can place your unscheduled wants on a standby list to be worked into your schedule as time allows.

High on your list of needed activities will be those which affect your health and those which affect your important goals. You will also want to give a high priority to promises you have made and to activities which concern the people you care about.

Consider your limitations and strengths
No one has more than twenty-four hours to spend on any day's activities. This absolute limit on available

COURTESY ST. LOUIS DISTRICT DAIRY COUNCIL

Good students usually give priority to time for study.

time is the reason for giving a priority rating to each of your activities. But there are other limitations which must also be considered as you plan your time schedule.

There are limits which come from outside schedules. Perhaps it would be more convenient for you if school would start at noon on one particular day or if the bus came five minutes later each morning. However, picture the real troubles which would develop if such schedules could be changed to suit the momentary wishes of each student or each bus rider.

Make a time schedule for preparing the following evening meal for your family:

Hamburgers
Buttered Peas   Baked Potatoes
Celery and Carrot Sticks
Chocolate Pudding
Milk

Plan the time at which you will begin each major step including preparing and cooking the various foods, setting the table, and cleaning up.

You may plan to use convenience foods and to do some of the tasks the previous day, but include these tasks in your schedule. If possible, prepare and serve this meal as planned, or plan and use another menu and time schedule. Evaluate your schedule and, if necessary, make recommendations for improving it for use at another time.

Bulletin board IDEA
Title: *Divide Your Time Wisely*
Directions: Make a picture of a large, red apple. Divide the apple into three parts. Label the apple sections *Work, Play,* and *Rest.*

Keep a time record of your activities for several days to determine whether you are getting enough sleep, rest, and exercise. If the record indicates that you should increase the time spent for one of these activities, suggest changes in your use of time that will allow for this necessary change.

As you go over your list of activities, make a note of those which must fit specific time schedules. List these activities in the order in which they occur throughout the day. Then you can fit in your other activities around these fixed schedules.

The needs of the other people in your family can limit the ways in which you schedule your time. If someone in the family goes to work at 8 P.M., the evening meal is often served early enough to allow him time to enjoy eating with the family. Even though you might prefer to eat at a later hour, as a responsible family member you will plan your time schedule to fit the family needs.

Your body makeup also limits your choices of wise ways to spend your time. Each person has different periods throughout the day when he can work more efficiently than at other times. At first it may seem to you that outside schedules will not let you make good use of some of these periods of high efficiency. But as you learn when your high-efficiency periods occur, you can take advantage of them at the same time that you adjust your total plan to your other limitations.

For example, you may find that you must struggle through your afternoon study period in order to finish tomorrow's math assignment. But you can easily do the same assignment in 15 minutes at home after the evening meal. Even though you can't change your school program, you can plan to spend your total study time wisely. Study the math at home when you can efficiently concentrate on it. Use the school study period for other subjects which require less of your concentration.

Even when outside schedules are not involved, it is wise to schedule

Energy can be conserved through the use of labor-saving equipment.

COURTESY WESTINGHOUSE ELECTRIC CORPORATION

your activities to match your periods of high efficiency. You might find that you spend 30 minutes straightening your room in the evening when you are tired. You can do a better job in 10 minutes in the morning when you are fresh. By scheduling this task for the morning, you can save 20 minutes.

Evaluate your schedule

Once you have made a time schedule and followed it for several days, it is time to evaluate it. How could it be improved? Does it need to be more flexible? What important activities did you forget to include? Each time you improve your plan you will learn how to make time schedules which are more satisfactory.

DISCIPLINING YOUR USE OF TIME

Perhaps your time schedule was a wise one but you failed to follow it effectively. Are you willing to interrupt your schedule for almost any reason? Perhaps each interruption seems important at the moment. Yet at the end of the day you find that many of your most important scheduled activities were never completed. Think of your time schedule as a tool which will help you reach your important goals. Then you will be able to judge whether it is wise to change it for a specific interruption. A flexible time schedule can be adjusted to include the interruptions which are truly worthwhile.

IMPORTANCE OF HABITS

By the time a person reaches school age, he has formed a great many habits. As he grows older, new habits are learned and old habits become stronger. In one way, all such habits save time. Think of the time you would spend if you had to go through the problem-solving process each time you brushed your teeth, took a bath, or made your bed. But habits such as these can also cause you to waste time. Perhaps you learned to make your bed when you were six inches shorter than you are now. Are you still making the bed the same way? How can you take advantage of your added height?

It is wise to evaluate your habits as you evaluate your time schedule. You may find you have some time-consuming habits which contribute very little to your well-being. You may find that you are doing some household tasks inefficiently because you haven't formed the habit of using available time-saving equipment. For example, which pieces of time-saving equipment does your family own which you have never learned to use?

At first, a new way of doing something may take longer than the old. This is because time must be spent to break the old habit and develop the new one. But if the new

For the most efficient use of your home study time, follow these guidelines:
Begin your studies before you are too tired to concentrate.
Select a quiet place.
Dress comfortably.
Choose a comfortable chair and a good light.
Alternate your favorite subjects with those you do not like as well. Be sure to allow time for each assignment.
Concentrate on what you are doing.
After about an hour of studying, take a short rest period, and then resume studying with renewed energy.

Analyze your study habits by considering the following points:
Look at yourself objectively. Are you wasting time? If so, why? Do you put off studying because you do not know how to study or do not understand the subject matter?
Set up a plan to correct the things you feel need improvement. Make a time schedule.
Choose a good place to study.
Have materials on hand and avoid distractions.

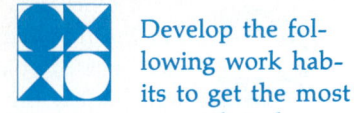

Develop the following work habits to get the most from your courses of study:

At School
Have the necessary tools.
Concentrate on the lesson.
Contribute to discussions.
Take notes accurately.
Ask questions when you don't understand.
Write down the assignments.
Use the school library.
Make up the assignments you miss.

At Home
Set definite times to study.
Have a quiet place and the right tools for studying.
Set goals for accomplishing something definite in the time allotted for your study.
Rest for a few minutes every half hour or hour when studying.

For Major Examinations
Start reviewing several days beforehand.
Get your regular amount of sleep on the night before the exam.
Eat a good breakfast on the morning of the exam.

habit is a useful one, the time spent in learning it is time well spent.

VALUING THE TIME OF OTHERS
Time is a resource which is often shared and sometimes misused. To waste another person's time is to use resources which are not one's own. A person may be justified in becoming annoyed when his time must be wasted waiting for someone who gave him an appointment for a given moment. In a sense, students who create disturbances which interfere with classwork are stealing the time of others. So is the person who talks unnecessarily at a meeting.

You probably know people who seem to have very few responsibilities. Such people sometimes make things difficult for their friends who are expected to use their time wisely. They may interrupt your work without being aware of it. Possibly their goals and those of their families are different from yours. If you wish to achieve your goals, you must let others know that your time is valuable. If you treat time as a valuable resource, your friends will respect your attitude. Whether or not time is important to them, they will recognize its importance to you.

If you have made a professional appointment or a social engagement, be sure to be there on time. Remember to leave promptly when the time is up. Many visits have been ruined because the guest didn't know when to go home. Leaving a professional appointment promptly may be even more important, since other people may be waiting.

If you ever need to break an appointment, do so as far in advance as possible. This will allow the other person to make new plans for the time which was scheduled for you.

USING LEISURE TIME
Many young people think of leisure time as free time, time when there is nothing to do. But leisure time includes more than that. It is time free from assigned duties. A good manager often plans leisure time so that it is balanced between *individual* and *group* activities.

Some leisure time should be free, or unplanned. This time can be used for relaxation. It is a time for unwinding when the pressure is off. A student with no free time in his schedule may be trying to achieve more than his abilities will permit.

Most people find that they do not want very much free time. The problem for them is to find enjoyable ways to use their leisure time. A part of this time can be used for self-improvement. There are many creative projects which can enrich one's life. Examples are drawing, writing, cooking, sewing, building things, taking photographs, and joining a musical group. Creative

A professional may choose to spend his leisure time helping others.

activities such as these give one a chance to express his inner self. Whatever your choice of leisure activities, caution should be practiced. When the desire for perfection exceeds the desire to have fun, leisure ceases.

Most people spend some of their leisure in social activities. It is good to be with other people. Those who work with an athletic team or join a group such as the Scouts are using some of their leisure time to meet their social needs. Many teen-agers enjoy using some leisure time for serving others. There are many chances to serve through community organizations. Have you also considered such service as an individual project? In most neighborhoods there are people who are cut off from others through old age or ill health. A phone call, a gift of home cooking, or simply an offer to run errands for such people can be a very effective way to use leisure time. You gain from the joy of helping others. They gain when their basic needs are met.

Attitudes about energy

Do you have friends who appear to have an unlimited supply of energy? To such people, no activity seems too much. You may have other

Report to the class how you have been able to use the following suggestions for improving your personal study habits:
1 Look over the entire assignment to get an idea of its length and difficulty.
2 Glance over all the assigned pages quickly. Do not try to read them carefully at this point.
3 Read the pages of the assignment carefully, studying charts, maps, and the captions under the pictures. Be sure you understand what you read.
4 Summarize the lesson in your own words. Determine the main points of the lesson.
5 Go over the parts that need to be remembered accurately. Be sure you can recall names, dates, and special points.
6 Make notes in a notebook or on cards if you are using a textbook which belongs to the school. If the textbook belongs to you, you may underline parts of the text or write important points in the margin.

Conduct a survey of your home or the homes of friends to find resources which can be used for leisure activities. Determine those which can be shared by all family members and friends and those which are for individuals only.

Conduct a survey to find the ways in which your friends spend their leisure time. What leisure-time activities are most popular?

Discuss how individuals and families of the past spent their leisure time. In what ways did their leisure-time activities differ from those of today? Explain these differences.

Discuss the reasons why mental-emotional fatigue might affect a person's level of efficiency.

Bulletin board IDEA
Title: *Balance Your Day*
Directions: Use a silhouette of a balance scale. On one side write *sleep, exercise,* and *nutrition.* On the other side write *study, recreation,* and *work.*

friends who are constantly tired. What causes this difference in people?

There appear to be real differences in the amount of energy available to different people. Some people have a greater capacity for work than do others. Not only do some people have more energy, but also each person shows a wide variation in his energy supply from time to time. As a person uses up his energy, he begins to experience *fatigue.* There are differences in fatigue levels just as there are in energy levels.

The energy-fatigue pattern is affected by many things. There are physical factors and mental-emotional factors. Some of these are under a person's control, and others are not. For example, most people can more or less determine that they will get eight hours of rest each night. But a family situation may require that a student has heavy home responsibilities as well as a full-time school work load. Before he can spend his energy wisely, he needs to identify the factors which determine his energy-fatigue pattern. At that point, a wise manager can make a plan suited to his individual situation.

YOUR PHYSICAL ENERGY PATTERN
There is a definite relationship between a person's eating habits and his energy supply. A person with poor eating habits may have more energy than a friend who is known to eat wisely. Even so, the person who makes poor food selections will find that he can increase his energy supply by improving his eating pattern. Regular amounts of sleep and rest and regular physical exercise can also affect his energy level. A good general health program, suited to his individual needs, will help anyone maintain his energy at its most productive level.

Energy patterns are also affected by physical makeup. Inherited patterns will determine, to a degree, whether you have a naturally high- or low-energy level. The size and shape of your body can further affect your total need for energy. More energy is needed to move a heavy body than a light one. Your physical makeup also determines the number of high-level energy periods you have each day. Nature sets a rhythm for these energy peaks.

Many people who have inherited low-energy levels have learned to use their energy so effectively that they accomplish more each day than some of their friends who have a more abundant supply of energy. People who have a natural energy pattern which produces late-afternoon energy peaks can learn to use these peaks effectively even though their school or work schedules require them to start work much earlier in the day. The type of energy pattern you have is partly inherited. How to use inherited energy patterns skillfully becomes an individual decision.

YOUR MENTAL-EMOTIONAL ENERGY PATTERN

Have you ever told yourself you were too tired to enjoy a party simply because you were worrying about something else? Have you ever felt exhausted just thinking about a distasteful school assignment? This lack of energy is real. It is not imagined. Your mental-emotional state affects your energy level. Negative attitudes seem to drain your energy, while positive attitudes seem to bring forth an additional supply.

Physical energy and mental-emotional energy may, on the surface, appear to be the same thing. Either can make you enthusiastic. Either can carry you successfully through a period of activity which requires energy. However, there are important differences between these two types of energy. People who mistake mental-emotional energy for physical energy can cause permanent damage to their health. For example, a person sapped of energy by a recent illness may use emotional energy to play in an important ball game. Everyone will mistake one type of energy for the other at times. The skillful manager learns to recognize and develop both types of energy to their full

COURTESY JELL-O GELATIN

A person who completes necessary tasks before enjoying leisure prevents the fatigue often caused by frustration.

positive levels. He uses them together to reach his important goals.

Managing your energy resources

No two people have exactly the same energy pattern. Therefore, your plans for managing your energy must be very personal. What is wise for you may be unwise for your best friend. This does not mean that you must work alone as you learn to manage your energy. Who among your friends and relatives can help you improve your management skills?

Give a demonstration to illustrate that with practice and experience you have learned to do some task more quickly and efficiently. This might be a task such as ironing a shirt, sewing on a button, or cleaning an oven.

Write a short story or paragraph entitled: *A Day in the Life of the Muscles of my Right* (or *Left*) *Arm.*

Discuss the factors which might have an obvious effect on your personal energy and production level.

Define *dovetailing* as it applies to housekeeping chores. Give examples to show how a homemaker may dovetail several jobs in order to conserve her money, time, or energy. For example, explain how several tasks which require the use of the iron and ironing board could be dovetailed in order to save resources.

Your career
Food or equipment demonstrator

Duties: Aids consumers in comparing new products with familiar products.
Where employed: Food and equipment companies.

205

Save time, energy, and money by caring for your possessions, using the following set of guidelines:

Decide where each article can be best kept when not in use, and make a practice of putting the article away in that special place.

Every week inspect the things you wear and use, and repair them if necessary.

Find ways to mark your belongings so they will not be confused with similar items belonging to your family and friends.

Consider the energy required for each of your planned activities. Then schedule high-energy tasks for periods in the day when you experience energy peaks. You can save energy for other uses by tackling required tasks early in the day. Mental-emotional fatigue can build up as you postpone necessary activities. Such fatigue can steal energy you need for enjoyable activities. The student who convinces himself that he can study most effectively after 2 A.M. is probably fooling no one but himself. The young mother who dreads bathing the baby would wisely schedule this activity for early morning. Such a plan would prevent the sapping of her emotional energy caused by practicing put-it-off tactics.

Plan to use your energy resources to meet your needs before you spend energy for your wants. As you develop skill in managing your energy resources, you will find that wise management allows energy supplies for both your needs and your wants.

You can replenish both physical and mental-emotional energy by alternating strenuous activities with more relaxed activities. For example, you might choose to mend your clothes after you have washed the bathroom floor. On the other hand, a fast game of catch might build up your energy after heavy mental activity at school. When you undertake a long, difficult project, you may find that you have worked until you can no longer think clearly. Take a short break. Spend ten or fifteen minutes in a completely different activity. If you choose the activity wisely, you will return from your break with a clear mind.

Check your activities to see if you are using your energy efficiently. Perhaps you can develop a dishwashing system that is better than the one you have established. Compare the ways you use both time and energy. How can you plan activities to make the best use of each resource? You may need to spend energy to save time at some

The arrangement of storage shelves and work tables often determines the amount of energy necessary for completing a given task.

COURTESY FARLEY MANNING ASSOCIATES, INC.

Spending money for needs before wants is a sound consumer practice.

point each day. How can you balance this with a period in which you spend time to save energy? How can you spend available money to save both time and energy? Energy is wisely managed when it is combined with available time and money to reach the greatest number of priority goals.

Attitudes about money

Most teen-agers have worried about money from time to time. To many people, money seems to be the biggest source of trouble in life. Perhaps you have friends who borrow money regularly in order to satisfy their wants and needs. Others will do without true necessities in order to save money. Some seem to spend all their money as soon as they can, with no thought for future needs.

Why do some of your friends seem to have all the money they need while others with a larger supply of money are always broke? Like time and energy, money is a basic resource which can be used poorly or well. It is valuable because it can buy goods or services.

Individual goals affect people's attitudes toward money. The ease with which money can be obtained

Discuss factors to be considered when choosing clothes for traveling. Add guidelines to the following list:
Clothes that are light in weight
Blouses, skirts, pants, and undergarments that can be laundered quickly and easily, that dry fast, and that need little if any pressing or ironing
Clothes that do not wrinkle easily
Clothes that will be suitable for the anticipated activities
Clothes that are interchangeable, such as separates for girls and extra coats for boys, and clothes that can be worn in a variety of ways with a change of accessories

Your career
Family budget consultant

Duties: Works with troubled families to plan the spending of their incomes for supplying needs before wants.
Where employed: Banks and loan companies.

Keep a record of the amount of money spent over a period of time for clothes cleaning or laundry care. Add this amount to the original cost of the garments in order to determine the total cost. Did some garments prove to be more expensive purchases than others? How will your findings affect your future clothing purchases?

Discuss the reasons why the percentage of money spent for different items varies greatly from one family to another.

As a class project, make reports on the care needed for such belongings as balls and bats, tennis rackets, or other athletic equipment. Discuss the relationship of money management to the care of belongings.

Bulletin board IDEA
Title: *How Do You Pocket Your Money?*
Directions: Tack up a cloth or paper apron with several pockets. Label the pockets with such words as *clothing, savings, gifts,* and *education*. Tuck play money into each pocket.

is also a factor in each person's attitude. For example, money may be spent freely when jobs are plentiful. But a business change which makes jobs hard to find may change a family's spending habits. In the same way, young people who have grown up in families which supply money for many of their wishes may feel that money is not important. On the other hand, their friends whose families must struggle to provide money for basic needs may value money highly. People who think of money in relation to the time and energy they have spent in order to earn it will probably have a different attitude than people who think only of the things which money can buy.

Managing your money

At some time in their lives, most people must consider two basic questions about money: "How can I get the money I need?" "How can I manage my money in order to reach my goals?"

SOURCES OF MONEY

People work to earn money. That is, they spend time and energy to furnish goods or services other people will buy. For their efforts they receive money. Most families depend on the money they earn on the job for their basic income.

People who have developed a good savings program can use their savings to earn extra money. For example, interest on savings accounts or government bonds can add money to a family's total income. Rent from property or dividends from business investments may also add to a family's basic income.

Teen-agers may have special sources of income which they must consider as they plan to use their personal money resources. Perhaps they are given money from the family income when they ask for it. They may earn extra money for special jobs. They may receive money as a birthday gift. Although money received in these ways is not part of a regular income, it is unwise to spend it wastefully.

Many teen-agers operate on an *allowance,* a definite amount of money which they receive on a regular schedule, such as once a week or once a month. Many parents feel that an allowance gives a teen-ager a chance to learn to manage money in a safe situation. Since the amounts of money involved are usually small, an allowance plan keeps down the cost of a beginner's mistakes.

The size of an allowance and the goods and services it is expected to provide depend on the individual situation. The number of people in the family and the total family income must be considered in determining each allowance. The age of a family member and his individual needs usually affect the size of his allowance. Family needs and goals will help determine the items each allowance is to cover. Individual experiences in handling money will also affect the size and purpose of each allowance. For example, some families have worked out effective allowances for free-spending money on the age-privilege plan. A child has perhaps 5 cents per week times his age to spend as he pleases. While the five-year-old child has 25 cents to spend each week, a more responsible ten-year-old receives 50 cents. School expenses and other activities affect the amount of money each person needs. For instance, the cost of transportation or lunches bought at school must be considered if allowances are to be workable.

MAKING A SPENDING PLAN

Some people seem to be afraid of the idea of planning how to spend money. Perhaps such people fear that a plan will prevent them from using their money as they wish. A *budget* is a plan for using available money for reaching your goals. In the long run a budget will provide money for more of your goals than will unplanned spending.

Consider your resources

How much money do you have? A realistic plan for managing your money will begin with a list of your available resources. Your list should include the sources of your income, the amount of money from each source, and the times when each amount can be expected. You will also want to note which amounts can be depended upon and which are estimates.

Are you certain you will receive a definite amount of money on a regular schedule? This will probably be true if you have a steady part-time job or receive an allowance. Plan your spending to match this regular basic income. You can

Discuss the advantages and disadvantages of various ways of keeping records of expenditures such as:
Keeping envelopes containing the cash allotted for food, clothing, utilities, and insurance payments
Using a notebook to record daily expenditures
Using checkbook stubs as balance sheets

A good spending plan helps a person use his resources for reaching his goals.

COURTESY FARLEY MANNING ASSOCIATES, INC.

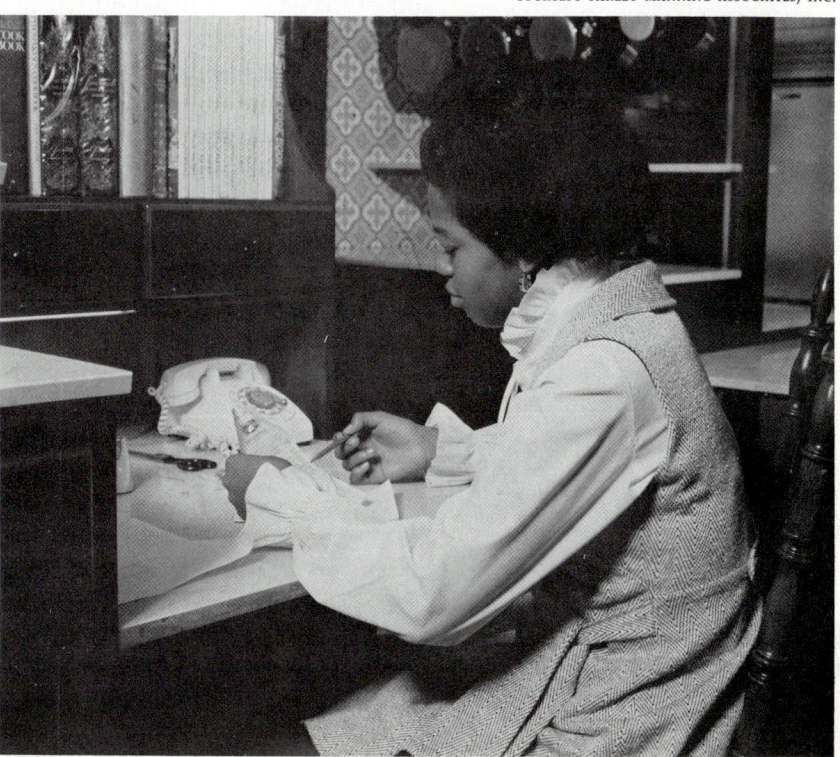

Keep a record of your income and expenses for a given period of time. You may use the form below or develop one of your own.

SAMPLE EXPENSE RECORD

I: *Income*
Allowance
Earnings
Gifts, loans, others
   Total income

II: *Fixed Expenses*
Lunch
Transportation
School supplies
Clothes
Contributions

III: *Flexible Expenses*
Recreation
Snacks
Cosmetics
Personal grooming
Bicycle repairs
Gifts
Club dues
Personal accessories
Sporting goods
Others
   Total expenses

IV: *Savings*

List the desirable features of any good spending plan or budget.

add any extra income to your total whenever you receive it. It is easier to adjust a spending plan to take advantage of extra money than it is to make adjustments for expected income which you do not receive.

Perhaps you do not have a regular income. You may be asked to baby-sit three times in one week but get no jobs the following week. In this situation you need to estimate your basic income. Can you determine your average weekly income over a fairly long period, perhaps the last six months or all of the last year? There may be some weeks when you earned nothing and other weeks when you earned $8 or $10. Perhaps your average income was $5 a week. Since it is relatively easy to adjust a spending plan upward, you may prefer to plan for a basic income of $4 a week. This estimate allows a small safety margin for times when your earnings are lower than usual.

Consider your expenses

What items must be covered by your basic income? You can begin your budget planning by listing all your expenses. Some of these expenses are for true needs. Others are for items and activities you want. Some of your expenses are fixed, and you cannot control their cost. Others are flexible. Which expenses have you forgotten that should be listed? Do you owe money? Did you include savings?

Does your list of expenses exceed your basic income? If you listed *all* your wants, it is certain to do so. Your next step is to adjust your list so that your spending plan agrees with your actual income. Your priority spending will be for those items which are true needs. Perhaps this includes money for lunch at school and money for bus fare to school or to work. Money for savings, money you owe, and contributions you have promised must also be included. If you and your parents have agreed that you are responsible for buying some of your basic clothing, your priority list will include these items.

Some items on your priority list will be fixed expenses. You cannot pay less than the regularly charged bus fare or buy food at school for less than the school charges. Sometimes it is possible to change the amount of these fixed expenses by spending some of your time and energy. For example, consider the possibility of walking to school. Consider taking lunch from home instead of buying it. Before you decide to make such substitutions, however, be certain that they will provide true savings. If you can buy a more nutritious lunch at school than the lunch you can prepare at home for the same cost, you are wasting some of your resources by preparing your lunch at home.

The other expenses on your priority list are usually more flexible.

Perhaps they can be lowered through careful buying. Wash-and-wear pants may cost a dollar or two more than a similar dry-cleanable pair. But the cost of dry cleaning may mean that the wash-and-wear pants save money in the long run. Try to decide whether you buy too many items of the same type. For example, how many shades of lipstick or nail polish do you really need?

Once again, compare your total expenses with your basic income. When your total planned expenses become lower than your basic income, your plan becomes workable. You may select items from your list of wants to include in your current spending plan. Your personal goals and values will determine which of your wants are most important to you. The most important of these can be added to your spending plan as soon as your resources permit. Your standby list will be helpful whenever you find that you have extra income.

What can you do if you find that your priority expenses are greater than your basic income? Perhaps you have mistaken some of your wants for true needs. Perhaps you have overlooked some of your resources. Look again at your resource list and your list of expenses. Did you overlook a source of income? How can you spend time and energy to save money? What skills do you have which can be used to earn money or to save your basic resources? Which of the expenses on your priority list are not absolutely necessary at this time? No one can afford to buy everything he wants, but as you grow more experienced in using your resources, you will probably begin to have money available for your most important wants.

Consider your savings

Perhaps you are wondering why savings are included in your list of priority expenses. Unless you include a definite amount for savings in your budget and take this out

Discuss the differences there might be in the amount of money you are allowed from the family income in each of the following situations:
1 Your mother works outside the home
2 Your brothers and sisters are of preschool age
3 You have a brother or a sister in college
4 You are an only child

A father's willingness to help with child rearing can free part of a mother's time and energy for wage earning outside the home.

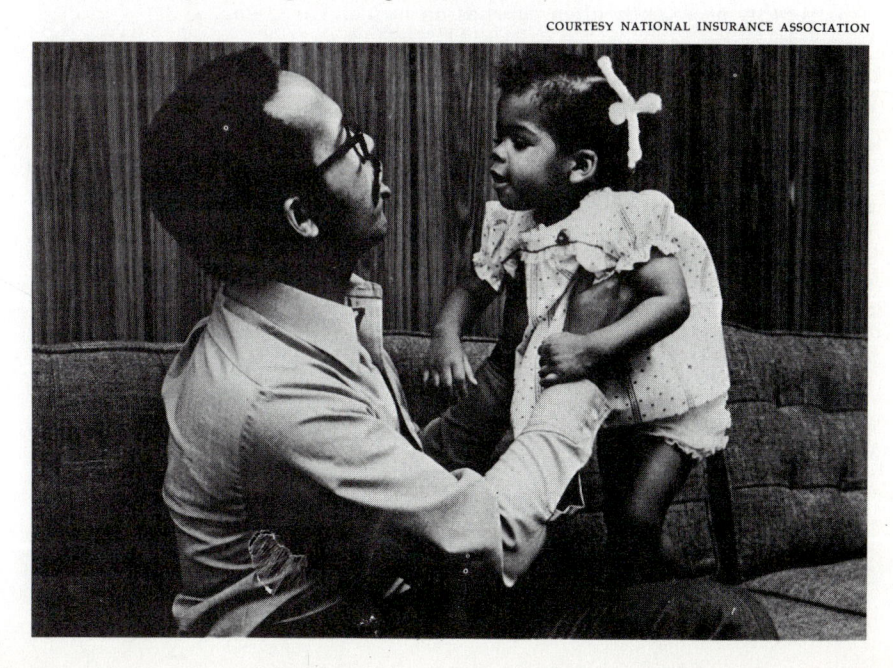

COURTESY NATIONAL INSURANCE ASSOCIATION

Keep a written record of your personal expenditures for two or three weeks. At the end of that time combine the expenditures into such groups as lunches, bus fares, clothes, magazines, cosmetics, and recreation. On the basis of your record, decide whether you need to improve your spending habits. If so, make a plan for improvement, follow it, and evaluate the results.

of your income regularly and promptly, you will probably find that you have no money left to save.

In the first place, savings help you meet emergency situations. For example, illness in the family could increase your necessary expenses at the same time your basic income drops. Everyone should try to save something for emergencies of this type. It is also wise to have money available for emergency wants such as ball-game tickets or costumes for special plays or parties.

How can you decide on the amount of money to be saved each week? There are several good plans. Some people decide that they will save a certain part of their total income, perhaps as little as one cent out of every dollar. Others begin by adding up their fixed expenses. They then decide how much of the rest of their income should be saved. This amount becomes a fixed expense. For good management it is important to begin a savings plan. Save some definite amount regularly. As you grow in savings experience, you will be able to select an amount which is best for your purposes.

When you have planned your savings program, you need to decide where to keep the money. Money kept in your home is available when you want it. This could be an advantage in case of true emergencies. On the other hand, savings which are so readily available are easily spent for wants which are not emergencies. If you place your savings in a savings account or use emergency money to buy government bonds, your savings will be earning interest which will increase your total savings fund. Since this type of saving is harder to spend, you will be less likely to spend it unwisely. On the other hand, you may find it difficult to make such money available in case of a true emergency.

Perhaps you can compromise. Many people keep a small emergency fund on hand. Money being saved for a special purpose in the near future is also kept at home. But the major part of their savings is

The security of a family often depends on its plan for saving.

COURTESY NEW YORK LIFE INSURANCE COMPANY

placed in an account where it will earn interest. Since such a savings plan is flexible enough to meet changing situations, it will tend to encourage the savings habit.

Evaluate your spending plan

After you have used your spending plan for a short time, evaluate it. What necessary expenses did you forget? Did you underestimate some of your expenses or overestimate some of your income? Mistakes such as these are common. Perhaps you think you are spending according to your plan, but find you don't know exactly where your money goes.

Try keeping a record of your actual spending. Many plans fail simply because the planner needs more information. Records are especially helpful when you plan for your flexible expenses. Perhaps you are actually spending some of your clothing money for after-school snacks. Perhaps you neglected to include some extra bus fare in your original plan. A record of your spending will help you adjust your spending to meet your *real* needs. Some people struggle with an unrealistic spending plan for a month or two, then give up the whole idea of budgeting. They say a budget won't work for them. In reality, such people are refusing to learn to manage a basic resource.

As you examine your records, you may find that you have spent money for items or activities which conflict with your important goals. The successful manager has learned to measure the cost of each purchase in terms of his values. He asks, "Will this expense help me reach my goals? Will I be spending extra money, or money which I had planned to use for another, more important purpose?"

Once you have developed a realistic spending plan, you may be tempted to follow it without further checking. It is true that a good plan can continue to serve you well. But your situation is likely to change from time to time. Your income may change. Needs can change quickly. Goals may change more slowly, but they do change from year to year. Even your *value scale* changes as you mature.

The wise manager checks his plans and his actual spending regularly. During these examinations, he decides whether his spending plan continues to meet his needs. You can evaluate your actual purchases in terms of their value to you and their relation to your goals. You can compare your use of money with your planned and actual uses of time and energy. Only in this way can you be sure that you are using all your basic resources for successful living.

Discuss the following situations. Try to determine the wisdom, or lack of it, in each situation.
1 Beverly gets paid for every top grade on her report card.
2 John's father punished him for disobedience by refusing him his weekly allowance.
3 Since David started delivering newspapers every afternoon, his mother feels that he should not receive his allowance.
4 Mark, age six, and Bill, age fourteen, receive the same allowance from their parents, who feel that they want to be very fair to both boys.

List possible ways and places to keep your savings. Give advantages and disadvantages for each of the following:
1 Giving it to your parents to keep for you
2 Having a bank in your room that cannot be opened easily
3 Putting it in a savings account
4 Buying United States government bonds

11 CHAPTER POSTTEST

Fill in the blank in each sentence with the *best* word to complete the statement. *Do not* write in this book.

1. The first step in planning a time schedule is to list all your __(1)__.
2. In making a time schedule, it is wise to separate the things you want to do from those things that you __(2)__ to do.
3. It is wise to plan your time so that you take advantage of the periods when you have more energy and, therefore, are probably more __(3)__.
4. After a time schedule has been made and followed for several days, it should be __(4)__ to see if it can be improved.
5. When you waste another person's time you are using a(an) __(5)__ that is not your own.
6. Time which is free from assigned tasks or duties may be thought of as free, unplanned, or __(6)__ time.
7. There are individual differences in energy and efficiency levels just as there are in the __(7)__ levels that occur as a person uses up his energy.
8. Physical, mental, and __(8)__ factors may affect a person's energy level.
9. There are real and important differences in the amount of money and __(9)__ available to each individual.
10. A person's attitude toward money is greatly affected by his values and __(10)__ in life.
11. People who have planned a good __(11)__ program can often use money to earn additional money.
12. The amount of money a child may receive from his parents on a regular schedule is usually called a(an) __(12)__.
13. Unplanned spending usually provides less money for reaching goals than does a(an) __(13)__.
14. The items which must be covered by your basic income are called your __(14)__.
15. Priority spending should be for those things which are real and basic __(15)__.
16. Money kept in a savings account earns extra income in the form of __(16)__.
17. Savings can be included in a spending plan when extra money is wanted or needed for a(an) __(17)__ situation.
18. Expenses which change and vary from time to time are called __(18)__ expenses.
19. A person's goals usually change more slowly than his financial situation, income, and __(19)__.
20. Sometimes a person can save money by spending his energy and __(20)__.

12 CHAPTER PRETEST

Fill in the blank in each sentence with the *best* word to complete the statement. *Do not* write in this book.

1. A person who buys and uses goods and services is a(an) __(1)__.
2. Buying certain brands, owning a special make of automobile, or living in a particular neighborhood may be important to a family seeking social position or __(2)__.
3. An advertisement that implies that you will be more charming or beautiful after using a certain product appeals to your __(3)__.
4. Instructions for the care of a product, suggestions for its use, and guarantees are often included on an attached tag or __(4)__.
5. A canceled check or a(an) __(5)__ is your record of payment.
6. Many stores have sales after an important __(6)__.
7. Goods with flaws, or imperfections, are called __(7)__.
8. Emergency buying allows little time to __(8)__ prices and quality.
9. Service stations, utility companies, and discount stores are examples of __(9)__.
10. A good credit rating is established by paying __(10)__ on time.
11. Thirty-day credit is often considered __(11)__ payment.

CHAPTER 12

Making consumer decisions

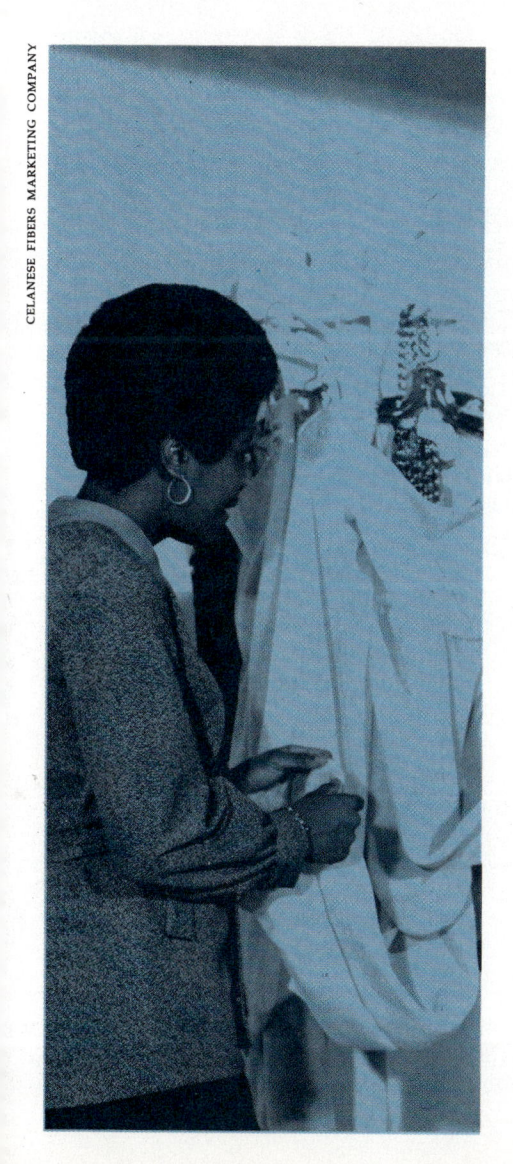

A consumer is one who uses goods. Because the use of goods is on the increase, the consumer is a big figure in the news. When people produced or made the things they needed and wanted at home, they were well informed about the content and quality of a product. This is no longer true. When today's buyers see consumer goods on display in a modern store, they need some background information in order to make wise buying decisions. What is a product made of? How long will it last? Will it serve my purposes? These are all consumer questions the informed buyer asks himself.

Learning how to produce needed or wanted goods has been, and will continue to be, an important part of the learning process. However, the average person today buys most of his material possessions as well as many services. The emphasis has changed from *doing* to *knowing*. Each person needs to learn how to make intelligent consumer decisions.

Spending money

Money is worthwhile only in terms of what it buys. The reason for

List desirable housing possibilities in your area for families of various incomes. Describe family situations in which each of the following might be the best choice:
Renting an apartment
Buying an apartment
Renting a home
Buying a home
Renting a mobile home
Buying a mobile home

Give examples to illustrate how the following may be a *need* for one person and a *want* for another person:
Motorcycle
High-fashion clothes
Sewing machine
Skis
Orange juice

Explain the meaning of the following statement:
It is just as important to know how to spend money as it is to know how to earn it.

Pretend that you are an advertising consultant for station PXYZ. Create advertisements that try to persuade different types of people to buy a product. Work up ads that appeal specifically and primarily to groups such as these:

Teen-agers
Boys or men
Girls or women
Parents
Grandparents

Bring to class or tell about advertisements that are eye-catching. Discuss the ways in which they could be misleading to a young reader or viewer.

On a bulletin board, make a display of grade labels and information tags. Discuss the reasons why such labels are of value.

Your career
Writer

Duties: Writes newspaper columns, technical publications, brochures, package directions, magazine articles, or equipment manuals which may help consumers get the best use from their resources.
Where employed: Publications and food and equipment companies.

The person who learns to read and understand hang tags is more likely to be able to select clothes which fulfill both needs and wants.

learning how to spend it wisely is to make your life a more satisfying one.

It has been said that it is just as important to know how to *spend* money as it is to know how to *earn* it. Many people can earn a great deal of money. Relatively few people learn how to spend it for worthwhile goals.

TO FULFILL NEEDS AND WANTS

You understand that *needs,* from a consumer viewpoint, are materials necessary to sustain life. *Wants* are those things or services which add pleasure and meaning to your life. Many consumers seem to face problems when they try to distinguish between needs and wants. As a result, wants are sometimes fulfilled while needs are neglected.

Consider the problem of transportation. Do you think of owning a car as a need? Some people do. When is a car a want? When is a car a need? When is car ownership in a city less necessary than in an isolated rural area? Can a want for one person be a need for another?

Perhaps closer to the lives of teen-agers is the problem of selecting between food needs and wants.

Do you have friends who drink only a soft drink for breakfast or who eat only a bag of potato chips for lunch? Anyone who understands the body's nutritional needs would assume that such practices are for the fulfilling of wants rather than needs. Your body needs certain foods if you are to enjoy good health and have plenty of energy. Meat, milk, fruits, vegetables, and cereal are food needs. Soft drinks and potato chips are more correctly classified as wants.

TO PROVIDE GOODS AND SERVICES

Money is spent in two major areas: goods and services. As the population increases, demands for both continue to rise. Many teen-agers have become accustomed to buying both goods and services. When buying ready-made clothes, teenagers practice buying goods. When they eat in restaurants or have their hair professionally styled, they are buying services. The problem-solving process will help you plan to include priority items when selecting goods and services.

In choosing between goods and services, a teen-ager might have a hard time deciding between a new record and a trip to the movies. A woman might need to decide between new shoes and a new hair style. Whether to buy a new car or to invest money in expensive repairs for an old one might be a man's typical problem. Perhaps a family would struggle with a decision between buying a new TV set and having their home painted. Goals and values usually influence such decisions. Some people seem to value material possessions, while others prefer to spend their money on services. It is possible for either to provide immediate satisfaction or lasting value. The success of any purchase is determined by the goals of the buyer.

Plan and give a sales talk trying to sell your classmates a particular household item. Ask the class members to analyze the *sales pitch* to determine what was said and done that might have influenced them to buy the product. What may have influenced them *not* to buy the item?

A family is buying a service when they hire a moving company to pack their belongings and move them to another home.

COURTESY UNITED VAN LINES

Define the term *status symbol*. Give some examples of status symbols in your school and community.

Find examples of emotional advertising in newspapers and magazines and on billboards, radio, or television. What does each advertisement imply to you as a consumer? Find factual advertisements that provide information which is helpful to you as a consumer. Locate advertisements that both appeal to your emotions *and* provide valuable consumer information.

Define the term *planned obsolescence*. Give an example to illustrate your understanding of the expression.

Your career
Tester and developer

Duties: Work to help develop and test new household products such as prepackaged foods, cleaning products, and small household equipment.
Where employed: Testing laboratories and research departments of various industrial companies.

TO PROVIDE STATUS SYMBOLS

When were you last tempted to buy a record, a tape, or an article of clothing because a friend had the same thing? You probably know adults who want to keep up with neighbors by buying things similar to those the neighbors have. Many wants are created by the possessions of others.

There are many ways in which people show status, or social position. For example, they might choose to live in a certain neighborhood, own a certain kind of car, or shop in a particular store. Students sometimes feel that one school has higher status than another. Other teen-age symbols of status may include athletic jackets, club pins, motor scooters, labels in clothes, and the brand or amount of makeup a girl carries in her purse.

The search for status sometimes reveals a weak self-concept. People who do not think well of themselves may go out of their way to present an image which looks successful. Unfortunately, these people feel that things, rather than their actions, show other people what they are. To buy status symbols, they may use money which would better be spent on needs.

AS A REACTION TO ADVERTISING

How many times have you gone to a store to look at an item you saw advertised on TV or in the newspaper? How much space in your favorite magazine is taken up by advertising? Does your mother read the grocery ads before she does her grocery shopping? In other words, in what ways is your life affected by advertising?

Advertising has contributed meaningfully to the American way of life. Other countries have produced goods similar in quality to those of the United States without attaining the standard of living reached by many American citizens. Why? Probably advertising, which provides knowledge and creates wants, contributes more than any other single factor to your desire for specific consumer goods. The nation's business people know how to *sell* through advertising. You reap the rewards of advertising when you learn how to use it wisely.

Advertising can be very useful when it makes people aware of the many new products available on the market. It can show people how to tackle problems in new and creative ways. Some advertising provides facts to use in comparing products. These facts might refer to such things as color, size, price, or materials contained in the product.

On the other hand, certain advertising can be misleading. Can you tell by reading ads carefully just what a certain company is trying to sell? It isn't always a product.

Often it is the idea that you'll be more attractive, desirable, or popular when using certain goods. Such advertising is sometimes called *emotionalized* advertising.

How can a young consumer learn to evaluate advertising? He learns to weigh advertising carefully by checking claims against reality. He uses factual information as he makes decisions. He learns to understand the difference between *emotionalized* and *factual* advertising.

Consumer responsibilities

Much is written and said concerning the various ways certain businesses and industries take advantage of consumers. An informed consumer is his own best protection against such practices. Staying informed on current consumer affairs, making comparisons, reading labels, returning faulty merchandise, keeping records, and paying promptly are all parts of your responsibility as a consumer. When each consumer takes his responsibilities seriously, all businesses will be forced to conform to the high standards most businesses expect of themselves.

STAYING INFORMED

Being an informed consumer is a continuous process. As products change, you must continually re-educate yourself in order to be a wise consumer. Although you may gain a basic understanding of consumer problems in school, there is a steady flow of new consumer information available. This information might be considered required reading for the person who wants to be well informed on the subject.

Does your family receive a daily newspaper? If not, there are probably several in your library. They offer education for consumers of various ages. Some of the best authorities in finance and consumer affairs write for the press and are quoted in the newspapers. Read what they have to say, and discuss such articles with your parents, friends, and teachers.

Magazines and journals are another excellent source of current information. Many have regular features concerning management of money and other resources. In addition, their articles on buying and caring for food, clothes, homes, and home furnishings are helpful.

A number of government and commercial publications are useful. They are particularly timely in terms of the specific products discussed. Such references may be found in public libraries. They can be consulted as a resource when you are trying to arrive at a consumer decision.

Mail-order catalogues are found in many homes. They are excellent sources of information on general prices and current styles of merchandise. They also answer ques-

Check which of these items in an advertisement for a bar of soap would be of real value to the consumer. *Do not write in this book.*

Endorsement by a famous person
Ingredients
Color
Size of the bar
Approval of physicians
Net weight
Price
How much it lathers in different kinds of water
What it can do for your social life
Kind of wrapper
Special features such as for dry or oily skin

Describe the buy of a lifetime which you have just found. Discuss whether or not others would buy it. Why, or why not?

Bulletin board IDEA
Title: *YOU Be the Judge*
Directions: Fasten a gavel at the end of the title. On one side of the bulletin board arrange play money and on the other side arrange mock credit cards. Below write:
   Cash or Credit?

Survey several products in a store to note the descriptive names used to designate the various sizes. Compare the descriptive terms used on several brands of the same type of product—from the smallest size to the largest size. What do these descriptive terms have in common?

Make a consumers' guide for various items frequently purchased by teen-agers. Examples might be blouses, bras, shoes, or cosmetics.

Brainstorm to find things, other than candy and food items, that can be bought for less than a dollar.

Develop a plan for teaching a 9-year-old child about the purposes and functions of a bank.

Your career
Consumer service representative

Duties: Checks products offered for sale in the area, writes consumer bulletins, and makes an effort to keep consumers informed by radio, TV, or newspaper contact.
Where employed: City, state, or national government agencies.

tions you might have about trends in future clothing styles and new household items. Some catalogues feature a consumer information section which describes various aspects of catalogue items. It answers many of the shopper's questions in regard to the merchandise advertised.

READING TAGS AND LABELS

Tags and labels are important to today's consumer. By throwing them away or leaving them in the store, you are overlooking the fact that they are provided for your information and protection.

Federal and state laws require that certain information appear on the labels of various products. This labeling applies to food, clothing, and many household items. Labels give information about content, fibers and finishes, amount, quality, additives, nutrients, and special instructions for using a product. Tags and labels may also advise you as to the care of the product and some of its possible uses.

Additional information includes warranties and guarantees. These should be read carefully before an item is purchased. Some are real money-back guarantees. Others are well-phrased paragraphs which promise nothing.

Remember the names of the manufacturer and of the store when an item is purchased. It may be necessary to have this information if goods need to be serviced or returned. You will want to buy other items from stores and manufacturers who provide satisfactory merchandise.

DETERMINING QUALITY AND QUANTITY

Your needs and available money should be your guides when deciding on the quality and quantity of an item to be purchased. For example, in regard to clothing, would you rather have only a few high-quality garments, or would you rather have many inexpensive things? In regard to housing, would your dream home of the future fit better into a small, but tastefully built apartment or into a large, old, repair-it-yourself house? Such concerns involve choices between quality and quantity.

In regard to food, there are many times when you may wish to buy a lower quality because of the way you plan to use the particular item. For example, fancy peach halves would not be the best buy if you were going to cut them up for a fruit salad. On the other hand, overripe bananas would not make an attractive salad. If you have the storage space, it might be wise to buy in quantity when prices are low. If the item is perishable, decide whether you could use it before it spoils. A bargain is not a bargain if you neither need nor want it.

To further complicate your decisions concerning quality versus quantity, many items are priced in groups of three, five, ten, or perhaps even twelve. Such grouping indicates that items are sold more cheaply in quantity. Other goods may be advertised as the *giant economy size.* Such information is frequently misleading. Analyzing packages sometimes reveals that the price per unit or per ounce is highest for the giant size.

PAYING PROMPTLY
In some places teen-agers may have credit extended to them. Responsibility is a vital part of a successful credit operation. If you fail to pay your bills, you will have a poor credit rating. This can be held against you later when you try to enter into new, and often more important, business transactions.

Prompt payment is a consumer's obligation. If you have a good reason for not paying a bill when it comes due, explain your problem to the person you owe. Most businesses will give you a chance to arrange for future payments. However, since most businesses can continue to operate only when they are paid bills due them, prompt payment should be made except in cases of real emergency.

KEEPING RECORDS
Think of the times you have watched your parents refer to their financial records as they determined

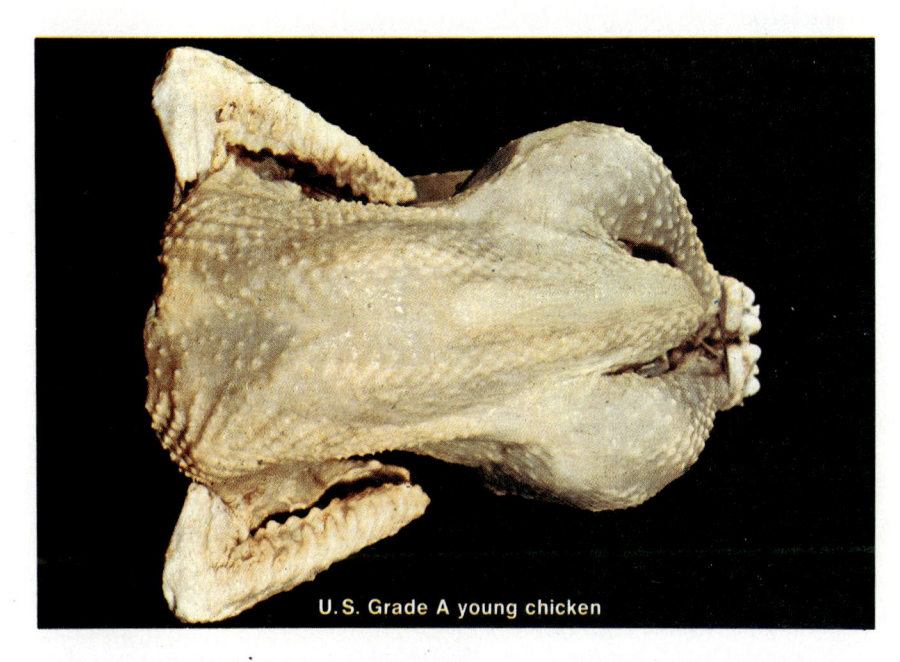

Government grading systems and information provided by food packagers provide useful guidelines for buying food.

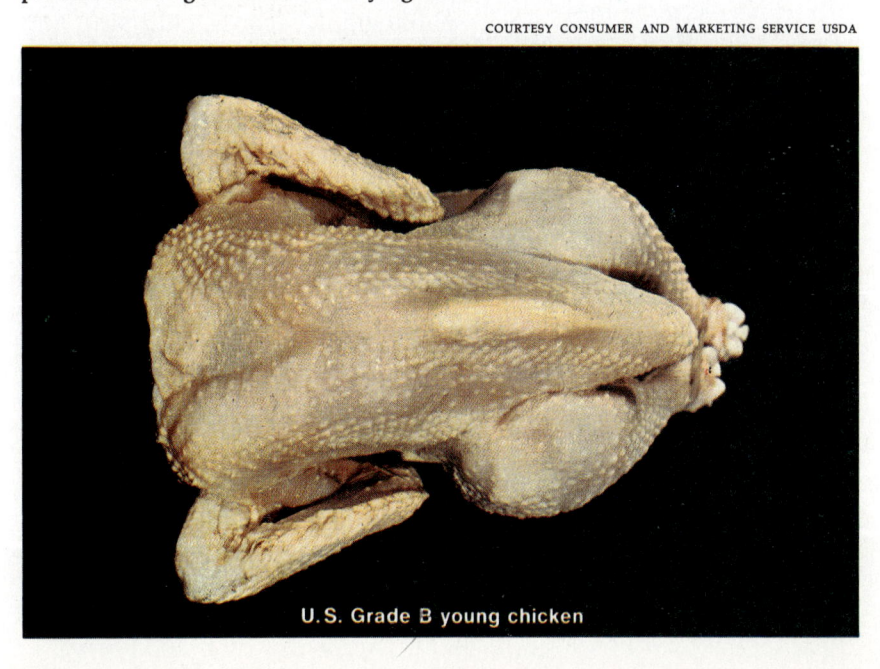

COURTESY CONSUMER AND MARKETING SERVICE USDA

Present skits showing desirable and undesirable shopping practices. Include situations that illustrate shopping with and without a list, using good and poor manners, returning merchandise, and seeking information about goods in order to make a wise selection. Discuss the characteristics of a salesperson from whom you enjoy buying. Discuss the reasons why a responsible consumer has many of these same qualities.

Observe consumers who act irresponsibly. What are some of the things shoppers do that show a lack of consideration for others? What effects do their actions have on businesses and on other consumers?

Write a *Code of Ethics for Consumers*.

In small groups, write and present mini-skits which show how an intelligent consumer shops for a specified item such as a kitchen tool, a small appliance, or a winter coat.

Pretend that you have taken a plane trip to a distant city and your suitcase was lost. Your insurance claim for $200 has been received. What would you buy? Why?

when a certain item was bought or when they paid for it. You probably wonder why it is necessary to keep so many records. Keeping accurate records is time consuming, but it is necessary in a complicated consumer economy. For example, records can tell your parents whether or not a large appliance is still covered by a warranty, or guarantee.

When you pay for something at school, your receipt is your record to share with anyone who may question your payment. If you get a medical prescription filled, the receipt is a record for tax purposes. It may be important when your parents account for deductions from their income taxes. Keep receipts of payment for school annuals, phonograph records, club pins, and other items which you may have ordered. You would not want to pay twice for the same article because careless records were kept.

HANDLING MERCHANDISE CAREFULLY

What do you notice when you look carefully at things piled on a counter during a clearance sale? You may find rips, heel marks, lipstick smudges, broken zippers, missing buttons, and other signs of damage. Who pays for such carelessness and destruction? You and other consumers. Such unnecessary damage is considered when prices are marked on goods throughout the store.

In self-service stores it is very important for shoppers to handle goods carefully, because items frequently receive little care from attending salespeople. If you step into a garment, first remove your shoes. If you are wearing lipstick, place a cleansing tissue over your lips before putting on or removing a garment over your head. When trying on a knitted garment, make sure your nails have no rough edges which would snag the fabric. If clothing is obviously too tight, avoid breaking the zipper. Do not force it closed. If a button comes off, give it to a salesclerk or drop it into a pocket of the garment. These are ways in which consumers show consideration when handling merchandise.

In what ways have you seen grocery shoppers show their lack of concern for others? Perhaps you have seen a man take the lid off the French dressing to sniff the garlic. There are those who squeeze many fruits and vegetables, then perhaps decide to buy none. People knock articles on the floor, ignore them, and go on. Sometimes a shopper may decide against keeping a carton of ice cream and leave it to melt among the canned goods. Who pays for such damage? Once again, you and other consumers absorb such costs in the total price you pay for food items. Only when all consumers learn to accept their responsibility in handling goods will

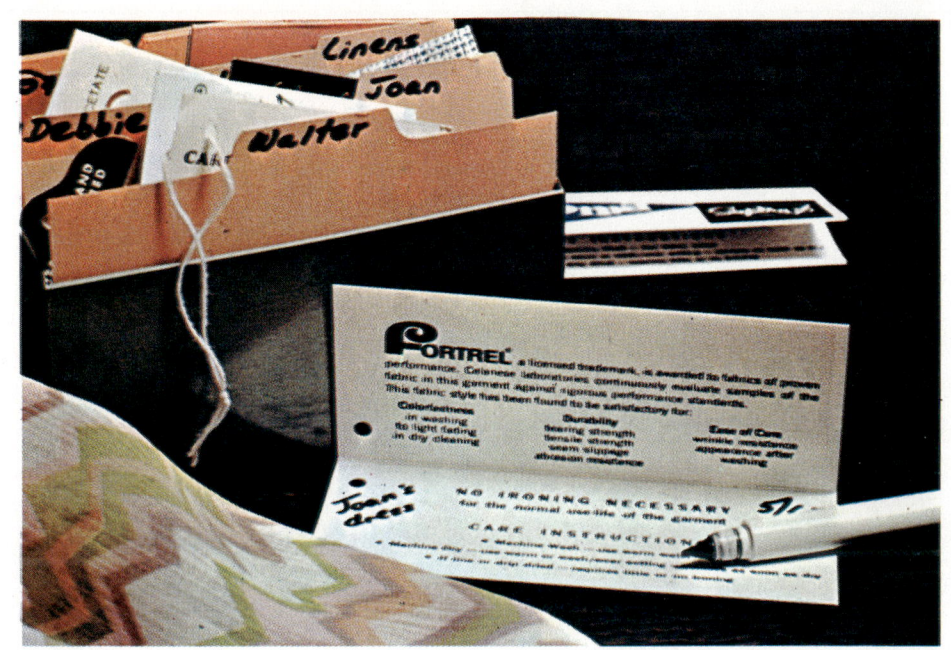

COURTESY CELANESE FIBERS MARKETING COMPANY

The date an item is purchased and special care instructions can be recorded on a tag which is stored for reference during the lifetime of the purchase.

the general public be relieved of such costs.

Consumer protection

As consumer problems increase and demands are made for protection, laws are enacted for this purpose. Many laws have been passed to protect consumers. For example, you feel that it is safe to eat packaged meat which bears a government stamp. Consumer protection extends from local rulings to international laws. You as a consumer should know what you are buying and be reasonably certain it is what you want before you buy it. If you find the product or service unsatisfactory, go immediately and explain your problem to the seller. Most of the time, an honest complaint is well received by conscientious businesses. They will usually refund the cost or replace faulty merchandise. Sometimes the retailer may advise you to write directly to the manufacturer.

In most states there is more than one agency assigned the responsibility of advising and protecting consumers. Nearly all states have

Suggest situations to show that buying the largest size of a product is not necessarily a good choice. Suggest conditions under which buying the largest size of a product would be best and conditions under which buying the smallest size of the same product would be best. Try to find a product for which one of the larger sizes actually costs the same or more per unit than a smaller size.

Examine tags and labels for information that can be of value to the consumer. Give examples to show how each of the kinds of information can be used.

Discuss the actual value of special offers such as trading stamps, gift china, or glasses intended to attract consumers to buy at a particular marketplace.

Your career
Home service representative

Duties: Demonstrates the use and care of various kinds of home equipment. May demonstrate to groups who visit company facilities, to schools, or to individuals in their own homes.
Where employed: Utility companies.

Consumer care guide for apparel

	When label reads:	It means:
MACHINE WASHING	Washable Machine washable	Wash, bleach, dry, and press by any customary method, including commercial laundering.
	Home launder only	Same as above, but do not use commercial laundering.
	No bleach	Do not use bleach.
	No starch	Do not use starch.
	Cold wash Cold setting Cold rinse	Use cold water from tap, or cold washing machine setting.
	Lukewarm wash Warm wash Warm setting Warm rinse	Use warm water (hand comfortable), 90° to 110° Fahrenheit.
	Medium wash Medium setting	Use warm water (medium washing machine setting), 110° to 130° Fahrenheit.
	Hot wash Hot setting	Use hot water (hot washing machine setting), 130° Fahrenheit or hotter.
	No spin	Remove wash load before final machine spin cycle.
	Delicate cycle Gentle cycle	Use appropriate machine setting; otherwise wash by hand.
	Durable press cycle Permanent press cycle.	Use appropriate machine setting; otherwise use medium wash, cold rinse, and short spin cycle.
	Wash separately	Wash alone or with like colors.
NON-MACHINE WASHING	Hand washable Wash by hand	Launder only by hand in warm water. May be bleached. May be dry-cleaned.
	Hand wash only	Same as above, but do not dry-clean.
	Hand wash separately	Hand wash alone or with like colors.
	No bleach	Do not use bleach.

This Care Guide was produced by the Consumer Affairs Committee, American Apparel Manufacturers Association. It will help you understand and follow the brief care instructions found on permanent labels in garments.

Such information is typical of efforts made by manufacturers and businesses which help make consumer goods more effective in use.

Consumer care guide for apparel —*continued*

When label reads:	It means:	
Tumble dry Machine dry	Dry in tumble dryer at specified setting (high, medium, low, or no heat).	HOME DRYING
Tumble dry Remove promptly	Same as above; but in absence of cool-down cycle, remove at once when tumbling stops.	
Drip dry Hang dry Line dry	Hang wet and allow to dry with hand shaping only.	
No squeeze No wring No twist	Hang dry, drip dry, or dry flat only.	
Dry flat	Lay garment on flat surface.	
Block to dry	Maintain original size and shape while drying.	
Cool iron	Set iron at lowest setting.	IRONING OR PRESSING
Warm iron	Set iron at medium setting.	
Hot iron	Set iron at hot setting.	
No iron No press	Do not iron or press with heat.	
Steam iron Steam press	Iron or press with steam.	
Iron damp	Dampen garment before ironing.	
Dry-clean Dry-clean only	Garment should be dry-cleaned only.	MISCELLANEOUS
Professionally clean only or Commercially clean only	Do not use self-service dry-cleaning.	
No dry-clean	Use recommended care instructions. No dry-cleaning materials to be used.	

Identify the Federal requirements for labels on foods, drugs, and cosmetics. Look for information in addition to the following:
1 The name of the product
2 The variety and style of the product, when applicable
3 The manufacturer's name and address
4 The quantity of the contents in net weight or volume
5 The common, or usual, names of the ingredients, listed in the order of their relative amounts
6 Information about the grade of the product and special directions for its use
7 When foods are enriched with nutrients, a statement of the percentages of these nutrients in terms of the recommended daily allowances suggested by the National Research Council
8 A statement of the presence of artificial flavoring or coloring, or imitations, or of a chemical preservative in the contents
9 Information concerning special dietary uses.

laws concerning consumer rights and responsibilities. State agencies provide materials explaining the laws to its citizens. Contacting the correct agency concerning misrepresentation of goods and services is a consumer responsibility.

Some of the federal consumer protection laws have been in effect for a long time, others are new, and still more are in the process of being enacted. Examples of existing laws determining rights of consumers are the *Federal Food, Drug, and Cosmetic Act*, the *Wool Products Labeling Act*, the *Textile Fiber Products Identification Act*, the *Fair Packaging and Labeling Act*, the *Wholesome Meat Act*, the *Wholesome Poultry Act*, and the *Truth in Lending Act*.

The United States Congress has given the Federal Trade Commission the responsibility of stopping unfair commercial practices. Suppose you buy a dress that is unwearable after the first cleaning. The FTC recommends five steps, the first four to be taken before seeking Federal assistance with such a consumer problem:
1 Compare before you buy.
2 Bring your complaint first to the seller.
3 Report false advertising to the media carrying it.
4 Report deception to local organizations concerned with business standards.
5 Write the facts to the Federal Trade Commission.

If these methods fail to bring answers to consumer problems, there are additional possibilities. You may wish to consult a family lawyer or seek advice from an organization such as a Legal Aid Society. This is a group in many communities which consists of lawyers who assist people with free or low-cost legal advice. In many areas, local businesses police their own ranks. Many newspapers publish a column devoted to justified consumer complaints. Few businesses can afford to be mentioned frequently in such a column.

In most instances where there is a sincere consumer complaint, there is a way to solve the problem. It may take time and it may take patience. However, time, patience, money, and energy are resources well spent if they are directed toward improving this consumer-oriented world.

Types of buying

There are a number of types of buying. In addition to general buying, there are bargain buying and emergency buying. A typical teenager will find it necessary to take part in all these types of buying from time to time. It is the person who plans ahead and knows in advance how to handle a given situation who usually comes out best both in the quality of goods and in the cost.

Cosmetics are available in a wide range of prices and colors to blend with every natural skin tone.

GENERAL BUYING

Most people buy something every day, every week, or occasionally. Buying know-how can be applied to any given situation. Buying can be profitable when a person learns to distinguish wants from needs and to use advertising to advantage. Knowing *when* to buy can also improve a consumer's buying skills.

At Christmas time, would you rather have a gaily wrapped gift under the tree or money to spend at the sales after the holiday? Would you rather buy your clothes at preseason and postseason sales or during the height of a certain season? Does your mother enjoy weekend shopping or does she prefer to buy groceries during the week? When you want fresh strawberries, do you buy them regardless of cost? Many products are less seasonal then they once were. Year-round production, refrigeration, and other modern technology make more products available more of the time. However, the season of the year still affects the price you pay for many items.

With buying experience, you will begin to notice the various times of year associated with special sales. If you learn to anticipate sales, you can save money for such purposes and thus make your income go further. Learn to judge value in order to take advantage of sales. Some

Suggest the time of year when the following types of merchandise are most likely to be sale priced:
Christmas ornaments
Bathing suits
Summer shoes and sandals
Toys
Linens (sheets, pillow cases, and bath towels)
School supplies
Why are prices on these items usually lower at that particular time of the year? What problems might be associated with buying one of these items on sale?

Distinguish among different types of stores and compare their goods and services.

Your career
Personal shopper

Duties: Aids elderly people, shut-ins, or people too busy to shop by taking orders and shopping for them. The ability to judge quality, to understand fair prices, and to accept individual preferences is necessary for this type of work.
Where employed: May be employed by individuals or by stores.

227

Tell the class about an unfortunate incident in which a person lost credit cards or had them stolen. In such cases, what should the credit card owner do?

Conduct a survey of lending agencies in which small loans may be obtained. Compare interest rates, repayment terms, security required, and the range of amounts available to borrowers. Summarize your findings in chart form. Share your findings with the class.

Visit a local bank. Find out how to start a savings account and how to fill out deposit and withdrawal slips. Practice filling out the slips.

Using a motorcycle, electric guitar, color TV set, second-hand car, or some other item of your choice, list the various ways in which a person might pay for it. Give the advantages and disadvantages of buying the item by each of the following methods:
1 Paying cash for it
2 Buying it on an installment plan
3 Borrowing money from a bank to pay for it
4 Borrowing money from a finance company to pay for it

sales may not be real sales at all, but a means of advertising.

BARGAIN BUYING

It has been said that the whole world loves a bargain. Shopkeepers understand this reaction on the part of customers. Often they try to make all sorts of merchandise look like a bargain. Did your family ever buy a home or rent an apartment because they were warned that the price would soon go up? Did you ever buy a coat in a summer sale, only to find that it didn't fit when winter came? Did you ever buy a $10 dress on sale for $8 and find one exactly like it selling in another store for a regular price of $7?

When is a bargain a bargain? Generally, a bargain is a bargain when a storekeeper can help you while helping himself. People are in business to make money. They certainly do not object to helping you if at the same time they can make a profit for themselves. Consider this list as possible bargain situations:

1 Bakery goods and fresh produce which may spoil on Sunday can frequently be bought at a good price shortly before closing time on Saturday.
2 Seconds, inferior merchandise bought at low cost from a factory, may be sold at greatly reduced prices in a local store. If flaws can be mended or do not matter, seconds are real bargains.
3 Summer clothing is often drastically reduced so it can be moved out to make room for fall clothing. Winter clothing is also reduced in early spring. Cars, refrigerators, TV sets, and other appliances are sometimes reduced when a new model is on the way. When you are more interested in performance than style, any of these items can be a bargain.
4 Sometimes a store will buy out a warehouse at reduced prices. These savings can be passed along to customers. When you find such items marked below the price you would usually pay, the purchases can be good buys.

When shopping for bargains, remember that there are real bargains and imitation ones. When tempted to take advantage of a bargain, make sure you understand all aspects of the proposition. Many so-called *specials* are on their way to being out of style.

EMERGENCY BUYING

Have you ever had a number of people drop in unannounced for an evening of visiting? If you have, you may have had to rush out and buy refreshments at the last minute. Have you ever experienced the happy feeling of being chosen to represent your school at a regional conference, only to remember that you had nothing suitable to wear? Perhaps you made a wise emergency purchase, but it is easy to make a mistake when you buy in a hurry. The rush often causes you to overspend or to buy items you would otherwise not choose.

Emergency buying usually does not give you time to compare prices as you might ordinarily do when shopping. You may even settle for inferior quality because you don't have time to look further. Knowing that time is valuable, can you think of ways to cut down on the cost of emergency shopping?

Where to buy

Places where people come together to exchange goods and services are called marketplaces. Although people can discuss the exchange of goods by telephone and goods may be sent through the mail, most frequently sales are made on a person-to-person basis. The choice of where to buy depends on who sells the goods or services you need and who sells the quality which suits your purposes.

TYPES OF MARKETPLACES

The American marketplace has undergone sweeping changes. The general store has become a department store, and the grocery store has been replaced by the supermarket. The pharmacy is now a drugstore, where medicines and prescriptions account for only a fraction of the sales each day. Other marketplaces include service stations, trading-stamp stores, utility companies, discount stores, bookstores, and countless other stores of both general and special natures. Your home becomes a marketplace when a door-to-door salesman calls on you.

The concept of going to town to shop is being rapidly replaced. Malls and shopping centers scattered conveniently near housing areas tend to be on the increase as downtown shopping declines. Available public transportation and free parking are strong attractions for the shopping center. Laundry and cleaning may be done by one member of the family in a laundromat, while other family members shop in an adjoining shopping center.

CHOOSING THE MARKETPLACE

There are a number of factors to consider when choosing a marketplace. Most people are interested in using their time, energy, and money wisely. All three can possibly be accomplished if the best marketplace is chosen.

Suppose you want to buy a popular record. You know they are sold in department stores, drugstores, music stores, and gift shops. If you have information regarding the kind

List the various types of credit available to consumers in your area. The following list may help you think of other types.
1 Credit accounts that can be used in only *one* place of business.
2 Credit accounts which can be used across the country, but only in branches of the same nationally organized business establishment.
3 Credit accounts which can be used nationwide in many types of business establishments.

Explain the meaning of the statement: *Your signature is your most valuable possession.*

Your career
Home extension aide

Duties: Works with small groups or individual homemakers to help them improve their food buying, food preparation, housekeeping, and money management skills.
Where employed: Various government agencies.

229

Discuss the rules of thumb given by many financial advisers concerning the amount of credit a family can safely accept.

1 At any one time, total installment debt (except for home) is not to be greater than 8 weeks' income.
2 Monthly installment payments are not to be above 13 percent of the monthly income.
3 Total unpaid charge accounts are not to be greater than 2 weeks' income.

Why are these called *rules of thumb?* Suggest situations and circumstances that might change the limits of safe credit for a particular family. Determine the limits of safe credit for typical families with $100 and $200 per week incomes.

Compare the actual cost of one hundred dollars' worth of merchandise financed by the following methods:
1 Paying by check
2 Charging goods to your account and paying the full amount within 30 days
3 Charging goods to your account and making equal installment payments for 18 months
4 Borrowing the cash from a finance company and repaying the loan in equal installments for 18 months

COURTESY CELANESE FIBERS MARKETING COMPANY

Many stores provide expert help for coordinating large purchases such as fabrics, papers, paints, and furniture for a given home.

of record you want, you may save time by telephoning the various stores for prices. This enables you to make a comparison without going from store to store.

It is always important to buy from a store you know to be reliable. There may be a variety of reliable stores. You might consider a store near your home or where transportation is convenient. If you're in a hurry, you may prefer a store with trained salespeople rather than a self-service market. The best selection of a store combines all the good aspects of shopping. You have made a wise choice of marketplaces when, with the least amount of time, energy, and money, you can buy the needed goods.

How to pay

Credit cards and checks have largely replaced currency in the marketplaces. An interbank charge card is another form of credit which can be used for buying goods on credit in a wide variety of stores across the country. Transportation systems and vending-machine owners in various large cities have developed plans for accepting tokens in exchange for services. The tokens may be bought at banks and various marketplaces.

Even with the trend toward credit buying on the upsurge, cash buying remains a form of buying by which millions of dollars' worth of trading is done each year. Buying situations vary. Either cash or credit may be used depending on the situation.

CASH PAYMENT

Have you known people who say they pay cash for everything? Often they seem proud to say that, if they can't pay cash for something, they won't buy it. Often such people are very successful shoppers. Debt-free families are usually happier than debt-ridden families. While they often have less material goods, many say their freedom from concern over debts offsets their lack of possessions.

While there are many advantages to cash buying, there are some disadvantages. People who pay cash, but keep few records, may have only vague ideas of how their money was spent. This makes it very difficult to evaluate spending habits. Also, since credit ratings are developed through payment habits, *cash-only* buyers actually have no credit rating. The lack of a credit rating may be a real problem if such a family decides to buy a home, car, or home appliance on credit.

USING CREDIT

Recent studies indicate that people who use credit have more material goods than families of equal income who don't. However, serious family problems can be traced to the overuse of credit.

From the time you first use credit, you are establishing a credit rating. Any time a person uses credit in a community, he establishes a credit-risk record. Further, families known for their steady payment of debts have established a good credit rating. This credit rating may be a real asset if such a family decides to make a large credit purchase. The record may be kept by a profit-making credit bureau, or it may be operated by a group of businesses. A good credit rating indicates that you pay your bills on time. Stores, banks, and insurance companies with whom you do business, and even prospective employers, may be interested in your credit rating.

Cost of credit

Understanding the costs of various kinds of credit helps you to understand when each can be used best to reach a certain goal. Perhaps you buy a pair of shoes, charge them to your parents' account in the store, and your parents pay for them less than a month later. Thirty-day credit is considered to be cash payment. No noticeable charges are made for this kind of credit. The

Supply words to complete the poem below about Careless Connie Consumer. *Do not* write in this book.

When Connie spends, she's
  not concerned.
The buying facts she has not
  ____.

Connie thinks it's one big bore
To check the price from store
  to ____.

When buying pounds or buying bags,
She seldom stops to read the ____.

If only she could get a loan,
Just think of all the things
  she'd ____.

She needs help, she does indeed,
To separate her wants from ____.

Connie fumes and Connie raves,
So far she can't learn to ____.

Things wouldn't need to look
  so bleak
If she'd put aside some every
  ____.

If she used resources with
  some care,
Her pockets wouldn't be so ____.

But every cent she ever earns,
Will soon be gone unless
  she ____.

Please help Connie. Suggest a
  few
Buying habits she ought to ____.

231

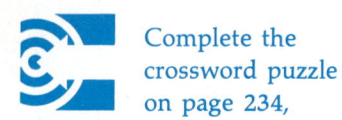

Complete the crossword puzzle on page 234, using a separate sheet of paper for the answers. *Do not* write in this book.

ACROSS

2. A penny is a small ____.
4. Instant credit is available with a bank credit ____.
5. Food is a(an) ____ for everyone.
8. The things you have to help you reach your goals are your ____.
11. Read the ____ of any contract.
13. In establishing priorities, you consider your needs and ____.
14. If you once got credit from a bank, the bank ____ you money.
15. It is difficult to have a credit rating if you pay ____ for everything.
17. What you have to pay is what you ____.
18. You settle a debt when you ____ your bill.
19. Some states have both income and sales ____.
23. In some families your allowance depends on your ____.
25. Air and water are ____ resources.
26. One of your basic resources is ____.
27. Currency is a form of ____.
28. Merchandise and products for sale are sometimes called ____.

cost of this service is absorbed by the store, which in turn pays for it by selling at higher prices. Your parents might decide to buy a car, finance it through a bank or automobile-finance corporation, and pay for it within a two- or three-year period. You may have relatives who buy a house, finance it through a savings and loan association, and agree to pay for it over a period of twenty-five or thirty years. Different situations call for different kinds of credit, each available at a different interest rate.

In general, the length of time goods remain resalable determines the cost of interest on money borrowed to pay for them. For example, the cost of credit for buying clothing and household goods is very high. Once used, they have very little resale value. Cars, which have a longer resale value than clothes, can be bought on cheaper credit terms. Real estate, which can be sold and resold year after year, can generally be bought on credit at lower interest than other purchases.

Unfortunately, some people do not have good credit ratings. If they must buy on credit, they are forced to go to lending agencies where very high interest is charged for the use of money. Often a person pays twice as much for the use of money borrowed from such lending agencies or on revolving store charge plans as he would pay if he were able to borrow at lower interest rates. It may become necessary to take advantage of poor credit terms from time to time. If you have any doubts about the real cost of credit in a given situation, ask for help. Particularly if you are being rushed to sign a contract, you will be wise to obtain the help of a free legal aide or some other trusted financial adviser.

Credit cards

Many department stores, motel chains, and oil companies send credit cards to large numbers of people. Such cards may be obtained for use in several stores in a single community or for use in a certain chain of stores all across the country. Some cards are secured by applying for them. When the applicant has a good credit rating, cards are sent promptly. There is no charge for the cards. Neither is there a charge for credit when bills are paid within thirty days of billing. Persons receiving credit cards they do not want should destroy them by cutting them into small pieces.

Bank credit cards may offer *instant credit*. Such cards may be used in service stations, beauty salons, department stores, restaurants, and many other marketplaces. The card owner uses it to make a purchase in a store. The store sends credit slips to the bank daily. The bank subtracts a given amount, perhaps

1 or 2 percent, from the credit slip, and deposits the rest to the account of the store. The bank then bills the credit-card owner at the end of the month with the amount of the sale. As in other forms of credit, stores offering to do bank-credit-card business must absorb the cost of the service. This cost is passed on to customers in the form of increased prices.

Advantages and disadvantages of credit cards are subjects of frequent discussion. Actually the problems often cited involve the users themselves rather than the credit cards. With the easy credit a card provides, some people overspend. However, many people feel the advantages credit cards offer offset the disadvantages.

No doubt there have been times when families have felt it was unsafe to carry large sums of money. With credit cards, they can carry small sums and still obtain the goods and services they need and want. Credit cards also offer security to persons away from home in the event of an emergency.

Many people prefer to have written records of all expenditures. Such people, if not tempted to spend recklessly, find credit-card services quite convenient. In addition, there are times when they may wish to buy something but will not have the money until payday. Rather than risk having someone else buy the item, they simply use a credit card. When using credit cards, avoid charging more than you have planned to spend, whether your money is in your pocket, in the bank, or in the form of unpaid wages.

Lost credit cards can be more serious than lost money. The finder of a lost credit card may charge things to the owner's account, and the owner is legally obligated to pay for them. In case of loss, the owner should immediately notify the company that issued the card, informing them by telephone *and* by letter. This will enable the company to stop all charging of goods or services to the old card number and to issue a new card. A card user is not obligated to pay for goods or services charged to a lost-card number after a company has acknowledged his loss.

Installment contracts

Such items as TV sets, furniture, and appliances are frequently bought on an installment plan. The buyer pays a certain amount of cash as a down payment and then signs a contract agreeing to pay the remainder, so much per month, during a stated period of time. In addition to the cost of the item, he also pays carrying charges. These charges include interest, credit charges, and perhaps insurance. Carrying charges add appreciable amounts to the real cost of installment purchases. Installment plans

DOWN
1 An advertisement is sometimes called a(an) ____.
2 Currency is used less than in the past because of the more frequent use of credit cards and ____.
3 Consumers buy and ____ goods and services.
4 Your payment habits will determine your ____ rating.
6 Rent is a fixed ____.
7 A self-service store with lower prices may be a(an) ____ store.
9 A bank is one place to keep ____.
10 Fatigue can be caused by ____.
12 The foods you eat affect your ____.
15 The price of an item is the same as the ____ to the consumer.
16 The largest expenditure many families ever make is for a(an) ____.
18 A budget is actually a(an) ____ for spending and saving.
20 Summer clothes may be placed on ____ in the early fall.
21 Intelligence and creativity are ____ resources.
22 If you do not read the fine print in a contract you may be very ____.
24 Interest is the money you ____ on a savings account.
26 Information about fiber content is found on a label or ____.

Defend the statement: *Honorable businessmen prefer to deal with informed customers.*

In your own words, define the following terms:
Consumer
Credit
Credit card
Fixed expenses
Flexible expenses
Goods
Interest
Installment contract
Services
Status symbol

Fill in the spaces by completing the statements found in the side columns on pages 232 and 233. *Do not* write in this book.

Reputable stores replace unsatisfactory purchases, returning faulty goods to companies that have manufactured them.

usually provide that, if the buyer fails to make payments, the merchandise can be repossessed by the seller.

Anyone using installment credit should read and understand the fine print in the contract. The buyer should consult a financial expert if he doesn't understand the conditions of the contract. Installment payments to be paid over an exceedingly long period of time are generally to be avoided. Often carrying charges paid over the years amount to more than the price marked on an item.

Business-consumer interaction

Perhaps after watching the operations of certain businesses and the misuse of their consumer rights on the part of some consumers, you wonder whether business can survive. Many consumers seem to buy without knowing, use without reading instructions, give very little thought to quality, avoid paying promptly, keep no record of when articles are bought, and misuse merchandise when shopping. To what degree is consumer protection deserved? How many of America's businessmen deal unfairly with consumers?

Most consumers are honorable purchasers. Most businesses are run by honorable businessmen. Laws have been enacted to protect the vast consuming public against a few businesses who might deceive them. All consumers and businesses should be equally interested in reforming the proportionately small number of consumers who practice poor consumer activities. Only when business and the consumer work together will both prosper. At that time, business can be profitable, and the consumer can get a dollar's worth of goods for a dollar spent.

12 CHAPTER POSTTEST

Number from 1 to 30. Beside each number indicate if the corresponding statement is true or false. *Do not write in this book.*

1. A consumer is a person who helps make or produce goods.
2. When a boy has his hair cut at the barber shop he is actually buying goods.
3. Spending money for status symbols may be a means of seeking security and acceptance.
4. The purposes of advertising are to sell goods and services, to provide information, and to create wants.
5. Advertising may be planned to appeal to the buyer's emotions rather than to his common sense.
6. Advertising that provides accurate information about a product is called factual advertising.
7. An informed and alert consumer can be his own best protection against business concerns that try to take advantage of him.
8. Federal and state laws designed to protect consumers apply only to clothing, foods, drugs, and cosmetics.
9. If a consumer has purchased faulty merchandise, the first thing he should do is to make a complaint to the Federal Trade Commission.
10. The season of the year affects the price and quality of many fresh produce food items.
11. Many stores have sales after Christmas and in mid-summer.
12. The time of the year when school clothes are least expensive is in late August, or just before school begins.
13. Seconds are usually sold at the same price as other merchandise if the flaws do not affect the usability of the goods.
14. If time and energy permit, it is a good consumer practice to compare the price and quality of merchandise before buying.
15. More sales are made through telephone calls and mail orders than through any other type of transaction.
16. Trading stamp stores, car-wash stations, and shopping malls are examples of marketplaces.
17. Credit buying has almost disappeared from the consumer economy.
18. The best way to establish a good credit rating is to pay for everything with cash.
19. Families that use credit often have more material possessions than families with similar incomes that do not use credit.
20. Bank credit cards can be used in many different types of markets.
21. A 30-day credit account is often considered cash payment.
22. The cost of credit when buying clothing is usually less than the cost of credit when buying a home.
23. The cost of obtaining a credit card is usually 2 percent of the total charged purchases made during the first month.
24. When families are traveling away from home, they may find that using credit cards is a real convenience.
25. One of the disadvantages of using credit cards is the possibility of overspending.
26. One disadvantage of paying cash for all purchases is the necessity for keeping fairly extensive written records.
27. A credit card owner is legally obligated to pay for merchandise charged to his account.
28. Carrying charges paid over a long period of time add little to the total cost of goods purchased through installment contracts.
29. The Truth-in-Lending Act requires that information on the true interest rate be available for the consumer.
30. A monthly finance charge of 1½ percent is the same rate as a yearly finance charge of 18 percent.

4
Your Home Economics Department

Looking at the department
Improving the department
Caring for the department

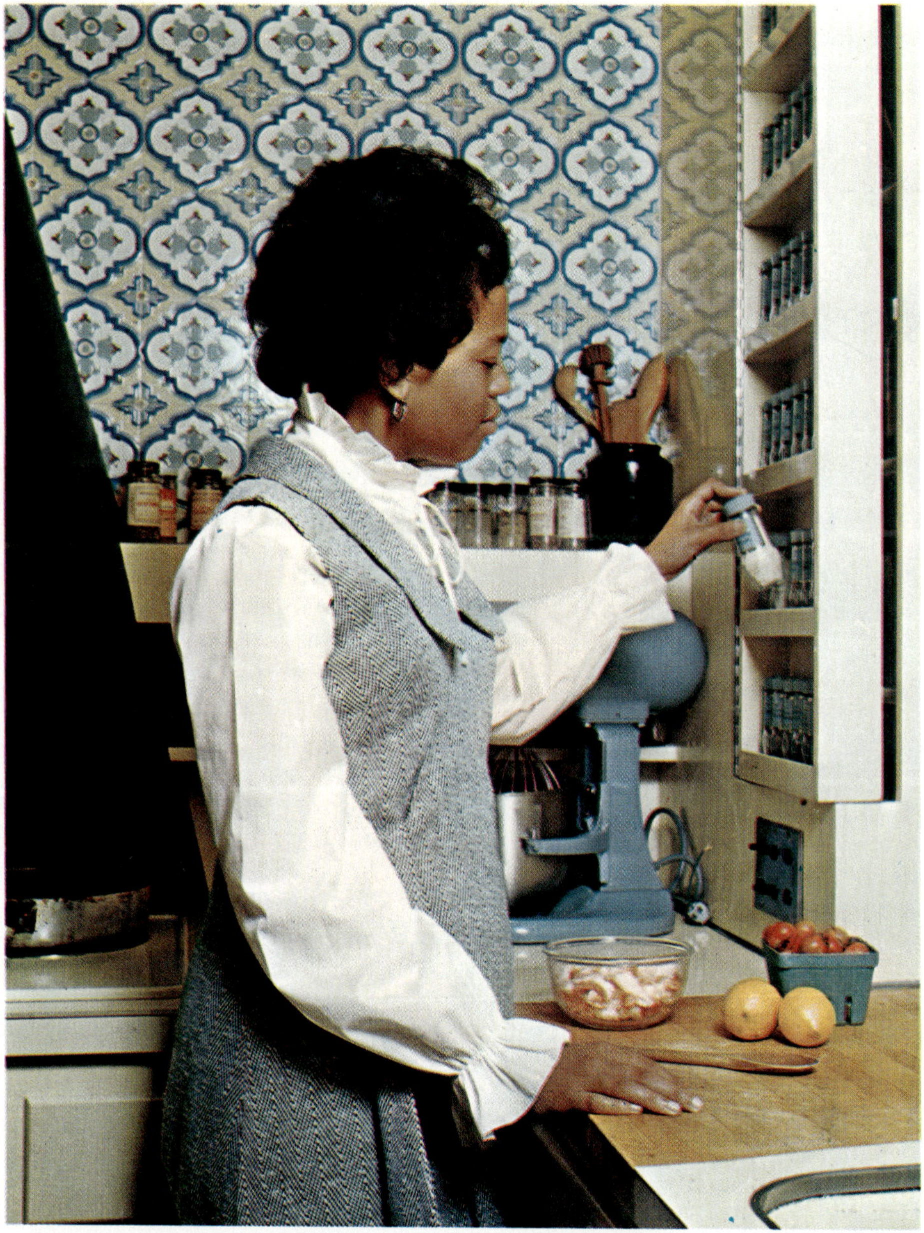

Your home economics department

Your career
Professional home economist

Duties: May develop, interpret, and apply principles of homemaking to promote health and welfare of individuals and families. May advise homemakers in selection and utilization of household equipment, food, and clothing, or interpret homemaker's needs to manufacturers of household products.

May write advertising copy and articles of interest to homemakers, test recipes, equipment, or new household products, conduct radio and television programs, or perform other public relations and promotion work for business firms, newspapers, magazines, or radio and television stations. May advise individuals and families concerning budget and other home management problems. May teach improved homemaking practices to homemakers and youths through educational programs, demonstrations, discussions, or home visits.

ARMSTRONG FLOORING

The home economics department is really very much like a home at school. It is more than just a classroom; it is a place where pupils may develop skills and attitudes for happier living both at home and away.

In the home economics department you may have many opportunities to learn to . . .

1. Understand yourself as a person and your family as people.
2. Respect and appreciate other people, especially those in your family and your school environment.
3. Manage your time, energy, and money.
4. Improve your health and grooming practices.
5. Help with the development of young children.
6. Help with the care of family members who are ill.
7. Select, make, and care for home furnishings.
8. Select, use, and care for home equipment.
9. Select, make, and care for clothing.
10. Select, prepare, serve, and care for food.

There are some differences between working in the home economics department and working at home. While at home you may frequently work alone, at school you work in groups, sharing activities and equipment. You learn how to get along with others of your own age, and you work with all class members rather than only with those that you know best.

At school, also, you may be required to budget your time and money more carefully than you have been doing at home. The things you work with at school may be very different from those to which you have been accustomed. You may find a greater variety in brands and models of equipment at school. The equipment may be better than, or possibly not so good as, that in your home. Both at home and at school, it is necessary to share equipment and materials.

Looking at the department

Home economics in your school will probably be taught in specially planned and equipped classrooms in the school building. The number of these rooms depends upon the size of the school and the number of students who take home economics courses. Some schools have a homemaking cottage or an apartment for the use of the pupils. In small schools the department frequently is a *multipurpose*, or *all-purpose*, room which provides facilities for many areas of home economics education. In larger schools there may be two, three, or more rooms with equipment grouped for more specific uses. There may be a room for food preparation and service, a room for constructing clothing and home furnishings, a living-dining area, a laundry and storage space, and a room equipped for teaching child development and care. In addition to these laboratories, there may be space for

May engage in research to explore family relations or child development. May develop new products for homes, search for facts on food or nutrition, or test serviceability of new materials.

Where employed: Schools, industry, government, equipment or utility companies, research division of food and textile companies, newspapers, magazines, or radio and TV stations.

Cured leaves and artificial flowers may be combined into attractive floral arrangements which are long-lasting, colorful additions to a learning center.

COURTESY BETTER HOMES AND GARDENS, © MEREDITH CORPORATION, 1967

Use the following set of guidelines to open the home economics department efficiently. While arranging the department, make a step-by-step plan for storing the equipment and supplies when the department is closed at the end of the school year.

1. Clean cabinets and reline with shelf paper.
2. Clean woodwork, walls, windows, mirrors, chairs, tables, and bookshelves.
3. Inventory entire department, and check each item against last year's inventory. Put utensils and equipment in convenient places. Report any missing items to the teacher.
4. Unpack and arrange books and illustrative materials.
5. Clean each piece of equipment, and check to see that it is in operating condition.
6. Oil and regulate sewing machines.
7. Launder linens and draperies if necessary before using them.
8. Wax and polish furniture; arrange for convenient use.
9. Polish metal accessories and equipment.
10. Hang pictures and place accessories attractively. Choose and begin care of growing plants which will make each area look attractive.

Most home economics departments provide modern equipment which students can learn to use and care for.

COURTESY WESTINGHOUSE ELECTRIC CORPORATION

240

consumer education, home management, and human development.

THE EQUIPMENT
In any arrangement of rooms, it is necessary to have certain basic equipment and furnishings in order to carry on the desired learning activities. For preparing meals, you may expect to find a range, a sink, a refrigerator, base cabinets, wall cabinets, tables, and chairs—all arranged in unit kitchens, each of which accommodates a group of several students working together. For clothing construction, there will be worktables, chairs, sewing machines, pressing equipment, and space for supplies and clothing projects. For learning about laundering, there will probably be an automatic washer and dryer and space for using all of the special laundering equipment. In these rooms, or in other rooms adjoining, there may be a place where you can practice hospitality by entertaining guests and learn how to care for children by watching and working with them in their activities. There may be child-size furniture and toys if you work with young children in a laboratory arrangement. Many departments provide a place for practicing care of the sick, personal grooming, and crafts.

THE STORAGE SPACE
A place to put things when they are not in use is necessary in a well-organized home economics department. In fact, provision for storage of equipment is just as important at school as it is at home. In your home economics rooms, you will probably find built-in or movable storage cabinets for small equipment. Aprons, cleaning materials, reference materials, and clothing under construction must be stored. Such storage space may be improvised, if necessary, at little expense, but some kind is needed.

Storage cabinets are needed in the foods laboratory as well as in the other parts of the home economics department. It is necessary to store staple foods as well as cooking utensils, tableware, linens, laundry supplies, and cleaning supplies. Tall cabinets with shelves, rods, or hooks are useful, and both wall cabinets and base cabinets should be included.

When planning storage, use the principle of *storage at point of first use.* According to this plan, supplies and equipment used in preparing food at the sink are stored close to the sink. Utensils used in cooking are stored at the range. China and flatware are stored near the serving center or dining room.

Improving the department

By studying your own department, you may note some ways in which it can be made more convenient and attractive. The convenience of a

Rate the arrangement of the equipment in your home economics department. To the following, add other suggestions which might apply to your own department.

1. Are students assigned to sewing machines and worktables which are located close to each other?
2. Are ironing boards accessible to worktables and sewing machines?
3. Are ironing boards and electric equipment placed out of the line of traffic and so that long extension cords are unnecessary?
4. Are sewing machines placed for effective lighting?
5. Are worktables in the food preparation center placed for effective use with the ranges and refrigerators?
6. Are the refrigerators easily accessible to the groups using them?
7. Are worktables placed for effective lighting and for use with the chalkboard during discussion periods?
8. Is the arrangement satisfactory for other types of classwork such as crafts or special assignments in various areas such as child growth or first aid?

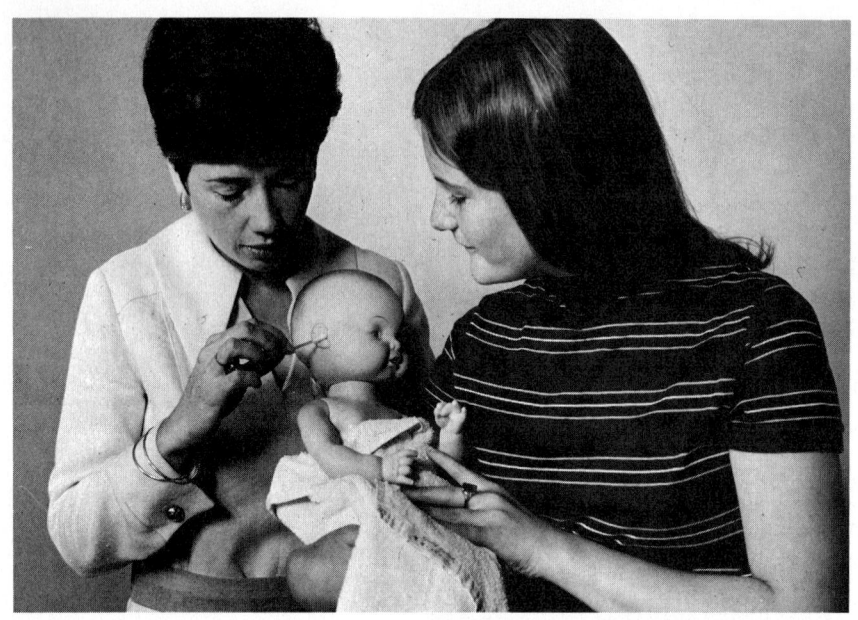

Special areas may be provided for the study of first aid, baby care, and child development.

department depends, to a great extent, on the placement of furniture and equipment. Attractiveness depends on *centers of interest,* or focal points, such as window groupings, bookshelves, or a bulletin board which will add color or interest to an area. The department will be a more pleasing place to work when interesting accessories such as pictures and dried or living plants are added, also. (See page 239.)

IMPROVING THE ARRANGEMENT OF THE FURNITURE

In any room the furniture can be more effectively arranged if comfort and convenience are considered. In a home economics department, as well as at home, it is necessary to consider ways to save time and energy. Some of the equipment is stationary and cannot be rearranged, so a plan which calls for moving furniture for convenience must also consider the pieces that must remain where they are now located.

The worktables

A convenient place for clothing-room worktables is near the sewing machines. In the food-preparation areas, or unit kitchens, the tables are convenient when placed near the range and refrigerator. Some thought should be given to table arrangements which allow students to face in one direction when discussion is in progress or films are being shown.

COURTESY VIKING SEWING MACHINE COMPANY

Clothing and textile experiences offer opportunities for students who want to make their own clothing as well as for those who want to learn a vocational skill.

The sewing machines
Location of sewing machines is determined by the sources of light and electricity. If possible, position sewing machines so that light falls naturally over the left shoulder of the person sewing. It is important that electric extension cords be placed so they will not interfere with traffic through the room.

The pressing equipment
For safety and convenience, locate pressing equipment near the sewing machines but out of the line of traffic.

The mirrors and fitting stands
Since students can learn by observing the fitting of garments, place mirrors and fitting stands in an area where students can observe as fitting is done. Of course, privacy for removing and putting on the garments is necessary. A screen may be used if a dressing room is not available.

WINDOWS AND WALLS
It is possible to use the wall spaces and window areas to make the home economics department seem pleasant and homelike.

Rate the appearance of your home economics department. If appropriate, make suggestions for improvement.

Is the housekeeping acceptable?
   Floors, lower parts of equipment, and mopboards clean; equipment and work surfaces clean; window, shades, blinds, and curtains clean; refrigerators and ranges clean; tables, chairs, and bookshelves dusted and in order.

Is the department in good repair?
   Paint free from stain and scaling; equipment in working order; water faucets and gas jets free from leaks; doors and drawers easy to open and close.

Are there signs of good management?
   Equipment efficiently arranged; supplies suitably stored and labeled; out-of-date materials discarded; sewing machines and other equipment protected from rain and sun.

Is the department attractive?
   Color scheme of room harmonious; windows suitably treated and curtained; furniture and accessories arranged for beauty and efficiency.

Your career
Home economics extension agent

Duties: Instructs and advises adults and teen-agers in developing programs to improve family life. Works with families of various sizes and incomes to provide for their food, clothing, housing, and child care needs. Visits homes to advise families on problems such as family budgeting and home remodeling. Organizes and advises clubs, and assists in discussions and demonstrations in subjects such as sewing, food preparation, and home decoration. May write leaflets and articles or talk over radio and television to inform the general public in areas of special interest such as consumer education or home management. Participates in community activities such as judging at rural fairs. May direct 4-H Club activities.
Where employed: State or county offices of the Federal, state, or state university extension service.

Windows
Many departments are built so that windows can become the center of interest in one or more rooms. The rooms may have entire walls of windows from the ceiling down to counter or floor level. Such windows may be tinted or curtained to cut down glare and to make the room more attractive. If curtaining the entire window area is too expensive, other decorating methods may be worked out.

Walls
Color can be added to walls in a variety of ways. Murals and wall hangings are effective. Wallpaper can be used to add interest to a single wall or to cover an unused chalkboard. Wall planters, too, are bright and attractive if they are well arranged.

Bulletin boards
Bulletin boards, or tack boards, can be both educational and attractive. They can be used to publicize events, to give information, to create and maintain interest in a class activity, or to display projects completed by class members.

In preparing a display on a tack board or elsewhere, it is important to arrange the materials neatly and artistically. Any item containing reading matter should be placed so that it can be easily read. When kept up-to-date by frequent changes, the bulletin board adds interest to the home economics department.

ADDING FURNISHINGS AND ACCESSORIES
The home economics department will be more attractive in appearance if colorful furniture, pictures, and other accessories are used. Choose furnishings and accessories to harmonize with those already in place. Try to choose accessories which are attractive and serve the purpose for which they are intended. It is important that furnishings and accessories be easy to clean.

Furniture finishing and refinishing
Often a club or class will decide to improve the appearance of the department by finishing or refinishing one or more small pieces of furniture. An unfinished bookcase, coffee table, or small cabinet may be painted, antiqued, or varnished to make an attractive addition to the room.

For help in finishing or refinishing furniture, consult books, government publications, or an expert, such as the teacher of industrial arts.

Slipcovers and cushions
Furniture may be slipcovered, or bright-colored cushions can be made at relatively small cost. If the slipcovers or cushions are well chosen, they will add color and in-

terest to the room and protect the furniture as well.

Pictures

Color and interest can be added to a room by hanging pictures. Several small pictures grouped interestingly together or one large picture can become a center of interest. Reproductions of good paintings or the original art work of talented students are inexpensive and pleasing. Pictures such as flower or bird prints may be cut from magazines, mounted on plywood or corrugated cardboard, and shellacked. Charts, finger paintings, or maps which blend with other colors in the room may be displayed.

Pictures look best if they are hung straight and at eye level. They should rest flat against the wall. If it is not possible to put the necessary hooks in the wall, it might be possible to hang the pictures from the ceiling molding by two parallel wires.

Flowers or growing plants

Probably no other effort adds more hominess to a department than the addition of cut flowers or growing plants. Any room becomes more pleasing with fresh flowers attractively arranged. (See page 239.) When fresh flowers are not available, green foliage, dried leaves or grasses, pine cones, and seeds make good substitutes. Bowls of fresh fruits and vegetables are colorful

and appropriate. Permanent arrangements of artificial plants and flowers are inexpensive and interesting.

Other furnishings and accessories

Your imagination and willingness to put forth effort are the limiting factors when determining ways to improve the attractiveness of the home economics department. A display of new fabrics, colorful dinnerware, lamps, a folding screen, a room divider, or a whatnot shelf may give warmth and life to a room. Color

Necessary equipment and supplies can be arranged to give the home economics department a homelike atmosphere.

COURTESY FARLEY MANNING ASSOCIATES, INC.

List the essential requirements for a good home economics department such as the following:
Adequate light, heat, and ventilation
Convenient, safe, and attractive arrangement of furniture and equipment
Adequate equipment and space for each area of study
Sufficient storage space

Check the bulletin board you have made for the home economics department. Answer the following questions to determine its effectiveness.

Does it serve any of the following purposes?
   Supplement classroom discussion
   Emphasize a concept
   Present a new idea
   Create interest, inspire, or motivate

Does it attract attention by one of the following methods?
   Catchy title through a play on words, unusual spelling, or interesting arrangement of letters
   Interesting textures such as burlap, corrugated paper, fishnet, flannel, or tissue paper
   Variety of shapes
   Real objects such as boxes, labels, grooming articles, or toys

Has color been used for one of the following purposes?
   To attract attention
   To create a mood
   To provide an association

may be added to bookshelves by covering a set of books with brightly colored adhesive paper. Other accessories too, such as mirrors, vases, pillows, bookends, and wastebaskets, if selected according to suitability and beauty, add to the appearance of a department.

Avoid having too many accessories in a room. A few good ones that are given adequate space are better than a great many which make a room look cluttered. Accessories may be changed and put away from time to time so that other things may be brought out.

Accessories that are in good taste can be bought for a small amount of money if an effort is made to find them.

PROTECTING FURNISHINGS
A class may work many weeks to make the home economics rooms attractive, only to find that in a very short time the furniture and accessories have become scarred, stained, or chipped. Since more people use the home economics department than the average home, care is necessary in the use of furniture in order to retain its attractive appearance and prolong its usefulness.

MAKING BEST USE OF STORAGE
It is necessary to have some place to put illustrative materials and pieces of equipment when they are not in use. Certainly nothing detracts more from the appearance of the home economics department than does the sight of unused materials and equipment left scattered around.

A plan for storing each article will be a valuable guide. In some home economics departments the students have planned with their teacher just where each article will be stored. They have considered where, and with what, the articles will be used, and they have tried to store them conveniently.

Time allowed in the daily schedule for putting things away will help to keep equipment in order. This is an important part of management.

Caring for the department

In every home economics department there are many routine housekeeping duties. Some must be performed before and after each class, some daily, some occasionally, and some seasonally. These duties can be rotated so that they can be shared by each member of each class. It is a good idea to make a chart on which duties are listed, together with the names of the class members, rotating the chores according to the plans made by the class and teacher.

DAILY HOUSEKEEPING
There are some jobs that need to be done each day if the department is to look its best.

COURTESY GREEN BAY WISC. PUBLIC SCHOOLS

Organization of storage shelves and cabinets is necessary so that a large number of students may locate and use the equipment which is provided.

Dusting
Tables, desks, sewing machines, bookshelves, window sills, chairs, and accessories require daily dusting. A clean, dry cloth, preferably chemically treated, should be used to pick up dust without scattering it. A feather duster only scatters the dust. A vacuum cleaner with special attachments is useful in removing accumulated dust from many of the pieces of furniture in the department.

Caring for the floors
Floors require daily care. To ensure beauty and to prevent damage, follow directions given for the particular flooring material in the room. Most schools provide custodial services for floors within a department. However, spilled water or food should be wiped up immediately in order to preserve the appearance of the floor and to prevent accidents. Asphalt tile or plastic tile can be dented or scratched if heavy furniture is dragged across it or if students make a practice of tilting back in their chairs.

Sweeping with a broom at the end of each class period is not recommended. It disturbs the class and stirs up dust. Sweeping so fre-

Is the lettering practical from the following points of view?
  Easy to read
  Appropriate to the subject
  Easy to render

Does it create a favorable impression when considered from the following points of view?
  Pictures attractively mounted
  Uncluttered appearance with only a few representative pictures or items
  No more than three main colors
  A worthwhile message of current value

Have the principles of design been used to provide the following?
  Pleasing balance
  Pleasing proportion and interesting treatment of space
  Good rhythm to lead the eye from one subconcept to another
  Effective emphasis with only one main center of interest
  Unity or harmony with only one theme, or central message

Is it practical?
  Reusable
  Easily stored
  Easy to put up and easy to take down

247

Follow these guidelines when arranging pictures in the home economics department.

1 Hang pictures so that they are related to a piece of furniture or a group of furniture pieces.
2 Consider as wall space the entire wall area between the ceiling and top of a piece of furniture placed against the wall. Also consider the width of the furniture or grouping.
3 For a vertical wall space, use a vertical picture or group of pictures to form a vertical panel within the space.
4 For a horizontal wall space, use a horizontal picture or group of pictures to form a horizontal panel within the space.
5 Hang small pictures, especially photographs, in groups.
6 Avoid hanging pictures in a stair-step arrangement unless there is a lamp, drapery, or some other item to lead the eye downward from the highest pictures.
7 Avoid hanging pictures so that the wire or hooks can be seen.
8 Study interior decoration magazines and books for good arrangement ideas.

COURTESY COLONIAL HIGH SCHOOL, ORLANDO, FLORIDA

The home economics student can learn commercial food preparation in cooperative courses set up by the school system and local business.

quently will not be necessary if scraps, pins, papers, and trash are kept off the floor or picked up at once. If custodial service is not available, class members may clean the floors at the end of the school day. A vacuum cleaner is preferred for this cleaning, but it is satisfactory to use a broom if the sweeping is done correctly. Sweeping compounds may be helpful. Pupils may wish to practice correct methods of floor care at school or as projects in their rooms at home.

Cleaning the chalkboards
Chalkboards require daily care any time they are used. Include the chalk trays and erasers in this cleaning detail. The school custodian can supply information about the best way to clean them.

Arranging books and magazines
Current magazines and reference books which are readily accessible and neatly displayed add to the usefulness and beauty of a room. Plastic covers help to protect them. Piles of old magazines and rows of tattered, out-of-date books are unsightly and should be discarded.

Attractive bookends may be made from painted bricks or wood. Inexpensive ones may be purchased.

Caring for plants and cut flowers

Plants and cut flowers require daily care if they are to add to the beauty of a room. Plants need frequent watering, and dead leaves should be removed. To keep cut flowers fresh, add fresh lukewarm water to the container each day. Often an entire arrangement of flowers will have to be discarded and a fresh one substituted. A plant, too, may occasionally need to be replaced. From time to time, plants should be fertilized, the leaves washed, and the flowerpot or container cleaned. Vinegar solution can be used to remove the rings from the inside of flower vases. If necessary, let vases stand in a hot mixture which is half vinegar and half water.

Cleaning lavatories and kitchen sinks

Sanitation requires that lavatories and sinks be cleaned frequently. Scraps of paper, soap, and hair should be removed from the lavatory. Rinse off the bar of soap after use, and return it to the soap dish. Keep paper towels in the container provided for them.

Any one of several good scouring powders on the market will be useful in cleaning the sink. Avoid scouring powder which will scratch or discolor the sink surface. Strong acids should never be poured into the sink. Grease may stop up sinks, especially those that do not contain waste-disposal units.

COURTESY FARLEY MANNING ASSOCIATES, INC.

Foods laboratories may provide well-arranged demonstration kitchens where students learn by watching, or unit kitchens where students work together.

COURTESY ARMSTRONG FLOORING

Demonstrate flower arranging with real or artificial flowers. Make some arrangements that can be used as table centerpieces during your study of foods and nutrition. Make other arrangements which are suitable accessories for use in other areas of the department. Find various items around the school that might be used to hold the arrangements.

Putting things in order
An entire room may look in disarray during a class session, but plans can be worked out so that it is left in order at the end of every class period. Students may decide to take turns in being responsible for checking the orderliness of the area when the session ends. It will help to have a chart listing the proper place for textbooks, illustrative materials, food supplies, tableware, cooking utensils, table accessories, and pressing equipment. Location of sewing machines, tables, and chairs can also be listed on the chart.

Laundering kitchen linens
Clean dish cloths are necessary for each work session in the foods laboratory. In order to provide this sanitary precaution, some method must be devised for washing the kitchen linens after each lesson in food preparation. An automatic washer and dryer are convenient. If the department does not have them, the towels can be sent to a laundry or washed in hot, soapy water, rinsed well, and hung to dry. If a dryer is not available in a department, care must be exercised to see that several sets of dish towels are available. This plan provides dish towels for classes who may need them while towels from earlier classes are drying.

Caring for the range and refrigerator
Spills and spots on the inside and outside of the range and refrigerator can be wiped off before a class period ends. Allow the range to cool before using a wet cloth on it. Surface elements and ovens in the range are usually cool enough for cleaning by the end of the class period. (See page 240.)

The refrigerator requires daily care. Its contents should be examined so that spoiled foods can

Many home economics departments provide laundry equipment with which students can learn to correctly wash and dry various kinds of fabric.

COURTESY CULLIGAN INTERNATIONAL COMPANY

be discarded and leftovers used promptly. (See page 240.)

Removing trash and garbage
Routinely check the trash and garbage containers. If there are several small trash containers or wastebaskets in the clothing room and a small garbage container in each unit kitchen, empty them after each class session. Place the waste in the large containers provided by the school. Wrap the garbage in paper before placing it in the large garbage can and replacing the cover. Reline the garbage cans in the unit kitchens with paper or paper bags. Many schools have electric garbage-disposal units to simplify the garbage-removal problem.

OCCASIONAL HOUSEKEEPING DUTIES
Many cleaning jobs do not have to be done every day but still require occasional scheduling. It is a good idea to have a plan for doing each job in the very best way. In some schools the pupils in home economics classes have listed on cards the various cleaning chores and the materials to use, as well as the time required, to complete each chore. Then on cleaning day each class member selects a card listing a job that will be a new experience.

In order to care for the equipment in the department effectively, the teacher and students set up and maintain a file of up-to-date information about all equipment. The instruction booklet that accompanied each appliance as it was installed is kept for use by those operating the appliance. Before using any appliance, it is important to learn how to use it.

SEASONAL HOUSEKEEPING DUTIES
In many schools the pupils take an active part in opening and closing the home economics department at the beginning and end of the school year. Many of the activities are similar to those necessary in opening and closing a house before and after an extended absence. (See the side column on page 240.)

COURTESY FUTURE HOMEMAKERS OF AMERICA

The home economics department is often used for Future Homemaker Projects.

Make suggestions for window treatments that might be used in the home economics department. Consider the following list and add other ideas.

Panels of suitable drapery fabric, lined or unlined, may be hung at the ends of the window area or on wall spaces between the blocks of windows in the clothing room or living-dining room.

Drapes or curtains may be made of muslin with designs made of textile paint, applique, embroidery, or rickrack braid. Feed sacks, tobacco cloth, colored cotton, or cotton prints are also inexpensive selections.

For the food-preparation area, cafe curtains may be hung across the lower section of the windows. Avoid hanging curtains over a range unless they are very short. They may collect grease or become a fire hazard.

A cornice board of wood across the top of the entire window area may be painted or covered with fabric to add unity, color, and interest.

Plywood or beaverboard may be shaped to frame the individual windows or the entire window area.

5
Your Clothes

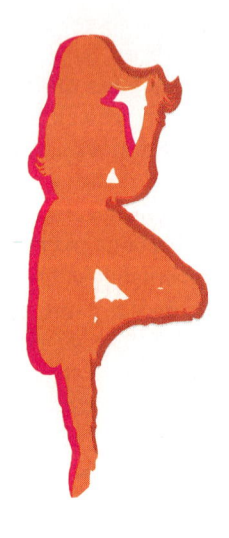

Chapter 13   Choosing clothes for you and your activities

Chapter 14   Buying clothes for use and fashion

Chapter 15   Maintaining your clothes for attractiveness

Chapter 16   Planning projects to match your ability

Chapter 17   Creating clothes to wear and enjoy

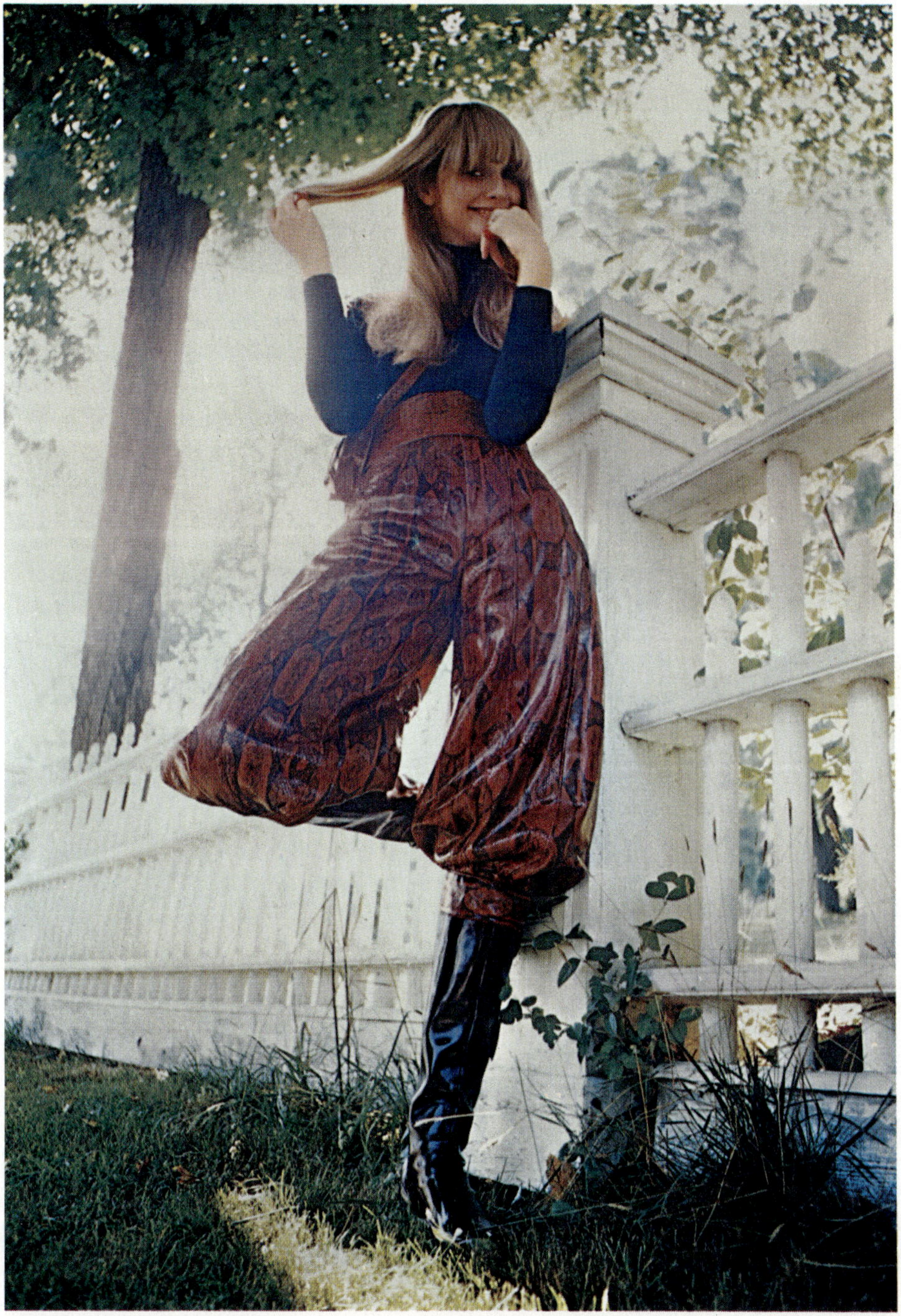

13 CHAPTER PRETEST

Fill in the blank in each sentence with the *best* word to complete the statement. *Do not* write in this book.

1. All skin colors are actually tints and shades of __(1)__.
2. The lightness or darkness of a person's skin color is determined by the amount of __(2)__ his skin contains.
3. In selecting a becoming color, you need to consider your skin, eye, and __(3)__ color.
4. The color which calls out the silhouette, or outline, of a figure most strikingly is __(4)__.
5. Accent colors are correctly used to call attention to your __(5)__ features.
6. The color which best suggests activity, energy, and gaiety is __(6)__.
7. Colors ranging between green and blue-violet are generally placed in a group called __(7)__ colors.
8. Yellow and violet color pigments mixed in equal amounts will produce a(an) __(8)__ color.
9. If you want to appear smaller, choose dark, cool, and __(9)__ colors.
10. The family name of a color is its __(10)__.
11. The brightness or dullness of a color refers to its __(11)__.
12. Colors opposite each other on the color wheel are said to be __(12)__ to one another.
13. The color which is located opposite blue on the color wheel is __(13)__.
14. Pink is a(an) __(14)__ of red.
15. Red, yellow, and orange are generally placed in a group called __(15)__ colors.
16. A single color scheme such as dark, medium, and light green is __(16)__.
17. Red, yellow, and blue make a(an) __(17)__ color scheme.
18. Yellow, yellow-orange, and orange make a(an) __(18)__ color scheme.
19. Colors chosen for clothing and interior decorating reflect an individual's __(19)__.
20. Gloves or a purse which contrasts with the color of your outfit tends to call attention to your __(20)__.
21. A small, narrow-brimmed hat of contrasting color adds __(21)__ to the apparent size of the figure.
22. A rough, nubby, thick fabric will make you look larger because it adds width and __(22)__ to the apparent size of your figure.
23. Light blue in denim, chambray, corduroy, or suede will appear __(23)__ than the same shade of light blue in satin or some other shiny fabric.
24. A person with a long, thin face should try to avoid wearing necklines which are extremely low and __(24)__-shaped.
25. The apparent size of your figure is affected by the line, design, fabric pattern, color, and __(25)__ of the clothes you wear on a particular day.

Match the *descriptions* given in List A with the *types of lines* given in List B. Use a line given in List B only once.

List A: **Descriptions**

A. Feminine
B. Masculine
C. Tall and/or slender
D. Short and/or wide
E. Tall or short depending on the angle

List B: **Types of lines**

1. Curved
2. Diagonal
3. Horizontal
4. Straight
5. Vertical

CHAPTER 13

Choosing clothes for you and your activities

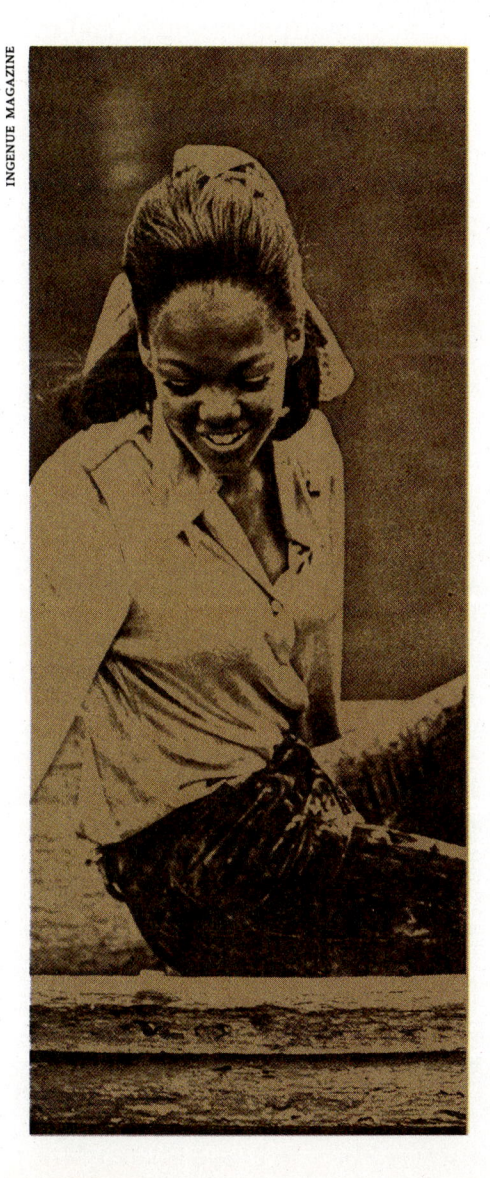

Clothes have long been a favorite topic of interest and conversation in the female world. In recent years the male population has developed a similar interest. History is repeating itself. Once again both sexes are interested in bright colors and clothing fashion.

This interest in clothes is easy to understand when you consider the importance of appearance to your feeling of worth. Ralph Waldo Emerson once said that being well dressed gives a feeling of inward tranquillity which all other forces are powerless to bestow. This is doubtless an overstatement. Nevertheless, if your appearance can bring a feeling of peaceful satisfaction and self-respect, doesn't it seem wise to draw upon every available tool to achieve that feeling?

On the surface it sounds a little shallow to say that clothes make the person. When you think about it, though, maybe clothes are more important than some people realize. If your suit or dress sags, your shirt or blouse is rumpled or soiled, or your shoes need polishing, isn't it natural for people to assume you are careless about other details?

Answer the following questions *Yes* or *No*. *Do not write in this book.*

Do you know . . .
How many clothes you really have?
Which of your clothes need repair?
Which of your clothes are out of style?
About how much money you spend on clothes each month?
Which of your clothes are most comfortable to wear?
Which are your most flattering colors?
Which are your most flattering styles?
What to consider in planning and selecting clothes?

Describe a personal experience in which a person made a good first impression because of his or her choice of clothing. Did your impression of this person change later? Why or why not?

List recent changes in boys' and men's clothing which reflect their interest in fashions.

Determine your own special interests from the items in the following list. Include only the items which you most enjoy.

Discussing why people dress as they do.
Wearing nice clothes.
Going to fashion shows.
Shopping for clothes.
Reading fashion magazines.
Planning what to wear.
Reading about fashion designers.
Buying clothes for others.
Daydreaming about new clothes.
Wearing new clothes.
Designing some of your clothes.
Choosing appropriate accessories.
Looking at pattern books.
Remodeling clothes so they will be in style or will fit better.
Giving good clothes you have outgrown to someone who needs them.
Reading about the clothes that famous people wear.
Reading about the history of clothing.
Looking at mail-order catalogues.

Does your list show that you value clothes? If you enjoy most of the items on this list you might be interested in choosing a career in the field of clothing and textiles.

COURTESY IBERIA INTERNATIONAL AIRLINES OF SPAIN

A good clothing plan allows a person to have suitable clothes for many occasions, whether traveling or staying at home.

Develop a plan

If you are a person who looks *just right* most of the time, you probably already know that, to be well dressed, one must spend a certain amount of time in careful planning. Such planning involves figuring out the kinds of activities you like and the kinds of clothes you need for those activities. Then, it requires that you choose colors, styles, and fabrics that look well on you and with the clothes and accessories you already have.

If you want to look your best and your supply of money is limited, perhaps you need to spend more time planning and less time buying. Start today and try following these suggestions:

1 List the places you go and the things you do.
2 Check the clothes you have. List the number and kinds of clothing according to color and style.
3 Mark the clothes that will need altering to fit properly. Use some other kind of mark for clothes that will need remodeling to be in style. Discard those which cannot be used.
4 Think again about the places you go and the clothes you would like to wear. This will help you decide exactly what clothes you need to buy or make. Write down a list of these clothes.
5 Decide how much money you will be able to spend on each new item. Put the major part of your clothing dollars into the clothing you expect to wear the most.
6 Shop in a number of stores and check several ads before you buy. This will help you know which styles are up-to-date and the price range you can expect to find.
7 Buy only the clothing that fits into your plan. Spur-of-the-

moment shopping should be curtailed, as it usually proves disappointing and expensive.
8 Learn how to select clothing and accessories best suited to your figure, coloring, and personality. A study of color, design, and texture of clothes will help.

Choose clothes for attractiveness

Wise decision making in buying requires several considerations. You want your clothes to be appropriate for your activities and to be in line with the current fashions. However, your greatest concern is how attractive they are on you.

You already know that when you wear certain clothes you feel much happier and more self-confident than when you wear others. The clothes you enjoy the most usually are the ones that are the most becoming to you. They make you look and feel attractive.

COLOR

Color brings vitality to your life. Not only does it affect your feelings but also it affects your looks. The colors you choose can make you feel and look perky, happy, or pretty, or they can make you feel and look droopy and tired.

The colors that you associate with the sun, fire, and warmth are called warm colors. These colors include reds, yellows, and oranges. They make you feel warm, gay, and energetic. The colors you associate with trees, sky, grass, water, and shadows are the cool, or restful, colors. The blues, greens, and purples fall into this category.

As you glance around the room, what are the things that catch your eye first? Doesn't the girl in the bright red dress catch your eye before the girl in the pale blue blouse

Choose three of your garments in which you feel you look your best. Decide why these garments are becoming to you.

Choose three of your garments in which you often feel self-conscious. Decide why they make you feel self-conscious. Determine common problems and discuss possible solutions.

The girl who is told she looks attractive can be reasonably assured that she has chosen clothes which compliment her physical features.

COURTESY SIMPLICITY PATTERN CO. INC.

257

Discuss how your choice of clothing can contribute to some of the following feelings. Name other feelings which can result from your choice of clothing.
  Security
  Confidence
  Poise
  Popularity
  Friendliness
  Attractiveness
  Satisfaction
  Comfort
  Creativity
  Individuality
  Femininity (for girls)
  Masculinity (for boys)

Your career
Fashion designer

Duties: Creates original designs for new types and styles of apparel including almost anything which is a part of the costume of men, women, or children. May design either outer or under garments, hats, purses, shoes, gloves, costume jewelry, scarves, or beachwear. **Where employed:** May work within the garment or accessory industry or for a manufacturer of paper patterns.

who sits next to her? Do you see the brilliant orange books on the shelf before you notice the green ones? Do the warm-colored objects seem to be closer and larger than the cool-colored objects? Do these observations tell you something about the effect colors give when you wear them? The warm colors will cause you to be noticed, they will help you to feel cheerful, and they may make you appear larger than you are. The cool colors will help you feel serene, they will cause you to blend into a group, and they will help you appear smaller than you really are.

Determining your skin tone
While colors are important for the effect they have on your apparent size and your emotions, their most important function is their effect on your appearance. Colors can clash with or compliment your personal coloring. Since rather large areas of your skin may be exposed in an outfit, your skin tone can be flattered or deadened by colors worn nearest your face. To determine the total effect a color will have on your appearance, the color of your hair and eyes should also be considered. Your most becoming colors will flatter all three: your skin, hair, and eyes. However, your prime concern is your skin coloring.

Boys as well as girls should consider color. When buying clothing, keep your skin color uppermost in your mind. With the wide selection of colors available, each person can choose colors from among those which look well on him.

There appear to be five basic skin colors: black, brown, red, white, and yellow. Actually, however, the colors found in all skins are tints or shades of orange—yellow, yellow-orange, red-orange, or orange-red. The amount of pigment in the skin causes the degree of lightness or darkness. The more pigment the skin contains, the darker it will be. In reverse, if skin contains very little pigment, it may appear to be creamy white.

When choosing becoming colors, undertones are a far more important consideration than the amount of pigment in your skin. Undertones are caused by the amount of red or yellow pigment present. Since all skins are colored by a mixture of red and yellow, the skin color of any individual is likely to veer toward either the yellow or the red side of orange. The red or yellow undertones divide people into two special groups. Their skin is either *warm* or *cool* in appearance. Redness tends to make skin look warm, while yellow skin has a cool look. This warmth or coolness determines, to a large degree, which colors look best on you.

The color of clothing can either emphasize or minimize warm or cool skin tones. To determine which effect you desire, you may need help in deciding whether your skin tone tends toward yellow or red. Once this is known, you will be able to choose colors which look well on you.

Choosing your best colors
The safest way to know what a certain color will do for you is to hold it close to your face in a good light and look at yourself closely. It is seldom true that a given color is always becoming to an individual. Because colors vary so much in lightness and darkness, you will be able to find some tint or shade which looks well on you. But there will be other tints or shades of the same color which are not becoming. You may be able to wear a tint of orange, while a deep shade of orange will bring out unbecoming undertones.

When you are checking a color for becomingness, be sure to use the kind of light under which you expect to wear it. If the garment will always be worn at night under artificial light, check it under artificial light. If the garment will usually be worn during the daytime, look at it under both artificial and natural light.

When shopping, it is sometimes inconvenient to hold every garment or piece of cloth up to your face to see what it does for you. If you know whether your skin tends toward red or yellow, you can determine the effect basic colors will

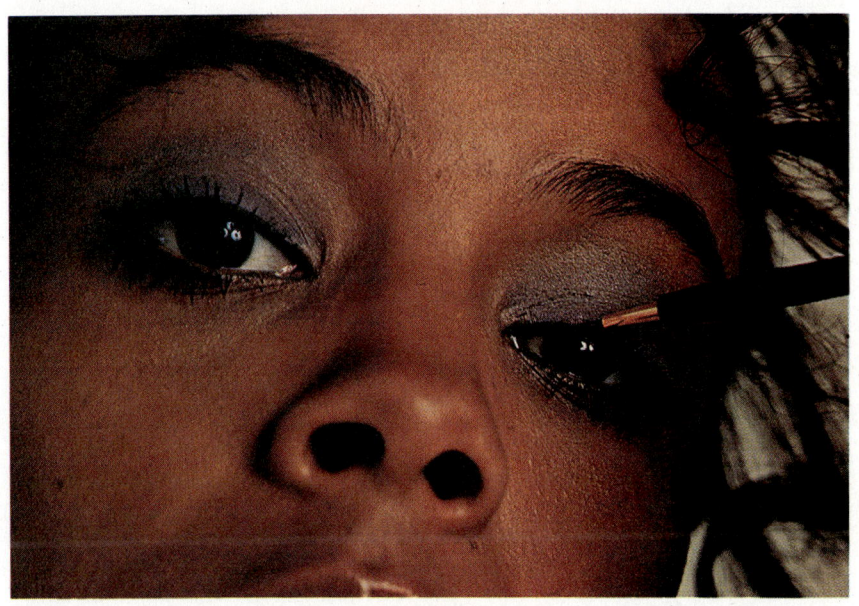

COURTESY AVON PRODUCTS, INC.

Whether your skin tone and hair coloring are dark or light, makeup and clothes are available in colors which will blend with your coloring.

COURTESY THE SAVINGS AND LOAN FOUNDATION, INC.

Make a flower color wheel, using the primary colors for the largest petals, the secondary colors for the middle-size petals, and the intermediate colors for the smallest petals.

Make a montage from pictures to illustrate both a particular color scheme and good use of the principles of design.

Bulletin board IDEA
Title: *Colors Have Families, Too*
Directions: Under this title place pictures illustrating monochromatic, analogous, and complementary color schemes.

have on it. This will help you to shop more selectively. Only final selection will need to be checked against the color of your skin.

Look at the color wheel. (See page 261.) Colors that are arranged opposite each other on the color wheel are called complementary colors. This means that these color pigments, if mixed together, will produce gray, or will neutralize each other. They are opposites, or complements. Placed next to each other, each makes the other look brighter. Thus, green and red Christmas decorations look much brighter when the colors appear together than when each color is used separately.

As you look at the color wheel, you see that the opposite of yellow is violet. People with yellowish skin will find that violet clothes tend to make their skin look even more yellow. Likewise, the greens and blue-greens emphasize the pink tones in the skin.

Colors may be emphasized in other ways. One way is by repeating the color in large amounts and in a deeper shade. Thus, pink in the skin will be emphasized by wearing a red dress or sweater.

Colors are also emphasized by repeating a small amount of the same color in a brighter intensity. Thus, a bright yellow collar will make yellow skin or hair look more yellow, while a bright pink collar will bring out the pink in the skin.

Colors may be made to appear less obvious by overpowering them with very bright colors or by combining them with a dull color of about the same *value* (no lighter or darker) and a slightly different *hue* (color). For instance, a person who is concerned with sallow, yellow skin might overcome the problem by wearing an outfit of snappy orange or red. A person with skin which is too red can overcome the problem by choosing a garment of medium-dull orchid or plum or perhaps by choosing pastel pink, which dulls the skin while highlighting the eyes. Colors that do not enhance your skin may be worn by using white or another becoming color at the neck of the outfit.

Using color accents
Many people find that their wardrobes are more flexible if outfits for various occasions are chosen in basic colors—neutrals such as brown, beige, gray, black, or white. By highlighting them with flashy scarves and pins and other bright-colored accessories, such clothes can be appropriate for a large range of activities. Colors vary in *intensity* (the brightness or dullness of a color), and a bright spot of color in an accessory can balance the larger area of dull color in a basic outfit.

Color plays tricks on your eyes. If used well, it helps cover up figure faults and attracts attention to your good features. You can use colors

COLOR WHEEL

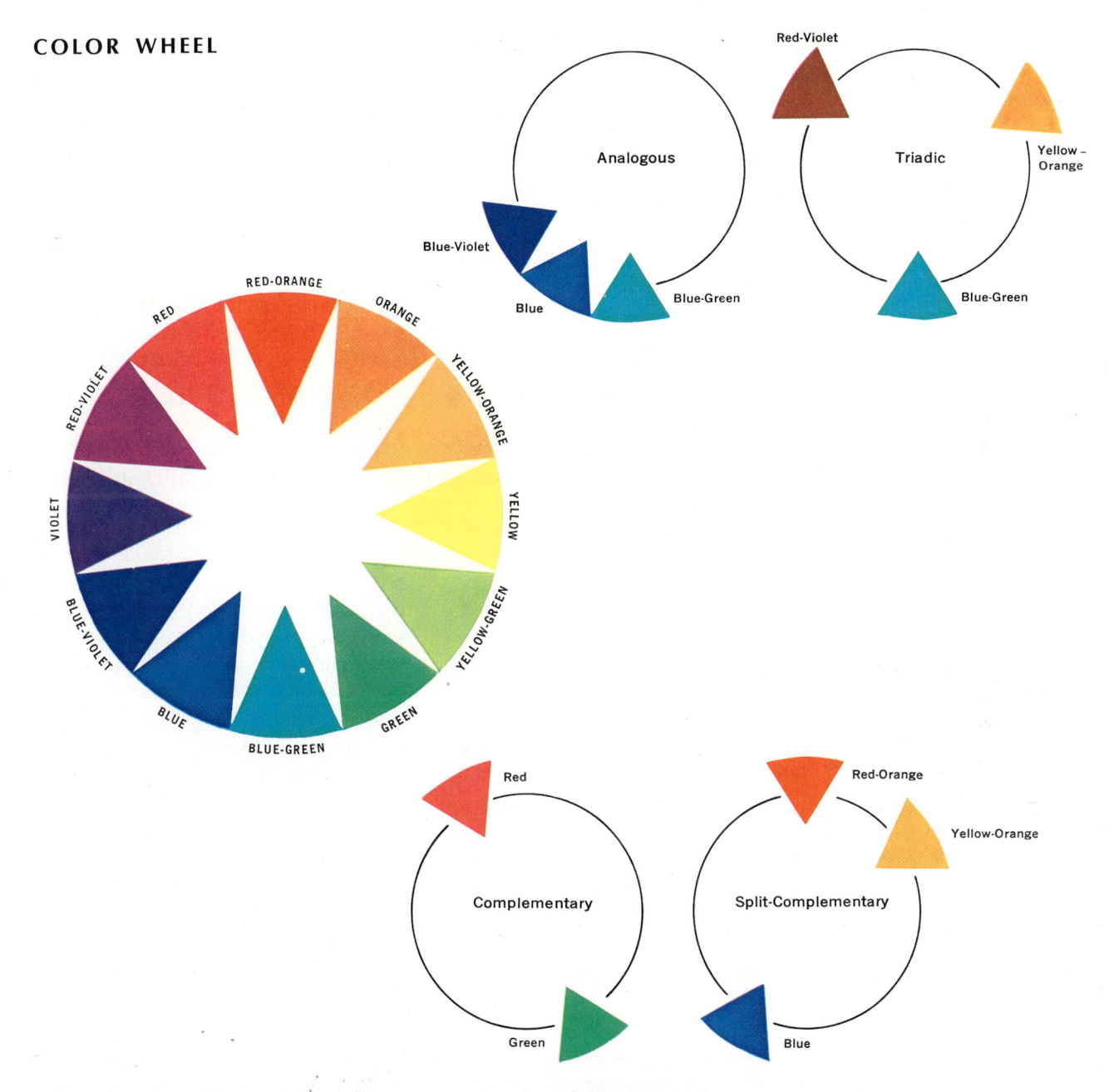

Basic colors can be chosen from the color wheel in varying shades or tints which combine well in costumes or room decorations.

261

Collect pictures which illustrate good uses of the color schemes described below. Or make your own illustrations for each color scheme.

1 Monochromatic: a single color with variations of value and intensity.
2 Analogous (neighboring): Two or three colors that are adjoining in their position on the color wheel.
3 Accented neutral: Large areas of dull color with one or more small areas of bright or intense color.
4 Complementary: Two colors that are located opposite each other on the color wheel.
5 Split complementary: A color used with hues from both sides of the opposite color.
6 Triad: Any three colors on the color wheel that are an equal distance from each other.

Considering hue, value, and intensity, list three colors that look well on you and three that are not becoming to you. Try to explain the reasons why in each case.

Suggest ways in which a large girl or boy may wear bright, warm colors without appearing larger.

COURTESY SIMPLICITY PATTERN CO. INC.

Outfits chosen in basic colors may be highlighted by the addition of scarves, collars, or jewelry which add color accents.

in ways which will make you look larger or smaller. Color can also be used to make you look shorter or taller. For example, white and pastels reflect light and make you appear larger. Dark, dull, or grayed colors absorb light and make you appear smaller. A one-color outfit will add height, while pants and sweater of contrasting colors will reduce your apparent height.

Black emphasizes your silhouette. It usually needs some contrasting color accent for a smart-looking effect. You can wear black well when your figure is in good proportion. On the other hand, black calls attention to a figure of poor proportion. A figure with large hips, large bust, or short waist attracts less attention when it is dressed in a dull or grayed color instead of black.

Since accent colors attract more attention than the basic, or background, colors, use them to call attention to your best features.

A hat of an accent color adds height. Select the size and shape of hat most becoming to you. Look at yourself in a full-length mirror before buying a hat. Purses of accent colors carry the eye to that part of the figure which they touch. A girl with a slender figure may wish to carry a purse of contrasting color, while a girl with large hips might well choose a bag to match her outfit. Select the size and shape of your purse in proportion to the size of your figure.

A spotty look is caused by the use of too many accent colors. Spots of a single color can have the same effect. When shoes, purse, gloves, and hat vary greatly in color or are identical, the eye jumps from one spot of color to the next. Try for a blend. There are two good ways to achieve a blend. Choose one accessory which matches either the basic outfit or blends with both the outfit and the other accessories. For instance, with a spring green coat and orange accessories try a perky, dark blue straw hat or scarf. If you can't find the right blue, try beige.

Use placement of color to advantage. You can add to or cut your apparent height by the arrangement of color on your body. Short, stout figures appear taller when dressed in one color. To add further height, use an accent color at the neck, on the head, or down the center of the figure. Two-piece outfits of different colors cut the apparent height. These may be worn if you are tall and slender or if you look slender. A belt of contrasting color is also good for the tall, slender figure. Certain placement of contrasting colors adds width to the figure. For example, white gloves worn with a dark dress add inches to the hips, because the eye jumps from one white hand to the other.

TEXTURE

The *texture* (roughness or smoothness) of a fabric surface affects its apparent color and the size of your figure. Rough surfaces reflect light in tiny accents and throw little shadows that dull the intensity of the color. If a piece of rough fabric and a piece of smooth fabric were dipped into the same dye bath, the rough fabric would appear to be duller in color because of the softening effect of the rough texture.

A smooth fabric such as chino, used in pants, adds less bulk to the figure than a rough fabric like corduroy and makes you look smaller when wearing it. But a smooth, shiny fabric such as satin will make you look larger. On the other hand, a rough, nubby texture, even though its color is dull, will make you look heavier because of its bulk.

FABRIC DESIGNS

The design, or pattern, of a given fabric affects the apparent size of the person wearing it. A person looking at large, splashy designs usually moves his eyes from one spot to the next. Such splashy spots give the impression of increased size. On the other hand, small designs are more restful to look at and blend into an all-over effect which makes the figure appear smaller. Thus, a garment made from a large-print or plaid fabric will make a person look heavier than will one with a small design.

Fragile, dainty designs may look out of place on a large individual, while large designs can be overpowering to a small person. Design is a question of relationships. One who is small in stature usually is wise to select small-scale designs in clothes rather than take a chance on being overwhelmed by the design itself.

In planning your outfits, try to determine which fabric designs relate best to your figure. You may choose large or small designs in some part of your costume if you work toward a unified effect.

List ways in which colors can be used to flatter your figure. Be able to demonstrate and explain how each color choice will affect your appearance. The following items will help you start your list.

To look taller choose . . .
1 Colors which are repeated up and down.
2 Bright necklaces or scarves.
3 Bright hats or hairbands.
4 High collars.

To look shorter choose . . .
1 Crosswise or horizontal contrasting color lines.
2 Contrasting color belts.
3 Contrasting band or trim at the hem.
4 Contrasting skirts and blouses.

To look thinner choose . . .
1 Darker shades.
2 Duller intensities.
3 One-color outfits.

To look heavier choose . . .
1 Bright colors.
2 Light colors.
3 Colors found in bulky textured fabrics.
4 Contrasting color lines which go around the figure.

Your career
Cloth designer

Duties: Originates designs for cloth, specifying weave, pattern, color, and thread to meet fashion demands. Develops new ideas for using fabrics through study of fashion trends and knowledge of textiles.

Where employed: Textile mills and chemical textile companies.

Blends of fabric textures and design can be attractive if selected to enhance a person's skin color and personality.

COURTESY SIMPLICITY PATTERN CO. INC.

LINES IN CLOTHES

You have noticed at some time or other that a certain outfit made you look taller and thinner than you thought you were. This might have occurred when you were trying on clothes in a store or when you were dressing at home. You may have tried on a garment that belonged to a friend and found that it didn't look so well on you as expected. Have you discovered why these things are true?

The becomingness of a garment depends upon where the seams fall, as well as on the color, texture, and design of the fabric. The style, or way the garment is put together, creates lines that catch the eye. The most important line is the outline (silhouette) of your figure. When people look at you from a distance or when the light is behind you, your silhouette is most apparent.

As people look at you from close range, the details of the construction of your clothes become more noticeable. The direction in which the eye is led by fashion lines determines the impression your garment gives. As you examine the lines of a garment, you will see that some of the lines go up and down the figure vertically. Some lines travel across the figure horizontally. Since vertical lines carry the eye up and down, it is natural that they make the person wearing them look taller and more slender. When the eye travels from one side to the other, the object naturally appears wider.

Other lines are formed where the different parts of the garment are put together. For example, the waistline, the neckline, and the lines made where sleeves are sewn into a garment all form fashion lines in an outfit. The hemline, the edges of the sleeves, and the collar and cuffs form other lines. Such things as pleats, rows of buttons, yokes, bows, and lines of trimming also create definite lines for the eye to follow.

The other fashion lines you find in clothes are more or less variations of the vertical or horizontal lines. Diagonal lines run from one side to the other on a slant. The more nearly vertical the line, the more slenderizing it is. V-shaped lines may be slenderizing or not depending upon how broad the V is. Curved lines add graceful width and softness to clothes.

Dominant, or outstanding, lines influence clothing appearance. Since the eye follows these dominant lines, choose designs to add height or width in the body areas where it is needed. Be sure these lines emphasize your best features and hide your faults.

If you have a round face and full neck, a round neckline will make your face look rounder and your neck fuller. In reverse, a narrow V-neckline will carry the observer's eye down away from your face and make your face appear longer. A wide belt will carry the eye around your figure at the waistline and make that part of your body look larger. If you have a small waistline, you may want to call attention to it with a brightly colored belt.

One of the most interesting ways to create lines is through the use of color. Stripes and plaids in fabrics create definite color lines for the eye to follow. The way a garment is cut from such fabrics will determine whether the lines add height or width to your figure. A tall person might choose horizontal lines, while vertical ones would be better for a short person.

Choose clothes for appropriateness

Knowing what to wear for each occasion is a skill developed through planning and practice. The person who puts forth the effort to dress appropriately is showing through his actions that how he looks is important. He is showing his

COURTESY GAY GIBSON

The lines in clothes combine with color and texture to make an outfit appear dressy or casual.

Tell why color is an extremely important factor in clothing selection. For example, color can be used to . . .
Express your personality.
Give clothing individuality.
Coordinate separate clothing items in a costume.
Give unity to an entire costume.
Create a center of interest.
Emphasize attractive features.
Create a desirable illusion of added height or fullness.
Outline forms and areas.

Discuss how the following factors can influence your choice of colors in clothing.
1 Your personality
2 Your complexion (skin, hair, and eyes)
3 Your size
4 Your age
5 Your activities (or the occasion)
6 The texture of the fabric
7 The effect of light

Bulletin board IDEA
Title: ool olor ombinations
Directions: Below the title, fasten attractive pictures or swatches of cloth which depict attractive color combinations.

Notice in the drawings below what happens as vertical lines are spaced farther and farther apart. Tell how such conclusions can be used in choosing clothing.

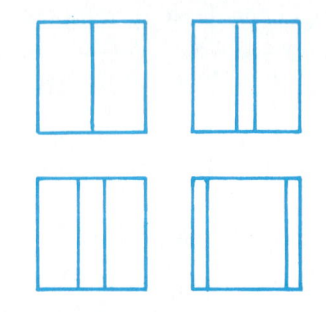

Your career
Tailor

Duties: Makes tailored garments such as suits, topcoats, overcoats, and dress clothes. May measure customers and record measurements. May perform any part of the making of tailored garments including designing, cutting, padding, shaping, fitting, and finishing. May perform the more difficult hand and machine tasks in the construction of garments while supervising less skilled workers.
Where employed: Garment factories or tailoring shops. May be self-employed.

awareness of the pleasure a well-chosen outfit brings, not just to himself, but mainly to others.

FOR THE INDIVIDUAL
Your personality along with your body build will determine what type of clothes you will look best in and enjoy wearing. Some young people enjoy athletics, are strong and muscular, and look and feel best when they are wearing casual, tailored clothes. Others look and feel better in dressy-looking clothes.

One way to help you decide on the type of clothes that is best for you is to think over the clothes you now have. Which clothes make you feel the best? Which type brings you the most compliments from your friends? Could it be that these clothes are best suited to your personality as well as to your coloring and figure type?

If you're a girl
One of the most wonderful qualities a girl possesses is her femininity. One of the most widely accepted ways of expressing your femininity is in the way you dress. From the time you were born, you probably were dressed in girls' clothes. Even as infants, most baby girls are dressed in pastel-colored outfits with lace and bows for trim. As a toddler, a little girl is likely to be dressed in shorts or slacks a great deal of the time. But even these play garments are apt to display designs and trim which make them different from boys' clothes.

Some girls look very well in ruffles, soft fabrics, and feminine lines. Such girls feel uncomfortable in severely tailored suits and dresses. Other girls are tall, queenly, and dignified. These girls find they look well in some of the rather extreme styles, and they often like clothing styles referred to as *high fashion.*

Today the pantskirt is a popular teen-aged girl's choice for many activities. Pants may be chosen for informal entertaining as well as for active sports. Few people would deny girls the casual and relaxed feeling these clothes provide. Even though feminine clothes of this type may seem to be tailored in imitation of masculine styles, they are designed with details which express the wearer's femininity.

If you're a boy
Boys are taught from infancy to be proud they are boys. Most boys learn to act rougher and tougher than little girls. To help them fit the role society expects of them, little boys are dressed in clothes in which they can actively project their masculinity.

The man's world of fashion is today filled with bright colors, splashy designs, and comfortable fabrics. A white shirt, tie, and dark suit are no longer the only accepted dress-up wear for young men. Some boys prefer wearing a soft knit shirt and comfortable slacks.

Another important difference noted in today's clothes for men is the matter of change. In the recent past, significant differences in men's fashions have come more slowly than in women's fashions. Now with increased leisure time and spending money, men are responding to fashion change much like women. It is important that boys understand the place of fads, fashions, and styles in clothing choices.

FOR YOUR AGE
Today's teen-agers can find clothes they like. They are not expected to wear styles that are either too childish or too mature looking for them. Nor are they expected to wear clothes which fail to fit their activities. As a matter of fact, it seems the clothing world is, to a degree, teen-oriented, since so many styles are keyed to the figures, personalities, and activities of teen-agers.

Fashion designers often seem to emphasize the older teen-ager. This sometimes creates problems for younger people. Have you ever bought something that you thought would make you look grown up, only to find that when you got home with your choice it was a disappointment? Perhaps your parents were also unhappy with your purchase.

Such clothes as swim suits, party clothes, and coats are kinds of clothes which require careful consideration before a final decision is made. Think about how fast you are growing. An outfit which is already skimpy might all too soon be outgrown.

Parents and teen-agers do not always agree on clothing choices. However, many realize that a good relationship between parents and teen-agers is more important than any one item of clothes on which they happen to disagree. Both you and your parents may need to compromise occasionally if your relationship is to be a happy one.

COURTESY EMILE BERNAT & SONS CO.

A girl learns to express her femininity with the clothes she chooses and wears.

Suggest ways in which the lines diagrammed below are used in clothing styles. Explain the effects of horizontal lines on apparent figure size. What happens to apparent figure size when horizontal and vertical lines are combined?

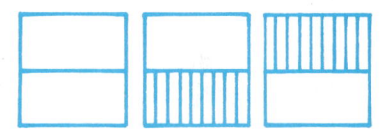

Using pictures of different dresses and sportswear, try to describe the personality of a girl who would choose each costume. What factors influenced your decisions?

Your career
Buyer for teen-age clothes

Duties: Buys teen-age clothes and accessories from manufacturers. Plans seasonal, quarterly, and special purchases. Buys at merchandise shows, through catalogues, or from manufacturer's sales representatives. Helps train employees to develop product knowledge.
Where employed: Large department stores and specialty shops.

Follow these guidelines when packing for a trip. Discuss in class other specific packing details which you know are useful.

- Make a list of the garments you will need. Include accessories.
- Put shoes and other heavy articles in bags. You can buy bags, make them, or use things from around the house, such as old socks.
- Place the heaviest things, such as shoes or purses, near the back and bottom of the suitcase so that they remain on the bottom whether the suitcase is standing on edge or lying flat.
- Avoid packing glass bottles. Transfer only as much liquid as you might need to a plastic bottle. Nail-polish remover is one item which should not be transferred from a glass container to a plastic one.
- If you must pack something that is in a glass bottle, wrap it in a piece of cloth, and then in a plastic bag. This will prevent other articles from being damaged in case of breakage.

FOR THE OCCASION

Different kinds of activities require different kinds of clothes. Some of these differences are due to the kind of activity itself, and some are due to social customs. Casual clothing is becoming more and more popular in today's informal way of living. It is no longer customary for girls to wear hats and gloves for a shopping trip. In fact, many communities no longer demand that they wear hats to church services.

A person can learn to choose becoming clothes which are suitable for a particular activity.

COURTESY OF TAMPAX INC.

Unfortunately, some people have misinterpreted the word *informal*. They feel that informal means sloppy. As a result, they seldom dress carefully for any occasion. People who reason and dress in this manner often forget that careless dress implies to others that they are generally careless people.

The value you place on your personal appearance is a part of the value you place on your own importance. The person who develops faith in his own worth will be able to accomplish more than the one who does not. Wearing clothing that is right for the occasion—sports clothes for active sports; casual clothes for school and shopping; dressy clothes for parties, dates, and church—will give you a feeling of confidence in your appearance and in yourself.

The person who is well dressed knows that when people turn to look at him on the street it is because he is neat and attractive. This is a far better feeling than one created when people stare because you are messy and peculiar looking.

Choose clothes for wearability

While the style and type of clothing you select should be appropriate for you and your activities, the selection of fabrics from which they are made is an equally important consideration. A pair of pants made from a fabric that stretches as you move and then returns to its original shape will be more comfortable and attractive than slacks that become baggy and shapeless after you have worn them for a short time. Too, they are more practical than pants that split in the crotch during their first wearing. A fabric that wrinkles as soon as you sit down in it can look mussed before you arrive at a party. The way a garment is made, its fiber content and fabric finish, and its care requirements are all a part of wearability.

Choose clothes for enjoyment

Sometimes you need to buy clothes just for fun. You may be shocked to read such a statement because you have heard so much about buying for wear, buying for care, buying for color, buying for many other good reasons.

Carefulness in buying can't be overemphasized. Timing, also, must fit into the family situation. Nevertheless, every girl needs, once in her life, to know that she is the prettiest one at the party. A boy, too, occasionally needs to know that he is the smartest dresser in the crowd. Clothes wear out, and money is always spent for something. But the feeling that you were special and looked the part remains with you forever.

There is no need to overdo it, but occasionally, buy something simply because you want to. Can you recall the feeling of buying something, not because you needed it, but because you wanted it badly? Such clothes add spice to your wardrobe and extra pleasure to everyday living.

COURTESY CAROUSEL FASHIONS, INC.

Almost everyone needs to learn how to choose something, whether a wig, a garment, or makeup, simply because it is fun to own.

Use cellophane tape to secure the lids and tops of containers for liquids and creams.

Pack suits, sweaters, skirts, dresses, or heavy clothing near the bottom. Place the lightest things, such as blouses, underclothes, and nightclothes on top.

Place plastic cleaner bags between the folds of clothing that is likely to wrinkle. Fold garments along the side seams or at the waistline to avoid wrinkling.

Roll up hose and bras and put them inside of shoes or purses.

Before you lock the suitcase, check to see that no clothing shows outside.

Identify your suitcase on both the inside and outside.

Collect pictures of various types of garments. Make a list of appropriate places and occasions where each might be worn.

Let one of the tallest girls in class stand while holding a large purse. Let one of the smallest girls in class hold a small purse. Ask them to exchange purses and note the effect.

13 CHAPTER POSTTEST

Fill in the blank in each sentence with the *best* word to complete the statement. *Do not* write in this book.

1. Small areas of bright color are usually used as ___(1)___.
2. If you want to appear larger, choose bright, warm, and ___(2)___ colors.
3. Colors that seem to advance are classified as ___(3)___ colors.
4. The lightness or darkness of a color refers to its ___(4)___.
5. Red and green color pigments mixed in equal amounts will produce ___(5)___.
6. Adjacent colors with one hue in common are ___(6)___.
7. When complementary colors are used together, each appears ___(7)___.
8. Navy blue and burgundy are ___(8)___ of blue and red.
9. Contrasting skirts and blouses make you look heavier and ___(9)___ than one-color outfits.
10. The roughness or smoothness of a fabric is called ___(10)___.
11. A smooth, shiny fabric like satin makes you look larger because it ___(11)___ light.
12. A person with a round face can wear the ___(12)___ neckline best.
13. Vertical lines make the figure appear slimmer and ___(13)___.
14. The clothes you choose should be appropriate for your personality, figure type, personal coloring, and ___(14)___.

Match the *placement of contrasting color* given in List A with the *emphasized feature* given in List B. Use each feature from List B only once.

List A: **Placement of contrasting color**

A Belt
B Neckline scarf
C Gloves
D Cuffs on short sleeves
E Commercial trim on hemline

List B: **Emphasized feature**

1 Bustline
2 Face
3 Hips
4 Legs
5 Waist

Match the *colors* given in List A with the *descriptions* given in List B. Use each description from List B only once.

List A: **Colors**

A Tan, gray, beige
B Red, yellow, orange
C Bright yellow-green
D White and light tints
E Blue, green, aqua

List B: **Descriptions**

1 Cool
2 Intense
3 Neutral
4 Reflect light
5 Warm

14 CHAPTER PRETEST

Fill in the blank in each sentence with the *best* word or words to complete the statement. *Do not* write in this book.

1. Fads and fashions are popular for a shorter time than ___(1)___.
2. Laws which protect buyers are called ___(2)___ laws.
3. Cotton, linen, wool, and silks are ___(3)___ fibers.
4. All chemical fibers can be classified into specific ___(4)___ groups.
5. Lycra, Dacron, Dynel, Orlon, and Herculon are ___(5)___ names.
6. Orlon, Creslan, and Zefran are man-made fibers which can be classified as ___(6)___ fibers.
7. Any process which changes the natural characteristics of a fiber is a(an) ___(7)___.
8. When two or more fibers are used to make a fabric it is called a(an) ___(8)___.
9. A fabric which has been treated so that it requires little or no ironing, will stay smooth, and keep sharp pleats will be labeled ___(9)___.
10. The best source of information about fiber content is the label or ___(10)___ attached to the garment.
11. The primary considerations in buying any garment are quality and ___(11)___.
12. Scarves, jewelry, hats, and handbags are classified as ___(12)___.
13. In buying a slip, choose one that is opaque and is ___(13)___ free.

CHAPTER 14

Buying clothes for use and fashion

The fashion industry is a big business. One of its jobs is to persuade you that you need new clothes. If this can be accomplished, the industry will become even bigger. When you understand that the fashion industry uses advertising techniques to create clothing wants, you can be amused by them. Then you can buy clothes to fit your *needs* rather than the *wants* advertising has caused you to have.

There are three terms to keep in mind in referring to clothing: *fads*, *fashions*, and *styles*. Fads come and go rapidly, usually lasting no more than a season. Fashions stay popular for a varying period of years. Styles last for many years in different fashionable versions.

Much of what people consider to be fashion is really *fad*. Fads fade more rapidly than fashion itself. Many people become slaves to fads. They are constantly buying articles of dress because they want the newest look. Fads frequently are poor buys. These highly popular items are usually quite expensive both in original cost and in cost per wearing. They usually pass out of popularity long before they are worn out.

Write a short paper or give a talk entitled either *Why I Would Prefer to Wear Fads* or *Why I Would Prefer to Wear Fashions.* Discuss some of the reports in class.

List popular fad items that can be purchased for a small amount of money. List similar fad items which could be made inexpensively at school or at home.

Ask your parents to describe several fashions that existed when they were your age. Discuss these descriptions in class.

Bulletin board IDEA
Title: *Accessories Add Accents*
Directions: Display pictures of interesting accessories. You may also use actual accessories for this display.

271

Select three pictures of fads and three pictures of fashions. Tell why each is an example of a fad or fashion.

Discuss in class or write a paper which supports or disagrees with the following statement: *Fashions in women's clothing have changed in relation to world change.*

Describe at least three fads which have grown into fashions. From fads which are now current, predict which will become a part of the fashion scene. Be able to defend your choice.

From pictures of garments, determine if each illustrates fad, fashion, or style.

Using illustrations from old pattern catalogues or magazines, select pictures which illustrate how a basic style such as the shirtwaist dress has been changed slightly through the years.

Collect pictures of current fad items. Discuss the major optical illusion created by each.

Discuss at least three reasons why fashions change.

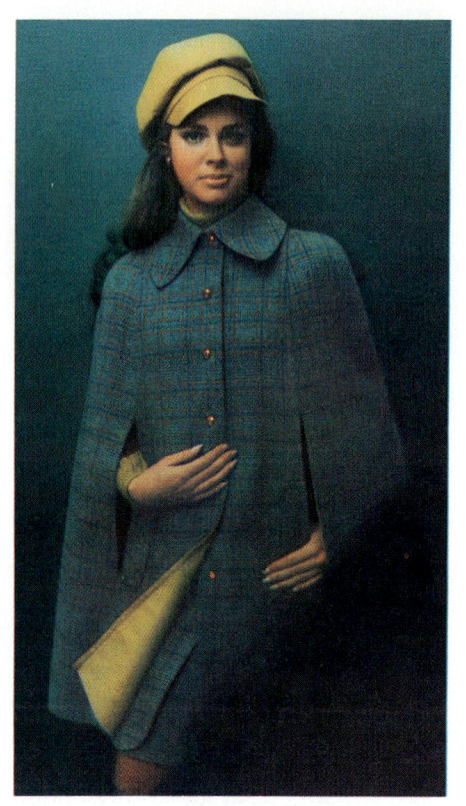

COURTESY PENDLETON WOOLEN MILLS

A garment of high-quality fabric and good design remains fashionable while fads come and go.

The term *fashion* refers to clothing trends that are currently in vogue. Such things as width of shoulders, length of skirts, and loosely belted, tightly belted, or beltless styles are all parts of the current fashion picture in a given season.

The *style* of a garment may refer to such things as shirtwaist style, princess style, double-breasted look, pleated skirt, and button-down collar. Styles tend to last longer than either fads or fashions. A style may go out of fashion, only to return at a later date.

The wise buyer learns which styles are personally becoming and then buys the fashionable adaptations of those styles. While fad items can be fun to own and can add spice to some of your outfits, they are wisely purchased with care and only when extra money is available.

Laws protecting consumers

Over the years several attempts have been made by the government to provide protection for the buyer by means of *consumer laws.* There are laws and regulations controlling the labeling of wool products, silk products, fur products, and flammable goods.

As the man-made fibers, such as nylon and the acrylics, came into the clothing picture, it became increasingly difficult for a consumer to tell by glance the content of a fabric. The Textile Fiber Products Identification Act, put into effect in 1960, was a real help to consumers. It provided that all garments and piece goods be labeled, stating the percentage of each fiber contained in the fabric. This act, however, controls only one aspect of clothing. That is the fiber. Fiber content *is* important in the performance of a garment. However, so are the construction of the yarn and the fabric, the type of dye used, and the finishes that have been applied to the fabric. Certainly, too, the garment construction affects the appearance and wear qualities of a garment.

As specified by the Textile Act, all fibers of similar chemical composition are grouped together into classifications called *generic* groups. The natural fibers of wool, cotton, silk, and linen are listed as such. The other fibers are known as polyesters, nylons, rayons, etc. When the law was passed, there were sixteen different generic fiber groups. Since then, other groups have been developed. The number keeps growing. (See the chart on pages 274–275.)

Perhaps you are thinking that you know the names of generic groups and have in mind Orlon, Acrilan, Creslan, and Zefran. These names do not refer to generic groups but rather are the trade names adopted by certain companies for single generic fibers. Thus, Orlon, Acrilan, Creslan, and Zefran are all trade names for individual members of one generic group, the acrylic fibers.

On a label you might read that the garment is made of 60 percent Orlon acrylic and 40 percent wool. Whether or not the manufacturer uses the trade name, Orlon, for the fiber, he is required by law to use the generic term *acrylic*. The charts in this chapter provide a better understanding of the characteristics and care of the individual generic fibers.

While more adequate clothing legislation is being considered, it is your responsibility, as a buyer, to check on the things you can see—the construction (firmness of weave) of the fabric and the construction of the garment itself. Such things as colorfastness, shrinkage, and special finishes usually cannot be determined by observation alone. For this information, you must rely on the reputation of the manufacturer or the store from which you buy. Read the labels and follow the instructions which are available.

Many manufacturers go beyond the requirements of law to help the buyer of their products. For example, even though only a statement of fiber content of the fabric is required by law, many manufacturers are providing much more information voluntarily. Calling attention to such qualities as shrinkage control and spot-resistant or durable-press finishes makes their goods seem more desirable. It is also to their advantage, as well as to yours, that you care for the garment properly. Therefore, many labels or hang tags now give you information such as:

1. Fiber content
2. Size
3. Brand name
4. Shrinkage expectancy
5. Special finishes
6. Care suggestions
7. Price

Make a file for your hang tags and labels. Begin with the labels you have already saved. Be sure that you mark each label in some way so that you can find the proper information for each item. Small labels may be fastened to file cards so that they will be more easily found. You may keep your file in a large box such as a shoe box. Or you may use an inexpensive file box to hold your labels. The dividers in the file box can be used to separate the items by type, such as dresses, sleepwear, blouses, coats, and so on. Keep your file up to date. Add new labels each time you buy a new item. Remove labels each time you discard items from your wardrobe.

Bulletin board IDEA
Title: LOOK
at the label!
Directions: Beneath the title, display labels and hang tags from various garments and bolts of fabric.

Textile fibers

Natural fibers

Fiber	Chief Uses (Home & Apparel)	Characteristics	Care
Cotton	Lightweight apparel—general Household fabrics—general	Versatile and durable Endures frequent laundering Easily ironed at high temperatures when damp Inexpensive	Limited only by finish, dye, and construction of item Special for durable press May be machine laundered Avoid risk of mildew
Linen	Women's and children's dresses and blouses Summer suiting Table linens and other household fabrics	Endures frequent laundering Does not shed lint Wrinkles easily unless treated Resists dye-type stains More expensive than cotton	Limited only by finish, dye, and construction of item Iron at high temperatures Avoid pressing in sharp creases Avoid risk of mildew
Silk	Light- and medium-weight clothing Accessories Some expensive upholstery and drapery fabrics	Strong, with natural luster Moderately resilient Resists wrinkling More expensive than man-made (filament) silky yarns	Dry cleaning usually preferred May be hand laundered in mild suds Avoid overexposure to light Can be attacked by insects
Wool	Outerwear Medium-weight clothing Bankets Upholstery	Springs back into shape Requires little pressing Great versatility in fabrics Insulating capacity which increases with fabric thickness	Dry cleaning usually preferred Will shrink and felt in presence of moisture, heat, and agitation, as in laundry Can be attacked by insects

Man-made fibers

Fiber	Chief Uses (Home & Apparel)	Characteristics	Care

Acetate
  Acele[1]
  Estron[1]
Triacetate
  Arnel[1]
	Light- and medium-weight clothing
	Drapery and upholstery fabrics
	Fiberfill
		Drapes well
		Dries quickly
		Subject to fume-fading
		Inexpensive
		Triacetate is wrinkle resistant
			Will glaze and melt if ironed or pressed at higher temperatures
			Dry cleaning preferred
			Triacetate is washable

Rayon
  Bemberg[1]
  Coloray[1]
  Avril[1]
  Nupron[1]
  Zantrel[1]
  H.W.M.[2]
	Light- and medium-weight clothing
	Drapery and upholstery fabrics
	Some blankets, throw rugs, and table coverings
		Absorbent
		Lacks resilience; wrinkles easily
		Flammability a danger in brushed or napped fabric
		Inexpensive
		H.W.M.—strong and resists laundry damage
			Dry cleaning often required
			Can be laundered
			Tends to shrink and stretch unless proper chemical finish is applied
			Washable

Rubber Lastex[1]	Foundation garments Swimwear	Stretch and recovery rate is high Damaged by oils and light Discolors	Frequent washing in mild suds Avoid constant overstretch and high temperatures

Spandex
  Clospan[1]
  Lycra[1]
  Vyrene[1]
	Foundation garments
	Swimwear
	Surgical hose
	Ski pants and other sportswear
		Stretch and recovery rate is high
		Resists abrasion and body oils
		Discolors
			May be machine laundered with warm water
			Dry on lowest heat, shortest cycle

Man-made fibers (*continued*): General characteristics of the following man-made fibers

Moderate to high strength and resilience Abrasion, moth, and mildew resistant Sensitivity to heat in ironing Resists stretching and shrinking Completely washable		Tends to accumulate static electricity Nonabsorbent; easy to wash; quick drying Resists non-oily stains, but body oils penetrate the fiber and are hard to remove Holds pleats because of thermo-plastic qualities	

Fiber	Chief Use (Home & Apparel)	Characteristics	Care

Acrylic
  Acrilan[1]
  Creslan[1]
  Orlon[1]
  Zefran[1]
  Zefkrome[1]
	Tailored outerwear
	Knitted wear
	Pile fabrics
	Blankets
	Carpets
		Resists wrinkling
		High bulking power
		Wool-like texture, if desired
		Soft hand
		Very resistant to effects of sunlight
			Remove oily stains before washing
			Waterborn stains easily removed
			Washable or dry cleanable
			Use medium ironing temperatures

Modacrylic
  Dynel[1]
  Verel[1]
	Deep-pile and fleece fabrics
	Carpets (in combination with acrylic)
		Soft and resilient
		Resists wrinkling
		Nonflammable
			May be ironed at extremely low temperatures only
			Hand washable

Nylon
  Antron[1]
  Blue C[1]
  Cediela[1]
	Hosiery
	Lingerie
	Sweaters
	Wind jackets
	Dress fabrics
	Carpets
		Exceptional strength
		Excellent elasticity
		Retains shape
		Woven fabrics often uncomfortable in contact with skin; textured yarns are less so
			Remove oily stains before washing
			Washes easily; wash with care to maintain whiteness
			Press at low temperatures
			Dry-cleanable

Olefin
  DLP[1]
  Herculon[1]
  Vectra[1]
	Seat covers for automobiles and outdoor furniture
	Carpets—indoor and outdoor
		No water absorption
		Low melting temperature
		Strong and abrasion resistant
			Shampoo with mild detergent and lukewarm water

Polyester
  Dacron[1]
  Fortrel[1]
  Kodel[1]
  Tough Stuff[1]
  Trevira[1]
	Wash-and-wear clothing—often in combination with other fibers, especially cotton
	Curtains
	Carpets
	Fiberfill
		Sharp pleat and crease retention
		Some are pill resistant
		Exceptional wrinkle resistance
		Reinforces cotton in durable press fabrics
			Remove oily stains before washing
			Washes easily; wash with care to maintain whiteness
			Needs little ironing or pressing
			Use steam iron at warm setting

Saran
  Rovana[1]
  Saran[1]
	Seat covers
	Screening and awnings
	Luggage
		Resists soil, stains, and weathering
		Flame resistant
			Blot stains; rinse with clear water
			Sensitive to heat

Vinyon	Mixed with other fibers for heat bonding	Resistant to chemicals and light Nonflammable Low melting temperature	Choose care practices suitable for fabrics which have been bonded with Vinyon

Each natural and man-made fiber has unique physical and chemical properties which translate into the special use and performance properties of interest to the consumer. However, these desirable properties are only achieved if the fibers are properly used in fabrics and if selected dyes and finishes are used to enhance the finished product performance.

[1]Trademark name   [2]High wet modulus

TEXTILE HANDBOOK/AMERICAN HOME ECONOMICS ASSOCIATION—ADAPTED BY CELANESE FIBERS MARKETING COMPANY

Role-play a situation where a person has washed a sweater with a hang tag which stated, *Dry-Clean Only*. The person tries to return the sweater for a refund at the store where it was purchased.

Make an ideal label or hang tag for:
A dress, pants, a coat, hosiery, or a bra.

This information is a real asset to those who use it. Learn to understand what a hang tag tells you. Then follow through with proper care. If the label tells you to dry-clean or hand-wash a jacket and you wash it in the washing machine with a load of machine-washable clothes, the label will be of no help to you. You will not be justified in returning such a garment to a store or manufacturer for a refund. On the other hand, you might hand-wash the jacket as the label suggests. If at this point you find the jacket zipper has shrunk so much that the jacket is short in front and puckers, it should be returned. A reputable store wants to know when its goods are not up to standard. The store will return the item to the manufacturer. This kind of cooperation between buyer, store, and manufacturer will help produce better goods.

Since the care instructions for each garment are easily forgotten over a period of time, it is a smart buyer who keeps this information handy.

Making quality judgments

Quality is one of the key factors to consider when buying clothing. Sometimes it is possible that poor quality is a wise buy. For instance, the quality of fabric in a Halloween costume is usually not very important. On the other hand, it is quite important that clothes which will be worn many times for a number of years be made of high-quality fabric. It is also important that the garment is smart looking, that the fabric can be cared for easily, that the fiber content is suitable for the garment, and that construction details have had careful attention.

APPEARANCE
Whether you are buying pajamas, a winter coat, or a party dress, ap-

Appearance is the key consideration in choosing clothing successfully.

COURTESY AVON PRODUCTS, INC.

276

pearance should be your first consideration. Money spent on unbecoming clothing is usually wasted money. Style, color, line, and fabric design are to be considered in relation to your skin color and figure type. (See pages 257 through 265.) When you find the correct blend of fashion characteristics, a garment will look well on you. Such a garment will be a good buy.

Some people can almost be correctly labeled *lucky*. They seem to have precisely the physical build and skin coloring the fashion designer had in mind when their clothing was designed and constructed. However, very few people have this ideal combination of body build and skin coloring. Rather than feel imposed upon by nature, it is best to make the most of the assets you have, whether they be looks or personality.

If your bustline is almost concave and your skin color out of tune with this year's fashion colors, use the problem-solving approach. Think through your problem squarely. Choose garments which flatter you most from among the styles which are currently fashionable.

You might be surprised to learn that someone else would gladly exchange problems with you. People with yellow skin tones may think reddish skin is far more attractive than theirs, and vice versa. Your own problems always seem biggest to you.

FIBERS AND FABRICS

Teen-agers buy a large proportion of the clothing sold in the United States. Most young people need to buy outer wear, undergarments, and accessories sometime during the year. Although each item has specific details that are to be considered before purchase, there are general fiber and fabric details which apply to most clothing items. Good questions to ask yourself before buying a garment include:

1. Are the fabric fibers suitable for the garment?
2. Is the fabric suitable for the garment?
3. Will the fabric performance be in keeping with that expected of the garment?
4. Are the fabric finishes desirable for the type of garment?

Suitable fibers

The fibers from which clothes are made fall into two main classifications—natural and man-made. The natural fibers come from plant or animal sources. The animal fibers most often used are silk and wool. The common plant fibers are cotton and linen.

Before the twentieth century, all the fabrics known to man were made from either plant or animal fibers. The natural fibers have both good and poor wearing qualities. For example, cotton is inexpensive, cool to wear, and easy to launder. On the other hand, it wrinkles

Research the history of dyeing. For example, find out how American Indians dyed fabrics. Bring to class illustrations of the clay, berries, or bark, or other similar things which they used for dyes.

After studying several garment labels and hang tags, list the types of information found on them which will be of the most help to consumers.

List types of garments such as undergarments or swimsuits where the quality of the fabric is a primary consideration. List types of garments where the wearability of the fabric would be of less importance.

List articles in which textile products are used, then list specific fabrics which would be suitable for making these items. Defend your choices.

Give several reasons why a manufacturer would blend two or more fibers into one fabric. Tell why the following might be blended:
　Cotton and acrylic
　Cotton and silk
　Cotton and wool
　Cotton and spandex
　Rayon and acetate
　Wool and nylon

◉ Select a fiber or several fibers which would be suitable choices for each of the following garments. Defend your selection.
- Winter coat
- Bathing suit
- Dungarees
- Dress for traveling
- Nurse's uniform

List manufacturer's names for variations of the durable-press or permanent-press finish. Discuss the factors to consider when buying these fabrics.

Bring to class several different blouses—all of similar style but varying in price. Cover the labels and prices. Rank the blouses from the most expensive to the least expensive. Uncover the labels and prices. Was price related to quality? What factors influenced the pricing of the blouses?

Find a relatively expensive garment that has been poorly constructed and make a list of the poor construction techniques. Find an inexpensive garment which has been made well and list the good construction features.

COURTESY GAY GIBSON

Fiber, fabric, and finish are vital considerations when purchasing garments. Such information is found on hang tags attached to ready-made garments and to bolts of fabric.

easily, soils readily, and doesn't stretch well with the movements of your body. Wool is warm, wrinkle-resistant, and can be tailored beautifully. However, it shrinks easily, it usually needs to be dry-cleaned, and it is attacked by moths. Similar kinds of advantages and disadvantages can be listed for all the natural fibers.

Just before the beginning of the twentieth century, man discovered that fibers could be made in the laboratory. Since the first of these fibers, rayon, was developed, the synthetic-fiber industry has changed the whole world of textiles. The first man-made fibers were made from natural products like cotton and wood and are called *semisynthetic* fibers. Now, many fibers are made entirely from chemicals and are called *synthetics.*

Most of the man-made fibers have very desirable qualities. However, they, too, have certain poor wearing qualities. So far, no fiber has been produced that is perfect for every use.

Suitable fabrics

Does this sound like something that happened to you? You bought a dress that looked wonderful in the store. The color looked well on you. The lines were becoming to your figure. The texture of the fabric was just what you wanted. Then, the first time you wore it, it wrinkled. Worse still, perhaps the first time you washed it, it faded and stretched out of shape or shrank. Maybe it held its shape fairly well, but when you wore it, you found that it was uncomfortably hot or it scratched. Perhaps you have had other problems similar to these.

Lost clothing dollars which tend to wreck the clothing budget can often be saved through a knowledge of fabrics. The fabrics from which your clothes are made will perform in certain ways, depending upon their fiber content, the way these fibers have been made into cloth, and the finishes applied.

Fabric performance

The fiber content will give you a good indication of the wear and performance you can expect from a fabric. Cloth made from a blend of two or more fibers performs more like the fiber which makes up the greater part of the fabric. Thus, if you find a blouse made of 65 percent Dacron polyester and 35 percent cotton, you can expect that it will have the wrinkle resistance and strength of Dacron but that to an extent it will be cool and absorbent because of the cotton. Also, you can expect this fabric to attract oil because of its polyester content.

If you have a skirt made of wool and Orlon, you can expect it to have the warmth of wool but to hold its shape and be less apt to shrink than pure wool because of the Orlon fibers.

Each fiber performs in its own way. Fabrics made of a given fiber can be judged before they are bought. If you have found garments made of a certain generic fiber, or fiber blend, to give desired wear, you will know what to expect from similar garments.

Fabric finishes

To overcome some of the natural disadvantages found in a given fabric, manufacturers have developed many finishes that are applied to the woven fabric or to the completed garment. A finish may prevent garments from wrinkling, staining, or shrinking. By reading garment labels, you can usually tell which finishes have been applied and whether such a garment will perform in a way that is useful for you.

Durable press and permanent press are terms frequently appearing on garment labels. Both refer to a shape-setting process which makes it possible for entire garments, if cared for properly, to be washed and worn many times with little or no ironing. This process can be applied to many types of fabrics and can be used on a wide range of fiber blends. The finish helps a fabric to stay smooth, and it helps pleats and creases to keep their sharpness. However, it has disadvantages. The chemicals used to produce the finish may weaken the fabric so that the garment will not wear as well. The durable-press finishes are cured, or baked, onto a fabric. Any wrinkles or construction creases that are in the fabric when the cloth is cured will probably remain in the fabric for life. This makes it difficult to alter durable-press garments to fit. Be sure that the length and size are both correct when you buy them. Too, the color of durable-press fabrics sometimes fades during laundering. Grease stains are

Wash fabrics woven from each of the natural fibers and evaluate the results. Vary the temperature of the water, the degree of agitation, and the method of drying.

Burn samples of selected man-made fabrics. Test other samples of the same fabrics with acetone. Evaluate the results in terms of wearability and safety.

Make a notebook which displays man-made and natural fibers. Each fiber should be displayed by using small swatches of fabrics. Include microscopic drawings and a brief description of the characteristics and the uses of the fiber.

Prepare a game or a crossword puzzle using fibers and their characteristics as the key words. Share the game or puzzle with class.

Illustrate the three basic weaves by weaving together thin strips of construction paper or heavy yarn. Relate the type of weave to durability of fabrics, light reflection, drapability, and the type of garment for which the weave is best suited.

279

Use a microscope to see how natural fibers, man-made fibers, and blends vary in appearance. Relate what these facts mean to the consumer in wrinkle resistance, washability, and warmth.

Make a poster about one fiber, trying to motivate a person to use that fiber.

Determine how yarn is made of fibers by untwisting yarns into fibers.

Arrange a display of nonwoven fabrics such as felt and Pellon. Discuss the uses of each. Compare the strength of woven fabrics and nonwoven fabrics by wetting tests, by abrasion tests, and by testing the weight that the fabrics will hold.

Make a crossword puzzle using the most common fabric finishes as key words.

Bulletin board IDEA
Title: *Peggy Pill, Suzy Stretch, Sheila Shrunk, and Ellen Enormous*
Directions: Use comic visuals to demonstrate each of the titles in relation to the care of a sweater.

difficult and sometimes impossible to remove.

In spite of what seems to be a long list of disadvantages, most people are buying durable-press fabrics. They feel that the no-iron feature outweighs the problems the finish causes. In fact, much of the clothing sold today has some form of durable-press finish.

Soil releasants were developed to overcome the tendency of some fabrics to hold on to oily soil. Such nonabsorbent fabrics as the polyesters and permanent-press fabrics have this tendency. A soil-releasant finish may be a film, or coat, which protects the fibers so that oil- or water-borne stains float away easily when a treated garment is washed. It may be a chemical which reacts with the fiber so that the nonabsorbent surface becomes absorbent. Fabrics treated with soil-releasant finishes should be laundered as no-iron fabrics. The oily spots can be pretreated with full-strength laundry detergent for an hour or so before laundering. Then a fabric softener can be used in the final rinse to help reduce the amount of static electricity.

Water repellents are applied to rainwear to keep the water out. Some of them, such as Zelan, react chemically with the fiber and will last through either dry-cleaning or laundering. Another type, called Aridex, will withstand several launderings. Then the fabric requires another treatment to restore the water repellency.

Soil and oil repellents protect wearing apparel and home furnishings from spills and stains. The fibers are coated with a finish which makes it difficult for stains to soak into the fibers. Any spill should be carefully blotted as soon as it is noticed, however. If rubbed in or neglected, a stain tends to be more difficult to remove. Scotchgard and Zepel are two common brands of soil- and oil-repellent finishes. Any fabric may be made soil- and oil-repellent by spraying with a home treatment.

Antistatic finishes prevent the tendency of many of the synthetic fibers, such as nylon and the acrylics, to collect static electricity. While harmless, this electricity buildup is irritating in that it can cause you to feel shock after walking across a rug or cause a skirt or pants to cling to you.

Some fabrics are permanently treated with chemicals so that they do not collect this static electricity. Garments which do not have antistatic finishes will cling less if a fabric-softening agent is added to the rinse water. These softeners coat the fibers and thus keep them from collecting static electricity.

CONSTRUCTION DETAILS

The way a garment is put together not only affects its looks when it is new, but also gives an indication of the wear you can expect. Learn to check each construction detail in a garment you are considering. Buy garments which are carefully constructed and finished. This will help you to have smart-looking clothes. Actually, you'll even feel better dressed when wearing them.

Good questions to consider before buying a garment include:

1. Has each piece of the garment been cut straight, or on the grain of the fabric?
2. Do any plaids, stripes, or prints in the fabric match at the seam lines?
3. Has the stitching been carefully done?
4. Are the seams well made and correctly finished?
5. Are the buttons of adequate quality and are the buttonholes well made?
6. Are closures, such as zippers, of good quality, well attached, and inconspicuous?
7. Are the hems of an even width and invisible?
8. Are the trimmings fashionable yet serviceable enough to last the lifetime of the garment?
9. If the garment is washable, are the linings, paddings, and interfacings made of washable fabrics? If the garment is to be dry-cleaned, are these items made of dry-cleanable fabrics? Are they well attached to the garment?

COURTESY R & K ORIGINALS, A DIVISION OF JONATHAN LOGAN

Check garments before purchase to assure yourself that they are cut on the straight of the fabric, that fabric designs match, and that seams are sturdy.

Grain

The yarns, or threads, from which a fabric is made are woven straight, or square, in a fabric. So that a garment will hang attractively when it is worn, each major piece of a well-made garment is cut on the square. The center of each garment piece is lined up with the vertical threads of the fabric. If the yarns in a finished garment slant to one side or curve downward across the body, the garment will generally hang unevenly. It has been cut

Demonstrate the technique of tie dyeing. Suggest items which could be brightened by tie dyeing such as curtains, tee shirts, and shorts.

Examine your wardrobe and decide which clothing items need to be renovated. Have a Dye Day and dye an article of clothing. If time and equipment permit, bring garments to school and share dye solutions, to dye similar garments such as pantyhose, shirts, or jeans.

Demonstrate proper methods for drying a garment with a durable-press or permanent-press finish so that it requires a minimum amount of ironing.

Illustrate a temporary finish by bringing to class a garment which has been heavily starched and one which has been heavily sized. Wash the garments and note the changes. Relate this experience to garments which you may have bought and washed.

Show pictures or actual garments which depend on trimming, such as buttons, for the major interest. Sketch the same garment with uninteresting buttons.

Develop a checklist to use in judging minimum-care garments. Add other points to the following list:
1. Do the labels and hang tags indicate that the garment was made by a reliable manufacturer?
2. Do the labels and hang tags indicate a high percentage of man-made fibers or a special finish for the natural fibers in the garment?
3. Are the seams deep, straight, and adequately finished to withstand washing or cleaning?
4. Are the trimmings either washable or removable?
5. Can the lining and paddings be cleaned in the same manner suggested for the outer fabric?
6. Was the garment stitched with appropriate thread? That is, was thread made of man-made fibers used on a fabric made from man-made fibers? Was mercerized cotton thread used on a garment made from cotton fabric?
7. Is the garment colorfast?
8. Will the garment hold its shape and be relatively wrinkle free with a minimum of pressing?

off-grain. Avoid buying improperly cut garments.

Matching pattern
In a garment made of patterned fabric, the designs correctly match at the waistline and center seams. Pockets should match each other, as should the sleeves and collars. All parts should look well in relation to the body of the garment. If plaids or stripes intersect at the side seams, these designs are carefully matched in a well-made outfit. Be certain that you are satisfied with the appearance before buying.

Hand or machine stitches
For a garment to wear well, stitches are small, even in length, neat, continuous, straight, and securely fastened at the end of seams. For the sake of appearance, thread used for stitching is carefully matched to the color of the garment.

Seams
Strong seams are important to the wear of a garment. Check to see that they are uniform in width and that they have been pressed as the garment was constructed. Wide seams are a mark of quality garments. They lie smoothly, wear well, and allow for alterations, which are often impossible in garments made with narrow seams. If the fabric ravels easily, the raw edges should be finished in some suitable manner which will prevent raveling.

Buttons and buttonholes
While the purpose of buttons is to hold a garment together, they can also add style. In buying washable clothes, try to consider whether the buttons will last when submitted to the water movement and heat of washing and drying. In dry-cleanable clothes, consider whether buttons will require removal for each cleaning. Leather-covered buttons or those which have jeweled insets may be poor selections because they would be injured in the cleaning process. Buttons so unusual that they could not be matched if one were lost might also create additional expense. Quality garments frequently have extra buttons attached to prevent this problem.

Buttonholes are correctly of a length neither too long nor too short to fit over the buttons easily. Check to see that they are cut on the grain of the fabric. Check also to see that they are evenly and firmly stitched or bound and have well-reinforced ends.

Closures
Check zippers and other types of fasteners to see that the placket opening is long enough to permit getting into and out of the garment without strain. Look, too, for a placket which lies flat and is unnoticeable. You can learn to tell by the appearance and movement of a zipper whether it will last under

continued use. Since a garment is unwearable until a broken zipper is replaced, avoid garments which contain poorly made zippers. Hooks and eyes, snaps, and buttons are securely fastened to most well-made garments.

Hems

Hems which are flat and even in width generally look well and hang well. The stitching is usually invisible on the right side of the garment hem. Generous hems permit lengthening unless the garment is made of a durable-press fabric. (See pages 279–280.)

Trimmings

Check all forms of trimming to see that they are securely attached. Try to determine whether they require the same care as the rest of the garment. Sometimes washable garments are trimmed with materials that must be dry-cleaned or that have been glued to the garments. These can be a total loss once they are soiled.

Linings, paddings, and interfacings

Any materials used to give a garment shape are correctly made of fabric which requires cleaning care identical to that needed by the rest of the garment. If you are in doubt about the cleaning care necessary for a jacket lining or shoulder pads, for example, ask the salesperson who is helping you. Usually, reports she has received from other customers who have worn similar garments, together with the information on the hang tag, will guide you in caring for your garment. Frequently, because of the linings in a garment, an otherwise washable garment requires dry cleaning. This additional cleaning cost should be considered when purchasing such a garment.

Buying outerwear

Outerwear garments are those seen by other people. They include blouses and shirts, pants and skirts, sweaters, coats and jackets, and dresses and suits.

In general, outer garments are of acceptable quality if they are made of an appropriate fabric and the construction details have been performed adequately. A garment weak in several construction details might still be a good buy, however. For example, poorly attached buttons or snaps can be quite easily fixed. Hems can be straightened, if necessary, and rehemmed with invisible stitches. On the other hand, if the fabric, style, or cut of the garment is poor, these defects can't be remedied. Try to avoid buying garments which have such built-in weaknesses.

It is important to try on clothes before you buy them. If possible, model them for someone whose

Develop a checklist to use in judging the quality of a skirt. Add other points to the following list:
1 Does the style suit my figure? If slender and short, is the skirt gathered, pleated, flared, or straight?
If slender and tall, is the skirt gathered, pleated, flared, straight, circular, or draped?
If plump, is the skirt slightly flared or does it have diagonal lines, or a side drape?
2 Does the size match my waist measurement or dress size?
3 Will the skirt fit without straining or wrinkling, especially at the hipline?
4 Does the waistband hold the skirt snugly in place?
5 Does the back of the skirt hang straight? A lining in the back helps to prevent wrinkling and stretching.
6 Is the lower edge straight and even?
7 Is the length becoming to me?
8 If the skirt is straight, is it lined or underlined?

Your career
Industrial seamstress

Duties: Operates a commercial sewing machine. The job usually involves making one particular item such as pockets, sleeves, collars, skirt seams, or darts, or applying zippers. May involve only the pressing operations. Pay is usually determined by the number of pieces completed per hour.
Where employed: Garment factories.

judgment you trust. Such a person will be able to point out features you cannot see for yourself. It is important that you feel comfortable in clothes you buy. It is also important that the clothes give you a pleasing appearance.

BLOUSES AND SHIRTS

Blouses or shirts make up a large part of most teen-age wardrobes. The key considerations in buying these popular garments are *fabric* and *fashion*.

Blouses and shirts can be a joy to wear and care for if they are made of carefully selected fibers. Usually blends of the man-made and natural fibers are wise selections. For example, a polyester-cotton blend is usually very successful because the polyester adds strength to a fabric which is comfortable to wear because of the absorbent qualities of the cotton. If the blend has been given a durable-press finish, the garment is even a better buy.

Fads come and go in the blouse and shirt field just as in all areas of the clothing industry. Try to buy *fashion*. If the collar, sleeves, and general body cut of a shirt or blouse are in current fashion, you can buy with some confidence that the garment you have chosen will remain smart looking during the years ahead.

Look, too, for sturdy, well-made seams, full cut through the shoulder area, sufficient length, well-made buttonholes, and buttons which will last through many washings. Blouses and shirts are worn often. Though it is seldom wise to buy the most expensive garment available, buy one of a quality adequate to give you reasonable wear. Often the decision to spend an extra dollar or so on this type of garment is a very wise decision.

PANTS AND SKIRTS

Pants and skirts are bought by teen-agers almost as frequently as are shirts and blouses. Most teen-

Choose a blouse that is easy to launder and one which will match a number of outfits.

COURTESY SPRINGMAID FABRICS

agers own fewer skirts and pants than blouses or shirts. This is probably true because pants and skirts can often be worn several times before cleaning or washing, while shirts and blouses usually need to be washed by the end of a day. Care qualities and wrinkle-resistance of pants and skirts weigh heavily in determining whether they are good buys. Check, too, to see that seams and hems are sturdy, that high-quality zippers are invisible, and that the fabric looks well and will wear well.

Fads hit even the skirt and pants industry. The well-dressed person occasionally buys one of these fad garments. Sometimes a fad grows into a fashion trend. Try to think through some of the new looks when they first appear in the stores. If a new skirt length is suddenly twelve inches shorter than current fashion, can you adjust the skirt if the new length later seems too short? On the other hand, if you buy a skirt several inches longer than current fashion, is all lost if your skirt turns out to be a fad? Can you shorten it and continue to wear it? The same kind of judgments can be made with pants. Wide or flared legs can be tapered if styles change. Long pants can be made into short ones. Wise decisions on your part can allow you to be part of the current fashion scene while preventing extreme waste through poor buying practices.

SWEATERS

Sweaters almost seem to be made for teen-agers, since they fit a wide range of teen-age activities. Their characteristic knit texture provides *give* qualities which adjust to the needs of active teen-agers.

Fiber content is a key consideration when buying sweaters. Read the label before buying. Today's sweaters are commonly made of treated and untreated wools, man-made fibers, and blends of these fibers. The cost of care makes the fiber selection vital. Some wools are machine washable. Most of the man-made-fiber sweaters can also be washed at home. Be careful, however, in considering dry-clean-only all-wool sweaters. They are beautiful, and they may be worth the price. Simply know what the total price is. Can you afford a white wool sweater which requires a two-dollar cleaning bill after one or two wearings? If so, fine. If not, by thinking ahead you might decide to buy an acrylic machine-washable sweater. Such planning might provide you with a clean sweater any day it is needed, instead of one which lies in your drawer a good deal of the time for lack of cleaning funds.

Another consideration in buying sweaters is the knit of the fabric itself. If the knit is extremely loose, it tends to stretch. Loose threads may hang and pull when you wear the sweater. Check to see that the

Develop a checklist to use in judging the quality of sweaters. Add other points to the following list:
1 Are the color, style, and type of trim becoming to my coloring and body build?
2 Do the color and texture of the sweater fit in well with garments that I plan to buy or those that are already in my wardrobe?
3 Does the sweater fit properly over garments with which I plan to wear it?
4 Does the sweater fit smoothly at the neck, across the shoulders, and through the back and chest?
5 Are the sleeves of a comfortable size and length?
6 Is any ribbing at the neckline, wrist, or lower edge firm but elastic?
7 Is the sweater of a fiber and knit which will be likely to hold its shape?
8 Is the sweater of a fiber which is relatively free of pilling and of a knit which is unlikely to allow threads to pull?
9 Is the sweater of a fiber and fabric which can be easily cared for?
10 Does the label or hang tag give specific directions for care of the sweater?

COURTESY SEARS, ROEBUCK AND CO.

When buying clothes for any member of the family, give serious consideration to fiber content, the quality of construction, and the ease with which garments can be kept in wearable condition.

BIOGRAPHY OF A BLOUSE

Fiber to Fabric

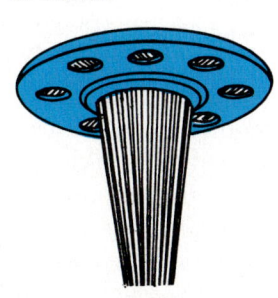

Man-made fiber is extruded from a spinnerette.

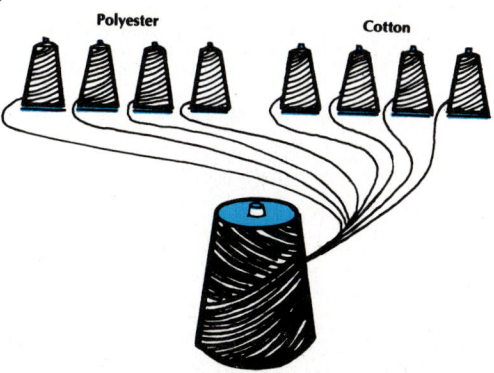

Yarn is made from a blend of man-made fibers and cotton.

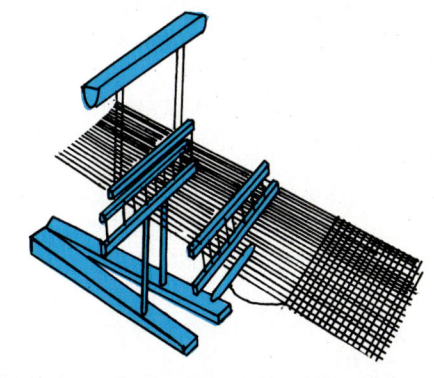

Fabric is woven from the blended yarn.

Fabric to Blouse

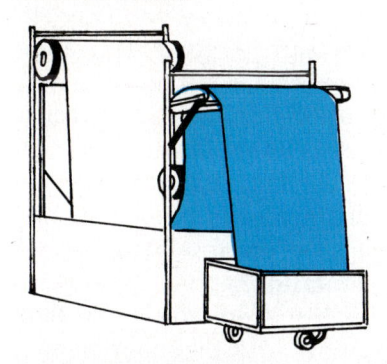

Dyeing and finishing are usually done at the fabric stage.

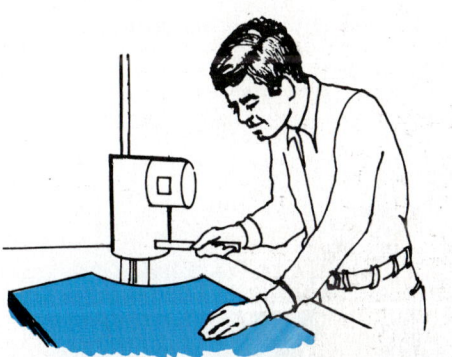

Cutting the blouse calls for skill and precision.

Sewing correctly includes use of proper thread and tension.

Blouse to Consumer

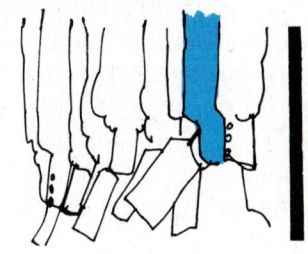

Hangtag gives fiber content and proper care instructions.

Consumer examines blouse considering her wardrobe needs.

Proper care is the final step in a successful purchase.

ADAPTED FROM MATERIALS PROVIDED BY CELANESE FIBERS MARKETING COMPANY

Your career
Alterationist

Duties: Changes already completed garments to fit an individual or alters the style of a garment.

Where employed: Specialty shops, department stores, or may be self-employed.

When buying school clothes, give particular attention to the mix and match characteristics of garments you are considering.

COURTESY SEARS, ROEBUCK AND CO.

sweater fits rather loosely through the chest or bust area. Seams of a good sweater are sturdy and finished to prevent raveling. Buttonholes are well-finished, and buttons are carefully attached.

COATS AND JACKETS

This group of clothes requires a combination of all your fashion know-how and buying skills. Each garment is a relatively expensive item. It will be worn many times; and when it is worn, everyone who sees you looks at it. There is no way to cover up a poor coat buy.

Most coats and jackets require dry cleaning. Knowing this, consider becoming colors which do not show soil easily. Wrinkle qualities of fabrics are also important. Since soil- and wrinkle-resistance are important, it follows that all-wool or wool–man-made-fiber combinations are fabrics to be considered.

Tailoring in coats and jackets is also important. This is, in a sense, unfortunate, because you may still need to learn a good deal about tailoring but need to buy coats now. When shopping, look between a coat and its lining. By doing so, you can tell whether a garment has been carefully made or poorly stitched together. To improve your knowledge of tailoring, go to a really high-quality store during a slack buying time. Ask the salesperson to show you the work in a coat or jacket which represents good tailoring detail. If you go alone or with an older person and show a polite interest in learning, a good salesperson will be flattered if you ask for help. With the quality guide lines she will give you, you can wisely choose coats and jackets in the price range you can afford.

DRESSES

Guide lines for buying dresses are difficult to establish. This is due to a large number of varying conditions. For one thing, there are many fabrics available. The list of activities to which a dress may be worn is also varied. Too, the body build and coloring of an individual should be considered when a dress is bought. (See pages 257–265.)

For the most part, dresses for home and school should be washable. Party dresses may or may not be made of washable fabrics. In all types of dresses, check to see that seams and hems are sturdy and well made. Buy dresses which are interfaced or trimmed only with materials that may be cleaned in the same way as the dress itself. And buy dresses which will be right for a variety of occasions. Very few people have enough money to buy a dress for each special occasion. The girl who thinks ahead to the kinds of activities she may be attending can own a few dresses which serve many occasions.

Buying undergarments

Selecting the proper undergarments can have a marked effect on both your comfort and the appearance of your outer garments. Since cleanliness is so important in undergarments, select fabrics which will hold their shape and appearance through many washings. Also, undergarments must have the ability to absorb moisture. Otherwise, they will be uncomfortable, particularly during hot weather.

UNDERPANTS
The comfort and fit of underpants are due largely to their cut, the quality of elastic used in the waistband, and the fiber content of the fabric. Before buying, measure your hips with a tape measure. Most underpants are sized 4, 5, 6, 7, or 8. Others are sized simply small, medium, and large. If you know your hip measurements, the salesperson can help you choose your correct size.

Underpants are usually available in knit fabric made of rayon, cotton, nylon, or a blend of these fibers. Rayon is generally inexpensive, nylon wears well, and cotton is absorbent. Knowing the strong feature of each fabric, you can choose underpants which best fit your needs.

BRAS
The proper fit of a brassiere is important both for comfort and health. It is not enough to go to a counter and choose a bra you *think* is your size. Try the bra on before you buy it. Preferably you should have the help of a trained salesperson to be sure you get the correct fit. As your body changes and develops, the bra size that fitted you six months ago may no longer be right for you. Also, bras marked the same size may vary because the styles or cuts are different. When correctly fitted, a bra will give support and protection to your figure. It will be com-

Develop a checklist to use in judging tailored garments such as boys' suits. Add other points to the following:

Does a coat have . . .
1 Smooth, unbroken shoulder lines?
2 A collar that fits close to the neck?
3 Lines which hang straight from the shoulders without wrinkling?
4 Smooth fit about the hips?
5 Neatly rolled lapels?
6 Well-fitting sleeves, ¼ to ½ inch shorter than long sleeved shirts?
7 Well-shaped and neatly finished lining made of fabric which can be cleaned in the same manner suggested for the outer fabric?
8 Tailoring which will withstand wear and cleaning?

Do pants have . . .
9 Smooth fit in the waist and hip areas?
10 A firmly woven fabric interfacing at the waist?
11 Creases made on the grain of the fabric?
12 Comfortable fit through the seat and crotch area?
13 Good quality buttons and zipper which are well attached?
14 Comfortable length?
15 A cut which is stylish?

Develop a checklist to use in judging the quality of a dress. Add other points to the following:
1. Will the fabric keep its shape, be easy to care for, and wear reasonably well?
2. Has the dress been cut on grain?
3. Were the pattern pieces matched carefully?
4. Does the design of the fabric match at the seam lines?
5. Are the stitches small and even?
6. Does the thread used in stitching match the color of the fabric? Is it strong enough so the seams will not break?
7. Are the seams wide, even, and flat? Are they finished to prevent raveling?
8. Are the zippers, hooks, snaps, and buttons securely attached?
9. Are the buttonholes well made?
10. Is the hem ample, even, and neat?

Choose a garment from a mail-order catalogue. Consider it from the viewpoint of price, style, and information given. If possible, order the garment. Compare it with the description given in the catalogue.

fortably snug without binding. Its straps are either adjustable or elastic.

SLIPS

The size of a full-length slip is based on the bust measurement or dress size. Half-slip sizes relate to the waist measurement. They usually are found in size small, medium, and large. It is best to try on a slip before buying it. Look for slips that are proportioned to your height or have adjustable straps.

Choose a slip made of either knitted or closely woven fabric. It should be lightweight, opaque, and static free. Try to determine before buying that the fabric is easy to care for and will not shrink when washed. If you are considering deep-colored lingerie, check the hang tag and consider whether the garment is colorfast to perspiration, laundering, and crocking, or rubbing off of color.

The adjustable shoulder straps of high-quality slips are attached to the body of the slip, not just to the lace trim. The trimming is durable, washable, and firmly attached. The seams are finished to prevent fraying.

Buying accessories

The accessories you select, such as shoes, hose, handbags, scarves, and jewelry, can change a rather dull outfit into something special. The knack for using accessories effectively takes a sense of adventure tempered by taste. Improperly chosen accessories can overpower your outfit. Carefully selected, they can make you look fashionable and well dressed.

The wise shopper buys accessories after major clothing needs have been met. This practice prevents overspending on less essential items and helps you choose accessories which go well with your clothes. When choosing accessories, keep your eyes open for ideas in store displays and in fashion magazines. Before choosing an accessory, ask yourself these questions:
1. Which outfit will it go with especially well?
2. Does it go with other outfits I own?
3. Does it go with me?

SHOES

Shoes are the best place to start in your accessory collection because they are a necessity. Too, they are expensive. Try to select them for practical use as well as for fashion. This is especially essential when you are selecting school shoes which are worn often. Buy school shoes of the best quality you can afford. It is smart to choose a neutral color that will harmonize with your school coat and most of your other clothes. Leather you can polish will be easier to maintain than suede.

Select a style that flatters your feet. T-straps and low-buckled styles will make your ankles look slim and your feet small, while chunky, heavy styles will increase your apparent foot size. Small-boned persons can look loaded down by shoes chosen to make their feet look bigger. Choose shoes for a general pleasing effect. When trying on a possible selection, study your total appearance in a mirror before making a decision.

Since fit and comfort are of utmost importance in shoes, these features should be checked with particular care. Shop for shoes after walking awhile to allow for normal foot expansion. Have both feet measured each time you buy new shoes. Shoes should be fitted to your larger foot. Try on both shoes and walk around for awhile. Stand with your weight on both feet to judge the shoe length and width. Then check the following points:

1. Is the shoe flexible enough for comfort when you walk?
2. Does the shape of the shoe conform to the shape of your foot, with the big toe pointing straight forward and the toe cap standing above, rather than pressing on, your toes?
3. Does the widest part of your foot correspond to the widest part of the shoe?
4. Is the shoe ½- to ¾-inch longer than your longest toe when you are standing?
5. Is the fit from the ball of the foot to the heel smooth and firm without pressure or gapping?
6. Does the heel section provide firm and comfortable support for your foot?

Try to think of each purpose a pair of shoes is to serve in your wardrobe—work, play, or dress. Decide what style, heel height, material, and color will best suit your purpose. Before buying, determine that both the style and materials used are appropriate for your wardrobe and that the shoes are becoming and comfortable.

HOSIERY

Your choice of stockings will depend upon your taste, wardrobe, and activities. It is a good idea to buy at least two identical pairs so that if one stocking is lost or worn, its mate can be used as a spare.

Correct size is a major point in getting good wear from hose. It is important to know both the width and length of your foot as well as the length and fullness of your leg. If your foot is wide or narrow, you may take a half size larger or smaller accordingly. If your leg is full, you might require a longer stocking length. Many stocking packages suggest the proper size for you according to your shoe size. Wearing stockings that are too short in the foot area can be as harmful to your feet as wearing improperly

Make a checklist to use in judging the quality of undergarments. Add other points to the following:

1. Is the general garment shape similar to the shape of my body?
2. Are the seams durable, stretchable, and overcast in the case of knits and elasticized fabrics?
3. Are shoulder straps attached to the body of the garment, rather than to the trimming?
4. Is the fabric of a type which is . . .
   Easily laundered and quickly dried?
   Wrinkle resistant?
   Stretchable for ease in motion?
   Absorbent?
   Opaque?
5. Is the fit smooth with no bunchiness?
6. Does a slip have the following desirable characteristics? Is it made of static-free material? Is the hemline 1 inch shorter than the skirt length with which it is to be worn? Is the silhouette similar to the outer garment with which it will be worn?
7. Are the straps of slips and bras stretchable or adjustable?

Divide the class into groups and ask each group to select and demonstrate suitable accessories for either the tall, slender figure; the tall, full figure; the slender, petite figure; the small, full figure; or the medium-size figure. Each group may use the appropriate guidelines to help them prepare the demonstration.

Tall and slender figure
- Large accessories of contrasting colors
- Bold, dramatic jewelry
- Wide belts
- Full skirts and bulky sweaters

Tall and full figure
- Large accessories which match outfits
- Plain but unusual jewelry
- Skirts with moderate flare

Slender and petite figure
- Small accessories which match outfits
- Small, dainty jewelry
- Shoes with high heels

Small and full figure
- Narrow belts which match garments
- Simple accessories
- Neatly fitting outfits of one color
- Accessories which emphasize vertical lines

Medium-size figure
- Accessories which emphasize your most pleasing characteristics

COURTESY THE RED EYE

Shoes, stockings, ties, scarves, and headbands are all a part of a teen-age girl's accessories. They can be chosen to make an outfit appear simple or dressy.

fitted shoes. Hose too short for you in the leg are unsightly and uncomfortable.

The term *denier* describes the fineness of the yarn used in making stockings. Small numbers refer to very fine yarn. To make the right stocking choices, buy hose according to the occasion for which you plan to wear them. Fine-denier (numbers 10 to 12) hose are suitable for evening wear. Heavy denier (number 30) is suitable for hose worn for work or walking. Numbers between 12 and 30 are those teenagers most often choose for school and dress-up wear.

Knit in stockings also affects their appearance. Most hosiery that you might choose can be bought in either regular or mesh knits. Since either knit usually wears well, your choice is mostly a matter of personal taste.

Besides ordinary hosiery, an entire line of fashion hose in a wide range of colors is available. These stockings can be color-keyed to many outfits. The same general points for buying ordinary hose apply when you are buying fashion stockings.

Many girls find they prefer *pantyhose* to regular hose for all kinds of occasions. Because pantyhose are pulled up to the waist like underwear, it is not necessary to wear a support belt or a girdle in order to hold them up. Another advantage is their smooth fit all the way to the crotch with no dark band showing in the upper leg area. This feature solves the problem of sitting without showing stocking bands if you are wearing either a short or a tight skirt. Pantyhose usually cost more than other hose of the same quality.

HANDBAGS

Handbags, often called purses, are more useful when chosen to look right with a variety of clothes—your shoes, your coat in winter, and your skirts or dresses during all seasons of the year. A neutral color is usually a wise selection. Try to buy handbags in relation to the size of your body and the length of your skirts. The items you need to carry will also affect the size of your bag. In general, huge bags look wrong with short dresses and small girls, just as tiny bags look wrong with large girls.

Regardless of your size, try to find a handbag designed to hold a variety of articles. A medium-size bag with several compartments or expandable sides will generally hold everything you really need to carry. Such a bag is more effective than a bottomless-pit type in which things are jumbled together and lost.

GLOVES

Gloves add a touch of glamour, or finish, to your fashion look. From this standpoint, gloves help complete any costume except perhaps the most casual of sport outfits. Keep your glove colors simple. A pair or two chosen for their neutral colors plus a pair of short white ones usually provide enough variety for a teen-ager. When used solely for warmth, gloves or mittens may be keyed to the color of your coat.

TIES, SCARVES, BELTS, AND JEWELRY

Accessory items can be chosen which are interesting to look at as well as becoming to you. Ties, scarves, belts, and jewelry are available in a wide variety of choices. Styles change almost from season to season. In this clothing area, the latest fads and ideas can frequently be enjoyed without wrecking your clothing budget, because each piece can be relatively inexpensive.

Accessories offer dozens of ways to give a costume a new look. You can look casual or dressed up, dramatic or conservative. Different effects can be achieved by the ways you select and use accessories with your outfits.

Develop a checklist to use in judging the quality of shoes. Add other points to the following list:
1 Is the style suited to the purpose for which the shoes will be used?
2 Are the shoes of a color which will go with several outfits?
3 Is the shape of the shoes similar to the shape of the foot, allowing toes to fall in normal position?
4 Are the shoes ½ to ¾ inches longer than the foot when I am standing in them?
5 Do the shoes fit in the instep, over the arch, and around the heel? Do they pinch or allow the foot to slide forward?
6 Are the shoes to be worn frequently? If so, are they of a quality which will stand wear?
7 Are the shoes to be worn only occasionally? If so, is it necessary to buy shoes of a quality to withstand wear?
8 Are the shoes made of leather or another material which will give good support?
9 Are the shoes comfortable?

14 CHAPTER POSTTEST

Number from 1 to 20. Beside each number indicate whether the corresponding statement is true or false. *Do not* write in this book.

1. Fashions are popular for longer periods of time than fads.
2. Styles are popular for longer periods of time than fashions.
3. The Textile Fiber Products Identification Act of 1960 requires that all garment labels contain the name of any finishes which may have been used on the fabric.
4. Acetate is a trade name.
5. Dynel is a trade name.
6. Modacrylic is a trade name.
7. A finish is a process which changes the natural characteristics of a fiber.
8. Garments with a durable-press finish present a special problem in lengthening.
9. Another name for durable press is permanent press.
10. Fibers which are made entirely from chemicals are called synthetics.
11. Fibers of similar chemical composition are classified together into generic groups.
12. The most useful source of information about the fiber content of a fabric is the salesperson.
13. Quality is more important in selecting a winter coat than in selecting a costume for a play.
14. Manufacturers blend two or more fibers to obtain the desirable qualities of each.
15. The fiber which can be tailored most easily is silk.
16. A garment which has been cut off-grain is more likely to stretch than one cut on-grain.
17. In buying hosiery, larger denier numbers refer to finer yarn.
18. Shoes with straps across the top make your feet look longer.
19. In buying shoes, you should try on both shoes in the pair.
20. Handbags should be selected in relation to the size of the person.

Choose the word or words which correspond to the *best* answer for each of the following questions.

1. Which of the following is a chemically made fiber?
   Angora, cotton, linen, nylon, or silk
2. Which of the following was the first man-made fiber?
   Acetate, nylon, Orlon, rayon, or silk
3. Which of the following is a polyester fiber?
   Acetate, Dacron, Dynel, rayon, or saran
4. Which of the following is an acrylic fiber?
   Kodel, Lycra, Orlon, Vinyon, or wool
5. Which of the following is *not* a finish?
   Colorfastness, Sanforization, spot and stain resistance, water repellency, or weave

15 CHAPTER PRETEST

Fill each blank with the *best* word to complete the statement. *Do not* write in this book.

1. If knitted garments are hung on hangers, choose __(1)__ hangers.
2. Soiled clothes can be stored in a laundry bag or __(2)__.
3. Buttons are sewn on a garment with a(an) __(3)__ thickness of thread.
4. General laundry cleaning agents are classed as soaps or __(4)__.
5. Separate your garments for laundering according to the amount of soil, the water temperature to be used, and their __(5)__ content.
6. Moth repellents should be used when storing __(6)__ fabrics.

Match the *use or characteristic* in List A with the *laundry aids* in List B. Use an item in List B only once.

List A: **Use or characteristic**

A. Used in final rinse water
B. Slow-acting presoaker
C. Should not be used with soap
D. Prevents formation of scum or curd on surface of water
E. Does not remove dirt, only stains

List B: **Laundry aids**

1. Bleach
2. Enzyme stain remover
3. Fabric softener
4. Water softener
5. Synthetic detergent

CHAPTER 15

Maintaining your clothes for attractiveness

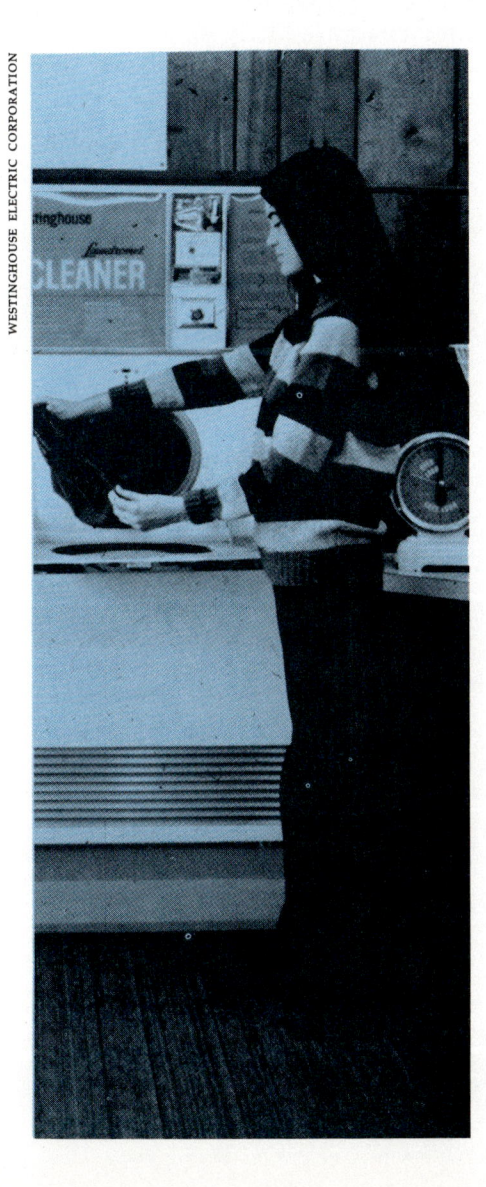

WESTINGHOUSE ELECTRIC CORPORATION

The difference between a well-dressed person and a poorly dressed person often lies in the care each gives his clothes. No matter how many outfits you have hanging in your closet or how becoming they were when you bought them, they can be worn and enjoyed only if they are in wearable condition. A rip in a seam, a missing button, a soiled neckline, or a spot can give the impression that you are a messy, careless person. Clothes more or less show those who look at you, "I care" or "I don't care what you think of me."

Taking good care of your clothes is one of the ways you can show your family that you are growing up and accepting responsibility. It may even be easier to persuade others that you are grown up enough to hold a job or go on social dates if you have first been a responsible person at home.

Daily care

Many teen-agers feel that weekly washing and ironing is the only care their clothes need. The laundry is frequently someone else's responsibility. Unfortunately, these young

Tell about an incident when a person was treated disrespectfully because of his or her personal appearance. Tell about a situation when a person may have been treated with respect because of his or her good grooming and choice of clothing. Specifically, why did others react to these people as they did?

Arrange on a flannel board pictures of people dressed in different kinds of attire. Discuss how you would react to each? Why would you react this way?

Discuss occasions when your appearance does *not* make any difference in the way people react to you. Do you feel that people as a whole make too much or too little of the way people dress? Defend your answer.

Bring to class fashionable garments which have been made over from previous years' clothes or from *hand-me-downs*.

295

Bring to class clothing which is in need of hand repair work. Choose an appropriate stitch from those shown below for repairing your garment.

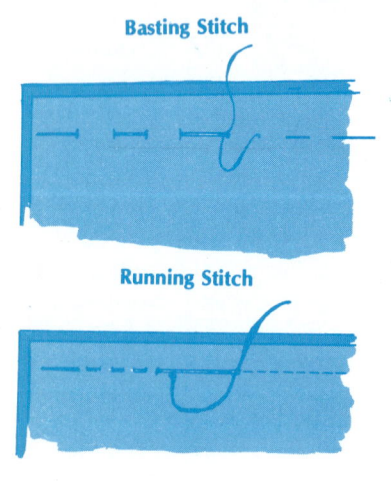

Basting Stitch

Running Stitch

Hemming Stitches

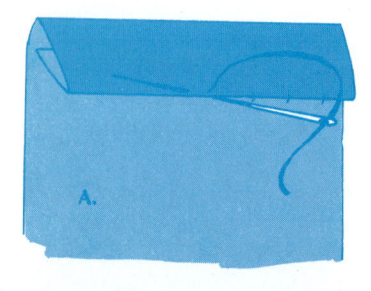

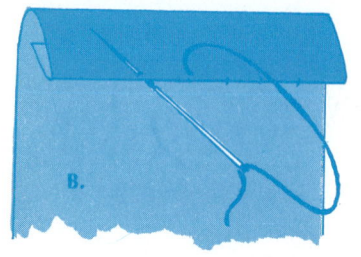

A.

B.

people don't know that their own daily care of their clothes will help make weekly care easier and more effective. If you brush your clothes and carefully return them to their proper places after each wearing, treat spots and stains, and repair rips, tears, and other damage as soon as possible, you'll find your clothes are generally in wearable condition and will look well when you are wearing them.

BRUSHING, HANGING, AND SORTING

As you hang each garment on the hanger, brush away any lint or dust that has accumulated. Hang clothes straight on hangers, and button or zip them so they won't slip off. It usually takes less than a full minute to find a hanger, fit a garment on it properly, and hang up the garment to air. This is a good time to check to see if there are any loose buttons, split seams, or spots resulting from the day's wear.

Some loosely knitted fabrics stretch if hung on hangers. It is better to air such knits and then fold them neatly in a drawer. If you wish to hang tightly knitted or double-knitted garments, use padded hangers. Be sure the shoulders are placed properly on the hanger so that the fabric is not poked out of shape. Wire hangers can be padded with plastic foam or strips of old towel wrapped around the upper curve of the wire.

Clothes which require washing before further wear, such as underwear and some blouses, can go directly into the clothes hamper or your laundry bag. Clothes that are left on the floor or carelessly thrown on a chair are likely to wrinkle and soil. If dirty, they will cause unpleasant odors in the room.

Many teen-agers wash their personal things, such as underwear, each evening as part of getting ready for bed. This is an excellent habit to develop. Clothes which are kept clean will last longer than those which are not. Too, such regular washing will ensure a clean supply of these clothes when they are needed.

SPOTS AND STAINS

The longer a spot or stain is allowed to remain in clothes, the more difficult it is to remove. Such stains as perspiration, soft drinks, and tea can become permanently set in the fabric. It should be noted also that insect damage is encouraged by certain food stains. There are inexpensive spot removers available in spray cans, bottles, and tubes, as well as the enzyme detergents and presoakers. Spots of most types can be easily and quickly removed if they are treated soon after a fabric is stained. If the fabric is one that must be dry-cleaned, take the garment to a dry-cleaner. Show him the stain, and if possible tell him what type of stain it is.

Sometimes a stain is not visible immediately but will become noticeable if it is allowed to remain in the garment. This is particularly true of perspiration and sugar stains. To avoid damage that will make the garment unwearable, wash or dry-clean your clothes often.

MENDING

When brushing and hanging clothes, you may find they need minor repairs, such as replacing a button, snap, hook, or thread loop. You should be able to do this type of mending yourself. (See the illustrations on pages 298–299.) If a seam has started to rip, a few stitches on the sewing machine can repair it. If you do not have a sewing machine at home, you can use small running stitches made with matching thread and an ordinary sewing needle.

Weekly care

When you get home each day, it's wise to change from your school clothes into something more casual. You may not have time to do much more than to brush, remove spots, and hang up your school clothes before another activity requires your attention. Sometime during the week, however, you need to set aside a certain amount of time for the care of your clothes. This care should include machine and hand laundry, taking items to the drycleaner, and ironing and pressing those garments which need such care. Take time during your weekly cleaning period to mend any garment which you discover needs mending.

MACHINE LAUNDERING AND DRYING

Many families find it is convenient and advisable to own an automatic washer and a dryer or a combina-

COURTESY LYSOL HOME SERVICE BUREAU

If garments are brushed and hung to air after each wearing and are occasionally sprayed with a bacteria-killing deodorant, they can often be worn a number of times before cleaning is necessary.

Practice threading a needle and tying a knot in the end of a thread. Follow the line drawings shown below.

a. Cut thread on the slant.

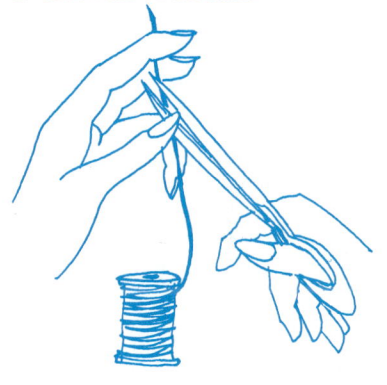

b. Slide thread through needle's eye.

c. Loop thread around finger and pull loop into a knot at the end of the thread.

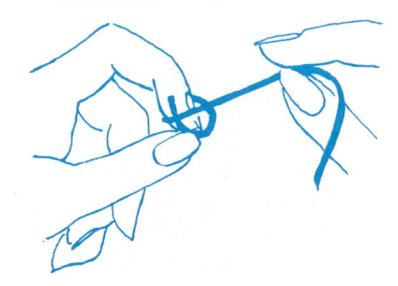

STEPS IN SEWING ON SNAPS

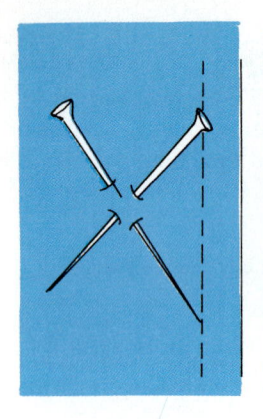

1. Mark location of snap, using two pins.

2. Take small stitch in position to be covered by snap.

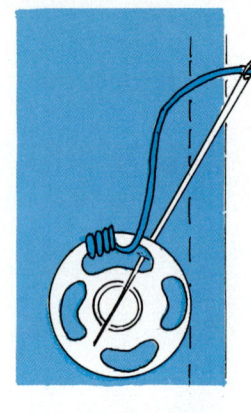

3. Placing stitches close together, go over the edge of the snap and into the fabric several times.

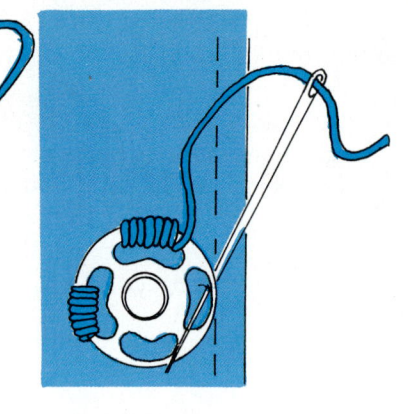

4. Insert the needle under the snap and into the next hole, and continue stitching. Fasten thread on wrong side under snap when finished.

STEPS IN SEWING ON HOOKS AND EYES

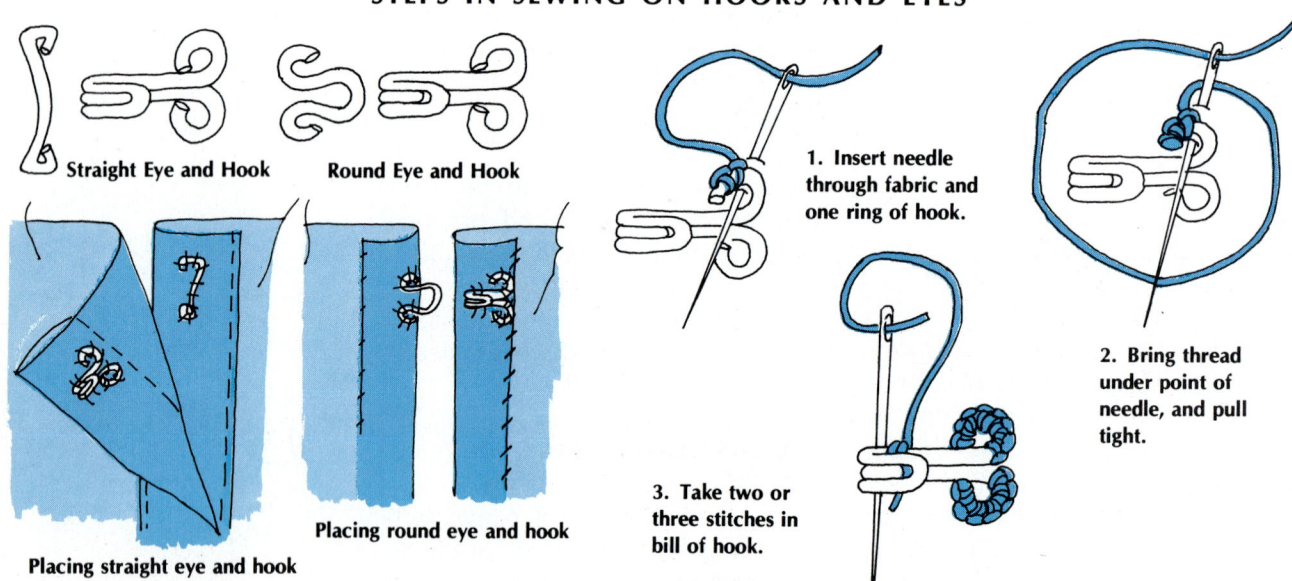

Straight Eye and Hook

Round Eye and Hook

Placing straight eye and hook

Placing round eye and hook

1. Insert needle through fabric and one ring of hook.

2. Bring thread under point of needle, and pull tight.

3. Take two or three stitches in bill of hook.

tion washer-dryer. A source of an additional water supply, perhaps a sink, is also desirable near the washing machine. Some families wash their clothes at home and dry them on lines. Other families find the inexpensive coin-operated washers and dryers at the neighborhood laundromat fit their purposes better. Most families will see a need for a steam-and-dry iron. Storage space for laundry supplies, such as detergents, stain removers, and bleaches, can be provided near the home laundry area. A hamper or cabinet for soiled clothes, a flat surface for sorting them, an ironing and pressing board, and a clothes rack for freshly ironed garments are all desirable laundry equipment.

Laundry aids

At most large stores you can choose from among an assortment of laun-

Experiment with various products and methods for removing spots and stains from a variety of fabrics. Try each method on stains such as blood, catsup, chocolate, grape juice, grass, grease, lipstick, and perspiration.
Make a chart indicating the products and methods that were most successful on the different types of spots and stains and on the different types of fabrics.

STEPS IN SEWING ON BUTTONS

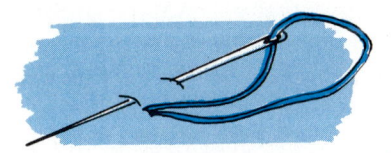

1. Using double thread, take one or two small stitches at the point where the button will be attached.

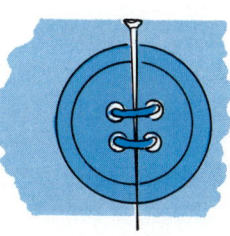

2. Hold a pin across the top of the button and take a stitch over it.

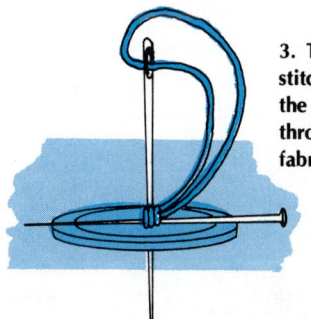

3. Take several stitches over the pin and through the fabric.

4. Remove the pin, and bring the needle and thread through the fabric.

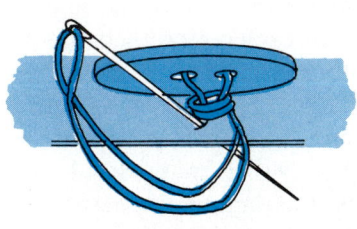

5. Wind the thread around under the button several times to make a thread shank. Fasten the thread on the underside of the fabric.

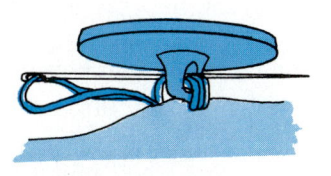

6. For a button with a shank, take several stitches over the shank and through the fabric. Fasten.

Write skits or role-play situations where family problems arise because one individual does not take care of his or her clothing. You may use one of the following situations for a skit or develop an idea of your own:
1. Leaving clothing items strewn around the house
2. Having nothing ready to wear when the family is ready to go out
3. Spending more than his or her share of the family budget for new clothes because old ones were abused
4. Having frequent emergency situations which call for new clothes

Discuss how such situations increase clothing costs and how they can be avoided.

Conduct laboratory experiments in which the fabric and water temperature remain the same and different detergents are used. Try cold-water detergents, enzyme detergents, and bar soap. Compare the results and costs, for each type of laundry aid.

Make a file of index cards telling how to remove common stains.

dry aids. For general laundry purposes, you will want to keep on hand both mild and all-purpose detergents, some kind of bleach, and perhaps an enzyme presoak powder. Some people, particularly those living in hard-water areas, also use water softeners and fabric softeners in their weekly laundry.

Detergents include a wide range of cleaning agents which mix with water to help remove dirt from fabrics. There are two main classes: soaps and synthetic detergents, or syndets. It is common practice, however, to speak of general cleaning agents as being either soaps or detergents.

Both soaps and detergents will help water as it acts to clean fabrics. However, it is the kind selected and the amount used that affect the cleaning process. The label on the package will give information as to when to use the product and how much of it to use. Soap and synthetic detergents cannot be used successfully in the same wash load, since each counteracts the work the other is capable of doing.

Bleaches are used to help remove stains from fabrics. While they are effective on many kinds of stains, they are generally hard on fibers. Weekly bleaching is seldom necessary if fabrics are washed frequently and correctly.

Enzyme stain removers contain enzymes which act to break up stains that cannot be removed by detergents alone. Since their natural action is slow, they should be given time to work. While some people simply add the presoak powder to the laundry water, others feel they get best results by soaking heavily stained items overnight.

Water softeners are compounds that are used for softening water in areas of the country where the water supply is *hard*. Hard water contains minerals that combine with soap to make a scum, or curd, on the surface of the water. Clothes cannot be washed clean in this scummy water. Water softeners combine with the water minerals to prevent the formation of this curd.

Fabric softeners are laundry compounds sometimes used in the final rinse water. As their name implies, they make the fabric soft and fluffy. They do so by covering the fabric yarns with an oily coating. Too, they help prevent the collection of static electricity in synthetic fabrics.

Steps in the machine-laundry process

Whether you have your own washing machine and dryer at home or use commercial laundry equipment, there are some things to remember in getting the clothes ready for laundering.
1. Separate items into piles according to their color, the degree of water temperature to be used, and the amount of soil. White fabrics are kept

separate from colored ones. Sheets, towels, and other items that need to be washed in hot water are separated from dresses, lingerie, or other fabrics that require warm water. Dark clothes, especially those that might lose some color during washing, are washed separately.

2 Check for spots, stains, and excessive soil. Most of these can be treated successfully by using either an enzyme presoaker or a full-strength detergent. Stains such as grass, perspiration, blood, and food can be removed with enzyme presoakers. Oily spots and stains, which are frequently found around collars and cuffs, respond best when treated with concentrated liquid detergent rubbed directly into the soiled area.

3 Use the proper water temperature for each type of fabric. Hot water and all-purpose detergent will give good results on ordinary cotton fabrics. Delicate fabrics, manmade fibers, and durable-press finishes respond best to warm water and mild detergents.

4 Load the washing machine according to the manufacturer's directions. Avoid overloading. If possible, wash white cotton clothes in hot water. Select warm or cool water for man-made fibers and colored fabrics.

5 Use the correct amount of detergent for the size of the laundry load. Too much detergent may cause suds to bubble out of the washing machine. Nonsudsing detergents are frequently recommended for automatic washing machines because they help avoid this sudsing problem. Use the amount suggested on the detergent box.

Your career
Clothing repair specialist

Duties: Mends broken seams; replaces buttons; replaces zippers; sews on hooks, eyes, snaps, belt carriers, and belt thread loops; replaces worn-out pockets, worn linings; reworks buttonholes.
Where employed: Laundries and dry-cleaners. May be self-employed.

Whether laundry is done at home or in a laundromat, effective results require that clothes be sorted into suitably sized wash loads of similar fabrics and colors.

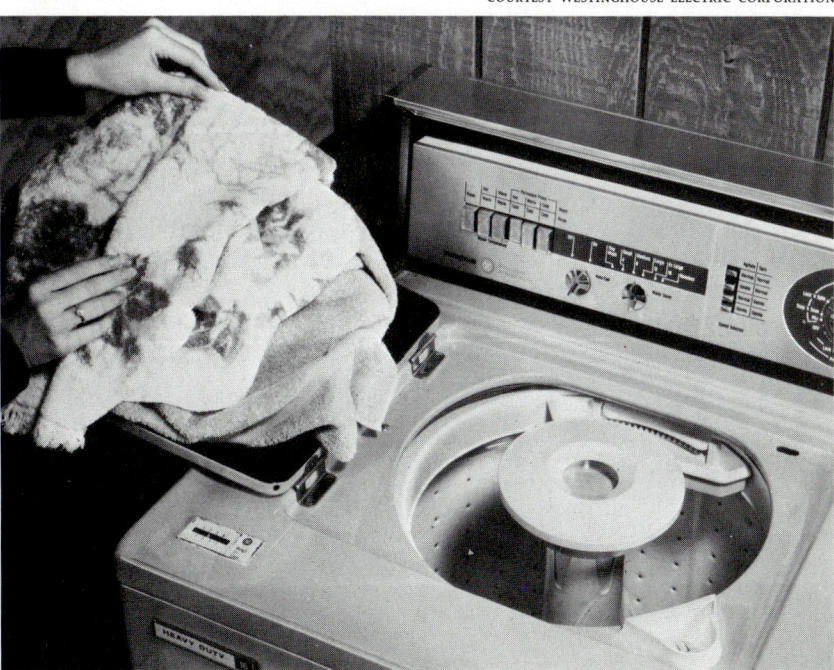

COURTESY WESTINGHOUSE ELECTRIC CORPORATION

Check the grocery store shelves and prepare a list of the descriptions used for various sizes of a single cleaning product. Perhaps other students can research other products. Make a chart which shows the type of product, the actual measurement of the contents for each size container, and the descriptions used to label each size. Give reasons which you feel explain why such products are labeled as they are. Do you feel these labels are effective?

Compare the cost of various washing powders, detergents, and bleaches. Design experiments to compare their effectiveness. Make some conclusions about how to buy laundry aids effectively.

Demonstrate ways of hanging various items on a clothesline to prevent stretching and puckering and to eliminate as much pressing as possible. Use items such as underpants, boys' slacks, and knit tee shirts.

Demonstrate washing clothes without using a washing machine or running water.

Care for clothes as you wear them

1 Avoid carrying bulky or heavy objects in your pockets.
2 Keep your hands out of your pockets.
3 Pull up a tight skirt or pants slightly before sitting down.
4 Protect your clothing from food stains or spots by wearing an apron when cooking, by using a napkin during meals, and by sitting up straight at the table. Before sitting down in a place where food is served, look at the chair seat to be sure that no food has been spilled on it.
5 Unfasten a fitted suit jacket when you are seated. To avoid wrinkling your suit, adjust or straighten your skirt or pants and the back of your jacket as you are seated.
6 Before lying down for a rest in your room, take off your dress or pants so that they will not be wrinkled.

---

6 When using a clothes dryer, dry clothes at the correct temperature. Untreated cotton can withstand high temperatures. Man-made fibers require low drying temperatures. A hot dryer will set wrinkles in a durable-press garment, while a warm one will remove wrinkles caused by wear or washing. When fabrics are overdried, they tend to lose their softness. Remove clothes from the dryer as soon as the drying cycle is finished. Fold flat items and hang other clothes on hangers while they are still warm.

HAND LAUNDERING

With today's up-to-date laundry equipment, practically all of a person's clothing referred to as *hand washable* could be washed by machine without injury. That is to say that fancy lace-trimmed blouses and underwear, girdles, hosiery, and handkerchiefs can be machine-washed effectively. There are, however, several *ifs* which make a knowledge of hand-laundering techniques essential for most people.

Many home-owned automatic washers and practically all of those found in laundromats have only one agitation speed. They are set to wash men's work clothes and such cottons as sheets and towels. This heavy agitation is hard on delicate fabrics. Many automatics are set for a hot-water wash and a warm-water rinse. Your delicate clothing will look better and last longer if it is washed in warm water and carefully rinsed in cool water. Also, it is a real temptation to mix fabrics and colors when you have only two or three delicate garments to wash. This mixing can easily cause your good white blouses and underwear to take on a gray or yellow look.

LAUNDERING MINIMUM-CARE FABRICS

Whether washed by hand or machine, minimum-care fabrics require special laundry attention. If handled correctly, these fabrics require little or no ironing.

Besides the knit and seersucker fabrics which have been worn for years, there are two new kinds of fabrics that should have minimum-care treatment:

1. Fabrics made entirely of man-made fibers or of blends of man-made and natural fibers.
2. Fabrics which have been treated with special resin, or durable-press, finishes.

Minimum-care garments require small washer and dryer loads to prevent wrinkling. Additional precautions include washing in warm—not hot—water and rinsing in cool water. Slow, gentle agitation during the washing period and a slow spin during the drying time are advised. If hung on a hanger to dry or if dried gently in an automatic dryer, these garments may require no ironing or perhaps just a touch-up with a slightly warm iron.

DRY CLEANING

If your clothing budget is limited, you will be wise to consider the cost of upkeep when selecting your clothing. The expense of dry cleaning can add greatly to your total clothing costs. Expensive clothes, silks, and noncolorfast items should be trusted only to your commercial dry-cleaner.

A quality dry-cleaner is up-to-date on the latest developments in fabrics. He knows the proper way to care for them. He can remove most spots and stains if he knows what they are made of. If a fabric loses body and becomes limp during the cleaning process, your dry-

Demonstrate ways of pressing clothes in a hotel or motel room where an ironing board is not available.

Demonstrate methods for mending worn stockings, sweaters, or other garments which require hand repair.

Bulletin board IDEA
Title: *Cure for Sick Clothes*
Directions: Display devices which ease clothing-wear problems. For example, you might display mending tape, a clothes brush, and iron-on patches.

Dry-cleanable clothes may be cleaned economically at a coin-operated dry-cleaner or sent to a dry-cleaning establishment. Choose either type of dry-cleaning system on a basis of the results desired.

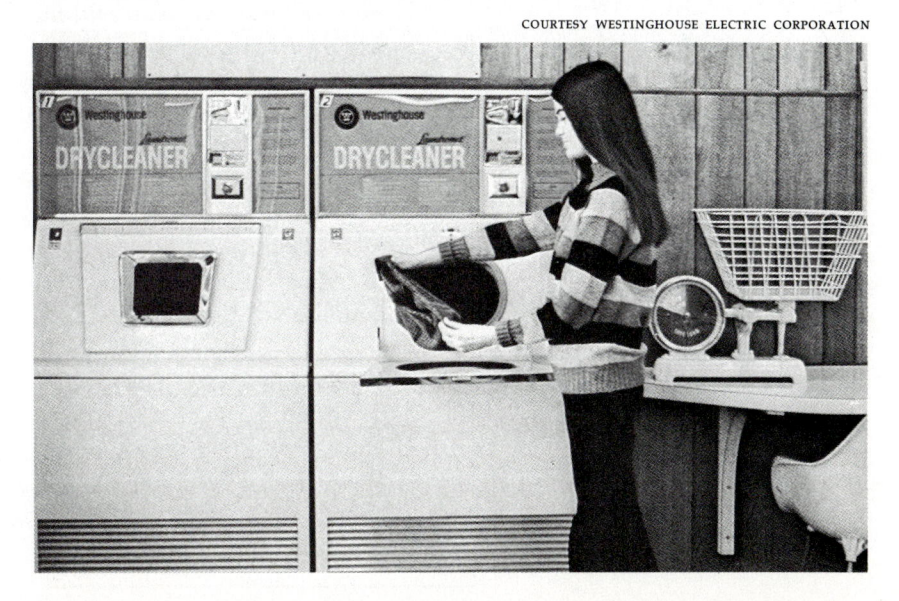

COURTESY WESTINGHOUSE ELECTRIC CORPORATION

Invite a guest speaker to come to class to demonstrate pressing and ironing blouses, skirts, dresses, men's shirts, and pants. A mother who does laundry would be a good choice as a guest. Bring clean articles from home which are difficult to iron. Get ideas and suggestions from the guest speaker about ways to iron these difficult items. Ask questions about handling specific fibers and fabrics.

Compare various brands and types of irons for cost, usability, and special features.

List reasons why it is desirable to make a habit of pressing garments from the wrong side.

Your career
Alterationist, men's wear

Duties: Alters men's wear of all types. May advise customers whether alterations are possible. Must understand tailoring techniques and the limitations imposed by fibers and fabrics.
Where employed: Men's shops, department stores, or may be self-employed.

How to wash clothes by hand

1. Remove your rings, and be sure that your hands are clean.
2. Look over the articles you plan to wash to be sure that all jewelry, ribbon, or other nonwashable trimming has been removed.
3. Sort the clothes as follows:
   a. Separate white and colored garments.
   b. Separate garments of man-made fibers, such as nylon, rayon, acrylics, polyesters, and spandex, from those made of natural fibers.
   c. Separate clothes that are slightly soiled from those that are dirty.
   Note: Give special treatment to heavily soiled areas by rubbing into them gently with the fingers or a soft brush a thick paste of soap or a liquid detergent.
4. Use water of the correct temperature for the fabric of the garment:
   a. For cotton and linen garments, use hot water.
   b. For man-made-fiber garments, use warm water.
   c. For woolen garments, use lukewarm water and handle the garments as little as possible in the washing to avoid shrinkage.
5. In a basin or bowl that is partly filled with water, dissolve enough soap flakes or detergent to make a good suds.
   Note: Garments labeled "wash-and-wear," "drip-dry," or "durable press" should be washed in a large container to prevent crushing.
6. Squeeze the sudsy water through each garment gently without rubbing or twisting the clothing. Badly soiled clothes may require more than one sudsing and a little rubbing on the soiled spots.
7. Rinse the garment two or three times in clear water to remove all traces of soap or detergent. Cotton can be rinsed in warm water, but minimum-care fabrics are generally rinsed in cool water.
8. Gently squeeze excess water out of the garment.
   Note: If the garment is made of drip-dry fabric, take special care not to wring or twist it. While it is still wet, place it on a rustproof hanger and allow it to drip-dry. Since drip-dry garments require little or no ironing, smooth the seams, cuffs, and collar while the garment is wet.
9. When you want a garment to dry quickly, spread out a bath towel, place the garment in it, roll up the garment and the towel together, and gently press out the excess water. Unroll them at once.
10. Hang clothes on a rack or clothesline in such a way that they will not stretch out of shape while drying. Place blouses on smooth, rustproof hangers. Hang stockings over rods, or pin them by the toe.

> **How to press a skirt**
>
> 1. Turn the skirt to the wrong side for pressing.
> 2. Slip it over the board with the hem toward the wide end.
> 3. Start pressing at the hem, moving the iron toward the waist.
> 4. Slip the iron under the skirt seams so that they will not make pressing marks on the right side of the skirt.
> 5. To press pleats, pin them in place at the hem and at the top, and press toward the waist.

cleaner can usually restore the original finish.

Many homemakers find that they can save money and also get good results from coin-operated dry-cleaning machines. To use them successfully, be sure to follow carefully the posted instructions. Avoid overloading the machine. It's a good idea to put the light-colored clothes in a nylon mesh bag separate from the dark clothes. Do not include noncolorfast items. Spots and stains should be pretreated before garments are placed in the machine. To prevent wrinkling of the freshly cleaned garments, be ready to remove them and hang them up to air immediately after the machine stops operating.

IRONING AND PRESSING

With the many synthetic fibers and special finishes used in today's wardrobes, there is little need for long hours spent on weekly ironing chores. However, since some ironing and pressing are necessary, the well-dressed person still needs to develop ironing and pressing skills. They can be used when a garment requires them. They include:

1. Sprinkle linen or all cotton clothing with warm water. Fold such clothes away in a plastic container, where they should remain for an hour or so before ironing.
2. Use a steam-and-dry iron to touch up or press durable-press clothing. Fill the iron with the type of water recommended by the manufacturer.
3. Use a well-padded board or table with a clean, heat-resistant cover.
4. Set the iron at the proper setting for the fabric you are ironing or pressing. (See page 225.)
5. Remember that it is the heat and the steam that remove wrinkles rather than the amount of pressure you apply.

Define dry cleaning. The following information may help you form your definition. Dry cleaning is the process of wetting and shaking a garment in a chemical solvent. The process is not actually *dry*. There are two general classifications of dry-cleaning solvents:
  Petroleum
  Synthetics of various chemical compositions
Solvents are chosen on the basis of the fibers and fabrics in the garments which are to be cleaned.

Answer these questions:
What are invisible stains?
What causes them?
Why is it important to identify spills, spots, or stains for a dry-cleaner when you know what they are?

Bulletin board IDEA
Title: *Be an I CARE Girl*
Directions: Display the title at the top of bulletin board. Underneath the title display pictures showing:
  Care of hands
  Care of hair
  Care of clothes
  Care of skin
  Care of teeth

Make a display showing a variety of storage accessories such as multiple skirt and blouse hangers; plastic garment bags; tie, belt, and shoe racks; and hanging shelves for purses. Discuss the advantages and disadvantages of each.

Develop a plan for hanging your clothes in similar groups. Rearrange your clothes this way and report on how well you like the system.

Put plastic cleaner's bags to use:
1 Line drawers with them to protect clothes from snagging.
2 Use them as dividers when packing a suitcase.
3 Use them under throw rugs to keep the rugs from slipping on the floor.

CAUTION:
Keep plastic bags away from small children to prevent death by smothering. Avoid using plastic bags to store out-of-season clothing because . . .
A Furs and suedes need air.
B Some fibers disintegrate in plastic bags.
C Some dyes discolor in airtight containers.

COURTESY WEST POINT PEPPERELL

Garment bags can be made of fabric. Other closet accessories can be covered with matching fabric or attractive combinations of fabric and adhesive paper.

6 Use a starch or silicon finish before ironing if such a finish is desired.
7 Press with the grain of the fabric (along the straight yarns) to avoid stretching the garment out of shape.
8 Press on the wrong side of the garment whenever possible.
9 If the fabric becomes shiny when touched with the iron, use a pressing cloth between the iron and the fabric.

Seasonal care

Most people like to dress in harmony with the seasons to at least some extent. Perhaps this desire is due to an inborn feeling. Perhaps it is due to training. But when the seasons change, almost everyone wants a change of clothing. A crisp, cool autumn day may trigger your desire for warm clothes in the fall colors of red, orange, gold, and brown. On the other hand, a sunny springlike day in February or March will make winter clothes seem dull and drab. You are ready for spring clothes in clear, bright shades of pink, green, and yellow.

It is this seasonal change which signals you that it is time to give your clothing a special kind of care. It is time to carefully clean and store the clothes from the season just ending. To make a place for them, remove from storage and put into shape those clothes which have been stored for the season just ahead.

STORING

Because so many buildings are climate-controlled, a number of your clothes can be worn all year long. These can be routinely kept in wearing condition. However, many summer clothes should be washed or cleaned and folded away in a drawer or box. Be sure that any stains have been removed before packing the clothes. Such stains may be almost impossible to remove if allowed to remain for a six-month storage period.

There will be less chance of discoloration if clothes are simply washed and dried before storage.

Both starch and heat from ironing tend to discolor clothes which are not being used regularly. Also, it is possible for starch-loving pests, such as silverfish, to eat holes in starched garments which are left in storage for several months.

When preparing to store your cold-weather clothes, be sure they, too, are absolutely clean. Holes can be eaten in them by moth larvae during the storage season. Garments containing wool should be protected with moth preventives of some kind. Some people prefer to use sprays, while others like to use crystal or cake types of moth repellents. Any one of these can be effective. Be sure that all clothes are carefully brushed and wrapped in tissue paper or plastic. This will lessen the chance of stain during storage and will help keep pests away from fabrics they are likely to damage.

REMODELING

Upon removing your clothes from storage for the new season, you may find that some of them need only pressing to be ready for wear. Others may not be in wearable condition. Perhaps hemlines need to be lengthened or shortened. A dress may have a good skirt, while its bodice is too tight. The jacket of a suit may be too tight or the wrong length for current fashion.

Imagination and *ingenuity* are the keys to successful wardrobe rebuilding. Can this skirt be combined with a different sweater or jacket? Could the jacket be used with a new pair of slacks? How about cutting off this dress to tunic length to be worn over several different skirts or pants? These are the kinds of questions you can ask yourself as you try on clothes left from last year's wardrobe. Remodeling can be a creative challenge. The wardrobe built on last year's selections tends to be larger, more adaptable, and less expensive than the one which is built entirely new each season.

Make storage accessories for your closet. You may wish to begin with one of the following:
1 Cloth shoe bags for the back of a closet door
2 Draw-string laundry bags
3 Skirt hangers made from wire hangers and clothespins or other clips
4 An additional skirt or blouse rod made from a broom handle attached with rope to the rod above

A closet or storage area which provides for storing garments in areas which are dust free will increase the wear life and appearance of garments.

COURTESY SEARS, ROEBUCK AND CO.

307

15 CHAPTER POSTTEST

Number from 1 to 27. Beside each number indicate if the corresponding statement is true or false. *Do not* write in this book.

1. Spots and stains should be allowed to set before attempting to remove them.
2. The condition of a person's clothes (their cleanliness, neatness, and state of repair) may reveal important aspects of his personality.
3. When taking stained clothes to be dry-cleaned, it is advisable to tell the dry-cleaner what the stains are.
4. A button should be sewn on a garment so that it is held closely against the fabric.
5. Soap and synthetic detergent should not be used in the same wash load.
6. Bleach may help remove stains and whiten fabrics, but it is hard on fibers if used in concentrated form or too frequently.
7. Fabric softeners help prevent the collection of static electricity in synthetic fibers.
8. Water softeners may be used in hard water areas to prevent the formation of a scum or curd on the surface of water.
9. Presoaking stain removers which contain enzymes react quickly.
10. Garments with durable-press finishes are dried at high temperatures.
11. Remove clothes from dryer as soon as the cycle is complete.
12. It is desirable to press dark fabrics from the wrong side.
13. Liquid chemical solvents are used for dry-cleaning.
14. Some stains cannot be seen until a garment has been cleaned.
15. Clothes should be clean before they are stored.
16. Many garments labeled *hand-washable* may be washed successfully by machine if agitated slowly, washed in warm water, and rinsed in cool water.
17. Drip-dry fabrics are correctly twisted and wrung tightly to remove excess water.
18. Press fabrics with the grain.
19. When drying stockings, hang them from the top.
20. Wash colored and white clothes in the same load.
21. Minimum-care fabrics are rinsed in hot water.
22. Spots should be pretreated before placing garments in coin-operated dry-cleaning machines.
23. Cotton fabrics can be ironed at higher temperatures than can cotton-polyester blends.
24. Garments should be starched before seasonal storage.
25. In sorting clothes for laundering, separate only according to color.
26. All stains are best removed from fabrics with soap and hot water.
27. Mending should be done before, rather than after, laundering.

16 CHAPTER PRETEST

Fill in the blank in each sentence with the *best* word or words to complete the statement. *Do not* write in this book.

1. In order to press and shape a garment to fit the curves of your body it is desirable to use a pressing ___(1)___.
2. When cutting a garment from fabric, it is advisable to use ___(2)___ which have bent handles.
3. For ordinary hand sewing, needles of size ___(3)___ are a good choice.
4. For machine sewing, number ___(4)___ thread is most frequently used.
5. The lengthwise yarns of the fabric are called the ___(5)___.
6. When the lengthwise and crosswise yarns of a fabric are *not* exactly perpendicular to one another, the fabric is ___(6)___.
7. A fabric which is guaranteed to shrink no more than 2% has been ___(7)___.
8. The two-toed part of the sewing machine which holds the fabric in place during stitching is called the ___(8)___.
9. The device which regulates the looseness and tightness of the top thread on a sewing machine is called the upper ___(9)___.
10. When a seam is stitched fast against a facing so the facing will lie flat against the garment, the process is called ___(10)___.

CHAPTER 16

Planning projects to match your ability

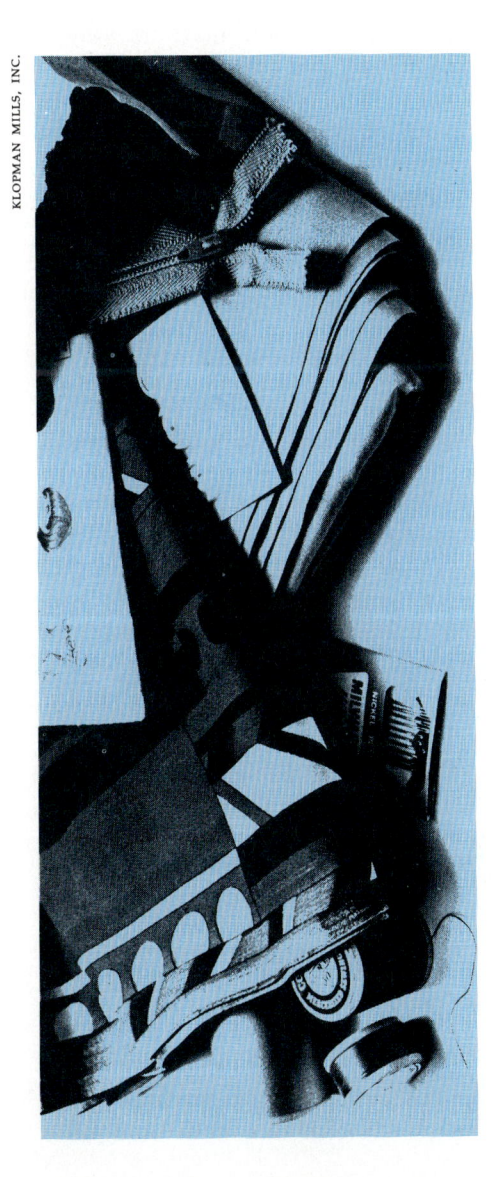

As the variety in ready-to-wear garments continues to grow, it may seem strange that there is also a growing trend toward home sewing. It was predicted that, as the variety of clothing available at popular prices increased, families would no longer find a need to sew. Yet the reverse seems to be true. The sale of fabrics, patterns, and sewing machines has grown at an even greater rate than has our population. It could be that the average person owns more clothes today than before. Can you think of other reasons for this unpredicted interest in home sewing?

Perhaps you think of home sewing as an economy. It is that. For the same amount of money, a person who has the time and ability to sew can have many more clothes than if buying similar clothing ready made. Also, one who sews can cut garments to fit particular figure problems. Are these, however, all the reasons for the growing trend in home sewing?

Many modern seamstresses will tell you that they like to sew. Rather than for fit or economy, they sew mostly for a feeling of *accomplishment*. They can express personal

List reasons why sewing is often part of a course in home economics. Discuss the reasons why a person might want to learn to sew. In addition to the reasons given in this book, what other benefits can be gained by learning to sew?

Interview at least one person who likes to sew. Ask this person why he or she enjoys it. As a class group, compile a list of reasons why people like to sew. What reasons were given most frequently?

Sponsor a class debate on the subject *Everyone should learn to sew.*

Bulletin board IDEA
Title: *Oceans of Notions*
Directions: Display various articles illustrating the numerous notions available for use in home sewing. Snaps, buttons, tape, ribbons, lace, zippers, and thread are examples of these sewing notions, or findings.

309

Select a dress which you would like to buy from a store. Note the price. Then, find a pattern which is similar to the dress. Select fabric and notions and make a list of the costs. Total the cost of the home-created dress. Compare the cost of the two dresses. Under what conditions is it economical to make your own clothes? Under what conditions would it be inadvisable for a person to decide to make her own clothes?

Suggest simple items a boy might make in class for himself. What will he learn from this experience that may help him in later life?

Bring an old nonelectric iron to class. Discuss the problems involved in using an iron of this type. How can these irons be used today as decorative items?

Suggest situations where an individual or a family may prefer a portable machine. Why would a portable machine best suit their needs? In what situations would a cabinet type machine be most practical? Why?

creativity through their selection and combination of styles, colors, and fabrics. They like to wear original, one-of-a-kind garments. Even if they never say it to anyone else, to themselves they can say, "I made it myself."

Sewing is not a skill to be enjoyed by women *only*. In fact, most of the best tailors and many dress designers throughout the world are men. A boy who senses he has an interest in this type of work can begin to use a sewing machine by making a barbecue apron, a vest, or some other masculine garment. Even if he loses interest in sewing as a vocation, the skills he learns can be put to good use when he leaves home for military service, college, or to live in a bachelor apartment.

Sharing the clothing construction center

Just as a carpenter or a mechanic needs tools for his trade, the seamstress needs tools for sewing. Part of learning to use tools, whether at home or at school, is learning to share the responsibility for keeping the tools in place and in good repair. For instance, if a school sewing machine fails to stitch, it becomes your responsibility to report the problem to an assigned student or the teacher. Too, courtesy suggests that you put away equipment you have used. Friendly cooperation between class members will help make the sewing laboratory serve all students more efficiently.

Most school clothing laboratories furnish the large pieces of equipment. These include the irons and pressing aids, hem markers, sewing machines, and other, similar equipment. It is your responsibility to avoid damaging any of this equipment. Time is also important. Sometimes several people may be waiting to use one set of ironing equipment. In such difficult situations, try to consider the time of other students as important as your own.

Selecting sewing equipment

Perhaps your family is considering equipping your home for sewing. If so, you will want to consider each type of equipment carefully. Your list may include a sewing machine and pressing equipment as well as sewing tools. Compare several brands of each before making a decision. However, if your interest is only in equipping your school sewing tray, learn how to choose quality sewing tools. You can learn at school how to use and operate the larger, more expensive sewing equipment.

LARGE EQUIPMENT
The sewing machine is the most expensive piece of sewing equipment. Machines can be bought in

SEWING LABORATORY EQUIPMENT

Padded Sleeveboard

Padded Ironing Board

Pressing Mitt

Steam Iron

Yardstick,

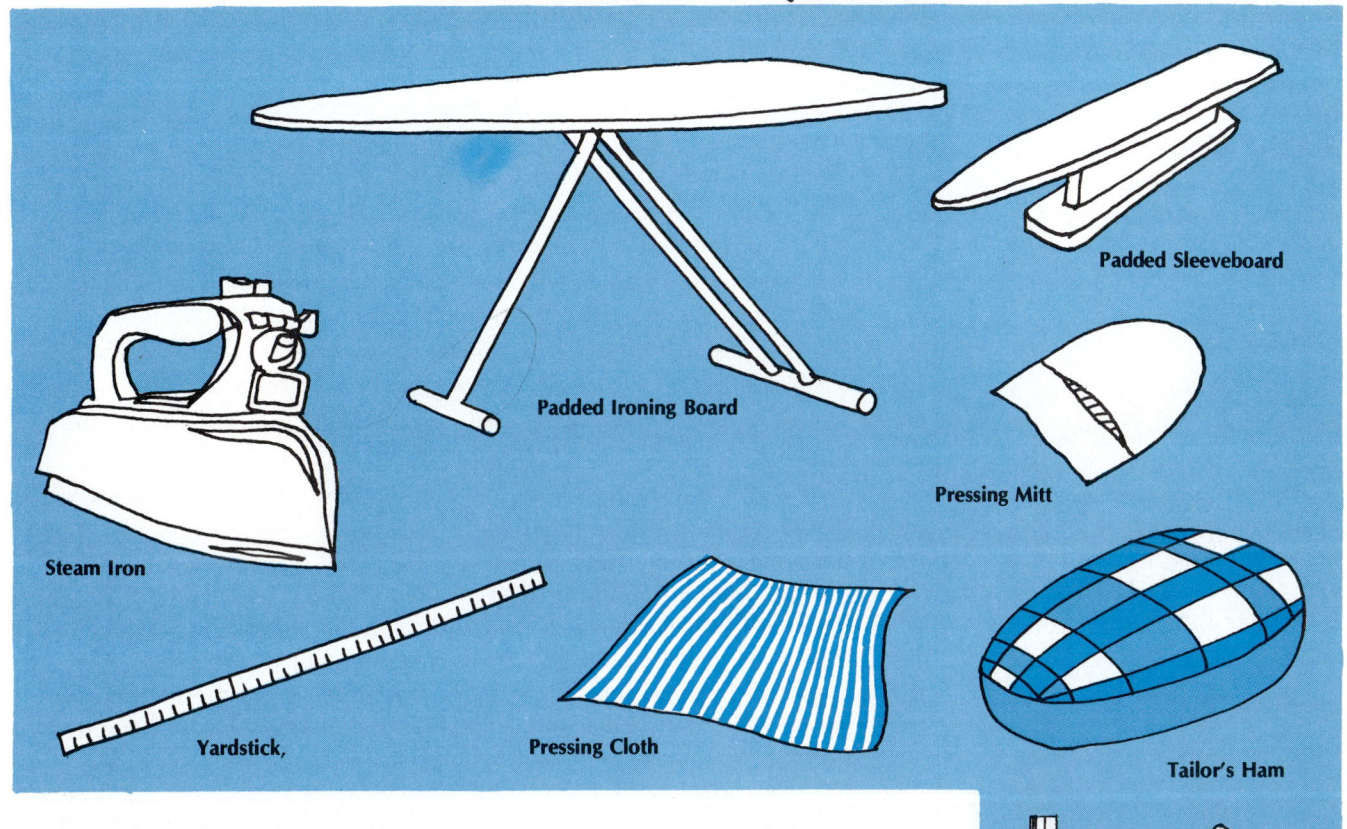

Pressing Cloth

Tailor's Ham

The large equipment needed in making simple sewing projects is usually kept in the home economics laboratory for school use.

Hem Markers

portable-case models as well as built-in desk or table models. Many may be used either way. Other equipment, sometimes called large equipment because it won't fit into a sewing tray, includes an ironing board, a steam-and-dry iron, pressing equipment, a yardstick, a hem marker, and a padded sleeve board. In clothing laboratories where advanced classes are taught, still other equipment may be used as students work on difficult fabrics and projects.

The sewing machine

You may find that the sewing machines in your school are all alike or of various brands and models. All brands of machines operate very much alike. Once you have learned to thread and operate one kind, you can generally, by reading the instructions, operate any machine. If

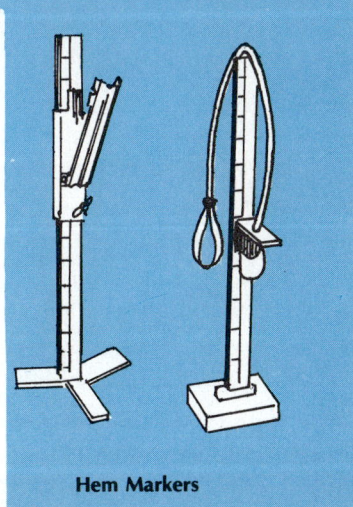

311

Observe stitches made on various sewing machines. Try to determine whether or not the tensions are adjusted correctly. Beginners can usually adjust the upper tension. Correction of the bobbin tension requires the attention of an expert.

Correct Tension Adjustment

When both tensions are in adjustment, the needle and bobbin threads are locked in the center of the fabric.

Tight Upper Tension

When the tension on the needle thread is too tight, the needle thread will lie straight along the upper surface of the fabric.

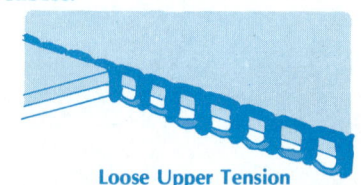

Loose Upper Tension

When the tension on the needle thread is too loose, the bobbin thread will lie straight along the under side of the fabric.

Parts of a sewing machine

1. *The head:* Metal portion of the machine which contains most of the sewing parts.
2. *The bed:* The flat base of the head which rests in the cabinet.
3. *The handwheel or balance wheel:* The wheel at the right of the upright section of the head, used in starting and stopping the machine.
4. *The bobbin:* The spool on which is wound the thread to be used as the lower thread in stitching. It fits into a *bobbin case*, or *shuttle*.
5. *The slide plate (or bed slide):* The metal plate covering the bobbin case, or shuttle, which carries the lower, or bobbin, thread.
6. *The spool pin and thread guides:* The pieces which hold and guide the thread to be used as the upper thread in stitching.
7. *The needle bar:* The piece that holds the needle and carries the upper thread down to it.
8. *The needle:* A needle with an eye and a point at one end. It is inserted into the needle bar and held in position with a clamp.
9. *The presser foot:* The piece which holds the fabric in place as you stitch. It is raised and lowered by means of a lever called a *presser-bar lifter*, found on the back of the machine. For stitching the presser foot is lowered gently, with the fabric in place, and then raised when the fabric is removed after the stitching is finished.
10. *The throat plate:* The metal plate directly under the needle.
11. *The throat-plate positioning lever:* A lever on the front of the bed of some sewing machines which regulates the up-and-down position of the throat plate for general sewing, darning, embroidering, or button sewing, and which unlocks the throat plate for removal.
12. *The feed or feed dog:* The part which keeps the material moving along toward the back of the machine as it is being stitched. It is a toothlike part located under the presser foot. It projects upward through the throat plate.
13. *The stitch regulator:* A device usually located on the upper portion of the head for lengthening or shortening the stitch.
14. *The thread take-up lever:* A lever through which the upper thread passes and which moves up and down as the machine is operated.
15. *The upper tension:* The device which regulates looseness and tightness of the stitch by controlling the pull on the thread as it comes from the needle. There is a similar tension on the lower thread of the bobbin.

you are thinking of buying a machine for home use, you will want to consider these points:

1. Buy from a dealer known for reliable service.
2. Choose a machine for the kinds of sewing you intend to do. Lightweight machines, usually less expensive than heavy ones, are easy to handle and are good for most ordinary sewing. Heavy machines should be considered if you are making slipcovers and heavy coats.
3. Avoid buying a machine filled with gadgets you will probably never need or use.
4. Compare desirable features of various brands in relation to prices.

The ironing board

An ironing board, which is generally thought of as laundry equipment, is almost as important to successful sewing as the sewing machine itself. An adjustable metal ironing board or table with a clean, well-fitted heat-resistant cover and pad will provide the necessary place for pressing large, flat areas of garments as they are being made.

The steam iron

Since moisture is necessary for effective construction pressing, a steam iron is also an essential part of your sewing equipment. A steam-and-dry iron, which can be used for general ironing as well as pressing, is a good selection.

The pressing cloth

Many fabrics develop an undesirable shine when they are touched by even a warm iron. For this reason, a small pressing cloth (usually made of a fabric similar to the garment) is used. It is placed between the outside of a garment and the iron when pressing is done during construction. For example, when a garment is pressed after the zipper is put in, the zipper area is covered by the pressing cloth.

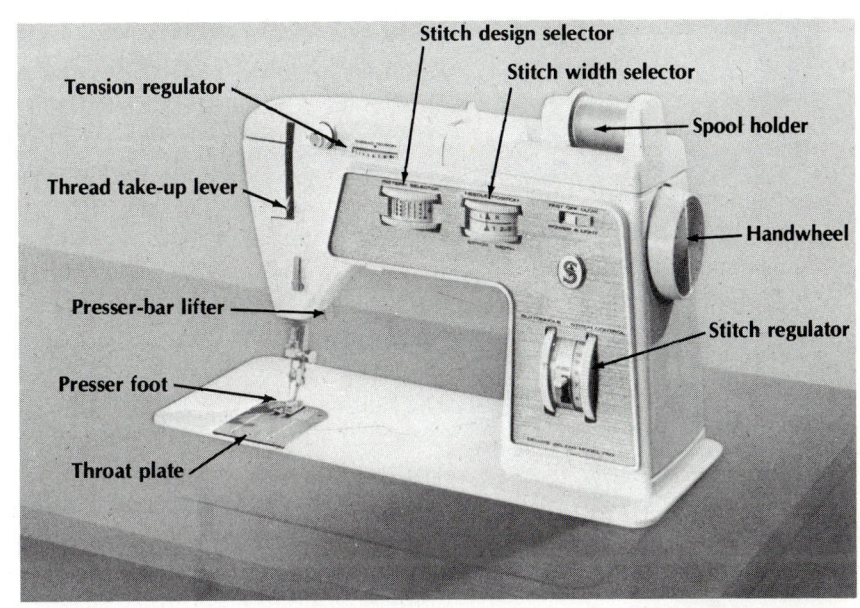

COURTESY THE SINGER COMPANY

Many modern sewing machines offer such features as self-winding bobbins, built-in buttonhole makers, dial-a-stitch mechanisms, special stretch stitches for knit fabrics, and the chain stitch for basting. Examine the features offered by several brands before making a final selection.

Bulletin board IDEA
Title: *Waiting for the Garment YOU Make*

Directions: Display an empty hanger on the bulletin board. Over the hanger drape fabric suitable for a simple garment. To the fabric fasten the small equipment and tools a student needs to bring to class for a planned project.

Show a garment which was the first project made by someone who is now an excellent seamstress. Also show something which this person made recently–a tailored coat or jacket, a dress made from an intricate pattern, or an entire ensemble. Discuss the progress an interested beginner can expect to make during one school year.

Divide a sheet of paper in fourths. In each rectangle list one type of equipment:
1 Large equipment necessary for sewing
2 Small equipment necessary for sewing
3 Large equipment desirable, but not absolutely necessary, for sewing
4 Small equipment desirable, but not absolutely necessary, for sewing

Suggest substitutions for the items listed as necessary.

Bulletin board IDEA
Title: SEW WHAT?

Directions: With brush strokes which resemble machine stitches, paint the title on poster paper. Below attach pictures of suitable garments for students to make.

The pressing mitt
Rounded or hard-to-reach areas of a garment can be pressed with the aid of a pressing mitt. The mitt can be placed over your hand or over a sleeve board. The garment is slipped over the mitt and covered with the pressing cloth. Then it can be steam-pressed into the desired shape.

The tailor's ham
A well-made garment is *blocked*, or steam-shaped, to fit your body. A tailor's ham is used with the ironing board and steam iron to create this shape. Darts, stitched in by machine, can first be carefully pressed on the wrong side and then shaped on the right side of the garment. By using the pressing ham, you can shape a garment to fit the curves of your body.

The yardstick
A yardstick is necessary for drawing long, straight lines. It is used to check grain lines and to mark hems during the construction of clothing projects. Most clothing departments keep several yardsticks for students to use.

The hem marker
An adjustable hem marker consists of a yardstick placed upright on a base of some kind. It may require the use of pins or chalk to mark a desired length from the floor. The pin marker is more accurate but must be used by a helper. You can use the chalk marker by yourself. Be careful, however, that the chalk marks are not dusted away as you pin the hem into the garment.

The padded sleeve board
The sleeve board can be used for much steam pressing during the construction of a project. A sleeve can be slipped over it wrong side out, and the seam easily pressed open. If the board is well padded, it can also be used when sleeve caps and other small circular garment areas are blocked into shape.

YOUR SMALL EQUIPMENT
Having your own sewing tools handy when you need them contributes to the success of early sewing experiences. Such tools include a supply of needles, pins, and thread, as well as scissors or shears, a thimble, a tape measure, and a 6-inch ruler or hem gauge. Mark each item with your name and class section. Misplaced items can then be returned to you.

Your teacher may suggest that you make a small sewing apron with pockets to hold all of your small pieces of equipment. If you put the apron on when you enter the classroom, you will have needed equipment with you at all times, whether you are in your seat, at the sewing machine, in the pressing area, or at the teacher's desk. (See directions beginning on page 326.)

SMALL SEWING EQUIPMENT

Sewing Box

Tote Tray

Wrist Pin Cushion

Shears

Tracing Wheel

Thimble

Emory Bag

Spools of Thread

Pins

Pin Cushion with Emory Bag

6-inch Ruler

Needles

Scissors

Sewing Gauge

Tape Measure

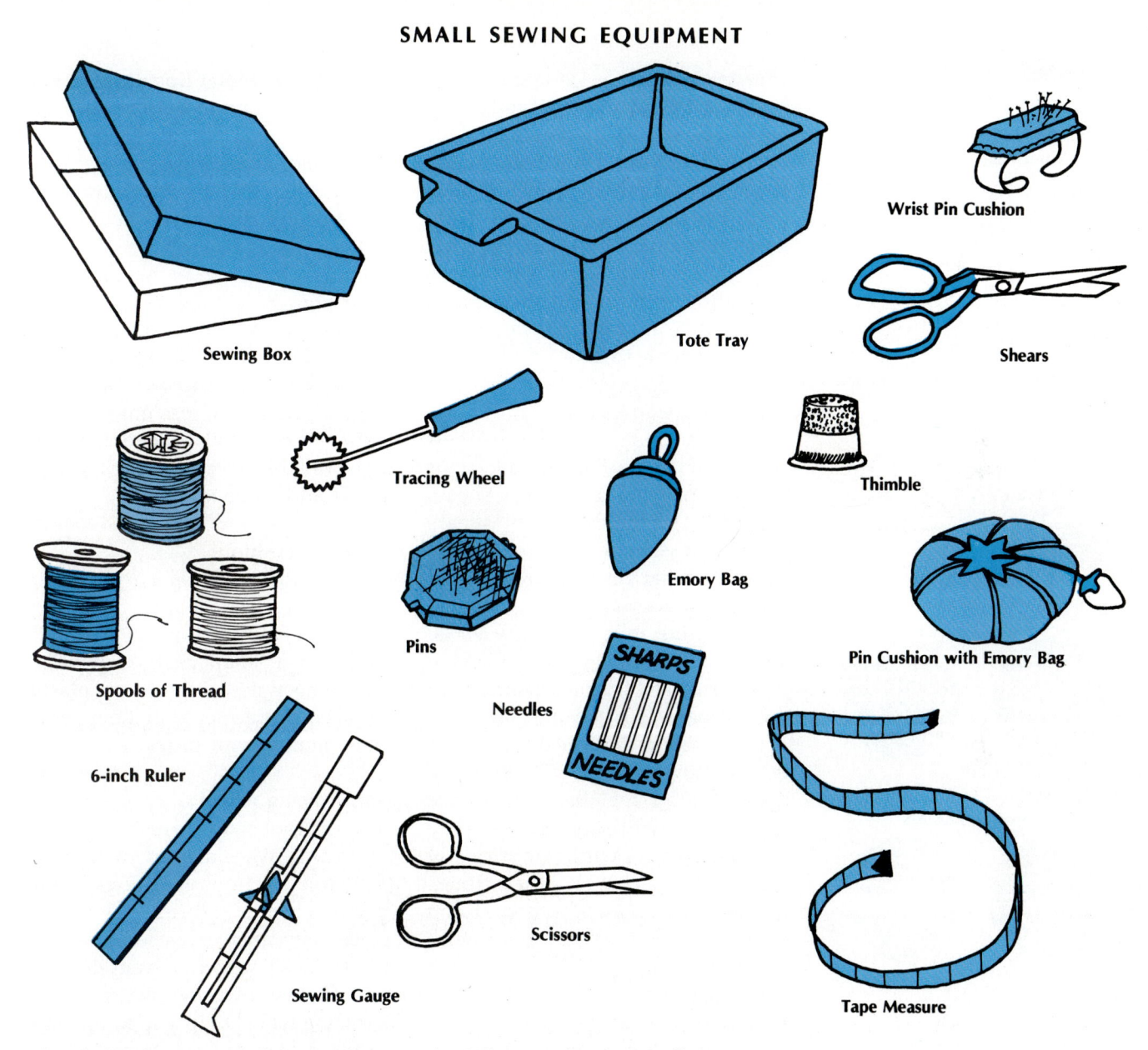

The small equipment needed in making simple clothing projects is usually owned by individual students and kept in boxes or tote trays provided by the school.

315

Identify the information found on the spool labels shown below. Which would be helpful to you as a consumer?

Silk

Synthetic

Mercerized Cotton

Heavy Duty

Your sewing box
Your teacher may assign you a tote tray to hold your belongings. This tray will fit into a specially made shelf. If your school does not have these trays, you will need to bring your own box. It should be large enough to store your equipment and fabric without crushing. Select a box that is easy to carry and sturdy enough to last.

Your scissors and shears
Scissors and shears differ in their sizes and uses. For cutting your garment from fabric, select shears with bent handles. Such shears make it easier to cut the fabric while it is flat on the table. Small sewing scissors are good for most small cutting jobs necessary while the garment is being made. Pinking shears are used to finish seams after the garment is fitted and stitched.

Both scissors and shears will keep their cutting edges well if they are made of good steel. Be sure they are sharp. They will stay sharp if they are used only for cutting fabrics, not for cutting paper or other things around the house and school. Keep them in a dry place and avoid dropping them.

Your tape measure
A tape measure is useful and necessary in accurate clothing construction. Select one made either of plastic or of a strong fabric that will not stretch when it is used. The tape should have metal tips on each end to protect it and to help in accurate measurements. For convenience in use, select a tape measure that is 60 inches long and clearly numbered in opposite directions on the two sides.

Your pins
Dressmaker's pins are thin and sharp. Because they are made of brass, they are rustproof. Size 17 is a good choice. Dressmaker's pins with either metal or plastic heads are available in paper packages or in ¼- and ½-pound boxes.

Your pin cushion
Pin cushions may be purchased in many sizes and shapes. They are also fairly easy to make. You will find that a small cushion that fits over your wrist with either a plastic or elastic bracelet will keep your pins handy at all times.

Your tracing wheel
Your school may furnish a supply of tracing wheels used to transfer the construction markings from patterns onto fabrics. However, since they are such useful sewing tools, most students want to buy one of their own. Marks made by a tracing wheel help you know how to put a garment together. Tracing wheels with very sharp teeth or smooth, round discs are available. However, most beginners find that a wheel which has rather blunt

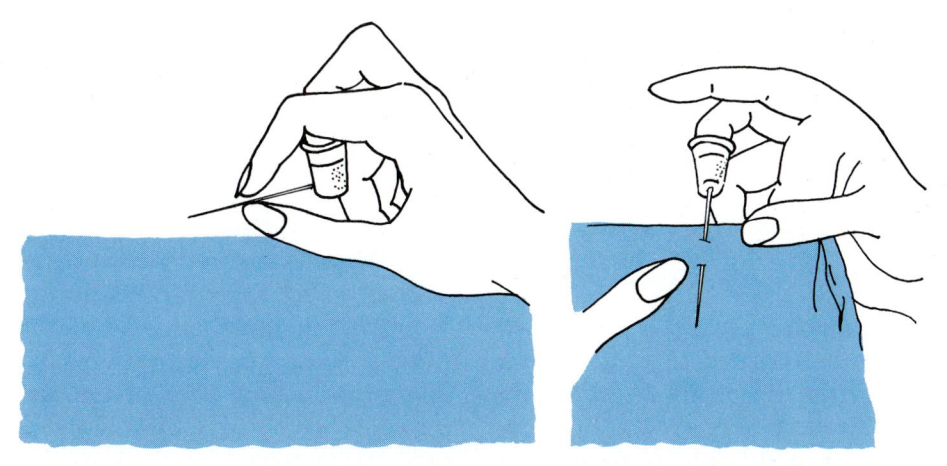

When learning to use the thimble, push against the eye end of the needle with the side of the thimble (left) and the end of the thimble (right). Push an unthreaded needle through the fabric for rapid beginning progress.

teeth works best for marking regular lightweight to medium-weight fabrics.

Your needles
Needles are sold in variety packages or in regular packages of twelve and twenty-four. They vary in size from 1 to 12. The smaller the number, the larger the needle. For ordinary sewing, size 7 or 8 needles are a good choice. Be sure they are sharp and rust free. To keep your needles sharp, you can use a small emery bag. These bags are filled with finely ground metal. Needles can be sharpened by slipping them into and out of the bag.

Your thread
Thread is made of different fibers and in a variety of sizes and colors. Cotton thread is very commonly used. It is sized by numbers from 8 to 100. The larger the number, the finer the thread. For ordinary machine sewing, number 50 is most frequently used. Number 40, or heavy-duty thread, is suitable for slipcovers and other heavy sewing. Numbers 80 to 100 are correctly used only for very sheer fabrics.

In addition to ordinary cotton thread, there are other kinds available. The list includes mercerized cotton, linen, silk, monofilament nylon, polyester, and cotton-covered polyester. As threads become stronger, there is a trend toward producing them in only one size.

In selecting thread for a specific project, choose synthetic thread for synthetic fabrics, silk thread for animal-fiber fabrics, and mercerized cotton for cotton fabrics. As nearly as possible, match the thread color to the predominant color in the

Relate an experience when a person should have used a thimble but did not. What happened? What have you seen people do in order to push or pull a hand needle through heavy fabric? Why are these methods undesirable?

Divide into groups to write and present skits which illustrate buying fabric and sewing equipment from well-informed and poorly-informed salespeople. Discuss the facts students need to know to successfully buy fabric and equipment from untrained salespeople.

Your career
Model

Duties: Models garments, such as dresses, coats, underclothing, swimwear, and suits for garment designers, buyers, sales personnel, and customers at fashion shows, private showings, and retail establishments. May inform prospective purchasers as to model, number, and price of garments and department where garment can be purchased.
Where employed: Department stores, fashion shops, fashion design studios, wholesale clothing outlets, modeling agencies, and TV stations.

Make a tailor's ham following the directions below. Discuss why the use of such equipment will improve the appearance of a garment you might make.

Make the ham with a wool cover on one side and a heavy cotton cover on the other side.

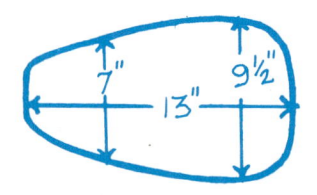

Cut two pieces of fabric according to the dimensions shown above. Sew the pieces together, right sides together, with a ⅜ inch seam. Leave a 2 inch opening at the large end. Press the seam and turn the cover right side out.

Stuff the ham as tightly as possible with clean builder's sand, pitch-free sawdust, or wool scraps. Hand-sew the opening together. The ham is correctly about 5 inches thick when finished.

fabric. In keying thread to fabrics, choose thread which, on the spool, appears slightly darker than the fabric itself. Thread looks lighter after you have stitched it into the fabric.

Your thimble
A thimble is used to protect your finger from the needle when you are hand-sewing. Some beginning sewers think a thimble is more of a nuisance than a help. In a way a thimble is a little like a pair of glasses. It may be hard to get used to, but after you have learned to use it you wonder how you ever got along without it.

In selecting a thimble, try several different sizes on the middle finger of the hand with which you sew. A thimble should fit comfortably. It should be tight enough to stay on your finger when you shake your hand, but loose enough not to crush or pinch the end of your finger.

Your sewing gauge
A sewing gauge is useful for measuring and marking hems, buttonholes, pockets, and seams. It may be made of metal or plastic and should have a sliding marker.

Choosing a project

Try to choose a first project which will give you plenty of opportunity to practice using the sewing machine. Be realistic as you search for a project. Choose something you are fairly sure you will be successful in making. Also, if possible, your choice should be something you'd like to own.

Sometimes students become discouraged about sewing and give up after their first attempt. There is no need to expect perfection on your first project. Don't be upset over mistakes. There is seldom one that can't be corrected.

TORN PROJECTS
The first thing you attempt to make should be simple enough to complete in a few class periods. Such a project can help you build self-confidence as well as skill.

If you elect to make something that does not require a pattern, but can be made by tearing the pieces into the proper shapes, you will save both time and effort. You can learn to handle the sewing machine before struggling with other problems, such as using patterns, marking fabrics, and fitting garments. The sewing apron described in this chapter is quick and easy to make, requires only a small amount of fabric, and will be very useful during the rest of your sewing classes. (See pages 326–329.)

PROJECTS REQUIRING PATTERNS
If you decide to use a pattern for your first project, try to find a very simple one. Probably your teacher

will suggest one or two patterns that will be suitable for the entire class to work on together.

You are more likely to be successful with your first project if you choose something simple. Consider making a beach poncho, a curler bag, a vest, or a blouse which has no more than two or three basic pattern pieces. The pattern you select should be marked with such words as *easy to make*.

Selecting fabric

Beginning projects require sturdy, easy-to-handle fabrics. In your rush to make something beautiful, you may find yourself wanting to buy a shiny, slippery fabric for a party dress. This is a serious mistake. Just one failure at the beginning could cause you to lose interest in sewing altogether.

Your first project is for learning to use the sewing machine. You may need to rip some stitches. You may need to tear the fabric into pieces. You may need to press creases which will stay in the cloth. Take all of these things into consideration. Try to choose fabric which will encourage success.

CHOOSE STURDY FABRIC

Don't be surprised if your family feel you should buy inexpensive fabric for your first project. They may feel you will become tired of your project and discard it after it is finished. Too, they may feel such fabric is fine to practice on. They may be right. On the other hand, low-quality fabric may not last long enough for you to complete your project. It could lose its shape while you are working on it. It might fade, stretch, or shrink the first time it is washed.

Since much of the fun and satisfaction of sewing is being able to wear or use something you made yourself, try to buy an attractive and sturdy piece of fabric. It can be discouraging if all your work in learning to sew is for practice only.

CHOOSE PRESHRUNK FABRIC

Some synthetic fabrics do not seem to shrink to any great degree when they are washed. But cotton, linen, and wool, the washable natural fibers, as well as rayon, have always given a certain amount of shrinkage trouble to both manufacturers and dressmakers. If you are considering one of these fabrics, or a blend of them, for a project, check very carefully for shrinkage-control guarantees before buying the fabric.

Most of today's fabrics are preshrunk. They have been treated in some way so that they will not shrink enough to make a garment unwearable after washing. However, it is wise to check the label before buying any fabric. Imported fabrics may or may not be labeled.

Sanforized is a trademarked shrinking process. It guarantees that

Show that you understand the following measurement terms: ⅛ inch, ¼ inch, ⅜ inch, ½ inch, ⅝ inch, and ¾ inch.

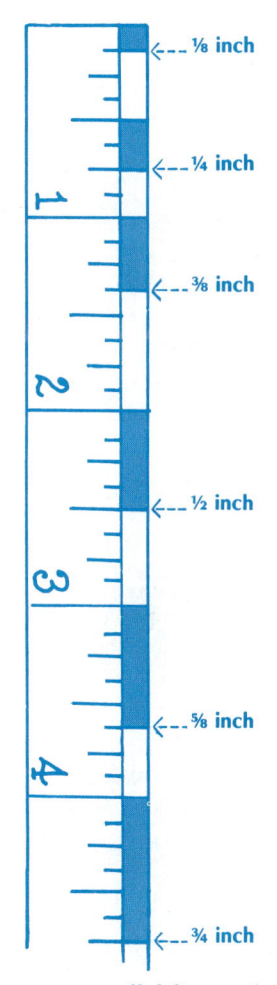

Draw two parallel lines which you feel are ⅝ inch apart *without* using any kind of measuring instrument. Measure the accuracy of your work.

Choose from the drawings below the one which best shows *balance of design* and attractive placement of *center of interest*. Defend your choice. How does the design of a fabric affect the amount of fabric necessary for a given garment?

a fabric will shrink no more than 1 percent. If a fabric is simply marked *preshrunk*, you need to know how much additional shrinkage to expect. Some preshrunk materials may still shrink enough to make them unwearable, while others are within the bounds of safety. If a label says a fabric will shrink no more than 2 percent, you can buy with assurance. Such a fabric will not need home shrinking.

Avoid fabrics which are not preshrunk. Home shrinking methods are bothersome, messy, and time consuming. By buying only clearly labeled, preshrunk materials, you, as a consumer, are encouraging manufacturers to shrink fabrics effectively before putting them on sale.

CHOOSE EASY-TO-HANDLE FABRICS

Fabrics vary considerably in the ease with which they may be handled. Try to determine before you buy that your fabric will be easy to handle. This means easy to cut, easy to stitch, and easy to press.

Some fabrics slip and slide around on the sewing machine and are difficult to stitch straight. Others will not tear and are difficult to cut. Some fabrics stretch while you are working on them and pucker at the seams. Some are so firmly woven that pin marks show, and when you rip out and replace stitches, the first needle holes continue to show.

Other fabrics tear when you are ripping out unwanted stitches. Still others are very loosely woven or have loops that catch on the presser foot of the machine while you are stitching.

In general, cotton or cotton-synthetic blends with a firm weave and dull finish are easy to work on. Try to find one of these materials for your beginning project.

Effects of fabric design on sewing projects

From year to year the kinds of designs in fabrics change with the current fashions. Sometimes large, splashy prints are popular. Sometimes plaids and stripes are big fashion news. Sometimes small all-over prints are very popular. Solid colors, however, are usually fashionable. Your choice of fabric will depend to some extent upon what is popular and available in the stores. In making your choice, consider these effects which fabric designs tend to have on the difficulty of a project:

1 Large designs must be carefully placed so that the finished garment will appear balanced. If there is a huge rose on one sleeve, the dress will look one-sided if the other sleeve is rather plain. A large design generally is more pleasing if centered in the garment or balanced in its distribution. Large designs are

difficult to work with, and extra fabric may be required because of the waste involved in balancing the design.
2. Stripes, plaids, and large checks are difficult designs for a beginner. Correctly, they are cut and stitched to match at the seamlines which fall at the center front and back and at the sides of a garment. It is best to wait until you have mastered many of the other sewing skills before you attempt this matching problem.
3. Plain fabrics might seem to be the best choice as there is no problem relating to matching designs. However, the loss of one problem creates another one. On plain fabric, all top stitching is very noticeable. This means that stitching must be straight. If you need to rip out stitches during your work, the marks of the old stitches are difficult to remove.
4. Small all-over designs are usually the easiest to work with. They do not require matching or balancing in a garment. Because stitches blend with the fabric, it is hardly noticeable if they are a little crooked.

Effect of fabric grain on sewing projects

Grain refers to the yarns with which the fabric is woven or knitted. In woven fabrics, the long lengthwise yarns that run parallel to the selvage edges are called the *warp*, or lengthwise, grain. The yarns that interlace with the warp yarns are called *filling*, or crosswise, grain. These yarns should be absolutely perpendicular to each other. If so, they are said to be *grain perfect*.

In the near future, with new fabric construction methods becoming common, the grain may not affect the way a garment hangs. But, for now, grain is still important to both the way the fabric will handle and the looks of the finished product.

Fabric which is properly prepared for cutting is grain perfect. As such, lengthwise yarns are absolutely perpendicular to crosswise yarns.

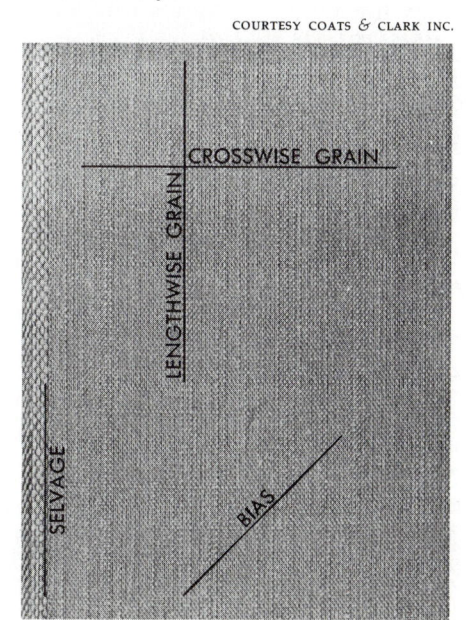

COURTESY COATS & CLARK INC.

Make a checklist of *construction* qualities to consider when buying fabric for a school project. Add other points to the following list:
1. Is the fabric firm, yet light in weight, and does it have body?
2. Is it straight?
3. Will it crease easily?
4. Can it be pressed easily?
5. Will it fray, or ravel, at seam edges?
6. Does the design present difficult matching problems?

Make a checklist of *care* qualities to consider when buying fabric.
1. Has the fabric been pre-shrunk?
2. Is it colorfast?
3. Is it easy to press?
4. Has it been sized, or starched, heavily?

Make a checklist of *comfort* qualities to consider when buying fabric.
1. Is the fabric absorbent?
2. Will it irritate my skin?
3. Does it soil easily?
4. Will it wrinkle easily?
5. Does it have stretch qualities?

Preshrink polyester and other fabrics which are not labeled *preshrunk* or *Sanforized*. Follow the steps in order.
1. Fold the fabric lengthwise with the wrong side out, so that the two selvages are even and the ends are even.
2. Use the longest stitch on the sewing machine and stitch across the ends through both layers of cloth. A few pins at intervals through the two selvages will help to hold these edges straight.
3. Fold the fabric crosswise several times so that it is a convenient size to handle.
4. Immerse the folded fabric in water, and let it remain for about 10 minutes.
5. Remove the fabric from the container and gently press out the water. Avoid twisting the fabric.
6. Roll it gently in a Turkish towel or heavy cloth to absorb excess water.
7. Spread the fabric out on a flat surface, smoothing out wrinkles as it dries.
8. Press before cutting. Some cotton fabrics may be preshrunk by pressing them with a steam iron until they are thoroughly dampened.

If something has happened in the manufacturing process to make the warp and filling yarns run untrue, or not perpendicular, the fabric is said to be *off grain*. Fabrics go through so many processes while the finishes, designs, and colors are applied that it is easy for them to become off grain. If this has happened to a fabric you are considering, check the label to see whether a durable-press finish has been applied over the fabric. If so, the threads will be permanently held in the off-grain position and cannot be straightened. If it does not have a durable-press finish, it can probably be made grain perfect with heat, moisture, or tension.

Sometimes the designs are crooked because they are applied after the fabric becomes off-grain. Check the selvage (woven edge) of the fabric to see that the design is straight along the edge and doesn't run off the cloth. Check the torn or cut end of the fabric for the same thing. If the design is printed crooked, buy from another bolt of fabric.

KEY POINTS IN BUYING FABRIC

A fabric is a good buy if you can answer yes to the following questions:
1. Ease of handling: Will fabric stay in place on the sewing machine or table and be easy to hold?
2. Sturdiness: Will fabric pull out of shape or stretch easily when worked on?
3. Strength: Will the fabric remain intact when ripping is necessary?
4. Shrinkage: Is the fabric guaranteed to shrink no more than 2 percent when laundered or cleaned?
5. Design: Will it be easy or unnecessary to match designs in putting the garment together? Can mistakes be hidden by the design itself?
6. Grain: Are the lengthwise and crosswise threads square, causing the fabric to hang straight?

PREPARING THE FABRIC

If fabric was carefully checked in the store before purchase, pressing may be all that is necessary before you begin your project. However, there may be reasons why you wish to use fabric which is less than grain perfect. An attractive bargain buy or a gift fabric may have become stretched on the bolt. There are ways to correct such imperfect fabrics, but they take time and energy. The more consumers demand grain-perfect fabrics, the more careful manufacturers will be about the fabrics they put on the market.

Straightening the grain

Before cutting into any fabric, check to see that it is grain perfect. To do so, fold the fabric down the center with the selvages straight along the edge of the table. Smooth out the wrinkles. If the fabric is straight, the torn or cut edges will fit together perfectly and the fabric will lie flat. If the fabric is stretched out of shape, one layer will be longer on the corner than the other. If the ends have been cut unevenly, you will need to straighten them by cutting along a pulled yarn. If the edges were torn but do not fit together, do not cut off the excess. Fabric tears along a straight thread; the trouble is stretched edges. Sometimes this stretching can be corrected by pulling the fabric by hand. To do so, grasp the fabric by the shorter end and pull it carefully.

Pin together the cut or torn edges at each end of the fabric, and pin the selvages. If the fabric does not lie flat with all of the edges pinned together, you will need to *block* it. Blocking is done with a steam iron. Gently lower the steaming iron to the fabric. Then lift, lower, lift, lower, until all the fullness and wrinkles have disappeared and the fabric is straight.

Using the sewing machine

Sewing machines come in many price ranges and styles. A variety of machines gives the student an opportunity to become acquainted with more than one type. However, using all one kind of machine makes it possible to interchange bobbins and other small parts, allowing you to use different machines on different days without the need for winding a new bobbin.

You will find it is easier to understand your teacher's directions if you take the time to learn the correct names of the various parts of the machines you will use. (See pages 312 and 313.)

THREADING THE SEWING MACHINE
Before attempting to thread the machine you plan to use, study the instruction booklet. Perhaps your teacher will have a large chart for you to follow. Every model of sewing machine is threaded in one particular way. However, there is a general procedure which is similar for threading most machines. It follows this order:

1. Raise the presser foot to the *up* position with the presser bar lifter, and, with the handwheel, raise the take-up lever to its highest position.
2. Put the thread on the spool pin.
3. Pull the thread through the top thread guide or guides.
4. Continue pulling it through tension control.
5. Find the next thread guide and secure the thread in it.
6. Feed the thread through the take-up lever.
7. Continue pulling the thread

Make fabric grain-perfect before cutting the pieces of a garment. When a fabric is off-grain, it cannot be folded straight. Either the torn edges will be uneven (a), or the selvages will be uneven (b). By pulling the fabric on the bias or by machine-stitching and steam-pressing, most fabrics, except durable-pressed ones, can be straightened (c).

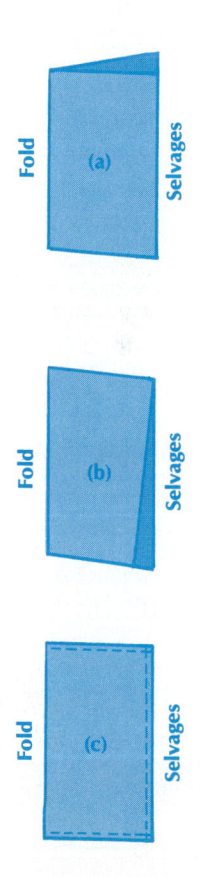

Create a SEWING MACHINE OPERATOR'S LICENSE. Try to earn your operator's license before beginning to construct your clothing project. Use the following ideas for a guide.

```
SEWING MACHINE
OPERATOR'S LICENSE
DATE          SCHOOL
NAME
ADDRESS
GRADE
     HOME ROOM
     TEACHER
THE STUDENT NAMED ABOVE
HAS MET REQUIREMENTS
FOR OPERATING THE
SEWING MACHINE
NONTRANSFERABLE
```

```
REQUIREMENTS
SATISFACTORY SKILLS
IN THE FOLLOWING:
1. THREADING THE MACHINE
2. THREADING THE BOBBIN
3. STITCHING A STRAIGHT
   LINE
4. TYING THREADS AT
   THE END OF STITCHING
5. BRINGING UP THE
   BOBBIN THREAD
   SAFELY
6. NAMING IMPORTANT
   PARTS
```

through any other thread guides that are present.

8 Thread the needle, being sure you put the thread into the side of the needle that has a groove running the full length of the needle. This groove is on the same side as the last thread guide.

9 Pull the thread through the needle for 4 or 5 inches.

TYPES OF BOBBINS

In general, there are two kinds of sewing machine bobbins. One is called the *conventional* bobbin because it has been used in various brands of machines for many years. The other is called the *self-winding* bobbin. As the name implies, this bobbin almost fills itself.

Filling the conventional bobbin

Most bobbins are filled on a special spindle on the surface of the machine head. The filled bobbin is then inserted into the lower part of the machine. It supplies a second thread so that the machine can make a durable locked stitch. To fill the conventional bobbin, follow these steps:

1 Disengage the balance wheel.
2 Place the bobbin on the bobbin winder, and snap it into position. (Check the instruction booklet accompanying your machine.)
3 Place the spool of thread on the bobbin thread pin, and pull the thread through the thread guide, which holds it firm. Then thread it through one of the small holes on the side of the bobbin, from the center of the bobbin to the outside. Hold this thread with your left hand.
4 Apply pressure to the knee or foot lever, or the speed control, and watch the thread wind evenly and smoothly. If it does not, recheck each step.
5 When the bobbin is full, it will snap out of the winding position automatically. Tighten the thumb screw in the balance wheel, and thread the top part of the sewing machine.
6 Place the bobbin in the bobbin case or shuttle according to the instructions in the sewing-machine booklet. Grasp the top thread in your left hand. With your right hand, turn the balance wheel, or handwheel, one complete turn. As the needle is lowered and raised, the top thread loops around the bobbin thread and pulls it back through the needle hole in the throat plate.
7 Pull the bobbin thread up and both threads to the back under the presser foot for about 4 or 5 inches.
8 Close the slide plate. You are ready to sew.

The self-winding bobbin

Certain sewing machines can be filled while the bobbin is fastened securely in the bobbin case in the lower part of the machine. Thread is supplied from the spool on top of the threaded machine. To fill the self-winding bobbin, follow these steps:

1. Open the slide plate and push the bobbin push button to the side.
2. Wrap the thread coming from the machine needle around the presser foot screw, and hold the thread tight.
3. Apply pressure to the knee or foot lever, or speed control, until the bobbin is filled to the desired fullness.
4. Close the slide plate. You are ready to sew.

WORK HABITS AT THE SEWING MACHINE

In learning to make straight stitches on the sewing machine, give attention to control of the speed. If you can stitch at a slow, even rate, you can better learn to handle fabric as it moves through the machine. At first you may want to stitch on lined paper.

Keep the bulk of the fabric to the left of the needle as you sew. Learn to watch the right side edge of the fabric rather than the needle. Guide the edge of the fabric along the seam guide lines marked on the throat plate of the machine. If your machine does not have lines on it, a piece of colored tape stuck on the throat plate may be used as a guide.

Posture

When machine-sewing, sit squarely and erectly in front of the machine with your feet flat on the floor. Choose a chair or stool which allows you to place your arms comfortably and easily on the bed of the machine. This will ensure free movement of both hands in the needle area of the machine and enable you to reach the handwheel easily with your right hand. Check to see that you are also able to reach the knee or foot lever (speed control) comfortably.

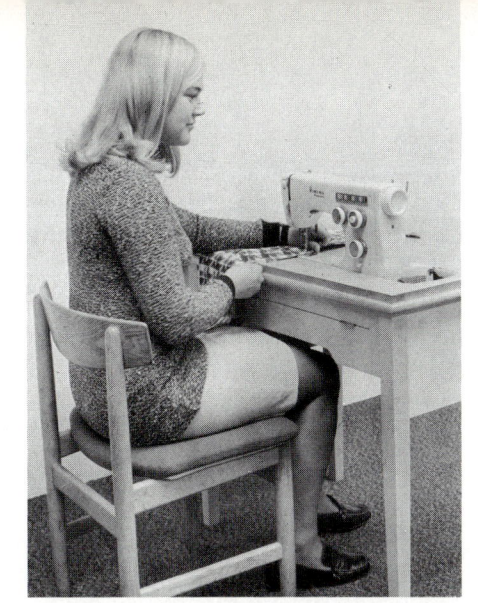

COURTESY VIKING SEWING MACHINE COMPANY

Correct posture while sewing allows a person to stitch accurately over an extended period of time with a minimum of fatigue.

Practice stitching *slowly* on the sewing machine. Explain why a beginning seamstress should operate a sewing machine with the same caution that a beginning driver is instructed to use in driving a car. Show and explain why stitching can be more accurate when a machine is operated at a slow-speed than at a fast one. Give three advantages of being able to stitch accurately.

Demonstrate both proper and improper posture at the sewing machine. Why are proper posture and adequate light important considerations when sewing?

If the plan seems workable, rearrange your sewing and pressing equipment to take advantage of both natural and artificial light. Consider also the placement of electric outlets.

Stitch your name or initials on a piece of notebook paper to learn how to guide the sewing machine. *Do not* use thread for the practice stitching.

Demonstrate the use of electric and battery-operated scissors. List the advantages and disadvantages of each.

Sturdy Fabric 1

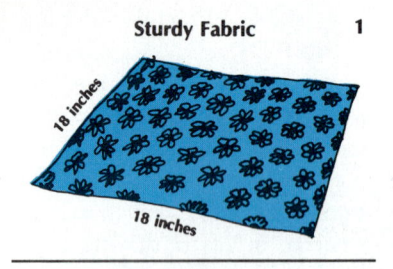

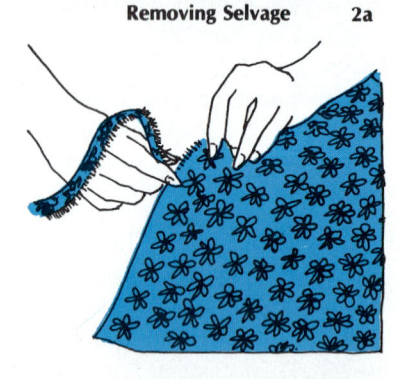

Removing Selvage 2a

Apron Body and Pocket Pieces 2b

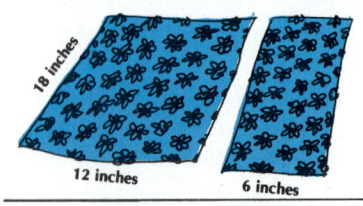

Straightening Fabric 3

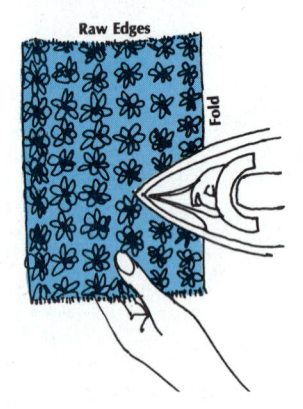

Lighting

Good lighting is necessary for accurate sewing results. While the small light on the machine helps by shining directly on the stitching area, it is not sufficient to prevent eyestrain. If possible, sew in a well-lighted room. Position the sewing machine so that light is projected over your left shoulder.

MAKING A SEWING APRON

Materials Needed:
½ yard cotton fabric (36" wide)
2 yards grosgrain ribbon (1 inch wide)
1 bolt matching single-fold bias binding
1 spool matching thread
1 medium-size snap

1. When choosing fabric for your apron, choose a very firmly woven (rather stiff) cotton fabric. If you choose a printed fabric rather than plain, your stitches will not be so obvious. One-half yard is enough fabric for two aprons. Perhaps you and your sewing partner will want to share the same half yard of fabric and spool of thread.

2. Tear the half yard in half lengthwise so that you have two 18-inch squares of fabric. Give one square to your partner or put it away. Clip ¼ inch in from the selvage, and tear off the selvage edge. Tear a 6-inch strip off the bottom of your square. You should now have one piece that measures 12 × 18 inches and one piece that measures 6 × 18 inches.

3. Fold the strips to see that the corners are square and not stretched out of shape. If they are pulled out of shape, you will need to block them with the steam iron to get them absolutely square. (See page 327, illustration at top left.)

4. Stitch ¼ inch from the edge along the top of the 6-inch strip. With the right side of the fabric up, fold the fabric underneath along the line of stitching, and stitch again as close to the fold as you can. This is called *clean finishing*. Turn under another ¼ inch, and stitch along the inside fold on the wrong side of the fabric to make a hem in the top of the apron pocket.

5. Lay the right side of the narrow pocket strip against the wrong side of the large strip on the bottom of the apron, and stitch them together ½ inch from the edge.

6. Turn the apron pocket over, and with the seam folded toward the apron section, understitch along the bottom of the apron section to keep the seam from rolling and to reinforce the bottom of the pocket. (See the illustration on page 327, lower left.)

7 Press the pocket section to the right side of the apron, and pin it in place with the edges of the apron and the pocket exactly together. Then stitch the entire edge of the apron from bottom to top, ¼ inch from the edge, catching the apron pocket to the apron. You will be stitching through two thicknesses of fabric through the pocket area. Stitch both sides of the apron this way.

8 With the right side of the apron up, turn the edge of the apron under along the side stitching line, and stitch along the fold as close to the edge as you can stay. Then hem the sides with a ¼-inch hem as you did the top of the pocket.

9 Fold and press the entire apron in half to find the center, and clip a small place in the top of the apron to mark the center front.

10 Fold the apron into fourths, and press a straight line from the top downward for about 3 or 4 inches. Clip the new folds to mark the apron in fourths.

11 At each of the two outside clips, make a small dart 2 inches long and ⅜ inch wide at the top. Stitch the darts so that they run off the cloth, making points. Tie the threads.

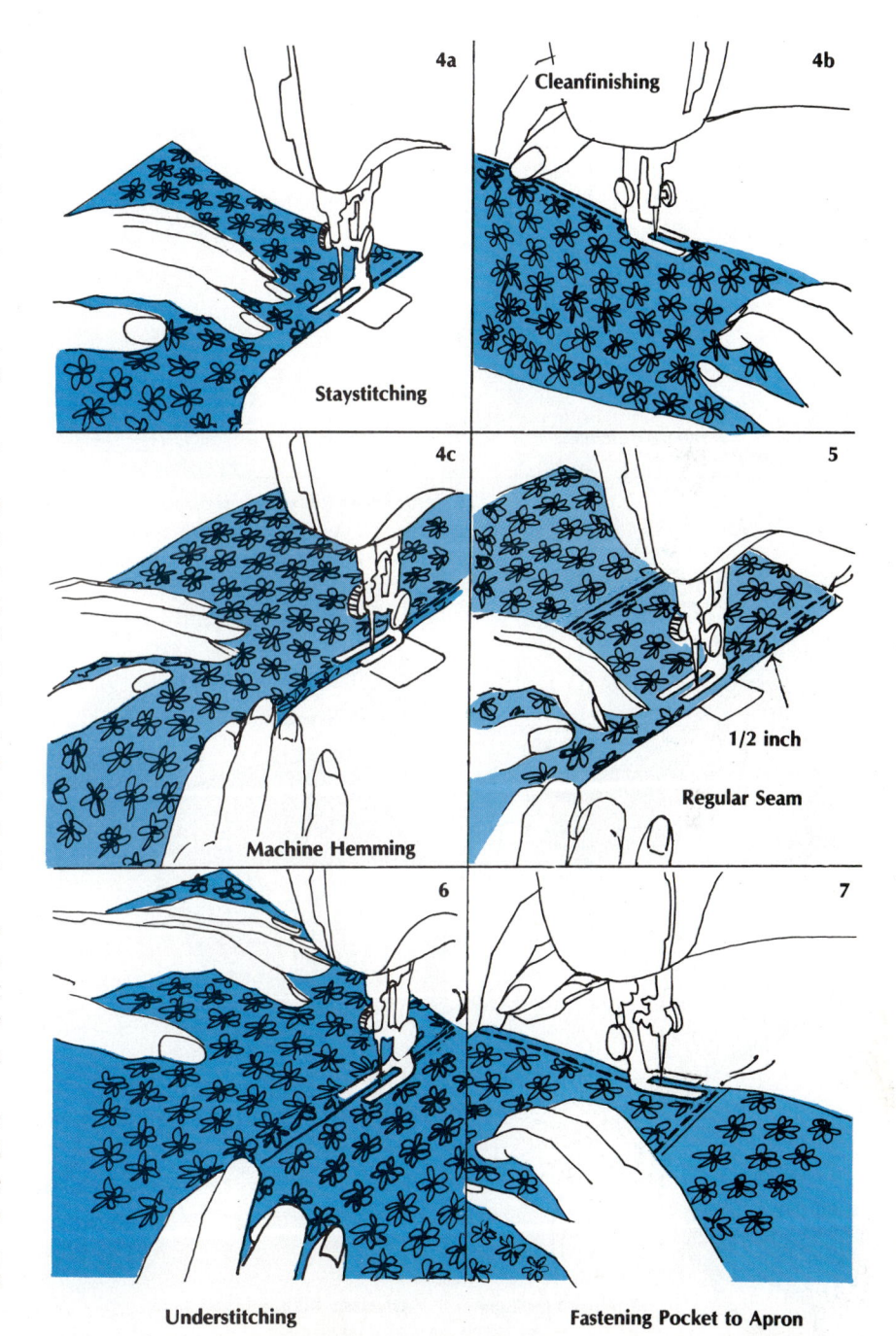

4a Staystitching

4b Cleanfinishing

4c Machine Hemming

5 Regular Seam — 1/2 inch

6 Understitching

7 Fastening Pocket to Apron

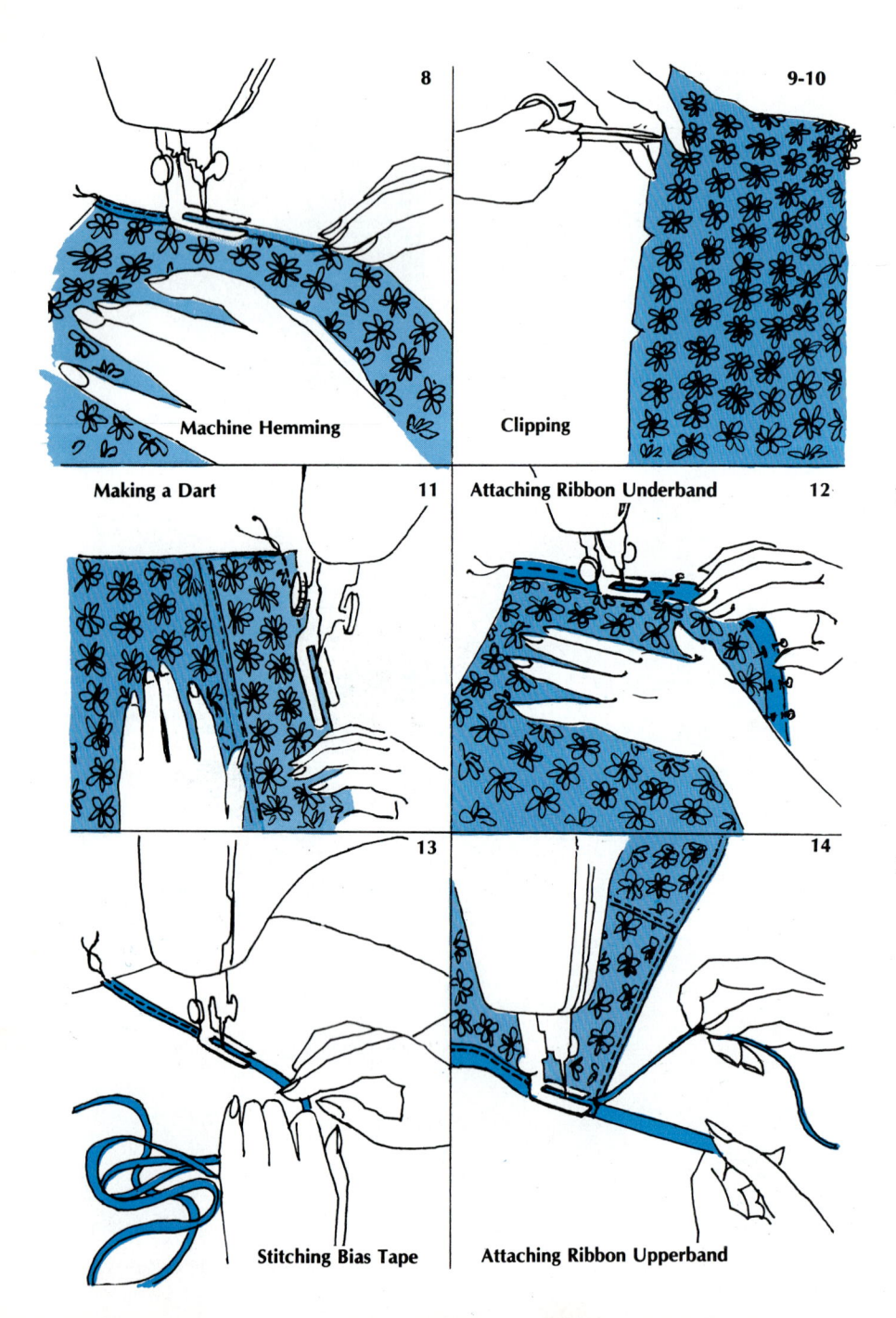

12 Cut a piece of the grosgrain ribbon 1 inch longer than the length of the top edge of your darted apron. Pin the ribbon to the back side of the top of the apron. Check to see that the edge of the apron top lies along the center of the ribbon. Allow the ribbon to extend ½ inch at each side of the apron. Fold the ends of the ribbon to the front to hide the raw edges. Stitch the ribbon to the fabric very near the top.

13 Cut a piece of the bias binding twice the length of your outstretched arm. Stitch to fasten the open side edges of the bias tape together, folding in the edges at one end for a finish. Put the unfinished end of this bias strip on the top of the ribbon at the right side of the apron top, if you are right-handed, or at the left side, if you are left-handed.

14 Pin the rest of the ribbon to the top of the apron so that the edges of the ribbon sections are together, making a double layer of ribbon along the apron top, with the center of the long piece of ribbon at the center of the apron. Stitch the ribbon together from the apron front along all sides of the shorter ribbon section, catching the end of the bias strip firmly between the two layers of ribbon.

Machine Hemming (8)

Clipping (9-10)

Making a Dart (11)

Attaching Ribbon Underband (12)

Stitching Bias Tape (13)

Attaching Ribbon Upperband (14)

15 Sew one side of a snap fastener to the loose end of the bias strip. Sew the other side of the snap to the ribbon where the bias strip is caught between the two pieces of ribbon. Cut the ends of the ribbon tie on a slant so that they will not ravel.

16 Sew a line of stitching 1½ inches from each edge of the apron from the bottom of the pocket to the top edge of the pocket. Backstitch at the bottom edge of the apron, and stitch a small triangle at the top to reinforce the top edge of the pocket. (See illustration at the upper right.)

17 Stitch another 1½-inch-wide pocket in the center of the apron. Measure ¾ inch from the center of the apron on each side of the press mark to find the places to stitch. This makes five small pockets out of the one large pocket.

18 Put the bias strip through the large ring in the handle of your shears. Snap the snap fastener together, and place the shears in the narrow pocket at the side of the apron.

19 The other pockets may be used to hold your tape measure, thimble, needles, thread, measuring gauge, tracing wheel, and other sewing equipment.

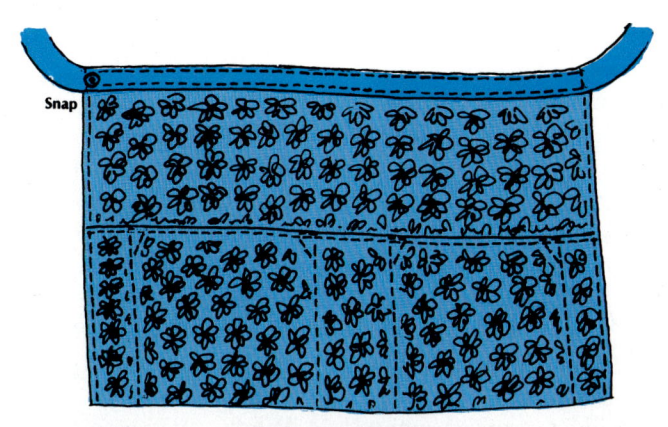

Pocket Stitching Plan 15-16

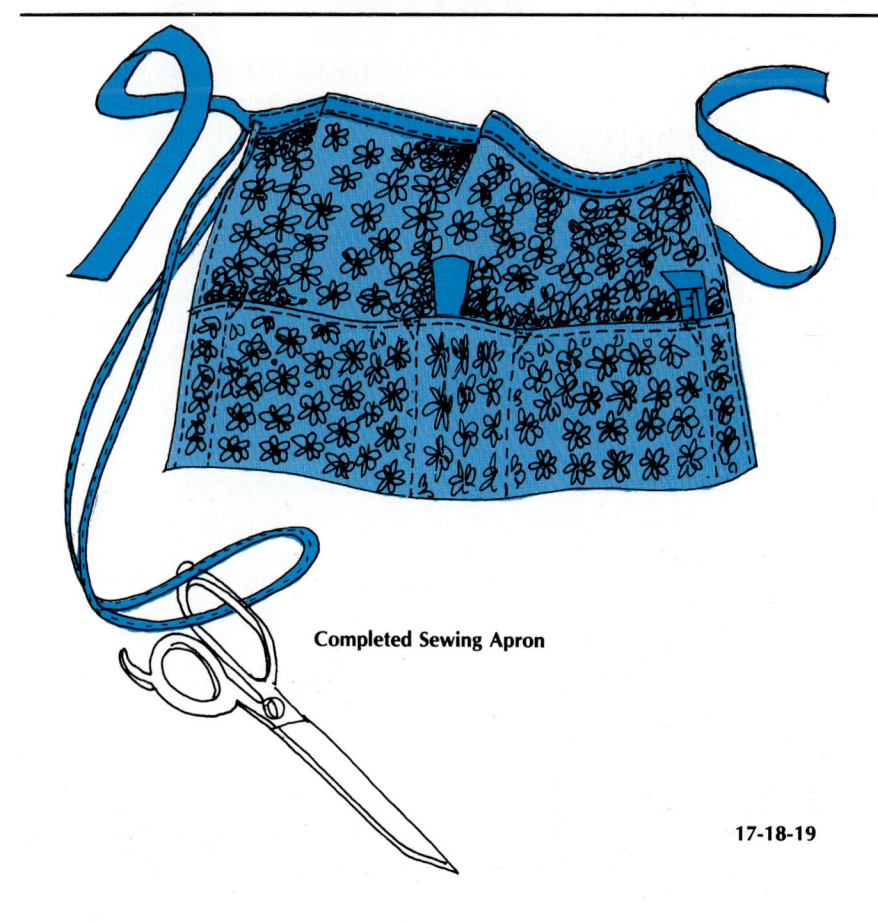

Completed Sewing Apron 17-18-19

16 CHAPTER POSTTEST

Fill in the blank in each sentence with the *best* word or words to complete the statement. *Do not* write in this book.

1. To prevent an undesirable shine on fabrics when using a warm iron, it is wise to use a(an) __(1)__.
2. Hem markers which consist of a yardstick placed upright on a base are made to be used with either pins or __(2)__.
3. The most expensive item of sewing equipment at school or at home is the __(3)__.
4. Small cutting tasks are done with __(4)__ which measure from three to six inches in length.
5. In transferring construction markings from a paper pattern to fabrics it is often possible to use a(an) __(5)__ wheel.
6. For sewing thick items such as slipcovers or coats, it is advisable to use heavy-duty thread number __(6)__.
7. A thimble should be worn on the __(7)__ finger of the hand with which you do hand sewing.
8. A trademarked finishing process which guarantees that a fabric will shrink no more than 1% is __(8)__.
9. For a beginning clothing construction project it is wise to select a fabric which has a firm __(9)__ and a dull finish.
10. The crosswise threads of the fabric are called the __(10)__.
11. Stripes or squares on a fabric are matched if they are wider than __(11)__ inch.
12. When the lengthwise and crosswise yarns of a fabric are absolutely perpendicular to one another the fabric is said to be __(12)__.
13. A fabric which is off-grain cannot be straightened if it has a(an) __(13)__ finish.
14. When straightening a fabric, blocking is done with a(an) __(14)__.
15. The toothlike part of the sewing machine which moves the fabric forward and backward is called the __(15)__.
16. In machine stitching, the spool which holds the lower thread is called a(an) __(16)__.
17. The part of the machine located at the right of the head which revolves once with each stitch is called the __(17)__.
18. On many sewing machine models there are seam guide lines varying from ⅜ to ¾ inch marked on the __(18)__ of the machine. (Be specific).
19. In selecting a spool of thread, choose one which is slightly __(19)__ in color than the fabric with which it will be used.
20. When machine sewing, the bulk of the fabric is kept on the __(20)__ side of the needle.
21. The process of stitching, folding, and restitching an edge is called __(21)__.

17 CHAPTER PRETEST

Fill in the blank in each sentence with the *best* word or words to complete the statement. *Do not* write in this book.

1. The pattern type which has odd numbered sizes such as 7, 9, and 11 is __(1)__.
2. Each pattern size provides exact measurements of the bust, waist length, waist, and __(2)__.
3. In buying a pattern for a blouse, select the size which best fits your __(3)__ measurement.
4. Directions for laying the pattern on various width fabrics are found on the __(4)__.
5. To determine which pattern pieces fit together, match the __(5)__.
6. The seam allowance is usually __(6)__ of an inch.
7. The amount of extra room provided in a pattern so that the body can move comfortably is called __(7)__.
8. Cutting with the grain of a fabric is called __(8)__ cutting.
9. Stitching ½ inch from the cut edge of the garment to prevent stretching is __(9)__.
10. The exact diagonal of the fabric which stretches is the __(10)__.
11. Stitching through the facing and both seam allowances so that the facing will roll toward the inside of the garment is called __(11)__.
12. The fabric used between the facing and the garment to add body and shape is called __(12)__.

CHAPTER 17

Creating clothes to wear and enjoy

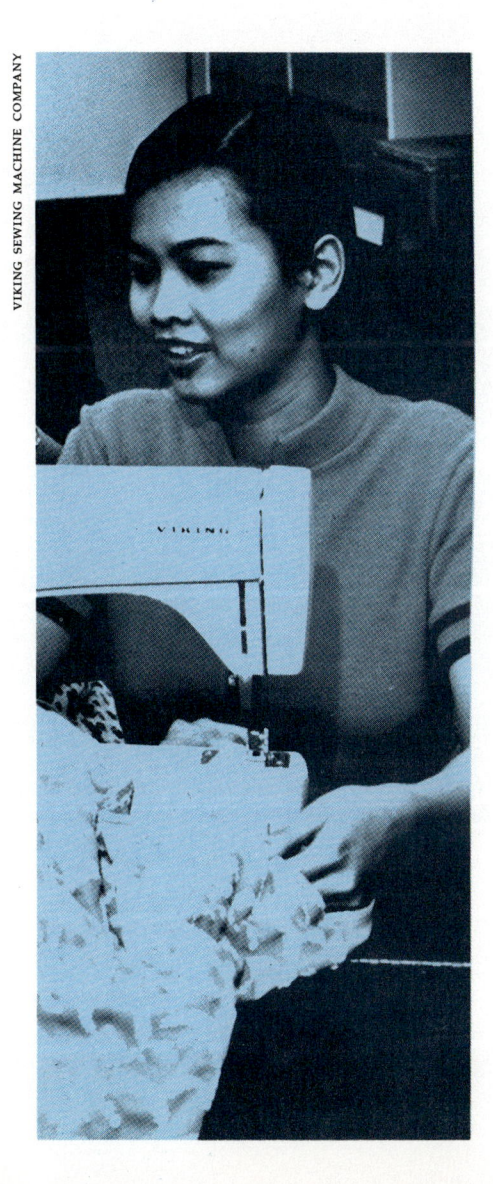

History suggests that people first learned to sew in order to put skins together as garments. These sewing skills continue to be useful today, but many people recognize sewing for another reason. It provides a means for them to create clothing they can enjoy.

The success of your first school project depends somewhat on how careful and patient you are as you learn to sew. Keep in mind that you are just beginning. Even if you have had some sewing experience, patient practice is necessary.

Just as in other activities, some days everything seems to go wrong in sewing. Other days everything will fall into its proper place. If your project is moving slowly, instead of hurrying, try taking only a step at a time. The use of sewing aids will also make your work move faster. Successful first projects are important because early successes contribute to your enjoyment of sewing.

Selecting a pattern

There are several brands of commercial patterns on the market. These patterns offer a wide choice

Make a list of the garments in your wardrobe by organizing them into categories. Select a garment to make on the basis of your needs.

Show a ready-made garment which was cut off-grain. What have been the results? How can you apply this information when cutting the pieces of your clothing project?

Explain the *stroke the cat* test to determine the direction in which a fabric should be cut and stitched.

Bulletin board IDEA
Title: *Your Work's Cut Out For YOU*

Directions: Below the title and cutouts of paper dolls, print words which describe work to be done in a clothing construction class. Include words such as fitting, marking, staystitching, and pressing.

C Work on the following series of projects while waiting for the sewing machine, other equipment, or your teacher's help.

Indicate which of the lines in Set A are best for you and tell why you made this selection.

Set A

| T ↑ Y

Indicate which of the lines in Set B are best for you and tell why you made this selection.

Set B

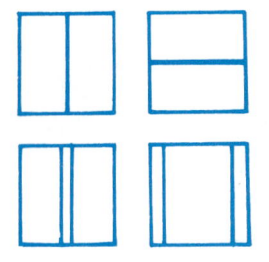

Look through pattern books for patterns which include several attractive garments: perhaps a blouse, a vest, a skirt, and a pair of pants. Discuss the advantages and disadvantages of choosing such a pattern for a beginning project.

CHOOSE PATTERN FOR FIGURE TYPE

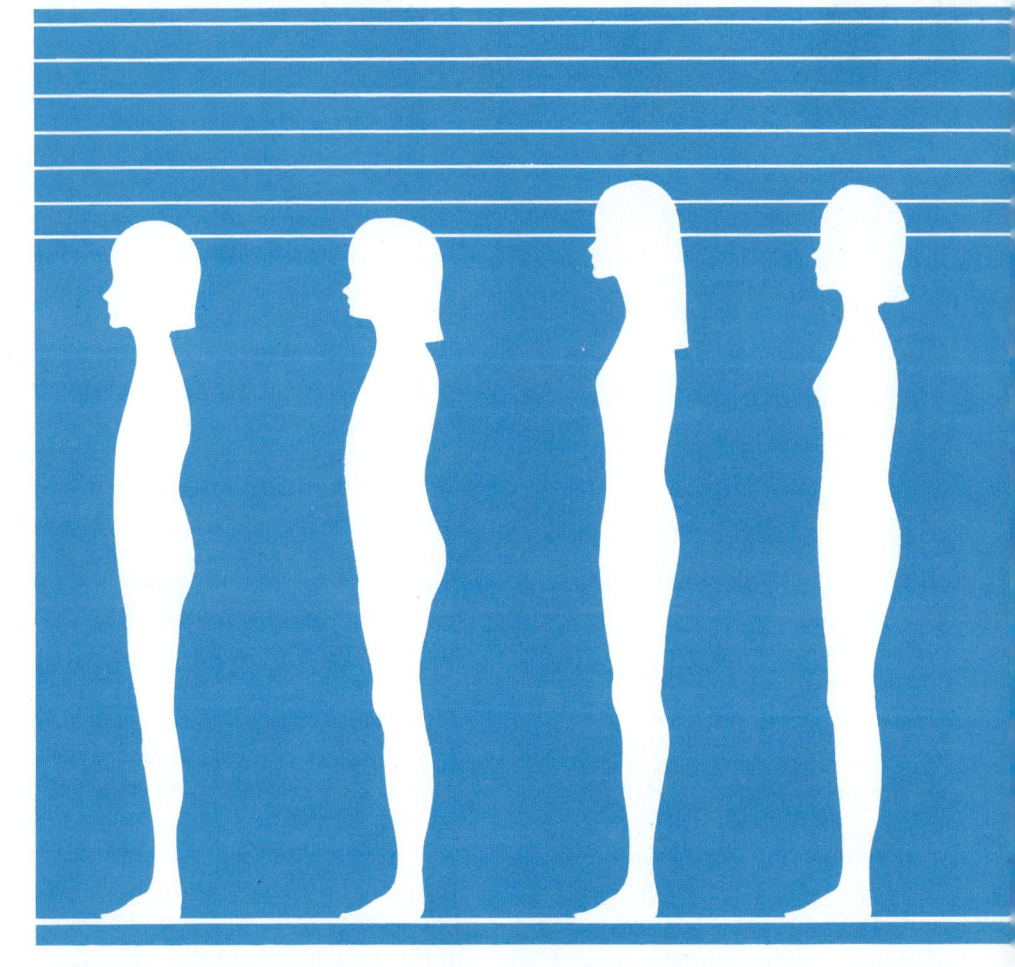

Girl (from 4'2" to 5'1") is the smallest of the eight figure types. Because the bustline is not defined on this just-developing figure, no underarm dart is needed in the dress bodice.

Chubbie (from 4'2" to 5'1") is the growing girl who weighs more than the average for her age and height. Girl and Chubbie patterns are the same height in comparable sizes.

Young Junior/Teen (about 5'1" to 5'3") designates the developing teen and pre-teen figure which has a very small, high bust with a waist larger in proportion to the bust.

Junior Petite (about 5' to 5'1") is a short, well-developed figure with small body structure and a shorter waist length than any other type.

332

Miss Petite (about 5′2″ to 5′3″) is a shorter figure than a Miss with a shorter waist length than the comparable Miss size, but longer than the corresponding Junior Petite.

Miss (about 5′5″ to 5′8″) is well-proportioned, well developed in all body areas, and is the tallest of all figure types. This type can be called the "average" figure.

Half-Size (about 5′2″ to 5′3″) is a fully-developed shorter figure with narrower shoulders than the Miss. The waist is larger in proportion to the bust than in the other mature figure types.

Woman (about 5′5″ to 5′6″) is a larger, more mature figure of about the same height as a Miss. The back waist length is longer because the back is fuller, and all measurements are larger proportionately.

COURTESY SIMPLICITY PATTERN CO. INC.

Mount pictures of garments which illustrate the lines drawn below.
1 Label each picture showing which line is illustrated.
2 Tell briefly what the line arrangement does to the apparent size of the figure.

Set A

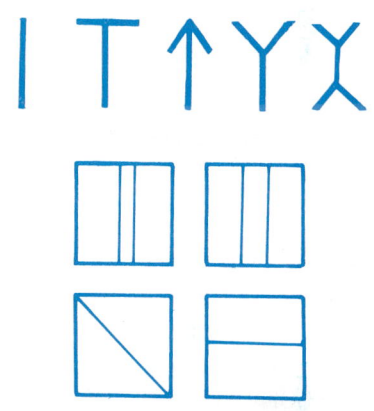

Set B

Look through pattern books for simple dresses which may be made to look like different outfits by adding detachable collars or jewelry. Discuss why such a garment might be a good clothing project.

Discuss the reasons for needing the following ease allowance for each specific area of the body:

AREA	EASE ALLOWANCE
Bust	3–4 inches
Hips	2 inches
Waist	1 inch

Make plans for every class member to get his fair share of help from the teacher(s). Try one of the following ideas or think of others:

1. The *number* system, which allows students to take numbers and be helped in systematic order.
2. The *list* system, which allows students to add their names to those on the chalk board for help in the order listed.

Bulletin board IDEA
Title:

Figure
your pattern size

Directions: Write the word *figure* with a tape measure twisted to form the letters and held up with pins. Show up-to-date fashions using pattern envelopes in Girls, Young Junior/Teen, Junior Petite, Miss Petite, and Misses sizes.

of up-to-date styles. Best of all, they are carefully drafted for accuracy, and they fit together with a minimum of trouble. The directions that come with the pattern tell you every step to take in putting a garment together. It is to your advantage to learn to understand the instructions and to follow them carefully.

Commercial patterns have been developed for many different figure types. You may find there are several students in your class who wear a size 8 pattern. Yet, if they all stood side by side, you would see that they vary in height, weight, and body development. Some students mature more rapidly than others and are larger in the shoulders and hips than their friends of the same age. Some grow tall before they mature in other ways. Naturally, it would be difficult for the same pattern to fit all of these figures the same way. So pattern companies, taking into consideration the many ways figures develop, have made patterns which will fit each figure type.

PATTERN TYPES AND SIZES

To accommodate all the different ways that girls develop, the pattern companies have worked out series of sizes for the various figure types. According to her development, a girl might choose a pattern from any of these series: Girls, Young Junior/Teens, Junior Petites, Miss Petites, Misses, Half-Sizes, and Women. A variety of patterns are also available in both Boys' and Men's sizes. Commercial pattern books have charts explaining all of these pattern types and sizes, usually in the back of the book.

As you study these charts, you will notice how to determine which type will best fit you. *Girls* patterns are for short girls who have not started to mature physically and require few darts for figure contours. *Young Junior/Teen* patterns are for tall girls who are just beginning to develop in the bust and hips. *Junior Petite* patterns are for girls who are short but well developed. *Miss Petite* patterns are for girls who are well developed but shorter than average from the shoulder to the waistline. *Misses* patterns are for medium-tall to tall girls with well-proportioned figures. *Half-sizes* are made for fully developed, short-waisted girls who are thick in the waist and hip areas. *Women's* sizes are designed for large figures.

Each pattern type is made in a range of sizes, such as 10, 12, 14, and 16. To distinguish Junior Petite from other patterns, their sizes are marked in odd numbers, such as 7, 9, 11, and 13. Young Junior/Teen sizes are marked 5/6, 7/8, 9/10, etc. Each pattern size allows for a definite measurement in the bust, waist, and hip area. The back waist length is also listed.

After you have determined which figure type you have, you need to decide which size will be best for you. It is to be expected that your figure size or type will change as you mature. The girl who wore a Young Junior/Teen size 9/10 last year may this year require a Misses size 8. Take your body measurements before buying the fabric and pattern for each new project. Very few people can buy a pattern that fits them exactly, but you can find one that requires few alterations.

Since patterns list the measurements for bust, hip, waist, and back waist length for the different sizes, it is necessary that you take measurement of your corresponding body areas. You may find they are almost identical to one particular figure type and size. If, however, they do not fit any size exactly, choose the size that is nearest to your bust measurement. The waist and hip sections of a pattern are much easier to adjust than the shoulder and bust areas. Of course, if the project you have chosen is a skirt, shorts, or slacks, your concern should be for the hip and waist measurements. Since the waist section of a pattern can be altered more easily than the hip section, buy such patterns to fit your hips.

STEPS IN TAKING MEASUREMENTS

To get accurate measurements, take them over well-fitting undergarments. Remove bulky dresses, sweaters, skirts, or pants. If the garment you are wearing fits you well and is not bulky, you may be able to measure over it. Be sure to stand straight and look straight ahead while your measurements are being taken. If you look down, you have a tendency to bend your body and the measurements may not be accurate.

It is preferable to have a partner take your measurements for you so that you can stand still and erect.

The bust
Place the tape measure around the fullest part of the bust. Be sure to keep the tape straight across the back shoulder area. The tape should be tight enough to stay in place but loose enough that you can place your finger underneath it.

The high chest
Some people are full busted but narrow through the shoulders. By using their high-chest measurement in place of the bust measurement, they can select patterns that fit them more accurately. To take this measurement, place the tape around the body, up high under the arms. Check to see that the tape is straight and firm but not too tight. If there is doubt about whether to use the bust or high-chest measurements, ask for your teacher's advice.

The waist
Place the tape around the natural waistline, holding it snug but not

SCRAMBLE GAME

Unscramble the seven words below, allowing one letter to each square. The unscrambled words describe essential steps in clothing construction. *Do not write in this book.*

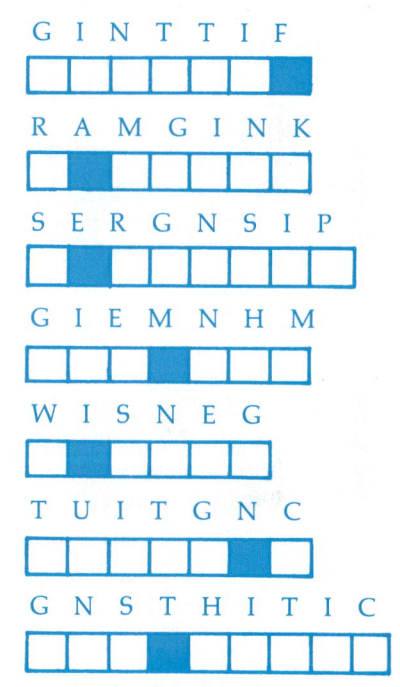

G I N T T I F

R A M G I N K

S E R G N S I P

G I E M N H M

W I S N E G

T U I T G N C

G N S T H I T I C

Now arrange the shaded letters to form the surprise word which describes the product of clothing construction efforts.

Discuss points to consider when choosing fabrics for garments to be worn for various occasions and activities.

For school: ease of care and durability, as in gingham, broadcloth, corduroy, gabardine, jersey, flannel, tweed, or hardy double knits.

For housework: washability, stretch, and comfort, as in stretch denim or special cotton polyester blends.

For sports: durability, comfort, and suitability to use, as in corduroy, denim, sailcloth, poplin, flannel, or tweed.

For lounging: comfort and crease-resistance, as in corduroy, jersey, flannel, challis, velveteen, seersucker, and soft quilted fabrics.

For nightwear: washability and comfort, as in batiste, nylon, rayon, broadcloth, or cotton flannel.

For dress: soft, delicate color, or bright gay color, attractive prints or solid colors, and pleasing texture, as in organdy, batiste, dotted swiss, velveteen, taffeta, crepe, faille, or polyester knits.

tight enough to squeeze the body. The natural waistline is located well above the hip bone in the narrowest part of the body.

The hip
The hip measurement is correctly taken around the largest part of the hips. For the teen-age figure, this is usually about 6 inches below the natural waistline.

The waist length
The waist length is measured from the bone you can feel at the back of your neck down to the natural waistline. Stand erect when this measurement is taken. Put your hands around your waist with the thumbs toward your back so that your partner can readily determine the location of your waistline.

The skirt or pants length
The skirt length is determined by measuring from the center back of the natural waistline to the floor. From this number is subtracted the number of inches you like to wear your skirts above the floor. If the garment you wore to school is of a becoming length, you may find it easier to measure it than to establish a new length. Be sure to add

For a beginning project, choose a simple pattern with only a few pattern pieces. To determine the amount of fabric to buy, draw a line *across* from your fabric width and a line *down* from your pattern size. Where the two lines cross, you will find the number of yards to buy.

COURTESY SIMPLICITY PATTERN CO. INC.

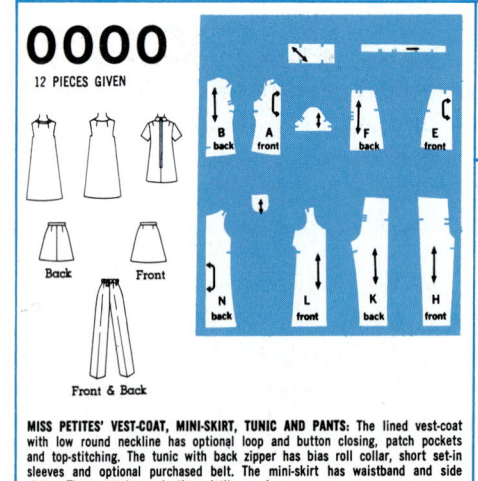

at least 2 inches for a hem allowance. Length for pants is determined in the same way except that the measurement is taken along the side of the body.

JUDGING PATTERN DIFFICULTY

As a general rule, the smaller the number of pieces in your pattern, the easier the garment will be for you to make. Styles that require careful fitting are more difficult than styles that fit loosely. Designs that feature scallops, points, tucks, gussets, and bound buttonholes require more skill and patience than beginners generally possess.

Many simple patterns are difficult because they do not fit correctly. Once you know your own body measurements, you can determine the type and size pattern to buy for your figure. Many classrooms have large charts posted on which you can locate the figure type and pattern size to buy for good fit. If you have any questions about the kind of pattern to buy, check with your teacher.

JUDGING BECOMINGNESS OF PATTERN DESIGNS

People are frequently disappointed with a finished garment because the style is not becoming to them. To avoid this disappointment, choose patterns with becoming lines. The lines in the pattern should be becoming to your figure as well as to the fabrics you choose. It might be

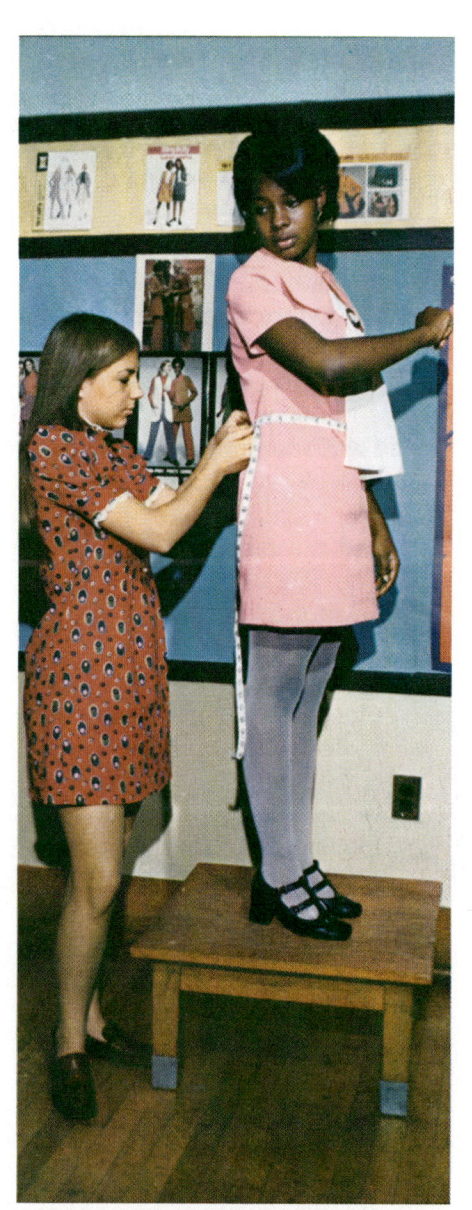

COURTESY DETROIT, MICHIGAN PUBLIC SCHOOLS

Measurements needed for buying and altering patterns can be taken easily and accurately when partners take and record measurements for one another.

Take care of your pattern by following these practices.

1. Write your name and class period on the pattern envelope.
2. Remove the pattern and check the pieces with the guide sheet to be sure all pieces are included.
3. Write your name and class period near the center of each pattern piece.
4. Before attaching the pattern to fabric, press all wrinkles from the pattern pieces with a warm, not hot, iron.
5. Handle the pattern pieces carefully to avoid tearing them.
6. Mend torn pattern pieces with cellophane tape.
7. Avoid tearing the pieces as you mark the garment.
8. Keep the pattern and the guide sheet in your sewing box during the construction of your garment.
9. Place related pattern pieces together immediately after use, and fold them together smoothly and neatly to a size similar to the shape of the envelope. Store them in the pattern envelope.
10. Store the pattern with other patterns in a suitable place for further use.

◔ Given a pattern envelope, determine the number of yards of fabric needed for various sizes, fabric widths, and views.

Make a report to the class of items that you would like to see on pattern envelopes that are not on them at present.

Discuss double-duty clothes you can make such as these:
Skirts: To be worn with both sweaters and blouses.
Blouses: To be worn with skirts, jumpers, shorts, pants, or knee pants.
Simple dresses: To be worn for school, spectator sports, afternoon parties, movies, and dates.
Dressy dresses: To be worn for church, parties, luncheons, and dinner parties.

Select a basic outfit from a magazine, store catalogue, or pattern book. Using this one outfit, find or draw pictures of accessories which would dress up and dress down this one garment for a variety of occasions such as:
  Party
  Football game
  School
  Club meeting

helpful to review the section on lines in clothes in Chapter 13. (See pages 264–265.)

UNDERSTANDING THE PATTERN ENVELOPE

The pattern envelope provides useful information. By studying it carefully before beginning a project, you gain basic information which helps in buying fabric and notions for your project. The following information is given on all brands of pattern envelopes:

1. The brand name of the pattern and the pattern number.
2. The size of the pattern in the envelope.
3. The number and shape of the pattern pieces. (The number of pieces to be used generally indicates the amount of difficulty you can expect in assembling a garment.)
4. Pictures of the way the garment will look when it is completed and the different versions of it you can make from the one pattern.
5. A list of fabrics from which the garment can be made successfully.
6. Easy-to-make markings on beginners' patterns.
7. A chart indicating the amount of fabric required to make the garment in each size.
8. A list of needed notions, such as buttons, zippers, tape and trimming.

UNDERSTANDING THE PATTERN INSTRUCTION SHEET

The instruction sheet inside the pattern envelope is your guide to easy sewing. You should refer to it often throughout the construction of the garment. It is poor management to spend a great deal of time trying to figure out how to put two pieces together when the directions on the instruction sheet explain every step.

In addition to step-by-step construction directions, you will also find directions for laying and pinning the pattern on various widths of fabric. Instructions for straightening fabric, transferring the pattern markings to the fabric, and general sewing directions are provided on most instruction sheets.

UNDERSTANDING PATTERN MARKINGS

The pattern pieces themselves are marked with lines, dots, and notches to show you where to alter, how to place the pattern on the fabric, where to cut, where to match pieces together, and where to sew. Darts, pockets, centers, fold lines, buttonholes, pleats, and tucks are all marked on the pattern. (See the illustration on the following page.)

ADJUSTING PATTERNS FOR FIT

Since few people have measurements exactly the same as any one pattern size, each person may find a need to change the size of a pattern in some area. However, if you

CONSTRUCTION MARKINGS

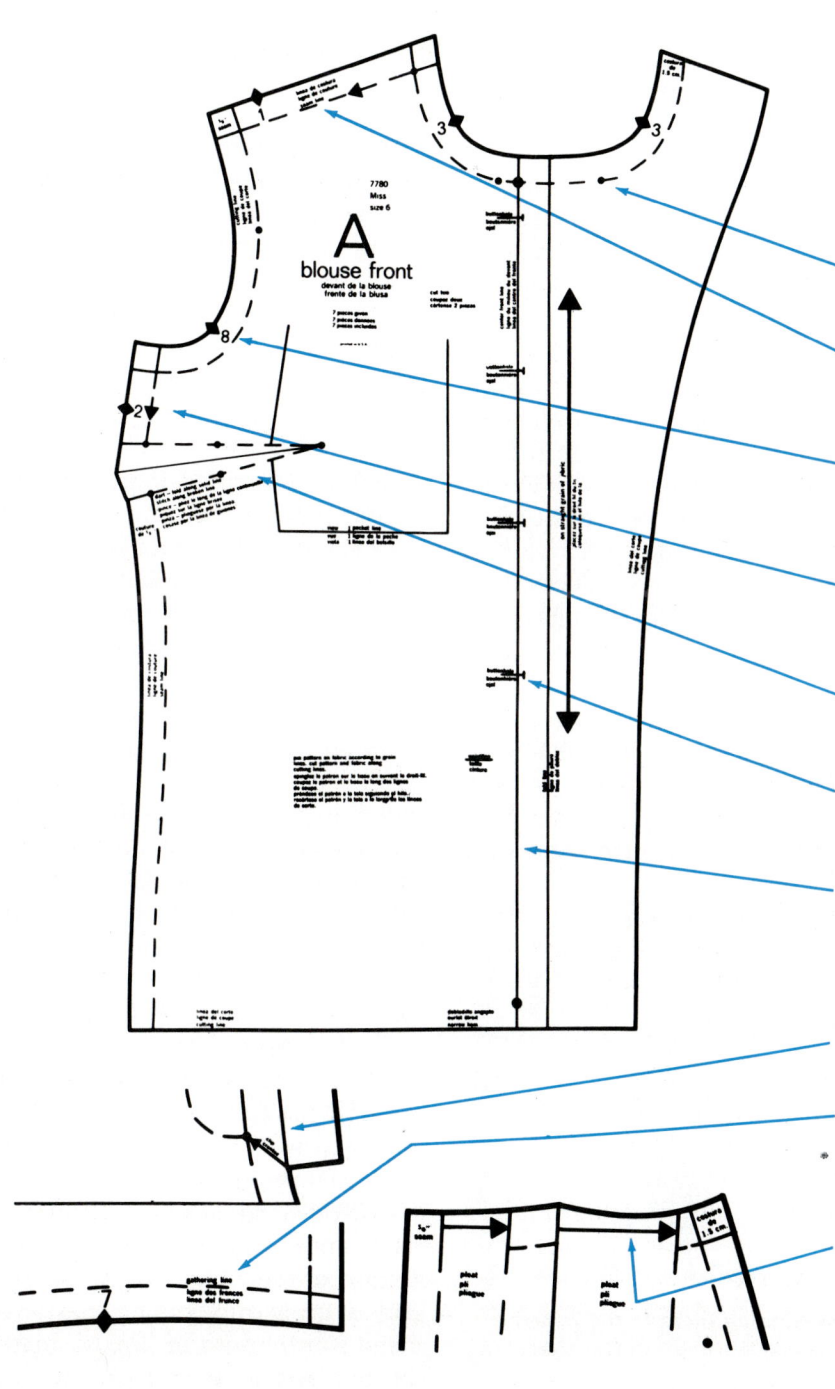

Construction markings are the guide posts for putting together and sewing your garment. Some patterns have many of these markings, others have only a few, depending on the design details of the style.

Dots are aids for matching seams and other construction details.

The seamline (stitching line) is indicated by a broken line. It is usually 5/8" from the cutting line, but it can vary in certain areas.

Notches are V-shaped symbols along the cutting line which aid in joining pattern pieces. Two or more notches are grouped together to form a block for easier cutting.

Arrows on the seamline indicate the direction in which the pieces should be stitched so as not to distort the fabric grain.

Darts are indicated by two broken lines for stitching and a solid line at center for folding.

Buttonholes are indicated by a solid line having a short line at right angles to one end when horizontal or at both ends when vertical.

Solid lines are used also to indicate center fold lines, some hemlines, placement for pockets and trimmings that go on the outside of the garment.

"Clip" with a short arrow indicates where to clip into the seam allowance to release it.

Gathering or **easing** is indicated by a broken line similar to a seamline, but labeled "gathering line" or "ease". Usually, you gather or ease between two points on the pattern.

Pleats are usually indicated by an alternating solid and broken line. Arrows show the direction of the pleating with the instruction "fold along solid line; bring fold to broken line".

Find the information listed on a pattern envelope which is helpful to the consumer.

Show how to choose a cutting layout for your construction project. Demonstrate folding the fabric as the layout directs.

Demonstrate the correct placement of pattern pieces on napped fabrics such as corduroy or velveteen. Show the effect improper cutting will give to a garment made from a napped fabric.

Using a sample of fabric which contains woven checks, plaids, or stripes, demonstrate the meaning of grain-of-fabric. Show also how to match plaids or stripes when cutting.

have selected your pattern carefully according to your measurements, you should not find it necessary to make many changes.

Because people vary widely in size and shape, you will want to check your pattern to see if it will fit *you*. If any part of the pattern is too long, too short, too large, or too small, adjust it to fit. It is much easier to make the necessary changes in the paper pattern than to change the pieces after they have been cut from cloth. Since your first project will be made with a pattern containing only a few pieces, you will probably find the changes easy to make.

Measuring pattern pieces
Use a tape measure to check your pattern for correct fit. Measure from seam line to seam line rather than from edge to edge in determining the length or width of a pattern. Since many pieces are cut double, they are measured from the fold line to the seam line. The number of inches is then doubled to determine the width of a pattern piece. By adding together the width of the back and front of a pattern, you have a good idea of the size of a garment made by it.

Ease allowance
Don't be surprised if you find the dress pattern you bought for a 32-inch bust line to be 36 inches when you measure it with a tape. You need this extra room in your clothes to allow for the movement of your body. If your clothes measured the same as your body, you wouldn't be able to get them on.

The amount of extra room you need in your clothes in order to move freely is called *ease allowance*. It is logical that you need plenty of room through the bust area so that you can move your arms without tearing out your sleeves. Most people find that 3 or 4 extra inches in this area is a good amount for comfort. Thus, if you measure 32 inches around the fullest part of the bust, you will want your dress or blouse to measure 36 inches in this area.

The next greatest need for ease allowance occurs in the hip area, where ample width must be provided for sitting down. Here you need a minimum of 2 extra inches in the width of a garment. The

STEPS IN ALTERING A PATTERN

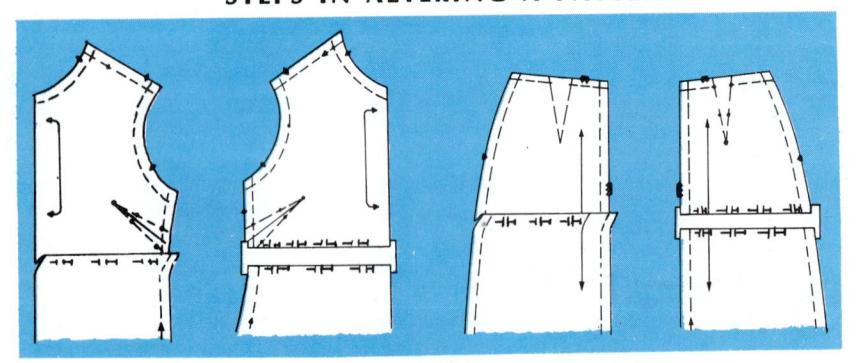

Simple alterations can be made in patterns by pinning tucks in the pattern pieces to make them smaller or by inserting strips of paper to make them larger.

340

waistline comes next with a requirement of 1 extra inch.

Do you notice that each ease requirement is exactly half the amount of the one before it? Thus, if you can remember that the bust area requires 4 inches for ease, it will be simple to remember the ease requirements for the hips and waist.

Choosing fabric to suit the pattern

Certain fabrics are much more suitable to certain patterns than others. Your pattern envelope will list several kinds of fabrics that are satisfactory to use for that particular garment design. If you do not recognize the fabrics which are suggested, ask the salesclerk to help you. A trained person should be able to help you decide whether the fabric you are considering will make a satisfactory garment.

Heavy, bulky fabrics do not do well in gathered, full, or tucked designs. Firmly woven fabrics work better for tucks and pleats. Soft fabrics gather and drape better than stiff ones. Printed fabrics do not show off seams and stitching details to their best advantage. Choosing material that is suitable for your design could mean the difference between satisfaction and unhappiness. Buy easy-to-handle fabric which will look well when made into your chosen design. (See page 320.)

COURTESY J.C. PENNEY COMPANY, INC.

Select fabric for your garment which will suit the pattern you have chosen. Choose thread and trimmings which will add to the appearance of the outfit.

Preparation for sewing

Buy only fabric which has been finished *on-grain.* It is far better to make a change in fabric selection than to correct fabric grain which has been pulled out of shape in the manufacturing process. (See pages 322–323.)

ALTERING, LAYING, AND PINNING THE PATTERN

As you prepare to lay your pattern on the fabric in readiness for cutting, follow these steps:
1 Study the instruction sheet to find the suggested layout for the size and version of the pattern you have selected and for your fabric width.
2 Separate the pattern pieces you will need, returning any unneeded ones to the pattern envelope.

Make a list of safety practices to follow when sewing. Add other practices to the following list:
1 Put pins and needles in a pincushion rather than in your mouth or clothes.
2 Pass sharp objects, such as scissors and shears, to others with the handle first.
3 Store scissors and other sharp objects in holders or in other secure places.
4 Keep blades of shears and scissors closed when they are not in use.
5 When pressing, keep your hands away from the steam.
6 Keep your fingers away from the path of the sewing machine needle.
7 Use slow speed while learning to use the sewing machine.
8 Locate the electric cord so that no one will stumble over it. Disconnect the cord from the wall or floor outlet before disconnecting it from the sewing machine.
9 Close the sewing machine carefully to avoid damaging the machine or the electric cord.
10 Keep the drawers or door of the sewing machine closed to avoid accidents.

C Define, in your own words, the following terms which are used on patterns. Discuss instances when knowledge of each definition would be necessary.

Bias fold. A fold along the diagonal line formed when fabric is folded so that the selvage is parallel to the crosswise threads.

Bodice. The waist portion of the pattern, usually not including sleeves.

Crosswise fold. A fold in the fabric along the crosswise threads by which each selvage is doubled over on itself.

Dart. A fold in fabric, usually stitched to a point at one end, placed so as to fit the fabric over a rounded surface.

Facing. A piece of fabric used to finish edges of the garment, usually curved edges, such as neckline and sleeves.

Gore. A shaped piece of fabric, usually a section of a skirt. Ordinarily a gore is narrower in width at the waistline than it is at the bottom of the skirt.

Gusset. A piece of fabric inserted in a garment to add fullness or to improve the fit.

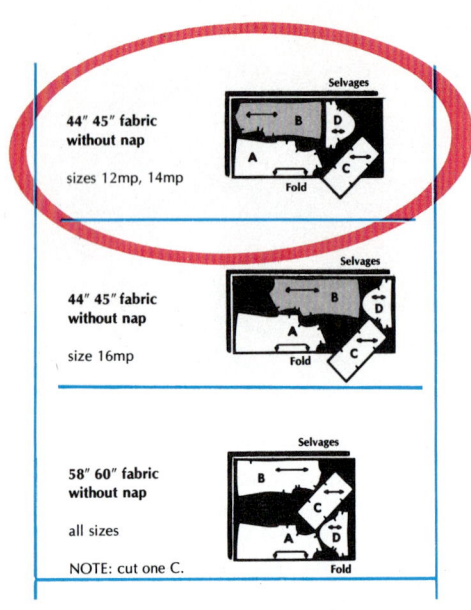

On the instruction sheet, circle the pattern layout which describes the instructions for laying your pattern on the width of fabric you have chosen.

3 Put your name on the body of each pattern piece, on your instruction sheet, and on the envelope.

4 Draw a circle around the cutting layout you have selected so that you will see it immediately each time you want to refer to it for help.

5 If the pattern pieces are wrinkled, press them with a slightly warm iron. Avoid pressing tiny wrinkles into the pattern pieces.

6 Measure in inches both the blouse front and the blouse back at the bustline. Add the measurements and double the sum. This tells you the total distance around the bodice top. Measure the length of the bodice from the shoulder seam to the waistline seam to be sure it is the right length. Measure the skirt front and back at the widest part of the hip area, and total the two measurements. Check the skirt length. Make any alterations which are needed to make your pattern fit your body measurements.

7 Double the fabric lengthwise, right sides together, and lay it out smoothly on a flat surface. Match the bottom and top selvages perfectly. If necessary, refold the fabric as suggested in the cutting layout, making sure the right sides of the fabric are together on the inside.

8 Place the pattern pieces on the fabric in the positions shown on the cutting guide to make sure they will all fit.

9 Make sure the grain lines on the pattern are placed on the grain line of the fabric. (See illustration on this page.)

10 Pin the pattern to the fabric at the point of each arrow shown on pattern pieces. Pattern grain markings, such as arrows, should be parallel with the edges.

11 Smooth the pattern, and put a pin in each corner. Be sure the pins are inside the cutting

PINNING PATTERN TO FABRIC

CUTTING GARMENT PIECES

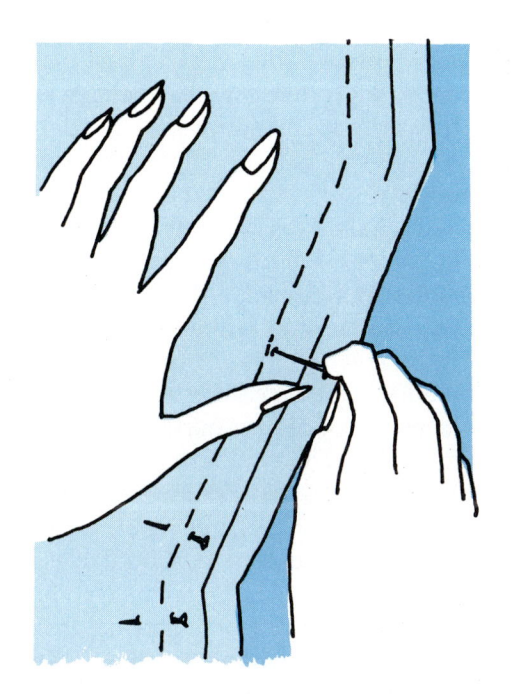

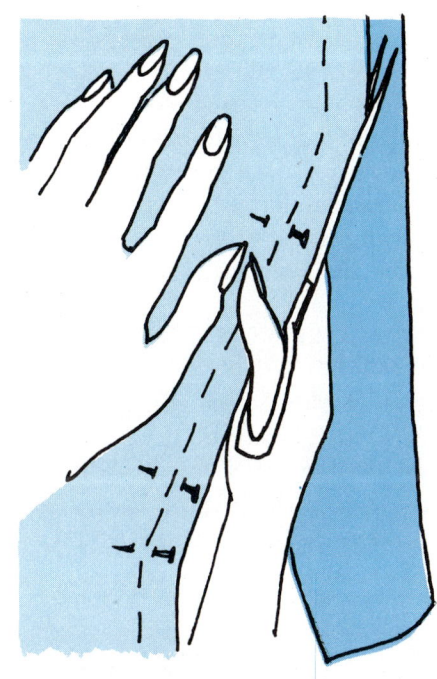

So that garment pieces will be shaped correctly, pin the pattern to the fabric and cut the garment pieces as they remain flat on a cutting table or cutting board.

line. Place enough pins around the edge to hold the pattern securely. Avoid using too many pins. One pin placed every 6 to 8 inches should be sufficient.

12. Recheck your complete pattern layout against the cutting layout on the instruction sheet. When you are sure all pieces are placed accurately and on the straight-of-the-fabric, you are ready to cut the garment.

CUTTING PATTERN PIECES

The word *directional* is used over and over in the study of clothing construction. This sewing term means *moving with the grain*. In cutting garment pieces from fabric, look at the pattern piece. You will notice that by cutting from the wide to the narrow part of a piece, you cut with less pull on the grain of the fabric. This is called *directional cutting*.

Use sharp shears to cut the fabric. Cut carefully along the cutting line

Define, in your own words, the following terms which are used in unit construction.

Baste stitching. A line of long machine stitches.

Clean-finishing. A finish in which the edge of a facing or hem is staystitched ¼ inch from the edge and the edge is turned to the wrong side on the stayline. The folded edge is stitched less than ⅛ inch from the folded edge.

Cutting to fit. Fitting the garment by altering the pattern before the garment is cut.

Directional stitching. Stitching in the direction of the grain.

Grain-perfect. Term used to describe fabric in which the threads cross each other at right angles.

Staystitching. A line of machine stitching on the off-grain edges of a single thickness of fabric to hold the grain, usually ½ inch from the cut edge.

Understitching. A stitching that is made after a facing is stitched to the garment by turning the facing back over the seam and stitching from the right side of the facing through the seam, close to the seam line.

C Select a fabric sample from a group of fabrics with varying weaves and textures. Identify which of the following seam finishes to use with your fabric. Defend your selection.

1 Plain seam: Used to join two pieces of fabric where special treatment is not required and where a flat, inconspicuous seam is desired.
2 Plain seam, pinked: For use on fabric which does not ravel easily.
3 Plain seam, edge-stitched, zig-zagged, or overcast: For use where the fabric will ravel or where extra strength is needed.
4 French seam: For use when a flat finish is not needed, when the fabric is sheer or transparent, or when the garment is to be laundered frequently.
5 Flat-felled seam: For use where a flat seam without a raw edge is needed or where strength is needed.
6 Lapped seam: For use where outside stitching is desired or where the two edges are curved or angular.
7 Beveled seam: For use on bulky fabrics where seams are turned in the same direction or are enclosed.
8 Bound seams: For use on bulky fabrics that ravel badly.

shown on the pattern. Use long, even strokes. Stop each stroke about 1 inch from the end of the blades of the shears. If you close the blades with each stroke, the resulting cut edge will be choppy and uneven. As you come to the *notches* (diamond-shaped marks) on the cutting line, cut around them away from the pattern.

TRANSFERRING PATTERN SYMBOLS

The markings on the pattern are there to guide you in putting the garment together. Carefully transfer these markings to your fabric pieces so they will be visible when you need them.

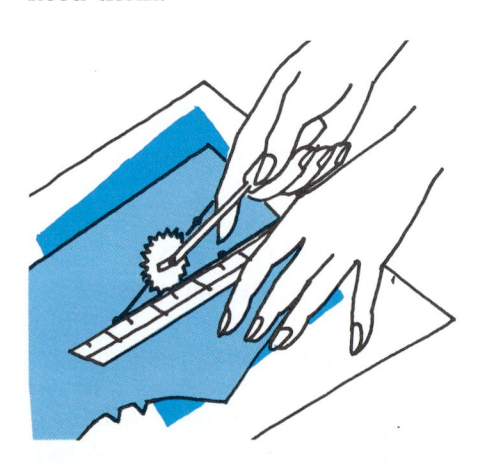

To use the tracing wheel and tracing paper, place one layer of paper, colored side down, between the pattern and the fabric. Place another layer of paper, colored side up, below the garment piece. Using a straight edge for a guide and the tracing wheel, trace marks onto the *wrong* side of the garment pieces.

Tailor's tacks, marks which are made of thread, have been used for many years. They are the best type of marks to use on white, sheer, or heavily napped fabrics.

Tailor's chalk and pins are used mainly for temporary markings. The chalk rubs off, but it is useful in places where stitches can be made immediately. Pins may drop out, but if they are inserted carefully and the sewing is done immediately, they can be used to mark locations of seams, darts, or buttonholes. You may find pins a satisfactory form of marking at home, but they are usually not permanent enough for use in a school class.

The tracing wheel can be used for all fabrics except light-colored, sheer, heavily napped, or loosely woven fabrics. To use a tracing wheel, place the special tracing paper face down between the wrong side of the fabric and the pattern itself. Then place another piece of tracing paper face up under the wrong side of the fabric. With the pattern in the proper place, hold a ruler along the line to be marked and run the tracing wheel along the line at the ruler's edge. The prongs of the tracing wheel will transfer bits of color from the paper onto the fabric in the desired areas.

Since the prongs on the tracing wheel might dig through the fabric into the table surface, be sure that some form of protection, such as an old magazine or heavy cardboard, lies between fabric and table. Too, because tracing marks can be very permanent, be careful to avoid marking on the right side of the fabric.

Mark the center front, darts, fold lines, buttonholes, and any other construction marks indicated on the pattern. You generally will find it unnecessary to mark the seam lines, since they can be stitched straight by using the seam guide on the sewing machine.

Assembling a garment

After you have completed the markings, you are ready to put the garment together. It is wise for beginners to leave each pattern piece pinned to the fabric until the piece is needed. Something which looks to you like an armhole facing may turn out to be a neck facing. The pattern will help you identify it. Also, the pattern acts as a tissue paper to keep the fabric from wrinkling when stored in your sewing tray.

UNIT METHOD OF CONSTRUCTION

The method of construction in most common use today is called the *unit method of construction*. This method will help you to attain professional-looking results in a minimum of time.

In the unit method, all possible construction is completed on each

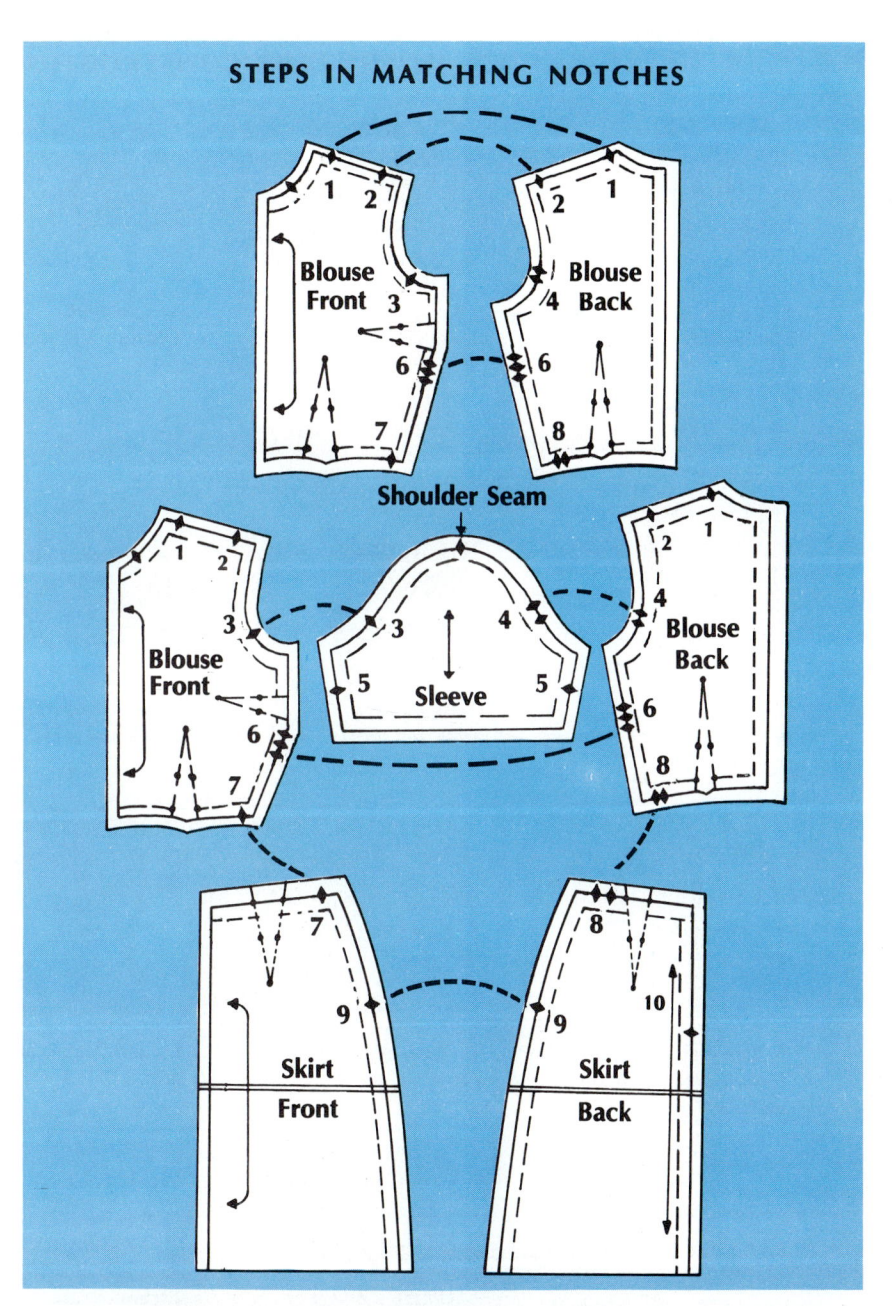

STEPS IN MATCHING NOTCHES

Look for numbered notches or groups of notches. They direct you to fit the pieces of a garment together correctly.

STEPS IN THE UNIT CONSTRUCTION METHOD

1. Complete front blouse unit.

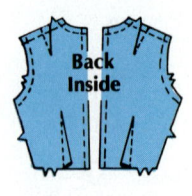

2. Complete back blouse unit.

3. Complete sleeves.

4. Complete neck facing and press.

5. Make shoulder seams and press.

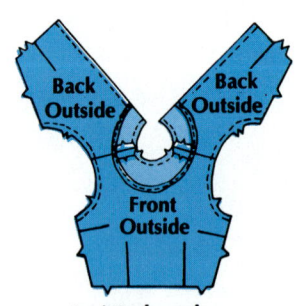

6. Attach neck facing and press.

7. Make underarm seams and press.

8. Attach sleeves and press.

9. Join seams in front and back skirt unit.

10. Press skirt seams.

11. Join blouse and skirt.

12. Attach zipper to garment.

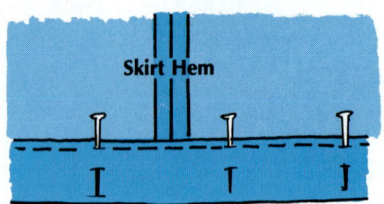

13. Measure, trim, and cleanfinish hem. Pin in place and attach to garment with invisible stitches.

section of the garment before putting the pieces together. For example, in making a dress, the staystitching, darts, tucks, pleats, and seams are put in the bodice front, back, sleeves, collars, and skirt pieces. All pieces are pressed carefully before they are joined together. Every seam must be pressed before it is crossed with another seam.

Construction details

Only a few construction details are needed to complete simple garments. These details can be practiced over and over as you make simple shifts and blouses, skirts, slacks, and many other garments worn by teen-agers. As your ability increases, you may want to learn still other skills for tailoring a coat or suit. However, when you have mastered the following skills, you can make most garments worn by today's teen-agers.

Staystitching is a line of stitching that keeps the edges of garment pieces from stretching out of shape while you are working on them. It is particularly important on bias and curved edges. It is done by stitching a single row of regular-size stitches ½ inch from the cut edge. Staystitching is done through a single thickness of the fabric before seams are stitched together. Since the purpose of staystitching is to hold the yarns of the fabric in place so that they will not stretch out of shape, the stitching should be done in the proper direction to achieve this. (See the illustration on this page.)

Darts and tucks are folds stitched into a garment to control fullness. While tucks have various shapes, a dart is stitched to a sharp point at one or both ends where fullness is needed. It is wide where fullness is to be removed. Darts point toward but do not extend over the fullest curves of the figure. Dress and blouse patterns frequently have darts at the waistline and at the shoulder and underarm seams to provide for fullness through the shoulder and bust area. Waistline darts provide for fullness in the hip area of skirts or pants. Darts are indicated on the patterns by lines

Practice using the points of small scissors for ripping. Hold the scissors near the points of the blade rather than by the handles. Cut through a stitch approximately every inch. Slip the small point of the scissors under one of the threads in the center of the cut section and pull out the thread. Continue in this manner to the end of the section to be ripped. Pull away the long thread on the underneath side.

Make a notebook illustrating different seam finishes. Under what circumstances would each be appropriate?

Staystitch garment pieces directionally as the arrows suggest to prevent their stretching out of shape.

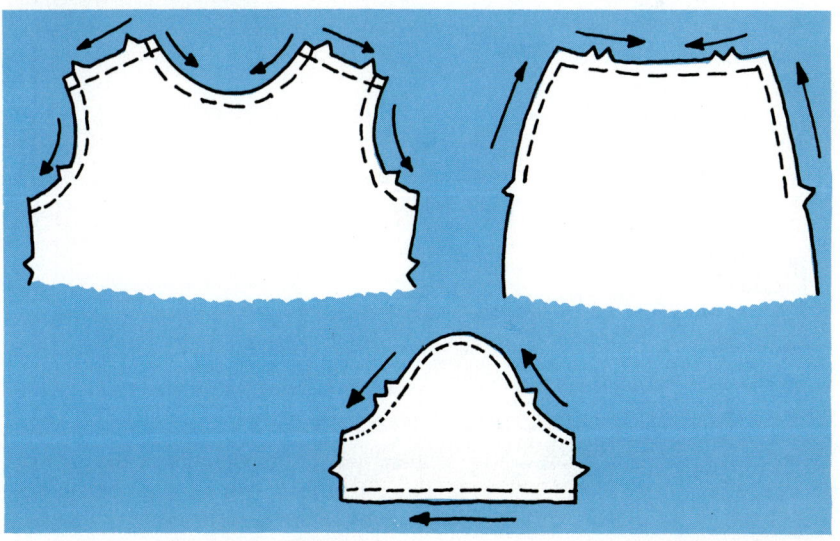

Follow these guidelines in construction pressing. Add other points you have found to be useful.
1. Try the iron on a sample of the fabric to check the effect of the temperature and moisture on the fabric.
2. Press with the grain, usually lengthwise.
3. Press by lifting and lowering the iron to avoid stretching the fabric.
4. Press on the wrong side whenever possible.
5. Plan construction procedures so that each difficult pressing task can be done on as small a section of the garment as is possible.
6. Press shaped parts over a tailor's ham and flat parts on a flat surface.
7. Remove shiny surfaces and basting thread imprints by steaming and then brushing.
8. Avoid seam prints by slipping strips of brown paper between the garment and the seam allowance.

Your career
Custom dressmaker

Duties: Making clothing for other people.
Where employed: A dressmaking shop, or may be self-employed.

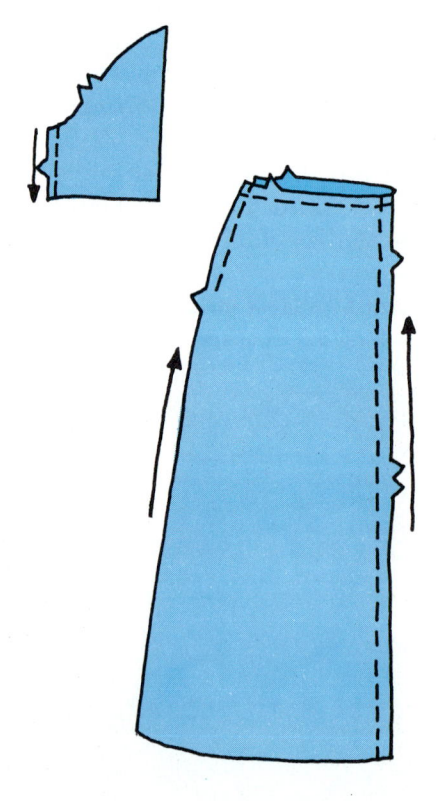

Stitch seams directionally as the arrows suggest so that your garment will hang correctly when completed.

which can be carefully transferred to the garment pieces. (See pages 344–345.)

Darts are pressed on the underside of the garment. Underarm darts are turned down toward the waistline as they are pressed. Shoulder and waistline darts are turned with the fold toward the center of the garment. Block darts carefully into shape by using a pressing ham and a steam iron.

Directional stitching of seams is a method for joining two pieces of fabric. When two pieces of fabric are sewn together with any kind of stitching, the resulting line of stitches is called a *seam.* Seams should be smooth and flat. While there are many kinds of seams, probably most of the articles you make at this time will require only plain seams.

Seams are correctly stitched with the grain of the fabric. This *directional stitching* prevents them from stretching or puckering. For example, in directional stitching, the side seams of a skirt are stitched from the wider bottom to the narrower top. The stitching direction is determined by the grain of the fabric edge. Most patterns show you in which direction to stitch. However, if you are in doubt, stitch from the wide toward the narrow area.

Facings and interfacings are garment reinforcements. A facing is an extra piece of fabric added to an edge, such as the edge of a neck or sleeve. It is used to reinforce and cover the raw edges. Facings that are shaped the same as the edges they are used to cover are called *fitted facings.* Another common kind is called a *bias facing.* This type of facing is made by cutting a strip of fabric from a diagonal area of a square of fabric. Bias-cut fabric is very stretchy and can be shaped to accommodate curved edges.

Interfacings are extra pieces of fabric, usually the same shape as a fitted facing. They are used between the body of the garment and the facing. Their purpose is to add firmness, thus helping the garment hold its shape during wear. Interfacings can be made of firmly woven or matted fabrics which are stitched into the garment. Some interfacing can be bonded onto a garment with the heat of an iron. Then the facing is *fused* (stuck) to the garment with heat.

Clean-finishing is a commonly used method of finishing the edges of sleeves, hems, and facings. By this method, the edge to be finished is first staystitched ¼ inch from the edge. Then with the right side of the garment piece face up, the edge of the fabric is folded under along the staystitching line. Stitching is made along the fold as close to the edge as possible. The bed of the machine holds the fold in place as the stitching is done. Excess fabric may be trimmed away when the stitching is completed.

Understitching is an extra line of stitching applied to the top side of any facing to make it fold under and lie perfectly flat. It is used on facing seams, collar seams, and cuff seams. When you want a facing to be invisible from the right side of the garment, fold the seam in the direction of the facing and top stitch through the facing and the seams.

Understitching is made on the right side of the fabric. Before understitching the seam, trim and clip the seam if necessary to make it lie flat. (See page 327.)

PRESSING
The importance of careful step-by-step pressing during the construction of a garment cannot be overemphasized. Often people

Press curved seams over a tailor's ham to mold them to fit your body. Press each group of seams before they are crossed by other stitching.

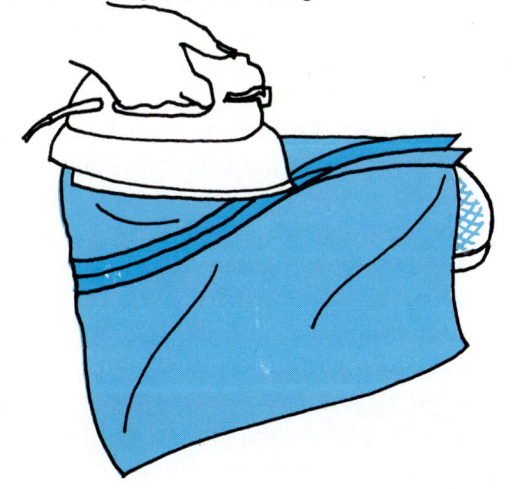

Follow these guidelines when pressing woolen garments. Add other points you have found to be useful.
1 Try the iron on a sample of the fabric to determine the effects of the temperature and moisture on the fabric.
2 Use moist heat in pressing—a steam or a dry iron with a damp cloth. Avoid pressing woolen fabrics completely dry. Allow them to air dry before further handling.
3 Press on the wrong side whenever possible. Use a press cloth even when pressing from the wrong side.
4 Press with a lowering and lifting motion. Do not apply pressure.
5 Flatten the fold edge of darts with the iron. Press vertical darts toward the center of the garment and horizontal darts downward. Use a strip of paper beneath the dart to avoid marking the garment.
6 Mold curved areas and dart ends over a tailor's ham.
7 Press with the grain, usually lengthwise, to keep the lengthwise and crosswise threads at right angles, unless doing special shaping or pressing slanted seams.

Pin and stitch samples of single-pointed and double-pointed darts. Steam press them into shape, using a tailor's ham.

SINGLE-POINTED DART

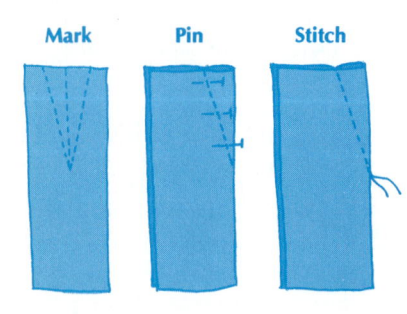

Mark   Pin   Stitch

DOUBLE-POINTED DART

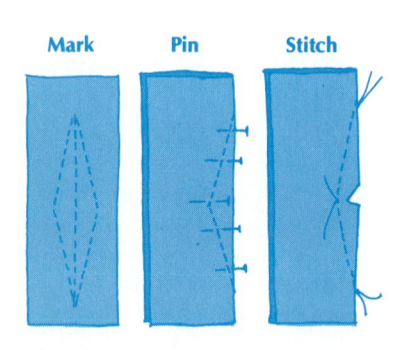

Mark   Pin   Stitch

think it is too expensive or too much bother to heat the iron to press every seam. They are tempted to wait until they have completed a garment before they press. This is false economy of time and money. Such people find their garment never looks so well as if they had pressed during the construction process.

Actually, the unit method of construction requires only three or four pressing sessions. Carefully press each section of the garment after the units have been completed. Press again after the shoulder seams, underarm seams, and skirt seams are stitched. Press again when the garment is stitched together and during the construction of the hem. Your trips to the pressing board are frequent enough if you press each line of stitching, or seam, before crossing it with another seam line. For example, darts must be pressed before side and shoulder seams are stitched. Side seams must be pressed before a skirt and bodice are joined.

Most of the fabrics used in beginning projects require only simple pressing. Put the garment on the ironing board wrong side out. First, press the line of stitching flat. Then, open the seam with the fingers of your free hand, and lay the steaming iron gently on the flattened seam. Lift, move forward one iron length, and lower the iron again. Continue this process for the entire length of the seam. It is the steam and heat that do the work, not the amount of pressure you apply. Remember to press rather than to iron. Perhaps your teacher will ask a student to demonstrate to the class the difference between ironing and pressing.

SPECIAL CONSTRUCTION SKILLS

Almost anyone who can operate a sewing machine can stitch darts and straight seams. It is the care given to the finishing details that will make a dress look homemade or give it a custom-made look. With a little extra care, you can learn to make clothes which you are proud to wear.

Trimming and clipping seams

Pattern companies usually have a full ⅝-inch seam allowance on all pattern pieces, even though they know you may have to trim some of the fabric away. In this way you have ample fabric to handle so that you can get a smooth stitching line. Also, it is easy to remember that all seams are stitched ⅝-inch from the edge and then trimmed where necessary.

It would be difficult to remember that side and silhouette seams are always at least ⅝-inch and that collar, facing, and belt seams might be narrow. When trying to decide whether to trim a seam, turn a similar garment wrong side out. Any seam which shows is left untrimmed. Those covered by facing and hems may be trimmed to remove bulk. Visible seams are the strain-bearing seams and need the width for strength. Hidden seams, such as those inside a collar or pocket, do not bear much strain and can be trimmed to give a garment a finished look.

Curved seams require clipping in order to have an attractive appearance. There are two kinds of curved seams: One curves in, while the other curves out. An inward curved seam, such as a neck edge, requires only simple clips in enough places to make it lie flat. Outward curved seams on the outer edges of collars may require wedge-shaped pieces clipped from the seam for a smooth finish.

Making collars

Well-made and well-attached collars lie smooth and wrinkle-free. The underneath layer is not visible. Collars vary in shape and size. Regardless of the type of collar you are making, your goal should be an underneath layer which does not show. The outside seam on such a collar lies absolutely flat. On some collars, the outer seam edge can be understitched for flatness.

To make a professional-looking collar, trim away excess fabric after the collar seam is stitched. Then follow the clipping directions given.

When preparing to join a collar to the neck edge, pin it accurately into place. To do this, pin one end of the collar to one end of the neck edge. Then pin the other end of the collar to the other end of the neck edge. Find the center of the collar. Depending on the type of garment, pin the collar center to either the center-front or the center-back neckline edge of the garment. Match the notches. Find the marks on the collar neck edge that show where it is to join the neck at the shoulder seams of the blouse. Pin the collar and neck edge together at both shoulder seams. Ease and pin the collar and neck edges together between the pinned points.

If the collar is smaller than the neckline, clip the edge of the collar at ¾- to 1-inch intervals down to the line of staystitching. If the collar is larger than the neck edge, clip the neck the same way. If you have been careful to make ⅝-inch seams throughout, you will find that the collar, neck edge, and facing will fit together accurately. If you have been careless about the width of seams, you may find that your pieces will not fit together as they should.

When pinning together two parts of a garment, first pin the ends together. Then pin the centers together. Then ease the rest of the seam area into place before pinning it together. In pinning any seam together, if you begin at one end of the seam and work toward the other end, one piece will usually turn out

Attach a collar to a garment according to the following guidelines. How are these directions different from those discussed under **Making collars**?

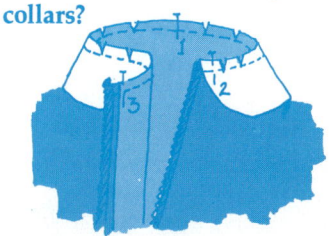

Single collar—Pin the center of the collar to the exact center front of the bodice. Pin both ends in place. Then fit the rest of the collar to the bodice.

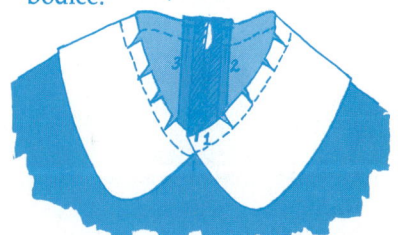

Double collar—Pin each collar piece to the center front of the bodice. Be sure that the collar pieces meet exactly in the center of the bodice where they will be sewn ⅝ inch from the cutting line. This means that the collar pieces may overlap above the ⅝-inch sewing line. Pin the ends in place. Then fit the rest of the collar to the bodice with pins. If necessary, slash the garment or collar to the staystitching so they will fit together.

Discuss the following common fitting problems and the causes. Explain why the suggested solutions will help improve the fit of garments.

Skirt side seams slant to the front—a flat posterior or a prominent tummy
　Take up the waistline in the back.

Skirt side seams slant to the back—a prominent posterior
　Take up the waistline in the front.

Hemline tilts—hips have different shapes
　Take up waistline on one side.

Skirt band rides up—skirt is too narrow across hips
　Raise skirt from the waistline.

Fitted dress bulges across the back—garment is too long waisted
　Relocate waistline or waistline darts.

Back zipper stands out from neck—bodice is too wide across the back
　Take in zipper seam.

Scoop neck gaps—bodice is too large in front
　Take in neckline slack at shoulder seams.

Front sleeve seams cut into upper arms—bodice is too tight across shoulder blades
　Let out sleeve seams.

Attractively simple dresses can be made by beginners. Such garments are suitable for school parties or other social events when dressy trimmings or accessories are chosen.

COURTESY SIMPLICITY PATTERN CO. INC.

to be longer than the other. Avoid this problem by pinning the ends together, then the centers, and finally the areas between these points.

Types of closures

Almost everybody looks and feels better if his clothes fit well. Did it ever occur to you just how difficult it would be to have well-fitting clothes without fasteners and closures? Of course, there are a few stretch garments, such as pantyhose and knit shirts, that can be slipped over the body. They are made without closings. Most clothes, however, look better longer if they have been made to include closures and fasteners, such as zippers, buttons, and snaps.

Zippers are the most common kind of closure used in clothing. There are two types of zippers on the market today. They include the traditional zipper and the invisible zipper, so called because the teeth are hidden behind a fold in the zipper tape. Either type of zipper might be a good choice for a particular project, and each can be considered well attached if the finished closing keeps the zipper invisible and the stitching is straight. Since there is such a wide variety of acceptable zipper application methods, follow the one on your zipper package. You will probably find that it gives you very satisfactory results.

Buttonholes are of three kinds: machine-made buttonholes, hand-worked buttonholes, and bound buttonholes. The type you decide to make might depend on your fabric, as well as on the equipment you have available.

In clothing for women and girls, buttonholes are placed so that the right side of the garment laps over the left. In men's clothing, the reverse is true. All buttonholes are made through two or more thicknesses of fabric. They are strengthened with interfacings, as those found in tailored garments.

The size of the button used determines the size of the buttonhole. The buttonhole should be just large enough for the button to pass through easily.

When making buttonholes by any method, follow the markings on the pattern which indicate where the buttonholes are to be made. Use machine basting stitches to transfer marks from the wrong to the right side of the fabric.

When making machine-made buttonholes, follow the directions given by the manufacturer for using the machine or its special attachments. When the buttonhole has been made, cut it open between the two lines of zigzag stitching.

When making hand-worked buttonholes, cut the marked buttonhole, and use the buttonhole stitch. This knot-type stitch keeps the cut edge of the buttonhole from raveling when a garment is worn or laundered.

A bound buttonhole can be made by a variety of acceptable methods. Since these buttonholes are used to best advantage in tailored garments, most beginners do not make them. If you are particularly interested in learning this sewing process, perhaps your teacher will give you directions for making a sample bound buttonhole.

Making and setting sleeves

Many students select sleeveless garments for beginning projects. These projects do not require set-in sleeves. However, since there are sleeves in so many of the garments teen-agers like to wear, most students decide to learn how to put sleeves in garments while they have help from a sewing instructor. Sleeves are really quite easily made and set into garments if this easy step-by-step process is followed:

1 Staystitch the top of the sleeve on the seam line. Use regular stitches from the sleeve edge to the first notch. Change the

Determine the cause of wrinkles in a garment.

Make the necessary alterations to eliminate them.

Vertical or near-vertical wrinkles mean a garment piece is too wide. Alter by taking a tuck, increasing the size of the seam or by adding an additional seam.

Horizontal or near-horizontal wrinkles indicate that the garment piece is too tight horizontally or too long.

(a) If tight, alter by letting out the vertical seams.

(b) If long, alter by recutting or by taking a wide horizontal seam.

Diagonal wrinkles are due to strain or excess length at one edge. If you will trace the wrinkle to the point, or points, of origin, you will locate the trouble.

a If due to strain, alter by letting out nearest seam to allow more fabric.

b If due to excess length at one side, alter by taking up nearest horizontal seam, increasing size of a dart, or adding an additional dart.

c If due to dart too small for size of bulge, alter by making dart bigger. Obtain needed length or width by letting out seam.

Set the sleeve into a garment following the guidelines below.

Make the sleeve and bodice. Machine-baste around the top edge of the sleeve.

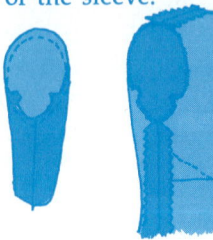

Slip the sleeve (right-side-out) into the bodice (wrong-side-out.)

Pull the thread of the machine basting so that the sleeve fits the armhole.

Block and pin the sleeve in place, checking the shoulder seam and underarm seam for accuracy of placement.

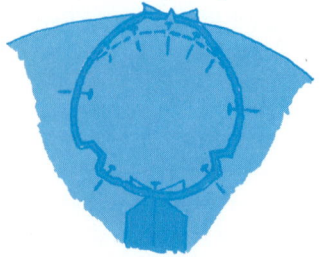

Machine-stitch the sleeve in place and press the seam into the sleeve area.

stitch length to a basting stitch, and continue stitching over the cap of the sleeve to the next notch. Return to the regular stitch, and continue stitching to the other edge of the sleeve.

2. If the lower edge of the sleeve is to be finished with a hem, staystitch it ¼ inch from the edge, and clean-finish it. (See page 349.)
3. Starting at the underarm, stitch the underarm seam, making a ⅝-inch seam, and press it open.
4. Turn the sleeve right side out.
5. With the garment wrong side out and held so that you are looking into the armhole, place the sleeve into the armhole with the notches matching.
6. Pin the sleeve seam to the garment underarm seam. Match and pin the top of the sleeve to the shoulder seam. Match the sleeve notches to the garment notches, and pin them together.
7. Adjust the sleeve to fit the armhole by pulling the machine basting.
8. Remove the sleeve, and block the cap to remove excess fullness.
9. Put the sleeve back into the armhole, and repin at the seams and notches. Add additional pins as needed.
10. Pin the sleeve into the armhole by placing pins rather close together and at right angles with the seam edge. Baste the sleeve in place, stitching with the sleeve side up. Avoid stitching puckers into the seamline if the sleeve has a smooth cap.
11. Try on the garment, and check the fit of the sleeve.
12. Stitch the sleeve into the garment, beginning at the back notches. Continue stitching under the arm to the front of the sleeve. Stitch around the entire sleeve, ending at the front notch. This provides double stitching in the underarm area.

Hems

The bottom edge of skirts, blouses, sleeves, and other parts of garments must be finished in some way to keep the raw edges from showing. The most common finish used is a hem formed by folding the fabric up and sewing it in place with invisible hand stitches. Hems vary in width depending upon the fabric and style of the garment. There are many suitable hemming stitches that may be used, but none should be noticeable on the right side.

A good hem is the same width all the way around, hangs evenly, and contains hemming stitches which are invisible from the top side of the garment.

17 CHAPTER POSTTEST

Number from 1 to 23. Beside each number indicate if the corresponding statement is true or false. *Do not* write in this book.

1. Young Junior/Teen pattern sizes are marked 5/6, 7/8, etc.
2. In buying a pattern for slacks, select the size which best fits your waist measurement.
3. The bust measurement is correctly taken below the bustline.
4. The waist length is measured from the bone you can feel at the back of your neck to the natural waistline.
5. In determining the hip measurement, place the tape measure around the hips 9 inches below the waist.
6. A pattern envelope will provide information about the number of pieces required to make that garment.
7. The pattern envelope contains a chart indicating the amount of fabric required to make the garment in various sizes.
8. In making a particular garment, use of a fabric which is 45 inches wide may require less yardage than use of a fabric which is 36 inches wide.
9. The cutting line on a pattern is indicated by a broken line.
10. Stitching lines show more on plain than on printed fabric.
11. A person who measures 36 inches around the hips requires a pattern which measures at least 38 inches in this area.
12. If your bust measurement is 34 inches, you need a pattern which measures between 37 and 38 inches in this area.
13. Pins should be placed 2 inches apart when pinning pattern pieces to fabrics.
14. In transferring pattern markings to fabric, the shiny side of the tracing paper is placed against the wrong side of the fabric.
15. Staystitching is done ¼ inch from the cut edge of a pattern piece.
16. The side seam of a blouse is stitched from the waistline toward the bustline.
17. The shoulder seam is stitched from the neckline toward the shoulderline.
18. The method in which all possible construction is completed on one section of a garment before it is attached to another section is called the unit method of construction.
19. Bustline darts extend ⅝ inch beyond the fullest part of the figure.
20. A fitted facing is made from a piece of bias fabric cut one inch wide.
21. Clean-finishing is done ¼ inch from the folded edge of the facing.
22. Understitching is done ⅜ inch from the seam line.
23. Horizontal bustline darts are pressed down before the side seams of a blouse are joined and pressed open.

Match the *description* in List A with the *pattern type* in List B. Use a pattern type from List B only once.

Column A: **Description**

A. For the short figure which has not yet started to mature physically
B. For the figure which is just beginning to develop in the bust and hips
C. For the short, well-developed figure
D. For the medium height figure which is shorter than average from the shoulder to the waistline
E. For the medium-tall to tall figure which is well developed and proportioned
F. For the fully developed, short-waisted figure which is narrow through the shoulders

Column B: **Pattern Type**

1. Girls
2. Half-Sizes
3. Junior Petite
4. Misses
5. Miss Petite
6. Young Junior/Teen

6
Your Foods

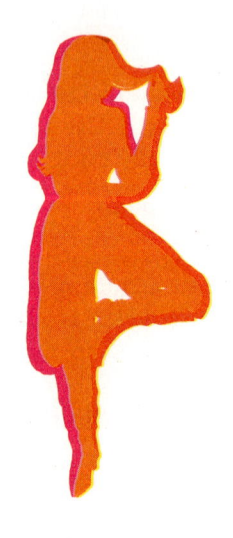

Chapter 18	Choosing food for health and vitality
Chapter 19	Buying food for economy and convenience
Chapter 20	Managing meals at home or school
Chapter 21	Preparing protein foods
Chapter 22	Preparing milk and milk-rich foods
Chapter 23	Preparing fruits and vegetables
Chapter 24	Preparing cereal products
Chapter 25	Preparing energy foods
Chapter 26	Enjoying food with family and friends

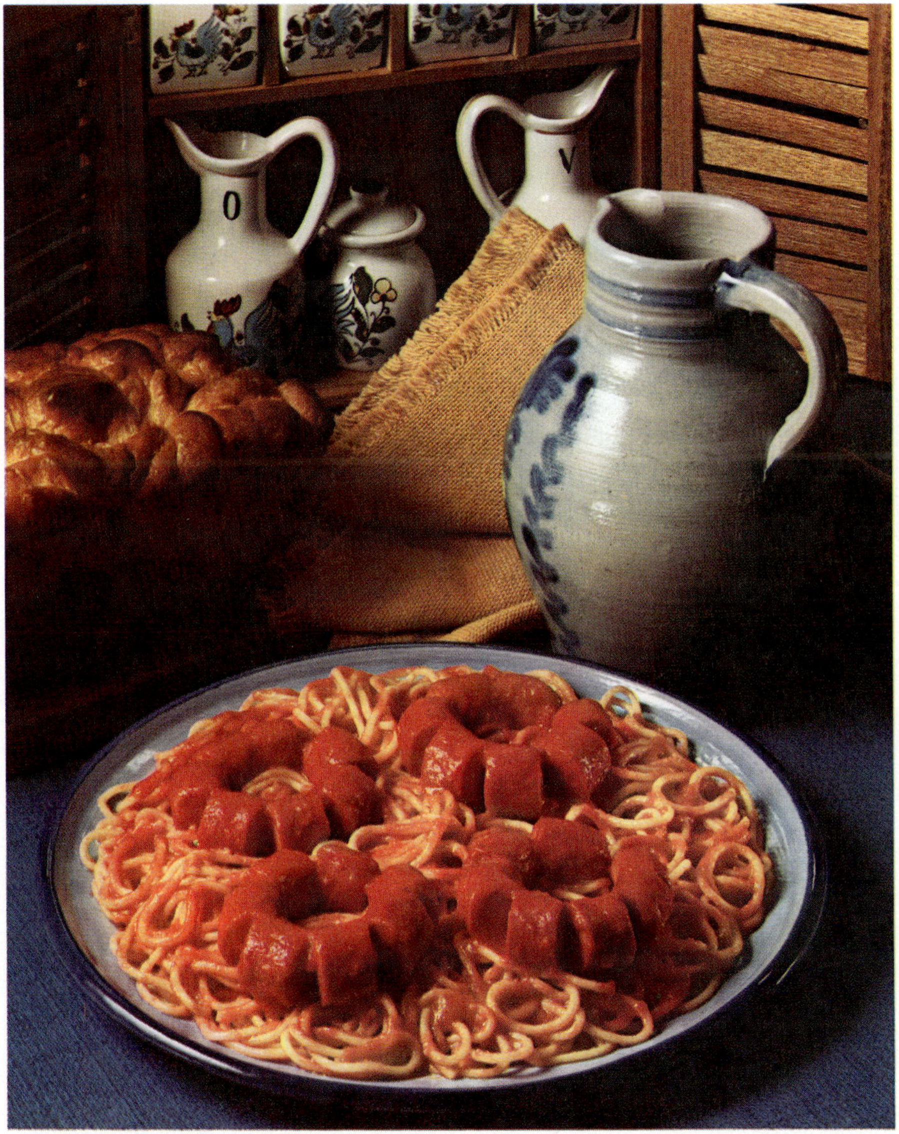
O
V

18 CHAPTER PRETEST

Match the *body functions* in List A with the *nutrients* which encourage them in List B. Use a nutrient from List B only once. *Do not* write in this book.

List A: Body Functions

A Helps prevents colds, sore gums, and easy bruising
B Helps prevent dry skin
C Helps in formation of strong bones and teeth
D Promotes tissue growth and repair
E Helps body utilize calcium

List B: Nutrients

1 Calcium
2 Protein
3 Vitamin A
4 Vitamin C
5 Vitamin D

Number from 1 to 13 on a piece of paper. Beside each number write the letter which corresponds to the *best* answer for that question.

1 Which of the following is the *best* source of calcium?
   a Meat   b Fruits
   c Vegetables   d Milk
2 Which of the following is the *best* source of vitamin A?
   a Skim milk
   b Sunshine
   c Leafy green or bright yellow vegetables
   d Steak
3 Which of the following lists of foods contains the *best* sources of vitamin C?
   a Citrus fruits, raw cabbage, and strawberries
   b Corn, carrots, bananas, and avocados
   c Lettuce, green beans, and spinach
   d Liver, pork, and fish
4 Which of the following lists of foods contains the *best* sources of *complete* protein?
   a Dry beans and dry peas
   b Enriched bread and cereals
   c Fish, poultry, cheese, and eggs
   d Citrus fruits, broccoli, and fresh strawberries
5 Which of the following lists of nutrients contains *all* fat-soluble vitamins?
   a Vitamins A, B, and C
   b Vitamins B, D, and E
   c Vitamins C, D, E, and K
   d Vitamins A, D, E, and K
6 For which of the following does the *Daily Food Guide* recommend two servings daily?
   a Meat group
   b Milk group
   c Fruit-vegetable group
   d Bread-cereal group
7 Which of the following are *minerals* which your body needs every day?
   a Thiamine and niacin
   b Starch and sugar
   c Ascorbic acid and riboflavin
   d Phosphorus, iron, and iodine
8 Which is *most* essential for good appetite and digestion?
   a Vitamin A
   b Vitamin B complex
   c Vitamin C
   d Vitamin D
9 Which of the following foods often contain empty calories?
   a Ice milk and ice cream
   b Fruit juices
   c Candy and soft drinks
   d Cheese dips
10 Which of the following are sources of *incomplete* proteins?
   a Cheese and eggs
   b Turkey and chicken
   c Beef and ham
   d Baked beans and pea soup
11 Which of the following lists of foods is *not* included in the bread and cereal group in the *Daily Food Guide*:
   a Pancakes and waffles
   b Potatoes and corn
   d Grits and rice
   d Biscuits and muffins
12 Which of the following does *not* affect the number of calories you need each day?
   a Your age
   b Your height
   c Your food likes and dislikes
   d Your activities
13 Which of the following is *not* a nutrient?
   a Carbohydrate
   b Calcium
   c Water
   d Fat

CHAPTER 18

Choosing food for health and vitality

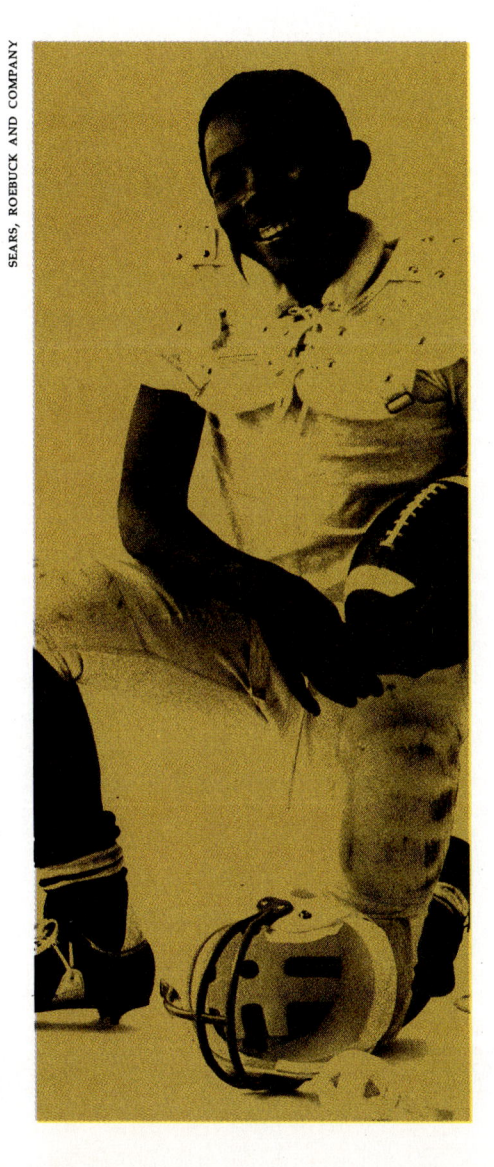

SEARS, ROEBUCK AND COMPANY

While some people may eat improperly, people who are both healthy and attractive have probably learned that certain foods, eaten in proper amounts, give their body the materials it needs for energy, growth, and repair. By choosing such foods, they tend to avoid those which cause them to become ill or overweight or to have skin problems.

Just as an engine cannot run without fuel, your body cannot continue to operate without food. Food provides your body with the fuel it needs. An engine may run along for a while on low-quality fuel. However, it will run better and longer if provided the type and amount of fuel intended by the manufacturer. In much the same way, your body can operate longer and more efficiently, when you provide it with the type and amount of food it needs.

Because you are a human being with emotional as well as physical needs, you may sometimes eat when you do not need fuel. The way you feel may cause you to consume food your body doesn't need. Emotional problems can cause people to eat in an effort to

Obtain nutritional facts for a week's time from television programs, commercials, advertisements, books, and personal interviews to answer the question: *Why do we eat?* Conduct a class discussion on the subject.

Discuss the ways in which your body is like a machine and the ways in which it is different from a machine.

Using a checklist, indicate the foods you eat often, eat occasionally, would never eat, and have never tried. Using all the students' answers, compile the results. Introduce foods in future laboratory lessons from the categories *would never eat* and *have never tried.*

Discuss observations you have made concerning the fact that some people eat to supply their emotional needs as well as their physical needs. Discuss the effect this habit may have on a person's personality and appearance.

Keep a record of what you eat for a day. Assign each food to its appropriate food group and total the number of servings in each group. Determine whether or not you ate enough servings from each food group in the *Daily Food Guide.* How can you improve your eating habits?

Plan and give to each class member a different menu for one day. Try to plan each menu so that foods in one group in the *Daily Food Guide* are missing. Let each student try to decide which food group is missing and suggest specific foods which might be included to improve the menu.

List reliable sources of food information such as the *National Dairy Council* or the *United States Department of Agriculture.* Find the addresses of these information centers in your library. Order pamphlets or other material useful in your study of nutrition.

Distribute pictures of a wide variety of different foods, giving one to each class member. Ask students who have pictures of foods belonging to the same group in the *Daily Food Guide* to collect themselves into a group. Discuss why various foods belong in a specific food group.

overcome nervousness or unhappiness. Food is often used as a substitute for love, security, or acceptance. For good health and vitality, however, it is important that you learn the real purpose of food. It will provide you with the materials you need for body energy, growth, and repair. When food is too frequently used as a substitute for other needs, your health, appearance, and vitality may suffer.

A guide to nutrition

People who study the content of foods are called *nutrition experts.* Through studies and experiments they have learned which foods contain materials for energy, growth, and body repair. To help you make wise daily food choices, government nutrition experts have divided the foods you need into four groups. By choosing daily from these four groups, you choose foods for good nutrition. Eating a wide variety of foods within each of the four groups offers further assurance that you are getting enough of each nutrient. (See page 362.)

FOOD GROUPS

The four food groups include meat, milk, fruits and vegetables, and cereal products. Together these four groups make up the foods included in the *Daily Food Guide.*

Nutrition experts have found that the healthy person who eats a certain amount from each of these four groups each day continues to be well fed. In other words, he has plenty of nutrients for energy, growth, and body repair. To round out meals and to satisfy his appetite, he uses some other foods.

By calling this plan *the 2-4-4-4 Food Guide,* you can easily remember your own food needs. Your body needs two servings of meat, four cups of milk, four servings of fruits and vegetables, and four servings of bread or other cereal products for good daily nutrition. A growing teen-ager may want more food, but this guide is the place to start. Eat these foods for good health. Add others if you need them for growth and energy.

The meat group

Nutrition experts include beef, pork, lamb, fish, poultry, cheese, and eggs in the meat group because they are excellent sources of body-building protein. At least two 3-ounce servings of these foods are needed daily. (See page 362.) They contain the building blocks necessary for body growth and repair. Milk, another animal product, is a valuable source of protein. But, because of its high bone-building value, it has been placed in its own separate food group.

Other foods, for example, dry beans, dry peas, lentils, and gelatin, contain protein. However, these foods do not contain all the essential protein building blocks. When several of these foods are eaten together, or when they are eaten in combination with meat or milk, your body can take from each of the different foods the materials needed for growth. Because these foods are substitute sources of the building blocks found in meat, they are sometimes called *meat alternates.* When the alternates are eaten, a smaller amount of meat is necessary for good nutrition.

The milk group
Milk and milk foods, such as cheese and ice cream, make up the milk group. Without milk in some form, it is almost impossible to get from the rest of your foods the minerals necessary for building strong teeth and bones. Teen-agers need at least four cups of milk each day served in drinks or in milk-rich foods. Milk and milk products are also important growth and repair foods.

The fruit-vegetable group
The fruit-vegetable group furnishes several special compounds called *vitamins.* These vitamins are necessary if your body is to use the foods you eat. In addition to helping your body use foods for growth and repair, the vitamins act as body regulators. They also help prevent diseases. Various vitamins are found in almost all foods, but fruits and vegetables are among the richest vitamin sources.

The fruits and vegetables also provide various minerals, sugar for energy, and the roughage needed for good digestion and elimination. Teen-agers need to eat four good-sized servings of fruits and vegetables each day. You may choose among raw, cooked, and liquid forms of these foods.

The bread-cereal group
Cereal foods provide energy. They also contain some of the proteins necessary for body growth and repair, as well as valuable vitamins. Include four servings of bread or cereal foods among your daily food choices.

The effects of nutrition on health

The food needs of teen-agers in general are higher than those of most children and adults. This is due to the fact that most teen-agers live at a busy, active pace while continuing to grow rapidly. In addition to actual growth, teen-agers are going through many physical changes.

The teen-age years are often the time when young people are given freedom to choose what they will eat. Since your looks, your energy, and your health are all, to a large extent, determined by your choice of foods, you have much to gain by learning to like foods included in the *Daily Food Guide.*

Explain in your own words the meaning of the term: *balanced diet.* Using the menu for a meal you prepare in the foods laboratory, plan the other meals which might be served that day to make the day's diet balanced.

Copy several menu offerings from a restaurant menu. Evaluate the menus on the basis of the *Daily Food Guide.* Were the meals good nutritional buys? Why or why not?

Arrange a *cafeteria* of food models from which you can select foods for a day. Check the quality of your selections against those recommended by the *Daily Food Guide.*

Discuss the *miles of motion* covered per day by the human body and the relative amount of fuel needed for this activity.

Bulletin board IDEA
Title: *Balance Your Diet*
Directions: Draw and cut out a clown balancing himself on a large ball while holding four balloons. On each balloon, write the name of one of the four food groups.

Meat Group

Milk Group

Fruit-Vegetable Group

Bread-Cereal Group

COURTESY NATIONAL DAIRY COUNCIL

The 2-4-4-4 Food Guide allows a person to choose from each of the four food groups the foods his body needs daily.

YOUR LOOKS

Most people want to look their best. Of all the factors you control, the food you eat probably affects your looks more than any other. For instance, your height and weight and the general health of your skin, hair, eyes, nails, and bones and teeth are all affected by the food you eat. No matter how carefully you choose your clothes or how much time you spend on grooming, you will look your best only if you eat the right foods.

YOUR ENERGY

Energy is provided by all of the food groups. Good food choices and abundant energy so often go together, however, that a person is more likely to feel energetic if he makes wise food choices.

Fruits, vegetables, and cereals, the main energy foods, also provide other health-giving nutrients. Knowing this, you may be encouraged to select these foods for health and energy, rather than candy or other sweet foods, which offer little except quick energy.

What are calories?

You have probably heard the word *calorie* many times. Do you know what a calorie really is? It is not something you can touch or see at all. Rather, it is a measure of the heat given off by food when it is burned. Your body can turn food into heat, or energy. The ability to produce heat determines whether a food is high or low in calories. For example, a spoonful of burning fat gives off a large amount of heat, while a spoonful of burning green vegetables gives off very little. This is the reason fat is called a high-calorie food, while green vegetables are said to be low in calories.

Your body needs food enough to provide a certain number of calories each day for energy and heat to keep you warm. If the food you eat contains more calories than you need, your body changes the food to fat, stores it, and you gain weight. If you eat fewer calories than your body needs, your body uses stored fat and you lose weight. (See side columns, pages 363–367.)

How many calories do you need? That depends on your sex, age, size, weight, and activities. There is one other factor, sometimes called metabolism, which affects your need for calories. Do you know someone who seems to eat anything and everything without gaining weight? Do you know other people who seem to eat much less but gain weight easily? How can this difference be explained? Differing rates of metabolism are often the answer. Because people with high rates of metabolism tend to burn up calories in nervous energy, they usually remain thin. On the other hand, because of low rates of metabolism, other people can remain warm and

Study the lists of foods shown in these five side columns and the number of calories each contains. Conduct a class discussion concerning the types of foods teen-agers need to choose each day. Consider the number of calories foods contain and the foods which are necessary for good health.

Daily Energy Requirements

Girls, 12–15	2500 calories
Girls, 15–18	2300 calories
Boys, 12–15	3000 calories
Boys, 15–18	3400 calories

Protein Foods

ITEM	CALORIES
Beef	
Beef liver (2 oz.)	120
Beef, roast (3 oz.)	255
Beef, steak (3 oz.)	330
Beef stew (1 cup)	250
Hamburger patty (3 oz.)	245
Eggs	
Eggs, boiled or poached (1)	80
Eggs, fried (1)	125
Eggs, scrambled (1)	110
Fish	
Bluefish, baked (3 oz.)	135
Crabmeat (3 oz.)	90
Fishsticks (5 sticks)	200
Shrimp, cooked (3 oz.)	110
Tuna (3 oz.)	170
Lamb	
Lamb chop (1)	130

(Continued on next page)

ITEM	CALORIES
Miscellaneous	
Bologna, large (1 slice)	100
Frankfurter (1)	155
Pork	
Bacon, broiled (2 slices)	95
Ham, sliced (3 oz.)	340
Pork chop (3.5 oz. with bone)	260
Poultry	
Chicken, broiled (3 oz.)	115
Turkey, white meat (1 slice)	100
Veal	
Veal cutlet (3 oz.)	185
Vegetable Protein	
Baked beans (1 cup)	300
Black-eyed peas (1 cup)	190

Milk-Rich Foods

ITEM	CALORIES
Butter (1 T.)	100
Buttermilk (1 cup)	90
Cheddar cheese (1 oz.)	115
Cocoa, all milk (1 cup)	235
Cottage cheese (2 T.)	30
Cream cheese (2 T.)	105
Custards, baked (½ cup)	150
Ice cream, chocolate (½ cup)	250
Ice cream, fudge sauce (½ cup)	400
Ice-cream soda (1 glass)	300
Ice cream, vanilla (½ cup)	200
Malted milk (1 cup)	280
Milk, skim (1 cup)	90
Milk, whole (1 cup)	165
White sauce, medium (¼ cup)	110

(Continued on next page)

COURTESY SEARS, ROEBUCK AND CO.

A growing young person burns up several thousand calories per day as he engages in many and varied activities.

active on far fewer calories. This type of person burns few calories as nervous energy and tends to store extra calories as fat. Such a person must be careful to make most food choices from the *Daily Food Guide* in order to remain trim and attractive.

What are nutrients?

In addition to calories, your body needs several kinds of materials to make it work properly. These materials are called *nutrients* because they nourish the body. The nutrients include proteins, carbohydrates, fats, vitamins, and minerals.

PROTEINS

Protein is necessary for body growth and repair. Without protein, your body is unable to grow or to repair its own bruises, cuts, broken bones, or injured muscles.

High-quality protein is found mostly in foods that come from animals. Therefore, meat, poultry, fish, cheese, milk, and eggs are considered the best protein sources. Because these animal products contain all of the necessary building blocks, they are called *complete proteins*. Most vegetable protein contains only some of the building blocks. Such protein is called *incomplete protein*.

CARBOHYDRATES

Plant foods which contain large amounts of starch or sugar are called *carbohydrates*. Your body can easily change both starch and sugar into a form which is usable as energy. Cereals, fruits, and vegetables are examples of carbohydrate foods. They come from plants, contain a large amount of starch or sugar, and are rich in energy.

Many foods that contain starch and sugar are good food choices because they are also rich in other important nutrients. On the other hand, some foods are almost pure carbohydrate with very few other nutrients. Since it is easy for your body to change carbohydrate into fat and to store the fat in your tissues, these are usually poor food choices.

To keep your weight in proportion to your height and body build, you will need to select carbohydrate foods wisely. For example, even though potatoes, corn, and fruit contain large amounts of carbohydrate, their minerals and vitamins are important to your health. Carbohydrate-rich snacks such as candy and soft drinks contain very few valuable nutrients. Since they have little real food value except energy, calories in such foods are often called *empty calories*.

FATS

Fats are high-energy nutrients found in both animals and plants. Cup for cup, they contain more than twice as many calories as pure sugar. The amount of fat you eat each day should be limited if you are to have a trim, attractive figure and a smooth, clear complexion. However, since fat is rich in certain vitamins and in energy, it is important to the diet of most teen-agers.

Recent studies indicate that certain fats, particularly animal fats, tend to damage the blood vessels of elderly people. Research also indicates that such damage begins early in life. If research continues to show danger connected with eating animal fat, perhaps you will want to limit the amount you eat. For the time being, however, include some butter or margarine in your daily diet.

VITAMINS

Vitamins help to regulate body processes. Without them, your body cannot function properly or use the nutrients in the food you eat. Although required in very small amounts, they are essential to life and health. For hundreds of years, scientists suspected that foods contained unknown life-giving elements. The actual discovery of vitamins, however, did not occur until the twentieth century.

During the Golden Age of Greece, physicians began to suspect that certain foods contained hidden particles necessary for good health. Various of the food-connected dis-

Fruits and Vegetables

ITEM	CALORIES
Fruits	
Apple, medium (1)	70
Banana (1)	85
Cantaloupe (½)	40
Grapefruit (½)	50
Orange, large (1)	70
Orange juice (1 cup)	100
Peach, medium (1)	35
Pear, raw (1)	100
Strawberries (1 cup)	55
Watermelon (1 wedge)	120
Vegetables	
Asparagus (6 spears)	20
Beans, green (1 cup)	25
Beans, lima (1 cup)	150
Beets (1 cup)	70
Broccoli (1 cup)	45
Cabbage, raw (1 cup)	25
Carrot (1)	20
Cauliflower (1 cup)	30
Celery, raw (1 stalk)	5
Collards, cooked (1 cup)	75
Corn on the cob (1 ear)	65
Lettuce leaves (2 large)	5
Onion, raw (1)	50
Onions, cooked (1 cup)	80
Peas, canned (1 cup)	110
Pepper, green (1)	15
Potato, baked or boiled (1)	90
Potato, French-fried (10 pieces)	155
Spinach (1 cup)	45
Sweet potato (1)	155
Tomato, fresh (1)	45
Tomato juice (1 cup)	50
Turnip greens (1 cup)	45

(Continued on next page)

Cereal Foods

ITEM	CALORIES
Biscuits, baking powder (1)	130
Bran flakes (1 oz.)	85
Bread, rye (1 slice)	55
Bread, white (1 slice)	60
Bread, whole wheat (1 slice)	55
Corn flakes (1 cup)	110
Corn grits, cooked (1 cup)	120
Coffee cake or bun (1 serving)	135
Crackers, graham (2)	55
Crackers, saltine (2)	35
Griddlecake (1)	60
Macaroni, cooked (1 cup)	155
Macaroni and cheese (1 cup)	475
Muffin (1)	135
Noodles, egg, cooked (1 cup)	200
Pizza, section (1)	350
Rice, cooked (1 cup)	200
Roll, dinner	115
Rolled oats, cooked (1 cup)	150
Sandwich, 2 slices bread, with meat or cheese filling (1)	300
Spaghetti, cooked (1 cup)	155
Waffle, 5-inch (1)	215
Wheat, shredded (1 cup)	100

(Continued on next page)

eases were described during that time and soon after. Early scientists learned that a certain disease could be prevented by eating a certain food. However, they could never find exactly what a vitamin was made of or what it looked like.

Early in this century, with the aid of improved laboratory techniques, scientists finally discovered the vitamins which man had partially understood for so long but had not been able to find. As each vitamin was researched, it was given a letter name. Thus the letters A, B, C, and D simply denote the order in which research work developed. As the complicated vitamin B was examined and found to consist of several similar vitamins, the group were named B_1, B_2, etc.

Finally, vitamins were isolated and their exact contents were determined. As scientists came to understand the content of each one, they were able to make that vitamin in the laboratory. Thus the vitamins fed to infants today are frequently laboratory products, produced as a result of centuries of research.

During early research, some people thought there were only two vitamins: one that dissolved in fat and one that dissolved in water. Then it became clear that there are several *fat-soluble* and several *water-soluble* vitamins. Because the vitamins within each of these groups have much in common, they can be studied as a large group. By studying vitamins according to solubility rather than according to letter order, you will be able to understand better where to find and how to care for each one.

The fat-soluble vitamins

The fat-soluble vitamins, A, D, E, and K, dissolve in fat rather than in water. As you might expect, they are found in the fatty parts of plants and animals. The fat-soluble vitamins which your body needs are taken directly from the foods you eat. Extra vitamins are stored in your body.

Since they do not dissolve in water, the body does not throw away vitamins A, D, E, and K in the food waste. It is therefore possible to get more of these vitamins than your body can use. An overdose of vitamins is very unlikely from simply eating vitamin-rich foods. However, it is altogether possible to get a bad vitamin reaction if you take large doses of pills containing vitamins which your body does not need.

Vitamin A helps to keep your skin in good condition. It also affects your eyesight. Without vitamin A, your eyes cannot adjust well to bright light or semi-darkness. For example, if you have trouble adjusting to the dim light of a movie theater when coming in from the light outdoors, you may need more vitamin A. If your skin is dry and rough, or if the linings of your nose,

Vitamins A, D, E, and K dissolve in fat. Each day choose foods rich in them which are served fresh, cooked in water, or broiled near direct heat.

COURTESY ST. LOUIS DISTRICT DAIRY COUNCIL

Energy Foods

ITEM	CALORIES
Cake, angel food (1 slice)	110
Cake, chocolate, iced, (1 slice)	400
Cake, sponge (1 slice)	125
Candy (1 oz.)	90–140
Candy bar (1)	300
Coffee or tea, plain	None
Carbonated beverages (1 cup)	80–100
Chocolate syrup, thin type (1 T.)	50
Cookies, plain, 3 inch (1)	110
Cookies, fruit-filled (1 small)	55
Doughnut (1)	135
Gelatin desserts (½ cup)	75
Gravy, meat, thickened, (3 T.)	50
Jelly (1 T.)	55
Margarine (1 T.)	100
Mayonnaise (1 T.)	110
Peanut butter (1 T.)	90
Peanuts (9 large)	100
Pie, apple (⅙ pie)	350
Pie, lemon meringue (⅙ pie)	300
Pie, pumpkin (⅙ pie)	260
Popcorn, plain (1 cup)	54
Potato chips (10 chips)	110
Shortening (1 T.)	110
Sugar, brown (1 T.)	50
Sugar, white (1 T.)	50

mouth, and throat are easily irritated, you may need more vitamin A.

Vitamin A is found in the fatty parts of animal products. For instance, cream, butter, cheese, and egg yolks are good sources of vitamin A. Animal liver is extremely rich in vitamin A because the unneeded vitamin an animal has eaten is stored in its liver.

Many bright-colored vegetables are said to be good sources of vitamin A. Does this statement seem surprising when you know that vegetables contain very little fat and that vitamin A is found in fatty foods? It can be explained this way: Bright-colored vegetables contain material your body can change into vitamin A. Therefore, when you eat bright green or bright yellow or orange vegetables and fruits, your body can manufacture its own vitamin A. Cantaloupes, carrots, broccoli, and spinach are rich sources of this provitamin.

Vitamin D is called the *sunshine vitamin*. It was given this name upon the discovery that the human body, when exposed to the direct rays of the sun, can make its own supply of vitamin D.

Vitamin D is essential to bone growth. Without it, the human body cannot use the minerals from milk

Divide into groups of three or four members. Let each group present a skit to the class about one nutrient. Draw slips of paper to determine which group will illustrate which nutrient. These skits should include the following information:
1. Sources of the nutrient
2. Its functions in the body
3. Interesting information about its history and discovery
4. Deficiency symptoms and diseases associated with an inadequate intake of this nutrient

Divide the class into teams for a *treasure hunt*. On the tack board place the names of the nutrients, leaving a place for pictures. Using old magazines from which to cut pictures, see which team can place the most foods under the correct nutrient in a given length of time.

Read references on nutritional needs of people in various age groups and occupations. Then compare the nutritional needs of the following: an elderly person, an expectant mother, a teen-age girl, a teen-age boy, a professional football player, a convalescent recovering from surgery, a preschool-age child, and an infant.

to build strong bones. Since a young child's bones grow at a rapid rate, it is vital that he receive vitamin D either in his diet or by exposure to sunlight.

Vitamin D is stored in the livers of many animals. The best-known form of this vitamin is found in fish-liver oil. In times past, children were fed cod-liver oil when they were young. Since scientists have learned to make this vitamin in the laboratory, the processed vitamin is fed to children either in drop form or as an addition to their milk supply.

Other fat-soluble vitamins include vitamins E and K. Vitamin E seems to provide protection for vitamin A, preserving it from destruction until your body can use it. It is definitely known that vitamin K helps the blood to clot if your body is injured. Both vitamins have many other uses, some of which have not been discovered.

Vitamins E and K seem to be found in many of the foods generally eaten for good health. Green leafy vegetables, fruits, and liver contain both vitamins. When enough of the foods are eaten to provide for general good health, plenty of vitamins E and K are included.

The water-soluble vitamins

The water-soluble vitamin group is made up of the vitamin B complex and vitamin C. Since these vitamins dissolve in water, they remain in liquid solution within your body. Thus, unneeded vitamins are discarded daily along with body waste.

The vitamin B family was found, upon research, to be indeed a complex group of vitamins. Some scientists feel there may be fifteen or more vitamins in the B complex. As each numbered vitamin was chemically understood, it was given a name related to its content. Among the group for which names have been established are *thiamine, riboflavin,* and *niacin.* It is not known whether every B vitamin is essential to human growth and health. These three, however, are very important.

The B vitamins help keep your appetite and digestion normal, your nervous system healthy, and your skin smooth. They are found in many foods. If you are careful to eat meat, milk, fruits and vegetables, and grain products included in the *Daily Food Guide*, most of the B vitamins will be provided.

Because the B vitamins are water soluble, they are not stored in your body but are discarded daily. This can be a problem, because you must eat vitamin B–rich foods daily.

Vitamin C might be called the escape artist. Because it, like the B complex is water soluble, the extra supply you might eat today may be discarded in the body waste before you need it tomorrow. Too, it is easily oxidized. In other words, it easily mixes with oxygen and thus

COURTESY ST. LOUIS DISTRICT DAIRY COUNCIL

Vitamins B and C dissolve in water. Each day choose foods rich in them which are served fresh, cooked in fat, or broiled near direct heat.

is no longer vitamin C. If a vitamin C–rich food comes in contact with a sodalike compound, or is left in the open air, much of the vitamin C is oxidized, or lost.

Vitamin C is a very essential vitamin found mostly in such fresh fruits and vegetables as oranges, grapefruit, lemons, strawberries, tomatoes, and broccoli. The person who fails to get enough vitamin C over an extended period of time may notice that he bruises easily and has frequent colds. His gums may bleed easily, his teeth may loosen, and his joints may become sore. Although actual death from lack of vitamin C is not common in the United States today, many people suffer vitamin C shortage. To prevent this shortage, try to include at least one citrus fruit, or a serving of tomatoes or strawberries among the four fruits and vegetables you eat each day.

MINERALS

You know minerals in the form of rocks and salts. Your body needs tiny amounts of certain of these

Study one of the nutrients and report to the class in an individual and creative way. Use a poster, make a bulletin board display, show a filmstrip, write a skit, or give a demonstration.

Devise a nutrition crossword puzzle. If possible, have the puzzle reproduced for class members to work out.

Discuss and evaluate the merit of old wives' tales such as these:
1 Don't eat fish and drink milk in the same meal.
2 Eating carrots will make your hair curly.
3 White eggs are more nutritious than brown eggs.
4 Eating onions will cure a cold.
5 Eat oysters only in months which have an *r* in their spelling.

Bulletin board IDEA
Title: *At 11:00 A.M.*
Are You a Lion
or a
Mouse?
Directions: Print the title and attach it to the bulletin board. In place of the words *lion* and *mouse*, pin up stuffed toys or cutouts to represent these animals.

Food is more appetizing to look at when the colors are bright and varied (left) than when they are dull and similar (right).

Foods seem tastier when they are chosen to complement each other (left) than when they have similar flavors (right).

COURTESY GREEN GIANT COMPANY

Foods are more interesting when their shapes vary (left) than when there is a sameness in their shapes (right).

COURTESY GREEN GIANT COMPANY

Foods are more palatable when their textures vary from soft, to chewy, to crisp (left) than when they are prepared to have similar textures (right).

371

Keep a record of the kinds and amounts of food you eat for a period of at least three days, including only one weekend day. Using the Calorie Table located in the side columns on pages 363 through 367 as a guide, and other charts if necessary, compute the calories supplied by the foods you ate each day. Was this about the right number of calories for you? How can you find out? How can you determine the number of calories you need to remain at your present weight? Why do some people require more calories than others?

Suggest several reasons why it is unwise to rely on vitamin pills for the nutrients your body needs.

Your career
Dietitian

Duties: Plans diets and menus, supervises food preparation and service, manages and administers food service activities, teaches dietetics and nutrition, counsels clients regarding proper nutrition, or does dietary research.
Where employed: Hospitals, nursing homes, the armed forces, or in other large food service operations.

minerals to function properly. Among the minerals you need every day are calcium, phosphorus, iron, and iodine. You need tiny amounts of a long list of minerals called *trace elements.* They include copper, sodium, potassium, magnesium, cobalt, chlorine, sulfur, and zinc.

Scientists are still searching to find exactly what the trace elements do for you. Although they have not yet determined exactly how much you need, they know that the person who eats plenty of the foods that contain calcium, phosphorus, iron, and iodine seems to get enough of the trace elements for good health.

Calcium and phosphorus
Two minerals, calcium and phosphorus, seem to work together as a team. The bones and teeth contain most of the calcium and phosphorus found in the entire human body. Milk and milk foods are extremely rich sources of calcium. Calcium and phosphorus are found together in similar amounts in many other foods. But your body needs more calcium than phosphorus. When bones and teeth are being formed, it is especially important to drink milk. During the teen years, if your diet includes four cups of milk a day in some form, you will have a good chance of remaining strong.

Vitamin D fits into the bone-making process. Without vitamin D, your body can't use the calcium and phosphorus you take in. Only when you have vitamin D, calcium, and phosphorus present in proper proportion are you able to build strong bones and teeth. (See page 367 for discussion of vitamin D.)

Iron
Iron, found in your red blood cells, combines with the oxygen you take into your lungs and carries it to all parts of your body. Without this iron-oxygen combination, you could not change the food you eat into the energy you need.

A lack of iron in the blood causes a disease called *anemia.* Whenever blood is lost, iron is lost.

Your body can store iron in the liver as well as in the blood. Therefore, you need not eat great quantities of iron-rich foods. If you eat meats, eggs, leafy vegetables, whole-grain cereals, and dried fruits and vegetables, you probably get enough iron for your needs.

Iodine
Your body uses iodine to help the thyroid gland produce the thyroid hormone. The thyroid hormone affects growth and weight. A lack of iodine in the body can affect the metabolism and slow the normal growth of children. In adults, it usually causes a lack of energy and a general tired feeling. The slowing down of body movement can cause a person to gain unwanted weight. If you do not get enough iodine, the

thyroid will enlarge in an effort to produce its hormone. This produces a condition called *goiter*. Goiter causes an unsightly swelling at the front of the neck. Today goiter hardly exists as a disease in this country. Most people avoid a shortage of iodine through the use of *iodized* salt.

Fish and seafood are among the best natural sources of iodine. If you frequently eat a variety of seafoods, you probably get all the iodine you need. Your body loses a little iodine every day, however, so you must constantly replace it with a new supply.

Water in the diet

Water is not actually a nutrient because it contains no nourishment. However, it is essential to life and good health. Your body uses water to carry the food materials to be used by the body. The body also gets rid of waste matter in the water it eliminates. Water helps to keep you cool as liquid perspiration evaporates from the skin. In fact, a person can live much longer without food than without water.

While you do not actually digest water and convert it to energy, your body cannot function without it. Most authorities agree that six to eight glasses of water are necessary for body maintenance and good health. However, water-rich foods, such as fruit juice, can replace a certain portion of your total water intake.

Nutrition—product of history, hope of the future

As you study nutrition, it may seem to be a difficult science. Indeed it is. When you consider that man studied more than 2000 years before he discovered vitamins, you grasp one of the difficult aspects of nutrition. Years and years of research went into each of the nutritional facts which today's students learn in their early school years.

During this long process of research and discovery, each nutrient had to be fitted into the total health picture. To put all the information together into a workable eating plan probably seemed like a giant jigsaw fact-puzzle to nutrition experts. Even the simple *Daily Food Guide* required research which spanned several centuries.

Scientists have shown us which foods to eat and how to produce food for all the world's peoples. They continue their research in an effort to keep the food production rate ahead of food needs. Can this goal be attained? Yesterday's scientists determined the foods you need. Tomorrow's scientists will be faced with producing these foods through methods not yet discovered.

Study possible situations such as overpopulation, lack of good soil, or colonization of space. Brainstorm to develop possible ways to provide food in these situations.

Explain and illustrate your understanding of the following statements:
1 Many kinds and combinations of food can lead to a well-balanced diet.
2 No one food, by itself, has all the nutrients needed for full growth and health.
3 Each nutrient has specific uses in the body.
4 Most nutrients do their best work in the body when teamed with other nutrients.
5 All persons, throughout life, have need for the same nutrients, but in varying amounts.
6 The amounts of nutrients needed are influenced by a person's age, sex, size, activity, and state of health.
7 The way food is handled influences the amount of nutrients it contains as well as its appearance and taste.

Bulletin board IDEA
Title: *You Are What YOU Eat*
Directions: Form a human-like figure out of pictures of a wide variety of foods.

18 CHAPTER POSTTEST

Match the *best sources* in List A with the *nutrients* in List B. Use a nutrient from List B only once. *Do not* write in this book.

List A: **Best sources**

A Meat, fish, poultry
B Carrots, spinach, egg yolk
C Sunshine, fortified milk
D Citrus fruit and raw tomatoes
E Milk and milk products

List B: **Nutrients**

1 Calcium
2 Protein
3 Vitamin A
4 Vitamin C
5 Vitamin D

Match the *functions* in List A with the *nutrients* which help maintain them in List B. Use a nutrient from List B only once.

List A: **Functions**

A Helps in the maintenance of a healthy nervous system
B Helps blood to clot
C Affects the red blood cell count
D Helps prevent goiter
E Provides the body with fuel for energy

List B: **Nutrients**

1 Carbohydrate
2 Iodine
3 Iron
4 Thiamine
5 Vitamin K

Fill in the blank in each sentence with the *best* word to complete the statement.

1 Food gives your body the materials it needs for good health, growth, repair, and ___(1)___.
2 The four food groups in the *Daily Food Guide* contain fruits and vegetables, bread and cereal products, meat, and ___(2)___.
3 The number of recommended daily servings from the bread and cereal group is ___(3)___.
4 The number of recommended daily servings from the fruit and vegetable group is ___(4)___.
5 The heat given off by food when it is burned in the body is measured in ___(5)___.
6 Carbohydrates contain large amounts of sugar or ___(6)___.
7 The fat-soluble vitamins are A, K, E, and ___(7)___.
8 The best-known B vitamins are riboflavin, niacin, and ___(8)___.
9 The B-complex vitamins and vitamin ___(9)___ are similar in that both are water-soluble.
10 All nutrients can be classified as proteins, carbohydrates, fats, vitamins, or ___(10)___.
11 The nutrients which best help to regulate body processes are ___(11)___.
12 The nutrient essential for body growth and repair is ___(12)___.
13 Although it is not a nutrient, ___(13)___ is essential for good health.

19 CHAPTER PRETEST

Fill in the blank in each sentence with the *best* word or words to complete the statement. *Do not* write in this book.

1 The cost of food is affected by the ___(1)___ available.
2 All foods which cross state lines are subject to regulation by the ___(2)___, which is administered by the Federal government.
3 It is required that all food labels contain the name and address of the producer, the name of the product, and the net contents of the container either in weight or in ___(3)___.
4 Shopping without a list, seeing foods which are displayed attractively, smelling foods which have appetizing aromas, and shopping when you are hungry may result in ___(4)___ buying.
5 The four grades of beef are standard, good, choice, and ___(5)___.
6 Even distribution of fat throughout meat is called ___(6)___.
7 The highest quality of eggs available is Grade ___(7)___.
8 When milk has been heated to kill harmful bacteria it has been ___(8)___.
9 The four forms in which foods may be purchased are dried, frozen, canned, and ___(9)___.
10 Cereal products to which thiamine, riboflavin, niacin, and iron have been added are labeled ___(10)___.

CHAPTER 19

Buying food for economy and convenience

Good nutrition is not determined entirely by the amount of money spent for food. Many families who spend a great deal of money are poorly fed without realizing it. Other families who plan carefully and spend less are well nourished. In most cases, the lower a family's cash income, the higher the percentage of income spent on food. Food spending is also related to a family's size, its stage in the family life cycle, and its special health needs and food preferences.

How does a family know how much money to spend on food? The first consideration, of course, is the amount of available money. The second consideration is resources other than money that a family may use to place food on the table. For instance, families who have gardens or farms that produce food usually spend less money than families who must buy all of their food. Government assistance in the form of food stamps or other such plans or meals provided at school or by an employer are also a part of a family's food resources.

The amount of money spent on food also may reflect the amount of time and energy available for food

Invite two men and their wives to visit your class to discuss how activities away from home affect the eating habits of a family. Try to include a family in which the wife is a full-time homemaker and a family in which the wife works outside the home.

List foods which are traditionally served at special holidays. Suggest new and different ways of preparing, garnishing, or serving these foods. Suggest ways by which a family could have turkey on Thanksgiving, even though the mother was required to work away from home that day.

Make a list of your family's favorite foods. Try to determine why these foods are especially liked.

Give reasons to justify the statement: *The higher a family's income, the smaller is the proportion of money spent for food while the lower a family's income, the greater is the proportion of money spent for food.*

Tell about different food customs which are unique in various parts of the country such as *sugar on snow* in New England or *fish and grits* in the South. Explain why there are regional preferences in foods.

Tell of a food custom which has become part of your family holiday tradition. How did this tradition develop?

preparation. Families whose members all work or attend school may buy many partially prepared or ready-to-serve items. This practice tends to increase the total cost of food. Busy families are also tempted to serve snack foods. Unless special attention is given to wise choices, some sacrifice is made in good nutrition.

Families have different customs with respect to food. No matter how families differ in cultural backgrounds, however, they all share the need for good nutrition. The person responsible for planning meals and buying food for the family becomes responsible, to a degree, for the health of family members.

Why food costs differ

From day to day and from week to week, food costs change. This change is due to a number of factors. Supply and demand, the cost of producing food, and the cost of shipping and storing it until it is sold all affect food costs. Because of rapid transportation and modern preservation and packaging methods, a wide variety of foods is usually available the year round. Still, the cost of a single item of food may vary greatly from one time of the year to another. Watch food prices. Compare them when you shop. You will gain a better idea of how much food costs change. You will be better able to recognize good buys and to take advantage of them.

THE SOURCE

Food produced and sold locally with no shipping costs involved is usually lower in cost than food that comes from far away. Thus, if you buy fruits or vegetables that were grown in your own community, they will cost less than those shipped in from another state.

While cultural backgrounds may influence specific food choices, the total nutritional program of a family affects both the physical and mental growth of its school-age children.

COURTESY THE CLOROX COMPANY

COURTESY KAISER ALUMINUM

Food costs in general are determined by the amount of handling, processing, and packaging necessary to provide a given food in the form in which you wish to buy it.

THE SEASON

When there is an abundance of locally produced food on the market, it is usually inexpensive. If the food has been specially handled, stored, or shipped from another part of the country where it was produced, it is usually expensive. Fresh strawberries and tomatoes, for example, are costly in the North during January and February but fairly cheap in Southern localities where they are in season at that time.

As facilities for storing foods are improved, more and more foods are available in markets all over the country at all seasons of the year. However, the total price paid for a food is affected by storage costs.

THE PACKAGING AND ADVERTISING

Each time food is handled, the price goes up. Fruits and vegetables that are prewashed, trimmed, and packaged cost more than those you buy in bulk and clean yourself. For example, cabbage by the head costs much less than shredded cabbage in a package or cole slaw in a plastic container. Buying in large quantity

List foods which may be less expensive in your part of the country than in other places. Tell why this is true.

Make a calendar of the year. On it show the fresh fruits and vegetables available each month in your area. Indicate the months in which the market supply is best.

Make a list of foods which vary considerably in price from one season to another. Beside the name of the food, indicate the time of the year when it is least expensive in your area. At what time of year is this food most flavorful?

List foods such as peas and potatoes which can be purchased in four forms: fresh, frozen, canned, and dried. Is the nutritive value the same for each at the time of purchase? What could cause changes in their food value after purchase?

Bulletin board IDEA
Title: *To Market, To Market*
Directions: Use a picture of a shopping cart with these captions:
  Make a spending plan
  Make a market list
  Compare prices and quality
  Read labels

377

Compare the same amount of a specified food in fresh, frozen, canned, and dried forms. Compare and contrast their cost, flavor, color, texture, appearance, and the time and energy involved in preparing them for eating.

List private brands of food items sold in different grocery stores in your area. Associate the private brand name with the food chain that sells it. List brand names which are sold in many different chain stores in a wide geographic area. Compare the cost and quality of private and nationally distributed brands. Which do you feel is generally a better buy? Why?

Your career
Food products tester

Duties: Develops new products, recipes, or ways of using a company's output. May do test kitchen supervision, research, experimental cooking, or promotion work. May be expected to travel widely to put on demonstration meals and programs for selected audiences. **Where employed:** Large food companies.

or in bulk form is usually a saving. One large box of cereal costs less, for example, than the same amount of cereal packaged in ten individual boxes. Foods that are sold in fancy display packages usually cost more than the same product sold in bulk form. Foods that have been highly advertised in magazines and on TV are often sold for more than similar, unadvertised foods. This possible difference in price may pay for the cost of advertising. On the other hand, advertising may increase the total sales to the point where no increase in price is necessary or perhaps the price is lowered.

Consumer information and protection

Consumer legislation has been passed to protect the buyer from misleading pricing and packaging. Many foods are also graded according to quality. Familiarize yourself with regulations and laws governing the production, grading, and marketing of each food item. If you know the laws, you will be a better food buyer. (See pages 223–226.)

All foods which cross state lines are subject to regulation by the United States Food and Drug Administration. Food packagers are required to provide labels which tell the name of the product inside, the name and address of the company producing it, and the net contents of the container, by weight or liquid measure.

Some labels also tell you the variety, style, and type of pack. For instance, a label might tell you that you are buying Blue Lake variety of green beans, cream style corn, or pear halves. Another label might tell you that you are buying peaches packed in water or in light or heavy syrup.

If there are additives such as preservatives, fillers, or seasonings, they must also be listed. If you are buying wieners, you can expect the label to tell whether the wieners are all beef, are all meat, or contain cereal.

Labels usually contain a picture showing how the product inside looks. Thus, if you are selecting pineapple for a salad, the pictures will show you whether a can contains slices, chunks, or crushed fruit. If you are buying peaches, you might want halves for a salad or ragged pieces for a pie. A label illustration will usually help you identify the desired form of the product.

Since you cannot see inside cans or packages, brand names are very important as you decide which package or can to buy. As you practice buying and using foods, you will learn which companies produce foods of the quality you desire. You will also learn which *store* or *house brands* offer good value for money spent. A dollar or so spent now and then on trial brand products is usually money well spent.

Becoming an informed shopper requires careful observation, reading, and practice. If at all possible, try to shop with the food shopper in your family. This will allow you to practice using consumer information under guidance.

Shopping for food

The wise shopper knows the types of food necessary for good health. (See pages 360–362.) By shopping for food needs, rather than whims, his food dollars go farther. In choosing a food market, consider convenience. If you must walk several blocks with heavy bags of food, it might be wise to sacrifice a small money saving in order to shop more conveniently in a store nearer your home. The kind of cooking your family does may also influence your selection of a market place. The family that has a great deal of time to spend on cooking may buy large quantities of flour, sugar, shortening, and other staples. They may also keep a large supply of frozen meats and vegetables stored at home. On the other hand, working families who must prepare the evening meal in a few minutes may form the habit of buying freshly cooked meats as they return home from the day's work. Other quick foods may be a part of their daily menu. All of these factors can influence the family's choice of a marketing place.

PLANNING THE SHOPPING TRIP

Try to plan your food shopping trip before leaving home. Then carry out your plans while shopping. Plans can be altered, if necessary, in the food store. However, a pre-planned trip is usually a more re-

Write and present to the class a skit illustrating how advertising may influence the homemaker to shop at a particular grocery store.

Bring to class advertisements of foods used for snacks. Discuss the effect of advertising on food choices, especially snacks.

Large food processing companies produce, process, and package a broad range of products. The foods are produced to fit company standards and to comply with laws which are made and enforced by government agencies.

COURTESY SWIFT & COMPANY

Use the following information when buying and preparing canned foods. Discuss in class how this information might help you.

A rusty can is safe to use unless the rust has caused a leak in the can.

If the ends of the can are bulged and swollen, the food should not be eaten.

The content of a dented can is safe unless the can is leaking.

Canned vegetables are safe to eat without further cooking.

It is safe to keep food in opened cans in the refrigerator.

Save and use the liquid in which fruits and vegetables are canned. It contains valuable nutrients.

Make a display of U.S. grades of canned goods. What factors would affect the selection of each of the grades?

FOR CANNED OR FROZEN FRUITS
U.S. Grade A or U.S. Fancy
U.S. Grade B or U.S. Choice
U.S. Grade C or U.S. Standard
U.S. Grade D or U.S. Substandard

FOR CANNED OR FROZEN VEGETABLES
U.S. Grade A or U.S. Fancy
U.S. Grade B or U.S. Extra Standard
U.S. Grade C or U.S. Standard
U.S. Grade D or U.S. Substandard

warding one. Before leaving home, make the following decisions:
1. Decide which foods are to be served in the meals ahead, and check to see which supplies are already on hand.
2. Decide which supplies are needed, and make a market list.
3. Choose the market carefully. Consider location, service, and advertised prices. Find out when the store gets its supply of fresh produce. Try to shop when food is fresh.

SELECTING THE FOOD

Regardless of your family's eating habits, decide what you will buy before entering the store. Plans will help you to avoid picking up something because it looks good rather than because you need it. This *impulse buying* increases the cost of food, usually without improving nutrition.

Before choosing a food, determine in the following manner whether it is a wise choice:
1. Check labels on packages. Look for information about number of servings, ways to prepare the food, and ways to store it. Compare brands for cost per pound and quality.
2. Keep in mind the way the food is to be used. Select the quality and quantity that are best for the purpose you have in mind.
3. Check to determine whether in-season locally produced foods are available at a good price.
4. Consider the amount that can be used or stored easily. If you shop for a small family or if storage space is inadequate, small purchases may be more economical than large ones.
5. Consider whether fruits and vegetables are more wisely bought by weight or by number.
6. Watch for new foods on the market. Decide whether new preparations can add pleasing dishes to the family menu at a saving in cost or time.

Buying food for good nutrition

There are a number of ways in which the nutritional value of a certain food can vary. The way in which the food is grown, stored, shipped or prepared may affect its nutritional value. To be sure you are buying foods rich in nutrition, you need to know how to judge the quality of the food you choose.

The protein, carbohydrate, fat, vitamin, or mineral content can vary from one sample of food to another. For instance, one tomato can have more nutrients than another of about the same size. The kind of seed that was planted, the climate

COURTESY PROGRESSIVE GROCER

From among thousands of food items found in a local market, the consumer needs to buy foods which fill his family's nutritional needs at a price he can afford to pay.

and soil in which the plant grew, and the time of year it ripened, whether spring or fall, all affect its nutritional value.

After a plant is harvested, the way it is handled between the field and the market can also affect its food value. Some nutrients are easily destroyed by exposure to air and light. Some nutrients are destroyed by heat but preserved by cold. Sometimes cold temperatures or moisture will make foods such as bananas and citrus fruits spoil quickly. Some foods, such as potatoes and apples, can be held in cold storage for long periods of time without damage. Other foods lose nutrients if they are held in storage.

Even after food is delivered to the store, nutrients may be lost. This happens when frozen foods are allowed to thaw, when fresh fruits and vegetables get warm, and when eggs, meat, milk and other dairy products are not kept refrigerated. Knowing this, try to buy food at stores that have up-to-date storage and refrigeration equipment. Try, also, to buy from a store that has a rapid turnover of perishable goods. This will ensure, to some extent, that the food you buy has been recently delivered.

BUYING MEAT

The word *meat* to most people means beef, pork, or lamb. Each can be bought more wisely if you have a general knowledge of meat. For

List foods which add to the cost of meals but sometimes contain little nutritive value. The list might include relishes, pickles, appetizers, jellies, garnishes, and whipped toppings. Suggest times when it might be worthwhile to use such items.

Compare several grades and brands of the same canned food product for appearance, flavor, texture, and cost. Suggest uses for each of the grades.

Compare the cost, time, and energy involved in using convenience foods. Plan and prepare simple meals using only convenience foods. Suggest situations when such a practice would be a wise use of a family's time and energy.

List 6 food products for which commercial mixes are available.

List 6 commercial products which are fully cooked *or* baked and frozen.

List 6 commercial products which are sold chilled and ready-to-bake.

List 6 commercial products which are sold frozen and ready-to-bake.

List 6 commercial food products which are stored at room temperature and are ready-to-heat-and-serve.

Role-play two situations—one showing a disorganized shopper who does not have a list and one showing an organized shopper who has made a list. Discuss the two kinds of shopping from the viewpoints of nutrition and cost.

Role-play situations illustrating both courtesy and thoughtlessness in grocery shopping. Include situations typical of shoppers and merchants. Develop a consumer code of behavior.

Compare methods of planning meals. Discuss the advantages and disadvantages of planning by the meal, by the day, and by the week.

Your career
Food chemist

Duties: Conducts experiments in chemistry of foods; experiments with natural and synthetic materials or by-products to develop new foods, food preservatives, antiadulteration agents, and similar products. Tests food samples to insure compliance with government food laws, and to determine that products meet standards of quality and purity.
Where employed: Government agencies and food companies.

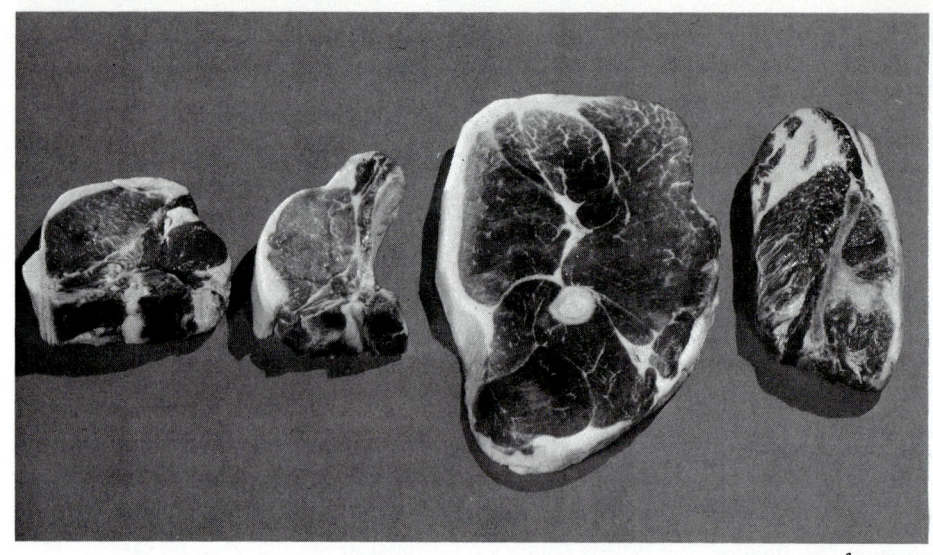

COURTESY SWIFT & COMPANY

When buying beef, veal, pork, or lamb, check it for firmness of texture, brightness of color, and distribution of fat.

example, all fresh meat is moist and of even color.

Meat which bears a round purple stamp shows that it has passed inspection by the Federal government. This stamp is required on all meat shipped across state lines. The stamp indicates that the meat was wholesome at the time it was inspected. Meat that is sold in the same state where it was processed is not required to pass the Federal inspection laws. However, it must be wholesome. If meat does not bear a government stamp, you have only the butcher's reputation and your own ability to recognize quality meats to use as buying guides. (See the photograph above.)

In addition to the Federal inspection stamp, meat also bears a grade stamp. Most meats are labeled *prime, choice, good,* or *standard.* Pork is graded simply *U.S. No. 1, No. 2, No. 3,* or *medium.* The terms *prime* and *U.S. No. 1* indicate highest quality. High grades of meat, except for that from young animals, have a thick outside layer of fat as well as an even distribution of marbling, or fat, throughout. High-quality beef is bright red, while pork is pink. The fat is nearly white, dry, and flaky. If the meat is dark and the fat is yellow and oily, the meat is probably from an old animal and therefore of poor quality. If you plan to use meat for stew or barbeque, low grades will usually serve the purpose more economically than high grades. If you plan to serve a tender oven roast or broiled steak, however, you will want to buy a higher grade of meat.

Because most *prime*, the highest-quality meat, is reserved for fine hotels and restaurants, the highest quality of meat available to the general public is labeled *U.S. choice*. Information concerning cooking methods for meats is found in Chapter 21.

Lamb comes from young sheep. Veal comes from young beef. These meats do not have the fat covering and marbling found in older beef and pork. High-quality pork has a heavy fat covering that may or may not be trimmed away by the butcher. If, however, pork is not light pink, or if it is watery and soft, the quality and flavor are usually poor.

When buying special meats, such as wieners, hamburger patties, or prebreaded meat cuts, check the label carefully. Find out how much meat and what kinds of meat are included. The reason some of these foods shrink excessively in cooking is that they contain a large amount of fat. High cereal content usually indicates a poor buy.

BUYING POULTRY

Poultry, as offered on the market, includes chickens, ducks, geese, and turkeys. In some markets you will also find Rock Cornish hens, guinea hens, and young pigeons, called squabs.

Like meat, plucked and cleaned, or *dressed*, poultry is graded by Federal and Federal-state programs. A label bearing the grade tells the quality of the poultry you are considering. (See page 221.)

In buying whole dressed poultry, look for a pliable breast bone, a good covering of fat, and a Federal or state grade label. In buying cut-up poultry, consider the color and size of the individual pieces and the price you are paying for convenience.

Generally, any poultry available in fresh form can also be found in frozen form. If you have freezer space available, frozen poultry is often an economy buy which can be kept on hand for days when long periods of time are available for cooking.

BUYING FISH

To choose fish for freshness, look for firm, elastic flesh, bright clear eyes, reddish-pink gills, and a light, pleasant odor.

A large variety of frozen fish is available on the frozen-fish market. It may be used just as fresh fish is used. Take care to keep fish frozen until shortly before cooking time. Do not refreeze frozen fish after it thaws.

When buying fresh shellfish, including shrimp, clams, crabs,

Given several sample menus, distinguish between low-cost meals and high-cost meals. Identify the factors which cause the difference.

Make a market list for your family following the guidelines below. Discuss in class the effectiveness of your marketing experience.

1 Plan the meals, check the recipes you will use, and make a list of the supplies needed. If possible, plan menus around items which are currently featured as *bargain* foods in the local grocery stores.

2 Check the supplies you have on hand.

3 List separately the foods you will buy at each store if you are going to shop at more than one.

4 Group together the foods that are alike or that will be found in the same location in a store.

5 Place such perishable items as frozen foods at the end of the list, so that you will buy them last.

6 Write the amount or size of the can or package you expect to buy. Also write any other specific information that will save time in the store.

Refrigerate perishable foods loosely wrapped or stored in containers. Buy only limited quantities since they spoil rapidly or lose food value. Use the following guidelines for judging the amount to buy.

ITEM	SAFE STORAGE TIME
Meat, Poultry, and Fish	
Meat, fresh	3 to 5 days
Meat, ground	1 to 2 days
Variety meats	1 to 2 days
Poultry, fresh	1 to 2 days
Poultry, stuffing	1 to 2 days, removed from roasted bird
Fish, fresh	24 hours
Shellfish, fresh	24 hours

(All fresh meat, fish, and poultry require loose wrapping. Store in the coldest part of the refrigerator.)

Eggs	
Fresh in shell	2 to 4 weeks
Fresh yolks	2 to 4 days
Fresh whites	2 to 4 days
Milk	
Fresh	5 days
Evaporated, can opened	3 to 5 days

oysters, lobsters, and scallops, choose those which have clean shells, good color, and a fresh, light odor. In some parts of the country, shellfish are sold alive in the shell; in other sections, they have the shells removed and are packed in containers for sale by liquid measure or by weight. Shellfish are sometimes cooked before marketing.

Heat-and-serve frozen fish dishes are also on the market. Since fish cooks quickly, the choice of these foods saves preparation time rather than cooking time.

Fish spoils easily. Keep all fresh or frozen fish ice cold until cooking time. Buy only fresh fish which is well refrigerated or frozen fish which is solidly frozen. Avoid refreezing any kind of fish.

BUYING EGGS

The Federal government sets the standards for grading eggs. Grade AA eggs are the highest quality available on the market. Grade A eggs are also considered to be of high quality. Both grades have a large amount of thick white that will stand up well around a firm, high yolk. Eggs with a thin, watery white and a flat yolk are not fresh. They are graded either B or C. Their flavor may be stronger and less pleasant than that of high-grade eggs. (See pictures on page 385.)

Eggs are also graded by size and weight per dozen, from *extra large*,

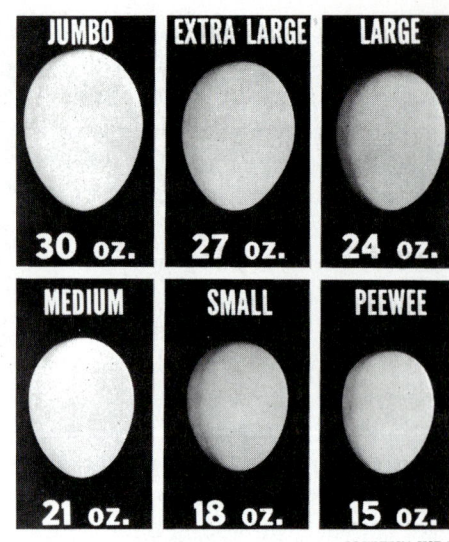

Federal regulations provide that eggs be graded according to size as well as by quality.

at least 27 ounces or over per dozen, to *small*, at least 18 ounces per dozen. The label on the egg carton tells you the grade, or quality, of the contents. When buying eggs, look for the letters *U.S.*, the grade letter and the size, all of which are given on graded eggs.

Shell color has no bearing on egg quality or flavor. There may be a regional preference for either white- or brown-shelled eggs which affects the cost and availability of eggs in that region. Flavor and freshness, rather than shell color, determine quality. Buy refrigerated eggs, since eggs retain their freshness best when kept in well-refrigerated storage areas.

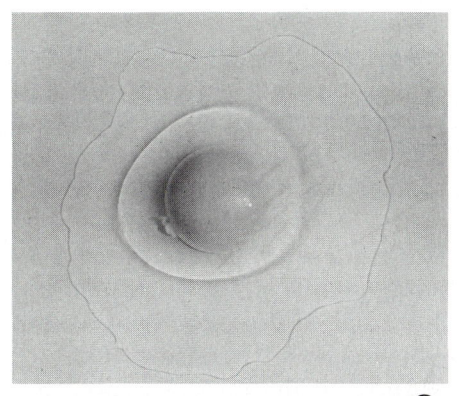

Grade AA

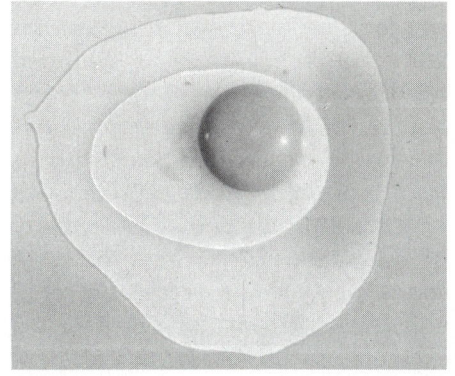

Grade A

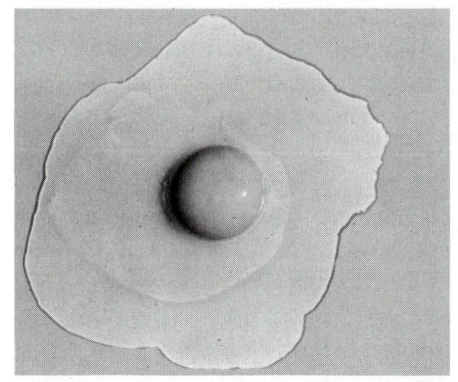

Grade B

COURTESY USDA

The quality of an egg may be determined by the amount the white spreads when the egg is cracked and by the profile of the yellow held suspended within the egg white.

ITEM	SAFE STORAGE TIME
Cheeses	
Cottage cheese	3 to 5 days
Other types of soft cheese	1 to 2 weeks
Hard cheeses	3 to 6 months
Cooked Milk Foods	
Custards and cream-filled cakes and pies	1 to 2 days on coldest refrigerator shelf

Store staple foods in a manner to retain their quality and nutrition.

Bread: Store in a breadbox that has a few holes for the circulation of air. Keep bread in its original wrapper, which is usually resistant to moisture. During hot weather, store bread in the refrigerator to retard the growth of mold.

Canned foods, unopened: Keep in a cool, dark place. If the storage conditions are good, canned foods may be kept indefinitely.

Potatoes: Keep in a cool, dark place where there is some circulation of air around them.

Sugar, flour, coffee, tea, and other dry staples: Place in airtight containers.

Take over the task of doing the family grocery shopping for one week. With your family, plan what to buy. Note the length of time it takes to do the shopping, the time of day when you go, and how many people are shopping at that time. Describe your experience in terms of what you might have done to save time and money. List suggestions to make shopping easy.

Experiment to determine the effects of different storage techniques on foods. For example, when fresh eggs are frozen, the yolk becomes gummy. After a period of time some spices become more potent and some less flavorful.

Observe mold as it develops and grows. Moisten a slice of bread, place it in a closed container, and leave it in a warm place for two or three days. How does this experiment show you the value of the bread storage guidelines given on page 385?

Consult your local market or the food section of the newspaper to compare the costs of protein-rich foods such as chicken, cheese, hamburger, steak, and fish. Compute the cost of one serving of each food. Which are the best buys?

BUYING MILK AND MILK PRODUCTS

Milk and milk products, such as ice cream, cheese, cottage cheese, and yogurt, are sold and used widely. Milk can be bought in many forms. They include homogenized milk, chocolate milk, skim milk, half-and-half, buttermilk, evaporated milk, and dried milk. The form of milk to choose depends partly on whether you plan to drink the milk or cook with it. (See pages 420–422.)

Milk spoils easily. Spoilage is caused by the growth of bacteria. Useful bacteria cause milk to sour, making the production of all kinds of cheese possible. However, harmful bacteria also are frequently carried by milk. Such diseases as tuberculosis and undulant fever can be contracted by drinking milk which is contaminated with these disease-bearing bacteria. For this reason, the quality of any milk supply must be carefully controlled. State, municipal, and county regulations and ordinances cover the production and handling of milk and milk products. Federal, state, and city inspections of cows, dairies, and dairy foods help to ensure a safe milk supply and to protect the consumer.

Most communities require that milk be pasteurized. Pasteurization protects consumers from the diseases that may be carried by raw milk. In pasteurization, milk is heated to 143 degrees Fahrenheit for 30 minutes, or to 161 degrees Fahrenheit for 15 seconds, and then cooled rapidly. This process kills harmful bacteria.

Grade standards for raw and pasteurized milk have been established by the United States Public Health Service, based on the bacterial counts. Grade A pasteurized milk has a low bacterial count, which makes it safe to drink.

Today many nondairy foods are used as substitutes for real milk products. You are probably familiar with nondairy forms of whipped toppings, coffee cream, sour cream, and milk. Many of these products are less expensive and keep better than real dairy products. They are vegetable products that have many of the same nutrients as the milk foods. They make acceptable milk substitutes in many cases. Read their labels in order to compare their food value with that of milk.

Buying frozen milk products

Many frozen milk products are available. They include ice cream, ice milk, sherbet, ice-cream cakes, frozen cream pies, and individual desserts. Products labeled ice cream must contain a given amount of fat. Other frozen desserts, such as ice milk and sherbet, contain lower amounts of fat. Frozen milk desserts are generally eaten for enjoyment rather than nutrition. Therefore, a certain amount of trial and error is necessary in order to

COURTESY NATIONAL DAIRY COUNCIL

1 Swiss	7 Blue	15 Queso Blanco	22 Cream Cheese
2 Cheddar	8 Baby Gouda	16 Camembert	23 Monterey Jack
3 Edam	9 Sliced Natural Brick	17 Breakfast	24 Cream Cheese
4 Processed American	10 Sliced Natural Cheddar	18 Schloss	25 Mozzarella
5 Processed Pimiento	11 Ricotta	19 Brie	26 Mozzarella Twist
	12 Cottage Cheese	20 Pimiento Cream Cheese	27 Salame Provolone
6 Gouda	13 Teleme	21 Cream Cheese	28 Boccini Balls
	14 Monterey Jack		

Learn to recognize cheese according to its type and to buy according to the recipe in which it is to be used.

get the best product for the amount of money you wish to spend.

Since the quality of a frozen milk product is harmed by melting, ask the grocery packer to place such items in insulated bags. Place frozen items in a freezer as soon as possible after buying them.

Buying cheese

Cheese is a milk food that is sold under several hundred different names. Although typed differently by different experts, all cheese may be grouped into five large classifications. They include *very hard* (Parmesan), *hard* (Swiss and ched-

Select convenience foods from an imaginary emergency shelf and plan menus using them in the following situations:

1 Dad calls to say that he is bringing his boss home for dinner. They will be there in thirty minutes.

2 A planned trip to the grocery store must be postponed until tomorrow. Your aunt from out-of-town will be passing through your area on her way home from a vacation trip. She is planning to stop at your house for lunch, but she can only stay a short time.

3 A friend asks if she may stay at your house tonight because her electricity has gone off. She will have to go to work very early in the morning and is accustomed to having a heavy breakfast before leaving.

4 Dad calls to tell you that Mother is coming home from the hospital earlier than had been expected. You had intended to have a *welcome home* dinner ready tomorrow but decide to carry through with your plans, even though it will have to be a day sooner and on short notice.

387

Discuss the factors which influence the choices a consumer makes while shopping in a grocery store. Discuss the techniques used by store personnel which may influence a consumer to buy.

Analyze the location and placement of staple foods, novelty items, and nonfood products in a grocery store in your area. What advantages are there in locating items where they have been placed? Where are the items that are most likely to be on your shopping list? Why are they there?

Obtain a copy of the foods needed for a week by a family. Get this from your mother, if possible. If not, your teacher might provide a list. Arrange items into similar categories for ease in shopping. Groups might include canned vegetables, meats, frozen foods, and fresh produce.

List special offers which are used by stores in your area to attract a consumer to shop at that particular store.

Present a skit in which two homemakers are shopping for food. One has a freezer and one does not. Show how this factor affects the quantity of food purchased, how often they shop, and their ability to take advantage of sale items.

dar), *semisoft* (blue and brick), *soft* (cottage and cream), and *processed* (a blend of cheeses which is pasteurized, mild, and soft). (See page 387.)

A great deal of the cheese produced today is marketed in foil, wax cartons, plastic wrapping, or glass jars. In buying cheese in any container, read the label to check the weight and description. Buy cheese according to texture or flavor or for the recipe in which it is to be used. Most cheese is a good buy because of its protein content.

BUYING FRUITS AND VEGETABLES

High-quality fresh produce is firm and heavy for its size but must be developed to a stage where ripening is assured. Fruits and vegetables that were picked too soon have a tendency to shrivel and fade before becoming edible. The color of high-quality fruits and vegetables is bright, and the skins are unmarred. Some fruits, such as bananas, peaches, pears, and other tree fruits, will continue to ripen after they are picked. Other fruits, such as melons, have better flavor if they are vine-ripened. Choose leafy vegetables which are crisp and are free from signs of insects and wilt.

Canned and frozen fruits and vegetables can be produced under a U.S. government grading system. If a producer prefers, he can market these products under his own grading system. Government grades in canned goods include grades A (fancy), B (extra standard), and C (standard). Frozen goods are simply labeled A or B.

The American public has never considered the grading of fruits and vegetables to be as important as the grading of milk, meat, and eggs. The reason for this thinking probably relates to the fact that few serious diseases are carried by processed fruits and vegetables. Too, many varieties and qualities are marketed under *brand* names. When you become acquainted with a certain brand and quality of tomatoes, for instance, your experience can tell you more than can government grading about the effectiveness of this food in the recipes you use.

BUYING CEREAL AND GRAIN PRODUCTS

Breads and cereals are foods that most families buy frequently. They are offered for sale in a wide range of varieties for many uses. Among the most popular cereal foods are all kinds of breakfast cereals, breads, biscuits, rolls, crackers, flours, grits, corn meal, and macaroni products.

Some people, concerned about the high starch, or carbohydrate content of cereal foods, avoid buying them. In doing so, they overlook the fact that cereals are one of the richest sources of the B vitamins. Cereals also contain protein and iron.

Select only breads, breakfast cereals, and mixes that are well packaged or wrapped. Good packaging offers protection against germs and moisture. Because the labels on most cereal products give information which you should use in making a selection, take time to read them.

Most American families keep ordinary bakery bread on hand at all times. Heat-and-serve rolls and breads and ready-to-cook biscuits and rolls are additional time-savers in busy homes. Various kinds of mixes are also available. The consumer will need to study nutritive value, number of portions, taste appeal, and time involved to decide which ready-to-serve or partially prepared products are good buys.

Breakfast cereals are sold in three forms:
1 Cereals which must be cooked before eating. You are probably familiar with oatmeal, which makes a hearty breakfast dish.
2 Cereals of the *instant* variety, which can be prepared merely by adding hot water or hot milk.
3 Cereals which have been precooked and are ready to eat just as they come from the package. Such cereals are more expensive than the uncooked cereals. In general, they supply less nutrition per dollar spent.

New cereal products appear on the market regularly. It is possible to buy noodles, macaroni, and rice packaged with tasty seasonings and sauces. By following the directions on the package, the beginning cook can add variety to cereal dishes.

BUYING FATS AND OILS

Fats and oils include butter, margarine, shortenings, and oils. Butter is made from cream and is valuable as a source of vitamin A. Margarine is manufactured from vegetable or animal fats other than butterfat. During the manufacturing process, margarine is *fortified* by the addition of vitamin A so that it is equal to butter in vitamin content. Margarine has the advantage of economy, while being as nutritious as butter and having the same number of calories. Buy only refrigerated packages of butter or margarine. Both, but especially butter, are likely to melt and to develop strong, unpleasant odors and flavors if stored at room temperature.

Many families keep both solid shortening and liquid vegetable oil on hand. Each can be used when called for in various recipes. The type of fat used may affect the quality of a given product. While similar in price and calorie content, food research indicates that vegetable oils produce fewer harmful health effects than either solidified vegetable fat or animal fats, such as hog lard.

List services which some grocery stores provide such as charge accounts, telephone order services, and delivery services. Suggest situations when it would be wise for a family to pay more for groceries because these services are available.

Define *impulse buying*. Make a list of factors which influence impulse buying such as:
1 Shopping when you are hungry
2 Smelling foods such as barbecue chickens which are being cooked in the store
3 Having young children with you

Bulletin board IDEA
Title: *Know the Facts*
Directions: Make a cartoon drawing of a talking can.

Below the cartoon list several facts which by law must be printed on can labels.

19 CHAPTER POSTTEST

Number from 1 to 27. Beside each number indicate if the corresponding statement is true or false. *Do not* write in this book.

1. Good nutrition depends entirely upon the amount of money spent for food.
2. Families with higher incomes spend a greater proportion of their money for food than do families with lower incomes.
3. Food prices remain stable from week to week.
4. The Food and Drug Administration requires that food labels contain a picture of the product.
5. The amount of money spent by a family for food may reflect the time available for preparation.
6. Unplanned purchases are often the result of impulse buying.
7. The amount of storage space available in a home influences the size of purchases.
8. All foods of the same size and variety have identical nutritional value when purchased.
9. Quick freezing is an effective method for preserving all foods.
10. The way in which a food will be prepared and served influences the quantity and quality which will be purchased.
11. A round, purple government inspection stamp on meat insures that it is wholesome at the time of purchase.
12. The four grades of beef are prime, choice, good, and standard.
13. High-quality beef is indicated by a dull red color and yellow fat.
14. High-quality pork is pink in color.
15. Veal comes from young sheep.
16. Cornish hen and duck are classified as poultry.
17. Fresh fish should be kept on ice or refrigerated until cooking time.
18. Oysters and shrimp are classified as shellfish.
19. Grade AA eggs are the largest size available on the market.
20. The nutritional value of eggs is determined by the color of the egg shell.
21. In a fresh, high-quality egg, the yolk is high and rounded and the white is thin and watery.
22. Six small eggs may be substituted for four large eggs in a recipe.
23. Grade standards for liquid milk are based on bacterial counts.
24. Cheese is a milk product.
25. The government grades for canned foods are fancy, standard, and substandard.
26. When purchasing lettuce by the head, it is advisable to select heads that are firm, heavy, crisp, and bright in color.
27. Enriched flours must contain established amounts of thiamine, riboflavin, and iron.

20 CHAPTER PRETEST

Number from 1 to 5 on a piece of paper. Beside each number write the letter which corresponds to the *best* answer for that question. *Do not* write in this book.

1. Which of the following is the most efficient kitchen arrangement?
   a L-shaped   b One-wall
   c Two-wall   d U-shaped
2. Which of the following appliances cooks by microwaves?
   a Browning oven
   b Ceramic range
   c Electronic range
   d Oil range
3. Which of the following equipment is used to make pie crusts?
   a Cabbage shredder
   b Egg whipper
   c Meat slicer
   d Pastry blender
4. Which of the following terms *best* describes the process of mixing ingredients by gently lifting the bottom of a mixture to the top?
   a Creaming
   b Folding
   c Kneading
   d Whipping
5. Which of the following terms *best* describes cooking in a small amount of water?
   a Braising
   b Dredging
   c Sautéing
   d Scalding

CHAPTER 20

Managing meals at home or school

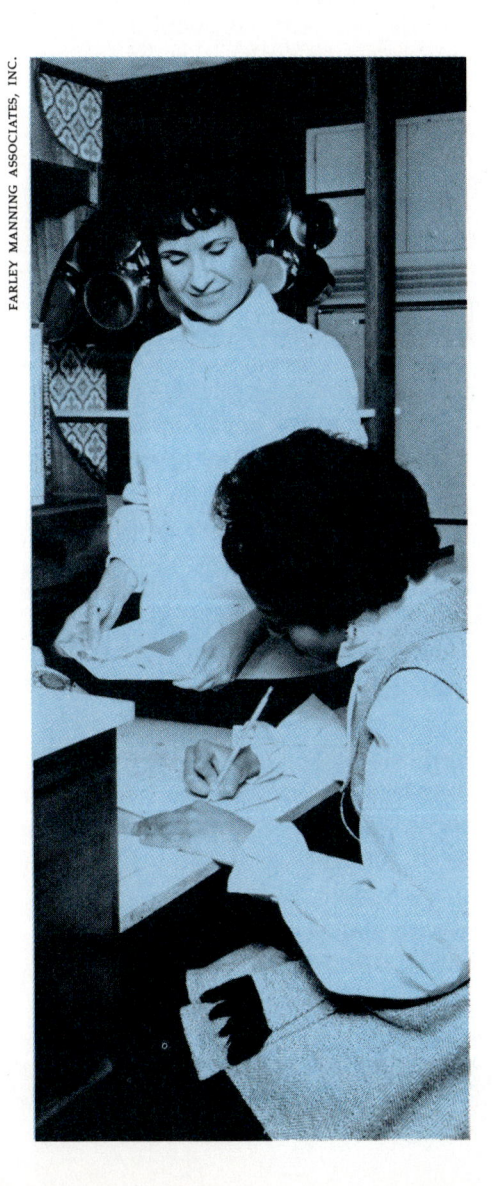

In the rush of daily living, the skill of putting a nourishing, appetizing meal on the table in minutes instead of hours is a real asset. If the homemaker has an outside job, this skill may be vital to the actual well-being of the family. Family health and happiness depend heavily on the quality of food prepared and the atmosphere which surrounds family mealtime.

There are few people who don't look forward to a well-prepared meal. Your ability to cook can give your family nourishing food they can enjoy together. When you take the time to plan meals that are nutritious, appetizing, and attractive, you show that you care about the well-being and happiness of your family.

If you help with meal preparation, you can understand the importance of time- and energy-saving methods at mealtime. If you know how to plan carefully and prepare food well, entertaining can also be easy for you and enjoyable for your guests. More important than the amount of time or money you spend on food, planning makes the difference between success and failure of a meal. When you make

Look at plans for U- and L-shaped kitchens and one- and two-wall kitchens. Locate and label the work centers in each. List the advantages and disadvantages of each type of kitchen. In which type of kitchen would you prefer to work?

Make a list of tools and equipment that would best be located at each of the kitchen work centers. Include the cleaning, storage, and cooking areas. Be practical and economical. Are there any small articles which could be duplicated at more than one center for convenient arrangement? If so, which ones?

Divide into groups and prepare identical meals in the different shapes of kitchens provided by your home economics department. Trace the steps of the cook on a scaled sketch of each kitchen. Measure the total length of the lines drawn. In which type of kitchen did the cook walk the least? Does that necessarily make this the best type of kitchen? Why or why not?

Make a Bingo card, replacing the usual numbers with names of small kitchen equipment. Include items available in your home economics department such as the corer, cheese slicer, tongs, ricer, meat tenderizer, vegetable divider, nut cracker, grapefruit spoon, whisk beater, pepper grinder, pizza cutter, tea strainer, baster, pastry brush, cake decorator, and radish rosette cutter. Duplicate the card so that every student has an identical one to use. Hold up objects so that students can see and cross out the square naming an item they recognize. The *winner* is the student who has the most squares correctly crossed out at the end of the game. Hold each item up a second time. Discuss its purpose and practicality. Also discuss acceptable uses for it other than those for which it is intended.

Place a number of slips of paper in a pan, each slip describing a food preparation task. Draw a slip of paper from the pan. Show a preferred tool for performing that task and then show other tools that might be used if the preferred tool is not available.

COURTESY FARLEY MANNING ASSOCIATES, INC.

The homemaker who learns to prepare a wholesome meal in a reasonable amount of time can become an asset to her family whether serving family meals or entertaining.

a careful plan, you will have the right food on hand and the right equipment to use. You will also have a tested recipe to follow. Working with others in a school foods class helps you further appreciate the importance of planning.

Whether at home or at school, there are several aspects of successful meal management. They include an understanding of the use of equipment and planning and cooking skills.

Getting acquainted with the kitchen

It has been said that the kitchen is the heart of the home, and this may also be true of a home economics department. A well-arranged kitchen, either at home or at school, makes meal preparation easy and enjoyable.

Ideally the kitchen is arranged so that the sink is placed between the range and the refrigerator with a work surface on each side. Usually, however, the home economics department has only one or two refrigerators placed so they are convenient to several kitchens. In your department you may find electric, gas, and oil ranges and refrigerators. It is desirable for each pupil to have the opportunity of working with more than one kind of fuel in the kitchens at school.

TYPES OF UNIT KITCHENS

Your home economics department will probably have more than one unit kitchen. These unit kitchens may be planned in several different ways, with different arrangements of the equipment.

The U-shaped kitchen

The U-shaped kitchen is generally the most efficiently arranged one. The equipment and cabinets are grouped on three sides of the kitchen with the sink in the center of the U. This arrangement has the advantages of grouping equipment conveniently and of eliminating the need for other class members to pass through the kitchen while work is in progress.

The L-shaped kitchen

The L-shaped kitchen probably ranks second in efficiency. The equipment and cabinets are placed on two adjacent sides. This arrangement saves steps and, consequently, saves time and energy. When possible, the sink and the range are placed at right angles to one another.

The two-wall kitchen

The two-wall, or double-wall, kitchen is economical to plan. The equipment is placed along two parallel partitions, or walls, separated by a passage which may be fairly narrow. Remodeled homemaking departments may be of this type because of space limitations. Meal preparation requires more walking and, therefore, more time and energy in the two-wall kitchen than in the U-shaped and L-shaped types.

The one-wall kitchen

The one-wall kitchen is simplest of all kitchens to plan. All equipment is placed along one wall. The person using this type of kitchen must take many steps and must retrace steps in preparing and serving a meal.

The aisle kitchen

The aisle-type kitchen is an innovation in some schools. Kitchens are placed in long rows, one after the other, with a narrow aisle between the rows of kitchens. The purpose of this type of unit kitchen is to give the teacher an opportunity to observe and direct students in six or eight kitchens during a single class period. One disadvantage of this type of arrangement is that there is little or no overhead storage space

Using one inch to represent one foot, make a scale drawing of your kitchen at home. Show windows and doors in their correct locations. Plan an arrangement of the range, sink, refrigerator, and cabinets that you think would be ideal.

Make a poster, bulletin board, or flannel board, showing the work triangle in a kitchen.

An island in a kitchen frequently adds work space conveniently near the dining area.

COURTESY WEAR-EVER ALUMINUM INC.

Discuss the meaning of the following cooking terms. Consider the types of recipes in which each might be found.

Bake: To cook in the oven by dry heat.
Baste: To spoon pan drippings, water, or sauce over food while it is roasting.
Beat: To add air to a mixture or to make it smooth by using a quick over-and-over motion with a spoon or fork or by using a rotary beater, electric mixer, or whisk.
Blend: To mix two or more ingredients.
Boil: To cook in boiling water or other liquid that is bubbling and steaming.
Bone: To remove the bones from fish, poultry, or meat.
Braise: To cook in a small amount of water in a covered container.
Broil: To cook directly under or over the source of heat.
Brown: To bake, fry, or toast a food until the surface is brown.
Caramelize: To heat dry granulated sugar to the melting stage.
Chill: To place in the refrigerator until cold.
Chop: To cut into small pieces.
(Continued on next page)

for dishes. Too, students are required to take many extra steps in carrying food and dishes back and forth, as tables are located in a different part of the room.

LARGE KITCHEN EQUIPMENT

When you prepare meals or clean up afterward, you will work sometimes at the sink and sometimes at the range, the refrigerator, or the cabinets. In each of these work centers, you will need to have a space in which to work and a place for storing things temporarily. You will store food, prepare it, serve it, and clean up at the end of the meal. As you work, you will use all the large pieces of kitchen equipment.

The refrigerator

The refrigerator is designed to preserve nutrients in foods and to keep food cold. A properly operating refrigerator keeps foods at a temperature of 38 degrees to 42 degrees Fahrenheit. Many refrigerators have special sections for storing eggs, raw fruits and vegetables, meats, and butter. There are trays for freezing ice cubes and desserts. Many feature automatic icemakers which are attached to a cold-water line. These icemakers usually continue to make ice until a storage bin is filled.

Most refrigerators have a separate freezer compartment for ice and for storage of a few days' supply of frozen food. Some refrigerators have large freezer sections located either beside or below the refrigeration area. Such freezers hold large quantities of food at a temperature low enough for safety for a few weeks or months.

Some models of refrigerators require periodic defrosting, but many defrost automatically. While more convenient, frost-free models cost more to buy and to operate than do ordinary refrigerators which require manual defrosting.

The freezer

The freezer is a piece of equipment used for storing frozen foods for a long period of time. Most foods remain safe from spoilage for six months to a year if kept at a temperature below 0 degrees Fahrenheit. It is important that foods be wrapped or packaged in airtight containers before storing.

A freezer needs defrosting only about once a year or when the frost deposit gets ½- to 1-inch thick. Defrosting should be done according to the manufacturer's directions. Many people prefer to buy frost-free freezers. Although such freezers require cleaning from time to time, it is not necessary to empty them for complete defrosting as is the case with conventional freezers.

The range

The range is usually a gas or electric model. Gas ranges heat by actual exposure of the cooking pan to the gas flame. Electric ranges have surface units which are heated as the electric current passes through them. A recent development in electric ranges features a surface area of ceramic material. This cooking surface appears to be a part of the counter top. Heating units are located beneath the tile surfaces. While the flat surface has the advantage of making it easier to wipe up spills and splashes, such units require specially made flat-bottomed pans to conduct the heat to the food.

The electronic range is a rather recent development in cooking equipment. It cooks the food by microwaves. The microwaves enter the food in the range oven and cause the molecules in the food to rotate so rapidly that they generate their own heat. The food cooks while the oven remains cool. However, since the food is cooked without heating, it never browns. Special browning units are added to electronic ovens so that roasts, pies, and other foods will look appetizing. Because electronic cooking is very rapid, it may become the main cooking method of the future.

The sink

The sink is used for washing food during its preparation, for washing dishes, and for general cleaning. Some sinks have single and some have double compartments, with drainboards on one or both sides. They are generally made of iron

Ranges with ceramic-covered cooking units add extra counter space for use whenever the range top is completely cool.

coated with porcelain or stainless steel.

A garbage-disposal unit may be a part of the sink. It is electrically operated and cuts the garbage into tiny pieces that can be washed through the drain into the sewer.

The automatic dishwasher

The automatic dishwasher is a convenience that is found quite frequently in home economics departments and in many modern homes. To obtain the best results, follow the manufacturer's directions carefully. Be sure to use a special automatic-dishwashing detergent. (See page 476.)

Combine: To mix or blend two or more ingredients.
Cream: To make a mixture soft and smooth by rubbing or beating it with a spoon, fork, wooden paddle, rotary beater, or electric mixer.
Cube: To cut into small, even-sided pieces.
Cut in: To distribute shortening or table fats in dry ingredients by chopping with a pastry blender or two knives until the fat is in tiny particles.
Dice: To cut into small cubes.
Dissolve: To cause a dry substance, such as sugar or salt, to pass into solution in a liquid.
Dot: To scatter small bits of a substance, usually fat, on top of a food.
Dredge: To coat the surface with flour, meal, or other powdery substance.
Fold: To mix ingredients by using two motions, cutting straight down through the mixture and across the bottom of the mixing bowl, turning the mixture over and over.
Fry: To cook in hot fat. The words *panfry* and *sauté* mean to cook in just enough fat to cover the bottom of the pan. *Deep-fry* and *French-fry* mean to cook in enough fat to cover food being fried.

(Continued on next page)

Glaze: To coat a food with syrup or jelly and then to heat or chill it.
Grate: To separate the food into tiny pieces by rubbing it on a grater.
Knead: To press dough with the palms of the hands, turning the dough slightly as it is reshaped.
Marinate: To allow a food to stand in a liquid (usually French dressing or oil and vinegar.)
Melt: To change a solid food to a liquid by heating it.
Mix: To combine ingredients, usually by stirring.
Mold: To place a food in a dish or mold until it congeals or hardens.
Panbroil: To cook uncovered in an ungreased or lightly greased frying pan, pouring off the fat as it accumulates.
Parboil: To boil in liquid until partly cooked.
Pare: To cut off the outer covering.
Peel: To remove or strip off the outer covering.
Poach: To cook in hot liquid, usually below the boiling point, taking care to retain shape.
Preheat: To heat an oven to the desired temperature before putting in food.
Purée: To press food through a sieve or ricer so as to make it smooth.

(Continued on next page)

SMALL KITCHEN EQUIPMENT

Any worker needs good equipment to do a good job. Good cooks are no exception. In the kitchen, small equipment is as important to cooking success as are such major appliances as the range and refrigerator. You will learn to know and use the small equipment available in your school kitchen. As you learn that a certain piece of equipment works well for a given job, you may be able to buy a similar one for use at home.

Choosing small kitchen equipment

Stop to think of all the jobs involved in preparing and serving meals. You will see how many kinds of equipment you need. You will see, too, the advantages of selecting multipurpose tools. A tool that can do more than one job saves space. Resist buying special-purpose gadgets that take up space and are rarely used. Discard or give to others gadgets which are seldom used.

In selecting small kitchen equipment, ask the following questions:

1 How much use will a tool get? If the item is one that will be used often, such as a paring knife, buy the best quality you can afford. You want it to last even with frequent use.
2 Will the tool be used in more than one place in the kitchen? If the item is not too expensive, consider buying one for each place it might be used. You often need mixing spoons and paring knives in more than one place in the kitchen.
3 Is it well-made of suitable material? The quality of construction and of material affects the usefulness of any tool. Look for rustproof, unbreakable materials.
4 Did a label or any other information come with the tool when it was purchased? Study the information. Keep it for later reference in caring for the tool.
5 Is there a guarantee? If so, keep it to be sure the materials and workmanship are of the promised quality.

Caring for small equipment

With proper care, good-quality equipment will give good service. Try to arrange space so that tools are easy to find and easy to put away. Drawer dividers help organize storage space.

Kitchen work requires sharp knives or knives with serrated edges. Serrated knives require no sharpening. Sharpen other knives as often as necessary to keep them easy to use. Sharp edges can cause injuries, however. To avoid injury, set aside a special place for sharp knives. To keep them sharp, store knives with the cutting edge protected. Plastic foam can be used for knife-edge protection. You can make a storage bed by cutting a piece of plastic foam to the desired size. Make slits in it in which the knife blades can be set.

Wash knives and forks carefully so that sharp edges and points are not dulled or nicked. Avoid soaking them in dishwater. Serious cuts can be caused by hitting a knife which was forgotten and left in the dishwater. Dry all knives and forks thoroughly. Pay special attention to those made of ordinary metal, since dampness causes rust.

It is especially important that you return small equipment to its proper place. Much time and energy can be wasted looking for misplaced tools. For example, keep measuring cups and spoons in their assigned places so that they will be easy to find.

Planning interesting meals

Colorful meals are more appetizing than dull ones. Most foods start out looking bright and colorful. You can keep them that way if you follow several general rules in meal preparation. Use the principles taught later in this unit to prepare food that is nutritious, appetizing, and colorful. (See Chapters 21–25.)

In order to add further interest to your meals, use these eight principles when they apply to the food you are preparing. Also study the colored photographs on pages 370 and 371.

1 Try to choose foods that make attractive color combinations. If the food itself has little color, plan to add a garnish such as parsley or a sauce such as cranberry.
2 Avoid repetition of flavors in a meal. For example, try to avoid serving tomatoes as a soup, salad, and sauce all in the same meal or apples in the form of cider, sauce, and pie in a single meal.
3 Select flavors that blend. Favorite go-togethers are roast pork and apples, turkey and cranberries, and lamb and mint jelly. Serve mild, or bland, foods with highly seasoned or strong-flavored foods. For example, bland spaghetti goes well with a highly seasoned meat sauce.
4 Avoid repetition of shapes in the foods served in a meal. For instance, meat balls, boiled potatoes, and whole buttered beets are all ball-shaped. Meat balls, mashed potatoes, and buttered shoestring beets provide varied shapes and more interest in the same meal.
5 Contrast the texture of foods served together. A meal is more interesting if some foods are soft and others are crunchy. For example, crisp cookies are a favorite with ice cream. On a vegetable plate,

Roast: To bake (usually meat) in an oven by dry heat.
Roll: To flatten to desired thickness by using a rolling pin.
Sauté: To cook in a small amount of hot fat.
Scald: To heat liquid to a temperature just below boiling point; to heat milk until a *skin* forms; or to pour boiling water over a food.
Sear: To brown quickly with intense heat.
Season: To add salt, pepper, or other substances that make the food taste better.
Shred: To cut or slice very fine.
Sift: To put dry substances through a sieve.
Simmer: To cook in liquid below the boiling point.
Slice: To cut into thin, flat pieces.
Sprinkle: To cover the surface of the food with particles of the substance.
Steep: To let stand in hot liquid in order to extract flavor.
Stir: To mix with a circular motion, using a spoon or a fork.
Toast: To brown by direct heat.
Toss: To mix ingredients lightly without mashing or crushing them.
Unmold: To remove from a mold.
Whip: To beat vigorously so as to add air.

SMALL KITCHEN EQUIPMENT

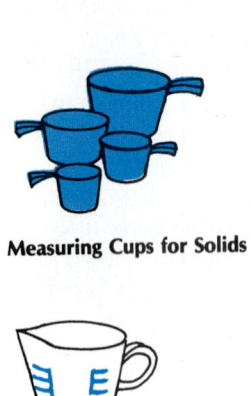

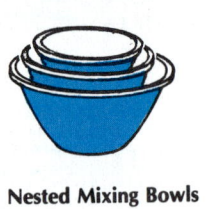

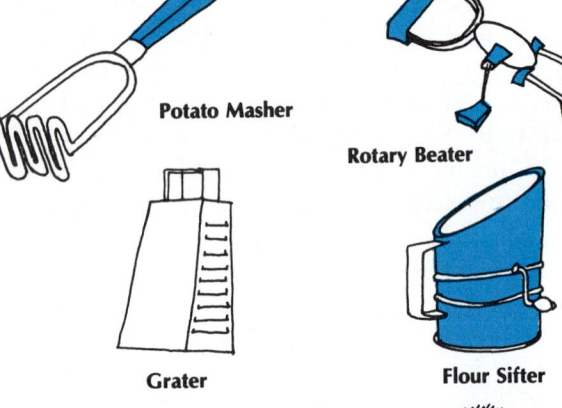

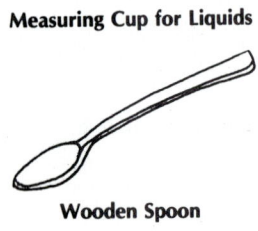

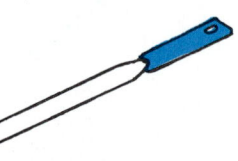

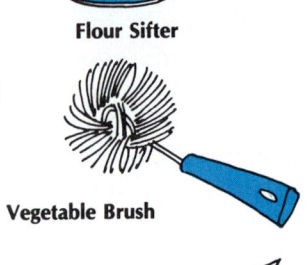

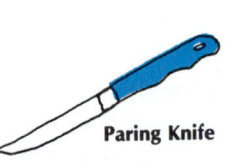

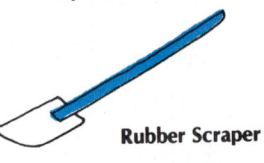

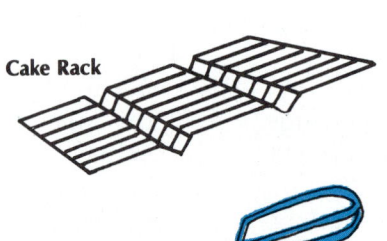

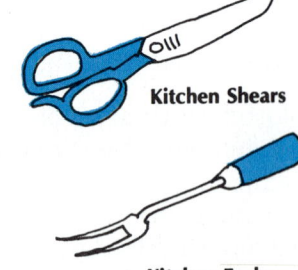

- Measuring Cups for Solids
- Measuring Spoons
- Potato Masher
- Rotary Beater
- Measuring Cup for Liquids
- Nested Mixing Bowls
- Grater
- Flour Sifter
- Wooden Spoon
- Spatula
- Rolling Pin
- Vegetable Brush
- Paring Knife
- Rubber Scraper
- Cake Rack
- Kitchen Shears
- Slotted Spoon
- Pancake Turner
- Vegetable Peeler
- Kitchen Fork
- Apple Corer
- Sieve
- Pastry Blender
- Can Opener

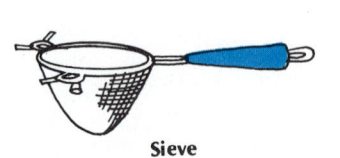

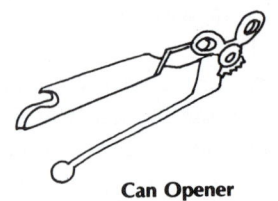

COOKING UTENSILS

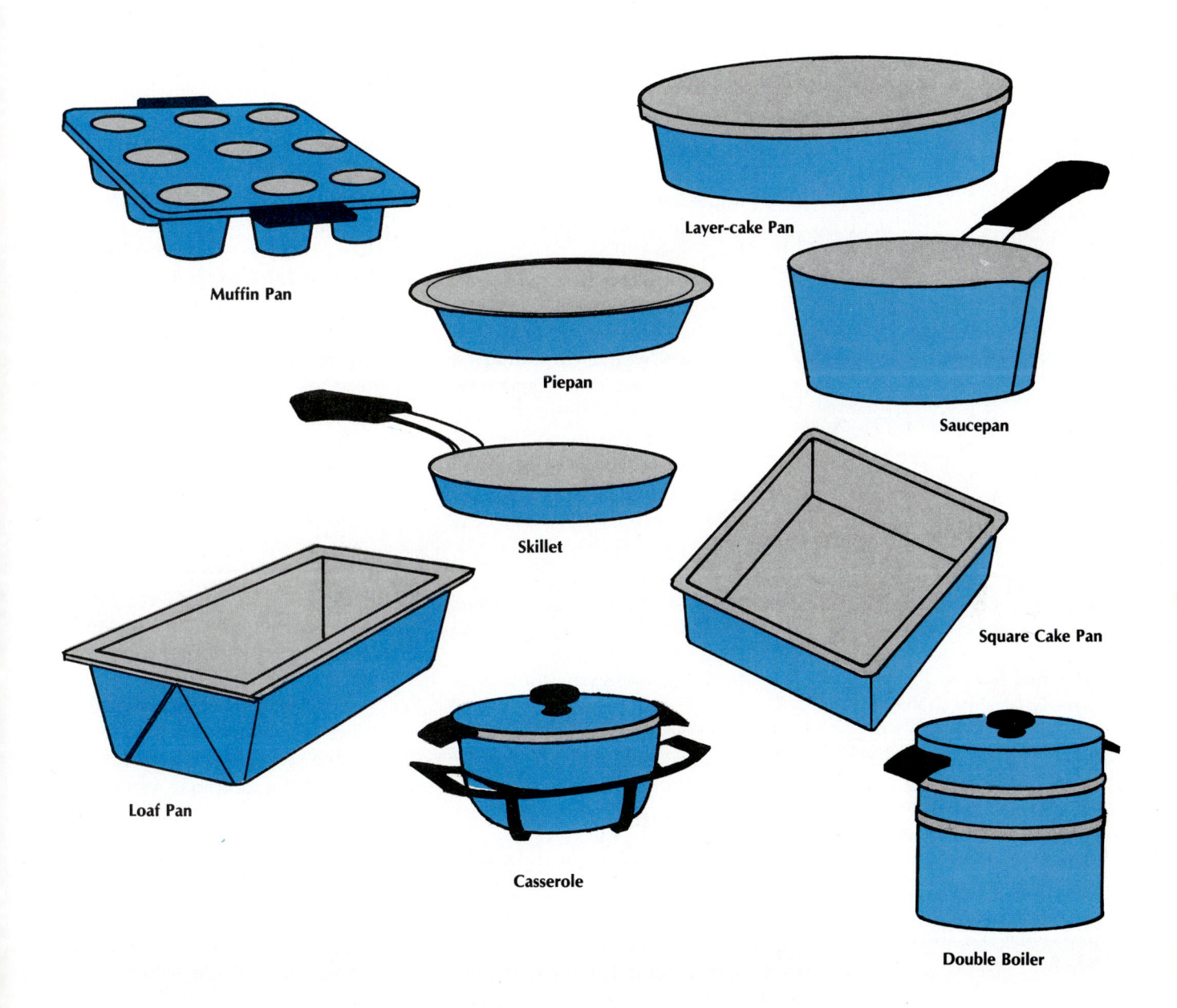

Muffin Pan

Piepan

Layer-cake Pan

Saucepan

Skillet

Square Cake Pan

Loaf Pan

Casserole

Double Boiler

Learn the common equivalent measures which are useful when dividing or doubling recipes. Practice measuring correctly the liquid, solid, and dry ingredients used in recipes.

3 t. = 1 T.
4 T. = ¼ C.
1 C. = ½ pint or 8 liquid oz.
4 C. = 1 quart
16 C. = 1 gallon
2 T. = 1 liquid oz.

2 C. = No. 303 can
3½ C. = No. 2½ can

2¼ C. firmly packed brown sugar = 1 pound
½ C. butter or margarine = 1 stick or ¼ pound
4 C. shredded cheese = 1 pound
1 oz. chocolate = 1 square chocolate
3½ C. confectioners' sugar = 1 pound
4½ C. sifted flour = 1 pound
9 coarsely crushed graham crackers = 1 C.
11 finely crushed graham crackers = 1 C.
1 lemon = 2½ to 3 T. juice
2½ C. raisins = 15 oz. package
2¼ C. uncooked rice = 1 pound
1 C. canned tomatoes = 1⅓ C. fresh tomatoes, simmered 10 minutes

a raw vegetable might be served as contrast in texture to the soft, cooked vegetables.

6 Use more than one preparation method for each meal. For instance, add a crisp, fresh salad to an oven meal made up of meat loaf, baked potatoes, scalloped tomatoes, and apple pie. Avoid serving a meal in which all the foods have been fried or all have been creamed.

7 Provide variety in the temperatures of the foods served. The hot oven meal would be improved in this respect by the addition of the cold salad and of ice cream on the pie. Except in very hot weather, an all-cold meal seems better when served with a hot beverage such as cocoa or coffee, hot bread, or hot soup.

8 In planning meals for guests, avoid foods or food combinations with strong, unusual flavors. Unless you know your guests' preferences, it is best to serve foods that are liked by most people.

Meal preparation

Whether at school or at home, learning to cook takes practice. It takes patience too. Successful cooking requires precision movements and timing. Skills come easily with a good plan, good equipment, and adequate practice. Expect some failures. You don't have to feel like a failure if the first things you try to make are not perfect. Every good cook learns from mistakes. You will too.

WORKING TOGETHER IN THE SCHOOL KITCHEN

In your school foods laboratory you will probably be working in groups of two or more. The number of workers in the group will depend on the size of your class and the way the work is organized. Successful results require cooperation in these areas:

1 The group needs a plan for the food-preparation lesson which they have worked out together. All should understand the reason for the work plan.

2 The group needs a schedule that can be followed easily and that distributes jobs fairly among the workers.

3 Each worker should accept responsibility for performing his job.

4 Each worker should understand the total plan so that he can help out in any emergency.

5 Each worker should understand what the other workers are doing in order that he can later repeat the activity at home or in the school unit kitchen.

Laboratory experiences are usually successful when students follow well-planned schedules and cooperate in their work.

SCHEDULING TIME

At school, certain tasks must be finished during a class period. Therefore, the schedule you make for work at school will not be the same as the one you would make to prepare the same meal at home. In each case, you will need to consider:

1. The time available.
2. The number of people in the work group.
3. The equipment available.
4. The time needed to prepare and cook the food to be served.
5. The time needed to eat and to clean up the dining and kitchen area.

DRESSING SUITABLY

On days you plan to work in the foods laboratory, wear clean, washable, comfortable clothes. Avoid clothes that absorb odors easily or require dry cleaning. As a safety measure, avoid fuzzy or long-sleeved garments, or any other clothing that might catch fire easily, or dangling jewelry that might catch handles of pots and pans.

A clean apron or smock is desirable, especially if you are wearing nonwashable clothing. Hair should be neatly combed before you start food preparation. Use bathroom or other grooming areas, rather than the kitchen, for this type of personal care. If you have a short, neat hair

---

Role-play the explosive effects of a situation when emotions get out of hand in a school kitchen laboratory. Replay the roles, showing better methods for handling the situation. For example, situations might include: needed equipment missing from the kitchen, two students wanting to do the same job, and one student refusing to accept a responsibility that is hers.

Prepare skits and act out scenes which illustrate the importance of group members planning and working together in the foods laboratory. These skits might represent a group of planners and a group of fumblers. Emphasize sharing privileges and responsibilities, and the ability to compromise when working with others.

Find cartoons and prepare a bulletin board display illustrating ways in which group members may show respect for the rights of others. Discuss the importance of being able to compromise.

Make a display of measuring tools and equipment. Discuss the value of the equipment in terms of recipes you plan to use in the laboratory.

Make a list of points to consider in planning any meal. Make a list of points to consider in planning a menu for a family lunch, the last dinner before the entire family leaves home for an extended vacation, and a luncheon for a six-year-old's birthday party.

Practice writing menus according to the accepted form. Include the points below when writing menus.
1 Write the menu so that dishes appear in the order in which they are served.
2 Begin names of dishes with capital letters, but do not capitalize prepositions and conjunctions.
3 Put the first dish or course first. If it is served alone, write it in the center. If two dishes are served together, write them on the same line.
4 When a starchy vegetable is served with the meat, fish, or poultry, write the two dishes on the same line.
5 When gravies, sauces, stuffings, or dressings accompany meat, fish, or poultry, write them on the same line.
6 When breads are served with butter or margarine, write them on the same line.

style, you probably won't need to do anything special to your hair. Long hair should be held back with a band, ribbon, or net. Loose hairs, so distasteful when found in food, can be avoided by these simple precautionary measures.

Once washed, your hands should be kept away from your hair and face. They can carry germs from your body to the food you are preparing.

USING RECIPES

You need good recipes to prepare good meals. If you learn to read recipes and to know what the terms mean, you can learn to prepare most any food.

A good recipe lists the kinds and amounts of ingredients needed in the order they will be used. It also gives step-by-step directions for combining ingredients. As a beginner, follow recipes exactly. Use the exact amount called for in the recipe, no more and no less. Accurate measuring is essential to success.

To follow directions, you must understand the words used in a recipe. You should know the meaning of such words as *cream, stir, beat, fold,* and *roll. Bake, fry, broil,* and *boil* are cooking methods you'll soon learn to recognize. (For definitions of these terms see pages 394–397.)

Some techniques in food preparation are not explained in most recipes because they are so basic. You will do well to know them before you start to cook. For example, you should know how to sift flour, separate and beat eggs, pare vegetables, wash leafy vegetables, and make basic white sauce. (See pages 422–424.)

MEASURING ACCURATELY

If you feel that measuring ingredients is a waste of time, you may never have had a real cooking disaster caused by failure to measure. Some people can't understand why others cook without stopping to measure. The fact is that experienced cooks *do* measure. Many have learned to estimate measurements correctly by *eye* or by *feel*. They also know which preparations require exact measures. That is, they can judge by looking at or handling a mixture whether it is the right texture, or consistency. This skill takes many hours, or perhaps years, of practice. With daily practice you, too, can learn shortcut measuring techniques with certain recipes. However, you will always need to measure ingredients for such foods as cakes and candies.

A beginner is wise to measure ingredients carefully both in classes and at home to ensure successful cooking results. By changing the proportions of ingredients by as little as a *dash* or a *pinch*, the end product can be altered. So minor a change sometimes explains why a dough meant for cake turns out to taste like biscuits or why a cake

COURTESY ST. LOUIS DISTRICT DAIRY COUNCIL

Accurate measurements increase your chances for cooking successes.

frosting is so thin that it runs off the cake.

Measuring tools

In order to achieve pleasing results, you need to use standard measuring cups and spoons. Cups and teaspoons used at the dining table come in various sizes. They are not used to measure ingredients because they are not standard and so are not accurate.

Measuring cups made of metal, glass, or plastic come in sizes of 1 to 4 cups. A 1-cup size holds 16 tablespoons. It is marked into divisions of halves, thirds, and quarters. A cup used to measure liquids should have a lip for pouring and its rim should be located slightly above the 1-cup line. These features help you avoid spilling when liquids are measured or poured.

Sets of measuring cups consisting of ¼-, ⅓-, ½-, and 1-cup measures that nest, or fit, together are useful in measuring dry ingredients accurately by the fractions of a cup. Sets may be made of metal or plastic.

Measuring spoons of metal or plastic usually come in sets of four. They are sized: ¼ teaspoon, ½ teaspoon, 1 teaspoon, and 1 tablespoon. One standard tablespoon

C Suggest ways to improve the following menus so that the meals are more appetizing:

Baked Perch   Mashed Potato
Cauliflower
Canned Pear Halves

Creamed Tuna on Noodles
Stewed Tomatoes   Applesauce
Chocolate Pudding
Chocolate Milk

Oatmeal
Toast   Jelly
Coffee

Peanut Butter and Jelly Sandwich
Vanilla Pudding
Chocolate Milk Shake

Fruit Cocktail
Waffles   Bacon   Syrup
Cocoa

Stewed Beef
Harvard Beets   Diced Carrots
Fruit Cocktail
Milk

Onion Soup
Lettuce and Tomato Sandwich
Peaches   Brownies
Cola Drink

Hamburger
Spinach   Broccoli
Devil's Food Cake
Chocolate Milk

Half Grapefruit
Pancakes   Syrup
Toast

403

Plan a *measure meet.* Set up the game at a long table with the students seated around it. In front of one girl, place a large tray containing dry, liquid, and fat ingredients and the necessary utensils for measuring them. Let each student measure the ingredients, using varying amounts. When the observers see a measuring mistake made, the tray goes to the next person.

Conduct the following experiment:
1 Sift flour directly into a cup.
2 Sift flour and then gently spoon it into a cup.
3 Put flour into a cup without sifting.
4 Pack flour into a cup without sifting.

Weigh each cup of flour to find differences. From what you have learned in this experiment, establish a procedure to be followed when measuring flour.

Make a file of low-cost recipes. Cover and decorate a cardboard box or accordian file to be used as a container for recipes. This might be given as a gift or used for recipes collected in class. Definitions of cooking terms might be included in the file.

measures the equivalent of three standard teaspoons.

Measuring dry ingredients
To separate particles of flour or other finely ground foods that may have packed together in the container, sift such ingredients before measuring. To measure flour, sugar, soda, or baking powder, fill the cup or spoon to overflowing. Run a straight edge, such as the edge of a spatula, across the top to level the measure.

Measuring liquids
To measure liquids, set the measuring cup on a level surface. Have your eyes level with the line on the cup. Pour in the liquid until the desired line of measurement is reached.

To measure spoonfuls of a liquid, dip the spoon into the liquid. If you pour the liquid into the spoon, hold the spoon above a cup or bowl to catch spills.

Measuring fats
A ¼-pound stick of butter or margarine is equal to ½ cup of fat. Some wrappers on sticks of butter and margarine are marked off into 1-tablespoon divisions. Cut through the wrapper line for the amount required. To keep hands clean, drop the fat directly from its wrapper into the mixing bowl.

Measure soft fat by pressing it into a nest-type measuring cup or spoon. Level it off as you would for dry ingredients.

Another way to measure solid fats is the water-displacement method. If, for example, a recipe calls for ⅓ cup of fat, or shortening, put ⅔ cup of water in the cup. Add enough shortening to make the water rise to the 1-cup mark, and pour off the water. For accuracy, you must press the shortening down under the water. Pour off water carefully before using shortening.

OBSERVING SAFETY RULES
In your unit kitchen or home kitchen, you must work with sharp knives, hot pans and dishes, boiling water, gas or electric ranges, and equipment with moving parts. It is easy to hurt other people. If there are young children or elderly people living in your home, kitchen safety rules become especially important. (See pages 158–159 and page 405.)

SAVING TIME AND ENERGY
One of the first lessons you learn in a foods class is that every minute counts. Most class periods are short. If a schedule is to mean anything, it must be followed to the minute. To make your schedule work, keep in mind these seven time- and energy-saving work habits.
1 As the class begins, go straight to your assigned place. Keep talk and confusion to a minimum.

Many convenient kitchens provide an area where family snacks and meals can be served.

Make a list of kitchen safety practices. Add other suggestions to the following list:

1. Avoid wearing clothes that might catch fire easily or become caught on the equipment.
2. Pin up long hair before working near a range.
3. Avoid standing with your back to a lighted range.
4. Avoid using saucepans that might tip over.
5. Use a knife with a sharp edge. Make cutting motions away from your body.
6. Before lighting a gas oven, open the door to allow any collected gas to escape, especially if the pilot light has gone out.
7. To light a gas oven, stand to one side, light the match, turn on the gas, and light it.
8. Turn handles of cooking utensils inward on top of the range or other work areas.
9. Handle hot pans with dry pot holders or mitts rather than with dish towels.
10. Remove the lid from a hot cooking utensil by lifting the far side first so steam is directed away from you.
11. Drain cooked foods while holding the kettle with one dry pot holder and the cover with another holder.

2. Keep each recipe card to be used and the work schedule to be followed where you can see them as you work. A rack or clip attached to a partition or cabinet makes a convenient spot. Copy recipes from books onto cards. Store all textbooks in a safe place away from the food-preparation area.
3. Gather all the utensils and supplies you need before beginning to work. Make as few trips out of your work area as possible. Use a tray and carry several food items at one time to save steps.
4. Use utensils correctly. Use the proper utensil for the purpose. Use only the equipment you really need.
5. Be aware of the clock and your schedule as you work.
6. Do your own work, and expect others to do theirs.
7. If things go wrong, check the plan. Offer your assistance in an emergency.

20 CHAPTER POSTTEST

Match the *definitions* in List A with the *cooking terms* in List B. Use a cooking term from List B only once. *Do not write in this book.*

List A: Definitions

A To cook in a small amount of hot fat
B To cook in water held just below the boiling point
C To cut off the outer skin of a fruit or vegetable
D To boil in liquid until partially cooked
E To cook in the oven by dry heat
F To make a mixture such as sugar and shortening soft and smooth by rubbing or beating it with a spoon or electric mixer
G To brown quickly with intense heat
H To coat the surface with flour or meal
I To beat vigorously to add air
J To cut into small cubes

List B: Cooking Terms

1 Bake
2 Cream
3 Dice
4 Dredge
5 Parboil
6 Pare
7 Sauté
8 Sear
9 Simmer
10 Whip

Give the following information on a separate sheet of paper.

1 List 5 characteristics of a well-planned menu.
2 List 3 different types of measuring equipment used in food preparation.
3 Study the kitchen types in the groups below. Rank the kitchens in each group from the most to the least efficient.
  Group 1
    a One-wall
    b Two-wall
    c L-shaped
  Group 2
    a L-shaped
    b U-shaped
    c One-wall
  Group 3
    a U-shaped
    b One-wall
    c Two-wall
4 Complete the following equations:
  3 t. =
  4 T. =
  2 C. =
  4 C. =
  2 pt. =
  4 qt. =
  1 stick of margarine =
  1 oz. of chocolate =
  1 liquid oz. =
  No. 303 can =
  3½ C. confectioners' sugar =

21 CHAPTER PRETEST

Copy the following list of protein-rich foods on a separate sheet of paper. Place the letter D beside those foods which are cooked by dry-heat methods. Place the letter M by those foods which are cooked by moist-heat methods.
  Arm roast of beef
  Hamburger patties
  Calf liver
  T-bone steak
  Catfish
  Lamb
  Tripe

Fill in the blank in each sentence with the *best* word or words to complete the statement.

1 The most important consideration in egg cookery is ___(1)___.
2 Roasting, panbroiling, and rotisserizing are examples of ___(2)___ cookery.
3 The toughness or tenderness of meat depends on the strength and amount of ___(3)___.
4 The two bone shapes found in many less-tender cuts of meat are the round and the ___(4)___ bones.
5 The meat from cattle which are butchered before they are a year old is either veal or ___(5)___.
6 Meat is a good source of protein, phosphorus, the B vitamins, and ___(6)___.

CHAPTER 21

Preparing protein foods

Do you enjoy adventure stories about people who lived before historical times? Meat was very important to such people. Stories tell of cavemen who created animal pictures on their cave walls. They thought these pictures would help the hunters find enough meat to feed the tribe. There were people who lived in lake regions where they could catch fish and birds for their food. Other groups kept herds and flocks so they could provide food for their tribes. These early people probably ate eggs whenever they found nesting birds. Milk and meat were easily available for those who tended flocks.

Since animal foods are *complete proteins* (see page 364), they continue to be important foods today. Meat, poultry, fish, shellfish, and eggs furnish a large percentage of the protein eaten in the United States. Milk and milk products provide the rest of the animal protein in the typical American diet.

It takes roughly ten times as much land to produce the animal protein to feed one person as it takes to raise enough cereal to keep him alive. For this reason, animal foods are expensive. In many coun-

Explain in your own words the meaning of the following terms which are used in the U.S.D.A. grading of meat.

USDA Prime: Has liberal quantities of fat *marbled* within the lean portion and is juicy and tender.

USDA Choice: Contains less fat than does the Prime grade but is of high quality.

USDA Good: Contains little fat, but the meat is relatively tender.

USDA Standard: Has very thin covering of fat, but is tender if properly prepared. The flavor is bland and the meat lacks juiciness.

USDA Commercial: Is from older animals. The meat requires long, slow cooking with moist heat to make it tender and juicy.

USDA Utility: Is from animals somewhat advanced in age. The meat lacks tenderness and must be chopped, ground, or prepared by pot roasting, stewing, or boiling.

Prepare a hamburger mixture using ground beef and a minimum of added ingredients. Divide the mixture equally into four small baking pans. Bake them in an oven set at 325° F. Remove one pan at each of four different times, when an injected thermometer reaches:

    145° F.
    160° F.
    170° F.
    185° F.

Compare the texture and appearance of the meat. Measure the amount of liquid which cooked out of each of the loaves. What conclusions can you make from having done this experiment?

Experiment with the following:
1 Cooking the same cuts of meat by moist- and dry-heat methods
2 Salting ground beef patties before, during, and after cooking

Report on what you learned while doing these experiments.

Find several pictures of common meat cuts. Label each picture with a number rather than a name. Practice until you can name each cut by looking at its picture.

COURTESY BIRDS EYE VEGETABLE

Hopping John is an economical protein dish made by combining rice with the vegetable protein found in black-eyed peas and the animal protein found in pork.

tries where land is scarce, farmers must use the land to grow vegetable crops so the people can survive. Even in countries with enough farm land for both plants and animals, the animal proteins tend to cost more at the market than other foods.

Some people cannot buy enough animal protein for an adequate supply of protein food. There are also various religious beliefs which lead people to avoid animal foods. The *Daily Food Guide* lists plant foods which can be used as meat alternates. Dried beans, lentils, dried peas, peanuts, and many nuts belong to this list. Since any of the common vegetable protein foods, except peanuts, contains only part of the total set of building blocks, the person who eats them in place of meat must eat different ones from day to day to remain healthy. Milk, a complete protein food, can replace meat protein in the diet.

Principles of protein cookery

What do you suppose causes some hamburger patties to be tender and juicy while others are tough and dry? Why does the cheese in one sandwich seem to be like stringy rubber bands while the cheese in another sandwich is creamy smooth?

Successful protein cookery depends on low cooking temperatures. The generally accepted temperature for cooking most protein-rich food is 300 degrees Fahrenheit. Protein-rich foods lose their juices and fats in high heat. They also shrink if overcooked. This makes them dry and tough. Since the juices and fats tend to hold many of the vitamins and minerals present in protein-rich foods, high temperatures can destroy these valuable nutrients, as well as cause the foods to be less tasty.

Vegetable proteins, such as dry beans and dry peas, also require low cooking temperatures. To keep them tender and help them retain their shape, simmer rather than boil them, or bake them slowly at a moderate or low oven temperature.

SELECTING THE COOKING METHOD

The tenderness and taste appeal of protein-rich foods are affected by other factors, too. For example, additional fat may improve such protein dishes as baked beans, while in a high-fat food such as sausage, removal of fat improves the food. The presence or absence of moisture during the cooking process is also of great importance. Meat, fish, and poultry products are frequently divided into those which are cooked by *dry-heat methods* and those which are cooked by *moist-heat methods*.

Dry-heat cookery

Dry-heat cooking methods are used with the more tender cuts of meat, fish, and poultry. These methods include broiling, roasting, rotisserizing, and frying.

Broiling is cooking by direct heat over coals or under an open flame or electric unit. Panbroiling is cooking food uncovered on a griddle or in a skillet on top of the range.

Broiling is probably the most popular form of dry-heat meat cookery. It is effective because it seals in the meat juices by quickly searing the surface of the meat. Because broiling is usually done at higher temperatures than other types of meat cookery, special care must be taken to avoid overcooking, toughening, or burning the meat. Precaution can best be achieved by controlling the distance between the heat source and the meat. Thick cuts of meat are placed farther from the heat than thin cuts. In this way each cut of meat can be cooked to the desired degree of doneness without toughening the meat or burning the surface.

Roasting is cooking food uncovered by dry heat, usually in an oven. Tender beef, pork, lamb, fish, and poultry may be roasted successfully if placed on a rack in an

Protein foods of all types are more tender and moist if cooked at a low temperature.

COURTESY OPEN PIT BARBECUE SAUCE

Demonstrate a variety of methods to use when tenderizing less tender cuts of meat. Include:
1 Grinding
2 Pounding to break the connective tissue
3 Cooking in liquid
4 Using a commercial tenderizing product

Evaluate the results in terms of flavor, tenderness, cost, and time and effort spent in the preparation.

Cook the same quality and amount of ground beef by frying, broiling, and char-broiling. After cooking, compare and contrast the meat patties for flavor, appearance, and size.

Using the same amount of meat and the same method of cooking, compare and contrast four differently priced varieties of ground beef. Measure the amount of fat collected from each of the meats. What conclusions can you draw from this experiment?

Collect and test unusual recipes using ground beef. Plan and prepare meals using these recipes.

Plan two low-budget dinners for a family of four. Explain how the family can have nutritious meals while using low grades and less expensive cuts of meat. Explain how the meat could be cooked to make it tasty and appetizing.

List common cuts of meat, arranging them in four columns. List each cut of meat according to tenderness and price:
   Tender cuts
   Less tender cuts
   Expensive cuts
   Inexpensive cuts
Explain the relationship between the cut of meat and its price per pound.

Make a chart showing prices of various cuts of beef in a certain grocery store. Information on prices can be obtained from advertisements or by visiting the store. Write a summary paragraph to accompany the chart.

Make a flannel board jigsaw puzzle by using different colors for the tender and less tender cuts of meat. Two colors of construction paper backed with flannel may be used. Fit the pieces together in the shape of an animal. Discuss the reasons why cuts are either tender or less tender.

COURTESY WESTINGHOUSE ELECTRIC CORPORATION

Dry-heat cookery is suitable for tender cuts of meat, young poultry, and fish.

ordinary oven. A low cooking temperature is required.

Poultry and ribs are frequently rotisserized by turning on a spit over or before direct heat. Most meats can be panfried successfully if cooked slowly and at low temperatures.

Moist-heat cookery

Moist-heat methods are used to cook the less tender cuts of meat and poultry. Fish and eggs, although tender, may also be cooked by moist-heat methods. These methods include braising, barbecuing, pot-roasting, poaching, and stewing. In moist-heat cookery the meat is simmered in liquids until the tough connective tissues are broken down and the meat is tenderized.

The amount and type of liquid used in moist-heat cookery vary in different recipes. In general, moist-heat cookery uses no more liquid than is necessary to tenderize the meat and prevent it from burning during the long cooking period. Sometimes the liquid used is somewhat acid, as in barbecue sauces. This acid helps to tenderize the meat. Vegetables, noodles, dumplings, or biscuits added near the end of the cooking time may add nutrients and absorb the extra liquid.

EXTENDERS

Foods which are regularly used in certain meat dishes are called meat extenders. They include sauces, noodles, spaghetti, rice, bread, bread crumbs, and other cereals. Extenders spread the meat flavor through the entire dish, causing the meat to be extended, or to go further. Meat extenders also serve in other ways. For example, bread crumbs mixed with ground meat to form a meat loaf help the meat to hold its shape during the cooking process. The crumbs will raise the nutritional value of the dish as well. You will find that many casserole

Less-tender cuts of meat may be browned before liquid is added to help tenderize the meat during moist-heat cooking.

Role-play a freezer-food drama in six short scenes. Divide the class into three groups representing three families. Let each group enact two scenes, one before and one after a freezer is placed in the home. Let one family show the rush hour in the morning, another family the hour before dinner, and the third family the day before an important holiday.

Make a bulletin board illustrating the following:
Foods to *Grow* On (Proteins)
Foods to *Glow* On (Vitamins and Minerals)
Foods to *Go* On (Carbohydrates and Fats)

Your career
Garde-manger

Duties: Oversees the breading of meat, fish, croquettes, and seafoods. Prepares salad dressings, cocktail sauces, and other cold sauces; prepares meat, fish, and seafood salads, parboils sweetbreads, cooks shrimp, prepares and decorates cold food; makes appetizers, canapés, and sandwiches.
Where employed: Large restaurants and institutional dining rooms.

dishes, stews, and ground-meat dishes include meat extenders. Actually, any meat dish which is made by combining meat with other foods is considered to be an *extended* dish.

Meat

To most Americans, the word *meat* means beef, veal, pork, or lamb. When the cost allows, meat is generally used for the main course in most meals. In addition to its pleasing taste and texture and its high protein content, meat is also a good source of iron, phosphorus, and the B vitamins.

Meats contain muscle, connective tissue, and fat. Toughness or tenderness depends on the amount and the strength of the connective tissue. Breeding, age, exercise, and feeding of the animal all affect the toughness of connective tissue. Meat from young animals, such as veal and lamb, is more likely to be tender than meat from older ani-

Plan meals for good nutrition while saving time and energy. The following suggestions may help you to think of others.

Choose recipes that require few steps in preparation.

Choose menus that have few different foods, and serve larger portions if necessary.

Occasionally prepare double amounts of meat dishes and casseroles, so there will be enough for more than one meal.

When coating chicken or fish with flour, meal, or crumbs, put all the ingredients in a paper bag and shake it.

Serve one-dish meals occasionally.

Use raw vegetables and fruits in salads and desserts.

Use prepared mixes or frozen or canned foods if their prices are within your budget.

Use wax paper instead of an extra bowl when measuring and sifting flour or sugar.

Try to make a cooking utensil or tool serve more than one purpose. For instance, by planning, you can use a measuring cup first for such dry ingredients as flour or sugar, and then without washing it, use it to measure milk or other liquids.

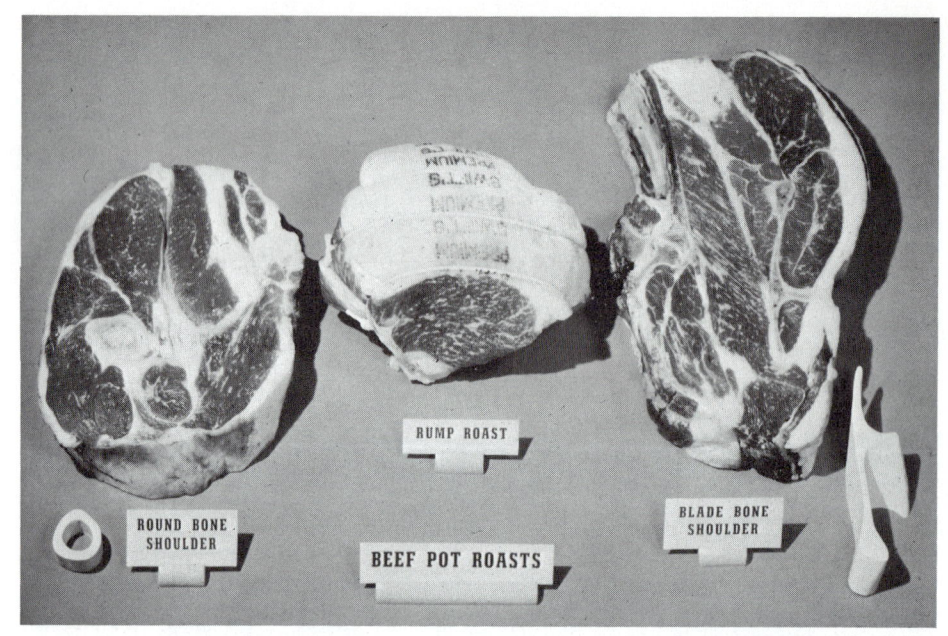

The tenderness of a cut of meat can be determined by the shape of its bone. Round and blade-shaped bones are found in less tender meat cuts while wedge- and T-shaped bones are found in tender cuts.

mals. The aging (handling and storage) of the meat in the packing plant sometimes breaks down connective tissues and thus helps to tenderize the meat.

MEAT CUTS

The part of the animal from which the meat is cut affects both the flavor and the texture of the meat. The *retail cuts*, or individual pieces of meat, sold by the butcher have been given special names. These names can help you tell the tenderness of meat cuts you are considering.

Meat can be divided into *tender* and *less-tender* cuts. The less-tender cuts are made up mostly of muscle tissue held together by strong connective tissue. This meat can be tenderized before cooking by grinding, pounding, or adding chemicals that break down connective tissues. Less-tender cuts can also be tenderized by cooking with moisture or acid foods, such as tomatoes.

Both tender and less-tender cuts of meat can be equally nutritious. If you choose a suitable cooking method, both types can be equally tasty. If you are able to determine whether a meat is a tender or less-tender cut, you can choose a proper cooking method.

One way to determine the tenderness of a meat cut is to look at the shape of its bone. Most animals have the same bone structure. Though cows, pigs, and sheep are of different sizes, their bones are much the same shape. Four general bone shapes are found in most meat cuts. One is *T*-shaped, one is *wedge*-shaped, one is *round*, and one is a rather thin *blade*. A fifth bone, the *rib*, is sometimes included.

The T-bone comes from the backbone and is found in the most tender cuts. The wedge is a part of the hip bone of an animal. It, too, is found in tender meat cuts. The round bone, which comes from the leg, and the blade bone, which comes from the shoulder, are both found in less-tender cuts. If the bone was removed before the meat was put on display, the name of the cut should be on the package, or the butcher will be able to tell you what shape of bone was removed.

Very bony cuts of meat, such as the neck, are less-tender cuts. Since these pieces are generally used for flavoring more than for their meat value, the tenderness of the cut is less important than in large pieces.

BEEF AND VEAL

Beef, the meat of cattle over one year old, is a favorite meat throughout North and South America. *Veal* comes from cattle butchered before they are three months old. *Baby beef* is meat from animals three months to one year old.

Although veal and baby beef are tender meats, they have a large amount of connective tissues in proportion to the amount of muscle tissue. Both veal and baby beef require cooking by moist-heat methods in order to break down these tissues. Veal has a pale color and a mild flavor. Herbs and spices can be used to add flavor to bland veal dishes. Baby beef is a deeper pink, contains more fat, and generally has more flavor than similar cuts of veal.

PORK

Pork comes from mature hogs. For this reason you might think the meat would be tough. However, hogs are usually fat animals raised in small pens. They do not move about to find food. This fact explains why most domestic pork is tender and can be cooked by dry heat.

Pork is always served well done. The reason is that hogs carry a parasite called *trichina* which is harmful to man. Authorities recommend cooking pork to an internal temperature of 170 degrees Fahrenheit so that it is safe to eat. While trichina is seldom found in pork sold in markets, most people feel that

Demonstrate cleaning fish and preparing it for cooking.

Follow these guidelines:
1 Place the fish on a large piece of paper which can be disposed of afterward.
2 Use a sharp knife to rub off the scales from the tail toward the head.
3 Skin the fish, if desired, by cutting through the skin of the back and abdomen, loosening it at the tail, and pulling it off.
4 Cut off the head.
5 Open the abdomen and remove the entrails.
6 Bone the fish, if desired, by slitting the flesh down the back, separating the flesh from the side bones, and pulling out the spine and other bones.
7 Wash the fish.
8 Wash the fish knife.
9 Wash your hands in cold salt water to remove the fish odor.
10 Store the fish at a very cold temperature for a minimum of time.

NOTE: Usually fish may be purchased at a lower price per pound if bought fresh but not dressed.

C Classify popular saltwater fish into two categories: finfish and shellfish. Add to the following list.

FINFISH	SHELLFISH
Bass	Clams
Flounder	Crabs
Halibut	Lobsters
Red Snapper	Mussels
Salmon	Oysters
Swordfish	Scallops
Tuna	Shrimps

Distinguish between freshwater fish and saltwater fish.

Name edible fish which can be caught in your area. Plan a menu in which one of these fish is served as the main dish.

Explain in your own words the following ways that fish are marketed.
Whole (as caught)
Drawn (with entrails removed)
Dressed (with scales, entrails, head, tail, and fins removed)
Steaks (cross-section slices)
Fillets (sides of the fish)

Suggest different methods of cooking and serving various types of fish.

Prepare some locally caught fish in a way other than frying.

good health is worth the extra time it takes to cook all pork thoroughly.

Cured pork products such as ham and bacon are very popular. Originally pork was cured as a means of preserving the meat. While modern meat processing techniques have made curing unimportant, the flavor of cured pork continues to appeal to most people. The curing process generally does not destroy the trichina parasite. Unless you are perfectly sure the meat is *fully cooked*, it is as important to cook cured pork as to cook fresh pork.

LAMB

Most of the meat from sheep used in the United States comes from young lambs. Because the meat is butchered at an early age, most lamb is tender and can be cooked by dry heat. The meat from older sheep, called mutton, is nutritious and strongly flavored. It is not popular in the United States, where the milder flavor of lamb is preferred.

VARIETY MEATS

In addition to the muscles, many of the internal organs of animals are also served as food. These products are called *variety meats*. They provide protein and are excellent sources of iron, phosphorus, vitamin A, thiamine, riboflavin, and niacin.

Variety meats include *liver, heart, kidney, brains,* and *tongue. Sweetbreads,* a gland from young animals, *tripe,* the stomach wall from beef, and *chitterlings,* the intestine from young pigs, are also included in the variety meats. When properly prepared, variety meats can provide tasty protein dishes, which are often low in cost.

Liver, kidney, brains, and sweetbreads are so tender they need little cooking. These cuts can be broiled, fried, or roasted. Tongue, heart, and tripe have a texture somewhat like the less-tender meat cuts. They require long cooking with moist heat.

Fish

Fish and shellfish are good sources of protein. Once people who lived near rivers, lakes, and oceans could depend on having fish or shellfish to provide the protein in their diets. Today water pollution has cut down the fish supply. Some types of fish cannot live in polluted waters. Other fish can survive in polluted water, but they are not safe to eat. Fish which is commercially transported across state lines is carefully checked for safety. Precaution must be taken in eating fish, clams, oysters, etc., which come from polluted waters. Consider the cleanliness of the water before eating fish you have caught from it.

Supplies of fresh fish can be carried safely over long distances in refrigerated trucks and freight cars. Canned and frozen fish can also be shipped to all sections of the country.

Because fish contains complete protein, it is as good a source of protein as any meat. Furthermore, fish is the richest known source of natural iodine, a mineral necessary for health. (See page 372.) It is also a source of the bone-building minerals, calcium and phosphorus.

Fish oil is chemically different from animal fat. It does not seem to damage human blood vessels. Fish such as salmon, mackerel, and tuna contain some fat. The unusual combination of protein and minerals along with vitamin-rich oils makes these foods worthy of consideration in meal planning. Many people try to include fish in the diet at least once a week.

Fish is a tender form of protein. It requires a short cooking period at a low temperature. It is ready to eat when a fork can easily pierce it and separate the flakes of flesh from the bone.

The amount of fat in a fish is an indication of the preferred cooking method. Moist-heat cooking methods keep lean fish from getting dry while it cooks. Lean fish such as cod, trout, bass, flounder, perch, and the shellfish are frequently cooked by steaming or poaching. To poach fish, wrap it in cheesecloth and lower it into simmering water for a short time. The cheesecloth helps preserve the shape of the fish while it is cooking.

For a quality end product, cook fish for a short time at a low temperature.

Fat fish such as salmon, catfish, and red snapper are tastier when prepared with one of the dry-heat cooking methods. Such fish are usually baked, broiled, or fried. To fry them, brush small fish or small pieces of large fish with beaten egg or milk. Then roll the moistened fish in cracker crumbs, cornmeal, or bread crumbs. This coating will help to hold the fish together while it fries. The coating will also absorb some of the cooking fat. This makes fried fish richer in fat than fish cooked in other ways. It thus raises the calorie content of fried fish, making it more fattening and harder to digest than other forms of cooked fish.

Explain in your own words the meaning of the following terms which are used in the U.S. grading of poultry. Discuss uses for each of the various grades.

The grading considers *fat covering of the bird, shape, pin feathers, cuts,* and *discoloration*.

U.S. Grade A: Poultry for table use

U.S. Grade B: Poultry for table use but graded lower on the items listed

U.S. Grade C: Poultry graded still lower on the items listed

Make a list of questions concerning nutritive values and methods of cooking eggs, meat, fish, and poultry. These questions should be ones which you think most of your classmates could answer. Give your list of questions to your teacher.

Divide into sides for a question and answer game. Play the game using rules similar to those used for a spelling bee.

Plan interesting menus for an entire day, using chicken and eggs for the main protein dishes. Discuss the advantages and disadvantages of using such menus often.

C Suggest situations in which you might want to purchase and use each of the four grades and sizes of eggs.

Grades

U.S. Grades AA and A: Eggs for table use, especially for cooking in the shell, poaching, or frying. They are top quality eggs.

U.S. Grade B: Eggs for table use, baking, and other cooking.

U.S. Grade C: Eggs for baking and other cooking.

Grade B and Grade C eggs are useful for many cooking purposes where appearance and flavor are not important.

Sizes

Extra large: Must weight 27 ounces per dozen.

Large: Must weigh 24 ounces per dozen.

Medium: Must weigh 21 ounces per dozen.

Small: Must weigh 18 ounces per dozen.

Determine the purpose for using eggs in the following products:
  Meat loaf
  Custard
  Angel food cake
  Croquettes
  Mayonnaise
  Pudding

COURTESY FARLEY MANNING ASSOCIATES, INC.

Young tender poultry can be either rotisserized or fried. Added garnishes make them suitable selections for company meals.

Poultry

The term *poultry* refers to the meat from various birds. The most popular poultry are chicken, turkey, duck, and goose. The lesser-known kinds are Rock Cornish hens, guinea hens, and squabs or pigeons.

Poultry is an important food because it contains complete protein, iron, and the B vitamins. Poultry generally costs less than other meats. It can be cooked in many tasty ways.

Just as do other protein foods, poultry stays juicy and tender if cooked at low temperatures. Young birds are tender and can be fried, broiled, rotisserized, and oven-roasted. Older birds are sometimes lower in cost than young ones, but they are tough and require long cooking by a moist-heat method. When used in soup, pot pies, fricassees, or stews, older birds become tender and their flavor improves.

Eggs

Eggs of many kinds are a favorite food all over the world. They may be served in some form at any meal. Eggs are generally a low-cost, easy-to-cook form of protein. They also contain phosphorus, iron, vitamin A, riboflavin, and fat. Most eggs sold in this country are produced by domestic chickens.

Eggs can be fried, scrambled, poached, baked, or cooked in the shells. They are often combined with other ingredients to form egg dishes such as omelets, soufflés, and custards. Like other protein foods, eggs should be cooked at low temperatures.

People refer to some shell-cooked eggs as *hard-boiled* eggs. These eggs are correctly called *hard-cooked* eggs. Eggs are correctly cooked in water below the boiling point (212 degrees Fahrenheit). Those that are actually boiled get tough and the texture is rubbery. The outside of the yolk darkens and the flavor is strong and unpleasant.

When cooking eggs in the shell, place them in cold water. Bring the water to a simmer and hold it at that

Egg dishes such as soufflés can be tasty and tender if baked at a low temperature.

temperature for the time needed for the desired degree of hardness. Soft-cooked eggs require about 3 minutes of simmering time. Hard-cooked eggs take 20 minutes of cooking in simmering water. When the eggs are hard enough for your purpose, pour off the hot water and add cold water at once. Fast cooling makes eggs easier to peel and helps prevent the discoloration and toughness caused by overcooking.

USES IN COOKING

Eggs are used in many ways in cooking. They thicken mixtures such as custards. They help to bind together mixtures like meat loaves. They are often used to add flavor and nutritive value to such foods as pudding. They act as leaveners in dishes such as chiffon cake and soufflé. In such dishes, it is the beaten eggs that make the product light and fluffy. Since egg protein hardens quickly with heat, it forms a kind of structure, something like plastic foam, that holds other parts of a mixture in place.

When you mix beaten eggs and a hot mixture, as in making sauces, the hot mixture *must* be added slowly to the eggs with constant stirring. Pouring eggs into a hot mixture cooks them immediately. Hard lumps form in the process. Adding the hot mixture to the eggs while stirring assures a smooth blend free from particles of cooked egg.

Demonstrate breaking an egg properly. Follow these guidelines:
1 Tap the shell sharply across the center with a knife blade or on the edge of a bowl.
2 Press your thumbs gently into the crack and pull the shell into halves.
3 Let the egg fall into a dish or bowl.

Demonstrate separating an egg white from the yolk.
1 Break the egg.
2 As the shell divides into halves, let the egg yolk remain in one half while the white runs out into a bowl.
3 Transfer the yolk to the other shell half so that more of the white runs out.
4 Place the yolk in a second bowl.
5 If more than one egg is to be used, separate each egg into small bowls before adding it to those already separated. This practice avoids getting broken yolk in the bowl of egg whites.
6 An egg separator may be used.

Display and demonstrate how to use small equipment associated with egg cookery. If possible, include a slicer, poacher, separator, whip, electric mixer, and rotary beater.

21 CHAPTER POSTTEST

Copy the following list of cooking methods on a separate sheet of paper. Place the letter D beside those methods which are examples of dry-heat cookery. Place the letter M by those methods which are examples of moist-heat cookery.

Oven roasting
Frying
Stewing
Charcoal broiling
Braising
Poaching
Rotisserizing
Barbecuing
Pot roasting
Baking

Copy the following list of food products on a separate sheet of paper. Beside each food indicate whether eggs serve primarily as a binding, coating, leavening, or thickening agent in that product. Use the following abbreviations:

   B for binding agent
   C for coating agent
   L for leavening agent
   T for thickening agent

Baked custard
Meat loaf
Sponge cake
Salmon croquettes
Soufflé
Fried perch
Chiffon cake

Fill in the blank in each sentence with the *best* word or words to complete the statement. *Do not* write in this book.

1. The key to successful cheese cookery is ___(1)___.
2. Meat is classified into tender and ___(2)___ cuts.
3. In moist-heat cookery, meat is cooked in a small amount of liquid in order to break down the ___(3)___.
4. The tenderness or toughness of meat is affected by the part of the animal from which the cut is taken and the animal's breeding, diet, amount of exercise, and ___(4)___.
5. The four general bone shapes in most meat cuts found in retail meat markets are T, blade, wedge, and ___(5)___.
6. Heart, brains, kidney, and tongue are classified as ___(6)___ meats.
7. Meat from cattle which are butchered before they are three months old is called ___(7)___.
8. Meat can be tenderized before cooking by grinding, adding chemicals, or ___(8)___.
9. The richest known source of natural iodine is ___(9)___.
10. Hard-cooked eggs are cooked in simmering water approximately ___(10)___ minutes.
11. Fish is a source of the bone-building minerals phosphorus and ___(11)___.

22 CHAPTER PRETEST

Match the *definitions* in List A with the *forms of milk* in List B. Use a form of milk from List B only once. *Do not* write in this book.

List A: **Definitions**

A. Whole or skim milk from which the water has been removed
B. Milk which has been artificially fermented
C. Milk from which about one-half of the water has been removed
D. Milk which contains as much calcium but less Vitamin A than whole milk
E. Milk which has been heated to kill the disease-causing bacteria

List B: **Forms of milk**

1. Buttermilk
2. Dried
3. Evaporated
4. Low-fat
5. Pasteurized

Fill in the blank in each sentence with the *best* word to complete the statement.

1. The solid part of milk is called the ___(1)___.
2. The *Daily Food Guide* recommends that teen-agers have the equivalent of ___(2)___ cups of milk every day.
3. White sauce is made from milk which has been thickened with cornstarch or ___(3)___.
4. Milk desserts in which eggs are used as a thickener are ___(4)___.

418

CHAPTER 22

Preparing milk and milk-rich foods

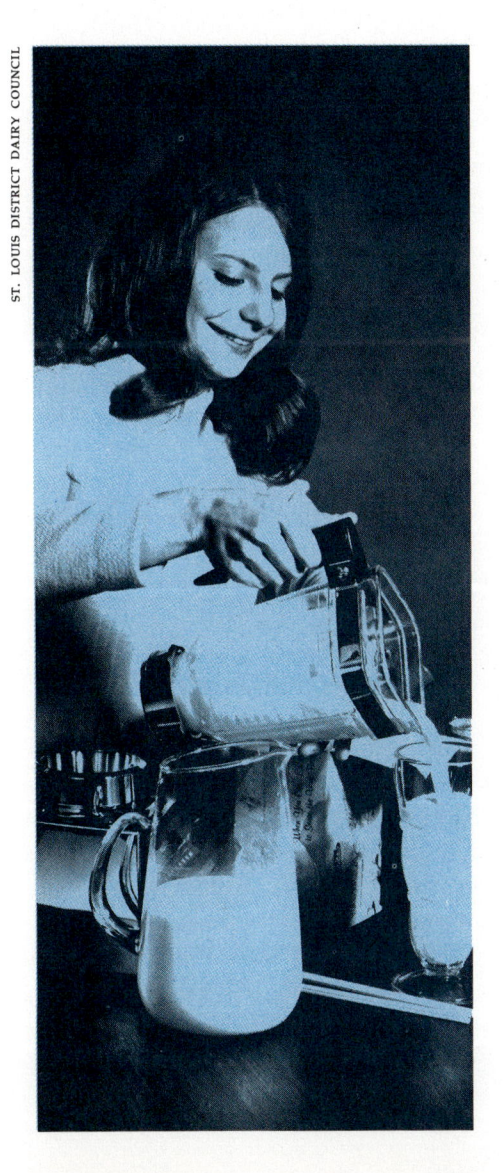

Milk has been an important food since early men first kept their flocks and herds. In many countries babies are transferred from mother's milk directly to some form of cow's milk. In other countries milk is supplied by goats, water buffalo, and reindeer, as well as by milk cows. Writers have suggested that the great sea mammals may become important suppliers of milk as people's need for milk outgrows the supply available from land mammals.

Milk is an excellent source of calcium and phosphorus. If vitamin D is added at the dairy, milk contains all three nutritive elements needed for bone-building. Milk also provides at least two of the important vitamins of the B complex, riboflavin and thiamine, and whole milk provides some vitamin A. Milk is also one of the best sources of complete protein. In fact, a quart of milk contains about half the protein a person needs for one day.

Since milk is such a good source of necessary nutrients, most families make sure that children include it in their daily diet. Teen-agers sometimes think it is not important to drink milk since their bodies

Discuss the meaning of the following statement: *Milk is nature's most nearly perfect food.* Does milk contain all the known nutrients? If not, what nutrients are missing? In what nutrients is milk especially rich? Does this vary according to the type of milk?

Tell of the problems which arise when young babies are allergic to milk. Discuss successful solutions to such problems in terms of illness, time, trouble, and expense.

Justify the following statement: *Iced tea, soft drinks, ades, and coffee may sometimes interfere with good teen-age nutrition.*

Bulletin board IDEA
Title: *YOU never outgrow your need for milk*
Directions: Below the title, mount pictures of attractive and healthy looking people at various stages of the family life cycle. Include babies, teen-agers, and older people.

Discuss the following terms which describe the various milk products. Determine which products are available in stores in your area.

Raw milk: Fresh, whole milk which has not been pasteurized.

Pasteurized milk: Milk which has been treated to kill the bacteria that cause diseases.

Homogenized milk: Whole milk in which the butterfat has been broken into tiny particles that will not rise.

Vitamin D milk: Whole milk to which vitamin D concentrate has been added.

Certified milk: High-quality whole milk which has very low bacterial count, used mostly for special diets.

Skim milk: Milk from which the butterfat and cream have been removed. Except for the fat which contains vitamin A, skim milk is just as nutritious as whole milk and is sometimes cheaper. In fact, the calcium content of skim milk is higher than that of whole milk.

Flavored milk: Milk to which chocolate or other flavors have been added. Chocolate milk is usually made from skim milk with cocoa added.

COURTESY ST. LOUIS DISTRICT DAIRY COUNCIL

Teen-agers can use milk as a snack food as well as a drink with meals, in order to fill their daily requirements for calcium and protein.

have almost reached full size. But growth is only part of the story. Bone and muscle cells continually wear out and die. They can be replaced only if your body continues to get the nutrients it needs. Since milk is one of the best sources of such nutrients, there is a great deal of truth in the expression *you never outgrow your need for milk.*

Milk in the menu

Milk can be served in many ways. In addition to its popularity as a drink, it is used as the basis for many cooked dishes. It can be used in sauces, gravies, custards, sherbets, and ice cream. Milk is often used as a binder to hold food mixtures together. Cheese, a milk food, can be used in meals to supply many of the same nutrients contained in meat.

MILK AS A DRINK

Most teen-agers like to drink plain milk with their meals and with between-meal snacks. Flavored milk, buttermilk, and fountain drinks such as milkshakes are also popular. Whole milk contains a good deal of butterfat. When chocolate is added, the fat content is further increased. The addition of flavorings such as chocolate and sugar also adds calories to the drink.

For those fortunate people who are not troubled with overweight or with oily skins, any form of milk is acceptable. Teen-agers who are bothered by weight or complexion problems should choose with care the form of milk they drink. Fat aggravates problem skin conditions and is high in calories. For this reason, low-fat milks, such as dried skim milk, bottled skim milk, and buttermilk are good choices. Vitamins are usually added when such milks are processed. If so, low-fat milk is just as rich as other milks in the vitamins, protein, and minerals necessary for body growth and repair.

The Daily Food Guide suggests that teen-agers need a quart of milk every day. You will usually be sure you are drinking plenty of milk if you drink a glass with each meal. The rest of the milk supply can be furnished by milk foods such as cheese and by milk-rich foods such as custards, gravies, and cream soups. Even bread, cake, and cookies often contain small amounts of milk.

Principles of milk cookery

However you plan to include milk in your menus, treat milk and cheese as protein foods. Like *all* proteins, they require low heat in cooking. Whether you are making cream soup, cocoa, cream sauce, cheese sauce, custard, or any other milk-rich food, use low cooking temperatures.

Many ranges may be adjusted to temperatures low enough for successful milk cookery. However, one of the best ways to be sure the temperature remains low is to cook milk over steam, as in a double boiler. The cooking dishes containing baked custards and soufflés are placed in a pan containing hot water, then set in the oven to bake. Thus the outside of the container holding the milk mixture will not get any hotter than the water surrounding it.

Milk and cheese mixtures scorch easily during cooking. To prevent the scorching of foods cooked on

Buttermilk: Milk produced from whole or skim milk which is soured by artificial fermentation.

Evaporated milk: Canned milk from which approximately one-half of the water has been removed before canning. Evaporated milk is available in both whole milk and skim milk forms.

Sweetened condensed milk: Milk from which approximately one-half of the water has been removed and to which sugar has been added before canning.

Dried milk: Milk from which the water has been removed. Dried milk is available in both whole milk and skim milk forms.

Half-and-half: A mixture of equal parts of milk and cream, usually homogenized.

Cream: A portion of whole milk with a high butterfat content. Kinds are *coffee cream, whipping cream,* and *heavy whipping cream,* grouped according to the fat content of each.

Sour cream: Cream that contains about 18 percent fat. It has been homogenized and then soured by the action of lactic acid bacteria.

Milk is marketed in a variety of forms to fit the tastes of consumers and the recipes frequently used in cooking.

COURTESY ST. LOUIS DISTRICT DAIRY COUNCIL

◆●◆ Prepare white sauce by each of the two methods suggested on this page. Compare the results as to smoothness, flavor, and ease of preparation.

List types of cream soups and creamed dishes.

List foods which when combined with white sauce can be used as a main dish. Suggest variations for serving these, such as in toast cups or poured over biscuits.

List the advantages of drinking skim milk. What are the disadvantages?

Compare the prices of one quart of milk sold in different forms. List ways in which you might use each of these forms of milk.

Since evaporated, condensed, and dried milk are not usually sold by the quart, determine the actual cost of a quart of each. Figure the costs of the amount of each necessary to make a quart of liquid milk.

Compare the price of fluid whole milk sold by the half-pint, the pint, the quart, the half-gallon, the gallon, and in multiple-gallon containers. Suggest situations when each would be the best buy.

top of the range, stir the mixture frequently during the cooking process. Cook baked milk dishes in an oven set at a low temperature to prevent scorching. Some milk dishes, such as custard, are cooked at a high temperature for a few minutes to start the cooking process. However, if the heat is not lowered rather quickly, the custard will break into tough protein clots surrounded by watery fluid.

BASIC WHITE SAUCE

White sauce is a sauce made from milk which is thickened with a starch, usually flour. Various spices and fats may be added for flavor. White sauces in various forms are used as the basis for cream soups, gravies, croquettes, and many other mixtures. If you can make a good white sauce, you can make a great variety of dishes just by adding other foods to it. Many cooks today use canned soups to replace white sauce in food mixtures. This is a good practice as long as you happen to have the right kind of soup on hand. However, if you know how to make your own white sauce, you will always be prepared for a wide assortment of recipes.

When you make white sauce, you are combining the principles of cereal cookery and protein cookery. Your object is to have a smooth product without lumps. To achieve this, the cereal, usually flour, is carefully mixed with some other ingredient before it is cooked. It can be mixed with unheated milk or melted fat. After milk is added to the sauce mixture, a low cooking temperature must be maintained.

Ways to make white sauce

Since white sauce consists of milk thickened by cooking with flour or cornstarch, it can be made in several ways. Cold milk can be mixed with flour and cooked over low heat. Then butter and seasonings are added to taste. White sauce can also be made by first melting butter or margarine in a pan, sometimes the top of a double boiler. The pan is then removed from the heat, and the flour is stirred into the fat until it is free of lumps. The milk is added slowly with constant stirring so the mixture will be smooth. Salt, pepper, and other desired seasonings are added at this time. Then the entire mixture is returned to low heat or to the top of the double boiler, where it is stirred while the starch cooks and thickens the sauce.

You can prepare a basic cheese sauce by adding grated cheese to a hot, thickened white sauce mixture.

The thickness of the finished sauce will depend upon the amount of flour or cornstarch used in proportion to the amount of milk. There are four different thicknesses of white sauce: *thin*, used in cream soups; *medium*, used in creamed dishes and gravies; *thick*, used in soufflés; and *very thick*, used as a

COURTESY NATIONAL DAIRY COUNCIL

White sauce is most frequently made by (1) melting fat, (2) mixing fat and flour, (3) adding milk, and (4) cooking the mixture until the starch is cooked and the mixture thickened. This mixture can be cooked over direct heat or in a double boiler.

423

Prepare various foods, using different types of milk. For example, you may prepare creamed soups or puddings. Make a chart showing your findings. Which foods can be prepared successfully using dried milk?

Prepare a milk dessert for a young child which might be garnished for a suitable adult party dessert.

Visit a local dairy to see how milk is processed.

Tell about one of the see-through test farms located in your area of the country. Describe the cleanliness of the machinery involved in a modern milking operation.

Make several puddings, using an instant pudding, a pudding mix, and basic ingredients. Compare them for flavor, texture, cost, and time and effort involved in the preparation.

Make ice cream by several different methods. Which did you like best, and why?

Arrange a display of different types of cheese. Compare costs and nutritive values. Suggest possible uses and make serving suggestions. Have a tasting party.

COURTESY ST. LOUIS DISTRICT DAIRY COUNCIL

Low cooking temperatures are necessary if dairy dishes are to be tender in texture and mild in flavor.

binder in making croquettes. A medium white sauce is made with two tablespoons of flour to a cup of milk. (See White Sauce recipe, page 490.)

MILK PUDDINGS AND CUSTARDS
Milk puddings are made in much the same way as white sauce. The flour or cornstarch is mixed with the sugar, and the cold milk is added slowly before the mixture is heated. Then the entire mixture is cooked, sometimes in the top of a double boiler, while being stirred. Eggs are added to most puddings for texture and flavor. (See page 417 for adding eggs to a hot mixture.) The addition of chocolate, brown sugar, or other flavoring determines whether the final result will be a chocolate, butterscotch, or otherwise flavored pudding. Milk pudding can be used in filling cream puffs, éclairs, or pie shells. It can be combined with fruits such as peaches, bananas, or berries to make a fruit-crème pie filling or a pudding.

Fewer steps are involved in making puddings from commercial pudding mixes than from basic ingredients. In these mixes the starch, sugar, and flavoring are usually in the package. You add only the milk before cooking. Some of the instant pudding mixes contain an enzyme, rather than starch, which thickens the mixture. For these mixes all you do is add the milk and stir the mixture. The dessert is then ready for eating without cooking.

A milk dessert that is thickened with egg instead of starch is called a *custard*. Egg-milk mixtures that are cooked on top of the range, with constant stirring to prevent scorching, are called *soft-custard* or *custard sauce*. They may be drunk from a cup or used as a sauce over cakes, fruits, or meringues. If the egg-milk mixture is cooked in the oven until it thickens, it is called a *baked custard*. Baked custard may be varied by the addition of different kinds of spices or sauces. It may be served hot or cold. Since custards contain many valuable nutrients and are easy to digest, they are favorite foods for small children, elderly people, and persons on special diets.

Cheese

Cheese is made from milk by the thickening, or coagulation, of milk protein. The *curd*, the solid part of the milk, is separated from the *whey*, or liquid part. This is done either by allowing the milk to sour, as in the case of cottage cheese, or by adding an enzyme to the milk, as in the making of hard, semihard, or processed cheeses.

COURTESY KAISER ALUMINUM

Cheese dishes are cooked at low temperatures to produce tender products with full cheese flavor.

CHEESE COOKERY

Care must be taken in cooking foods containing cheese. If too high a temperature is reached, the cheese becomes tough and stringy. As with all protein foods, a temperature of 300 degrees to 325 degrees Fahrenheit is best for baking cheese mixtures.

Macaroni with cheese is a favorite main dish. Cheese is also combined with eggs, another protein food, to make cheese soufflé. (See recipes for Macaroni and Cheese and for Baked Cheese Fondue on page 491.)

Your career
Dietitian's aide

Duties: Works under the supervision of a registered dietitian in a hospital or nursing home, or may be under the direction of a supervisor who is under a consultant dietitian. Aids the dietitians in carrying out their duties.
Where employed: Hospitals or nursing homes.

22 CHAPTER POSTTEST

Match the *definitions* in List A with the *forms of milk* in List B. Use a form of milk from List B only once. *Do not* write in this book.

List A: **Definitions**

A Milk which has been heated to kill the disease-causing bacteria
B Fresh milk which has not been processed in any way
C Whole milk which has been processed to reduce the size of the fat globules so that the butterfat does not rise to the top
D Milk which contains less calories than either low-fat or whole milk
E Usually the least expensive form in which either whole or skim milk can be purchased

List B: **Forms of milk**

1 Dried
2 Homogenized
3 Pasteurized
4 Raw
5 Skim

Number from 1 to 20. Beside each number indicate if the corresponding statement is true or false.

1 The liquid part of milk is called the whey.
2 Milk has been nicknamed *nature's most nearly perfect food* because it contains plenty of every nutrient a person needs.
3 Both evaporated and condensed milk are sold in cans.
4 Milk products should be cooked at low temperatures because milk scorches easily.
5 Milk and milk products are one of the richest known sources of calcium.
6 Evaporated milk has been sweetened with sugar.
7 Milk is fortified with Vitamin C.
8 Elderly people do not need milk.
9 The thickness of white sauce depends on the proportion of flour or cornstarch used in relation to the amount of milk.
10 Cottage cheese can be made from sour milk.
11 Milk can be used as a binder to hold food mixtures together.
12 Skim milk has the same nutritional value as whole milk.
13 A temperature of 350° F. to 375° F. is best for cooking cheese mixtures.
14 The term *nonfat dry milk solids* refers to dried skim milk.
15 The whipping quality of cream is related to its butterfat content.
16 Most large grocery stores sell raw milk.
17 The standards for the production of certified milk are the same as those for pasteurized milk.
18 Certified milk is usually used only on a doctor's recommendation.
19 Cheddar cheese is a good source of vitamin A.
20 Soft custard, which is sometimes called custard sauce, is cooked on the top of the range.

23 CHAPTER PRETEST

Give the following information on a separate sheet of paper. *Do not* write in this book.

1 Name five leafy vegetables.
2 Name three root vegetables.
3 Name one stem vegetable.
4 Name one flower vegetable.
5 Name one seed vegetable.
6 Name five fruits which grow on trees.
7 Name two fruits which grow on vines.
8 Name two fruits which grow on bushes.
9 Name two vegetables which can be purchased fresh, frozen, canned, and dried.
10 Name two fruits which can be purchased fresh, frozen, canned, and dried.
11 Name two vegetables which are among the richest sources of vitamin A.
12 Name three fruits which are rich sources of vitamin C.
13 Name the three most common methods for cooking vegetables.
14 List five principles to apply when cooking vegetables.
15 Give one procedure which may be used to lessen the browning of certain peeled fruits, such as apples and bananas.
16 Name three salads which can be served as the main dish at lunch or supper.
17 Give one essential procedure to follow when using unflavored gelatin.

CHAPTER 23

Preparing fruits and vegetables

Historians do not know as much about man's early use of fruits and vegetables as they do about his use of meat. Along with hunting stories, there are some legends about farming, but most of these stories are concerned with the growing of grains. Perhaps it was so natural for man to eat the plant life about him that he did not think it important to record such.

Can you imagine a hunter watching birds pecking at the berries in the thicket where he was hiding? Perhaps he nibbled a few of the berries and discovered that the juicy fruit satisfied his thirst and made him less hungry. The berries were good to eat and easy to harvest. They could partially satisfy his need for food.

Many people in modern times take fruits and vegetables for granted. Most cooks and menu planners do not pay so much attention to fruits and vegetables as they do to protein foods. Yet fruits and vegetables are a very important part of a generally well-planned diet. They add a wide range of flavors, colors, shapes, and textures to menus. They are rich in vitamins A, B, and C. Many also contain

List all the vegetables you can think of for each letter in the alphabet. Discuss the varieties of the vegetables that have been listed. Discuss different methods of preparing them and of combining them.

List fruits and vegetables that can be purchased in four ways: fresh, frozen, canned, and dried. List ways to preserve nutrients when preparing and cooking them.

Make a list of guidelines for buying various fruits and vegetables.

Compare the cost and flavor of canned, fresh, and frozen orange juice and grapefruit juice.

Bulletin board IDEA
Title: *Sprinkle Your Diet with Fruits and Vegetables*
Directions: Below the title, fasten a cutout of a sprinkling can. Arrange small pictures of fruits and vegetables to appear as if they are falling from the sprinkler to plates below.

Experiment by cooking samples of the same vegetable for various lengths of time. Observe the differences and compare the flavors, textures, and appearances.

Follow these procedures so that boiled fresh vegetables will retain nutrients and quality.

1. Wash vegetables and pare or peel them if necessary, removing only a very thin layer of the skin.
2. Cut them into large pieces or leave them whole in order to preserve as many nutrients as possible.
3. Cook as soon as possible after preparing. Do not soak the vegetables after they have been prepared for cooking.
4. Place a small amount of water in a saucepan so that very little water will be left after cooking.
5. Add salt, usually one-half teaspoon for each cup of water.
6. Add the vegetables. Bring the water back to a boil, and cook until the vegetable is just tender.
7. Cover the saucepan to hasten the cooking and to preserve nutrients. Some strongly flavored vegetables, such as cabbage, may be cooked uncovered.

important minerals. Fruits and vegetables are the main source of the fiber and acid which help with the elimination of wastes and so help keep your body regulated.

Available forms of fruits and vegetables

You can buy fruits and vegetables in many forms. They may be bought fresh, frozen, canned, and dried. Some are best served raw. As such, they are particularly popular as between-meal snacks. Some seem to taste better cooked, while others are delicious either way.

Fresh fruits and vegetables may lose part of their vitamin content when exposed to heat or air. For this reason they contain more food value when they are garden fresh than at any other time. When fruits and vegetables are shipped over great distances, or when they are stored for a long time, valuable nutrients may be lost. Knowing that vitamins are easily lost, food processors often build their plants near the place where the fruits and vegetables are grown. The ripe foods are picked and taken immediately to the plant. Foods which have been picked, prepared, and canned or frozen at a nearby plant frequently contain more nutrients than they would if sold as fresh produce in the market.

Fruits and vegetables may be dried for future use. Water can be removed in various ways. For instance, foods can actually be freeze-dried in a vacuum to remove moisture while keeping the nutrients. Many of these dried foods have distinctive flavors which make them more suitable for certain dishes than other forms of the same food. Dried apricots, prunes, and raisins are popular in desserts. You find dried vegetables in soup mixes and sauce mixes or in forms such as instant potatoes. Dried beans have long been popular as the basis for protein-rich main dishes.

KINDS OF VEGETABLES

There are several recognized ways of classifying vegetables. Perhaps one of the most useful ways is to group vegetables according to the part of the plant used.

Leafy vegetables

You probably know many of the leafy vegetables. Among the best known are spinach, collards, turnip greens, mustard greens, beet greens, kale, and chard. Salad greens such as lettuce, cabbage, curly endive, parsley, watercress, romaine, and escarole are also leafy vegetables. Many of the leafy vegetables are generally eaten raw, while others may be served raw in one dish and cooked in another.

The leafy vegetables contain varying amounts of vitamins A and C. In general, the deeper green the color, the richer the vitamin content, particularly the vitamin A content. For example, broccoli provides more vitamins than lettuce.

Root vegetables
Some of the more common root vegetables are carrots, turnips, beets, radishes, parsnips, potatoes, sweet potatoes, and onions. Potatoes are sometimes classed separately as *tubers*, meaning they are only the thickened section of the plant root. Onions, which also grow underground, are classed as *bulbs* rather than roots. The underground vegetables are formed to help supply the plant with food. They are the plant's storage bin.

Since root vegetables grow under the ground and do not contain green color, you might expect that they would not be good sources of vitamin A or C. However, if you look at a chart that shows all the nutrients in the different foods, you will see that carrots and sweet potatoes contain a great deal of vitamin A. Like any other bright yellow or orange fruit or vegetable, these vegetables are rich sources of this vitamin. In fact, it is fairly safe to say that the deeper green or yellow the color of a fruit or vegetable, the higher its vitamin A content. The paler the color, the poorer the source of vitamin A. Thus, sweet potatoes and carrots are good sources of vitamin A, while white potatoes and onions contain only a trace.

COURTESY GOOD SEASONS SALAD DRESSING MIX

Leafy vegetables are frequently combined in a wide variety of tossed salads.

A study of a chart showing nutrients in vegetables might further surprise you. While white root vegetables, such as potatoes, parsnips, and turnips, contain very little vitamin A, they are relatively rich in vitamin C. If cooked correctly, a serving of one of these vegetables can provide up to one-fourth of your daily requirement for this vitamin.

Stem vegetables
While the stem is eaten along with the leaf of many vegetables, such as spinach, chard, and turnip greens, there is another group of

Practice several new ways of preparing vegetables. With what other foods would you serve them? Why would you choose these combinations?

Follow these procedures so that canned vegetables will retain their nutrients and quality.
1. Pour off the liquid into a saucepan.
2. Boil the liquid until it is reduced by one-half.
3. Add the vegetables and the seasonings to the remaining liquid.
4. Heat the vegetables, and serve as soon as possible.
5. Garnish the vegetables with chopped parsley, mint, butter, paprika, sesame seeds, cheese sauce, or toasted nuts.

Follow these procedures so that boiled frozen vegetables will retain nutrients and quality.
1. Put the amount of water indicated in a flat-bottomed pan and bring it to a boil.
2. Add salt as directed.
3. Add the frozen vegetables.
4. Bring the water back to a boil, and cook as directed on the package, breaking up the vegetables with a fork as they cook.
5. At this point, follow seasoning and serving directions given on the package.

Search for ways in which vegetables can be prepared attractively by using special herbs and garnishes. Discuss your findings in class.

Play a spell-down game, naming fruits and vegetables. Choose sides. The teacher will name a nutrient such as vitamin A, vitamin C, or iron. If you do not answer at once with the correct name of a fruit or vegetable which is a good source of that nutrient, you are down. A fruit or vegetable may be named only once.

Classify 20 vegetables according to the part of the plant from which they come:
  Stem
  Leaf
  Root
  Seed
  Flower
  Fruit
Compare the groups for nutritive values.

Bulletin board IDEA
Title: *Start the Day with a Bang*
Directions: Place a large exploding firecracker in the center of the bulletin board. Attach four clouds of smoke containing the words *FRUIT, PROTEIN, MILK,* and *CEREAL.*

COURTESY BIRDS EYE VEGETABLE

Carrots are classified as *root* vegetables while the *flower*, or *bud*, of broccoli is eaten.

vegetables used primarily for their stems. This group includes asparagus and celery. Many people are willing to pay more for blanched, or whitened, asparagus and celery than for a bright green vegetable. This is not a nutritionally wise practice, since green stem vegetables contain more nutrients than the white ones do. The deeper the green, the richer is the vitamin content in practically any green vegetable.

Flower vegetables
Broccoli and cauliflower are two familiar plants eaten in the flower, or bud, stage. Broccoli, a deep green vegetable, is much richer in vitamins A and C than is the white cauliflower. Actually, the leaves of cauliflower have much more food value than do the white buds. Unfortunately, people have not developed a taste for the leaves and usually throw them away.

Seed vegetables
The seeds and seed pods of plants are probably the largest single group of vegetables. Beans, peas, and corn, which so many people enjoy as vegetables, are plant seeds. Okra, cucumbers, squash, pumpkins, tomatoes, sweet peppers, and green beans contain plant seeds,

although these vegetables are eaten more for their covering than for the seed itself. The nutritional values of seed vegetables vary greatly. While seeds tend to be rich in the B vitamins, many of the seed vegetables are very rich in vitamins A and C.

KINDS OF FRUITS

Almost everyone enjoys fruit of some kind. A wide selection of fresh fruits is available during most seasons of the year. Fresh fruits probably vary in price more than any other type of food. Like vegetables, fruits add a variety of color, flavor, and texture to meals. They are valuable sources of vitamins and minerals. Dark yellow fruits, such as apricots, peaches, cantaloupes, mangoes, and persimmons, are good sources of vitamin A. Fruits such as the citrus fruits, cantaloupes, and strawberries are valuable sources of vitamin C. So valuable are these C-rich fruits that the *Daily Food Guide* encourages each person to eat some of them daily to ensure a good supply of this vitamin. (See pages 368–369.)

Fruits, like vegetables, can be classified in a number of ways. Sometimes they are classified according to food values, and other times according to the texture or shape of the fruit. Probably the most common classification, however, is according to the plants which bear them. Many, many fruits grow on trees. These include apples, pears, cherries, peaches, oranges, grapefruit, lemons, dates, limes, mangoes, figs, persimmons, plums, and tangerines. Fruits which grow on vines include melons, grapes, and some kinds of berries. Other fruits grow on bushes. Most bush fruits are berries, like blueberries, cranberries, and raspberries. Pineapples and strawberries grow on plants which remain rather close to the ground. Papayas and bananas grow on short-lived tree-like bushes. These bushes grow rapidly but must be replaced after a few seasons.

Consult tables of food values. Compare the nutrients and calories in vegetables such as spinach and collards with vegetables such as potatoes, corn, parsnips, red cabbage, peas, and beans. Compare and contrast the nutrients and calories in such fruits as oranges and strawberries with fruits such as bananas and avocados. Which fruits and vegetables do your findings cause you to recommend most highly? Why?

A broad range of fruits are available during the year that add variety to meals and vitamins to the diet.

COURTESY GOOD SEASONS SALAD DRESSING MIX

Fry several samples of a vegetable such as potatoes in fat at different temperatures. Use the same amount of vegetable and fat for each sample. Compare their appearance, flavor, and texture after cooking. Determine the amount of fat each test group of vegetables absorbed by measuring the amount of fat left after frying. Prepare a set of guidelines for frying this vegetable.

Cook several fruits and vegetables different ways and compare their appearance, texture, and flavor.

Principles for cooking fruits and vegetables

Of all the food groups, fruits and vegetables are the most susceptible to vitamin loss, as well as to changes in flavor, texture, color, and shape. Knowing this, an informed cook selects and prepares fruits and vegetables with three main goals in mind: to preserve nutritive values, to preserve or enhance food flavors and textures, and to retain attractive colors and shapes.

VEGETABLES

Vegetables may be cooked by many different methods. The most common methods are boiling, baking, and frying. Often vegetables are combined with other foods in casseroles. No matter what method you use to prepare them, there are ten sets of facts which, when applied, will make cooked vegetables both appetizing and nutritious:

1 The B vitamins, vitamin C, and minerals dissolve readily in water. Therefore, the less water used in vegetable cookery, the less will be the vitamin and mineral loss.

2 The B vitamins and vitamin C are easily destroyed by exposure to heat and air. By cooking vegetables containing these vitamins in a closed container, more of the vitamins are retained.

3 Since vitamins B and C are destroyed by exposure to oxygen, boil the cooking water a few minutes before adding the raw vegetables. This will allow excess oxygen to escape from the cooking water and prevent a certain amount of vitamin loss during the cooking period.

4 Vitamins A, D, and E dissolve in fats. Therefore, they are drawn out into the cooking liquid when fats such as bacon drippings or butter are added to vegetables during the cooking period.

5 The more surface of the vegetable exposed to water and air, the greater will be the

When vegetables are cooked in their see-through containers, B and C vitamins are held in the bag rather than lost in the cooking water.

COURTESY BIRDS EYE VEGETABLE

nutrient loss in cooking. Cook vegetables whole or in large pieces.

6 Many of the vitamins are concentrated near the surface of the vegetable. If the vegetable must be pared, remove as little of the vegetable as possible with the peeling.

7 Many vegetables, such as cabbage and spinach, contain acid which will destroy the color during the cooking process. To prevent this color loss, cook these vegetables as rapidly as possible and leave the pan uncovered so that the acid may pass off in the steam.

8 Baking soda will destroy some vitamins. It should not be added to vegetables, even though it will shorten the necessary cooking time.

9 To preserve food value and flavor, cook vegetables only until they are tender.

10 Overcooking of vegetables such as cabbage and onions will cause the flavor to become strong and unpleasing.

These ten sets of facts may include too much information for you to understand at this point. Some principles may even sound contradictory. You may find yourself wondering how to preserve the nutritive values in a certain vegetable while enhancing the flavor. If this is the case, use the following

COURTESY BIRDS EYE VEGETABLE

When vitamin A-rich vegetables such as carrots and broccoli are cooked in casseroles, their vitamins remain in usable form.

simplified set of rules as you continue to learn more about vitamins and cooking.

1 Leave vegetables whole when cooking them, or cut them into large pieces only.
2 Do not soak vegetables, especially after peeling.
3 Cook vegetables in a very small amount of water, but watch them to prevent burning.
4 Cover the pan as the vegetables cook, except for strong-

Experiment with the effects of different spices and other flavorings on vegetables. For example, try lemon juice on broccoli or nutmeg on spinach.

Prepare vegetables using one of the following variations:
Add unusual spices, seasonings, and herbs, such as a sprig of fresh mint, bay leaf, basil, whole cloves, thyme, rosemary, or dill.
Prepare with vegetable juice, bouillon, or meat stock in place of water.
Cook two or more vegetables together.
Add bits of crisp bacon or shredded nuts to Brussels sprouts or green beans; add onion rings to peas or beans.
Cut the vegetables into small pieces and cook them very quickly in a small amount of water, stirring constantly as the vegetables cook.
Braise the vegetables by heating in a little fat until partly done. Add a small amount of liquid, cover tightly, and allow to steam over low heat.
Bread the vegetables and deep-fat fry them. Vegetables should be at their peak of quality if they are to be prepared in this way.

Cook two groups of apples to produce apple rings and applesauce. The following facts will help:

Fruit will retain its shape during cooking if:
- It is cooked with sugar.
- It is cooked at a boiling temperature.

Fruit will make a sauce during cooking if:
- It is cooked in water without sugar.
- It is cooked at a low temperature.
- Sugar is added after the fruit is cooked.

Bring to class favorite recipes or samples of homemade jellies, jams, relishes, or pickles.

Prepare salad dressings using the same recipe but different kinds of vinegar: cider, tarragon, distilled white, and wine vinegar. Use the dressings on salads and compare their flavors.

Bulletin board IDEA
Title: *Toss Up a Summer Appetite*
Directions: Below the title attach a mock salad bowl with salad greens coming out of it. Cut the vegetable pictures from construction, crepe, or tissue paper. Around the salad bowl mount pictures of a variety of appealing salads.

COURTESY BIRDS EYE FRUITS

Fruits can be served separately or combined with pudding or pastry in a wide variety of dessert combinations.

flavored vegetables and those in which you especially wish to preserve the bright color.
5 Start vegetables in rapidly boiling water, and cook them as quickly and briefly as possible.
6 Avoid adding baking soda or fat to vegetables during the cooking period.
7 Serve the cooking liquid with the vegetable, or save it to use in sauces or soups.

FRUITS
Since many of the principles for vegetable cookery also apply to fruits, once learned, they can be applied to both foods. Fruits, like vegetables, are commonly cooked by boiling, baking, or frying. The following simplified rules apply more directly to fruits than to vegetables.

1 Cook the fruit as quickly as possible after peeling, since vitamins are easily lost by exposure to heat and air.
2 Dip peeled fruits, such as apples and peaches, into a slightly acid liquid, such as citrus juice, pineapple juice, or a salad dressing such as mayonnaise, to prevent browning. Since the protective coating may dissolve some of the nutrients, plan to serve the coating with the fruit. A commercial preparation which prevents discoloration may be sprinkled over a cut fruit to protect its appearance during serving and eating.
3 Cook fruits to prevent spoilage, to make them easy to digest, to change the flavor, to add variety to the menu, or to combine them with other foods.
4 Add sugar to the cooking water to help preserve the shape of a fruit. If you are cooking fruit to use in a salad or as a garnish, add the sugar early in the cooking process. If you are making applesauce, add the sugar after the fruit has cooked to a softened state.

Principles for preserving fruits and vegetables

Although fruits and vegetables may be purchased on the market in a wide variety of forms, people sometimes take special pleasure in the home preservation of fruits or vegetables. In all forms of food preservation, the bacterial growth is slowed or stopped so that the food may be kept for an indefinite period of time. Whether there is an oversupply of a given food produced at home or an especially good buy at the marketplace, most of today's home preservation is done for creativity rather than for economy.

Most preservation is done by freezing and canning. However, many families have treasured recipes for pickles, relishes, jellies, or fruit preserves. They enjoy making a quantity of these items to serve as a specialty of the house.

Vegetables may be preserved for future use in the following ways:
1. Fresh vegetables may be frozen after cleaning and blanching (heating in water).
2. Fresh vegetables may be canned either by following the hot-water-bath method or by cooking them under pressure in sealed jars or cans.
3. Vegetables may be preserved with the addition of salt, vinegar, sugar, or a combination of these ingredients.
4. Vegetables may be dried.

Fruits may be preserved for future use in several ways:
1. Fresh fruits may be frozen, with or without sugar.
2. Fruits may be canned by either the open-kettle or hot-water-bath method.
3. Fruits may be prepared, packed in suitable jars or cans, sealed, and processed in a pressure cooker.
4. Fruits may be cooked with a large proportion of sugar to make preserves, conserve, or marmalade.

Your career
Vegetable cook

Duties: Directs the cleaning, preparation, and cooking of vegetables and fruits which are used with the regular meal. May sometimes direct the salad-making procedures.
Where employed: Large restaurants, institutional dining rooms, and large school cafeterias.

Many families have favorite recipes for jellies, jams, or relishes which they take pride in making and serving on special occasions.

COURTESY CERTO FRUIT PECTIN

Unmold gelatin, following the steps below.

Then discuss common problems involved in making gelatin molds and how each can be overcome.
1. Run a knife around the inside edge of the mold.
2. Dip the mold quickly in and out of hot water.
3. Cover the top of the mold with a platter, invert, and remove mold. Garnish.
4. Chill in the refrigerator to set before serving.

Small pieces of fruits and vegetables can be combined in a gelatin mold to provide colorful additions to otherwise bland or colorless meals.

COURTESY APPLE INSTITUTE

5. Fruits may be dried.
6. Fruits may be candied. Citron, orange peel, lemon rind, pineapple slices, and cherries are often candied and used as garnishes or in baking.

Principles for serving raw fruits and vegetables

Because many of the vitamins and minerals supplied by fruits and vegetables are lost during the cooking process, a daily serving of raw fruits or vegetables is an important contribution to good health. Fruit and vegetable juices can also add important nutrients to the daily diet. Raw fruits and vegetables may be added to a cooked food as a garnish. These garnishes tend to make the dish pleasing to the eye. They also add interesting texture contrasts which make the food appetizing.

MAKING SALADS

Salads are high on the list of food favorites of many people. They may be made of fruits or vegetables or a combination of both. Almost any type of food may be used as an ingredient in a special salad. In addition to fruits and vegetables, meat, fish, poultry, cheese, or bread cubes appear frequently. Salad ingredients may be cooked, fresh, frozen, or canned, but most salads contain raw fruits or vegetables.

Small pieces of fruits and vegetables may be served in molded gelatin salads. Carrots, cabbage, and celery, as well as numerous canned fruits and vegetables, are favorites in gelatin molds. Such salads may stretch a small amount of food to make satisfying servings for everyone. This may be especially useful at times when certain fruits and vegetables are unusually expensive. These relatively inexpensive molded salads can add flavor and color to an otherwise uninteresting meal. (Study the recipe for Gelatin Mold, page 496.)

When using unflavored gelatin, soften it in a small amount of *cold* liquid before adding it to the other liquid ingredients. Most flavored gelatin mixes have been pretreated to make them dissolve easily. Package instructions direct you to dissolve these flavored mixes in *hot* water before adding cold liquid. Other ingredients are usually added when the gelatin begins to jell.

Salad making is a form of art. With practice, you can combine various shapes and colors of foods in interesting arrangements which look loosely artistic rather than rigidly hand-placed.

A few simple principles will help you to prepare salads which are colorful, tasty, and nutritious. Use the principles which apply to the type of salad you are making.

1. Plan flavor, color, and texture combinations which are pleasing in themselves and which complement the other foods in the meal.
2. Select cold, clean, crisp, fresh fruits or vegetables.
3. Pare or scrape fruits and vegetables only if necessary, and then remove only a thin outer coating, in order to avoid loss of nutrients.
4. Cut fruits and vegetables only moments before serving time if possible.
5. Keep prepared fruits and vegetables in tightly covered containers until serving time.
6. To cut down on loss of nutrients, avoid soaking salad ingredients in water.
7. In general, use fruits and vegetables that are dry or that have been thoroughly drained.
8. Arrange the base, or salad greens, to prevent their hanging over the edge of the salad plate.
9. Hand-tear salad greens into bite-size pieces to avoid bruising them with a knife.
10. In general, add the seasonings and salad dressing at the last possible moment so that the salad will remain crisp and fresh looking.

COURTESY KRAFT KITCHENS

A well-planned salad, hot or cold, is pleasing within itself and complements other foods with which it is served.

Your career
Food service manager

Duties: Manages a restaurant, cafeteria, school lunchroom, or short-order drive-in. Is responsible for hiring, training, and supervising the employees. Selects food, supplies, and food equipment; keeps accounts and records; plans or approves menus; enforces sanitation regulations; and deals with the customers.
Where employed: Local restaurants, cafeterias, drive-ins, or schools.

23 CHAPTER POSTTEST

Match the *vegetables* given in List A with the *parts of plant* given in List B. Use a part of a plant given in List B only once. *Do not* write in this book.

List A: **Vegetables**

A Cabbage
B Carrots
C Asparagus
D Broccoli
E Peas

List B: **Parts of plant**

1 Flower
2 Leaf
3 Root
4 Seed
5 Stem

Number from 1 to 21 on a piece of paper. Beside each number indicate if the corresponding statement is true or false.

1 Fruits and vegetables are the main source of the cellulose fibers which keep the body regulated.
2 Freeze-dried foods are processed in a vacuum to remove moisture while retaining nutritional value.
3 Canned and frozen foods consistently have less nutritional value than the same food product sold in the fresh-produce department of a grocery store.
4 Vitamin A is more easily destroyed by exposure to heat and air than vitamin C.
5 The two most widely used methods for preserving food are freezing and drying.
6 Instant potatoes are a form of dried vegetable.
7 Potatoes are a richer source of vitamin C than apples.
8 The B vitamins dissolve in fats more readily than vitamin D.
9 Vitamins are in greater abundance near the surface of a fruit or vegetable.
10 Overcooking vegetables may lessen their nutritional value.
11 Cabbage becomes bland and tasteless if it is overcooked.
12 To prepare vegetables for cooking, cut them into small pieces.
13 It is advisable to soak peeled vegetables in water for one-half hour before cooking them.
14 Cook vegetables in a small amount of water.
15 To lessen browning, freshly peeled peaches can be dipped in orange juice.
16 Adding sugar to the cooking water helps to preserve the shape of fruits.
17 Pickling is a form of food preservation.
18 Fresh vegetables are cleaned and blanched before canning.
19 All salad ingredients are served raw.
20 It is necessary to pare apples for a fresh salad.
21 Unflavored gelatin is softened in hot water before combining it with other ingredients.

24 CHAPTER PRETEST

Copy the following list of food products on a separate sheet of paper. Beside each food indicate whether it is made from a dough, a pour batter, or a thick batter. Use the following abbreviations:
   D for dough
   P for pour batter
   T for thick batter

Food products
Doughnuts
Pancakes
Muffins
Rolled biscuits
Waffles
Drop cookies
Yeast rolls
Pie crust
Popovers

Fill in the blank in each sentence with the *best* word or words to complete the statement.

1 The basic ingredient which is used in all breads, cakes, pastries, and cookies is ___(1)___.
2 Cereals such as oatmeal often can be purchased in quick-cooking, regular, and ___(2)___ forms.
3 Breads are classified as either quick breads or ___(3)___ breads.
4 The three leaveners are air, steam, and ___(4)___.
5 Two chemical leavening agents are baking soda and ___(5)___.
6 When flour is mixed with water, the protein in flour forms ___(6)___.

CHAPTER 24

Preparing cereal products

Since the dawn of civilization, man has cultivated the cereals and harvested their seeds to use as foods. In early days these cereal grains were pounded or ground to a powder, or meal, mixed with liquid to form a paste, and cooked as little cakes or crackers. Modern breads such as *tortillas* from Mexico, *chapati* from India, and *brods* from Sweden are still made in this primitive manner.

At first the whole grain was used in bread, just as it sometimes is today. But there are two problems involved in making breads from whole grain. While whole-grain flours make delicious, nutritious breads, the breads are somewhat dark and coarse in texture. Also, whole-grain cereals are apt to spoil rather quickly because of the relatively high fat content of the seed germ.

As the manufacturing process continued to develop, ways were found to remove the *bran*, which is the hard outer coating of cereal grains. Milling techniques were also developed to remove the *germ*, or life-giving portion of the seed. These milling techniques leave a soft, whitish grain center which can

Compare the labels on several cereal boxes for valuable information. Try to determine which boxes give the most reliable facts concerning nutritive values.

Compare instant, quick-cooking, and regular varieties of a particular cereal. Consider each type of cereal from the viewpoint of cost, flavor, ease of preparation, and the time involved in preparation. Discuss your findings.

Compare the cost of one serving of the same brand of ready-to-eat cereal when purchased in small, large, and individual packages. Is the larger size always a better buy? Why?

Bulletin board IDEA
Title: *Start Your Day With a Song*
Directions: Cut out a bass and treble clef from black construction paper. Use pictures of attractive breakfast foods arranged on lines representing the staff.

Prepare and serve a cooked cereal that is new to your family. Report to the class how well your family liked it.

Draw a diagram of a single whole grain. Label the parts.

Make a list of the various kinds of flour available in the grocery store where your family shops. Which kind of flour seems to be stocked in greatest quantities? Why?

be ground into very fine particles. The finely ground product is then called white flour, or *refined flour*. Since the germ of grain contains fat, and therefore spoils rather quickly, refined flours keep better than whole-grain flours. They also produce breads which have a much finer texture than those made with whole-grain flours.

Bran and germ contain most of the B-complex vitamins, iron, and roughage that are present in cereals. Most of this food value is removed during the milling of refined flours.

Therefore, it is necessary to return these nutrients to food products if they are to be nourishing. When the iron and vitamins of the bran and germ are restored to the flour in concentrated form, this treated flour is called *enriched flour*. Except for roughage, enriched flour contains all of the value of a whole-grain product. The Federal government has set standards for this enrichment, and manufacturers who use the word *enriched* must follow government standards.

Because of the high food value of the wheat germ, it is packaged and sold separately in small quantities. Many people buy wheat germ to sprinkle on cereals or fruits or to add to baked products.

Types of cereal foods

Many people think of cereal as a breakfast food only, but it is hard to plan a meal which does not include some cereal product. Rice, macaroni products, and all breads are cereal foods. Sauces and gravies depend on cereals as thickening agents.

BREADS

Breads are the most frequently eaten cereal products. Modern breads come ready-prepared, partially prepared, or in the form of mixes. These breads save time, have uniform quality, and add variety to meals. However, many cooks have

Bread products, rich in the B vitamins, are made most frequently from enriched white flour.

COURTESY KITCHENS OF SARA LEE

one or two favorite recipes for breads prepared from flour. These homemade breads are easy to make if you understand the basic principles involved. Cookbooks separate breads into *yeast breads* and *quick breads,* or those which do not use yeast for leavening.

BREAKFAST CEREALS

Many people in the United States feel that a breakfast must include a cereal in order to be complete. The cereal foods which are customarily served for breakfast have therefore come to be known as *breakfast cereals.* While it is true that these cereals are good foods to use at the start of the day, their use need not be limited to breakfast.

Some of the breakfast cereals on the market have already been cooked. These are called *ready-to-eat cereals.* When you buy ready-to-eat cereals, you pay extra for the precooking. These cereals provide a convenient and time-saving way to serve breakfast.

Oatmeal and various wheat cereals are common forms of the *hot breakfast cereals.* These cereals are cooked in water or other liquids. Rice may also be served for breakfast. Many of the hot cereals have been processed to cook in a very few minutes. When buying such cereals, notice whether the package is labeled *regular, quick-cooking,* or *instant.* The process used in preparing a cereal for the market affects the texture of the finished product as well as the amount of time required to prepare it.

OTHER CEREAL FOODS

Macaroni, spaghetti, lasagne, and noodles are cereal products. They are frequently used in the main dish served at lunch or supper. Rice and other cereal grains such as buckwheat and barley are used in similar dishes. Like the macaroni products,

COURTESY ALUMINUM ASSOCIATION

Cereal foods such as noodles, spaghetti, and macaroni are cooked by stirring the cereal product into rapidly boiling water. They are then combined with protein foods and used as the main dish in a meal.

Your career
Pastry chef

Duties: Supervises the pastry department, writes the dessert menus, orders supplies, decorates cakes, makes ornamental pieces, works on new recipes, and figures production costs.
Where employed: Bakeries, dining rooms, and hospitals.

Try the two methods given below for combining flour with a liquid. Decide which method is easier.
1. Mix the flour with some of the cold liquid, as in making cornstarch pudding.
2. Melt butter or margarine and stir in the flour to make a smooth paste before adding any of the liquid, as in making white sauce.

Make test recipes of white sauce using equal amounts of flour and cornstarch. How can you use information gained from this experiment when making sauces and puddings?

these cereals are popular in the preparation of many casserole dishes.

Principles of cereal cookery

The main purpose of cereal cookery is to adequately cook the starch content for easy digestion. Correct cooking procedures will help you achieve the texture and appearance which are considered desirable for a given product.

BREADS

Breads are made from a mixture of cereal products and liquid. Other ingredients commonly used in bread are leaveners, shortening, sugars and other flavoring ingredients, and eggs. If you understand the functions of these different ingredients, you can expect good results in your baking.

Flour mixtures are usually classified by the amount of flour they contain in proportion to the amount of liquid. Mixtures thin enough to be stirred by a spoon are called *batters.* Batters may be thin enough to be poured or thick enough to be spooned out in a soft mass. Griddle cakes, popovers, and waffles are examples of quick breads made from pour batters. Muffins, drop cookies, and drop biscuits are popular baked products made from thick batters.

Mixtures which contain a high proportion of flour are called *doughs.* Doughs are so thick that they cannot be mixed entirely with a spoon. The final mixing must be done by hand. Yeast breads, rolled cookies, and regular baking-powder biscuits are among the familiar baked products made from doughs.

Flour

Flour is the basic ingredient of yeast breads, quick breads, cakes, pastries, and cookies. While flour can be made from many grains, the most commonly used flours are made from wheat, rye, or barley. Flour can be coarse, as in whole-wheat flour, or very fine, as in pastry flour. Probably the finest flour of all is made from tapioca. This

Pancakes are made by pouring a thin batter onto a heated grill or skillet. The pancakes are turned and browned on both sides.

COURTESY ALUMINUM ASSOCIATION

flour, used occasionally at home, is employed extensively as a thickener in quantity cookery and frozen foods.

Since the kind of flour selected has a decided effect on the finished product, you need to understand something about the differences in flours. Wheat flour contains a protein known as *gluten*. It is this protein which hardens during the cooking process, giving shape to the finished product. Have you ever looked closely at a slice of yeast bread and noticed the small bubbles, or cells? The walls of these bubbles are formed by the gluten. Cake slices contain cells, too, but they are not so distinct as those in bread. Since most people want soft, fine-textured cakes, they choose a different type of flour for cake than for bread making.

The flour which bakers use for bread is made from hard wheat. This flour, which has a high gluten content, is commonly called bread flour. The flour which bakers use for cakes is made from soft wheat. This flour, which has a low gluten content, is commonly called cake, or pastry, flour. Most homemakers prefer a product called *all-purpose flour*, a combination of the hard and soft wheat flours. Self-rising flour, all-purpose flour to which salt and leavening have been added, is also used in many homes. Cake made from all-purpose or self-rising flour will not be so fine as cake made from cake flour, but the product will be acceptable. In bread making also, results with all-purpose flour are not so good as if bread flour had been used. However, bread made from all-purpose flour is acceptable.

Think for a moment about the real differences between all-purpose and bread and cake flours. Isn't it that all-purpose flour and bread flour contain more gluten than cake flour? That being the case, by cutting down on the amount of all-purpose flour in a cake, you can cut down on the gluten and make a more tender cake. And by adding more all-purpose flour than the amount of flour called for in a bread recipe, you can in-

Muffins are cereal products made by dropping a thick batter into muffin tins. Muffins are baked in a hot oven.

COURTESY KELLOGG COMPANY

Make a list of foods which can be substituted for others in a recipe. Add your list to those given below. Explain why each food can be effectively substituted for the other.

FOR 1 cup self-rising flour
USE 1 cup all-purpose flour plus 1½ t. baking powder and ½ t. salt

FOR 1 cup sifted cake flour
USE 1 cup minus 2 T. all-purpose flour

FOR 1 cup bread flour
USE 1 cup plus 2 T. all-purpose flour

FOR 1 t. cornstarch
USE 2 t. flour

FOR 1 t. baking powder
USE ¼ t. soda plus ½ t. cream of tartar

FOR 1 whole egg
USE 2 egg yolks (in a custard)

FOR 1 cup fresh sweet milk
USE 4 T. dried milk plus ⅞ cup water

FOR 1 cup sour milk
USE 1 cup fresh sweet milk plus 1 T. vinegar or lemon juice

FOR 1 cup honey
USE ¾ cup sugar plus ½ cup liquid

(See page 479 for more equivalents)

Compare three of the same type of products (muffins, biscuits, or pancakes), one made from a commercial mix, one made from a master mix, and one made from a conventional recipe. Compare and contrast them for flavor, texture, appearance, keeping quality, cost, time required in preparation, and ease of preparation.

Using a cookbook, list a variety of quick breads. What do they all have in common?

crease the gluten and improve the quality of the bread product.

A good general rule to remember is to remove two tablespoons of flour from each cup when substituting all-purpose flour for cake flour. Add two extra tablespoons per cup of all-purpose flour when substituting it for bread flour. Your results may not be exactly the same as those you could obtain from using the kind of flour called for in the recipe, but they will be acceptable. Most modern recipes are planned for all-purpose flour, so you will not need to change the amount of flour unless bread or cake flour is specified in the recipe.

The texture of cake is more tender than that of bread because it contains either weaker gluten or a smaller amount of gluten.

COURTESY KRAFT KITCHENS

Liquids

Water and milk are the liquids most commonly used in flour mixtures, but vinegar, sour milk, fruit juices, and even soups are sometimes used. The liquid helps bind the mixture together. It releases the carbon dioxide from certain leaveners, produces steam when heated, and adds flavor.

Leaveners

If you have ever made a cake or muffins and forgotten to include the baking powder, you are already familiar with the function of a leavening agent. It causes a flour mixture to rise. There are three types of leaveners: carbon dioxide, air, and steam. They inflate baked products and make them light and fluffy.

The leavener used in the greatest number of foods is *carbon dioxide.* Baking powder, baking soda, and yeast, when handled properly, all produce carbon dioxide. Carbon dioxide may be formed in two ways. When liquid is mixed with the chemicals contained in baking powder or baking soda, carbon dioxide gas is released. When yeast plants grow and multiply, they give off carbon dioxide. When either the chemical or plant is present in a warm flour-liquid mixture, released carbon dioxide causes the mixture to rise.

Both *single-acting* and *double-acting* baking powders are available. Since the carbon dioxide in single-acting baking powder is released when it is moistened, its effects are lost fairly rapidly if the batter is left standing after mixing. It will also be lost if the batter is overmixed. Double-acting baking powder acts once when moistened and again when heated. This double action makes for more general success in preparing breads and cake products than does single-acting baking powder.

The longer yeast plants are allowed to grow, the more carbon dioxide they will produce. In fact, if a yeast dough is left too long, the carbon dioxide will stretch the gluten until it breaks. At that point, a yeast bread falls.

Air is incorporated into a mixture by means of beating or whipping. By adding beaten egg whites, which hold air, large amounts of air can be folded into a mixture. Angel food and sponge cakes are leavened with air.

Steam is used as a leavener in such baked products as popovers and cream-puff shells. A hot oven is used during the first minutes of baking so that the liquid in these batters is quickly turned to steam. The steam causes the batter to puff up. The heat then sets and cooks the gluten and the egg proteins, causing the walls to harden. After the protein has set, the heat in the oven is reduced for the duration of the baking period so that the protein will remain tender.

Shortening

Any type of fat used in a flour mixture is called shortening. Commonly used shortenings are oil, margarine, lard, and hydrogenated vegetable fats. Shortening is added to a flour mixture to improve the flavor, to aid in browning, and to increase the tenderness. Thus, there is a much higher proportion of fat to flour in a tender product such as pie crust than in a firmer product such as yeast bread. Fats vary in shortening power. The animal fats, such as butter and lard, are considered *shorter*, or more concentrated, than the vegetable fats. In spite of this variation, the solid fats can

Prepare quick breads, allowing students in one unit kitchen to follow the recipe accurately. Let students in other unit kitchens make the same recipe, leaving out one ingredient, over- or undermixing the dough, or baking the mixture at the wrong temperature. Compare the results and keep a record of your findings. How can such information be useful?

Prepare a basic quick bread recipe adding various ingredients to create interest and add variety.

Cream puffs rise while cooking because liquid in the batter balloons as steam, causing the soft dough to rise.

COURTESY JELL-O PUDDING AND PIE FILLING

Give the reasons for the following procedures used in making quick breads:
1. Sifting the flour before it is measured
2. Measuring the ingredients accurately, using standard measuring cups and spoons
3. Sifting the dry ingredients together
4. Adding the liquid all at once
5. Using the size of baking pan called for in the recipe
6. Filling the muffin cups only two-thirds full of batter when making muffins

usually be successfully substituted for one another in a recipe. Liquid shortenings should not be substituted for solid fats unless the amount of liquid in the mixture is cut down accordingly.

Sugars and other flavoring ingredients

While it is true that sugar adds a sweet flavor to a product, it also serves other purposes. Sugar helps to tenderize the gluten in the flour and gives yeast its growing power. For example, since coffee cake has a softer texture than bread, it requires a larger proportion of sugar. Actually, the main use of sugar in yeast breads is not for either tenderness or flavor. Rather, sugar provides the energy needed by the yeast plants as they grow to produce the carbon dioxide for leavening.

Ingredients such as spices and flavoring extracts are added only for flavor. They have little effect on the texture of the finished product.

Eggs

Eggs are added to many flour mixtures. The egg proteins harden during the baking process, adding to the structure of the final product. The air which is beaten into the eggs helps make many baked products lighter. And eggs give additional flavor to baked products.

USING A BISCUIT MASTER MIX

In your foods class or at home, you might like to experiment with using a master mix. A master mix is a basic recipe that can be varied to produce several products. (See the recipe on page 502.)

Make a half recipe of the master mix in your school kitchen or at home. This will give you an opportunity to practice careful and accurate measurements. It will also give you a chance to practice cutting a recipe in half. If you make the master mix correctly, most of your products will be successful.

You might try making biscuits from the master mix to experience handling, rolling, and cutting dough. Later you may decide to make muffins or a coffee cake. These two

The Biscuit Master Mix, like many quick breads, is made by cutting together flour and shortening. Liquid is added later.

COURTESY WHEAT FLOUR INSTITUTE

products take the same ingredients but in different proportions. Perhaps your teacher will want to first demonstrate these products so that you can see what happens when muffins without extra sugar are stirred too much and the gluten starts to develop. You might find holes and tunnels in the finished muffins. In making coffee cake with extra sugar, you can stir much more vigorously and still produce a tender product. These experiments should help you see that accurate measurements are important. Too, they will help you understand the actual functions of the various ingredients in bread products.

BREAKFAST CEREALS

Hot breakfast cereals are cooked in boiling water or other liquid. After a certain amount of cooking, the cereal starch softens and swells as it absorbs the liquid. This is the reason cornstarch pudding, white sauce, oatmeal, and other cereal mixtures thicken when they are cooked.

Softened starch granules tend to stick together, making a lumpy mixture. The softened starch also tends to stick to the sides and bottom of the cooking pan, where it will scorch unless constantly stirred back into the mixture.

The lumping of cereal can be prevented in a number of ways. The cereal can be added slowly to boiling liquid while being stirred vigorously. It can be mixed with cold liquid to make a smooth paste before being combined with boiling liquid. To cut down on stirring, many people prefer to cook cereal mixtures over steam, as in a double boiler.

OTHER CEREAL FOODS

Macaroni products and cereal foods such as rice and barley are cooked in the same way as hot breakfast cereals. They are added to boiling salted water and cooked until tender. As they cook, they absorb water and swell to greater bulk. Use the exact amount of water given in recipes for preparing each of these foods. As in cooking breakfast cereals, it is important to prevent these foods from sticking to the pan and scorching.

COURTESY HOUSEHOLD FINANCE CORPORATION

Most breakfast cereals are cooked by gradually adding the cereal product to boiling water and stirring until the cereal starch is well cooked.

Demonstrate making a master mix. Make a wide variety of products from the mix such as coffee cake, waffles, brownies, cookies, and biscuits.

Find commercial products which are actually master mixes. Try some recipes contained on the packages of these commercial master mixes using your own homemade master mix instead of the commercial mix.

Make flour mixtures which are leavened by each of the following:
  Air
  Steam
  Carbon dioxide

Make a standard pizza sauce. Use different items for the pizza crust such as English muffins, half of a hamburger bun rolled thin, or canned biscuits which have been flattened.

Bulletin board IDEA
Title: *It's Pizza Time*
Directions: Place a cutout of a large round pizza in the center of the bulletin board. With yarn stretched from a pin in the center, divide the pizza into four large wedges. In each wedge, group pictures of the ingredients for a variation.

24 CHAPTER POSTTEST

Number from 1 to 12 on a piece of paper. Beside each number write the letter which corresponds to the *best* answer for that question. *Do not* write in this book.

1. What is the name of the hard outer coating of cereal grains?
   a Flour   c Rice
   b Germ   d Bran
2. Which of the following must be restored to enriched flours?
   a Vitamins A and C
   b B vitamins and iron
   c Vitamins A and D
   d Thiamine and calcium
3. With which of the following ingredients are quick breads most frequently leavened?
   a Egg yolk or egg white
   b Sour milk or buttermilk
   c Baking powder or baking soda
   d Dry granular yeast or compressed yeast
4. Which of the following ingredients has the greatest effect on the tenderness of a baked product?
   a Shortening   c Egg
   b Vanilla extract   d Milk
5. Which type of flour contains salt?
   a Pastry
   b Self-rising
   c All-purpose
   d Whole wheat
6. Which of the following types of flour spoils most easily?
   a Cake   c Tapioca
   b All-purpose   d Whole wheat
7. Which type of flour contains the least protein?
   a Cake
   b Bread
   c All-purpose
   d Self-rising
8. Which of the following is *not* a grain?
   a Rice
   b Rye
   c Gluten
   d Barley
9. Which of the following is *not* a leavener?
   a Carbon dioxide
   b Steam
   c Air
   d Flour
10. Which of the following is *least* likely to be made from a master mix?
    a Coffee cake
    b Yeast rolls
    c Brownies
    d Drop biscuits
11. Which of the following is *not* classified as a cereal or cereal product?
    a Macaroni
    b Cornbread
    c Noodles
    d Soufflé
12. Which of the following cereals is served hot?
    a Regular oatmeal
    b Corn flakes
    c All-bran
    d Puffed rice

25 CHAPTER PRETEST

Give the following information on a separate sheet of paper. *Do not* write in this book.

1. List three advantages of using commercial mixes.
2. List three different types of fats used in preparing food.
3. List three different types of sugar used in preparing food products.
4. List three different types of cookies.

Fill in the blank in each sentence with the *best* word or words to complete the statement.

1. The chief function of sugar in the diet is to provide ___(1)___.
2. Both starches and sugars are classified as ___(2)___.
3. The principle leavener in angel food cake is air which is beaten into the ___(3)___.
4. Bread dough generally contains less liquid, sugar, and ___(4)___ than cake batter.
5. The two common methods for mixing cakes made with solid shortening are the conventional method and the ___(5)___ method.
6. The two principle methods for frying foods are panfrying and ___(6)___ frying.
7. The two qualities most generally desired in pastry are shortness and ___(7)___.

448

CHAPTER 25

Preparing energy foods

BAKER'S CHOCOLATE

Perhaps you have been wondering about the place of sugars and fats in the daily diet. Do you need fats and sugars at all? Many delicious foods such as cakes, candies, and doughnuts seem to be missing from the *Daily Food Guide.* What place do they play in your total eating program? Actually sugars and fats serve two purposes: They are enjoyable to eat, and they provide energy.

There are two important points to remember as you plan to include these foods in your menus. First, make selections from the *Daily Food Guide* for your basic nutritional needs. Then, knowing that your body can store excess energy foods as fat, eat them with a certain amount of caution. Eat energy foods for needed energy. Avoid them when they cause you to gain unwanted weight.

So many packaged energy-food mixes are available on the market today that it really isn't necessary for a cook to spend long hours in the kitchen if she doesn't want to. These commercial mixes have several advantages:

1 They may be kept for an indefinite period ready for use when needed.

Discuss the advantages and disadvantages of displaying the desserts first, as is done in many cafeterias. Is it a good idea from the standpoint of selling food? Is it a good idea from the standpoint of buying food? Why did you answer the questions as you did?

Write on the chalkboard the names of snacks which are suitable for different occasions. Consider snacks for TV time, after a game, after school, after a dance, or when friends drop by. Discuss why the snacks you choose are appropriate for each occasion.

Bulletin board IDEA
Title: *Then YOU Shall Have Some Pie*
Directions: Under the title, place magazine cutouts of three kittens and pictures of a variety of kinds of pie. Arrange the kittens wearing construction paper mittens and holding slices of pie.

Plan a basic menu for a day. Alter the menu to meet the needs of each individual family member. Let the family include:

Sarah, the mother, who needs to lose weight and is trying to cut down on the number of calories she eats.

John, the father, who has a desk job and gets a moderate amount of exercise.

Bill, a teen-age son, who is on the football team and practices regularly every day after school.

Judy, who is an active, fast-growing seven-year-old.

Distinguish between the following:

All-purpose, self-rising, cake, and bread flour
Granulated, confectioners', light brown, and dark brown sugar
Jelly and jam

Your career
Cake decorator

Duties: Decorates cakes, cookies, and sandwiches with icing or cheese mixtures for special occasions.
Where employed: Catering services, bakeries, hotels, restaurants. May be self-employed.

2 They save time and effort.
3 They make it unnecessary to keep on hand the separate ingredients that may be included in a conventional recipe.
4 Good results are assured if the directions on the package are followed carefully.
5 They make it very easy for the homemaker to add variety to her menus.

Some of the commercial mixes do not have the homemade flavor families have learned to like in their quick breads, cakes, and cookies. Also, they may be more expensive than food made from basic ingredients. For these reasons many homemakers make their own mixes. With an all-purpose mix as a base, and with the addition of other ingredients, many kinds of energy foods can be prepared quickly. (See the recipe for the Biscuit Master Mix and the chart "How to Use the Biscuit Master Mix" on pages 502 and 503.)

Types of foods

Energy food falls into three main groups: sugar, fat, and flour. These groups tend to overlap. For example, pastry is made of fat and flour, while cake is a combination of all three. The energy foods have been grouped here simply so they can be studied one at a time. Flour is considered a cereal food and is described in Chapter 24.

SUGARS AND OTHER SWEET FOODS

Sugar, as sold at the grocery store, is pure carbohydrate. It furnishes energy to the body, but nothing else. Honey, table syrups, jams and jellies, and similar sweet spreads are also largely carbohydrate. Candy, cakes, cookies, puddings, ice cream, and similar desserts are all high-carbohydrate foods. Although some contain useful nutrients, their chief function in the diet is to provide energy.

Sweet dishes are traditionally served at the end of the meal. A small amount of sweet food may occasionally be served along with the main dish as a contrast to other flavors. For example, jelly on a hot biscuit may enhance the flavor of roast beef. Generally, however, if sweet foods are eaten before the end of a meal, they tend to destroy the appetite.

FOODS THAT CONTAIN FATS

The fats used most frequently in preparing meals are butter, margarine, lard, and hydrogenated vegetable shortening. Corn oil, olive oil, and peanut oil are commonly used liquid shortenings. These fats and oils are used in preparing such foods as pies, breads, and salad dressings. They add flavor to many foods, such as bread and cooked vegetables.

Fats are also used in frying foods. Meats, eggs, and some fruits and vegetables are sometimes panfried, or sautéed. This type of frying requires a small amount of fat. Most types of food can be fried in deep fat. Foods fried by either the panfry or deep-fry method contain more fat than if prepared another way.

SNACK FOODS

The snacks that most people serve after a game or skating party are chiefly energy foods. Corn puffs, pretzels, and crackers are largely carbohydrate. Potato chips, salted nuts, and spreads and dips, because of their high fat content, are also high-energy foods.

Principles of cookery

Cakes of fine texture and delicate flavor are more delicious than coarse, strong-flavored products. Creamy candies and frostings are more appetizing than coarse, grainy ones. Tender, flaky pie crust is preferred over a tough, chewy one, as are crisply fried foods over soggy, heavy ones. Through study and experience you can gain an understanding of the functions of fats and sugars in food mixtures. This will help you achieve satisfactory results in beginning cooking projects.

SUGARS AND OTHER SWEET FOODS

Cakes and cookies are called sweet foods because they contain a large amount of sugar. However, their sugar content is proportionately far less than that of candies and frostings. Sometimes candy and frostings are termed simply *sugar cookery*.

Candies and frostings

Granulated sugar, used in most cooked frostings and candy, consists of large grainy crystals which dissolve in liquids such as water and milk. When a sugar solution is cooked and then cooled, as in making frosting or candy, the syrupy mixture hardens to a crystalline form. If the crystals are small, the frosting or candy is creamy. If the crystals are large, the frosting or candy is coarse and

COURTESY BAKER'S CHOCOLATE

Many families make special candies during holiday seasons to use for family entertaining or to give as gifts.

Make candy from a recipe that directs you to test the doneness of the candy by using the cold-water method. Use the directions given here.

1. Have ready a cupful of cold water.
2. Drop several drops of the boiling hot candy syrup into the water, removing the pan of candy from the heat while making the test.
3. Form the drops into a ball between the fingers to check for the stage desired.

Soft-ball stage (234° F. to 238° F.): The drops just barely form a ball but will fall apart when removed from the water.

Medium-ball stage (238° F. to 245° F.): The drops form a firm ball that does not keep its shape out of the water.

Firm-ball stage (245° F. to 250° F.): The drops form a firm ball that keeps its shape when removed from the water.

Hard-ball stage (250° F. to 265° F.): The drops form a hard ball that makes a sound when dropped on a plate.

Hard-crack stage (300° F. to 310° F.): The drops separate into hard and brittle threads.

Discuss the reasons why your ability to follow the steps discussed below will help you make cakes successfully. Select a tested recipe. Have ingredients at room temperature.

Use the right kind and size of cake pan or pans.

Prepare the cake pan according to the directions given in the recipe.

Use the oven temperature given in the recipe.

Be sure the oven racks are adjusted correctly and are level.

Measure and combine all ingredients carefully.

Alternate placement of pans in the oven so that no pan is directly over another pan.

Watch for signs of doneness: Butter cakes shrink from sides of pan. If done, all cakes spring back into place when touched with the finger.

Place pan on cooling rack for 5 to 10 minutes before removing cake.

For angel food and sponge cakes: Handle the batter gently so as to keep the air in it, since air is the leavener. Allow the cake to remain in the inverted pan for 1 hour after removing from the oven.

grainy. The aim of sugar cookery is to obtain a creamy product.

Four general procedures will help you make creamy products:

1. Add corn syrup, egg whites, marshmallows, or cream of tartar to the mixture before cooking.
2. Cover the pan to help prevent the formation of crystals on the sides of the pan during cooking. Before and after cooking, wipe away any sugar crystals which are left sticking to the sides of the pan.
3. Cook the syrup to exactly the right stage, or temperature. This means following the directions of the recipe exactly.
4. Cool the syrup slowly without stirring until it has cooled.

Cakes

Cakes are very popular as desserts for family meals, as between-meal snacks, and as refreshments for social occasions. Cakes are usually divided into two groups: those which contain some form of shortening and those which contain none. Most cakes are leavened, or made light, with such chemicals as soda and baking powder. However, chiffon and angel cakes are leavened mainly by the air which can be beaten into egg whites.

Many good cake mixes are available in the market. You may enjoy using them because of their time- and energy-saving qualities. Many cooks prefer to make cakes from flour and the other basic ingredients. Since cakes are a leavened flour mixture, many of the principles which apply to bread making also apply to cakes. However, since cake mixtures usually contain more sugar and eggs than bread doughs, these ingredients suggest a different method of preparation than that used for most breads.

Cakes with shortening may be made with a solid shortening, such as butter, margarine, lard, or hydrogenated vegetable shortening, or they may be made with a liquid shortening. There are two general methods for mixing cakes made with solid shortening: the *conventional method* and the *one-bowl method*. Chiffon cakes, made with liquid shortening, are mixed by a third method.

In the conventional method the shortening is creamed with the sugar, and then the eggs or egg yolks are added. Next the liquid and mixed dry ingredients are added alternately. The egg whites, if beaten separately from the yolks, are added last.

In the one-bowl method the ingredients are combined in one bowl and stirred until mixed. This is the method called for in commercial cake mixes. (See the recipe for Quick-mix Gold Cake, page 508.)

Chiffon cakes are made by combining the oil, egg yolks, and flavorings; adding the dry ingredients;

and folding in the beaten egg whites. (See the recipe for Lemon Chiffon Cake, page 508.)

Cakes without shortening, such as angel food and sponge cakes, are leavened mainly by the air beaten into the mixture. The egg whites are beaten thoroughly, and then the egg yolks, if used, are folded in. Finally, the sifted dry ingredients are folded in gently to prevent the escape of air from the egg-white mixture.

Cookies

Cookies are popular throughout the world. Each country may have its national favorites. These versatile sweets may be served as lunch-box or picnic desserts. They are popular as between-meal snacks and as refreshments at teas and other parties. Boxes of fancy cookies are frequently given as gifts for special holidays. Cookies may be a useful source of nutrients or simply an energy food, depending upon the ingredients used.

A cookie recipe may be much like a cake recipe, with some changes in the proportions of the ingredients. Cookies are sometimes separated into seven types, according to content and the way the dough is shaped for baking. (See recipes for Peanut Butter Cookies, Fruit Blossom Cookies, and Chocolate Pinwheels on pages 505–507.)

Drop cookies have a soft consistency. They are dropped from a spoon onto a baking sheet, about 2 inches apart. Sometimes they are flattened, sometimes not. They usually spread and flatten as they bake.

Pressed cookies are made from a dough soft enough to pass through the openings in a cookie press and drop onto a baking sheet in fancy shapes.

Refrigerator cookies are made from a soft dough that is rich in shortening and sugar. The dough is

COURTESY ALUMINUM ASSOCIATION

Chiffon, sponge, and angel cakes (above) are leavened mainly by the air which is beaten into egg whites, while cakes made from mixes or conventional recipes (below) are usually leavened with baking powder.

Discuss the differences between frostings and icings. From the descriptions given below, determine how they are alike and how they are different.

Frostings

Frostings are used on cakes only. They are thicker than icings and may be cooked or uncooked.

Butter frostings are uncooked and are made of butter, confectioners' sugar, liquids, and flavorings.

Cooked frostings are mixtures of sugar and liquid, cooked like candy. Examples are brown-sugar frosting and chocolate fudge frosting.

Icings

Icings are used on cakes, breads, coffee cakes, and sweet rolls. They are thinner than frostings.

Fluffy icings are cooked mixtures of sugar, corn syrup, or other syrup, water, and unbeaten raw egg whites.

Thin icings are uncooked mixtures of confectioners' sugar and liquid, of a consistency that spreads easily. A very thin icing may be poured onto a pastry.

List the precautions that should be observed in cooking a sugar syrup to prevent crystallization during cooking. Give a reason for each.

Cookies of a wide variety of shapes, flavors, and ingredients are used at many types of social get-togethers throughout the year.

COURTESY BAKER'S CHOCOLATE

Your career
Baker

Duties: Bakes breads, rolls, hot breads, and muffins. Regulates temperature of ovens, sets and kneads the dough, and is responsible for the operation of the bakery department.
Where employed: Bakeries, dining rooms, and schools.

shaped into rolls or blocks, which are chilled in the refrigerator for several hours. Slices are then cut from the roll and placed on a baking sheet for baking.

Bar cookies are baked as a sheet in a shallow pan, cooled, and cut into squares or bars.

Molded cookies are made by forming the dough into small balls which are flattened with a fork or other utensil to form designs on top.

Rolled cookies are made from a stiff dough. The dough is rolled on a lightly floured board, cut into circles, squares, or fancy shapes, and baked. The cookies may be decorated before or after baking.

Rolled cookies may be cut into interesting shapes such as hearts, stars, bells, trees, turkeys, and bunnies, according to the season. When frosted with white or colored icing, the plain rolled cookie may carry out the theme of a party.

Pinwheel cookies are especially attractive. They are made by placing a portion of thinly rolled cookie dough on top of another portion of cookie dough of a contrasting color—for example, chocolate dough on top of plain white dough. The two portions of dough are rolled together and placed in the refrigerator to chill. Later the roll is cut into thin slices and baked.

Filled cookies are layer cookies. Each cookie is made from two pieces of thinly rolled cookie dough. Jelly, jam, cooked fruit, or other filling is placed between the two pieces of dough. Then the edges of the dough are pressed, or sealed, together. Cookies made with fruit fillings add valuable nutrients to snacks.

FOODS THAT CONTAIN FATS

Fats are added to foods to improve the flavor or to control the texture. Satisfactory results can depend on the type of fat used and the way in which the food is prepared. Be sure the fat is fresh. Fats, especially butter, become *rancid* with age. No matter how carefully the food is prepared, rancid fat will give it a disagreeable flavor.

The texture of many baked foods depends in part on when the shortening is added to the mixture and how it is incorporated. For example, pie crust has a tender texture because shortening is mixed with flour *before* a liquid is added. Pancakes have quite a different texture because shortening is added *after* the flour and liquid have been combined. Recipes specify the method which will give the desired result for a given product.

Making pie crust

Pies have worldwide appeal. They taste good and satisfy hunger. They can add valuable nutrients to the meal, depending upon the pie filling. Most of the popular dessert pies have either fruit fillings or fillings made of some form of egg and milk mixture. Pastry crusts are sometimes used with meat, egg, or cheese mixtures to make main dish casseroles.

Pastry for pies is made by mixing flour and fat together before adding liquid. This covering of the flour particles with fat helps prevent the formation of gluten when liquid is stirred into the flour mixture. Thus, a short, tender pie crust can be produced. Packaged mixes and already prepared pastry dough are available. Frozen shells are also available. However, they may be more expensive or less desirable than homemade products.

There are several good ways to make pastry. The *conventional method*, or *cold-water method*, produces a very flaky crust. However, dough made in this manner is sometimes hard for a beginning cook to handle. The *hot-water method*, the *paste method*, and the *oil method* are easier to master. All of these methods produce satisfactory pies and pastries. (See the recipes for Pie Crust, pages 510 and 511.)

Keep cookies in suitable containers to retain freshness.
Follow these directions:
Store crisp cookies and soft cookies in separate containers. They will keep for as long as a week, and longer if stored in a refrigerator.
Freeze cookies in air-tight containers or wrappers.
If the cookies become soft on storing, place them on an ungreased baking sheet in a slow oven for a few minutes to restore crispness.

While many pies are both delicious and nutritious, the quality of a pie is generally determined by the tenderness of its crust.

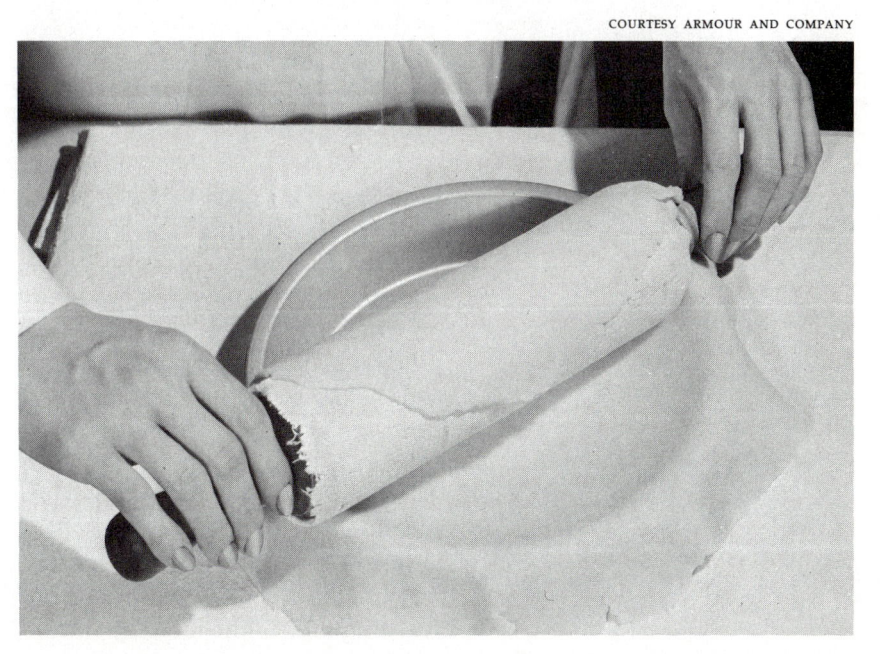

COURTESY ARMOUR AND COMPANY

◆◇◆ Check foods for fat content. For example, place mashed, hard-cooked egg yolk and chopped celery on pieces of notebook paper. Place each in the sunlight or heat them over a warm light bulb for a few minutes. Remove the foods and hold the papers up to the light. Any food which contains fat will leave a grease spot on the paper.

Make an exhibit of available fats and oils. Use several of them in the preparation of pie crusts. Use the recipes on pages 510 and 511. Compare the results as to taste, appearance, and cost.

Let each laboratory group make an original party dip. Have a tasting party. Judge the dips as to taste, cost, and nutritive value.

COURTESY ALUMINUM ASSOCIATION

Doughnuts, while made mostly of flour, are considered fat-rich foods because of the fat they absorb during the deep-fat-frying process.

Using fats and oils in frying

Well-fried foods are crisp but not hard. Some fats, particularly butter, burn easily. These burned, or decomposed, fats give a bad flavor to foods fried in them. If the frying fat is too hot, the outer portion of the food may overcook or burn, while the inner portion is undercooked. If the fat is not hot enough, the food tends to soak up the fat, making it soggy, greasy, and generally unappetizing.

Panfrying requires a heavy, flat-bottomed skillet, or frying pan. Choose a pan that is large enough to hold the pieces of food without crowding them. The fat used should be one that will not smoke or brown at low temperatures. (See recipes for Fried Eggs and Beef Stew, pages 487 and 484.)

Deep-fat frying is a popular method for preparing French-fried potatoes, doughnuts, fritters, and croquettes. This method of frying is quick and easy. However, accidents can occur unless a degree of care is taken during the cooking process. The following precautions will help avoid spills, burns, and kitchen fires:

1 Fill the pan to no more than one-third of its capacity.
2 To prevent spattering, dry the food thoroughly before putting it into the fat.
3 Use kitchen tongs to turn food or to remove it from the hot fat.
4 Watch carefully to prevent the fat from overheating or catching fire.
5 If a kitchen ventilation fan is available, use it.

SERVING SNACK FOODS

Snack foods are easy to serve, but they are more attractive and appetizing when served on colorful plates, in baskets, or in bowls than when served directly from packages. Foods like potato chips and pretzels are intended to be crisp and crunchy. The contents of fresh packages is usually acceptable. Occasionally, on opening a package, you may find its contents wilted and soggy. If this happens, spread the food in a shallow pan and place it in a warm oven for a few minutes. Usually this will freshen any type of pretzel or chip, even those which have been left in an open package.

The attractive appearance and taste qualities of spreads and dips depend on their temperature and consistency. Most of these mixtures are served cold, so you may wish to keep them in the refrigerator until time to serve them. Spreads should be firm but soft enough to spread easily. Dips are much softer than spreads. Avoid making dips so thin that they drip from chips or vegetables.

Many appetizing spreads and dips can be bought in ready-to-serve form. If you make your own, you may be able to serve special flavor combinations which are different from commercial varieties. Be sure that these spreads and dips are carefully mixed, so that their consistency and flavor are the same throughout the mixture. Prepare them ahead of serving time so that the flavors have time to blend.

Recipes for spreads and dips are very similar. By adding more moisture to a favorite spread, you can often turn it into an appetizing dip. Or by adding more cheese, peanut butter, or meat to a dip, you may develop a new, appetizing spread. (See the recipes for Peanut Butter Spread and Bacon Spread, page 512).

COURTESY BAKER'S COCONUT

Colorful cakes for use in celebrating the athletic season can be made by preparing a cake mix, cutting it to shape, and icing it for the occasion.

Make a heart-shaped cake for Valentine's Day. Use one square cake pan and one round cake pan. Check to see that both pans measure the same across the center. After cooling, cut the round cake in half and arrange as shown below.

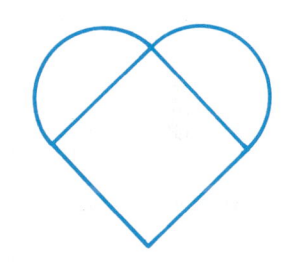

Frost and decorate the cake in an original fashion.

Tortilla-wrapped weiners and chili can be combined for a hot party snack after a ball game or a winter skating party.

COURTESY RICE COUNCIL

25 CHAPTER POSTTEST

Match the *examples of cookies* given in List A with the *types of cookies* given in List B. Use a cookie type from List B only once. *Do not* write in this book.

List A: **Examples of cookies**

A Cookies cut into shapes with a cookie cutter
B Tollhouse cookies
C Fig Newtons
D Brownies
E Balls of cookie dough which are flattened with a fork or glass

List B: **Types of cookies**

1 Bar
2 Drop
3 Filled
4 Molded
5 Rolled

Number from 1 to 20 on a piece of paper. Beside each number indicate if the corresponding statement is true or false.

1 The three main groups of high-energy foods are sugar, flour, and fat.
2 An appetizer served at the beginning of a meal should be sweet in flavor.
3 There are both animal and vegetable fats which can be used in preparing foods.
4 Granulated sugar is a good source of essential minerals.
5 A very fine powdery sugar used in making icings is confectioners' sugar.
6 Icings are thinner than frostings.
7 In sugar cookery the pan should be covered.
8 A sugar syrup should be stirred constantly while cooling.
9 In the conventional method of making a cake, the shortening and sugar are creamed together before the eggs are added.
10 Sponge cakes contain fat.
11 Chiffon cakes contain fat.
12 Angel food cakes contain baking powder.
13 Remove cakes from their baking pans immediately after removing them from the oven.
14 Butter burns at a comparatively low temperature.
15 In making pie crust by the conventional method, the fat is cut into the flour.
16 The amount of fat absorbed by a fried food is related to the temperature of the fat in which the food is fried.
17 When deep-fat frying, dry the food before putting it into the hot fat.
18 In deep-fat frying, fill the cooking utensil no more than one-third full.
19 The ingredients for dips are correctly mixed just before serving them.
20 Humid weather may affect the crispness of crackers.

26 CHAPTER PRETEST

Fill in the blank in each sentence with the *best* word or words to complete the statement. *Do not* write in this book.

1 Because knives, forks, spoons, and serving pieces are not necessarily made of silver, they are preferably called ___(1)___.
2 The most expensive and durable kind of dinnerware is ___(2)___.
3 When you are through eating soup which has been served in a cup, you leave the spoon on the ___(3)___.
4 Bread is buttered, a small piece at a time, with either a knife or a(an) ___(4)___.
5 Corn chips, pretzels, carrot sticks, radishes, olives, and corn on the cob are usually eaten as ___(5)___ foods.
6 The type of table service where the food is placed on a serving table and guests help themselves is called ___(6)___ service.
7 A reception is more formal than a tea and includes a(an) ___(7)___ where guests may meet the host, hostess, and special guests.
8 When dining at someone else's home, do not begin to eat until the ___(8)___ has begun.
9 When washing dishes by hand, wash the ___(9)___ first.
10 When washing dishes in an automatic dishwasher, place bowls so that their openings are toward the ___(10)___ of the machine.

CHAPTER 26

Enjoying food with family and friends

An appetizing, well-prepared meal can look even more inviting if it is attractively served. Because an attractive table improves the atmosphere for dining, the way the table is set and the way food is served make a real difference in mealtime enjoyment. Table manners and rules for table setting are intended to make dining relaxing and comfortable. By learning and following a few simple rules, you can enjoy your meals and contribute to the happiness of others.

A table setting provides the background for a meal. You probably have helped many times with setting the table for family meals. Simple arrangements of flowers or greenery, either fresh or permanent, provide a special touch for an ordinary table. A freshly baked cake placed as an attraction in the center of the table can delight the youngest family member as well as the oldest. You can express your own creativity in simple tasks such as table setting.

Choosing and using tableware

A table can be attractive whether set with the most expensive or the

Choose pictures of flatware, dinnerware, and glassware that look well together. Defend your selections. Suggest a tablecloth or other table covering which would go well with your choices.

Distinguish between the following kinds of dinnerware:
    Chinaware
    Earthenware
    Pottery
    Plastic
List the advantages and disadvantages of each.

Distinguish between the following kinds of flatware:
    Stainless steel
    Silver plate
    Sterling silver
List the advantages and disadvantages of each.

Give the advantages and disadvantages of linen, cotton, and plastic tablecloths and place mats. What other types of materials are used? What are their advantages and disadvantages?

BASIC STEPS IN TABLE SETTING

Set a table to fit the menu you are serving. Napkins can be placed either at the left of the forks or in the center of the dinner plates.

Location of knife and spoons

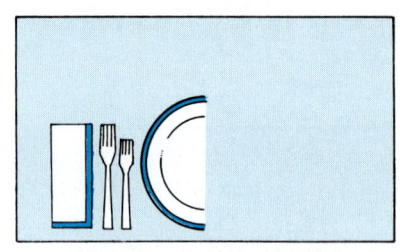

Location of napkin and forks

Location of bread-and-butter plate

Location of salad plate

Location of salad plate with bread-and-butter plate

Location of drinking glasses

Location of cup and saucer

simplest tableware. The idea that each family must have sterling silver, crystal, and china in order to have a complete home is out of date. Most of today's young families are aware that people are more important than things. The casual living they enjoy allows them to use any tableware they happen to have. Through their choice of colors, shapes, and textures, they produce table settings which show their interest in beauty. Cost becomes relatively unimportant.

SETTING THE TABLE
A few simple rules for table setting serve as a guide for most occasions. Common practices for table setting and food service have developed because they make sense. Tableware includes the china, glassware, flatware, table coverings, and table decorations. These are all placed on the table to make the meal easy to serve and easy to eat.

Table coverings
A covering on the dining table not only looks attractive but helps to protect the table surface. It adds color, keeps the tabletop clean, and adds to the picture you are trying to create.

Coverings are made in a wide variety of materials. Many modern materials used for tablecloths or mats can be wiped clean with a damp cloth. They require no laundering. Other cloths come in permanent press or other fabrics that do not need to be ironed after laundering. Since modern covers are so easy to keep clean, there is really no need to use table covers that are soiled or spotted.

A place mat is usually about 16 to 18 inches long and about 12 to 14 inches wide. When used on the table, the rectangular mat is placed so that one long edge is even with the table edge. A round mat can be placed close to the table edge or allowed to hang over just a little. Set the mats an equal distance apart and at the same distance from the table edge. This creates a neat and pleasing effect.

A cloth which allows the table edge to show is unsightly and may prove awkward when dishes are moved during a meal. One that hangs down too far gets in the way when people sit at the table. A full-size cloth should hang about 4 to 6 inches over the sides and ends of the table.

Napkins
Napkins are used to keep your hands and face clean while eating and to protect your lap from spilled food. To tuck a napkin under the chin suggests that a person may not be sure of his dining habits. For some special foods, such as spaghetti and lobster, your hostess may provide a bib. But bibs are usually reserved for children. Napkins are made of different fabrics and in

Set several covers with different types and patterns of flatware, dinnerware, glassware, and table covers. For example, place together dainty flowered dinnerware, very modern-looking stainless steel flatware, and glasses which are decorated with cartoon characters. Arrange them together on a strawlike place mat. Decide why certain choices do and do not go well together. Then from the items which are available, set a cover which is pleasing. Prepare a set of guidelines to use in combining table appointments effectively.

Make simple place mats. Use string dishcloths, burlap, Pellon, oil cloth, or shelving paper. Or make place mats by pressing leaves between two sheets of waxed paper. Scallop the edges.

Use a flannel board with construction paper cutouts to represent plates, knives, forks, spoons, and glasses. Set the table for a variety of breakfast, lunch, and dinner menus. Discuss your arrangements and improve on them if necessary.

Pretend that you know the life-style you will live when you are an adult. Find pictures of tableware you will choose.

Compile a notebook with pictures of various table settings. Write by each picture the kind of meal or occasion for which each table setting is appropriate.

Choose between chinaware, earthenware, pottery, or plastic for a given situation. Defend your choice.

different sizes. They may match or contrast with the table covering. For everyday meals, paper napkins are often used because they can be discarded after the meal.

The size of a napkin varies with the occasion. Cloth napkins are usually preferred at a formal tea party. Because they are used only for the lips and finger tips, they are quite small, usually 12 by 12 inches. For family breakfasts, lunches, or dinners, larger napkins about 17 by 17 inches give more protection. For formal dinners or banquets, napkins are 24 inches square. While napkins of a certain size may be customary for certain occasions, a family is not required to have a napkin wardrobe to entertain successfully.

In setting a table, the folded cloth or paper napkin is usually placed with the open edge nearest the left side of the fork, 1 inch from the edge of the table. For formal service the napkin may be placed on the service plate or on the tablecloth where the plate will be set when the meal begins.

Flatware

The knives, forks, spoons, and serving pieces used at the table are known as *flatware.* Flatware can be made of sterling or plated silver and is often called silverware. Other metals used for flatware are stainless steel and a mixture of metals that looks like gold. Plastic flatware is popular and practical for outdoor meals, picnics, and other informal occasions. Families place different values on the importance of flatware. Some invest a good deal of money in it. Others may use an assortment of knives, forks, and spoons rather than trying to keep matched sets, particularly while their children are young and pieces of flatware may be lost or misplaced.

The kind of flatware your family uses is determined by the amount of money they decide to spend for such things, the kinds of meals they serve, and the kinds of dishes they

Today's informal living allows for the use of paper napkins, cups, and dishes, and stainless steel flatware when other equipment is not available or when time is limited.

COURTESY FARLEY MANNING ASSOCIATES, INC.

use. So long as it is clean and properly placed, any flatware can add to the attractiveness of the table. (See chart on page 460.)

Dinnerware

The plates, cups, saucers, bowls, and dishes used to serve meals are called *dinnerware.* The kind and amount of dinnerware each family owns vary according to personal taste and budget. Family size, family customs, the amount of entertaining to be done, and the amount of money to be spent all reflect dinnerware choices.

Earthenware and *pottery* are made of clay. They are rather thick and heavy, but usually colorful and gay. Earthenware, sometimes called semiporcelain, is slightly more delicate than pottery and usually more expensive. Both kinds of dinnerware are suitable for casual and informal occasions. Some may be used in more formal settings.

Chinaware, or porcelain, is made of very fine white clay. It has been heated to an extremely high temperature in a special oven called a kiln. This process makes it more durable than earthenware. The extra care required to manufacture china explains why it costs more than earthenware.

In addition to earthenware, pottery, and chinaware, *plastic dinnerware* is popular because it is lightweight and practically unbreakable. A good grade of plastic withstands the heat of dishwashing and is resistant to scratches if handled with care. Plastic is available in many styles and colors at different prices. Some families who can afford more than one set of dishes keep china for special occasions and use plastic or pottery for everyday.

Attractive combinations of dinnerware add interest to any meal. Whether you select earthenware, chinaware, plastic dinnerware, or some of each, dinnerware can be placed on the table in a way to make the table look attractive.

When selecting dinnerware, try to imagine how it will look with food served on it. Odd colors or highly decorated pieces often fail to harmonize with food colors. The effect may be very unappetizing. For example, can you picture in your mind steak, spinach, and beets on a plain black plate?

Glassware

The goblets, tumblers, and glass dishes used on the table are referred to as *glassware.* Fine glassware is called crystal. Even inexpensive glassware can add sparkle to a table setting. Attractive break-resistant plastic glasses are made to use with plastic or earthenware dishes.

Glassware in many sizes, shapes, and colors is available. When you choose glassware, consider the flatware and dinnerware with which it will be used. Fine crystal looks well with china and silver, while heavy,

Suggest items that can be used for centerpieces.
Try to think of several usable items which are on hand in your home or school. The list below may give you ideas.
Candles in floral rings
Flowers
Plants
Figurines and porcelain objects
Fruits and vegetables
Shells and driftwood
Dried flower arrangements
Seasonal materials:
    Christmas evergreens or balls
    Thanksgiving turkeys or horns of plenty
    Easter eggs, hats, or umbrellas

Discuss reasons why the following guidelines are helpful when using candles.
Use enough candles to light the table sufficiently unless they are supplemented by electric lights.
Place the candles so they do not shine in the eyes of the diners.
Burn the wicks slightly before displaying the candles.

Visit stores that sell flatware, dinnerware, and glassware. Compare varieties of each for cost. What are the reasons for these cost differences?

Write the word CENTERPIECE on the chalkboard arranging the letters in a vertical line. Beside each letter write a word or words which might describe a desirable table centerpiece. For example:

C Colorful, cheerful, casual

E Enjoyable, economical

N Noticeable, neat

T

E

R

P

I

E

C

E

Without spending any money, make an appropriate centerpiece for a gift or for a family surprise. Autumn leaves, holiday materials, wild flowers, or fruit may be used.

Make new candles from old candle stubs by melting them and pouring the liquid into waxed cartons. Colored crayons can be melted and mixed with paraffin to make candles. Make a colorful flower- or evergreen-ring to complete the arrangement.

When you place flatware

1. Place each knife, fork, and spoon 1 inch from the edge of the table.
2. If the meal requires the use of more than one knife, or fork, or spoon per person, arrange the pieces so that the piece to be used first is placed farthest from the plate.
3. Place knives and spoons at the right of the plate.
4. Place the knife next to the plate, with the cutting edge toward the plate.
5. Place the forks at the left of the plate, with the tines, or prongs, turned up.
6. Place the forks or spoons for dessert when that course is brought to the table.
7. Place the fork at the right if it is the only flatware to be used during the meal. If a spoon is also used, place the fork at the left and the spoon at the right of the plate.
8. A cocktail fork may be placed to the right of the spoons or across the cocktail plate. A butter spreader or butter knife is placed across the top of the bread-and-butter plate at right angles to the other flatware with the cutting edge toward the plate. It may also be placed on the rim of the bread-and-butter plate parallel to the other flatware.

When you place dinnerware

1. The plates should be set at the center of each place, 1 inch from the edge of the table.
2. Place the cup and saucer at the right of the spoons, with the handle of the cup turned to the right.
3. Place the salad plate at the left of the dinner plate, outside the forks.
4. Place the bread-and-butter plate at the tip of the forks.

When you place glassware

1. Place the water glass at the tip of the dinner knife.
2. Place the milk or juice glass slightly to the right of the water glass.

casual-looking glassware seems to fit better with pottery or plastic dinnerware.

Accessory items

Among the additional items useful in serving a complete meal are serving dishes, platters, a salt-and-pepper set, a sugar bowl, a cream pitcher, bowls for gravy and other accessory foods, a bread dish or tray, a butter knife, a gravy ladle, a sugar shell, a pickle fork, and serving spoons. Flatware is placed on the table to the right of the dish for which it is intended. Once used, serving pieces should stay with the appropriate dish or platter.

The centerpiece

One way to add a bright touch of color to the table is by using a *centerpiece.* Although called a centerpiece, it may be placed anywhere on the table.

Fresh flowers from a florist or your own yard, vegetables, fruits, wild flowers, or weeds can be used as a centerpiece. When flowers are too expensive or are not available, artificial flowers of plastic, cloth, or paper can add color and interest to the table. Bowls, vases, and candlesticks in many styles are also popular table decorations.

It is rather annoying when you must look over or through a centerpiece to see and talk with people on the other side of the table. Therefore, you'll want to keep table centerpieces low enough to see over. Also, some kinds of flowers, such as gardenias or magnolias, have strong odors. Avoid using such flowers at mealtime since their fragrance may interfere with the aroma of good food.

Planning and arranging a centerpiece gives you a chance to be creative with a wide variety of mate-

Suggest menus and write them on the chalkboard. Arrange a table setting which is appropriate for each menu. Let the class discuss each menu, the way it is written, and the table setting arrangement which you have made.

A bright relish tray made of fresh vegetables can serve as an edible centerpiece at a teen-age party.

COURTESY KRAFT KITCHENS

465

◉ Discuss reasons why the following guidelines are effective when people are being seated at a table.

Allow room enough for convenient service and for pulling out chairs easily.

Place the hostess at one end of the table, usually near the kitchen.

Place the host at the opposite end of the table.

If the situation allows, arrange the seating so that each guest can talk with both men and women.

If the guest of honor is a man, place him at the right of the hostess.

If the guest of honor is a woman, place her at the right of the host.

Seat each person from the left side of the chair.

After the hostess sits down, let each boy seat the girl on his right. In doing so, he pulls the chair back, waits for her to get in front of it, and pushes the chair under her as she sits down.

Seat boys after girls have taken their places.

Practice seating yourself and rising from a dinner table. If there are boys in the class, let them practice helping the girls with their chairs.

rials. Table decorations can be formal or informal. They are successful when they are both attractive and in keeping with the meal.

Table manners

Your consideration for other people can be shown by your manners. Since eating is such a close-range activity, others notice your table manners very quickly. Table manners tell whether or not you are interested in the happiness of others.

To some people good table manners are to be put on when company comes and removed when they leave. However, good manners should be automatic, and they are more effective if used daily. Slouching at the table, grabbing food, talking loudly, eating noisily, speaking when your mouth is full, quarreling at the table—any of these unattractive actions may be unconsciously performed in the presence of others if they are a part of your day-to-day table manners. Careless habits spoil dining pleasure for others, while good habits increase mealtime happiness.

GETTING READY FOR THE MEAL

As a matter of courtesy, everyone in the family should be ready a few minutes before a meal is served. This makes it possible for everyone to be seated at once and for food to be served when at its best.

Your appearance can affect the happiness of a meal. When you come to the table, be sure that your hands and face are clean and that your hair is neat. If you have been doing heavy or dirty work, come to the table in fresh clothes. An untidy person shows lack of respect for others at the table.

Your place at the table

Unless you have a regular place, as you probably do at home, pause at the table until the hostess tells you where to sit. Stand behind your chair until each person has been placed and the hostess, or your mother, tells you to sit down. It is proper for a boy to help seat the girl who is at his right. Confusion is prevented if everyone is seated from the left side of the chair. This is especially important if the room is small or crowded or if chairs are close together.

At home or in public, a boy helps his mother with her chair. This is one way to show respect, kindness, and appreciation. It also gives him practice so that he can be at ease when helping a guest. Of course, if he is assigned to help another person with her chair, he may assume that his father or another man is available to help his mother.

To help with a chair, a boy pulls the chair back, then pushes it forward as the girl sits down. At the end of the meal he can help her by standing behind her chair and pulling it slowly back as she rises and steps to the side. If no boys or men are present, a girl may help an older woman with her chair.

YOUR CONTRIBUTION TO MEALTIME CONVERSATION
After you are seated, sit quietly in your chair with both feet on the floor. Keep your hands in your lap. If grace is offered, wait courteously until the prayer is over. Do not start to eat until the hostess has started.

During the meal enter into the table conversation. Mealtime should be a relaxed time. Family arguments or unpleasant subjects can be saved for another time. Unpleasant table talk can ruin a meal and actually upset a person's digestion.

If you can't think of anything pleasant or interesting to say, eat quietly and let others talk. If you are a guest in someone's home, you'll be surprised how welcome a nod or smile can be at the right time. After all, good conversation requires a good listener, too.

USING TABLE EQUIPMENT
A table set with more flatware than you ordinarily use can make you feel awkward. However, the use of table equipment is based on common sense. If you follow your hostess' example, you will act in a way which is acceptable. At home, or at the home of close friends, ask for the directions you may need.

Using the napkin
Since the napkin is folded with the open edge facing the fork, it is easily picked up with your left hand, partially unfolded, and placed on your lap. If the napkin has been left free, with no flatware lying on it, it may easily be picked up without disturbing the other things on the table. Use a patting or blotting motion with the napkin when removing food from your mouth or chin. Great wipes or swabbing motions are to be avoided.

Passing food
When passing food from one person to another, pass it to your right. The person on your right can then accept the dish in his left hand. His right hand is free to lift food onto his plate. If you are serving from a standing position, offer the food from the person's left so that he can take it comfortably with his right hand.

Using flatware
You will gain assurance in eating if you learn to know and practice the correct use of a knife, fork, spoon, and other special pieces of flatware. The use of each is described here.

The knife is used to cut pieces of food on the plate and, if there is no butter spreader, to spread butter, cheese, or jelly on bread. To use the knife for cutting, hold it in your right hand with the handle resting in your palm and with your thumb

Discuss why the following guidelines have developed for serving family and guest meals.
1 Place and remove plates from the left of the person being served. Hold the plate in your left hand. If you are carrying two plates, place first the one in your left hand, then move the other plate to your left hand, and place it before the next person.
2 Place and remove beverages from the right, with your right hand. Avoid filling cups or glasses too full.
3 Refill glasses or cups from the right, leaving them in position on the table.
4 Avoid touching surfaces of plates and rims of glasses. Handle silverware by the handles.
5 Offer food to the guest from his left, holding it low enough so that he can serve himself with his right hand.
6 Avoid reaching in front of a guest when serving or removing dishes.
7 When a course is finished, remove all dishes used in that course.
8 Avoid stacking dishes which are removed while guests are seated at the table.

Prepare skits showing what to do when some of the following situations occur. First show common errors and then show acceptable table manners.
1. A fork is dropped on the floor.
2. You have a bone or seed in your mouth.
3. Something is passed which you do not like.
4. You would like a serving of a food that is located across the table.

Fondue parties are simple parties in which a melted fondue is the central attraction in the meal.

COURTESY MAZOLA CORN OIL

and last three fingers steadying it. Place your forefinger on the back of the blade as you cut. When the knife is not in use for cutting or spreading, lay it across the back of your plate with the cutting edge toward you. Since *used* flatware should not touch the table, avoid accidents caused by resting the tip of your knife or fork on the edge of the plate.

The fork is used, with tines up, to carry solid food to the mouth. Food which is extremely soft or watery, however, requires a spoon. You may use the side of a fork to cut soft food, such as vegetables, cake, or pie.

The fork also holds in place food being cut with a knife. In this case it is held in the left hand with tines down. Brace it with your forefinger near the bottom of the handle. After cutting a bite or two of food and placing the knife across the plate, transfer the fork to the right hand with tines up and use it to carry the food to your mouth. To cut the next bite, change the fork back to the left hand and again pick up the knife with the right hand. In some countries the custom is to keep the fork in the left hand and the knife in the right throughout the meal.

Use a salad fork with the tines up to carry food to the mouth. If the salad requires cutting, try to cut it with the side of the salad fork. If the fork is ineffective, use your table knife as you would to cut food on the dinner plate. If there is no salad fork, a dinner fork is permissible.

The spoon is used for dipping and carrying soft or liquid food to the mouth. Hold the spoon in your right hand much as you would hold a pencil. Take only as much food onto the spoon as you will put into your mouth in a single bite. Eat from the side of the spoon. Between bites or after the food has been eaten, place the spoon on the saucer or plate that is under the bowl or cup. Leaving the spoon in a bowl or cup may cause it to tip. In eating soup or other liquid foods, dip the spoon into the soup with the spoon bowl tipped *away* from you—not toward you. Allow the spoon to drip back into the bowl before moving the spoon to your mouth.

Use your spoon for stirring or for testing beverages. Remove the spoon from the beverage before starting to drink. Place it on the saucer or service plate. This position looks better and helps prevent accidents.

The butter spreader is used to butter the bread. You may use the butter knife at your place or your dinner knife as a butter spreader. The butter knife that is passed with the butter is not intended for this purpose. It is used to cut off a portion of butter and to place the portion on your plate.

When you eat bread, break off a moderate-size piece with your fingers. Hold it on the edge of the bread-and-butter plate or the dinner plate, and spread butter on it with the butter spreader. Buttering a slice of bread held in the palm of the hand looks awkward and may soil your hand.

Flatware or fingers?
Particularly when eating away from home, you may find yourself wondering which piece of flatware should be used for a particular food. In general, use a knife to cut and spread. Use a fork for anything that can be picked up with a fork—that is, anything that is not too liquid. Use a spoon for soft, liquid foods. Use a fork or spoon, not your fingers, for all juicy, greasy, or sticky foods.

Some foods are awkward to eat, and it is a good idea to find out how to eat them correctly. Foods such as fried chicken may be eaten with the fingers if your hostess is eating in this manner. Such foods as corn on the cob, potato chips, crisp bacon, grapes and whole radishes are definitely finger foods. Use your napkin to clean your fingers after handling these foods.

WHEN THE MEAL IS FINISHED
When you have finished eating, place the knife and fork across the center of your plate. This lets your

COURTESY FARLEY MANNING ASSOCIATES, INC.

Many hostesses plan party foods which can be eaten with the fingers.

Decide which of the lists below would include suitable topics for table conversation. Why is one list suitable while the other is not?
LIST A
Activities of the day
News items
Anecdotes and stories
Hobbies
LIST B
Operations and medical or dental experiences
Controversial subjects
Unpleasant happenings
Illness and death

Suggest ways to make mealtime at home more enjoyable. Plan ways in which the breakfast period can be made pleasant for all family members.

Tell about a situation when a carefully prepared meal was ruined because of the table conversation. Discuss the circumstances and what might have been done to improve the situation.

Role-play family situations to show how problems of disruption and tension can be caused during mealtime by unpleasant table conversation, arguments, unexpected or long telephone calls, or discipline problems.

Discuss reasons why the following actions are considered acceptable table manners.

- Sitting comfortably straight with your feet on the floor, far enough back in your chair so that your body does not touch the table, but not so far from the table that you are likely to drop food
- Leaving the flatware alone unless you are using it in eating
- Placing all used flatware on the plate rather than the table
- Placing the fork with the tines up and the knife with the blade toward the fork when the plate is passed
- Accepting and eating some of each food
- Following the hostess' lead in passing food and helping yourself
- Waiting for the hostess to offer second helpings
- Avoiding such acts as chewing with your mouth open, picking your teeth at the table, tucking your napkin into your clothing, and reaching across the table
- Refusing additional food with a simple, *No, thank you*
- Asking to be excused if it is necessary to leave before the meal is finished

hostess know that you have finished eating. Also, it makes an easier task of carrying the used tableware away from the table.

At the end of the meal, fold or crumple your napkin, depending upon whether it is to be used for another meal. Place it on the table to the left of your plate. When you use a cloth napkin at home, you will probably fold it for use at another meal.

Types of meal service

There are several types of meal service. Food can be placed on the table in bowls and served to each person by the host and hostess. It can be placed on a buffet table, where each person helps himself to the food. It can be served directly from the cooking utensils onto plates before they are brought from the range to the table. There are also many variations of these types of service. Choose the type that suits the particular occasion. If foods are served at the proper temperatures, you may be sure that you have chosen an appropriate type of meal service.

FAMILY SERVICE

Families set their own styles in dining. There are several types of service used for regular meals. A family can choose the one it prefers.

In one type of service the food is placed on the table on platters and in bowls to be passed around the table. Food dishes and serving pieces are placed where they can be easily reached by the person who is to start passing them. The serving dishes are passed to the right, and each person is allowed to help himself. The serving spoon or fork is placed on the table at the right of the dish and is put into the food as serving begins.

In some families the host carves and serves the meat. The hostess may serve the salad and the beverage from the other end of the table. Vegetables may be served with the meat or passed in serving dishes.

Many busy families put the food onto plates in the kitchen and then serve the filled plates to each person at the table. This form of service saves time in table setting and dishwashing. However, it is necessary that someone carry each plate to the kitchen for refilling if second portions are to be served.

BUFFET SERVICE

One good way to serve a large group of people is to provide a buffet service. In this type of service the food is placed on one large table, and guests are asked to help themselves to the foods they want. Since few people have dining rooms large enough to seat a great many people, the buffet service has become very popular among people who do group entertaining. Many restaurants refer to their buffet service as a *smorgasbord*, the Swedish name for a similar type of meal service. Usually, at a smorgasbord, people are allowed to help themselves to a wide assortment of cold meats and fishes, cheeses, salads, and relishes.

When planning a buffet, put the serving table as near the kitchen as housing arrangements will allow. This makes for easy removal of empty dishes and refilling of empty serving plates and bowls. At home or in the classroom, place the table to allow for a free flow of guests past it without confusion. Arrange it so that guests pick up their plates at one end of the table and move in an orderly manner from one dish to another, picking up flatware and napkins last. The meat or main dish is generally placed first. Then come the vegetables, breads, relishes, and salad. The serving piece needed for each dish is placed next to that dish on the tablecloth. Once used, it stays with the food. Guests help themselves to food and move to some other area to eat. Guests are usually expected to help themselves to food as often as they like, without a special invitation from the hostess.

Card tables may be provided where four or more people are asked to sit. Some people provide guests with lap trays or TV trays. Young people can ease the crowded condition of a large party by sitting on the floor or on stairsteps.

In planning buffet menus, try to use foods that are easy to serve, those that give guests a choice, and those that do not run together on the plate. Since a guest may carry a filled plate, flatware, napkin, and sometimes a beverage to the place where he will eat, plan food that can be eaten with a single piece of flatware.

The next time you ask permission to entertain, you might plan a buffet. Planning such a meal in your foods class will give you a chance

Your career
Caterer

Duties: Plans, prepares, and serves special food for large group or home entertainment. Confers with a client to determine the time and place of the affair, menu desired, number of guests to be served, and the cost involved.
Where employed: Special catering agencies, or may be self-employed.

A buffet type party allows a hostess to prepare most of the food before her guests arrive and to spend part of the time during a party visiting with the guests.

COURTESY THE DOW CHEMICAL COMPANY

Collect recipes for foreign dishes that Americans like. Try some of these recipes at home. Report on your family's reaction to them. See recipes given in this book on pages 485 and 486.

Plan and prepare laboratory meals using foreign dishes. Each group might prepare one part of the meal. Combine them for an international buffet. Decorate the table and room appropriately.

Role-play situations where you are a guest. Also practice serving as host or hostess for the various types of meal service. Include greeting guests, handling coats and wraps, making introductions, and other general courtesies expected of those who entertain.

Use different types of table service for various laboratory experiences.

Write a menu which you think would be ideal for a buffet service. Prepare and serve a simple meal using this type of service.

Practice eating foods such as fried chicken with a knife and fork. You might use food that your teacher has prepared in a demonstration.

to practice making up menus for a buffet, arranging a buffet table, organizing a work schedule, working together as a group, and exercising good manners.

TEA OR RECEPTION SERVICE

Another way to entertain a large group is by giving a tea or a reception. A tea offers light refreshments in an informal way. A reception is more formal. It includes a *receiving line*, where guests meet the host, hostess, and special guests. They shake hands and exchange brief greetings. Either service may be used for showers or friendly get-togethers at clubs or with friends. If you learn how to plan and carry out the appropriate service, you will enjoy giving and attending such functions.

A tea is much like a buffet. The food, however, is fancier and lighter. Tea, coffee, or punch may be served. Small decorated cakes, fancy cookies, nuts, candies, and tiny finger sandwiches are considered appropriate for a tea. The table is planned to be as attractive as possible. A tea affords an opportunity to use a beautiful cloth, your prettiest dishes, and your most decorative centerpiece. A bowl of colorful punch surrounded by greenery can be used as a centerpiece. If a tea or reception is held after five o'clock in the afternoon, candles are considered to be an appropriate part of the decorations.

Preparing refreshments for a tea requires careful planning and scheduling. With packaged mixes available, preparation time can be saved. For a school tea or reception, one group can make fancy cakes, one can make cookies, one can make finger sandwiches, and one can make the tea or punch. If guests must stand while eating, plan food that can be eaten with one hand while a small plate with a tea or punch cup is held in the other.

Arrange the table so that guests can receive their beverage from the hostess or her helper, serve themselves refreshments, and move away from the table. The plates are placed at one end of the table with the napkins. China and glass cups and plates are considered formal. Paper goods are acceptable and can be used to carry out a special theme. Paper goods also offer a possible solution where dishwashing is a problem. The trays or plates of food are placed near the front edge of the table center, and the beverage is located at the end. If both a hot and a cold beverage are served, one is placed at each end of the table. The centerpiece is usually placed near the back of the center of the table.

Unless you are planning a small informal tea for just a few people, you will be wise to ask some special friends to assist you. Your friends may serve the beverage, remove the used dishes and wash them for a second using, refill the plates of refreshments so that they always appear to be attractively filled and inviting, and help you greet and entertain the guests. At a large tea many people may not know each other. Plan to have extra hostesses to introduce the guests to each other and to see that they enjoy the occasion. Try to arrange for enough helpers so that each one works only 30 to 45 minutes before being relieved by another friend. That way, your helpers too will enjoy the party.

A tea or reception is a come-and-go party. Guests are expected to arrive between the times given on the written invitation, visit a short time, enjoy the food, and leave to make room for others. They are not expected to stay for the whole time.

Both receptions and teas are dress-up occasions. In some communities, women wear hats and gloves to teas. When hats are worn, they are kept on throughout the visit. Gloves, however, are removed before greeting the hostess or before eating. Sport clothes seem out of place at a tea. Dressy suits or simple party dresses seem more appropriate for the occasion.

SERVING SNACKS

Many people like to show hospitality by serving refreshments, or snacks, to guests. Suppose your family has given you permission to entertain a group of friends. What foods would you serve?

When planning foods for a snack party, try to choose those that you can prepare earlier in the day. If you do, you will be free to enjoy your own party. Choose foods that can be eaten easily—perhaps finger foods. Choose foods that appeal to both boys and girls. Teen-agers enjoy eating, so you will want to have plenty of food. Consider the cost of different menus when you plan. Try to serve foods that are not messy so that clean-up chores do not take you away from the fun of your own party.

Some parties are planned so that snack foods can be prepared and eaten by the guests.

Bring some sample restaurant menus to school. Act out the parts of the restaurant personnel and the ideal customer. Practice ordering, making requests of the waitress, and tipping.

Role-play an imaginary travel day. Make stops at various types of eating places. Include a roadside park, a restaurant, and a drive-in. Show acceptable manners in each type of location.

COURTESY BEST FOODS

473

List and discuss points to be considered in buying different types of dishwashing equipment.

Discuss the reasons for installing or excluding a dishwasher when a new home economics department is built.

Make a checklist for studying the dishwashing practices of groups in your homemaking class. Let each group tell the class about weaknesses they found in their own dishwashing practices.

Foods for a snack party often include sandwiches, potato chips and dips, cookies, cupcakes, and fresh fruit. Raw vegetable strips to eat with dips are also used. Soft drinks and colorful fruit punches are always welcome.

You might plan a snack party in your class with each kitchen group preparing one item for the class party.

ENTERTAINING OUTDOORS

Indoor-outdoor living offers many opportunities for next-to-nature entertaining. Outdoor barbecues or picnics can be enjoyed by most everyone. Everything about this kind of party, even the clothing, can be casual. Outdoor entertainment is in order when small children are included among the guests.

If you are planning a picnic where food will have to be carried quite a distance, there are several points to keep in mind. Choose foods that do not spoil easily and that you can keep at the proper temperature. Plan foods that are easy to serve and that require little preparation just before serving. Choose foods that require very little use of flatware, since you may be eating while sitting on the ground with your plate in your lap. When possible, include easy-to-eat finger foods.

The most common choices for picnics are sandwiches, hamburgers, hot dogs, fried or barbecued chicken, baked beans, potato chips, and roasted corn. Pickles, relishes, fresh fruit, cookies, and cakes add the finishing touches.

Use as many disposable dishes as possible for a picnic. You can make good use of paper goods and of the foil pans saved from ready-to-eat foods. Bowls with plastic covers and covered pans are available in the stores. All are especially good for picnics. Make a checklist of everything you will need to carry along for your picnic. Be sure to include salt-and-pepper shakers, drinking cups or glasses, a bottle opener, and any utensils necessary for serving or eating the food.

Whether planned for the park or the back yard, an outdoor barbecue usually allows for good nutrition as well as fun with family or friends.

COURTESY RICE COUNCIL

Washing dishes by hand

1. Carry the dishes from the dining table to the sink. Using a tray saves time and energy.
2. Scrape and rinse the dishes, grouping together those of the same type and size.
3. Stack them on the right side of the sink or on a table nearby. Arrange them for washing from right to left if possible.
4. Half-fill the dishpan with *hot* water. The water can be still hotter if you use a dish mop, gloves, or a dishwashing spray attachment.
5. Use liquid or granular detergent, soap flakes, or soap powder to prepare a suds. Use enough soap or detergent so that suds will last until the dishes are washed.
6. Wash the dishes in the following order: glassware, flatware, cups, plates, saucers, small dishes, serving dishes, baking dishes, and pots and pans which have been soaking. Wash sharp-edged tools and fragile articles separately.
7. Use both hands in washing dishes. Reach for the dish with one hand, and hold it while you swab with the other hand. Pass the dish through the rinsing water, and turn it up to drain in the draining rack. Another method is to place dishes in the second sink compartment for rinsing.
8. Rinse with clear, hot water. If you have enough hot water, pass each dish under the hot-water faucet on the way to the draining rack. Otherwise, dip the dishes in the rinsing pan or place them in the drainer and spray them with hot water. When cups and glasses have been rinsed, turn them upside down to drain.
9. Use a clean towel to dry glassware, flatware, pots and pans, and any dishes that are not allowed to dry in the rack.
10. Use a tray to carry the dishes and flatware to their storage places, carrying several pieces each trip.
11. Wash and dry the dishpans, sink, and drainboard.
12. Wash and dry dish towels and dishcloths.
13. See that the floor around the sink is free from grease and water.

Discuss the advantages and disadvantages of drying dishes with a towel and the advantages and disadvantages of letting dishes drain. What factors would affect the method which is generally used by a family? What circumstances might affect the method used on a particular day?

Put a small amount of grease on the inside of two glasses. Wash one by holding it under the faucet, using hot water and no soap. Wash the second in hot water with detergent. Allow both glasses to air dry. Hold each glass to the light. Discuss the effectiveness of the two glass-washing methods.

Bulletin board IDEA
Title: *Are You Ready For a Cookout?*
Directions: Below the title, display outdoor cooking accessories such as long-handled spatulas, tongs, salt-and-pepper shakers, chef's aprons, and special pot holders. Discuss whether these items are necessities or luxuries.

Discuss different ways of starting a charcoal fire outdoors, including liquid chemical starters, electric appliances designed for this purpose, and *do-it-yourself* methods. Which seems to be the quickest, the slowest, the most expensive, the least expensive, and the best all-round selection? Why?

Compare and contrast different types of outdoor grills. For what type of situation is each best suited?

Suggest suitable foods for outdoor cooking, such as foil-wrapped potatoes or corn, graham crackers with melted chocolate, or hot dogs wrapped in biscuit dough.

Plan several inexpensive picnic menus. Divide into family-size groups to prepare and serve your picnics. When are picnics appropriate in your area of the country? What arrangement can be made to have fun when weather interferes with picnic plans?

Washing dishes with the automatic dishwasher

1. Rinse dishes under running water, scraping them lightly with a brush or a rubber spatula.
2. Load the dishwasher according to the manufacturer's instructions. Usually, however, load the bottom level first, placing pots, pans, and bowls to the outside with their openings to the center. Then alternate small and large plates.
3. Load the top level, placing cups in the outer section, openings to the center. Place glasses upside down in the center section. Place flatware, handles down, in the flatware basket in the top or bottom section.
4. Add the detergent according to the directions given for the particular machine.
5. Proceed to close the door and add the water according to directions.
6. Remove the dishes when they have been washed and dried.

Cleaning

One of the main responsibilities of a host or hostess is cleaning up after a meal. Whether you are having a party at home or school, cleaning up and putting things away takes organization and care. Your family will be much more willing to let you entertain your friends if you leave your home in good order after the fun is over. In class or in public places, you are obliged to leave the facilities ready for the next group to use.

Try to leave things just the way you would want to find them. This means you will wash dishes and put them back where you found them. Put away any other items that have been removed from their customary place of storage. Wipe up spills, pick up litter, and sweep the floor. (For directions on dishwashing, see charts on pages 475 and 476.)

26 CHAPTER POSTTEST

Number from 1 to 44. Beside each number indicate if the corresponding statement is true or false. *Do not write in this book.*

1. Expensive table appointments are essential for an attractive table arrangement.
2. A tablecloth should extend over the edges of the table about 4 to 6 inches.
3. A napkin used for a tea is smaller than one used for a formal dinner.
4. In setting the table, the folded napkin is placed to the left of the forks with the open edge toward the dinner plate.
5. At the end of a meal, place your napkin on the chair on which you were sitting.
6. Tableware made of sterling silver is more durable than that made of stainless steel.
7. Chinaware is more durable than pottery.
8. A cover is made up of all the tableware needed by one person for a particular meal.
9. Tableware consists only of flatware, dinnerware, and accessory items.
10. If they are needed for a meal, place knives and spoons to the right of the dinner plate.
11. Place the cutting edge of the knife toward the dinner plate.
12. If it is the only flatware to be used, place the fork to the right of the dinner plate.
13. Place the bread-and-butter plate at the tip of the fork.
14. Place a milk or juice glass to the right of the water glass.
15. Place the cup and saucer at the tip of the knife.
16. Place a butter spreader on the bread-and-butter plate diagonal to the other silver.
17. Place the cup on the saucer so that the handle is turned to the right and is parallel to the edge of the table.
18. When eating soup, dip the spoon into the bowl away from you.
19. Take only as much food on a spoon as you can eat in one bite.
20. Leave the spoon in the cup while drinking.
21. After finishing with a soup spoon, leave it in the bowl.
22. After finishing a meal, leave the knife and fork across the center of the plate.
23. After a bowl of gravy has been passed around the table, leave the gravy ladle in the bowl.
24. When entertaining mealtime guests, only fresh flowers should be used as a centerpiece.
25. Avoid using strongly scented flowers for a centerpiece at the dining table.
26. Good table manners are as important at home as they are when eating out.
27. A boy helps seat the girl on his left.
28. At a banquet, be seated from the left side of the chair.
29. If in doubt about which piece of flatware to use, observe which piece the hostess is using.
30. Food is passed to the right.
31. Butter an entire slice of bread at one time.
32. A butter knife remains on the butter dish when it is passed.
33. In buffet service, the flatware and napkins are picked up last.
34. Smorgasbord is a Swedish type of buffet service.
35. Guests stand while eating at a meal which has been served buffet style.
36. A reception is more formal than a tea.
37. At a tea the guests help themselves to the beverage.
38. Candles are an appropriate table decoration for a tea or reception if it is held after five o'clock in the afternoon.
39. Entertaining outdoors is ideal for large groups because there is no cleaning up to do afterwards.
40. For ease in cleaning up after a picnic, plan menus which require little flatware.
41. A successful picnic usually requires careful planning and preparation.
42. When washing dishes by hand, wash sharp knives with the glassware.
43. When washing dishes by hand, wash the pots and pans last.
44. It is desirable to alternate large and small plates when loading an automatic dishwasher.

7 Your Recipes

Substitutions

1 cup fresh milk	=	½ cup evaporated milk + ½ cup water
1 cup fresh milk	=	½ cup condensed milk + ½ cup water (reduce sugar in recipe)
1 cup fresh milk	=	4 tablespoons powdered whole milk + ⅞ cup water
1 cup fresh milk	=	4 tablespoons powdered skim milk + 2 tablespoons butter + ⅞ cup water
1 teaspoon baking powder	=	¼ teaspoon soda + ½ teaspoon cream of tartar
1 tablespoon cornstarch	=	2 tablespoons flour (as thickening)
1 tablespoon potato flour	=	2 tablespoons flour (as thickening)
1 cup pastry flour	=	1 cup all-purpose or bread flour less 2 tablespoons
1 square chocolate	=	3 tablespoons cocoa + 1 teaspoon to 1 tablespoon shortening (less for Dutch type cocoa)

Measurements and weights

A few grains or a dash	=	⅛ teaspoon or less
3 teaspoons	=	1 tablespoon
16 tablespoons	=	1 cup
¼ cup	=	4 tablespoons
⅓ cup	=	5 tablespoons + 1 teaspoon
⅜ cup	=	6 tablespoons
½ cup	=	8 tablespoons
1 cup	=	16 tablespoons
2 cups	=	1 pint
2 pints	=	1 quart
4 quarts	=	1 gallon
1 oz.	=	2 tablespoons
8 oz.	=	1 cup
1 pound (fats and liquids)	=	2 cups

Oven temperatures

Very slow oven	250° F. to 275° F.
Slow oven	300° F. to 325° F.
Moderate oven	350° F. to 375° F.
Hot oven	400° F. to 450° F.
Very hot oven	475° F. and up

Capacity of canned-food containers

8 oz.	=	1 cup
Picnic	=	1¼ cups
No. 1	=	1⅓ cups
No. 1 (tall)	=	2 cups
No. 2	=	2½ cups
No. 2½	=	3½ cups
No. 3	=	4 cups
46 oz.	=	5¾ cups
No. 10	=	13 cups

PROTEIN FOODS

BAKED HAMBURGERS

4–6 Servings

1 pound ground beef
2 tablespoons chopped onion
½ cup soft bread crumbs
¼ cup milk
1 teaspoon salt
⅛ teaspoon pepper

1. Place all ingredients in mixing bowl, and mix thoroughly.
2. Press into greased muffin pans.
3. Bake in moderate oven (350° F.) for 25 to 30 minutes.

VARIATIONS

Broiled: Shape into individual patties. Place on greased rack in broiler pan, and place pan in oven with patties 3 inches from broiling unit. Broil for 5 to 8 minutes on one side. Turn, and broil for 3 to 5 minutes on other side.

Grilled: Shape into individual patties. Cook on rack over coals, turning once.

Panfried: Shape into individual patties. Melt butter or margarine in skillet over low heat. Add patties, and brown on both sides, turning once.

Note: Broiled, grilled, or panfried hamburgers may be served in toasted hamburger buns with catsup or relish, if desired.

THE HAMBURGER MASTER MIX

5 Meals or 1 Meal (4 Servings Each)

5 MEALS	1 MEAL
1 tablespoon butter or margarine	1 teaspoon butter or margarine
5 pounds ground beef	1 pound ground beef
2½ cups chopped onion	½ cup chopped onion
1 cup chopped green pepper	3 tablespoons chopped green pepper
5 cups chopped celery	1 cup chopped celery
5 cans tomato soup, undiluted	1 can tomato soup, undiluted
5 15 oz. cans tomato sauce	1 15 oz. can tomato sauce
5 teaspoons salt	1 teaspoon salt
½ teaspoon black pepper	Dash of black pepper

1. Melt butter or margarine over low heat in 8 quart skillet or pot.
2. Crumble beef into skillet, increase heat, and cook until red color disappears.
3. Add onion, green pepper, and celery. Cook until beef is brown and vegetables are tender.
4. Add soup, tomato sauce, salt, and pepper.
5. Cover and simmer for 30 to 45 minutes, stirring occasionally.
6. Cool and divide equally into five freezer containers. Freeze. May be thawed and used for a variety of family dinner meals.

Note: Use a 12″ skillet when preparing Hamburger Mix for one meal.

HOW TO USE THE HAMBURGER MASTER MIX

Product	Mix	Other Ingredients	Directions
Beef-aroni	1 freezer container	1 7 oz. package elbow macaroni	Heat meat mix. Cook macaroni (see page 491). Mix meat and macaroni and serve hot.
Chili	1 freezer container	2 cups drained canned kidney beans 1 t. chili powder	Heat meat mix. Add beans and chili powder and simmer covered for 10 minutes.
Pizza	1 freezer container	Biscuit or yeast dough (canned biscuits may be used) 1 teaspoon Italian seasoning Olives, frankfurters, pepperoni, or sliced Italian cheese Parmesan cheese, grated	Add Italian seasoning to meat mix and simmer meat sauce until it thickens. Line pizza pan with thinly rolled dough. Spread meat sauce over dough and garnish as desired. Sprinkle with Parmesan cheese and bake in moderate oven (375° F.) for 15 to 20 minutes. Cut and serve at once.
Spaghetti	1 freezer container	1 8 oz. package spaghetti 1 t. Italian seasoning Parmesan cheese, grated	Cook spaghetti according to directions on package and drain. Heat meat sauce. Add Italian seasoning and simmer for 15 minutes. Mix meat and spaghetti and sprinkle with Parmesan cheese.
Spanish Rice	1 freezer container	3 cups cooked rice	Heat meat sauce. Add cooked rice. Cover and simmer 5 to 10 minutes.
Sloppy Joe	1 freezer container	1 package of 8 hamburger buns	Simmer meat sauce for about 1 hour or until thick. Toast buns. Serve meat sauce in hot toasted buns.

FRANKFURTER-BACON SPIRALS

8 Spirals in Rolls

8 hot-dog rolls
8 frankfurters
8 pieces American cheese, 2 inches by ¼ inch by ¼ inch
8 slices bacon

1. Wrap rolls in aluminum foil, and heat in oven.
2. Make 2-inch slit in each frankfurter, and insert piece of cheese.
3. Wrap slice of bacon spirally around each frankfurter, and fasten at each end with toothpick.
4. Place on rack in broiler pan, and place pan in oven with frankfurters 3 inches from broiling unit.
5. Broil for 5 minutes on each side, or until bacon is lightly browned.
6. Remove toothpicks, and place frankfurter-bacon spirals in hot rolls.
7. Serve immediately.

BROILED BACON

4 Servings

8 slices bacon

PAN-BROILED

1. Place bacon slices close together in hot skillet over medium heat.
2. Turn bacon as it broils. Pour off fat as it accumulates.
3. Drain on absorbent paper before serving.

OVEN-BROILED

1. Place bacon slices close together in shallow pan, and cook in moderate oven (350° F.), turning once, until brown.
2. Drain on absorbent paper before serving.

COOKED ON BROILER

1. Place bacon slices close together on rack in broiler pan.
2. Place pan in oven with bacon 3 inches from broiling unit.
3. Broil for 2 minutes on each side, turning once.

CHICKEN SALAD

4 Servings

1 cup chopped cooked chicken
1 cup chopped apple
3 tablespoons lemon juice
½ cup chopped celery
3 tablespoons mayonnaise or cooked salad dressing
Salad greens

1. Place first 5 ingredients in mixing bowl, and mix lightly.
2. Chill.
3. Serve on salad greens.

VARIATIONS

Add ½ cup chopped ripe olives.

Add ¼ cup chopped pecans, walnuts, or almonds.

Substitute 1 cup drained canned pineapple tidbits or chunks for 1 cup chopped apple.

BROILED LIVER WITH BACON

4 Servings

4 slices calf or lamb liver, ⅓ to ½ inch thick
2 tablespoons melted butter or margarine
Salt and pepper
4 slices bacon

1. Brush liver on both sides with melted fat.
2. Place on rack in broiler pan, and place pan in oven with liver 3 inches from broiling unit.
3. Broil for 6 minutes on one side.
4. Turn, and broil for 3 minutes on other side.
5. Season with salt and pepper.
6. Serve on hot platter with Broiled Bacon.

BROILED FISH

4 Servings

1½ pounds fish steaks or fillets
1 teaspoon salt
⅛ teaspoon pepper
3 tablespoons butter or margarine
1 tablespoon hot water
Lemon wedges

1. Rub fish with salt and pepper.
2. Melt butter or margarine in the hot water.
3. Place fish, skin side up, on greased rack in broiler pan, and place in broiler, 3 inches from heat unit.
4. Brush with melted butter or margarine, and broil for 11 minutes on one side.
5. Turn, brush with melted butter or margarine, and broil for 3 to 7 minutes on other side.
6. Serve with lemon wedges.

TUNA FISH CASSEROLE

4-6 Servings

1 teaspoon salt
1 quart water
1 cup uncooked noodles
1 tablespoon butter or margarine
½ cup chopped onion
1 can cream of celery soup, undiluted
½ cup milk
1 cup canned tuna fish, drained and flaked
½ cup cooked peas
½ teaspoon salt
Few grains pepper
½ cup grated American cheese

1. Add 1 teaspoon salt to water, and bring to rapid, rolling boil.
2. Add noodles gradually so water does not stop boiling.
3. Cook, uncovered, stirring occasionally to prevent sticking, for 10 minutes, or until fairly tender.
4. Drain in colander.
5. Melt butter or margarine in skillet over low heat, add onion, and cook until brown.
6. Add soup, milk, tuna fish, peas, ½ teaspoon salt, pepper, and noodles.
7. Pour into greased baking dish, and sprinkle with grated cheese.
8. Bake in moderate oven (350° F.) for 25 minutes.
9. Serve hot in dish in which it was baked.

VARIATION
Add 2 hard-cooked eggs, sliced or chopped, to mixture before baking.

BEEF STEW

4 Servings

2 tablespoons shortening
1½ pounds beef neck, chuck, or brisket, cut into 2-inch cubes
3 cups hot water
½ teaspoon salt
4 medium onions, sliced
4 medium carrots, halved
4 medium potatoes, quartered
Salt and pepper
2 tablespoons flour
½ cup water

1. Melt shortening in large saucepan.
2. Add meat, and brown on all sides.
3. Add hot water and ½ teaspoon salt, and bring quickly to boiling point.
4. Cover, and simmer for 2 hours, or until meat is very tender.
5. Add vegetables 30 minutes before meat is done, and cook until tender but not broken.
6. Season with salt and pepper.
7. Pour off liquid, measure, and add hot water, if necessary, to make 2 cups of liquid.
8. Mix flour and ½ cup water by shaking in a small covered jar, and add to liquid.
9. Return liquid to stew, and stir until it has boiled for 1 minute and is thickened.
10. Serve on hot platter or in vegetable dish.

VARIATIONS

Lamb: Substitute 1½ pounds lamb for beef.

Veal: Substitute 1½ pounds veal for beef.

Add 1 cup tomatoes for additional flavor.

Substitute turnips for half the carrots.

DUMPLINGS FOR STEW

4 Servings

1 cup sifted all-purpose flour
1½ teaspoons baking powder
¼ teaspoon salt
2 tablespoons shortening
½ cup milk

1. Sift together flour, baking powder, and salt.
2. Cut in shortening with pastry blender or two knives until mixture looks like coarse corn meal.
3. Add milk, and stir lightly until flour mixture is just moistened.
4. Drop dough from spoon into boiling liquid.
5. Cover, and cook over low heat for 15 to 20 minutes.

Note: If dumplings are to be served with a stew, add about 20 minutes before removing the stew from heat, being sure that dumplings rest on pieces of meat or vegetables so they will cook in the steam.

PERUVIAN CORN PIE

6 Servings

6 or 7 ears corn
1 pound hamburger
3 large tomatoes
2 onions
1 sweet pepper
Salt to taste
20 ripe olives, pitted
½ cup raisins
2 hard-cooked eggs

1. Cut corn from cob and set aside.
2. Chop tomatoes, onions, and sweet pepper.
3. Combine meat, tomatoes, onions, and sweet pepper and cook until tender.
4. Chop olives, raisins, and hard-cooked eggs and add to cooked meat. Add salt to taste.
5. Pour half of the corn into a baking dish. Cover the corn with the meat mixture, and top with the remaining corn.
6. Bake in a moderate oven (350° F.) for 1 hour.
7. Serve hot.

CHINESE SWEET AND SOUR PORK

4 Servings

1 egg
½ cup flour
½ teaspoon salt
3 to 4 tablespoons water
1 pound pork shoulder, cut into 1 inch cubes
Oil for deep frying
1 cup canned pineapple cubes
1 green pepper, cut into 1 inch strips
½ cup vinegar
¼ cup brown sugar
1 tablespoon molasses
¾ cup water
1 tomato, cut into 4 to 6 pieces
2 tablespoons cornstarch
¼ cup water

1. Beat egg and add flour, salt, and water to form a thin batter.
2. Pour batter over pork to coat pieces.
3. Fry, piece by piece, in deep fat until browned.
4. Drain the pork.
5. Mix the pineapple, green pepper, vinegar, brown sugar, molasses, and water in a saucepan and stir until mixture boils.
6. Add the tomato.
7. Mix cornstarch with ¼ cup water and stir into sauce.
8. Cook until sauce has thickened.
9. Add pork and stir.
10. Serve over hot cooked rice.

HAWAIIAN CURRY DINNER

4–6 Servings

2 to 2½ pounds chicken
Water
3 tablespoons margarine
1 cup grated coconut
1 teaspoon finely chopped onion
1 teaspoon finely chopped ginger root
3 tablespoons flour
1 teaspoon curry powder
½ teaspoon salt

1. Place chicken in saucepan, add water to cover, and simmer until it is tender.
2. Remove chicken from broth and set aside to cool.
3. Melt margarine, and add coconut, onion, ginger root, flour, curry powder, and salt. Cook to form a smooth paste.
4. Add chicken broth and heat to boiling, stirring constantly to form a sauce.
5. Remove chicken from bones and heat the meat in the sauce.
6. Serve hot over cooked rice with any or all of the following accompaniments.

ACCOMPANIMENTS
1 cup mango chutney; ½ pound chopped peanuts or almonds; ½ pound crumbled crisp bacon; 2 finely chopped hard-cooked eggs; 1 cup shredded coconut; ½ cup chopped preserved ginger; 1 chopped green pepper; 1 cup chopped green onion; 1 cup raisins; or 1 cup sweet pickle relish.

PANFRIED CHICKEN

4 Servings

2½ to 3 pound broiler-fryer chicken, cut up
½ cup flour
1 teaspoon salt
½ teaspoon paprika
¼ teaspoon pepper
Shortening

1. Wash chicken and pat dry.
2. Mix flour, salt, paprika, and pepper.
3. Melt solid shortening, or pour liquid shortening into a large skillet, to a depth of ½ inch. Heat.
4. Coat chicken with flour mixture.
5. Cook chicken in oil over medium heat 15 to 20 minutes or until it is light brown, turning once.
6. Reduce heat.
7. Cover the skillet and cook the chicken for 30 to 40 minutes or until thickest pieces are fork-tender.
8. Turn chicken once or twice to ensure even cooking.
9. Remove the cover during the last 5 minutes of cooking time so the chicken will become crisp.

SOFT-COOKED EGGS

4 Servings

4 eggs
4 cups water

COLD-WATER METHOD
1. Place eggs in saucepan with **cold** water, and bring to boiling point.
2. Turn off heat, cover, and let eggs remain in hot water for 3 to 5 minutes.

HOT-WATER METHOD
1. Place eggs in saucepan with **boiling** water.
2. Cover, and let eggs remain in hot water for 4 minutes without heat.

HARD-COOKED EGGS

4 Servings

4 eggs
4 cups water

COLD-WATER METHOD
1. Place eggs in saucepan with **cold** water, and bring to boiling point.
2. Reduce heat, cover, and simmer for 15 minutes.
3. Place eggs in cold water immediately to cool.

HOT-WATER METHOD
1. Place eggs in saucepan with **boiling** water.
2. Cover, and let eggs remain in hot water for 15 minutes without heat.
3. Place eggs in cold water immediately to cool.

FRIED EGGS

4 Servings

2 tablespoons butter or margarine
4 eggs
Salt and pepper

1. Melt butter or margarine in skillet over low heat.
2. Break eggs, one at a time, into saucer, and slip egg from saucer into hot butter or margarine.
3. Cook eggs slowly for 3 minutes, or to desired doneness.
4. Sprinkle with salt and pepper.
5. Serve immediately.

POACHED EGGS

4 Servings

2 cups hot water
4 eggs
Salt and pepper

1. Grease skillet or saucepan, and add water.
2. Place over low heat, and cook until water simmers.
3. Break eggs, one at a time, into saucer, and slip egg from saucer into simmering water.
4. Cover, and cook for 3 to 5 minutes, or until desired doneness.
5. Remove each egg with slotted spoon, and place on toast, hash, or vegetables, if desired.
6. Sprinkle with salt and pepper.
7. Serve immediately.

SCRAMBLED EGGS

4 Servings

4 eggs
¼ cup milk
½ teaspoon salt
Few grains pepper
1 tablespoon butter or margarine

1. Beat eggs slightly.
2. Add milk, salt, and pepper, and stir.
3. Melt butter or margarine in skillet over very low heat, and add egg mixture.
4. Cook slowly, scraping mixture from bottom of pan, until eggs are soft and creamy.
5. Serve immediately on heated platter.

VARIATIONS

Add ½ cup grated sharp cheese, 3 tablespoons chopped cooked ham, or 4 tablespoons chopped cooked bacon to beaten eggs.

BLACK-EYED PEAS AND RICE (HOPPING JOHN)

4–5 Servings

½ cup dried black-eyed peas
Water
⅛ pound salt pork, diced
½ red pepper pod
2 tablespoons chopped celery
1½ cups cooked rice
Salt
Pepper

1. Soak black-eyed peas overnight in enough water to cover.
2. Combine in large, heavy kettle the black-eyed peas, soaking water, and diced salt pork. Add red pepper pod and celery, if desired.
3. Simmer until peas are tender, but still whole.
4. Add cooked rice.
5. Add salt and pepper.
6. Cook, covered, until liquid is absorbed and peas and rice are hot through.
7. Remove pepper pod before serving.

Note: Red pepper and chopped celery may be omitted. One-half cup uncooked rice equals 1½ cups of cooked rice.

MILK-RICH FOODS

MILK SHAKE

4 Servings

4 cups milk
3 tablespoons sugar
1 cup finely chopped ice
1 cup vanilla ice cream

1. Place all ingredients in tightly covered container and shake, or place in blender and mix.
2. Pour into tall glasses.
3. Top with additional ice cream before serving, if desired.

VARIATIONS

Banana: Add 2 large bananas, mashed, and ¼ teaspoon vanilla.

Chocolate: Add ½ cup chocolate syrup.

Maple: Add ¾ cup maple syrup.

Strawberry: Add 1½ cups sweetened, crushed strawberries.

Vanilla: Add 4 teaspoons vanilla.

COCOA

4–5 Servings

4 tablespoons cocoa
6 tablespoons sugar
Few grains salt
1 cup hot water
3 cups milk
½ teaspoon vanilla

1. Place cocoa, sugar, and salt in top of double boiler, and mix well.
2. Add hot water slowly, stirring constantly, and cook over direct heat for 3 minutes.
3. Add milk, and stir.
4. Place over boiling water in bottom of double boiler, and cook slowly, stirring constantly, until milk is hot.
5. Remove from heat, and beat with rotary beater or fork for 1 minute.
6. Add vanilla, and stir.
7. Serve hot.
8. Top with marshmallows or whipped cream, if desired.

WHITE SAUCE

1 Cup

THIN
1 tablespoon butter or margarine
1 tablespoon flour
½ teaspoon salt
Few grains pepper
1 cup milk

MEDIUM
2 tablespoons butter or margarine
2 tablespoons flour
½ teaspoon salt
Few grains pepper
1 cup milk

THICK
3 tablespoons butter or margarine
3 tablespoons flour
½ teaspoon salt
Few grains pepper
1 cup milk

VERY THICK
4 tablespoons butter or margarine
4 tablespoons flour
½ teaspoon salt
Few grains pepper
1 cup milk

1. Melt butter or margarine in top of double boiler over boiling water in bottom of double boiler.
2. Add flour, salt, and pepper, and stir until smooth.
3. Add milk slowly, stirring constantly.
4. Cook slowly, stirring constantly, until smooth and thickened.

Note: White sauce may also be made in a saucepan over direct heat.

MUSHROOM SAUCE

Make 1 cup Medium White Sauce. Heat 1½ tablespoons butter or margarine in skillet, and add ¾ cup drained canned mushrooms or ½ pound sliced fresh mushrooms, and 1 teaspoon chopped onion. Cook until onion is golden brown, stirring 2 or 3 times, and add to white sauce.

CHEESE SAUCE

Make 1 cup Thin White Sauce. Add 1 cup grated American cheese, and stir until melted.

EGG SAUCE

Make 1 cup Medium White Sauce. Add 2 hard-cooked eggs, coarsely chopped, and 2 teaspoons chopped pimento, and stir.

ASPARAGUS-EGG CASSEROLE

4 Servings

2 tablespoons butter or margarine
2 tablespoons flour
¼ teaspoon salt
¼ teaspoon pepper
1⅔ cups evaporated milk, undiluted
2 cups canned asparagus, drained and cut into 1-inch pieces
3 hard-cooked eggs, sliced
1 cup grated American cheese
¼ cup chopped toasted almonds

1. Make White Sauce with first 5 ingredients.
2. Arrange half of asparagus, eggs, cheese, and almonds in alternate layers in greased baking dish.
3. Repeat layers, using other half of ingredients.
4. Pour white sauce over entire mixture.
5. Top with additional chopped almonds and grated cheese, if desired.
6. Bake in moderate oven (350° F.) for 20 minutes.
7. Serve hot in dish in which it was baked.

MACARONI AND CHEESE

4 Servings

2 quarts water
2 teaspoons salt
1 cup uncooked macaroni
2 tablespoons butter or margarine
2 tablespoons flour
½ teaspoon salt
⅛ teaspoon pepper
1 cup milk
1 cup grated sharp American cheese
½ cup dry bread crumbs
1 tablespoon butter or margarine

1. Place water and 2 teaspoons salt in saucepan, and bring to a rapid, rolling boil.
2. Add macaroni gradually so water does not stop boiling.
3. Cook, uncovered, stirring occasionally to prevent sticking, for ten minutes, or until fairly tender.
4. Drain in colander.
5. Make Medium White Sauce with 2 tablespoons butter or margarine, 2 tablespoons flour, ½ teaspoon salt, ⅛ teaspoon pepper, and 1 cup milk (page 490).
6. Add grated cheese to white sauce, and stir until cheese melts.
7. Place macaroni in greased baking dish, and pour cheese sauce over it.
8. Cover with bread crumbs, and dot with 1 tablespoon butter or margarine.
9. Bake in moderate oven (350° F.) for 15 to 20 minutes, or until crumbs are brown.
10. Serve hot in dish in which it was baked.

BAKED CHEESE FONDUE

4 Servings

1 cup soft bread crumbs
1 cup grated American cheese
½ teaspoon salt
Few grains pepper
1 tablespoon butter or margarine, melted
3 eggs, separated
1 cup milk

1. Place bread crumbs, cheese, salt, pepper, and melted butter or margarine in mixing bowl, and mix well.
2. Beat egg yolks until thick and lemon-colored, and add milk.
3. Add to bread-crumb–cheese mixture, and stir.
4. Beat egg whites until stiff, and fold into mixture.
5. Pour into greased baking dish.
6. Set in pan containing hot water up to about two-thirds depth of baking dish.
7. Bake in moderate oven (350° F.) for 30 to 40 minutes, or until firm.
8. Insert tip of knife in center of fondue, and if knife comes out clean, fondue is done.
9. Serve immediately in dish in which it was baked.

Note: This cheese fondue may be made in less time if baked in individual baking cups.

BAKED CUSTARD

4 Servings

2 eggs
6 tablespoons sugar
⅛ teaspoon salt
2 cups milk, scalded
½ teaspoon vanilla
Few grains nutmeg

1. Beat eggs slightly in mixing bowl.
2. Add sugar and salt, and mix well.
3. Add scalded milk slowly, stirring constantly.
4. Add vanilla, and stir.
5. Pour into custard cups, and sprinkle with nutmeg.
6. Set cups in pan containing hot water up to about two-thirds depth of cups.
7. Bake in moderate oven (350° F.) for 30 to 45 minutes.
8. Insert tip of knife in center of custard, and if knife comes out clean, custard is done.
9. Cool, and serve in cups in which it was baked.

VARIATIONS

Caramel: Caramelize ½ cup sugar, and pour it into custard cups before pouring in custard.

Chocolate: Add 1½ squares unsweetened chocolate, finely cut, to scalded milk.

Coconut: Add ½ cup flaked coconut at same time vanilla is added.

SOFT CUSTARD

4 Servings

2 eggs
4 tablespoons sugar
⅛ teaspoon salt
2 cups milk, scalded
½ teaspoon vanilla

1. Beat eggs slightly in mixing bowl.
2. Add sugar and salt, and mix well.
3. Add scalded milk slowly, stirring constantly, and return to top of double boiler in which milk was scalded.
4. Place over boiling water in bottom of double boiler, and cook slowly, stirring constantly, until mixture coats a spoon lightly.
5. Add vanilla, and stir.
6. Chill.
7. Serve in chilled dishes.

VARIATIONS

Substitute ½ teaspoon lemon or almond extract for ½ teaspoon vanilla.

Top with shredded coconut, chopped nuts or fruits, or whipped cream.

FRUITS AND VEGETABLES

BAKED POTATOES

4 Servings

4 medium potatoes
4 tablespoons butter or margarine
Paprika

1. Scrub potatoes thoroughly, and dry.
2. Place in shallow pan or directly on oven rack.
3. Bake in moderate oven (350° F.) for 45 to 60 minutes, or until potatoes are soft when pressed.
4. Remove from oven, and holding each potato in a towel, squeeze to loosen skin.
5. Make crossed gashes in skin to allow steam to escape, and press potato open.
6. Insert pat of butter or margarine in each potato, and sprinkle with paprika.

VARIATION

Stuffed Baked Potatoes: Scoop out the potato from hot baked potato halves and prepare as for Mashed Potatoes. Stuff potatoes back into shells and return to hot oven (400° F.) for 8 to 10 minutes, or until top is browned. Sprinkle tops with grated American cheese, chopped parsley, or chopped crisp bacon, if desired.

Notes: 1 Metal skewers inserted lengthwise in potatoes will speed the time of cooking.
2 Potatoes wrapped in aluminum foil will bake more quickly and will be less mealy.
3 Rubbing outside of potatoes with oil or butter before baking will soften skin.

MASHED POTATOES

4 Servings

4 or 5 medium potatoes
1 cup water
½ teaspoon salt
Salt and pepper
2 tablespoons butter or margarine
⅓ cup hot milk

1. Wash, pare, and quarter potatoes.
2. Place water and ½ teaspoon salt in saucepan, and bring to boiling point.
3. Add potatoes, cover, and bring to boiling point again.
4. Reduce heat, and cook for 20 to 25 minutes, or until potatoes are tender when pierced with a fork. (There should not be any liquid left, but if there is, save it for soups or sauces.)
5. Shake pan over heat for a moment to dry potatoes.
6. Mash potatoes with a potato masher or a fork.
7. Season with salt and pepper, add butter or margarine and hot milk, and beat until snowy white and fluffy.
8. Serve immediately.

VARIATIONS

Savory: Add 2 teaspoons chopped watercress and ⅔ teaspoon finely cut mint just before beating.

Spanish: Add 2 teaspoons chopped pimento just before beating.

TIMETABLE FOR COOKING GREEN VEGETABLES[1]

Vegetable	Servings per Pound of Fresh Vegetable[2]	Approximate Number of Minutes to Allow after Water Returns to Boil — Fresh	Frozen
Asparagus	4 (4 or 5 whole spears)	10–20	5–10
Beans (Green or String)	6	15–30	12–18
Beans, Lima	2	20–30	6–10
Beet Greens	4	5–15	6–12
Broccoli[3]	3 to 4 (2 or 3 stalks)	10–20	5–8
Brussels Sprouts	5	10–20	4–9
Cabbage	4 to 5 (cooked, shredded)	3–10	—
	4 (cooked, quartered)	10–15	—
Chard	4	10–20	8–10
Collards	4	10–20	—
Dandelion Greens	5	10–20	—
Kale	4 to 5	10–25	8–12
Mustard Greens	4 to 5	20–30	8–15
Okra	4	10–20	—
Peas	2	8–20	5–10
Spinach	2 to 3	3–10	4–6
Turnip Greens	4 to 5	10–30	8–12

Notes: 1 Boil green vegetables in lightly salted water. Bring water to a boil, add vegetables, and cover pan. When water boils again, reduce heat, and begin to count cooking time.
2 Approximate number of ½ cup servings of cooked vegetable.
3 Heavy stalks, split

Adapted from Home and Garden Bulletin No. 41, U.S. Department of Agriculture.

GREEN BEANS

4–6 Servings

1 pound green beans
1 cup water
½ teaspoon salt
Salt and pepper

1. Wash beans, and cut crosswise into 1-inch pieces or lengthwise into strips.
2. Place water and ½ teaspoon salt in saucepan, and bring to boiling point.
3. Add beans, cover, and bring to boiling point again.
4. Reduce heat, and cook for 15 to 30 minutes, or until tender. (There should not be any liquid left, but if there is, save it for soups or sauces.)
5. Season with salt and pepper.
6. Serve with melted butter or margarine, if desired.

VARIATIONS

Almonds: Arrange cooked green beans in greased baking dish. Add ½ cup Medium White Sauce (page 490). Cover with slivered almonds, and bake in hot oven (400° F.) until almonds are brown.

Cheese: Arrange 2 cups cooked green beans in greased baking dish. Sprinkle with ½ cup grated American cheese, and add ¼ cup heavy cream. Dot with 1 tablespoon butter or margarine, and bake in moderate oven (350° F.) until cheese melts.

Peanuts: Add ½ cup salted peanuts at same time seasoning is added.

Polonaise: Reheat beans with ¼ to ½ cup cream, and sprinkle with buttered bread crumbs or crushed corn flakes.

SLICED ORANGES

4 Servings

4 medium oranges

1. Wash and dry oranges, and chill.
2. Place each orange on cutting board, and remove peel by cutting off in strips from top to bottom.
3. Slice oranges crosswise ⅛ to ¼ inch thick as desired.
4. Arrange slices attractively on small plates, and serve immediately.

AMBROSIA

4 Servings

3 medium oranges
4 tablespoons sugar
½ cup flaked coconut

1. Wash and dry oranges.
2. Pare, remove all white membrane and seeds, and section oranges over bowl to save juice.
3. Cut sections in half, and place in bowl.
4. Add sugar and ¼ cup coconut, and mix lightly.
5. Top with remaining ¼ cup coconut.
6. Chill.
7. Serve in individual serving dishes as dessert.

VARIATIONS
Add 2 sliced bananas or ½ cup crushed pineapple.

GELATIN MOLD

4–6 Servings

1 package fruit-flavored gelatin (lemon, orange, cherry, raspberry, etc.)
1 cup hot water
1 cup cold water or fruit juice

1. Place gelatin in mixing bowl, add hot water, and stir until gelatin dissolves.
2. Add cold water.
3. Pour into mold, and chill until gelatin sets.
4. Unmold, and serve as a salad or dessert.

VARIATIONS

Fruit: Substitute ¾ cup fruit juice for 1 cup cold water. Add 1 cup grape halves, drained canned pineapple (crushed or diced), cherries, orange sections, sliced bananas, or combinations of fruits, and ¼ cup chopped nuts, if desired. Add fruits when gelatin has partially thickened, and return to refrigerator until gelatin sets.

Vegetable: Use lemon-flavored gelatin, and add 1 cup chopped cabbage, chopped celery, grated carrots, or a combination of vegetables. Add vegetables when gelatin has partially thickened, and return to refrigerator until gelatin sets.

Vegetable-Fruit: Use lemon-flavored gelatin, and add ½ cup grated carrots and ¼ cup drained crushed pineapple, or add ½ cup chopped cabbage and ½ cup chopped apple. Add vegetables and fruits when gelatin has partially thickened, and return to refrigerator until gelatin sets.

Note: To unmold, dip mold to rim in warm water, and shake it slightly. Then cover mold with a plate, turn plate and mold together, and lift off mold.

BAKED APPLES

4 Servings

4 medium apples
4 to 6 tablespoons sugar
Boiling water

1. Wash and dry apples, and remove cores about seven-eighths of the way down.
2. Slit skin around middle of each apple.
3. Place apples in ungreased baking pan or dish, and fill centers with sugar.
4. Pour boiling water into pan or dish to depth of about ¼ inch.
5. Bake in moderate oven (350° F.) for 30 to 40 minutes, basting often with liquid, until apples are soft when pierced with a fork.
6. Serve hot or cold in individual serving dishes with cream, if desired.

VARIATIONS

Substitute brown sugar for white sugar, or use half brown sugar and half white sugar.

Place cinnamon, nutmeg, lemon juice, raisins, or shredded coconut in center of apples with sugar before baking.

APPLESAUCE

4 Servings

4 medium apples
¾ to 1 cup water
4 tablespoons sugar
½ teaspoon cinnamon

1. Wash, quarter, and remove core from apples.
2. Place in saucepan, and add water.
3. Cover, and cook over low heat for 20 minutes, or until apples are tender.
4. Mash through colander or coarse strainer.
5. Add sugar and cinnamon, and mix.
6. Cool until ready to serve.

VARIATION
Add 1 teaspoon lemon juice or 1 stick crushed peppermint-stick candy just before cooling.

POTATO SALAD

4 Servings

2 cups cubed cooked potatoes
1 teaspoon grated onion
½ cup chopped celery
1 teaspoon salt
¼ cup French dressing
1 hard-cooked egg, sliced
¼ cup mayonnaise
8 leaves crisp lettuce
1 tablespoon chopped parsley

1. Place potatoes, onion, celery, and salt in mixing bowl.
2. Add French dressing (page 513), mix well, and let stand for 15 minutes.
3. Add egg and mayonnaise, and mix carefully.
4. Arrange in large bowl on lettuce leaves, and sprinkle with chopped parsley.

FRUIT PUNCH

24 Punch-cup Servings

2 cups sugar
1 cup hot water
4 cups grape juice
1½ cups orange juice
1¼ cups lemon juice
2 cups crushed pineapple, undrained
4 cups cold water or cold tea
Block of ice or ice cubes
Slices of orange or lemon
Mint leaves, maraschino cherries, or berries

1. Place sugar and hot water in saucepan, and stir until sugar dissolves.
2. Place over heat, bring to boiling point, and boil for 1 minute.
3. Cool.
4. Add fruit juices and crushed pineapple, and chill until ready to serve.
5. Add cold water or tea.
6. Serve in punch bowl with block of ice or ice cubes.
7. Garnish with slices of orange or lemon and mint leaves, maraschino cherries, or berries.

VARIATION
Substitute 1 quart ginger ale for water.

BROILED GRAPEFRUIT

4 Servings

2 grapefruit
4 tablespoons brown sugar
4 teaspoons butter or margarine

1. Wash and dry grapefruit.
2. Cut in half crosswise.
3. Cut pulp away from membrane in each section with small, sharp-pointed knife.
4. Cut out membrane at core with scissors or grapefruit corer.
5. Sprinkle each half with 1 tablespoon brown sugar, and dot with 1 teaspoon butter or margarine.
6. Place on rack in broiler pan, and place pan in oven with grapefruit 3 inches from broiling unit.
7. Broil for 5 to 10 minutes, or until sugar melts and top of grapefruit is slightly browned.
8. Top with maraschino cherry, raisins, or chopped nuts, if desired.
9. Serve hot as first course or dessert.

VARIATION
Substitute 4 teaspoons of honey or maple syrup for brown sugar.

Note: Instead of broiling, grapefruit may be baked in hot oven (400° F.) for 15 minutes, or until sugar melts and top of grapefruit is slightly browned.

TOSSED GREEN SALAD

4 Servings

1 piece celery
½ carrot
2 small tomatoes
½ medium head lettuce
½ teaspoon salt
¼ cup French dressing

1. Wash vegetables, drain, and chill for ½ hour.
2. Slice celery crosswise.
3. Scrape carrot, and cut it into very thin slices.
4. Cut the tomatoes into wedges.
5. Tear lettuce into pieces.
6. Put celery, carrot, tomatoes, and lettuce in a salad bowl. Add salt.
7. Pour French dressing (page 513) over vegetables slowly.
8. Toss lightly with two forks until vegetables are coated with dressing.
9. Serve in bowl to be passed or on individual salad plates.

VARIATIONS
Use any mixture of salad greens, such as chicory, watercress, endive, romaine, young tender spinach leaves, and cabbage with such raw vegetables as radishes, green peppers, onion, chives, cucumbers, and raw cauliflower, or such cooked vegetables as string beans, lima beans, peas, or carrots.

Add slices of hard-cooked egg or crumbled American Roquefort, or blue, cheese.

WALDORF SALAD

4–6 Servings

3 medium apples, preferably red
½ cup chopped celery
2 to 3 tablespoons mayonnaise
⅛ teaspoon salt
Salad greens
¼ cup chopped nuts

1. Wash, quarter, and remove core from apples.
2. Pare, if desired, but if red apples are used, skin may be left on to add color.
3. Place apples on cutting board, and dice.
4. Place apples, celery, mayonnaise, and salt in mixing bowl, and mix lightly.
5. Arrange on salad greens, and sprinkle with chopped nuts.

VARIATIONS

Add raisins or dates.

Add nutmeg or a little lemon juice.

Note: If salad is not to be served immediately, apples should be sprinkled with lemon juice before mixing to prevent their turning brown.

COLE SLAW

4 Servings

¼ cup light cream or evaporated milk
1 tablespoon vinegar
½ teaspoon salt
2 teaspoons sugar
⅛ teaspoon dry mustard
Few grains pepper
2 cups shredded cabbage

1. Place cream, vinegar, salt, sugar, mustard, and pepper together in mixing bowl, and mix well.
2. Add shredded cabbage, and mix lightly with two forks.
3. Serve immediately.

VARIATIONS

Substitute ½ cup chopped green and red pepper and ½ cup drained canned pineapple tidbits or chunks for 1 cup shredded cabbage. Mix green and red pepper, pineapple, and remaining cup of shredded cabbage.

Substitute 1 cup grated carrots for 1 cup shredded cabbage.

CEREAL FOODS

OATMEAL

4 Servings

2 cups water
½ teaspoon salt
1 cup rolled oats

1. Place water and salt in top of double boiler over direct heat, and bring to a rapid, rolling boil.
2. Add rolled oats to boiling water gradually, stirring constantly, so water does not stop boiling.
3. Cook for 5 to 10 minutes, stirring constantly.
4. Place over boiling water, cover, and cook slowly, stirring occasionally, for 15 minutes.
5. Serve hot with cream or milk and sugar as desired.

CORN GRITS CEREAL

4½ Cups

1 teaspoon salt
5 cups water
1 cup corn grits

1. Add salt to water and heat to boiling.
2. Stir in corn grits slowly.
3. Lower heat and stir until thickened.
4. Cook 15 minutes longer over low heat, stirring to keep from sticking.
5. Serve hot.

OVEN-COOKED RICE

4 Servings

1 cup uncooked rice
2 cups water
1 teaspoon salt
1 tablespoon butter or margarine

1. Place rice, water, salt, and butter in baking dish, and stir.
2. Cover, and bake in moderate oven (350° F.) for 30 minutes.
3. Serve hot as desired.

VARIATION

Add beef broth or chicken broth in place of water. Mushrooms may be added to the beef or chicken broth.

TOAST

4 Servings

4 slices bread
2 tablespoons butter or margarine, softened

OVEN METHOD
1. Place bread on baking sheet.
2. Bake in hot oven (400° F.) until light brown, turning once.
3. Remove toast, and spread with butter or margarine.
4. Serve immediately.

BROILER METHOD
1. Place bread on rack in broiler pan.
2. Place pan in oven with bread 3 inches from broiling unit.
3. Toast until light brown, turning once.
4. Remove toast, and spread with butter or margarine.
5. Serve immediately.

VARIATIONS

Cheese: Place toast on baking sheet, sprinkle with ¼ cup grated sharp cheese, and heat in oven for 1 to 2 minutes.

Cinnamon: Place toast on baking sheet. Mix 1 teaspoon cinnamon and 4 tablespoons sugar, sprinkle over buttered toast, and heat in oven for 1 to 2 minutes.

Milk: Place 2 cups milk, 2 tablespoons butter or margarine, and ½ teaspoon salt in saucepan, and heat until hot but do not boil. Pour over toast, and serve immediately.

Orange: Place toast on baking sheet. Mix ¼ cup orange juice, 2 teaspoons grated orange rind, and 4 tablespoons sugar in saucepan, and simmer for 2 minutes. Spread mixture on buttered toast, and heat in oven for 1 to 2 minutes.

Note: If toast is made in an automatic toaster, set control to desired brownness.

FRENCH TOAST

4 Servings

2 eggs
¼ teaspoon salt
½ cup milk
4 slices white bread
3 tablespoons butter or margarine

1. Beat eggs slightly in shallow bowl, and add salt and milk.
2. Dip each slice of bread into egg mixture, first on one side, and then on the other.
3. Melt butter or margarine in skillet over low heat.
4. Place slices of egg-coated bread in melted butter or margarine, and cook until golden brown, turning once.
5. Serve immediately with jelly or syrup, or lightly dusted with powdered sugar, as desired.

Note: Raisin or whole-wheat bread may also be used.

THE BISCUIT MASTER MIX

13 Cups

9 cups sifted all-purpose flour
⅓ cup baking powder
1 tablespoon salt
2 teaspoons cream of tartar
4 tablespoons sugar
1 cup nonfat dry milk
2 cups shortening which does not require refrigeration

1. Sift together 3 times the flour, baking powder, salt, cream of tartar, sugar, and dry milk.
2. Cut in shortening with pastry blender or two knives until mixture looks like coarse cornmeal.
3. Store in covered containers at room temperature.

Note: To measure the Master Mix, pile it lightly into cup and level off with spatula.

CORN BREAD

12 Servings

1¼ cups cornmeal
¾ cup sifted all-purpose flour
¼ cup sugar
1 tablespoon baking powder
½ teaspoon salt
1 egg
1 cup milk
¼ cup vegetable oil or bacon drippings

1. Sift together cornmeal, flour, sugar, baking powder, and salt.
2. Beat egg well, add milk and fat, and mix thoroughly.
3. Pour liquid mixture into flour mixture, stirring lightly until flour mixture is just moistened.
4. Fill greased pan (square, round, or muffin) one-half to two-thirds full.
5. Bake in hot oven (400° F.) for 20 to 25 minutes, or until brown.
6. Cut as desired, and serve hot.

BAKING POWDER BISCUITS

12 Biscuits

2 cups sifted all-purpose flour
3 teaspoons baking powder
¾ teaspoon salt
4 tablespoons shortening
⅔ cup milk

1. Sift together flour, baking powder, and salt.
2. Cut in shortening with pastry blender or two knives until mixture looks like meal.
3. Add milk gradually, stirring to make a soft dough.
4. Place dough on lightly floured board, knead gently 6 to 10 times, and roll ½ inch thick.
5. Cut dough with biscuit cutter dipped in flour.
6. Place biscuits on ungreased baking sheet.
7. Bake in very hot oven (450° F.) for 12 to 15 minutes, or until brown.
8. Serve hot with butter or margarine, jelly, preserves, or syrup as desired.

HOW TO USE THE BISCUIT MASTER MIX

Product Amount	Mix	Sugar	Water	Eggs	Other Ingredients	Amount of Mixing	Temperature/time
Biscuits (15–20)	3 cups		⅔ to 1 cup			Until blended. Knead 10 times.	400° F. 10 minutes
Muffins (12)	3 cups	2 T.	1 cup	1		Until ingredients are just moistened	400° F. 20 minutes
Coffee cake	3 cups	½ cup	⅔ cup	1	For topping: ½ cup brown sugar, 3 T. butter, ½ t. cinnamon	Until blended.	400° F. 25 minutes
Griddlecakes (18) or Waffles (6)	3 cups		1½ cups	1		Until blended.	
Gingerbread (8 × 8 inches)	2 cups	4 T.	½ cup	1	½ cup molasses; ½ t. cinnamon; ½ t. cloves; ½ t. ginger	Add half of liquid and beat 2 minutes. Add rest of liquid, and beat 1 minute.	350° F. 40 minutes
Oatmeal Cookies (4 dozen)	3 cups	1 cup	⅓ cup	1	1 t. cinnamon; 1 cup quick rolled oats	Until blended.	350° F. 10–12 minutes
Drop Cookies (4 dozen)	3 cups	1 cup	⅓ cup	1	1 t. vanilla; ½ cup nuts or chocolate bits	Until blended.	350° F. 10–12 minutes
Yellow Cake	3 cups	1¼ cups	1 cup	2	1 t. vanilla	Add two-thirds liquid, and beat 2 minutes. Add rest of liquid, and beat 2 minutes.	350° F. 25 minutes
Chocolate Cake	3 cups	1½ cups	1 cup	2	1 t. vanilla; ½ cup cocoa	Add two-thirds liquid, and beat 2 minutes. Add remaining liquid, and beat 2 minutes.	350° F. 25 minutes

MEAT SALAD SANDWICHES

4 Sandwiches

½ cup chopped cooked meat (chicken, ham, pork, or beef)
2 tablespoons chopped celery
2 tablespoons chopped olives
1 hard-cooked egg, chopped
¼ cup mayonnaise
8 slices thin sandwich bread
4 tablespoons butter or margarine, softened

1. Place meat, celery, olives, egg, and mayonnaise in mixing bowl, and mix thoroughly.
2. Trim crusts from bread, and place slices in two rows for spreading.
3. Spread all slices with softened butter or margarine.
4. Spread one row of slices with filling evenly to edges of bread.
5. Cover with other row of slices, and cut into halves, thirds, or quarters.

TUNA FISH ROLLS

6 Rolls

1 cup canned tuna fish, drained and flaked
¼ teaspoon grated onion
¼ cup chopped celery
⅛ teaspoon salt
Few grains pepper
3 tablespoons mayonnaise
6 oblong rolls

1. Place tuna fish, onion, celery, salt, pepper, and mayonnaise in mixing bowl, and mix lightly.
2. Split rolls lengthwise about two-thirds of the way through.
3. Fill with tuna fish mixture.

Note: Each roll may be wrapped in foil and heated in oven before serving, if desired.

ENERGY FOODS

TAFFY APPLES

6 Taffy Apples

6 medium apples
6 wooden skewers
1½ cups sugar
⅓ cup corn syrup
⅓ cup hot water
½ tablespoon vinegar

1. Wash and dry apples.
2. Insert wooden skewers in blossom ends.
3. Place sugar, corn syrup, water, and vinegar in saucepan, and stir.
4. Place over low heat, and cook to hard-crack stage (300° F.), or until syrup separates into threads which are hard but not brittle when dropped from spoon into cold water.
5. Remove from heat, and add red coloring, if desired.
6. Dip apples into hot mixture, and draw out quickly, twirling until taffy covers apples evenly.
7. Stand on end on well-greased tray so apples do not touch each other as they drain and cool.

Note: To prevent taffy from hardening in saucepan while dipping apples, place pan in boiling water or use double boiler.

PEANUT BUTTER COOKIES

5–6 Dozen Cookies

1¼ cups sifted all-purpose flour
¾ teaspoon baking powder
¼ teaspoon baking soda
¼ teaspoon salt
½ cup butter or margarine
½ cup sugar
½ cup peanut butter
½ cup brown sugar
1 egg, well beaten

1. Sift together flour, baking powder, baking soda, and salt.
2. Cream butter or margarine, and add sugar, peanut butter, and brown sugar gradually, creaming after each addition until light and fluffy.
3. Add egg, and mix thoroughly.
4. Add flour mixture gradually, beating after each addition until smooth.
5. Drop mixture, 1 teaspoon at a time and about 2 inches apart, onto ungreased baking sheet.
6. Press with tines of fork until very thin, making crisscross marks.
7. Bake in moderate oven (350° F.) for 8 to 10 minutes, or until cookies are brown.
8. Remove cookies with spatula immediately to cool.

FRUIT BLOSSOM COOKIES

2 Dozen Cookies

2¼ cups sifted all-purpose flour
1½ teaspoons baking powder
¼ teaspoon salt
⅔ cup shortening
¾ cup sugar
1 egg, slightly beaten
½ teaspoon vanilla
2 tablespoons milk
Fruit filling

1. Sift together flour, baking powder, and salt.
2. Cream shortening, and add sugar gradually, creaming after each addition until light and fluffy.
3. Add egg and vanilla, and beat until light and fluffy.
4. Add flour mixture to creamed shortening mixture in three portions alternately with milk in two portions, beginning and ending with flour mixture, and beating after each addition until smooth.
5. Divide dough into two parts, and chill both parts until firm enough to roll.
6. Place one part of dough on lightly floured board or wax paper, and roll until ⅛ inch thick.
7. Cut into circles with floured 2-inch scalloped cookie cutter, and place circles on greased baking sheet.
8. Place ½ teaspoon filling in center of each cookie.
9. Place other part of dough on lightly floured board or wax paper, and roll until ⅛ inch thick.
10. Cut into circles with same cutter, and cut out centers with 1-inch round cutter.
11. Place open circles on top of filled circles, and press edges with a fork.
12. Bake in moderate oven (350° F.) for 10 to 12 minutes, or until cookies are brown.
13. Remove cookies with spatula immediately to cool.

FRUIT FILLING FOR COOKIES

½ Cup

½ cup chopped seedless raisins
1 teaspoon grated orange rind
2 tablespoons orange juice
1 teaspoon lemon juice
8 teaspoons water
4 tablespoons sugar
1 teaspoon flour
¼ teaspoon salt

1. Place all ingredients in saucepan, and cook over medium heat for 5 minutes, stirring constantly until thickened.
2. Cool, and use as filling for cookies.

VARIATIONS

Apricot: Substitute chopped dried apricots for raisins, add 3 teaspoons orange juice, ½ teaspoon lemon juice, 6 tablespoons water, and 2 teaspoons flour.

Fig: Substitute chopped dried figs for raisins.

CHOCOLATE PINWHEELS

3 Dozen Cookies

2 cups sifted cake flour
1 teaspoon baking powder
½ teaspoon salt
½ cup butter or margarine
⅔ cup sugar
1 egg, slightly beaten
1 tablespoon milk
1 square unsweetened chocolate, melted

1. Sift together flour, baking powder, and salt.
2. Cream butter or margarine, and add sugar gradually, creaming after each addition until light.
3. Add egg and milk, and mix thoroughly.
4. Add flour mixture gradually, beating after each addition until smooth.
5. Divide dough into two parts.
6. Add chocolate to one part of dough, and mix thoroughly.
7. Chill until firm enough to roll.
8. Roll each part of dough between wax papers into rectangles ⅛ inch thick.
9. Remove top wax paper from each rectangle of dough, and place plain dough on top of chocolate dough with wax paper on outside.
10. Remove wax paper from top and bottom, place on lightly floured board, and roll up, starting from the long side of the dough.
11. Chill until firm enough to slice.
12. Cut into slices ⅛ inch thick, and place on ungreased baking sheet.
13. Bake in moderate oven (350° F.) for 10 minutes, or until cookies are brown.
14. Remove cookies with spatula immediately to cool.

Note: Rolls of dough may be stored in refrigerator or freezer, and sliced and baked as needed.

COCOA FUDGE

1½ Pounds

½ cup cocoa
2 cups sugar
⅛ teaspoon cream of tartar
⅔ cup milk
2 tablespoons butter or margarine
1 teaspoon vanilla

1. Place cocoa, sugar, cream of tartar, and milk in saucepan, and mix well.
2. Place over low heat, and cook, stirring constantly, until sugar dissolves.
3. Cover, and cook for 2 minutes longer.
4. Uncover, and cook to soft-ball stage (234° to 240° F.), or until mixture forms a soft ball when dropped from spoon into cold water.
5. Remove from heat.
6. Add butter or margarine, but do not stir.
7. Cool to lukewarm without stirring.
8. Add vanilla, and beat until creamy, or until shine disappears.
9. Pour into greased cake pan.
10. Mark into squares when mixture has set.
11. Cut when cool, and serve.

VARIATION
Add ½ cup chopped nuts or ½ cup chopped dried fruit during last beating strokes.

QUICK-MIX GOLD CAKE

Two 8-inch Layers

2¼ cups sifted cake flour
2½ teaspoons baking powder
1 teaspoon salt
1¼ cups sugar
¾ cup softened shortening
1 cup milk
2 eggs
1 teaspoon vanilla or 2 teaspoons grated orange rind

1. Sift together flour, baking powder, salt, and sugar.
2. Add shortening, ½ cup milk, and unbeaten eggs, and stir lightly until flour mixture is dampened.
3. Beat vigorously with mixing spoon or in an electric mixer at medium speed for 1 minute.
4. Add remaining milk and vanilla or grated orange rind, and beat for 2 minutes.
5. Pour into 2 greased cake pans.
6. Bake in moderate oven (350° F.) for 30 minutes, or until top of cake is brown and springs back to the touch.
7. Cool pans on cake rack.
8. Remove cake, and cool on cake rack before frosting.

VARIATIONS

Cupcakes: Make about 12 cupcakes. Fill each greased muffin pan one-half full. Bake in moderate oven (350° F.) for 25 minutes, or until tops of cupcakes are brown and spring back to touch.

LEMON CHIFFON CAKE

10-inch Tube Cake

2 cups sifted cake flour
3 teaspoons baking powder
1 teaspoon salt
1½ cups sugar
½ cup salad oil
¾ cup water
1 tablespoon grated lemon rind
7 eggs, separated
½ teaspoon cream of tartar

1. Sift together flour, baking powder, salt, and sugar.
2. Add oil, water, lemon rind, and unbeaten egg yolks, and beat until smooth.
3. Place egg whites in bowl, add cream of tartar, and beat with electric mixer at high speed or with rotary beater until stiff.
4. Pour flour–egg-yolk mixture into beaten egg whites.
5. Fold in lightly until just mixed.
6. Pour into ungreased 10-inch tube pan.
7. Bake in slow oven (300° F.) for 55 minutes, and then raise heat to moderate (350° F.) for 15 minutes, or until top of cake is brown and springs back to the touch.
8. Remove from oven, and invert pan on cake rack to cool.
9. Loosen with spatula around edges when cool to remove cake from pan.

UNCOOKED FROSTING

For 2-layer Cake

1 cup butter or margarine
2 teaspoons vanilla
6 cups sifted confectioners' sugar
¼ cup light cream or evaporated milk, undiluted

1. Cream butter or margarine, and add vanilla.
2. Add confectioners' sugar and cream alternately to creamed butter or margarine until mixture is of a consistency to spread.

VARIATIONS

Lemon: Substitute ¼ cup lemon juice for ¼ cup cream, and add 1 tablespoon grated lemon rind. Omit vanilla.

Mocha: Substitute ¼ cup cold, strong coffee for ¼ cup cream, and add 3 tablespoons cocoa.

Orange: Substitute ¼ cup orange juice for ¼ cup cream, and add 1 tablespoon grated orange rind. Omit vanilla.

Pineapple: Substitute ⅓ cup drained crushed pineapple for ¼ cup cream. Omit vanilla.

TEN-MINUTE FUDGE

1¾ Pounds

3 squares unsweetened chocolate
4 tablespoons butter or margarine
½ cup corn syrup
1 tablespoon water
1 teaspoon vanilla
1 pound confectioners' sugar
⅓ cup nonfat dry milk
½ cup chopped nuts

1. Melt chocolate and butter or margarine in top of double boiler over boiling water in bottom of double boiler.
2. Add corn syrup, water, and vanilla, and stir.
3. Sift together confectioners' sugar and dry milk, and add gradually to mixture in double boiler, stirring constantly until smooth.
4. Remove from heat, add nuts, and stir.
5. Pour into greased cake pan.
6. Mark into squares when mixture has set.
7. Cut when cool, and serve.

VARIATION

Substitute 1 cup marshmallow pieces or miniature marshmallows for ½ cup chopped nuts.

CHOCOLATE SAUCE

½ Cup

1 square unsweetened chocolate or 3 tablespoons cocoa
½ cup water
1 tablespoon butter or margarine
1 cup sugar
⅛ teaspoon salt
½ teaspoon vanilla

1. Place chocolate or cocoa in saucepan, add water, and cook over low heat, stirring constantly, until smooth.
2. Add butter or margarine, sugar, and salt, and cook, stirring constantly, until sugar dissolves.
3. Add vanilla, and stir.
4. Serve with ice cream or pudding.

PASTRY (Hot Water)

One 8- or 9-inch Pie Crust

1 cup sifted all-purpose flour
½ teaspoon salt
⅓ cup shortening
2 to 3 tablespoons boiling water

1. Sift together flour and salt.
2. Place shortening in mixing bowl.
3. Gradually add boiling water to shortening, creaming with a fork until well mixed.
4. Add flour to shortening mixture and shape into a ball.
5. Chill, roll, and bake as conventional pastry.

PASTRY (Conventional or Cold-water)

One 8- or 9-inch Pie Crust

1 cup sifted all-purpose flour
½ teaspoon salt
⅓ cup shortening
2 to 3 tablespoons cold water

1. Sift together flour and salt.
2. Cut in shortening with pastry blender or two knives until mixture looks like small peas.
3. Sprinkle with 1 tablespoon cold water, and mix lightly with a fork.
4. Continue adding cold water gradually and mixing quickly until dough holds together.
5. Chill dough for 5 minutes.
6. Place dough on lightly floured board or between two 12-inch squares of wax paper.
7. Roll dough to desired thickness (about ⅛ inch) in a circle 1 inch larger than pie pan.
8. Place circle of dough in pie pan, trim edge so there is ½ inch of dough beyond rim of pan, and fold under and flute as desired.
9. Prick small holes in dough with a fork before baking unfilled shell.
10. Bake in hot oven (400° F.), for 8 to 10 minutes, or until brown.

PASTRY (Paste)

One 8- or 9-inch Pie Crust

1 cup sifted all-purpose flour
½ teaspoon salt
⅓ cup shortening
3 tablespoons tap water

1. Mix flour and salt together. Save out one-fourth cup of the flour mix in small bowl.
2. Cut together the remaining three-fourths cup flour mix with the shortening until flour is meal-like in texture.
3. Make a paste of the one-fourth cup flour and water.
4. Stir the paste into the flour mixture and shape into a ball.
5. Chill, roll, and bake as conventional pastry.

PASTRY (Oil)

One 8- or 9-inch Pie Crust

1 cup sifted all-purpose flour
½ teaspoon salt
¼ cup salad oil
2½ tablespoons cold water

1. Sift together flour and salt.
2. Combine oil and cold water and beat with fork until creamy.
3. Pour, immediately, over flour mixture.
4. Toss and mix with fork.
5. Form into ball.
6. Chill, roll, and bake as conventional pastry.

PUMPKIN PIE

One 9-inch Pie

¾ cup brown sugar
1 tablespoon flour
¼ teaspoon salt
2½ teaspoons pumpkin pie spice
1 egg, slightly beaten
1½ cups canned pumpkin
1⅓ cups evaporated milk, undiluted
Pastry shell
1 tablespoon butter or margarine
2 tablespoons brown sugar
1½ teaspoons grated orange rind
½ cup chopped pecans or walnuts

1. Place ¾ cup brown sugar, flour, salt, and pumpkin pie spice in mixing bowl, and mix well.
2. Add egg, pumpkin and evaporated milk, and stir.
3. Pour into unbaked pastry shell.
4. Bake in very hot oven (425° F.) for 15 minutes.
5. Reduce heat to 325° F., and bake for 15 minutes longer.
6. Remove pie from oven.
7. Mix butter or margarine, 2 tablespoons brown sugar, orange rind, and nuts, and spoon around edge of filling.
8. Return pie to oven, and bake at 325° F. for 15 minutes, or until filling has set.
9. Serve hot or cold as desired.

VARIATION

Sweet Potato Pie: Substitute mashed sweet potatoes for the pumpkin.

CHERRY TARTS

6 or 8 Tarts

Pastry
¾ cup sugar
3 tablespoons flour
⅛ teaspoon salt
1 can (No. 2) sour pitted cherries
2 tablespoons butter or margarine

1. Roll pastry (pages 510–511), and cut into rounds large enough to cover cups of inverted muffin pan.
2. Place rounds on muffin cups, shape to fit, and prick with a fork.
3. Bake in hot oven (400° F.) for 10 minutes, or until very light brown.
4. Cool slightly before removing from cups.
5. Place sugar, flour, and salt in saucepan, and mix well.
6. Add juice drained from cherries slowly and butter or margarine, and mix thoroughly.
7. Place over low heat, and cook, stirring constantly, until mixture is smooth and thickened.
8. Add cherries, and bring to boiling point.
9. Remove from heat, and cool.
10. Pour into baked pastry shells.
11. Serve with whipped cream, if desired.

BACON SPREAD

1¼ Cups

½ cup chopped crisp bacon
3 hard-cooked eggs, chopped
2 tablespoons chopped sweet pickle
⅛ teaspoon horseradish
½ teaspoon salt
1 tablespoon French dressing
1 tablespoon mayonnaise

1. Place all ingredients in mixing bowl, and mix thoroughly.
2. Use as sandwich filling, or serve on crackers or toast.

PEANUT BUTTER SPREAD

2 Cups

1 cup peanut butter
1 cup chopped raisins
2 tablespoons orange juice
⅛ teaspoon salt

1. Place all ingredients in mixing bowl, and mix thoroughly.
2. Use as sandwich filling, or serve on crackers.

FRENCH DRESSING

1½ Cups

1 cup salad oil
¼ cup vinegar
1½ teaspoons salt
⅛ teaspoon pepper
¼ teaspoon paprika
¾ teaspoon sugar
1 tablespoon lemon juice
1 teaspoon Worcestershire sauce
1 garlic clove (optional)

1. Place all ingredients in tightly covered jar, and shake vigorously.
2. Remove garlic cloves.
3. Store in refrigerator.
4. Shake vigorously each time just before using.
5. Serve with vegetable salads.

VARIATION

Roquefort Cheese: Add ½ cup crumbled Roquefort, or blue, cheese.

THOUSAND ISLAND DRESSING

About 1 Cup

½ cup mayonnaise or cooked salad dressing
1 tablespoon chili sauce
1 tablespoon chopped stuffed olives
1 teaspoon minced chives
¼ teaspoon paprika
1 chopped hard-cooked egg
Dash pepper
Few grains salt

1. Place mayonnaise in small mixing bowl.
2. Add all ingredients and toss lightly.
3. Store in covered container in refrigerator.

VARIATIONS

Blue cheese dressing: Crumble small package of blue, or Roquefort, cheese into mayonnaise or cooked salad dressing.

Sour cream dressing: Mix ½ cup sour cream with ½ cup mayonnaise. Add 2 teaspoons chopped chives for flavor and color.

Student Bibliography

Teen-age Relationships

Bailard, Virginia and others. *Ways to Improve Your Personality.* McGraw-Hill Book Company, New York. 1965

Beery, Mary. *Manners Made Easy.* Webster Division, McGraw-Hill Book Company, St. Louis. 1966

Haupt, Enid A. *The Seventeen Guide to Your Widening World.* The Macmillan Company, New York. 1968

James, Barry. *Call Me Mister.* Milady Publishing Company, Bronx, N.Y. 1966

McGinnis, Tom. *A Girl's Guide to Dating and Going Steady.* Doubleday & Company, Inc., Garden City, N.Y. 1968

Menninger, William C. *How to be a Successful Teen-ager.* Sterling Publishing Co., Inc., New York. 1966

Sorenson, Herbert and others. *Psychology for Living.* Webster Division, McGraw-Hill Book Company, St. Louis. 1971

Uggams, Leslie. *Beauty Book.* McGraw-Hill Book Company, New York. 1966

Whitcomb, Helen and others. *Charm for Miss Teen.* McGraw-Hill Book Company, New York. 1969

Home and Family Living

Ames, Louise Bates. *Child Care and Development.* J. B. Lippincott and Company, Philadelphia. 1970

Baker, Katherine Read and others. *Understanding and Guiding Young Children.* Prentice-Hall, Inc., Englewood Cliffs, N.J. 1967

Clayton, Nanalee. *Young Living.* Chas. A. Bennett Co., Inc., Peoria, Ill. 1970

Craig, Hazel T. and others. *Homes with Character.* D. C. Heath and Company, Boston. 1970

Cross, Aleene. *Introductory Homemaking.* J. B. Lippincott and Company, Philadelphia. 1970

Fleck, Henrietta and others. *Exploring Home and Family Living.* Prentice-Hall., Inc., Englewood Cliffs, N.J. 1971

Hurlock, Elizabeth B. *Child Growth and Development.* Webster Division, McGraw-Hill Book Company, St. Louis. 1968

Landis, Judson T. and others. *Personal Adjustment, Marriage and Family Living.* Prentice-Hall, Inc., Englewood Cliffs, N.J. 1970

Landis, Paul H. *Your Marriage and Family Living.* Webster Division, McGraw-Hill Book Company, St. Louis. 1969

Lewis, Dora S. and others. *Teen Horizons at Home and School.* The Macmillan Company, New York. 1970

McDermott, Irene E. and others. *Homemaking for Teenagers—Book I.* Chas. A. Bennett Co., Inc. Peoria, Ill. 1970

Morton, Ruth and others. *The Home: Its Furnishings and Equipment.* McGraw-Hill Book Company, St. Louis. 1970

Osborne, Ernest G. *Understanding Your Parents.* Association Press, New York. 1966

Reiff, Florence M. *Steps in Home Living.* Chas. A. Bennett Co., Inc., Peoria, Ill. 1966

Shuey, Rebekah M. and others. *Learning about Children.* J. B. Lippincott and Company, Philadelphia. 1969

Consumership and Resource Management

Britton, Virginia. *Personal Finance.* Van Nostrand Reinhold Company, New York. 1968

Caplovitz, David. *The Poor Pay More.* The Free Press, New York. 1967

Lewis, Dora S. and others. *Housing and Home Management.* The Macmillan Company, New York. 1969

Schoenfeld, David and others. *The Consumer and His Dollars.* Oceana Publications, Inc., Dobbs Ferry, N.Y. 1970

Smith, Carlton and others. *Time-Life Book of Family Finance.* Time-Life Books, New York. 1969

Starr, Mary Catherine. *Management for Better Living.* D. C. Heath and Company, Boston. 1968

Thal, Helen. *Your Family and its Money.* Houghton Mifflin Company, Boston. 1968

Clothing and Textiles

Carson, Byrta. *How You Look and Dress*. Webster Division, McGraw-Hill Book Company, St. Louis. 1969

Dunn, Lucile and others. *Steps in Clothing Skills*. Chas. A. Bennett Co., Inc., Peoria, Ill. 1970

Erwin, Mabel D. and others. *Clothing for Moderns*. The Macmillan Company, New York. 1969

Garrett, Pauline G. and others. *You Are a Consumer of Clothing*. Ginn and Company, Boston. 1967

Gawne, Eleanor J. and others. *Dress*. Chas. A. Bennett Co., Inc., Peoria, Ill. 1969

Sturm, Mary Mark and others. *Guide to Modern Clothing*. Webster Division, McGraw-Hill Book Company, St. Louis. 1968

Todd, Elizabeth and others. *Clothes for Teens*. D. C. Heath and Company, Boston. 1969

Vanderhoff, Margil. *Clothes: Part of Your World*. Ginn and Company, Boston. 1968

Foods and Nutrition

Carson, Byrta and others. *How You Plan and Prepare Meals*. Webster Division, McGraw-Hill Book Company, St. Louis. 1968

Cote, Patricia. *People, Food and Science*. Ginn and Company, Boston. 1968

McDermott, Irene E. and others. *Food for Modern Living*. J. B. Lippincott and Company, Philadelphia. 1967

Shank, Dorothy E. and others. *Guide to Modern Meals*. Webster Division, McGraw-Hill Book Company, St. Louis. 1970

Tannenbaum, Beulah and others. *Understanding Food: The Chemistry of Nutrition*. McGraw-Hill Book Company, New York. 1962

Women's Day Magazine. *Women's Day Encyclopedia of Cookery* (12 volumes). Fawcett Publications, Inc., New York. 1965, 1966

The World of Work

Anderson, W. and others. *World of Work Kit*. Webster Division, McGraw-Hill Book Company, St. Louis. 1969

Andrews, Margaret E. *Opportunity Knocks Series*. McGraw-Hill Book Company, New York. 1968, 1969

Famularo, Joseph J. and others. *The Executive Profile: The Young Man's Guide to Business Success*. McGraw-Hill Book Company, New York. 1967

Feingold, S. Norman and others. *Occupations and Careers*. Webster Division, McGraw-Hill Book Company, St. Louis. 1969

McDermott, Irene E. and others. *Opportunities in Clothing*. Chas. A. Bennett Co., Inc., Peoria, Ill. 1968

The Turner Career Guidance Series. Follett Educational Corporation, Chicago. 1967

Audio-Visual Materials

Learning about Drugs. Filmstrip and record combination distributed in the United States by Webster Division, McGraw-Hill Book Company, St. Louis. 1970

Grieser, Edwina H. *Clothing Construction Film Loop Series*. Super 8 mm. Webster Division, McGraw-Hill Book Company, St. Louis. 1968

Sturm, Mary Mark and others. *Clothing Transparencies: Line and Color in Clothes. Design in Clothes*. Webster Division, McGraw-Hill Book Company, St. Louis. 1968

Food Preparation Film Loop Series. Super 8 mm. McGraw-Hill Films, McGraw-Hill Book Company, New York. 1970

Index

A

ability to learn, 51–52
acceptance, need for, 44, 85
accessories, in clothing, 290–293
   in furnishings, 244–246, 271
acetate, 274
acrylics, 272, 273, 275
additives, 378
adjustments, making of personal, 56
   in patterns, 338–340
adolescence, 41–42, 54, 85
   (see also teen-agers)
advertising, 216, 218–219, 271
   emotionalized, 64, 218, 219
   factual, 64, 219
   of foods, 377–379
air, as a leavener, 444–445
alcohol, use of, 63–64
allergies, 50
   to milk, 419
allowances, 208–209
alterationist, 288, 304
altering, of patterns, 341–343
AMBROSIA, 495
American National Red Cross, 164–165
anemia, 372
anger, 53
antiperspirant, 67
antistatic finishes, 280
appearance, 51, 255, 295
   aids to attractiveness, 64–74
   of clothing, *276–277*
   and nutrition, 363
APPLES, BAKED, 496
   cooking of, 434
   TAFFY, 505
APPLESAUCE, 497
appliances, 173–174, 179
   safety of, 164–165
appreciation, need for, 44

apron, sewing, 318, 326–329
aptitudes, 52
ASPARAGUS-EGG CASSEROLE, 490
assembly, of garments, 345–354
assistance, sources of, 80–82
attitudes, 52–53, 130
   about energy, 203–204
   and job choice, 93
   about money, 207–208
   about time, 197
attractiveness, aids to, 64–74

B

babies, caring for, 142–144
baby food specialist, 133
baby-sitting, *79*, *138*, *141–145*
bacon, 414
   BROILED, 482
BACON SPREAD, 512
BAKED APPLES, 496
BAKED CHEESE FONDUE, 491
BAKED CUSTARD, 492
BAKED HAMBURGERS, 480
BAKED POTATOES, 493
baker, 454
baking, 394
   of fruits, 434
   of vegetables, 432
baking powder, double-acting, 444–445
   single-acting, 444–445
   substitutes for, 479
BAKING POWDER BISCUITS, 502
barbecue, 410, *474*
bargains, buying of, 228
barley, cooking of, 447
baste stitch, 296, 343
bathing, *66*
   of babies, 143
   of young children, 144–145

bathroom, *155*
   care of, daily, 171
   weekly, 174–175
batters, 442
BEANS, GREEN, 495
   dry, 408–409
bedrooms, care of, daily, 171
   weekly, 176–177
beef, 381–383, 413
   cooking of, 413
   cuts of, 410
BEEF-ARONI, 481
BEEF STEW, 456, 484
behavior, in dating, 90–91
   patterns of, establishing, 141
   in public, 62–63
belts, 293
bias fold, 342
BISCUIT MASTER MIX, *446–447*,
   502–503
BISCUITS, BAKING POWDER, 502
BLACK-EYED PEAS AND RICE, *408*,
   488
bleaches, 299–300
blemishes, skin, 71–72
blend, of colors, 262
   of fibers, 277, 279
blocking, 314, 323
blouses, buying of, 284
bobbins, filling of, 324–325
   types of, 324
bodice, 342
body build, 49, 289
   and color choices, 260–265
body language, 61
boiling, 394
   of fruits, 434
   of vegetables, 432
bones, structure of, 49
brain, 51
braising, 410

bran, 439–440
brands, of canned goods, 388
   of food, 378–379
bras, buying of, 289–290
bread, buying of, 388–389
   ingredients used in, 442–447
   quick, 441–442, 445, 446
   types of, 440–441
   yeast, 441–442
bread-cereal food group, 361
breakfast, cereals for, 447
bridal consultant, 90
brods, 439
BROILED BACON, 482
BROILED FISH, 483
BROILED GRAPEFRUIT, 498
BROILED LIVER WITH BACON, 483
broiling, 409
brushing, of clothing, 296–297
budget, evaluation of, 213
   family, 112
   planning of, 209–213
budget consultant, family, 207
buffet, 470–472
bulbs, 429
bulletin boards, in home economics
       department, 244, 246–247
   ideas for, 20, 28, 29, 32, 34, 39, 45,
       48, 54, 55, 59, 61, 68, 77, 81, 86,
       94, 99, 109, 114, 122, 124, 135,
       145, 149, 150, 156, 160, 162, 167,
       171, 186, 189, 198, 199, 204, 208,
       219, 260, 265, 271, 273, 280, 303,
       305, 309, 313, 314, 331, 334, 361,
       366, 369, 373, 377, 389, 419, 427,
       430, 434, 439, 447, 449, 475
butter, 389
butter spreader, use of, 469
buttonholes, 282, 353
buttons, 282
buyer for teen-age clothes, 267
buying, bargain, 226, 228
   cash, 231
   on credit 221, 228–234
   emergency, 228–229

buying, general, 227–228
   on impulse, 380, 389
   on installment, 223–234
   seasonal, 227

C

cake decorator, 450
cake mixes, 452
cakes, angel, 452–453, 457
   chiffon, 452
   leavening in, 452–453
   methods of mixing, 452–453
   recipes for, 503, 508
   sponge, 453
   steps in making, 452
   texture of, 444
calcium, 372, 419–420
calories, 363–365, 372, 389
   requirements, 363–367
candles, 463–464
candy, cooking of, 451–452
   recipes for, 507, 509
   testing for doneness, 451
canned foods, 380
   capacity of containers, 479
capacity, mental, 51
carbohydrates, 365, 388, 450
carbon dioxide, as a leavener, 444–445
career, choice of, 91–94
   in home economics, 92–93
career opportunities, 74, 75, 78, 82, 84,
   90, 92, 93, 111, 129, 131, 133, 137,
   138, 140, 153, 187, 190, 205, 207,
   216, 218, 220, 223, 227, 229, 238–239,
   244, 258, 264, 266, 267, 284, 288,
   301, 304, 317, 348, 372, 378, 382,
   411, 425, 435, 437, 441, 450, 454,
   471
carpets, care of, 175, 178–179
Carver, George Washington, 104
casseroles, 432–433
   recipes for, 483, 490, 491
caterer, 471

cells, sex, 48
center of interest, 242, 244
centerpieces, 463–466
cereal cookery, principles of, 442–447
cereal foods, recipes for, 500–504
   types of, 440–442
cereals, 361–362, 365
   basic food group, 361–362
   breakfast, 447
       forms of, 389
   buying of, 388–389
   preparation of, 439–447
chapati, 439
characteristics, acquired, 48, 50
   and appearance, 51
   individual, 52
   inherited, 50
   physical, 48
charcoal, firing of, 476
charge accounts, 231
checkups, medical, 160–161
cheese, 361, 364, 367, 421–422, 424
   buying of, 387–388
   classifications of, 387–388
   cooking with, 425
   safe storage time for, 385
CHEESE SAUCE, 490
CHERRY TARTS, 512
chicken, recipes for, 482, 486
   (see also poultry)
CHICKEN SALAD, 482
child development, 124–130
children, caring for, 141–145
   clothes for, 130–133
   position in family, 106–108
   special needs of, 130–141
children's clothes designer, 131
CHILI, 481
chinaware, 459, 463
CHINESE SWEET AND SOUR
   PORK, 485
chitterlings, 414
chocolate, substitutes for, 479
CHOCOLATE CAKE, 503
CHOCOLATE PINWHEELS, 507

517

CHOCOLATE SAUCE, 510
choices, basis for, 151
    making of, 54–55
    vocational, 91–93
chores, household, 99, 113–114, 167–180
cigarettes, use of, 63–64
citizenship, responsibilities of, 19, 21–23
citrus fruit, 431
clean-finishing, 343
cleaning, after meals, 476
cleanliness, bodily, 66–67
    in the sickroom, 163
clique, 85
closets, cleaning of, 179
closures, 282–283, 352–353
cloth, see fabric
clothing, buying of, 271–293
    for children, 130–133
    choosing of, 255–269
        for age, 267
        for appropriateness, 265–267
        for attractiveness, 257–264
        for enjoyment, 269
        for occasion, 268
        for wearability, 268–269
    daily care of, 295–297
    seasonal care of, 306–307
    weekly care of, 297–306
clothing repair specialist, 301
coats, buying of, 288
cocoa, substituting for chocolate, 479
COCOA, 489
COCOA FUDGE, 507
COFFEE CAKE, 503
cold-water method, for making pastry, 455
    (see also PASTRY Recipes, 510–511)
COLE SLAW, 499
collars, attaching, 351
    sewing of, 351–352
color, in clothing, 257–263
    complementary, 260
    considering, in clothing selection, 259–263, 265

color, in food, *370*
    hue of, 260
    intensity of, 260
    placement of, 263
    of skin, 258–259, 277
    value of, 260
color accents, 260–263
color schemes, 262
color wheel, 260–261
comfort, organizing for, 168
commitment, to family members, 37–38
communication, barriers to, 61–62
    in family living, 35–*36*
    need for, 45
    nonverbal, 60
    verbal, 60
    written, 61
community, 18–19
    services of, 19, 25
companionship, with family members, 38–39
compromise, 56
concern, for family members, 36–*37*
confidence, and family living, 36
conflicts, brother-sister, 105
    of family, in mobility, 34
consideration, for family members, 39
construction, of clothing, details of, 280–281, 283, 347–350
    unit method of, 345–346
consumers, 215
    complaints of, 223–226
    as a family group, 33
    interaction of, with business, 234
    protection of, 223–226, 272–276, 378
    responsibilities of, 219–233
consumer service representative, 220
consumership, 155, *207*, 211, 215–234, 271–293, 310
contact lenses, 68
contracts, installment, 233–234
convalescent, caring for, 162–164
conventional method, of mixing cakes, 452
    of making pie crust, 455

conversation, at mealtime, 467, 469
cookies, recipes for, 505–507
    storing of, 455
    types of, 453–454
cooking, methods of, see individual foods and food groups
    terms in, 394–397
cooperation, in family living, 34–35
core family, 25–26
CORN BREAD, 502
CORN GRITS CEREAL, 500
cornstarch, substitutes for, 479
cosmetics, 72, 73, 227
cosmetologist, 74
cottage cheese, 425
cotton, 274
counselors, 81
courtesy, *63*
    in dating, *89*
    notes, 117
    toward parents, 103
cream puffs, 445
creativity, *192*
credit, 228–234
    cost of, 231–232
    prompt payment of, 221
    use of, 231
credit cards, 230–233
credit rating, 231
crosswise fold, 342
CRUST, FOR PIES, 455, 510–511
crystal, 463
crystallization, 451–453
culture, and food customs, *376*
curd, 425
custard, 421–422, 425
    recipes for, 492
custom dressmaker, 348
customs, of family, 27
    in food, 376
cutting, of pattern pieces, 343–344
    directional, 343–344
    to fit, 343
cycle, of family life, 29–33

D

Daily Food Guide, 360–361, *362*, 364, 368, 373, 420, 431, 449
day care centers, *19*
darts, 342, 347–348, 350
dating, *83*, 86–91
decisions, 75, 147
    acting on, 152–153
    consumer, 215
    making of, 54–*55*, 152–153, 188–189, 193
decorator, 153
decorating, for special occasions, 118
deep-frying, 451, 456
    safety rules for, 456
defrosting, 174, 394
denier, 292
dentifrice, 69
deodorant, 66–67
design, of fabric, 263, effect on sewing projects, 320–321
    of patterns, 337–338
designer, 264
designer, interior, 92, 153
detergents, 299–300
development, human, 93
    personal, *28*
    social, *102*
diabetes, 51
diet, balanced, 64, 361
dietitian, 82, 372
dietitian's aide, 425
differences, individual, 45–48
dinnerware, 459, 463–464
    placement of, 464
dips, 457
directional cutting, 343–344
directional stitching, *348*
discipline, children's need for, 140–141
diseases, childhood, 160
    contracted, 50–51
    inherited, 50–51
dishwasher, 474, 476

dishwashing, by hand, 474–475
doughnuts, *456*
doughs, 442
    for cookies, 453–454
dresses, buying of, 288–289
    judging quality of, 290
dressing, salad, recipes for, 513
DROP COOKIES, 453, 503
drugs, use of, 63–64
dry cleaning, 297, 302–*303*, 305
drying clothes, 297, 299
DUMPLINGS FOR STEW, 484
durable press, or permanent press, 278–280
dusting, 175–176
dyeing, 277, 281

E

earthenware, 459, 463
ease allowance, 334, 340–341
eggs, 364, 367, 372
    adding to hot mixtures, 417
    buying of, 384–385
    cooking of, 416–417
    FRIED, 456, 487
    grading of, 384–*385*, 416
    HARD-COOKED, 416–417, 487
    POACHED, 487
    safe storage time for, 384
    SCRAMBLED, 488
    separating of, 417
    SOFT-COOKED, 417, 487
    uses, in cooking, 417
        in flour mixtures, 446
EGG SAUCE, 490
elderly, the, 108
elimination, 68
emergencies, medical supplies for, 164
emotions, basic, 53–54
empathy, 39
endurance, 50
energy, 50
    attitudes about, 203–205

energy, conservation of, *200*, 404–405
    in cooking, 404–405
    levels of, 204–205
    management of, 187–189, 205–207
    and nutrition, 363
    sources of, 361
energy foods, cooking of, 449–457
    recipes for, 505–513
    types of, 450
entertaining, of family friends, 115–117
    meal service for, 470–474
    outdoor, 474
    planning for, on dates, 88
    safety in, 118
environment, 16
    natural, 18
    and physical needs, 42–43
    and physical traits, 48–49
    teen-age, 16–18
enzymes, 299, 300
equipment, cleaning, 170
    for family fun, 114
    in home economics department, *240–241*
    kitchen, 391
        care of, 396–397
        large, 394–395
        small, 392, 396–397
    for pressing, 243
    for sewing, 314
        large, 310–314
        small, 314–318
    for table, use of, 467–469
equipment demonstrator, 205
equivalents, 443, 479
ethnic groups, 27, *376*
etiquette, in dating, 87–88
evaluation, 75, 153
exercise, 65–66
    and appearance, 49
    and health, 160–161
expenditures, family, 111
expenses, considering, in budgeting, 210–211
    fixed, 234
    record of, 210

expressions, facial, 61, 63
extenders, of meat, 410–411
eyes, care of, 68–69

F

fabric, buying of, 322, *336*
  care of, 274–275
  choosing of, 277–280, 319–322, 336
    for pattern, *341*
  considering, in buying clothing, 278–280
  design of, 257–265, 277
  durable press, or permanent press, 278–280
  finishes of, 278–280
  folding, 323, 342
  making grain perfect, 323
  minimum care, 282
  performance of, 279
  preparation of, for sewing, 322–323
  preshrunk, 319–320, 322
fabric softener, 280, 300
face, daily care of, 70–72
facings, 342, 348–349
facts, collection of, in problem-solving, 149–151
fads, 271–272, 285
failure, learning from, 57
families, 18
  activities in, 112
  budget of, 112
  changes in, 30–34
  differences in, 26–27
  fun in, 114–115
  life cycle of, 29–32
  older members in, 109–111
  possessions of, 112–113
  resources of, 27, 111–113
  special occasions in, 113
  types of, 25–30
family budget consultant, 207
family living, 99–119
  and home management, 147

family living, seven "C's" of, 34–39
family service, of meals, 470
fashion, 266, 271–272, 284–285
fashion designer, 258
fatigue, 204
fats, 365
  adding to mixtures, 455
  animal, 445–446
  buying of, 389
  in foods, 450–451
  use of in cooking, 454–455
  vegetable, 445–446
fear, 53
Federal Trade Commission, 226
feeding, of babies, 143
  bottle, 133–134
  breast, 133
  of young children, 144
feet, care of, 73–74
femininity, in dress, 226–*227*
fibers, animal, 277
  chart, 274–275
  generic, 273–275
  man-made, 272–275, 278
  natural, 274, 277–278
  plant, 277–278
  semisynthetic, 278
  synthetic, 278
figure type, and clothing selection, 257–265, 277
  in patterns, 334–335
filled cookies, 454, 506
finfish, 414
finger foods, *469*, 473–474
fingernails, care of, 72–73
finishes, of fabrics, 278–281
  of seams, 344
first aid, 161, 164–165
fish, 364, 373
  BROILED, 483
  buying of, 383–384, 413, 414
  cooking of, 414–*415*
  freshwater, 414
  safe storage time for, 384
  saltwater, 414

fish-liver oil, 368
fitting, problems in, 352
flatware, 459, 462–464
  placement of, 464
  types of, 462
  use of, 467–469
floors, care of, 174–175, 178–179
  in home economics department, 247–248
  waxes for, 175
flour, all purpose, 443–444
  cake, 443–444
  combining with liquid, 442
  as an energy food, 450
  enriched, 440
  pastry, 443–444
  refined, *440*
  self-rising, 443–444
  substitutes for, 479
  wheat, 442–443
  whole-grain, 439–440
flowers, arrangement of, 250
  in centerpieces, 465
  in home economics department, 245
  care of, *245*, 249
FONDUE, *468*, 491
food chemist, 382
food demonstrator, 205
food groups, 360–362
food products tester, 378
food service manager, 437
food stamps, 375
food values, 431
foods, advance preparation of, 114
  buying of, for nutrition, 380–381
  for children, 133–134
  convenience, 381, 387
  factors affecting cost of, 376–378
  forms of, 377
  nutrients in, 364–373
  preparation of, 449–457
  research, *92*
  seasonal, 378
  selection of, 380
  shopping for, 379–380, 388

foods, storing of, 384–386
   traditional, 375
fork, use of, 468
FRANKFURTER-BACON SPIRALS, 482
freezer, 394
   foods for, 411
freeze-drying, 428
FRENCH DRESSING, 513
FRENCH TOAST, 501
FRIED EGGS, 456, 487
friendship quotient, 91
friendships, 22–23, 83–91
   boy-girl, 78–79
   establishing, 84
   maintaining, 84
   qualities of, 81–82
   values of, 85
frosting, butter, 453
   cooked, 453
   cooking of, 451–452
   UNCOOKED, 509
fruit, 361, 365, 367, 369, 372
   basic food group, 361–362
   buying of, 388
   canned, grading of, 388
   cooking, principles of, 432, 434
   frozen, grading of, 388
   forms of, 428
   kinds of, 431
   raw, serving of, 436–437
   recipes for, 493–499
FRUIT BLOSSOM COOKIES, 506
FRUIT FILLING FOR COOKIES, 506
FRUIT PUNCH, 497
fruit-vegetable food group, 361–362
frying, use of fat and oils in, 450–451, 456
   of fruits, 434
   of vegetables, 453
FUDGE, COCOA, 507
   TEN-MINUTE, 509
fungus, 73–74
furniture, arrangement of, 154–156
   for children, 131
      safety of, 131

furniture, in home economics
   department, 242–246
      caring for, 246–250
   planning of, 154–156
   polishing of, 176
   for storage, 156

G

games, for children, 137
gangs, 128
garbage disposal, 171, 395
garde-manger, 411
garment bags, 306
gelatin, 436–437
GELATIN MOLD, 496
germ, of wheat, 439–440
gifts, 118–119
GINGERBREAD, 503
glassware, 463–465
   placement of, 464
gloves, buying of, 293
gluten, 446
goals, 16, 57, 75, 152, 213
   choosing of, 55–56
   educational, 94
   family, 27–30
      achievement of, 30
   group, 189–190
   individual, 189–190
   long-range, 190
   occupational, 83
   personal, 83
   realistic, 189
   relating to problems, 148
   setting of, 82
   short-term, 190–193
   substitution of, 56
   unrealistic, 185
going steady, 87
goiter, 373
goods, buying of, 217
gore, 342
grading, 221

grading, of canned goods, 380, 388
   of eggs, 384–385, 416
   of frozen foods, 380, 388
   of meats, 382–383, 407
   of poultry, 415–416
grain, cereal, 441–442
   of fabric, 281–282, 321–322, 341
      straightening of, 322–323
grain-perfect, 322–323, 343
grandparents, 108, 109–111
GRAPEFRUIT, BROILED, 498
gratification, postponement of, 56
GREEN BEANS, 495
GREEN VEGETABLES, time chart for, 494
GRIDDLECAKES, 442, 503
groceries, shopping for, 386
   lists for, 383
grooming, 64, 75
   and health, 161
groups, social, 85–86
growth, emotional, 52
   mental, 52
   patterns of, 122–130
   physical, 44, 123–129
   rates of, 124
   social, 43, 52, 123
   vocational, 91–94
guarantees, 220
guidance, 80–82
guide, food, see daily food guide
gusset, 342

H

habits, of study, 203
   as time-savers, 201–202
hair, brushing of, 69
   daily care of, 69
   removal of, 70
   shampooing, 69–70
   styling of, 70–71
hairbrush, care of, 69–70
ham, 414

ham, tailor's, 314, 318, *349–350*
hamburger, 408, 480
HAMBURGER MASTER MIX, 480–481
handbags, buying of, 293
handicaps, 53
   environmental, 104
   physical, 50–51
hands, care of, 72–73
hang tags, 216, 273, 277
hanging, of clothing, 296–298
HARD-COOKED EGGS, 487
HAWAIIAN CURRY DINNER, 486
Head Start Programs, 19
health, in the home, 158, 160–165
heart, 414
hem marker, 314
hemming stitches, 296, 354
hems, 283, 354
heredity, 48–52
hobbies, 192–193
home, the, and family living, 99–119
home economics, areas of, 93–94
   careers in, *92–93*
home economics department, 238–250
   improvement of, 241–245
   kitchens in, 392–393
   opening efficiently, 240
home economics extension agent, 244
home economist, 238–239
home extension aide, 229
home-lighting adviser, 187
home service representative, 223
homemaker, visiting, 93
homemaker's aide, 111
hooks and eyes, 283
HOPPING JOHN, *408,* 488
hosiery, buying of, 291–293
hospitality, 115–117
hostility, 53–54
hot-water method, of making pastry, 455
house mother, 78
household items construction, 190
housekeeping, 167–180

housekeeping, seasonal, 177–179
   daily, in home economics department, 246–250
housing, 25, 215, 220

I

ice cream, 361, 386–387
icings, 453
illness, childhood, 134–135
   reporting of, 162
   signs of, 162
image, impact of, 74–75
   improvement of, 59–60
   positive, 59–60
impediments, in speech, 62
impressions, first, 59
independence, 48, 54, 57, 130
   as a goal, 193
   need for, 44–45
industrial revolution, 32–33, 42
industrial seamstress, 284
infants, growth and development of, 124–125
inoculations, 160
installment buying, 223–234
instruction sheets, in patterns, 338
intelligence, 51–52
interests, 192–193
   in clothing, 255–256
interfacing, 283, 348–349
interior designer, 92, 153
international recipes, CHINESE SWEET AND SOUR PORK, 485
   FRENCH DRESSING, 513
   FRENCH TOAST, 501
   HAWAIIAN CURRY DINNER, 486
   PERUVIAN CORN PIE, 485
iodine, 372–373, 415
iron, 372, 388, 411, 414, 416
iron, steam, 299, 305, 313, 349
ironing, 303–306
ironing board, 313

J

jackets, buying of, 288
jam, *435*
jealousy, 54
jellies, *435*
jewelry, 293
jobs, part-time, 90, 142, *151*
(also see career and career opportunities)

K

kidneys, 414
kindergartner, 137
kitchens, arrangement of, 392
   cleaning of, daily, 170–171
   weekly, 172–174
   shapes of, 391–393
knives, care of, 396–397
   use of, 467–468

L

labels, 220, 272, 277
   on clothing, 272–276
   on detergents, 300
   on food, 378–379
   on thread, 316
lamb, 381–383
   cooking of, 414
landscape gardener, 84
language, development of, 138–139
laundering, by hand, 302–304
   by machine, 297–302
   aids for, 299–300
   steps in, 300–302
   of minimum care fabrics, 303
layout, of patterns, 340–343
leaveners, types of, 444–445, 447
Legal Aid Society, 226
leisure, 202–203

LEMON CHIFFON CAKE, 508
life span, 109
life style, of teen-agers, 16
lighting, for sewing, 243, 325-326
linen, 274
linens, changing of, 176-177
   laundering of, 250
lines in clothes, 264-267, 333
linings, 283
liquids, in flour mixtures, 444
liver, 367, 414, 483
living areas, daily care of, 171-172
loan agencies, 232
love, need for, 42-44, 53

M

macaroni, 441
   cooking of, 447
MACARONI AND CHEESE, 491
makeup, emotional, 52-54
   facial, see cosmetics
   mental, 51-52
   physical, 48-51
management, of the home, 93, 147-165
   problem-solving in, 148-153
   of household tasks, 167-180
   of meals, 392
   of resources, 185-193
manicure, 74
man-made fibers, 272-275, 278
mannerisms, 62-63
manners, 62-63, 78
   of elementary school child, 128
   at the table, 466-470
margarine, 389
marketplaces, choosing of, 229-230
   types of, 229
masculinity, in dress, 266-267
MASHED POTATOES, 493
MASTER MIX, BISCUIT, 446-447,
      450, 502-503
   HAMBURGER, 480-481
maturity, 52, 121

maturity, achievement of, 54-57
   physical, 85, 127
   types of, 49
   and vocational opportunities, 77
meals, planning of, 370-371, 397-400
   for nutrition, 412
   preparation of, in foods laboratory,
      400-402
   serving of, 467
meal service, types of, 470-474
measurements, of cooking ingredients,
      402-404
   of dry ingredients, 404
   equivalents, 400-401, 478
   of fats, 404
   of liquids, 404
   tools for, 403-404
   in sewing, 335-337
   of pattern pieces, 340
   taking personal measurements,
      335-337
   terms for, 319
meat, 360-362, 364, 372, 411-412
   alternates for, 361
   basic food group, 360-362
   buying of, 381-383
   cooking of, 407-416
      by dry heat, 409-410
      by moist heat, 409-411
   cuts of 412-413
   determining tenderness of, 412-413
   grades of, 382-383, 407
   safe storage time for, 384
   variety, cooking of, 414
MEAT SALAD SANDWICHES, 504
medicine cabinet, 164
mending, 296-297
men's wear, alterationist for, 304
menus, 450
   writing of, 402
merchandise, handling of, 222-223
metabolism, 363-364, 372-373
milk, 360-362, 364, 372
   basic food group, 360-362
   as a beverage, 420-421

milk, buying of, 386-387
   cooking with, 420-421
   forms of, 386, 420-421
   fresh, substitutes for, 479
   grading of, 386
   need for, 419-420
   products of, 420-421
      frozen, 386-387
   safe storage time for, 384
   substitutes for, 386
milk-rich foods, recipes for, 489, 492
MILK SHAKE, 489
minerals, 369, 372-373
mix-and-match clothing, 288
mixes, commercial, 447, 449-450, 452
   homemade, 446-447, 450, 480-481,
      502-503
mobility, of families, 33-34
modacrylics, 275
modeling, 92, 317
mold, 386
molded cookies, 354
molded salads, 436-437
money, attitudes about, 207-208
   management of, 187-189, 208-213
   sources of, 208-209
   spending of, 215-219
      in reaction to advertising, 216
      to provide goods and services, 217
      to provide status symbols, 218
      to satisfy needs and wants,
         216-217
moods, 54
moth damage, prevention of, 307
mothers, working, 27, 32, 105-106, 211
MUFFINS, 443, 503
multipurpose room, 239
MUSHROOM SAUCE, 490
mutton, 414

N

napkins, paper, 462
   placement of, 462

napkins, sizes of, 462
  use of, 461–462
natural fibers, 274, 277–278
nearsightedness, 68
needles, 317
  threading of, 297
needs, 56
  for acceptance, 44, 85
  for appreciation, 44
  and budgeting, 211
  combined, 43
  emotional, 43
    of children, 139–141
    and the home, 99, 153–154
    meeting with food, 359–360
  for love, 43–44
  mental, 43
    of children, 135–139
    and the home, 100, 153–154
  physical, 42–43
    of children, 130–135
    and the home, 99, 153–154
  real, 55
  in relation to priorities, 191
  for security, 44
  separating from wants, 55
  social, 43
    of children, 139–141
    and the home, 100, 153–154
  special, of children, 130–141
  for variety, 44
niacin, 368, 414
nondairy products, 386
noodles, 441
notches, 344–345
nursemaid, 140
nursery, 134
nutrients, 364–373
nutrition, 49, 67–68
  buying food for, 380–381
  for children, 133–134
  effects on health, 361
  planning meals for,
nutrition experts, 360
nylon, 272, 275

O

OATMEAL, 500
OATMEAL COOKIES, 503
obstetrician, 122, 134
occasions, special, celebrating of, 117–118
occupation, 20
  choice of, 91–94
  part-time, 90, 142, *151*
  (see also career opportunities)
oil method, of making pastry, 455
oil repellents, 280
old age, changes accompanying, 109
olefin, 275
one-bowl method, for mixing cake, 452–453
ophthalmologist, 68
opportunities, in communities, 18–19
  for learning, in home economics department, 238–250
  occupational, 90, 91–94, 142, *151*
  (see also career opportunities)
  social, 77–78
optician, 68
ORANGES, SLICED, 495
organizations, belonging to, 21
outerwear, buying of, 283–289
outings, family, *113*, 115
OVEN-COOKED RICE, 500
oven temperatures, 478
oxidization, 368–369

P

packaging, of food, 377–378
packing, for trips, 268–269
padding, 283
pancakes, 442, 503
  (see also griddlecakes)
PANFRIED CHICKEN, 486
panfrying, 451, 456
pants, buying of, 284–285

pantyhose, 292–293
parents, getting along with, 103
  problems of, 103
  responsibilities of, 100–105
parties, family, 117–118
  fondue, *468*
  (see also entertaining)
paste method, for making pastry, 455
pasteurization, of milk, 386
PASTRY, 455, 510–511
pastry chef, 441
pattern envelopes, 338, 340
patterns, adjustment of, 338–340
  altering of, 341–343
  care of, 337
  choosing of, 318–319, 331–334
  cutting out by, 341–343
  judging difficulty of, 337
  markings on, 338, 344–345
    transferring of, 344–345
  measuring for, 335–337
  of mental-emotional energy, 205
  pinning of, to fabric, 341–343
  of physical energy, 204–205
  terms on, 342
  types and sizes of, 334–335
PEANUT BUTTER COOKIES, 505
PEANUT BUTTER SPREAD, 512
peas, dried, 408–409
pediatrician, 134
permanent press or durable press, 278–280
personality, 48, *51*
  building of, 52
  clothes to suit, 266
personal shopper, 227
PERUVIAN CORN PIE, 485
philosophy of life, 57
phosphorus, 372, 411, 414–416, 419
picnics, 474, 476
pictures, in home economics department, 245
  arrangement of, 248
PIE CRUST, 455, 510–511
  fats and oils in, 456

pin cushion, 316
pinning, of pattern to fabric, 341–343
pins, 316
PIZZA, 447, 481
place mat, 461
plastic, use of in dinnerware, 459, 463
play, 136–138
  space for, 137–138
play equipment, outdoor, 144
playthings, 136–138, 142
  safety of, 137–138
POACHED EGGS, 487
poaching, 410
polishing, 176
pollution, of water, 414
polyester, 275
porcelain, 463
pork, 381–383
  cooking of, 413–414
posture, 64–67
  at sewing machine, *325*
POTATO SALAD, 497
POTATOES, BAKED, 493
  MASHED, 493
pottery, 459, 463
poultry, buying of, 383
  cooking of, 415–416
  grading of, 383, 415
  safe storage time for, 384
pregnancy, 121–122
preschooler, growth of, 125–127
preserving, of fruits and vegetables, 435–436
pressed cookies, 453
pressing, of clothing, 303–306
  in clothing construction, 348–350
pressing cloth, 313
pressing mitt, 314
pressure, social, 15–16
priorities, establishing of, 190–193
problem solving, 148–153, 277
problems, personal, 63–64
  in housekeeping, 177–178
products, housekeeping, 173
programs, TV, 142

projects, sewing, planning of, 309–329
protein foods, recipes for, 480–488
proteins, 388,
  cooking, principles of, 407–417
  complete, 364, 407, 415–416, 419,
  incomplete, 364
  sources of, 360–361
puberty, 85, 127–129
puddings, 424–425
PUMPKIN PIE, 511
punch, fruit, 497
punishment, 128, 141
purses, buying of, 293

Q

quality, determination of, 220–221
quantity, determination of, 220–221
quarreling, 108, 127–129
quick breads, 441–442, 445, 446
  recipes for, 502–503
QUICK-MIX GOLD CAKE, 508

R

range, care of, 173, 175, 250, 394–*395*
  types of, 394–395
rayon, 274
rebellion, 57
receptions, 472–473
recipes, 480–513
  substitutions in, 443–444, 445–446, 479
  use of, 402
records, financial, 221–222
  of spending, 213
recreation, opportunities for, *42*, 53, 58
  resources for, 18
redecorating, 156, 177–178
refrigerator, care of, 173–174, 250, 294
refrigerator cookies, 453–454
relationships, learning, 139–*140*
religion, 18
  and customs, 27

relishes, *435*
remodeling, of clothing, 307
repair, of clothing, 296–297
repellents, 280
resolutions, 79
resources, 150–151
  basic, 186–189
  combination of, 186
  community, 19
  consideration of, in budgeting, 209–210
  of energy, 186–189, 205–207
  of family, 27, 80, 111–112
  human, 16, 185–*187*
  management of, 185–193
  material, 186–*187*
  of money, 186–189, 208–213
  national, 185
  natural, 16, 185–*186*
  technical, 16
  of time, 186–189, 197–202
  types of, 185–186
  use of, 195–197
responsibility, 77
  acceptance of, 45, 56–57
  for children, 141–145
  of family, 48
  of parents, 100–105
rest, 68
riboflavin, 368, 414, 416, 419
rice, 441
  cooking of, 447
  recipes for, 481, 488, 500
roasting, 409–410
roles, changing, 32–33, 99, 103
  of family members, 103–111
  sex, 20–21
  teen-age, 21–23
rolled cookies, 454
rooms, arrangement of, 155–156
rubber, 274
rules, for family living, 35
running stitch, 296
rural families (see families, differences in)

S

safety, 134–135
  in children's furniture, 131
  in deep-fat frying, 456
  in entertaining, 118
  in the home, *158*–160, 167
  in the kitchen, 405
  in sewing, 341
  in use of appliances, 164–165
SALAD, CHICKEN, 482
  dressings for, 513
  making of, 436–437
  MEAT, 504
  MOLDED, *436–437*, 496
  POTATO, 497
  TOSSED GREEN, 498
salesperson, 75, 129
Sanforization, 319–320
saran, 275
sauces, custard, 425
  recipes for, 490, 510
  WHITE, 422–424, 490
savings, 211–213
scarves, 293
scheduling, evaluation of, 201
  of household tasks, 168–169
  use of time, 195, 197–201
school, clothing for, 268
  role in, 22
scissors, 316, 325
SCRAMBLED EGGS, 488
seafood, 373
seams, 282, 344, 347–348
  clipping and trimming of, 350–351
  finishes for, 347
seating, at the table, 466–467
security, *102*
  and the home, 100
  need for, 44
  providing, to children, 139–140
self-care, learning of, 135–136
self-concept, 41, *48*, 57
  development of, 125

self-concept, negative, 59, 63
  and status, 218
self-confidence, *53*
self-feeding, 134
selvage, 321–323
semisynthetics, 278
service, to community, 18
sewing, general directions for, 309–354
sewing apron, 314, 318, 326–329
sewing box, 316
sewing gauge, 318
sewing machine, 243, 310–313
  buying of, 313
  parts of, 312
  tension adjustment of, 312
  threading of, 323–324
shampoo, *69*
shape, of foods, *371*
  of kitchens, 391–393
  of muscle and bones, 49
shears, 316, 343–344
shellfish, 383–384, 414
shirts, buying of, 284
shoes, buying of, 290–291
  care of, 73
  judging quality of, 293
shortening, 445–446
  buying of, 389
sick, caring for, *162*–164
  meals for, 164
sickroom, supplies for, *163*–164
silhouette, 264
silk, 274
silverware, 462–463
sink, 395
  cleaning of, in home economics department, 249
sitter services, 138
skills, development of, 77
  learning of, 52
  muscular, *127*
  social, 78–79
skin, problems with, *71*–72
  and Vitamin A, 366–367
skin tone, 258–*259*, 277

skirts, buying of, 284–285
  judging quality of, 283
slang, 60
SLAW, 499
sleep, 68
  for babies, 143–144
  for young children, 145
sleeve board, 314
sleeves, making and setting, 353–354
SLICED ORANGES, 495
slide fastener, or zipper, 282–283, 352–353
slipcovers, 244–245
slips, buying of, 290
SLOPPY JOE, 481
smorgasbord, 471
snacks, 449
  serving of, 456–457
snaps, sewing on, 283, 352
social work, *92*
SOFT-COOKED EGGS, 487
SOFT CUSTARD, 492
soil releasants, 280
soil repellents, 280
sorting of clothing, 296
soufflés, 421, 425
SPAGHETTI, 441, 481
spandex, 274
SPANISH RICE, 481
specials, in buying, 228
spending plan, or budget, 209–213
spoon, use of, 468–469
spot removal, 296–297
spreads, 457
  recipes for, 512
stages, of family life cycle, 31–32
stains, removal of, 296–297, 299–300
standards, setting of, 193
status symbols, 218
staystitching, *343*, 347
steam, as a leavener, 444–445
steam iron, 299, 305, 313, 349
stewing, 410
stews, 484

stitches, 282, 296, 343, 354
   on sewing machine, 312
storage, arrangement of, 156–157
   of clothing, 306–*307*
   of foods, 384–386
   in home economics department, 241, 246–247
   in the kitchen, 170
   seasonal, 179
straightening fabric, 322–323, 326
strength, 50
stress, emotional, 54
style, of clothing, 272, 277
substitutions, 443–444, 445–446, 478
suburban families (see families, differences in)
success, learning from, 57
sugar, in foods, 450
   in bread products, 446
   (see also energy foods)
supplies, medical, 164
sweaters, buying of, 285–286
   judging quality of, 285
sweetbreads, 414
synthetics, 278, 280
syrup, sugar, cooking of, 453

T

table coverings, 461
table manners, 466–470
table setting, 461–465
   basic steps in, *460*
tablecloths, 459, 461
tableware, 459, 461
   accessory items in, 465
TAFFY APPLES, 505
tags, 216, 220, 223, 273, 277
tailor, 266
tailoring, 288–289
tailor's chalk, 344
tailor's ham, 314, 318, *349–350*
tailor's tacks, 344

talent, development of, 52
tape measure, 316
tapioca, 442–443
TARTS, CHERRY, 512
tasks, developmental, 122–*123*
   household, sharing of, 113–114
      management of, 167–180
   organization of, 186
   outdoor, 180
teas, 472–473
teen-agers, 15–23, 42
   growth patterns of, 54, 85, 129–130
   roles of, 20–23
teeth, care of, 68–69
telephone, use of, 60–61
temperature, body, 162
   for cooking protein products, 408–410, 413
   oven, 478
tenderization, of meat, 409–*411*
TEN-MINUTE FUDGE, 509
tensions, sewing machine, 312
tensions, social, 15–16
tester and developer, 218
Textile Act, 272–273
textile research, *92*
textiles, see fabric
texture, of fabrics, 263
   of foods, *371*
thermometer, 162
thiamine, 368, 419
thimble, *317*–318
THOUSAND ISLAND DRESSING, 513
thread, 317–318
thyroid, 372–373
ties, 293
time, attitudes about, 197
   discipline of, 201
   leisure, 202–203
   management of, 186–189, 197–202
   record of, 200
   scheduling of, 195, 197–201
      in school kitchen, 401
   valuing, of others, 202

time, wise use of, in foods laboratory, 404–405
TIMETABLE FOR COOKING GREEN VEGETABLES, 494
TOAST, 501
toddlers, development of, 124–125
toenails, care of, 73–74
toilet training, 135–136
toothbrush, 69
torn projects, 318
tortillas, 439
TOSSED GREEN SALAD, 498
toys, 136–138, 142
trace elements, 372
tracing paper, 344–345
tracing wheel, 316–317, 344–345
traditions, family, 27
traffic, pattern of, 156
traits, inherited, 48–51
triacetate, 274
trichina, 413–414
trimmings, 283
tuberculosis, 51, 386
tubers, 429
tucks, 347–348
TUNA FISH CASSEROLE, 483
TUNA FISH ROLLS, 504
twins, 107–108

U

UNCOOKED FROSTING, 509
undergarments, buying of, 289–290
   judging quality of, 291
underpants, buying of, 289
understanding, of yourself, 57
understitching, 343, 349
undertones, of skin, 285
undulant fever, 386
unit method of construction, 345–346
urban families (see families, difference in)
U.S. Food and Drug Administration, 378

527

V

vacuum cleaner, use of, 171, 175–*177*
values, 16, 57, 77, 213
   consideration of, 192
   of family, 27–29
   identifying, 55
   in problem solving, 152
variety, need for, 44
variety meats, cooking of, 414
veal, 381–383
vegetable cook, 435
vegetables, 361, 365, 367, 369, 372
   basic food group, 361–*362*
   boiled, 428
   buying of, 388
   canned, grading of, 388
     preparation of, 429
   cooking, principles for, 432–434
     variations in, 433
   flower, *430*
   forms of, 428
   fried, 432
   frozen, grading of, 388
     preparation of, 429
   leafy, 428–*429*
   raw, serving of, 436–437
   recipes for, 493–499
   root, 429–*430*
   seed, 430–431
   stem, 429–430

vegetables, TIMETABLE FOR COOKING GREEN VEGETABLES, 494
vinyon, 275
visiting homemaker, 93
Vitamins, A, 133, 366–367, 389, 414, 416, 419, 427–432
   B complex, 368–*369*, 388, 411, 427, 431–432
   C, 368–*369*, 427–432
   D, 133, *367*–368, 372
   E, 366–368
   K, 366–368
   sources of, 361, 365–366
   fat-soluble, 366–368
   water-soluble, 368–369

W

WAFFLES, 503
WALDORF SALAD, 499
walls, caring for, 177–178
   in home economics department, 243–244
wants, 55, 56, 191
   and budgeting, 211
   fulfilling, 216
wardrobe, developing plan for, 256–257
warp, of fabric, 321
warranties, 220
wastes, disposal of, *171,* 249

water, in the diet, 373
water repellents, 280
water softeners, 300
waxing, of floors, 178
weights, equivalents, 478
whey, 425
WHITE SAUCE, 422–424, 490
windows, in home economics department, 243–244
wool, 274
work, of the family, 113–114
   professional, 91
   and sex roles, 20–21
   skilled, 91
working mothers, 27, 32, 105–106, *211*
work-study, 80
worktables, 242–243
world, living in the, 15–16
writer, 216

Y

yard, care of, 180
yardstick, 314
YELLOW CAKE, 503

Z

zippers, 282–283, 352–353